ROGUES' GALLERY

ROGUES' GALLERY

-=·=-

The Birth of
Modern Policing
and Organized Crime
in Gilded Age New York

JOHN OLLER

DUTTON

DUTTON

An imprint of Penguin Random House LLC
penguinrandomhouse.com

LIBRARY OF CONGRESS CATALOGING-IN-PUBLICATION DATA
Names: Oller, John, author.
Title: Rogues' gallery : the birth of modern policing and
organized crime in Gilded Age New York / John Oller.
Description: [New York, New York] : Dutton, [2021] |
Includes bibliographical references and index.
Identifiers: LCCN 2020051815 (print) | LCCN 2020051816 (ebook) |
ISBN 9781524745653 (hardcover) | ISBN 9781524745677 (ebook)
Subjects: LCSH: New York (N.Y.). Police Department—History—19th century. |
Police—New York (State)—New York—History—19th century. |
Organized crime—New York (State)—New York—History—19th century. |
New York (N.Y.)—History—1865-1898. | New York (N.Y.)—Social conditions.
Classification: LCC HV8148.N5 O55 2021 (print) |
LCC HV8148.N5 (ebook) | DDC 363.209747/1—dc23
LC record available at https://lccn.loc.gov/2020051815
LC ebook record available at https://lccn.loc.gov/2020051816

Printed in the United States of America
1 3 5 7 9 10 8 6 4 2

BOOK DESIGN BY KRISTIN DEL ROSARIO

To my mother

CONTENTS

CONTENTS

CONTENTS

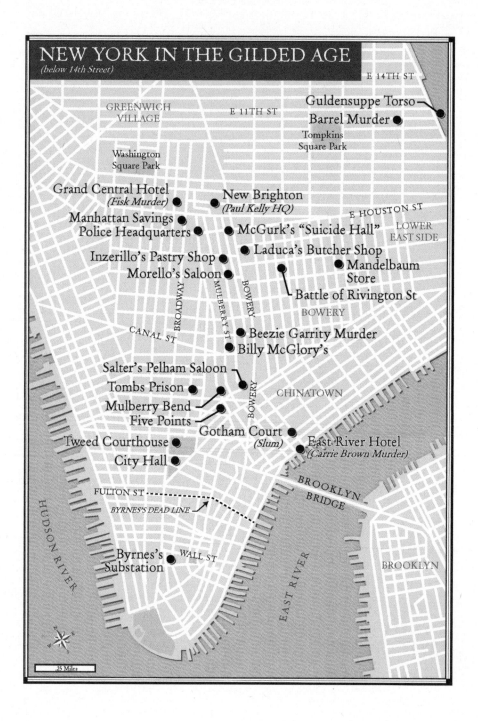

NEW YORK IN THE GILDED AGE
(below 14th Street)

E 14TH ST

GREENWICH VILLAGE

E 11TH ST

Guldensuppe Torso
Barrel Murder

Tompkins Square Park

Washington Square Park

Grand Central Hotel
(Fisk Murder)

New Brighton
(Paul Kelly HQ)

E HOUSTON ST

LOWER EAST SIDE

Manhattan Savings
Police Headquarters

McGurk's "Suicide Hall"

Inzerillo's Pastry Shop
Morello's Saloon

Laduca's Butcher Shop

Mandelbaum Store

Battle of Rivington St

BOWERY

CANAL ST

BROADWAY

MULBERRY ST

BOWERY

Beezie Garrity Murder
Billy McGlory's

Salter's Pelham Saloon

Tombs Prison

Mulberry Bend
Five Points

BOWERY

CHINATOWN

Gotham Court
(Slum)

Tweed Courthouse

East River Hotel
(Carrie Brown Murder)

City Hall

BROOKLYN BRIDGE

FULTON ST

BYRNES'S DEAD LINE

HUDSON RIVER

EAST RIVER

BROOKLYN

Byrnes's
Substation

WALL ST

.25 Miles

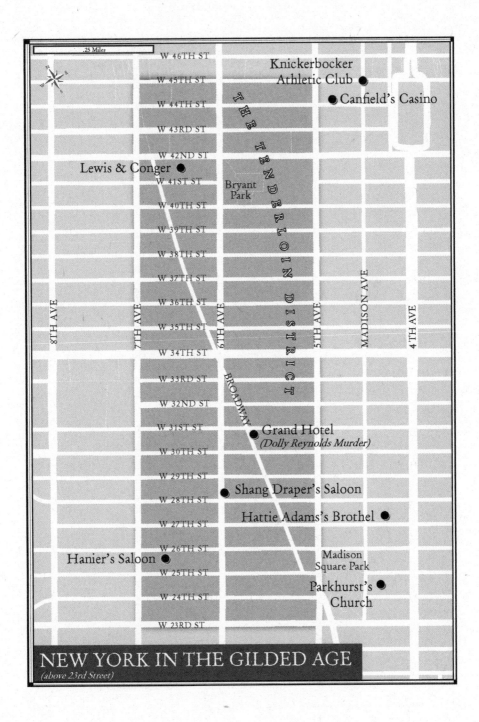

.25 Miles

W 46TH ST
W 45TH ST
W 44TH ST
W 43RD ST
W 42ND ST
W 41ST ST
W 40TH ST
W 39TH ST
W 38TH ST
W 37TH ST
W 36TH ST
W 35TH ST
W 34TH ST
W 33RD ST
W 32ND ST
W 31ST ST
W 30TH ST
W 29TH ST
W 28TH ST
W 27TH ST
W 26TH ST
W 25TH ST
W 24TH ST
W 23RD ST

8TH AVE
7TH AVE
6TH AVE
5TH AVE
MADISON AVE
4 TH AVE

BROADWAY

THE TENDERLOIN DISTRICT

Knickerbocker
Athletic Club ●
● Canfield's Casino

Lewis & Conger ●

Bryant
Park

● Grand Hotel
(Dolly Reynolds Murder)

Shang Draper's Saloon ●

Hattie Adams's Brothel ●

Hanier's Saloon ●

Madison
Square Park

Parkhurst's ●
Church

NEW YORK IN THE GILDED AGE
(above 23rd Street)

ROGUES' GALLERY

◂•▸═◉ ◉═◂•▸

FORMING THE PICTURE

The torso was found first: the headless upper part of the body of a well-built man bobbing in the East River on a hot summer day in New York City in 1897. Wrapped in floral-patterned red oilcloth, the type used to cover kitchen tables and line cupboards, the tightly tied package was pulled from the water by a group of boys playing near the pier at the foot of East Eleventh Street. The man's chest was sawed off just below the rib cage and was missing a sliced-out hunk of flesh.

The following day, ten miles away, a man and his two sons were out picking berries in the woods in a sparsely settled part of the Bronx, near the High Bridge Aqueduct, when they stumbled upon the lower part of the body, minus the legs. This bundle, too, was wrapped in red oilcloth.

Three days later, the severed legs showed up in another package near the Brooklyn Navy Yard, where sailors from the USS *Vermont* fished it from the river.

All that was missing now was the head.

Among the first New York police detectives assigned to the case was thirty-one-year-old Arthur Carey, a boyish-faced, Staten Island–born

Detective Arthur Carey, the "Murder Man" who led the investigations of many sensational homicide cases and headed the New York Police Department's first homicide squad.

son of an Irish cop. A veteran of the central detective bureau in Lower Manhattan, Carey specialized in homicide cases. But lately he had been patrolling the beat in "Goatville," the Bronx precinct where the lower torso had been discovered in the woods. Like Russians banished to Siberia, police officers who fell out of favor during one of the department's periodic political shake-ups were reassigned to Goatville, where nothing much ever happened.

That had been Carey's fate, in 1895, after his mentor, police chief Thomas F. Byrnes—the most famous cop in America—was forced into retirement by Theodore Roosevelt, the new head of the Board of Police Commissioners. The reformer Roosevelt had taken office in the wake of a highly publicized legislative investigation that unearthed rampant police corruption in New York City. Although Carey was not personally implicated in the scandal, the fallout was enough to get him sent to Goatville, where he'd been languishing for almost two years.

Carey's career would change dramatically beginning on June 27, 1897, when the package containing the limbless midsection was brought into the Bronx precinct station. Carey and his partner unwrapped the bundle to find, in addition to layers of brown paper and burlap, red-and-gold-patterned oilcloth that matched the type enclosing the partial corpse found in the East River the day before. The two pieces of wrapping even fit together. Carey now dismissed the initial police theory that mischievous medical students had cut up a cadaver and dumped it in the river to create a mystery. Instead, the matching oilcloth suggested a carefully coordinated crime by the same hand. He also noted, as confirmed later by city morgue doctors who fit the body parts together like a jigsaw puzzle, that the body appeared to have been crudely hacked with a saw, not a precision medical knife. Carey was sure this was no joke. Despite his exile to Goatville, "Murder followed me here," Carey would later recall.

As he continued examining the body, Carey spotted something else: a small ink stamp on a piece of wet brown wrapping paper stuck to the man's back, which read, "Kugler & Wollens Hardware, 277 Bowery." Carey guessed that the saw had been purchased there. So, he took the

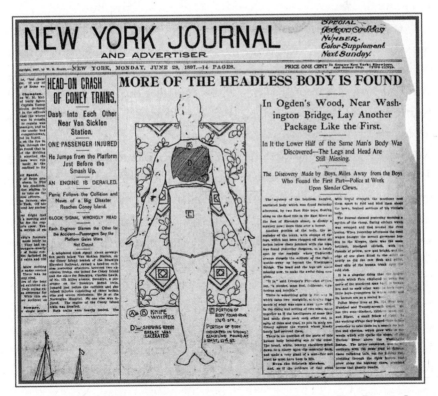

A newspaper illustration of a man's headless torso pulled from the East River in June 1897. Other parts of his body were found in a Bronx wood and in a river near the Brooklyn Navy Yard.

Third Avenue elevated train down to the corner of Bowery and Houston, near the central headquarters station at 300 Mulberry Street, where he had begun his detective career under Byrnes.

The Bowery was the seediest part of town, filled with concert saloons, brothels, dime museums, gambling dens, vaudeville houses, shooting galleries, and pawnshops. Low-rise tenements and flophouses also lined the muddy, garbage-strewn streets where a mélange of impoverished immigrants dwelt: Germans and Irish who had arrived in droves in earlier decades, as well as Chinese and, increasingly, Italians and Jews. Packs of neglected and homeless children, many of them once and future pickpockets and thieves, ran wild through the streets. They shared the crowded spaces with drunks who lay along the curb and doorways next to empty beer kegs.

At 295 Bowery, just across the street from Kugler & Wollens, was the most sordid dive in New York: McGurk's saloon, a combination dance hall and whorehouse frequented by thieves and lowlifes. Two years later, McGurk's would become known as "Suicide Hall" after a series of prostitutes jumped from the saloon's fifth-floor windows or imbibed carbolic acid to end their lives. The waiters at McGurk's drugged patrons to steal from them, and the bouncer, an ex-prizefighter nicknamed "Eat 'Em Up" Jack McManus, was considered the toughest brawler in New York. He got his nickname when, after confronting someone whose conduct he disapproved of, he "criticized the offender with his teeth." His knife-scarred face gave him a caveman look, made worse by a missing ear, chewed off in a fight.

At the hardware store, Carey found sheets of brown paper used for packaging, the same as the kind that covered the torso. He then tracked down a Bowery neighborhood fabric supplier who recognized the manufacturer of the red oilcloth pattern: A. F. Buchanan & Sons, pattern number Diamond B-3220. It had been distributed to fifty-some stores in the city, each of which now had to be canvassed.

Assisted by tabloid newspaper reporters who were eagerly pursuing the same leads, Carey soon ascertained that a stout German midwife named Augusta Nack had bought the oilcloth from a dry goods shop in the Long Island City neighborhood of Queens a few days before the body parts had started showing up. Mrs. Nack, estranged from her husband, lived in a Hell's Kitchen boardinghouse at Thirty-Fourth Street and Ninth Avenue and occasionally sublet part of her flat to others. One of her roomers, a German immigrant named William Guldensuppe, had been missing from his job as a Turkish-bath masseur since the day before the murder. Coworkers confirmed he had a tattoo of a girl in the spot carved out of the victim's chest, and they identified the reassembled body at the morgue as that of Guldensuppe.

It turned out that Guldensuppe had been Augusta Nack's lover until she jilted him in favor of a former roomer, a barber named Martin Thorn. The rivals had tangled on several occasions; Guldensuppe had twice beaten Thorn senseless, after which the barber moved out. It appeared that Thorn had a motive for revenge.

"The police machine began to grind," Carey recalled later. The keeper of a duck farm in Woodside, Queens, not far from the Long Island City shop where the oilcloth was purchased, reported that, for some days, the water in his duck pond had taken on a peculiar reddish substance that had made his ducks sick. Detectives traced the blood to a sewer line connected to a bathtub in a vacant cottage nearby.

Neighbors confirmed that a heavyset woman, accompanied by a man in a dark suit and brown derby, had recently rented the place under the names of "Mr. and Mrs. Braun." They were later identified as Augusta Nack and Martin Thorn. The two were duly arrested, and Nack eventually made a full confession. Nack had lured Guldensuppe to the vacant rental, where Thorn sprang from hiding to shoot him. The couple proceeded to dismember him in the bathtub, after which they disposed of the body parts. Only the head, encased in plaster of paris, had managed to stay submerged after being tossed in the river. Nack received a twelve-year prison sentence, while her lover, Thorn, was convicted at trial and given the electric chair in Sing Sing, the state prison on the Hudson River in Ossining, New York.

In his memoirs, Carey wrote that the "Case of the Scattered Dutch-man" had taught him certain fundamentals: first, that in a murder case, "there is no one obvious clue but that all clues are good if they are direct," and, second, that the police detective machine, though small at the time, "functioned with precision and relentlessly, from patrolmen on the beat to executives at headquarters," as they gathered and assessed bits of evidence coming in piecemeal from hundreds of different sources.

Carey was different from most cops: quiet, patient, and analytical. A plainclothesman, he dressed nattily and spoke eloquently. He never appeared too eager for information lest he inspire fear or reticence in a suspect. His manner could switch instantly from soothing and sympathetic to harsh and demanding. Carey's reputation for helping crack the Guldensuppe case soon won him a transfer back to the central detective bureau, where he focused almost exclusively on murder cases. A decade later, he would be made head of the NYPD's first homicide squad.

Carey's diagnostic style was what it took to solve complex cases back then. In 1897 fingerprinting as a standard crime-solving tool was still several years away. In vogue was the Bertillon system, endorsed by Roosevelt for the police force two years earlier. It recorded anatomical measurements of suspects, such as the circumference of the skull and the distance from the elbow to the fingertips, for future reference. But it was hardly reliable.

Medical examiners could detect poison well enough: in a well-publicized case in 1892, noted toxicologist Rudolph Witthaus, a professor at New York University's new Loomis Laboratory, had helped Carey prove that Dr. Robert W. Buchanan poisoned his second wife with morphine to inherit $50,000 just before remarrying his first wife. Consulted by Carey in the Guldensuppe case, Witthaus implicated Martin Thorn by identifying blood on the washboard and bathroom floor at the Woodside, Queens, cottage where the victim was murdered. But at that time, forensic science could not definitively distinguish between human and animal blood, much less group human blood into different types. Those breakthroughs would come around 1900.

A murder detective therefore had to rely on his wits, his deductive faculties, and whatever clues came his way.

Upon reaching a crime scene, Carey tried first to develop a picture of what had probably happened. He had guessed correctly that Guldensuppe was murdered on Long Island by at least two persons, and that the killers dumped the first piece of him off a ferry they took at night, then went back and loaded the heavier piece into a wagon, drove it over a bridge to the Bronx, and deposited it in a deserted wood.

The practice of forming a mental image of the crime was something Carey had learned from Thomas Byrnes, who used the expression "Here's the picture I get" when discussing a crime, or "Now, this is the picture I want you to get" when he assigned a detective to a case. It was just one of the many innovations pioneered by Byrnes, the father of the modern detective bureau and the most celebrated policeman of the Gilded Age.

Legendary detective Thomas F. Byrnes, longtime head of the NYPD's detective bureau and the most famous cop in Gilded Age New York. Byrnes pioneered such police practices as the rogues' gallery, the daily lineup, and the third-degree interrogation method. He later served as superintendent (chief of police) from 1892 to 1895 until forced by Police Commissioner Theodore Roosevelt to resign.

❖━━◗ ◖━━❖

The Gilded Age, during which first Byrnes, then Carey, forged their reputations, ran from the early 1870s until about 1910. It was a time of explosive, immigrant-fueled growth that saw the city's population, including Manhattan and the boroughs later consolidated with it, rise from one and a half million to nearly five million people. By 1910, 40 percent of New Yorkers were foreign-born, and almost three in four were immigrants or children of immigrants. Far different from today's rainbow demographics, New York was more than 95 percent white throughout the period. African Americans accounted for less than 2 percent of the population, while Asians and Hispanics/Latinos constituted negligible portions.

The city grew skyward during this time, culminating in the seven-hundred-foot Metropolitan Life Insurance Company Tower completed in 1909. Familiar icons such as the Brooklyn Bridge (1883), the Statue of Liberty (1886), and Ellis Island, which opened in 1892 to replace the old Castle Garden immigrant landing station in Battery Park, were added as well.

It was also a period of rapid technological change. The telephone, invented in 1876, brought New Yorkers closer together, as did mass transit: the elevated train in the 1870s, the cable car in the 1890s, and, finally, the subway system in 1904. Edison's electricity began lighting the city's streets in 1880 and turned Broadway into the Great White Way.

The most distinguishing characteristic of the Gilded Age, though, as its name implies, was its extreme wealth, concentrated in the hands of plutocrats such as Cornelius Vanderbilt, John D. Rockefeller, and J. P. Morgan. Known as the robber barons, they took advantage of unbridled capitalism, industrial expansion, and economic growth to amass fortunes that were conspicuously on display in the marble and granite mansions they built for themselves on upper Fifth Avenue and elsewhere.

The era took its name from Mark Twain's and Charles Dudley Warner's 1873 satirical novel *The Gilded Age: A Tale of Today*. Its leitmotif was that all the ostentation was merely a thin layer of gold; a wasteful façade that masked the era's greed, political corruption, and underlying social problems.

Among those social problems was the abject poverty that, especially in New York, stood in stark contrast to the plutocrats' affluence. In 1870 more than half of all Manhattanites still lived below Fourteenth Street, mainly crammed into squalid Lower East Side tenements. Social welfare legislation to ameliorate poverty's effects was minimal to nonexistent until late in the era. Crushing economic depressions following the Panic of 1873 and a similar one in 1893 overwhelmed private charity and stifled much of the progress that was made.

Another major social problem was crime—generally related to poverty, but not always so. New York, like other big cities, had its share of individual, sensational crimes: shocking murders of the type that Art Carey specialized in investigating. Often, these were crimes of passion, not profit, and were just as liable to be committed by the well-to-do as the poor. Over time, modernizations in policing techniques, coupled with the more mundane but necessary legwork that cops such as Carey learned to perform, would help increase the solve rate for crimes of this type.

But the era also saw the birth of a new breed of criminal: the organized crime figure. For many people today, the term "organized crime" conjures images of Al Capone and other Prohibition-era mobsters, as well as Mafia dons in later decades. Yet the origins of organized criminal enterprises can be traced to Gilded Age New York.

For Gilded Age gang members and thieves, crime was just business. The new criminals were low-life mirror images of the more exalted robber barons, who cut corners to earn their untold riches. Making money was more important than how one made it—or took it. And with so much money there for the taking, criminals saw no reason to deny themselves their rightful share of the growing economic pie.

The birth of organized crime posed new challenges for the city's police. As the crooks grew in sophistication and professionalism, the police struggled to keep pace. At times they failed, but they were mainly up to the challenge, despite rampant, never-ending corruption both high and low within the force. And the cementing of the NYPD's reputation as "New York's Finest" was largely attributable to the towering, controversial figure of Thomas Byrnes, whose ascent began at the very dawn of the Gilded Age.

CHAPTER ONE

❖⟶ ⟵❖

MAKING A NAME

Police captain Thomas F. Byrnes was at the corner of Broadway and East Eighth Street, near Astor Place, when he heard the news of the shooting. The word was spreading like wildfire through Lower Manhattan: just after four o'clock on the afternoon of Saturday, January 6, 1872, "Jubilee Jim" Fisk Jr., the roguish stock speculator and robber baron, had been gunned down at the Grand Central Hotel, the largest in America and among the most luxurious. His assailant was his erstwhile business partner turned archenemy, Edward "Ned" Stokes, a rival for the affections of Fisk's mistress, a voluptuous failed actress named Josephine Mansfield, better known as Josie.

The hotel, located at the corner of Broadway and Amity Street (now West Third), fell within Byrnes's jurisdiction—the Fifteenth Precinct—of which he had been made captain two years earlier. It was a mixed but mostly respectable neighborhood encompassing Greenwich Village and parts of the East Village.

Byrnes raced to the Fifteenth Precinct station house on Mercer Street, where he found Stokes already in custody. At just under six feet tall, broad-shouldered, with piercing, almost frightening eyes and a flowing walrus mustache, the thirty-year-old Byrnes cut an imposing figure. He sought to interrogate the prisoner, but the slender, handsome, impeccably dressed Stokes, the same age as the captain, would answer no questions beyond giving his name. Byrnes ordered him placed in a cell and left the station for the crime scene, less than a block away, arriving there about 4:20 P.M.

As Byrnes reached the second-floor hotel suite where Fisk lay dying, details of the incident began emerging. The adversarial relationship between Fisk and Stokes was already well known to the public and was blaring daily from newspaper front pages: once business partners in a Brooklyn oil refinery, they became enemies when Fisk ousted Stokes over a charge of embezzlement. In the meantime, the married Stokes had entered into an illicit relationship with the twenty-four-year-old divorcee Josie Mansfield, who preferred him to her rich benefactor.

The older (thirty-seven), short, rotund, cherubic-faced Fisk held little appeal for the "Cleopatra of Twenty-Third Street" beyond the money, jewelry, and Chelsea brownstone he had lavished upon her. Virtually all the largesse Fisk amassed was a product of unscrupulous business dealings. Together with his financial partner Jay Gould, Fisk had employed stock manipulation and bribery to wrest control of the Erie Railroad from Cornelius Vanderbilt, the Commodore, a few years earlier. Fisk then used his political connections with the notorious Boss Tweed, head of New York's corrupt Tammany Hall machine, to gain favors—and buy judges—to further the Erie's interests. In 1869 Fisk and Gould infamously cornered the market on gold during a financial panic, known as Black Friday, that ruined many investors, scandalized the administration of President Ulysses S. Grant, and enriched Gould and Fisk.

Unlike the dour Gould, Fisk wore his wealth on his sleeve, dressing ostentatiously in colorful velvets and silks and adorning his fingers with large diamonds. He sported a finely waxed red mustache. For vanity's sake, he underwrote a New York state militia regiment and had himself elected colonel.

Ruthless in pursuit of his enemies, Fisk publicly accused Stokes and Mansfield of blackmail when they conspired to give the newspapers the love letters he had written Josie before she jilted him—letters that the couple said would reveal Fisk's many past financial improprieties. Mansfield sued him for $50,000 for money she claimed he owed her and for libel, prompting Fisk to countersue. He also used his influence to procure a grand jury indictment of Stokes for extortion.

Earlier on the day of the shooting, Mansfield and Stokes had appeared in court to testify in her suit against Fisk, who did not attend. After a withering cross-examination, Mansfield broke down in sobs, but Stokes held his own and afterward went to Delmonico's, the city's most fashionable restaurant, for a late lunch of oysters and beer with his lawyers.

Stokes's good mood changed when he learned of the grand jury indictment. Enraged, Stokes hired a carriage to help him track down his antagonist. He stopped first at Fisk's Erie Railroad office in the Grand Opera-house at Twenty-Third Street and Eighth Avenue. Upon learning that Fisk had gone to the Grand Central Hotel to visit friends, Stokes had his driver take him there.

Stokes combed the hotel in search of Fisk but did not find him. Then, as Stokes stood on the landing of the ladies' staircase, he saw Fisk ascending the stairs below. At point-blank range from about five stairsteps above, Stokes shot Fisk twice with a newly manufactured, four-chamber Colt House revolver; it was destined to become known as the Jim Fisk pistol. The first bullet pierced Fisk's abdomen, and the second struck him in the arm. He turned away and tumbled down the stairs. Doctors quickly concluded that the stomach wound was mortal.

After finishing the deed, Stokes flung away his gun and looked to make his escape. A hotel doorman and bellboy had witnessed the shooting, while other onlookers heard the shots and saw Stokes take flight. When the hotel proprietor called out, "Stop that man!" Stokes ran downstairs to the hotel barbershop. He slipped and fell on the shop's marble floor and was overcome by several men, including some guests who leapt from their barber chairs with lather and towels still covering their faces.

NEW YORK CITY.—ASSASSINATION OF COLONEL JAMES FISK, JR., BY EDWARD S. STOKES, AT THE GRAND CENTRAL HOTEL—THE SCENE OF THE TRAGEDY—SEE PAGE 227.

The 1872 murder of financier and robber baron Jim Fisk Jr. by Ned Stokes, on a stairway in the luxurious Grand Central Hotel in Greenwich Village, as depicted in *Frank Leslie's Illustrated Newspaper*. The case brought the first public attention to investigating officer Thomas Byrnes, then a young police captain.

The arresting officer on the scene was Henry McCadden, one of Byrnes's Fifteenth Precinct patrolmen. Informed by hotel employees that Stokes was the shooter, McCadden took the prisoner up to the victim's suite, where Fisk was surrounded by doctors and friends such as Gould and Boss Tweed.

McCadden asked Fisk whether Stokes was the man who shot him, to which Fisk responded affirmatively. The *New York Herald* misidentified McCadden as Byrnes and spelled his name as "Burns," a reflection of how little known Byrnes was at the time.

When Byrnes got to the hotel a few minutes after McCadden, he took control of the investigation and began questioning witnesses. Per common practice at the time, he had them arrested and held at the station house until they could make their statements. Byrnes spent the next several hours shuttling back and forth between the hotel and the precinct station, a two-minute walk from one to the other. In his cell, Stokes asked for some cigars, and being a chain cigar smoker himself, Byrnes indulged the prisoner's request. Stokes lit cigar after cigar and smoked furiously, flinging them away one by one.

At the station around seven o'clock, Byrnes was told that Fisk was not going to survive. Although witnesses had orally identified Stokes as the assailant—and Fisk had as well—Byrnes thought it important to obtain a written statement from Fisk before he died. Courts demanded the strongest of evidence to convict one of murder in those days, when the death penalty beckoned. Byrnes therefore summoned the city coroner, who customarily recorded the victim's "antemortem" statements, and took him to the hotel, where an informal jury of hotel residents was impaneled to hear Fisk's testimony. Fisk attested that Stokes was the man who shot him.*

Around the same time, a hotel clerk gave Byrnes the Colt revolver that a female guest had found on a sofa in the women's parlor. Byrnes

---

* Coroners in nineteenth-century New York were quasi-judicial elected officers (not necessarily medical doctors) who were the only officials who could first touch the remains of a homicide victim. In addition

placed a mark on it so it could be identified later at trial and showed the gun to several people in the hotel to impress it upon their memories. He also retrieved a bullet that was found on the stairs and matched it to the Colt pistol. "Matched" is probably an overstatement, though, since forensic ballistics did not yet exist. A law enforcement officer could eyeball a bullet from a crime scene and say whether, in general, it could have come from the type of firearm found there, but there was no way to determine definitively that *this* bullet was fired from *that* gun.

Fisk died the next morning at ten forty-five and, despite his widespread reputation as a crook, was mourned by thousands. Byrnes took possession of the body pending the coroner's arrival. He then transported Stokes from the precinct station cell to the Tombs, the notoriously dank jail and court complex built in the Egyptian style over a poorly drained swamp pond that previously had served as the city's main water supply. On the way over, Byrnes rejected Stokes's request that they stop for a drink at a bar.

Stokes was held at the Tombs pending his trial for murder, at which Byrnes testified about the arrest, the gun and bullets, and Fisk's antemortem statement. Stokes's lawyers presented three theories: that he acted in self-defense, believing Fisk would shoot him first; that Fisk died due to poor medical treatment; and that Stokes was temporarily insane. Although Stokes claimed Fisk had a gun, no other witness had seen him with one, and Byrnes testified that a thorough search of the premises had found no such second weapon.

The first trial ended with a hung jury, and the second produced a first-degree murder conviction, for which Stokes was sentenced to be hanged. But the conviction was overturned on appeal due to a technicality: a new witness came forward to claim—falsely—that he had seen a gun in Fisk's hands. In the third trial, the jury compromised on a verdict of third-degree manslaughter, and Stokes was sentenced to four years in state prison.

---

to performing autopsies with the aid of a coroner's physician, coroners conducted inquests, assisted by a jury, into the causes of suspicious deaths.

The notorious Tombs prison complex in Lower Manhattan, where criminals were held pending trial and condemned prisoners walked to the gallows across the "Bridge of Sighs."

Jim Fisk was the most famous private citizen murdered in American history to that point; as an assassination, its notoriety was exceeded only by Abraham Lincoln's seven years earlier. And although Thomas Byrnes's role in the affair was modest—Stokes was identified and in custody before Byrnes was at the scene—it did bring him public notice for the first time.

Four months after the murder, the still relatively unknown Byrnes was back in the papers. On May 24, 1872, one of his detectives, William Henderson, was shot and nearly killed by a man he was in the process of arresting just outside the Mercer Street station. Cop killers were hunted down by men in blue as relentlessly then as now, so when the assailant, Robert Crawford—who happened to be the brother-in-law of Commodore Vanderbilt—fled the scene and hid out in Vanderbilt's home, Byrnes personally led a posse of his men to apprehend him. They found all entrances to the Commodore's massive redbrick mansion at 10 Washington Place barred and the inhabitants denying that Crawford was concealed there.

Though not in possession of a warrant, Byrnes obtained police chief James Kelso's permission to forcibly enter the Commodore's edifice if he was satisfied the fugitive was hiding in there. After Byrnes told Vanderbilt he was prepared to break down every door if necessary and search the entire premises, Crawford was produced and taken into custody.

The next day, Byrnes arrested Paul Lowe, the twenty-two-year-old son of the ex-governor of Maryland, for shooting three men, including one of his own friends, in a Saturday-night melee on Mercer Street. After interviewing several of those involved, Byrnes tracked down Lowe, who was preparing to escape to Maryland, and obtained his confession.

A month later, Byrnes was in the headlines again, praised for quickly solving the burglary of the Van Tine silk manufacturing company just below Union Square. Acting on a tip, Byrnes and Detective Henderson, since recuperated from his shooting, staked out a pair of locations on Wooster Street and arrested coachmen carrying trunks of stolen silk dresses and ladies' apparel. All $4,000 worth of the pilfered goods was recovered. This time, in its report on the incident, the *New York Herald* got Byrnes's name right. It would not be misspelled again.

⊷⊱⫶⊜⫶⊰⊷

CHAPTER TWO

A COP IS BORN

O r maybe the *New York Herald* had gotten Byrnes's name half right the first time. The future star policeman was born on June 15, 1842, in County Wicklow, Ireland, just south of Dublin, the youngest of three sons of a man listed as William "Burns" in census records and city directories.

William Burns was born in Ireland between 1805 and 1810 and married Rose Doyle, a woman the same age or a little younger. They emigrated with their three sons to America in 1845, crossing the Atlantic on the freight and passenger ship *Yorkshire*, in steerage, with the toddler Thomas on board. The family of five thereby joined the multitudes of fellow countrymen who left their native land in the wake of the great Irish potato famine. Three daughters would follow, all born in New York between 1845 and 1852.

Contrary to the only biography of Thomas Byrnes, which heavily fictionalizes his early years, his parents were not named James and Ellen; they did not settle in the fetid Five Points neighborhood of Lower

Manhattan, the worst slum in America;* his mother was not a laundress; and his father was not a garment worker and labor agitator who became a drunken bartender and left the family. Byrnes did not have a younger brother, Deven, who died of cholera at age twelve, nor did one of his sisters hold on to her job as a housemaid "by giving in to the sexual demands of the master of the house." There was no kindly Father Coogan of St. Patrick's Cathedral, then located on the Lower East Side, who provided comfort and support to the family.

The reality is less sentimental. William Burns, a laborer and porter, moved his family into the old Fifth Ward of Manhattan adjoining the Hudson River, the area now known as Tribeca. Though far from the fashionable neighborhood of expensive lofts and fine restaurants it would become a century and a half later, it was not a place of squalor. Rather, it was transforming from a primarily residential area to a center for textiles and dry goods, buoyed by the growing shipping business along the Hudson River piers. The Washington Market at Chambers Street was the city's premier open-air venue for wholesale produce.

In 1855 the Burnses were living with five other families in a five-story brick dwelling at 30 Jay Street, near the original warehouse headquarters of the American Express Company, then an express mail and package delivery service. All thirty-seven of the inhabitants, including the eight Burns family members, were either born in Ireland or were of Irish parentage. By that time, 25 percent of the city's population of six hundred thousand were Irish-born, and more Irish lived in Manhattan than in any city in the world except Dublin. Viewed by many as rowdy drunkards, the Irish faced severe discrimination.

Any family of eight would have felt crowded and without privacy in what were three or at most four rooms, some of them windowless.

---

* So named because the convergence of Orange Street (now Baxter Street), Cross Street (later Park Street, now Mosco Street), and Anthony Street (now Worth Street) created a five-cornered intersection. The area, today including Columbus Park in Chinatown, is adjacent to the Daniel Patrick Moynihan US Courthouse at 500 Pearl Street.

Almost certainly the Burnses lacked running water; at best, they may have had access to a nearby tap connected to the relatively new Croton Aqueduct reservoir at Forty-Second Street and Fifth Avenue, where the main branch of the New York Public Library and Bryant Park now stand. But indoor toilets in such tenement houses were still years away. Lacking central heating, the buildings were cold and damp in winter, while they baked during New York's hot, humid summers.

The Burnses counted themselves among the working poor. Yet the conditions they faced were not as dire as those in the worst tenements in the city. In the Five Points and similar enclaves, the population density was rivaled only by that in the poorer sections of London. More than a hundred people were commonly crammed into 24 two-room apartments in wobbly wooden structures. One five-story brick tenement house along the East River, the notorious Gotham Court at 38 Cherry Street, had 112 families and up to 800 people living in its 120 two-room apartments.

By 1860, the Burnses had moved just around the corner to 10 Caroline Street, a short lane running between Duane and Jay Streets that no longer exists. There, five families totaling twenty-eight people—twenty-three Irish and five German—lived in a three-story frame house with stores below it.

Now eighteen, Thomas had managed to find employment as a gas fitter, helping light the city's lamps in the age before electricity. A trade job that paid more than what menial workers earned, it required extreme care and attention due to the ever-present risk of explosion.

Typical of many Irish youths, Thomas also became a volunteer firefighter in his neighborhood. (New York had no city fire department until 1865.) The volunteer fire companies were essentially fraternal organizations, formed as much upon ethnic ties and local camaraderie as out of civic devotion; often, as with Boss Tweed, they served as springboards into politics. The companies were popular hangouts for gangs, and rivalries were so intense that sometimes buildings would burn down while the companies who had raced to get there first tenaciously fought each other for the right to extinguish the blaze.

It was likely through their volunteer activities that both Byrnes and his oldest brother, Edward, a fire engine company foreman before the Civil War, came to enlist in the famous New York Zouaves shortly after the fall of Fort Sumter in April 1861. Officially the First New York Fire Zouaves, Ellsworth's Zouaves, as they were known, were a volunteer infantry regiment organized at the outset of the war by the dashing, idealistic Colonel Elmer Ephraim Ellsworth, a young Illinois lawyer who had clerked for and befriended Abraham Lincoln back in Springfield.

The Zouaves were drawn from the ranks of the city's many volunteer firefighters, who were viewed as tough and hardy adventurers well suited to military service. Flashily dressed to resemble the French colonial light infantrymen serving in Algeria, and to distinguish them from ordinary bluecoats, the Zouaves were issued bright-red firemen's shirts and red fezzes with blue tassels, along with light gray French-style chasseur jackets with dark blue and red trim, colorful blue sashes, and baggy gray cloth pants with a blue stripe.

But the Zouaves lost their popular namesake commander on May 24, 1861, when Ellsworth was killed while descending the stairs of an Alexandria, Virginia, hotel after removing a Confederate flag that had been flying from the building's rooftop. The hotel proprietor, an ardent secessionist, blasted him in the chest with a shotgun. The martyred Ellsworth's body lay in state in the White House, then was taken to city hall in New York, where thousands of supporters came to see the first Union officer killed in the war.

Because the Zouaves were already camped and drilling in Washington, D.C., it is unlikely that twenty-three-year-old Edward Byrnes, the elected head of Ellsworth's Company B, or his younger brother Thomas, a member of that unit, were among the mourners at city hall. But they were with the Zouaves who carried the rallying cry "Remember Ellsworth!" into the First Battle of Bull Run, at Manassas, Virginia, on July 21, 1861, just two months after his death. After boldly advancing, they were routed by the Confederates, led by, among others, Stonewall Jackson and Jeb Stuart, after which the Zouaves turned and ran, having suffered more casualties than any other Union regiment. Many years later, Byrnes admitted with a smile that he had run as fast as anybody that day.

The demoralized Zouaves, scapegoated and ridiculed in the press, were eventually sent back to New York in June 1862 and mustered out of service. Thomas Byrnes, now twenty, returned to volunteer firefighting with the Hudson Hose Company No. 21, headquartered at 304 Washington Street. He participated eagerly in the "scrimmages" between rival companies, and in one such fracas put the future president of the paid fire department, Cornelius Van Cott, out of commission. As Van Cott recalled later when chatting with then police chief Byrnes about the old days, he had been decked by a lanky, black-mustached fellow of the rival company, prompting Byrnes to confess that it had been him.

Byrnes left the fire company when, on December 10, 1863, he was appointed to the New York Metropolitan Police Department as a patrolman in the Fifteenth Precinct. It was a coveted job, notwithstanding that a police officer's hours were long: sixteen-hour days split between patrol and reserve duty, with hundred-hour weeks not uncommon. The station house was the officer's home away from home, where he slept along with hundreds of homeless vagrants who routinely received shelter elsewhere in the same building. A later cop, Cornelius Willemse, would memorably describe "on reserve" living conditions under the two-platoon system:

> Picture a great barracks of a room twenty-five by forty feet, with only two windows in the front for ventilation. In the winter time there was no heat except a big pot-bellied stove downstairs in the back room, the windows were kept closed, and with thirty men sleeping there, their thirty pairs of shoes and boots, well-worn socks, none too clean, damp cloths hanging along the walls beside every bed, roaches and bedbugs by the million, fetid air, thick with smoke combined with body odors. . . . In the summer it was equally vile, for the uniforms were hot and the sun was blistering, and we

didn't have electric fans to air the place out. . . . The Board of Health would not have tolerated such conditions in cheap lodging houses, nor would prison supervisors have stood for them in jails.

The work could also be stressful. But the pay was good. A patrolman in 1864 made $1,000 a year, and in 1866 the salary went up to $1,200, where it remained for many years. Although less than the $2,000 average salary for New York's middle-class, white-collar employees, it was somewhat more than what skilled manual workers made. And it was almost double what Byrnes's father, as a common unskilled laborer, could expect to earn. Applicants for police positions always exceeded the number of openings.

Just past the age of majority, Thomas Byrnes had already made good in the New World. But the police department he joined had a checkered, inglorious history, marked by inefficiency, instability, and ineffectiveness.

The New York Municipal Police Department, as it was called originally, was established in 1845 as the city's first full-time paid police force and is among the nation's oldest. It was a military-style organization with hierarchical ranks (captain, sergeant, patrolman) and career officers.

Modeled on London's beat system, which stressed patrolling by day and night, the Municipal Police Department replaced the old constable system, which consisted of part-time civilian night watchmen and a small full-time force of elected and appointed constables and marshals. The amateur watchmen, known as "leatherheads" for their helmet material, were paid a small daily stipend and had no authority beyond making citizens' arrests. Constables had full police power but were unsalaried; they worked for fees and privately offered rewards.

In theory, the change to a salaried, full-time force augured a more professional outfit. But while the new department was an improvement over the old system, its performance did not live up to expectations. For one thing, it took nearly a decade for the Municipals to agree to wear uniforms, which offended their sense of independence. Uniforms were considered emblems of a servant class or a standing army. The early police were issued only a star-shaped copper badge, which they could wear or conceal as they pleased.* It was not until 1853 that the Municipals were persuaded that blue frock coats with brass buttons not only created an impressive look but also made it easier for them to be identified by the public, and by one another, at crime scenes.

Uniformed or not, the Municipals had difficulty coping with the city's rising immigrant population and crime in the pre–Civil War years. Unlike the London force, the New York police were under local, rather than national, government control, and were appointed by elected ward aldermen. Police officers' terms were limited to one or two years; as a result, politics played a greater role in the selection and retention of cops than did merit. (In 1853 employment became continuous, subject to the usual firing for just cause or bad behavior.) And with no physical or medical requirements or age restrictions, many police officers were too old or infirm for the work.

The roughly thousand-man force in the mid-1850s was also short-handed, relative to London, which had more than twice as many bobbies per inhabitant and a more homogenous, less unruly populace to control. Absenteeism and graft within the New York force were common. And, as under the old constable system, it was hard for civilians to induce police officers to investigate thefts or seek to recover stolen property without the promise of a substantial reward. Detectives would end up splitting the reward money with the thieves and their criminal "fences," who returned the stolen goods in exchange for immunity from prosecution. It was an arrangement that compounded the original crime instead of curbing it.

The uptown propertied classes, consisting of old-line New York Anglo-Saxon Protestants, came to view the increasingly Irish police force with suspicion. Rural upstate New Yorkers and adherents of the anti-immigrant,

---

* Whether the badge was the origin of the term "coppers" or "cops" as applied to police officers is unsettled; "copper" as slang for a policeman appears in print as early as the 1846 *Oxford English Dictionary*, likely based on the verb "to cop," derived from the French *caper* and the Latin *capere*, meaning to seize or capture.

anti-Catholic American Party (better known as the "Know Nothings") also distrusted the immigrant-heavy force. By the mid-1850s, almost two-thirds of the cops in the "Bloody Sixth" Ward, home to the Five Points, were Irish.

The Irish police were seen as cronies of Tammany Hall, the city's Democratic political machine, and its controversial partisan mayor, Fernando Wood, who used patronage to control the police and the immigrant vote. Blue-blooded Knickerbockers believed that Wood's Municipal Police were unwilling to crack down on gambling, prostitution, and drinking for fear of antagonizing the Catholic, foreign-born, Democratic dwellers of Lower Manhattan.

It did not help when, in 1855, the nativist brawler William "Bill the Butcher" Poole (the character played by Daniel Day-Lewis in the 2002 Martin Scorsese film *Gangs of New York*) was shot and killed in a saloon by an Irish ex-cop. "I die a true American" were Poole's famous last words, a not-so-subtle jab at aliens. The martyred Poole's funeral was the largest in New York to that point. Mayor Wood's police department was lax in pursuing Poole's killer, who was eventually discharged after three straight hung juries. Native New Yorkers were further convinced that the Municipals were in the pocket of the Irish Tammany clique.

Matters came to a head in 1857 when the new Republican, rural-dominated legislature in the state capital of Albany abolished the city's Tammany-dominated Municipal Police Department and replaced it with a revamped Metropolitan Department. It was now to cover an enlarged area including New York City, Brooklyn, Staten Island, and Westchester County. The Metropolitans were placed under the control of a civilian board of police commissioners appointed by the Republican governor.

Mayor Wood refused to recognize the authority of the new department. He perceived it as merely designed to transfer patronage from one political party to the other. On June 16 he famously rejected an arrest warrant served on him at city hall by police captain George Walling, a former Municipal who had gone over to the Metropolitan camp. (Walling would later serve as police superintendent, the name for the chief of police in those days.)

After Walling tried to forcibly remove Wood from the building, rioting broke out on the steps of city hall between more than three hundred Municipals stationed there—mostly foreign-born cops loyal to Wood— and fifty outnumbered Metropolitans, largely Anglo-American in origin, who had arrived to assist Walling. Many Metros were severely beaten and injured. Only the fortuitous intervention of New York's Seventh Regiment National Guards (state militia), who had been parading down Broadway en route to a boat bound for Boston, managed to restore order.

For the next several weeks, as Wood remained defiant, the rival police forces let criminals escape as they vied for the right to arrest them, much

New York's earliest police force had an unpromising start. In 1857, rival groups of policemen—Municipals and Metropolitans—battled one another on the steps of city hall in a contest for authority. In the ensuing confusion, the city's downtown gangs went on a bloody spree, known as the Dead Rabbits Riot, that police were powerless to quell.

as competing fire companies fought for the privilege to put out flames. Then, after New York's highest court upheld the constitutionality of the Metropolitan police force on July 2, 1857, Wood finally acquiesced and disbanded the Municipal Police Department.

During the confusion, the city's criminal elements went on a spree. It started with a Fourth of July barroom raid by the Irish Dead Rabbits gang of the Five Points (the Leonardo DiCaprio group from the Scorsese film, and supporters of Mayor Wood). They attacked the clubhouse of two nativist gangs at 42 Bowery: the Atlantic Guards and the Bowery Boys (or "B'hoys"). The latter had been affiliated with Bill the Butcher and now sided with the Metropolitans. At least, that was according to initial newspaper reports and *Gangs of New York* author Herbert Asbury, whose seminal 1928 book often prefers myth to fact.

Other accounts hold that the principal antagonists of the Bowery gangs were not the Dead Rabbits but a different Five Points gang called the Roach (or Roche) Guards, of which the Dead Rabbits were an offshoot. Some indignant letter writers to the newspapers claimed the Dead Rabbits no longer even existed.

Whatever their true identities, the Irish Five Points gang started things off by invading the Bowery area and attacking some of the new Metropolitan police, perceiving them to be anti-Catholic nativists. The nativist Bowery gangs came to the Metros' defense, and general mayhem ensued, spreading to other downtown areas where gangs took the opportunity to loot and vandalize. Amid the chaos, it was often impossible to tell who was fighting whom. At times, rival Irish gangs—political enemies—battled one another until the Metropolitan Police arrived, whereupon the belligerents dropped their private feud and turned on the authorities.

The most violent scenes took place around Bayard, Mott, Mulberry, and Elizabeth Streets, where the Five Pointers pummeled and bloodied any Metro they could spot. Men, women, and children sympathetic to the Irish gangs poured a fusillade of objects—bricks, stones, pots, and kettles—down upon the helpless police. The Bowery gangs pulled out pistols and rifles and shot a number of Rabbits/Roach Guards.

The inexperienced and outnumbered Metros were unable to quell the violence. The old Municipals, who previously had kept order in the area and knew the local Irish gangs, were out of commission and unwilling to help. There were even reports that they encouraged the mob to resist the Metros. Accounts differ on whether the militia finally stopped the riots or whether the gangs simply ran out of gas.

The official toll in the Dead Rabbits Riot, as it came to be known, was eight to twelve dead and between thirty and forty wounded. But many believed casualties were much higher because the Five Points gang buried its dead in secret alleyways and ramshackle tenement basements. The one certainty is that the Metropolitan Police Department, in its first major test, had utterly failed to keep the city safe.

It was another riot six years later, this one the bloodiest and most violent in the nation's history, that began the rehabilitation of the New York Police Department's reputation. It started on a sweltering and breezeless July 13, 1863, sparked by antagonism toward the draft lottery conducted under the new military conscription law passed by Congress. Angry mobs of poor and working-class New Yorkers, most of them Irish immigrants, took to the streets to protest. They resented being forced to fight a war to free black men who might compete for their unskilled labor jobs, while wealthy white men could pay $300 to avoid the draft.

Eventually swelling to fifteen thousand, the crowd burned and smashed the windows of the draft office and many other buildings and churches symbolizing the establishment, as well as the private homes of police officials, Republican politicians, and the rich. The offices of newspapers that supported the war came under siege and had to be barricaded. The rioters ripped up streetcar and train tracks and cut telegraph lines to prevent police communication.

Any living thing—cop, soldier, horse—standing in the mob's way was mercilessly attacked. Upon recognizing the sixty-year-old head of the police, Superintendent John Kennedy, one of the rioters shouted, "There's Kennedy!" He was beaten and trampled into a "mass of gore" and dumped in a deep mudhole, left for dead until a friend rescued his limp body.

The violence soon turned into a race riot. African Americans were tortured, lynched, burned, and dragged through the streets. At the Colored Orphan Asylum at Fifth Avenue and Forty-Third Street, home to two hundred children under the age of twelve, the mob set the building on fire and obstructed volunteer firefighters who sought in vain to tame the blaze. The terrified children somehow managed to escape out the back door; according to *The New York Times*, it was a young Irishman named Paddy McCaffrey, who was either one of the firemen or a coach driver, who escorted them to safety.

The children were brought—the smaller ones upon the backs of the larger—to Captain George Walling's Twentieth Precinct station house at Thirty-Fifth Street and Eighth Avenue. Walling, who seemingly was everywhere throughout the four-day riot and would be hailed as one of its heroes, ensured their protection at his station. At length, they were conveyed to a temporary refuge on Blackwell's (now Roosevelt) Island, then the site of a prison and insane asylum complex.

With the state militia having been sent to aid the Union army at the Battle of Gettysburg, the roughly two-thousand-man Metropolitan police force (which had since absorbed or reinstated many former Municipals) was left to handle the riot on its own. And, as in the Dead Rabbits Riot, the police were hopelessly outnumbered. Unlike in 1857, though, when they yielded to the mob, this time the cops carried the fight to the rioters. Small groups of policemen, strategically deployed against much larger mobs, fought the rioters in pitched battles. And as Walling recalled, whenever the police and the mob came into one-on-one contact, the police were victorious.

It took the return of the Seventh Regiment from Gettysburg, and thousands of federal troops who followed, to end the unrest on the fourth day. More than a hundred civilians had been left dead, countless injured, and millions of dollars in property destroyed. But the police came in for high praise, including the many Irish cops who had had risked their lives to protect the city from their Irish brethren. For perhaps the first time, New Yorkers had a police department of which they could be proud.

It is possible that Thomas Byrnes played a role in the draft riots. The New York Zouaves, who had been partially reconstituted in May 1863, assisted the police and military in suppressing the rioters. The Zouaves' new colonel, Henry O'Brien, was among those murdered, tortured, and hanged from lampposts by the mob. Afterward, the Ellsworth Zouaves broke up for good.

There is no documentation, though, of Byrnes's participation, if any, in the July 1863 riots. In any event, he did not engage in the heroics credited to him by his biographer, who claims it was Byrnes who, as a New York police officer, rescued Superintendent Kennedy from the mudhole, as well as a uniformed Byrnes who, at gunpoint, led the poor, frightened children of the Colored Orphan Asylum to Captain Walling's police station. In this telling, Byrnes is also supposed to have joined with several other police officers who stormed a barricaded house on Thirty-First Street and forced the rioters inside to surrender. These would have been neat tricks, considering that Byrnes did not join the police force until December 1863.

⋆⇒◯ ◯⇐⋆

Byrnes rose quickly through the police ranks. Soon after being assigned to patrol duty in the Fifteenth Precinct, he was transferred to the Third Precinct, its station house, at 160 Chambers Street, a three-minute walk from where the young single policeman lived at 328 Greenwich Street. Now, if not before, he was spelling his name "Byrnes," and it seems that his parents, William and Rose Burns, died around this time.

In October 1868 Byrnes was made a roundsman in the Third Precinct. It was a supervisory position, in the nature of a spy, who checked up on patrolmen to make sure they were at their posts. The roundsman had the authority to "dido" (write up) his colleagues for disciplinary charges.

Byrnes held this rather unpopular job for about a year before he was promoted to sergeant in 1869. Less than a year later, on July 1, 1870, he was made a captain, the next rung up the ladder. (The rank of lieutenant did not exist then, sergeants serving as the rough equivalent.) New York police officers seldom became captains before the age of thirty; Byrnes was twenty-eight.

The department's thirty-some captains, one for each precinct, reigned supreme in their jurisdictions. Given their vast discretionary power to enforce the laws (or not) as they saw fit, they enjoyed greater power, within their realms, than their boss—the superintendent of police. Four inspectors (one for each of four inspection districts) ranked higher than the captains, but the captains exercised almost limitless day-to-day authority in their respective precincts.

In 1870, the same year Byrnes became a captain, home rule over the police force was reestablished. With the Democrats back in power in Albany, Boss Tweed pushed through a new city charter restoring control of the police to New York City proper (soon to include the West Bronx), with Brooklyn, Staten Island, and other surrounding areas to have their own municipal police departments. The thirteen-year experiment in state control was over.

The renamed Police Department of the City of New York was governed by a bipartisan four-person board of commissioners appointed by the mayor. By custom, the four police commissioners were split evenly between Democrats and Republicans. In fact, the commissioners were responsive to the political machines of the respective parties and were subservient to them, not to the public at large. And the two Republican members, because they were generally appointed by Democratic mayors, tended to be Tammany friendly or at least Democratic friendly. (During these years, Tammany vied for control with some rival, reform-minded Democratic factions that helped expose Tweed's corruption in 1871.)

In addition to possessing overall supervisory authority over the police department, the commissioners had the power to appoint, promote, transfer, discipline, or dismiss police officers. Per custom, each commissioner had a quota of patronage appointments reserved for him. Typically, patronage was dispensed on the recommendation or approval of local politicians.

Byrnes began his captaincy in the lightly populated Twenty-Third Precinct, covering Yorkville and the far Upper East Side, then was soon transferred to the more stimulating Twenty-First. Running from Twenty-Sixth to Forty-Second Streets on the East Side, it included luxurious mansions along Park Avenue and squalor and petty crime nearer the East River.

It was while captaining the Twenty-First Precinct in 1871 that Byrnes received his first big test. In July, Protestants from Northern Ireland, so-called Orangemen, paraded down Eighth Avenue under police and state militia escort, jeered and hissed at by Irish Catholics who lined the streets. Five hundred New York police officers under the command of Inspector George Walling, and thirteen precinct captains, including Byrnes of the Twenty-First, were on hand to clear the street for the marchers.

When the procession reached Twenty-Fourth Street, someone fired a shot at the parade from a second-story window along the route and struck a member of the Eighty-Fourth Militia Regiment. Acting without orders, panicked members of the militia returned volleys in that direction. When the smoke lifted, eleven corpses lay on the sidewalk.

In all, more than sixty civilians were killed or fatally wounded that day, at least a hundred civilians and fifty police officers and militia were injured, and three guardsmen died. At the Sixteenth Precinct station house on West Twentieth Street, thirteen bodies were found in the hall, among them a girl of about twelve who had entered the street at the sound of drums beating and the sight of flags waving. She was struck in the head with a ball, killing her instantly.

One of the militiamen killed was the business manager of Jim Fisk's opera house. He fell at Twenty-Sixth Street while standing next to Fisk, who nominally commanded the Ninth Militia Regiment he had bought for himself. Fisk was knocked down by the mob, injured his ankle, and was rescued in a carriage by his business partner Jay Gould. Fisk escaped death that day, but it would find him six months later at the hands of Ned Stokes.

It became known as the Slaughter on Eighth Avenue. Many New Yorkers criticized government officials for calling out hundreds of armed police and militia to protect a trivial little parade. But the police—as opposed to the trigger-happy militia—were generally commended for guarding the marchers' freedom of religion and assembly. "The Police were the admiration of all law-and-order-loving citizens," wrote *The New York Times*, which listed Byrnes and a dozen other captains as among those to whom honor was due.

The faithfulness of the Irish Catholic police to their duty was especially noted. "To defend Protestant Irishmen against Roman Catholic friends and perhaps relatives is a severe test of fidelity," wrote one contemporary chronicler, "but the Irish police have stood it nobly."

After the Fisk murder the following year, Byrnes remained captain of the Fifteenth Precinct until 1874, when he was detailed to the Twenty-Fifth Precinct, known as the Broadway Squad. It directed traffic, an important function in an age before traffic lights or even rules. It also protected pedestrians along the fashionable Ladies' Mile shopping district, home to grand department stores such as Lord & Taylor and A. T. Stewart's Cast Iron Palace. Members of the specially picked Broadway Squad were all over six feet tall, "well proportioned . . . generally handsome" and "always polite to the ladies—especially to those who are young and pretty," observed *Harper's Weekly*.

Perhaps that is how Byrnes met his wife, for in 1875 he married twenty-three-year-old Ophelia Jennings, ten years his junior, the New York–born daughter of a Varick Street bartender. The newlyweds set up home on Greenwich Street near Trinity Church and the following year had the first of their five children, all daughters.

In 1876 Byrnes was back to captaining the Fifteenth Precinct. He

pursued and arrested sundry small-time burglars, swindlers, and embez-
zlers, conducted occasional raids on gambling houses and brothels, and
was considered, but passed over, for promotion to inspector. He was a
competent and efficient administrator and investigator, but there was
nothing especially noteworthy about his tenure. At least until October
1878, when he was handed the case of a lifetime.

-⊷⊶⊙⊶⊷-

CHAPTER THREE

HEIST OF THE CENTURY

Thomas Byrnes was still in his Sunday best on the morning of October 27, 1878, when he heard that the Manhattan Savings Institution had been robbed. It was unimaginable that this venerable bank, located at the corner of Bleecker Street and Broadway, within Byrnes's own Fifteenth Precinct, had been breached. Thought to be an impregnable fortress, it featured a maze of bolts, locks, and thick steel doors that opened to a steel vault with a separate safe within. In addition to holding millions in cash and securities, the bank was a repository for the money, jewelry, and other valuables of wealthy New Yorkers.

Just as astonishing was the reported haul: nearly $3 million in securities and cash, equivalent to $70 million in 2021 dollars. It was, and remains, the greatest bank robbery in the city's history.* Conducted during daylight, it was also, opined *The New York Times*, the most audacious.

---

* According to the website WorldAtlas, only 1972's $27 million robbery of New York's Pierre Hotel, equivalent to $160 million in 2021, and that same year's $30 million robbery of the United California Bank in Laguna Niguel, worth $180 million in equivalent dollars, rank higher in American history.

When newspapers, in subsequent months, referred in headlines to "The Great Bank Robbery," no one needed to be told what that meant.

Byrnes arrived at the scene around eleven, along with his boss, George Walling, who'd been promoted from inspector to police superintendent in 1874. Byrnes personally took charge of the investigation. The first witness he questioned was the bank's janitor, fifty-year-old Louis Werckle, a German immigrant and "little old man," as the *Times* described him, who had worked at the bank for twenty years.

Just before ten in the morning, Werckle had burst into the barbershop in the bank's basement and shouted out that the bank had been robbed. The barber then ran to police headquarters on Mulberry Street to report the crime.

Listening to the excited janitor's story, Byrnes was, by contrast, the very picture of self-confidence. A man of military bearing, he wore an expensive, dark cutaway coat, tie, and wide-brimmed derby, and puffed constantly on an ever-present cigar.

Janitor Werckle, who lived in a second-floor apartment above the bank, told Byrnes that just after six in the morning, a group of masked robbers in business suits entered his apartment and bound and gagged him, his sickly wife, and his feeble mother-in-law. They forced him at gunpoint to give them the combination to the bank's outer vault door (30-9-25) and threatened to return and kill him if he gave them the wrong numbers. Then they took the keys to the bank's entrance that were laying on Werckle's table and let themselves into the lobby.

Inside the bank, the burglars opened the vault doors with the combination and confronted the steel safe. Using jimmies and wedges, they ratcheted the safe door open and sledgehammered and chiseled their way into the inner compartments. The burglars stuffed as much as they could into satchels and exited the bank, somehow unnoticed by anyone on the street, around nine-thirty.

Upon inspecting the vault, the police found the floor littered with jewelry and silverware and broken tin deposit boxes. The thieves also left behind an elaborate set of the newest, state-of-the-art burglar tools that cost several thousand dollars to collect. The cops called it the cleanest job they'd ever seen; no blasting had been done. This was the work of professionals.

Counterintuitively, the burglars had raised the shades on the bank's side windows, partially exposing themselves to view, so that their guards could signal to them the approach of any beat patrolmen. When the Werckles' milkman showed up to make his morning delivery, one of the watchmen told him not to bother because the family had gone out of town.

So, who *were* these guys? They had left no solid clues. But Thomas Byrnes knew that there were only about six "yeggs," or heist men, in the entire country capable of pulling off a theft of this complexity and magnitude. And he had some names in mind.

⟶⟹ ⟸⟵

Professional criminals in the 1870s and 1880s formed a hierarchy. At the bottom were common, everyday thieves: shoplifters, pickpockets, highway robbers (street muggers), and house burglars, known as sneak and house thieves. Others on the lower end of the totem pole were the river thieves—desperate, brutish types who preyed upon immigrants or seamen just off the boat—and butcher cart thieves, who jumped off their horse-driven wagons to grab hogs in the street or carcasses in a butcher shop before making off with them.

But most run-of-the-mill thieves aspired to what Byrnes called "the higher walks of predatory industry." Criminal occupation, he explained, "is, like everything else, progressive."

Further up the chain were forgers and counterfeiters—skilled artisans who preferred to work in secret. Confidence men, or "con" men, used their wiles to swindle well-heeled and gullible tourists. Pretending to be an acquaintance or nephew of a friend from back home, the con man greeted his mark in the street and persuaded him to loan him some cash for a few minutes, after which he disappeared into the crowd. Or, he lured the dupe to a card or dice game of bunco (originally known as banco) in which the bettor is allowed to win successive rounds or draws with small amounts at risk until, told he must put up several hundred dollars more to save what he has already won, he draws the "blank" and loses all.

Hotel and boardinghouse thieves were respectable-looking types who scanned the newspapers for the comings and goings of wealthy travelers. They would chat up the hotel desk clerk or landlady to gather as much information about the lodgers as possible. Then, while the fashionably attired guests were at breakfast or dinner, the thief would sneak into their room, having effortlessly picked the door's lock.

Bank sneak thieves were likewise well-dressed gentlemen and smooth and entertaining talkers. Working in pairs or threes, they diverted bank tellers and cashiers with interesting conversations while one of their number slipped behind the counter to capture the cash box or a bundle of bonds.

Store and safe burglars, near the top grade of criminals, were expert at cracking the safes of business establishments at night and making off with cash and coin, or diamonds, jewelry, silks, and other valuables. They would drill, break, or blow their way into the safe or the room in which money was stored.

The cream of the crime world, though—the aristocrats of thievery—were the bank burglars. "The professional bank burglar," Byrnes once wrote, "must have patience, intelligence, mechanical knowledge, industry, determination, fertility of resources, and courage—all in high degree."

They formed a small fraternity, beginning around the end of the Civil War, often working alone or with a single accomplice if necessary. Out west, Jesse James and other outlaws and vigilantes, many of them ex-Confederates, were robbing small, local banks and, later, payroll and express trains. But with the dawn of the Gilded Age in the 1870s, professional bank burglars—a more apolitical lot—turned their attention increasingly to big-city banks back east. A surfeit of stocks, bonds, and commercial paper, issued to support industrialization, were being stashed away in urban bank vaults. And with the huge amounts of money to be made, the best of the bank robbers joined with one another to tackle the most challenging jobs.

Many professional bank burglars were from educated, middle-class backgrounds or, if humbly born, had transformed themselves into men of refinement and culture. On the surface, they could pass for a broker or prosperous businessman. Often they lived double lives and were model husbands and fathers at home.

They shied from using violence in their bank jobs, not so much for ethical reasons but because it drew more attention to the crime and led to longer prison sentences if they were caught and convicted. "Instead of the clumsy, awkward, ill-looking rogue of former days," wrote famed private detective Allan Pinkerton in 1873, "we now have the intelligent, scientific and calculating burglar, who is expert in the uses of tools, and a gentleman in appearance, who prides himself upon always leaving a 'neat job' behind him."

An early prototype was Maximilian Schoenbein, better known as Max (or Mark) Shinburn, a German-born mechanic who came to New York around 1860 in his early twenties and became, according to Byrnes, "probably the most expert bank safe burglar in the country."

A debonair, even dandified figure, Shinburn associated with sporting men and gamblers and always stayed in the best hotels. He thought violent methods were for brainless brutes, and he looked down on the common thieves he sometimes was forced to associate with. Haughty and arrogant, he fancied himself an aristocrat to the point that in 1870 he took his ill-gotten riches to settle in Europe, where he purchased a title of nobility as Baron Schindle of Monaco and, later, a castle.

Shinburn was a talented jailbreaker and getaway artist who could slip out of handcuffs without the key. He once crawled across a slippery, half-built, wooden-planked bridge high above the Niagara River during a nighttime blizzard, while carrying on his back bags of cash stolen from a Canadian bank.

But his greatest renown was as a safecracker. His specialty was making wax impressions of bank and safe keys that he stole from bank officials' pants pockets as they slept in their homes. He'd take the keys to a more convenient location for copying and return them the same evening so that the victim awoke with no knowledge that they'd ever been missing.

Once inside the bank vault—either that night if circumstances dictated or, preferably, at a later date—he'd break open the safe with his set of tools. If that proved too difficult, he'd resort to gunpowder, the weapon of choice for most safe burglars in the 1860s and the most effective for quick work. (Dynamite, first used in 1875, did not reach perfection until the early 1890s and was soon replaced almost exclusively by nitroglycerin.)

After the Civil War, a spirited competition began between burglars and safe makers in the nature of an arms race. Manufacturers came up with stronger, thicker safes, and yeggs developed new ways and tools to overcome them. It seemed that as soon as a bank pronounced its safe "burglarproof," the burglars would prove it wrong.

Increasingly throughout the 1860s and into the 1870s, banks protected their vaults and safes with a combination lock on the outer doors. The thieves could always try to extort the combination from a bank employee, but short of that, they developed a variety of ways to unlock the doors.

The early, simple locks introduced in 1860 by the Lillie Safe Co. had just three numbers on the dial knob. Expert thieves could determine the combination by listening to the clicks of the tumblers underneath (at least according to legend). Shinburn, who obtained a job with Lillie under an assumed name, was credited with this hearing ability. So was noted bank burglar Langdon Moore, who visited safe manufacturers to receive tours and explanations about how their safes were constructed. He then purchased safes on which he could experiment.

When Lillie went to a dial with the numbers 0 to 100, beating the lock got trickier. Around 1868, Shinburn took on a partner: a formerly respectable Massachusetts hotel owner named George White (alias Bliss, alias Miles), who came up with an ingenious device to ascertain the combination. He called it the "little joker." (Whether it was White's invention, as he claimed, or Shinburn's, as suggested by Byrnes and Allan Pinkerton, is unclear.)

The instrument consisted of a small piece of wire attached to a disc of paper or tinfoil. The burglar would remove the dial knob to the lock, insert the paper or tin wheel underneath it, then replace the knob. When bank officials turned the knob the next day to open the vault or safe, the wire would make a puncture mark in the disc at each tumbler number point where the dial stopped. On returning to the bank, the burglar could discover the combination by examining the marks made by the wire; all that remained was to figure out the sequence of the numbers, which was easily done through trial and error.

This did require entering the bank at least twice while no one was there—once to insert the little joker and replace the knob, and a second time to check the markings. But there was usually some way to get into the bank after hours, whether with a key duplicated from a wax impression or with the aid of a bribed bank employee.

Shinburn and White scored several coups with the little joker, using it to carry out bank robberies in Vermont, Connecticut, and Maryland. But its utility was short-lived. In 1869 they were preparing to rob New York's Ocean National Bank, at Greenwich and Fulton Streets, where they anticipated employing the joker device. While planning that operation, they used the joker to set up a robbery of a New Jersey bank, only to have bank officials stumble upon their handiwork. After that, Lillie altered its locks to make them joker-proof, which White recalled ruefully had greatly interfered with his previous easy access to bank vaults. The Ocean National vault would have to be won by other means.

White bought a facsimile of the Ocean National's new Lillie lock, enlisted a corruptible clerk inside the bank, then trained him how to estimate the numbers on the dial while watching from a few feet away as someone else was turning the knob to unlock the vault. The clerk figured out the first two numbers and was close enough on the third that when he let White in one night, the future jailbird was able to nail down the last one. How White obtained Ocean National's vault combination remained a mystery until he revealed it in his memoirs in 1905.

To get into the bank on the night of the burglary, the thieves adopted another common tactic, renting a room below, where they established a fake business as a base of operations. From there, they cut through the ceiling to gain entrance to the bank floor.

White and Shinburn made off with an estimated $800,000 to $1.2 million in the Ocean National heist. Neither was caught, and the case was never solved officially, though both were widely named as suspects, and White admitted to the robbery in his memoirs. He claimed that $100,000 of the haul went to pay off a ring of crooked New York cops.

By the early 1870s, the preferred method for breaching combination locks became to drill a hole in the lock using new diamond-tipped drills capable of cutting through steel. From there the burglar could place an explosive in the lock. Or, if he was mechanically adept, he could insert a stiff steel wire in the hole, pick up the tumblers, and throw them into the unlocked position. It required the dexterity of a concert maestro's fingers on the keys of a piano. If he needed to come back to finish the job, he'd return the tumblers to their original positions and fill the drilled hole with putty to prevent the bank from discovering the breach. Lillie locks became so easy to pick that the company was brought into disrepute and forced into bankruptcy.

⊰⊷⊜⊶⊱

As Thomas Byrnes was turning over the tumblers in his own mind, the New York newspapers were mocking the police for being clueless as to the perpetrators of the Manhattan Savings robbery. "All at sea" and "completely outwitted," said the *Times*, which thought the impunity with which the burglary was committed a disgrace to the city and a severe blow to public confidence in the safety of money in banks.

Bank officials were bracing for the usual: a ransom offer of compromise by the perpetrators. The haul from big bank heists was generally in the form of bonds and other securities, which were risky for the thieves to try to trade or cash. It became customary for the thieves to return the stolen bonds in exchange for some amount of cash less than their face value. The robbers would give the police 10 percent of the value of the loot in exchange for immunity from prosecution.

In 1872 crusading journalist Edward Crapsey wrote that this "brokerage in crime" needed to be stopped and that "the attention of the police officer must be diverted from the property stolen to the person stealing it." Thomas Byrnes agreed. He found the practice distasteful and hoped to end it if he ever got the chance. He wanted to catch and convict the culprits.

By the time of the robbery, Max Shinburn was living the life of a baron in Europe with the riches gained from the Ocean National heist, so he was not a suspect. George White was in jail in Vermont, serving a twelve-year sentence for the robbery of the Barre Bank. Langdon Moore was in Chicago; besides which, he would have nothing to do with jobs that involved tying up a bank employee. And William Sharkey, a sporting man and ace burglar previously associated with Shinburn and White, was on the lam, his whereabouts unknown. Imprisoned in the Tombs, where he was awaiting execution in 1873 as a convicted murderer, he'd escaped—disguised as a woman—to the considerable embarrassment of police and prison authorities.

Although janitor Werckle was quickly eliminated as a suspect, Byrnes was convinced that the burglars had inside help. The first thing he did was to put a tail on the night watchman, Patrick Shevlin. Then he went looking for the suspected ringleaders.

The first arrest came on December 13, 1878, seven weeks after the robbery. Accompanied by two of his precinct detectives, Byrnes personally arrested John "Red" Leary and John McCarthy outside a house in Yorkville at Ninety-Second Street and Second Avenue. McCarthy was an insignificant thief, but Leary was a real catch. Along with his wife, "Red Kate" Leary, a renowned Coney Island pickpocket, John Leary was an ace at that vocation, too. Arrested for pickpocketing at the 1867 Paris

Exposition (world's fair), he spent three years in a prison in the French city of Brest, then returned to America to launch a bank-robbing career. As his day job, he ran a saloon in Brooklyn and kept a safe there as a standing joke.

When Byrnes apprehended him, Leary was wanted for a Northampton, Massachusetts, bank robbery in January 1876, in which the thieves absconded with $1.6 million in mostly commercial paper and some cash. In gross amount, it was the biggest bank heist up to that time.

Leary's involvement in the Northampton robbery made him a natural suspect in the Manhattan Savings job, given the similarities between the two crimes. In the Massachusetts heist, seven masked men entered the home of the bank cashier around midnight, bound and handcuffed him and his family, then choked and beat him until he gave them the combinations to the bank's vault and safe. After the robbery, the bank ordered a $400 Yale time lock, capable of being opened only at preset hours, so that kidnapping the cashier would do no good. The Manhattan Savings bank did not make a similar investment.

Byrnes had no real evidence tying Leary to the Manhattan Savings burglary, but he threw him in the Ludlow Street Jail, where the disgraced Boss Tweed had died earlier in 1878, on the chance that Werckle would be able to identify him. Leary would not stay in Ludlow for long, though; in May 1879 his wife, Kate, engineered a dramatic rescue by renting a tenement house next door and having accomplices tunnel through to Red's prison bathroom.

Byrnes said later that it was not actually Leary he'd been looking for when he surrounded the Yorkville house but another notorious burglar and prison breaker, Jimmy Hope, who Byrnes felt certain was part of the Manhattan Savings gang. The forty-two-year-old Hope (known as "Old Man Hope," to distinguish him from his son Johnny, a budding thief) was short, stout, balding, and full-bearded. Originally from Philadelphia, where he ran a disorderly dance hall during the Civil War, he was known as a clever burglar. He also was another of the many two-faced robbers: he had a wife and children in one part of New York and a fashionable

Six members of George Leslie's famous bank robbery gang, several of whom participated in the spectacular heist of the Manhattan Savings Institution in 1878. Thomas Byrnes "solved" the $3 million burglary, launching his storied career. Clockwise from upper left: Johnny Hope, Jimmy Hope, Johnny Dobbs, "Banjo Pete" Emerson, Billy Porter, and "Sheeny Mike" Kurtz.

apartment in another, where he posed as a businessman and kept a circle of prosperous friends.

Ostensibly, Jimmy Hope preferred brains to brawn to accomplish his aims, but he wasn't averse to mixing the two. In the 1871 robbery of the South Kensington Bank in Philadelphia, which he helped plan, the burglars posed as uniformed cops to gain entrée to the bank, then bound and gagged the watchmen while they stole $100,000. Hope was also implicated in the violent February 1878 Dexter (Maine) Savings Bank heist. In that robbery, too, the thieves tied up a bank employee and demanded the combination to the safe. But in that case, the Dexter Bank's treasurer, John Barron, refused. The robbers beat him senseless and left him bleeding inside the vault; he died the next day.

Hope could not be found anywhere after the Manhattan Savings robbery—he'd gone to San Francisco—so Byrnes wasn't able to surveil him in New York. But informants said they'd seen him around the bank on the morning of the robbery, and, since that day, several offers of compromise had been made to bank officials through a man closely linked to Hope.

A further clue came when thirty-year-old Abe Coakley, Hope's senior lieutenant, was questioned by a detective shortly after the Manhattan Savings theft. Coakley, the son of a New York cop, admitted his participation in the theft and promised to tell all. He revealingly blurted out, "Every time Jimmy Hope gets in trouble, they want me, too."

From there, things began falling into place for Byrnes. Two witnesses identified Hope's son Johnny as the man who'd told the milkman not to bother delivering to janitor Werckle's family that morning. Another witness placed Johnny Hope at the scene. In February 1879 Byrnes had the younger Hope arrested and charged.

Then in May, Johnny Dobbs, another regular Jimmy Hope partner, was arrested in Philadelphia by agents of Allan Pinkerton's Pinkerton National Detective Agency while trying to negotiate $5,000 in bonds of the Manhattan Savings bank. Raised in the Fourth Ward slums of New York, the son of a Water Street oyster saloon owner, the forty-three-year-old Dobbs had ascended from river thief to become associated with the cream of bank burglars.

A machinist by trade, Dobbs was, in Byrnes's words, "a first-class workman." Others considered him a desperate, violent criminal; he had once shot a New York cop in the leg. He was part of the gang that, disguised as police, robbed Philadelphia's South Kensington Bank after overpowering the watchmen, and he was suspected of having shoved the Dexter bank's treasurer inside the vault and left him to die.

Byrnes went to Philadelphia, where he immediately identified Dobbs—five foot five, round face, slight English accent—and matched the bonds to those stolen from the Manhattan Savings bank. Byrnes discussed with Robert Pinkerton, Allan's son, what to do with the prisoner. They agreed that neither could hold his head up if Dobbs managed to escape, as he was known to do. That night, Pinkerton and Dobbs went to bed manacled to each other at the ankles while Byrnes, who held the key, slept on a sofa.

Asked by a reporter how long he had known that Dobbs was one of the Manhattan Savings robbers, Byrnes smiled slyly and said ever since the original Sunday morning. Informed of Dobbs's arrest, Johnny Hope, confined in the Tombs, quipped, "The more of them that are caught, the better it will be for me."

There were bound to be a few more. If Jimmy Hope, Coakley, and Dobbs were in on the theft, then Byrnes could figure that the perpetrators also must have included Banjo Pete Emerson (real name Peter Ellis). A tall, thin former Union army sharpshooter, Emerson joined a minstrel company after the war and became a member of the professional bank robbers' fraternity.

Another likely suspect was "Worcester Sam" Perris, a notorious criminal "of undoubted nerve," as Byrnes described him. Like Dobbs, Perris was wanted for the murder of treasurer Barron of the Dexter Bank.

And if Red Leary was involved in the Manhattan Savings theft, then surely Thomas "Shang" Draper, Leary's bosom friend and accomplice in the Northampton Bank robbery, had a hand in it somewhere. Draper's reputation as an A1 burglar was at its height in 1878, although his stretch at bank robbing would prove relatively brief, sandwiched in the middle of one of the more varied criminal careers of the post–Civil War era.

Born in Ireland in 1843, Draper was the black sheep of his family, which ended up disowning him. His father, John, was a respected, successful cotton broker in Brooklyn, and his older brother, William, followed in the same line of work. But like so many urban-dwelling young men of his generation, Thomas was looking to make it big quick. He found himself unable to resist the romance and potential riches of the criminal life. Not every ambitious, adventuresome young man in the Gilded Age could become a robber baron, but he could always become a robber.

Before turning to bank robbery, Draper had forged a reputation running prostitution cons. He'd operated several panel houses, where women enticed strangers who were fleeced during the sex act by accomplices who reached through secret sliding panels in the rooms to pinch their wallets. In a variation called the badger game, Draper employed young girls to lure drunken patrons to a brothel hotel. While both were undressing, Draper or his henchmen, posing as the girl's husband or outraged parents, would break into the room and shake down the startled john for his money and valuables.

Whether these "shanghai" operations are what gave Draper his nickname, or whether, as some claim, it was his six-foot-tall, lanky appearance, reminiscent of a long-legged Shanghai chicken, is not certain. But they made him a small fortune—an estimated $200,000—and allowed him to strut up and down Broadway in the early 1870s dressed in the finest broadcloth with a large diamond cluster pin attached. They also won him a wife esteemed for her beauty, although it's not clear they were legally married. Trained as a panel thief by a previous husband, whom she "divorced" while he languished in prison, Jennie Mooney became Draper's wife, whether legally or de facto. Later, she would play a fateful role in the Manhattan Savings heist.

After the police broke up Draper's panel thieving business in the Eighth Precinct (present-day Soho), he joined a gang that robbed the Northampton Bank and a string of others, possibly including the Dexter in Maine. Later, he would run a popular Midtown saloon and, after that, a fashionable casino near Fifth Avenue, where he reigned as a gambling kingpin.

So, Thomas Byrnes had his list of suspects and a picture of the crime—a top-notch job done with inside help and some rough tactics. But who was the insider, who played what roles, and who had organized the crime? Those answers would begin to emerge with the confession of the night watchman, Patrick Shevlin, the man Byrnes had put under surveillance.

CHAPTER FOUR

❖❯═══◉ ◉═══❮❖

THE THIRD DEGREE

P at Shevlin was not a well-to-do man. At the time of the Manhattan Savings robbery, the thirty-eight-year-old was a horse and truck driver at the Washington Market, making $1.25 a day. He served as a part-time watchman at the bank, working Sunday afternoons and weekday evenings. Married with six children, he barely made ends meet. Thus, when he began to show signs of sudden wealth right after the robbery—dressing better, drinking more, always possessed of ready cash—Byrnes's suspicions grew. He wouldn't arrest Shevlin yet but would continue to have his men watch him wherever he went.

Shevlin was seen spending a lot of time in an East Village saloon at Avenue C and Seventh Street in secret conversation with the bartender, Patrick Ryan. One day, Ryan introduced him to William "Billy" Kelly, a brawny criminal who passed about $1,600 in cash into Shevlin's hands.

Kelly had been spotted across from the bank at the corner of Bleecker Street and Broadway on the two Sunday mornings before the burglary. He was also unexplainedly absent from his all-night bartending job from about two o'clock Saturday morning until around noon Sunday on the

day of the heist. After the robbery, Kelly quit his job and began frequent-
ing the racetracks. With that information, Byrnes decided he had enough
to arrest Shevlin, who was hauled in for questioning at the end of May
1879, just before the trial of Johnny Hope, charged with the crime in
February, was to begin.

Shevlin initially denied any complicity in the robbery. But by Saturday morning, May 31, after spending three nights in a cell at Byrnes's
Fifteenth Precinct station house, he decided to make a clean breast of
everything.

Exactly what transpired during Shevlin's confinement can only be
surmised, as he gave his confession to Byrnes alone in the latter's private
office. Shevlin testified later that his wife urged him to just tell the truth
if he knew anything, but on June 2 *The New York Times* reported crypti-
cally that "Shevlin's story was forced from him." That was likely a euphe-
mism for the interrogation method for which Byrnes would become
famous: the so-called third degree.

Despite what many have claimed, Byrnes did not invent this tech-
nique. Ever since crime has existed, authorities have resorted to physical
force and even torture to extract confessions from suspects. Nor was the
practice unknown to the New York Police Department before Byrnes
began using it. But it was Byrnes who would give the phrase "the third
degree" its special cachet in the annals of American policing.

When he deemed it necessary, Byrnes did not hesitate to use pitiless
tactics. He was known to keep an arrestee in solitary confinement for
long periods with little food or water, usually supplied by unseen hands.
For brutish thieves, he'd engage in what author Jacob Riis, a police reporter early in his career, called "a little wholesome 'slugging.'" Byrnes
once allowed as how he had seen many tears flow from those he questioned, adding, "But all the crying is not done by the fair sex."

For more cerebral or nervous criminals, Byrnes preferred using psychological warfare. He'd promise them leniency or claim they were about
to be ratted out by their coconspirators, whether true or not. He'd sometimes show them the bloody evidence of their crime, as in the case of sea

captain Edward Unger, who killed his roommate during a quarrel, cut him up, and shipped the mutilated remains in a trunk to Baltimore.

Convinced of Unger's guilt, Byrnes had the contents of his apartment and the murder weapon, an iron poker, transported to a room in police headquarters, where he repeated the grisly details of the crime in Unger's presence. Byrnes brought in the trunk and placed it before Unger, pulled out the bloody articles of clothing one by one, and asked whether he had ever seen them before. At this, Unger began to break. Finally, when the horror-stricken prisoner realized he'd been seated on the blood-spattered sofa on which he had slaughtered his friend, he broke down and confessed.

On other occasions, it was said, Byrnes produced wax figures of murder victims, complete with bloody wounds, to play with a suspect's mind. "It is not remorse that makes the hardened criminal confess," he maintained, "it is anxiety, mental strain."

In a retrospective article on Byrnes's career in 1908, *Harper's Weekly* said there was nothing mysterious about the third degree. "It was simply the work of a master mind in reading the guilty secret of an accused person, studying his mental makeup, and choosing the surest way of forcing him to tell it." A Gilded Age New Yorker in Jack Finney's 1970 time-travel novel *Time and Again*, in which the twentieth-century protagonist meets Byrnes in 1882 New York, speaks approvingly of the famous detective's methods: "I don't expect he minds knocking a man about a little when he knows he's guilty. As why shouldn't he? . . . Would you have him let a criminal go scot-free, to society's peril, for want of a little persuasion?"

For many suspects Byrnes adopted a threatening tone; as one contemporary magazine writer noted, "His very manner, the size of him, the bark in his voice, his menacing shoulders and arms would terrorize the average crook." For other thieves, Byrnes would start chatting casually about innocuous subjects—family, work; anything but the actual crime— gradually mixing in detailed bits about the deed in question in order to unnerve his man. Muckraking journalist Lincoln Steffens, a grudging admirer, called Byrnes "a man who would buy you or beat you, as you might choose, but get you he would."

He got Pat Shevlin, as *The New York Times* reported, by impressing upon him how much the police already knew from shadowing him. Byrnes might have offered him immunity, or at least leniency, if he talked, although Shevlin denied it later. And Byrnes may have engaged in a bit of mockery: Shevlin was upset that he'd been promised a quarter million dollars if he helped the burglars but ended up with less than $1,500 for his cooperation. Although unaware of the $250,000 offer, Byrnes, guessing that Shevlin had been underpaid, allegedly told him that he'd been a sucker for accepting a measly $10,000 for his efforts. Shevlin responded by shouting that was a lie: he'd received far less, an incriminatory admission that led him to make a full confession.

Byrnes's interrogation methods may seem retrograde today, but they were ahead of their time in 1878 and lasted well into the twentieth century. Indeed, as late as the 1960s, police manuals routinely encouraged the use of psychological isolation and deception, if not physical browbeating, to induce suspects to confess. As the US Supreme Court would observe in its landmark *Miranda* decision in 1966, the manuals highlighted the need to isolate the person in custody in unfamiliar surroundings. Cops were instructed "to display an air of confidence in the suspect's guilt and, from outward appearance, to maintain only an interest in confirming certain details." Such tactics were "designed to put the subject in a psychological state where his story is but an elaboration of what the police purport to know already—that he is guilty. Explanations to the contrary are dismissed and discouraged."

Although Gilded Age police did not have the benefit of modern forensics, they had fewer restraints on their evidence gathering. It would be a century before suspects in custody for violations of state law were granted Miranda rights (the right to remain silent, etc.).

In theory, nineteenth-century defendants could keep a confession out of evidence by proving it was "involuntary." But since police interrogations were not recorded then, and cops rarely admitted to using coercive tactics in a specific case, courts generally gave police the benefit of the doubt and allowed the confession.

Shevlin proceeded to lay out the story of the Manhattan Savings robbery, which Byrnes would supplement with information gathered from other sources. It turned out that the job had been in planning for three years and had been masterminded by a man with the best alibi of all.

CHAPTER FIVE

KING OF THE BANK ROBBERS

Of all the elite bank robbers of nineteenth-century America, George Leonidas Leslie, also known as Western George, George Howard, C. G. Green, and other aliases, is the only one whose image has not been preserved in photograph, drawing, or painting. Perhaps that is fitting, for no other member of his profession is surrounded by so much mystery, or romantic legend, as the man often referred to as the King of the Bank Robbers.

It was not that he was braver or more daring than his brethren. He never dug a tunnel to pull off a heist, as noted burglar Adam Worth did in 1869 when he robbed the Boylston National Bank in Boston by burrowing in from a building he'd rented next door. Nor did Leslie ever spring someone from jail, like the friends of Red Leary had, or escape prison himself, via disguise or otherwise. And he wasn't necessarily smarter or cleverer than, say, Jimmy Hope, or more entrepreneurial than Shang Draper.

Other first-class burglars, such as Max Shinburn and George White, were just as resourceful when it came to beating vaults and safes. In fact, despite many claims to the contrary, there is no evidence that Leslie ever used, much less invented, the little joker, which had become obsolete around the time Leslie's career was taking off. Leslie was certainly mechanically gifted and knew his way around a combination lock as well as anyone, but no more so than Langdon Moore and perhaps others.

And he lacked the killer instinct of a Johnny Dobbs or Worcester Sam.

George Leslie's special gift was as a big-picture man. Like a film director who visualizes the screenplay and controls the actors, set design, and technical crew to fulfill that vision, Leslie was the creative force behind many of the biggest bank robberies of his time. At the peak of his career, he acted as a "putter-up," planning the jobs that other men executed. He'd target a bank or store, select the burglar team, and assign them their roles. A telegram might summon him from New York to Baltimore, or Kalamazoo, Michigan, or Macon, Georgia, to look over a scheme for a burglary to be carried out by others. Or he might be sought out to arrange with criminal fences for the disposal of what had already been stolen.

Like the best corporate CEOs, Leslie combined strong executive skills with a deep knowledge of the hands-on, nuts-and-bolts aspects of the business. He designed the latest and best burglar tools. A skilled lock picker and safecracker, he bought new models of safes and locks or created replicas, then practiced on them at his leisure. For the trickiest locks, he'd do the work himself.

His forte was studying the architectural plans of a building until he knew every nook and corner of the premises. According to author Herbert Asbury, Leslie went so far as to fit up rooms to resemble the interior of a bank, then had his gang members feel their way to the safe in the darkness and open it while Leslie critiqued their performance.

Superintendent George Walling estimated that 80 percent of all the money stolen from banks in the two decades before the Manhattan Savings robbery was pilfered by members of the Leslie gang. That figure is undoubtedly overstated, as Leslie's earliest known bank job wasn't until

1869. And the list includes some large robberies, such as of the Ocean National Bank that same year, which Leslie probably had nothing to do with.

Nonetheless, he is credited with having planned or consulted on the robberies of the South Kensington (Philadelphia), Northampton (Massachusetts), and Dexter (Maine) banks and several others. The composition of his gang would change from job to job, although there were repeat accomplices such as Jimmy Hope, Shang Draper, and Banjo Pete Emerson. But owing to his shrewdness, coolness, and talent for directing others, Leslie became the de facto chief.

More than any other thief, George Leslie turned bank robbery into a form of organized crime. And the Manhattan Savings, a job three years in the planning, was to be his masterpiece.

⌁⇒◯⇐⌁

The details of Leslie's life are hard to pin down, in large part because next to nothing was written about him until after his death. Virtually all of Leslie's crimes, including the Manhattan Savings robbery, were first credited to him only posthumously. And yet today he is considered one of the premier criminals of the nineteenth century.

He was born between 1840 and 1842 in the western part of upstate New York, where his father first settled after emigrating from England. The family moved to Cincinnati, where Mr. Leslie opened a brewery business and where George attended a local university, graduating with high honors (though assertions that he earned an architecture degree are unsubstantiated). At some point, his father died, and his mother remarried—although it may have been the other way around; in either event, the wicked stepparent supposedly drove young Leslie from the household and into a life of crime.

From there his story becomes even murkier. Some sources say he became a Civil War bounty jumper, while *The New York Times*, writing in 1878, said he joined a group of bushwhackers (guerrilla fighters) in Missouri and Kansas who robbed from both the Union and Confederate sides.

Some claimed he ran a business in Milwaukee and a hotel in San Francisco before establishing himself in Saint Louis.

Allan Pinkerton, who operated his detective agency out of Chicago, claimed that Leslie did some counterfeiting in that city and joined a gang of safecrackers. According to Pinkerton, Leslie tried to talk his Windy City confederates into robbing a prominent local banking house by gagging and binding the watchman, and a cop if necessary, but they balked at the prospect.

While in Chicago, Leslie picked up a mistress, known to history only as "Red-headed Lizzie," who would remain in the picture to the end of his days. A New York paper noted dryly that Leslie "was a great favorite with women of a certain sort and made the most of his favoritism." He was about five foot eight, well built or heavyset, short-haired or balding, and, by all accounts, despite a scarred face, quite handsome.

Leslie came east to Philadelphia in 1869, where he acquired the moniker Western George. He shows up in the 1870 federal census as thirty-year-old George W. Howard, living at 508 Locust Street in a boardinghouse run by Mary E. Coath, an aristocratic woman of thirty-five whose husband had deserted her sometime earlier. Her fifteen-year-old daughter, Mary Henrietta (known as Molly), reputedly married George later that year. One might easily imagine that Mrs. Coath, closer to Leslie's age, was his real partner, but later records confirm that it was Molly who both married and lived with George Leslie.

When they first met in 1869, George told Molly that he was a federal Internal Revenue Service agent, a representation she accepted for several years. He was suave and well-tailored, had polished manners, and spoke three languages, so she had no reason to doubt him. "His address was insinuating and wholly deceptive," is how one newspaper put it.

Leslie fit easily into the high society world that Molly's mother inhabited. True, he'd be absent for periods, but he could always claim it was secret government work. In fact, he was off robbing Philadelphia-area banks and jewelry stores as a member of a gang known as the Blue Shirts. In most of his thefts, he was protected from arrest by his friend Josh

Taggart, a corrupt, high-ranking Philadelphia detective who helped ne-gotiate offers of compromise between the robbers and the banks.

In May 1870 Leslie had his most harrowing—and perhaps only—serious brush with the law. He and two associates were caught trying to rob a jewelry store on the main street of Norristown, Pennsylvania. The incident, if true, belies the reputation for nonviolence that many have tried to bestow on him. Eleven shots by the police missed the fleeing Leslie; one of his, in return, hit an officer in the foot. He was caught, put in jail, and bailed out by Red-headed Lizzie. He jumped bail, failed to appear for trial, and resumed his society life, still under Taggart's pro-tection.

Over the next few years, Leslie was involved with several more thefts of major banks and stores in Philadelphia, Illinois, and elsewhere. Ap-parently, his doings were an open secret, yet somehow he always man-aged to avoid conviction or even mention in the newspapers as a suspect. Partly this was because he kept his distance from the crime scene, but he also made it a practice of quietly settling with detectives with whom he shared the spoils.

Around the fall of 1874, though, Leslie had a falling-out with his protector Taggart over the split of profits. With things too hot in Phila-delphia, he decided to remove himself and his young wife to New York. They took up residence on the third floor of a house at 478 Fulton Street in Brooklyn under the listing of George L. Howard.

Here Leslie continued his double life: on the one hand, he was a bon vivant who fancied the theater and opera, the music academy, and old bookstores; he was said to have amassed a collection of more than a thou-sand books, mostly on precious stones, metallurgy, mining, and machin-ery. He dressed as a gentleman, carrying a gold watch and chain, and owned the finest, most expensive dogs: an Italian greyhound, a Scottish terrier, and a black-and-tan coonhound.

His lavishly furnished apartment indicated a man of ample means. He socialized with popular actor and songwriter Sam Devere, who lived a floor below and was the manager of the minstrel company in which Banjo Pete had performed. Commenting on Leslie, New York's *The Sun* observed that there was "nothing vulgar in his manner nor conversation."

But he was an unreconstructed thief. In Brooklyn, he turned his attention initially to silk robberies, his easy, gentlemanly manner allowing him to enter stores and warehouses to discover their vulnerabilities. Silk, he found, brought a higher percentage payment by criminal fences than did jewelry, which was more easily traced to the rightful owner. One did need to remove the monograms or other identifying marks from the stolen fabrics, but savvy thieves and fences knew to take this precaution.

In his spare time, from the privacy of his library, Leslie continued to study the construction of locks and tinkered with improvements in burglary tools. And more and more, he began hanging out with his Brooklyn neighbor Shang Draper and Draper's circle of hardened criminals. They included not only Red Leary, Johnny Dobbs, Banjo Pete, and Worcester Sam, but also a couple of fearless desperadoes named Billy Porter and Johnny Irving, who would attain infamy in the coming years.

Porter, a good-looking man of twenty-eight, was really William O'Brien, a native of Boston. He was swarthy, curly haired, with a scowling face, daggers for eyes, and tattoos on both arms. Irving, a little younger and a native New Yorker, was an energetic, hotheaded thief who'd stolen since he was a boy. He sported a dark mustache and beard and was described as good-hearted underneath it all.

Porter and Irving were leaders of the Patchen Avenue Gang, so named because those two best of pals lived together in an elegant three-story mansion at 152 Patchen Avenue in Brooklyn, near the current Stuyvesant Heights neighborhood. Just down the street, at 176 Patchen, was their compatriot Shang Draper, who had enlisted them in the Northampton Bank and other robberies.

Surrounded by shrubbery, flowers, and a croquet lawn, the heavily fortified house at 152 Patchen was the main gathering place for the Brooklyn bad guys Leslie consorted with. It was also inhabited by two beautiful molls—one, Porter's wife; the other, Irving's sister Babe—and frequented by a third, the equally attractive Jennie Draper, the reputed wife, or mistress, of Shang. George Leslie, a hopeless womanizer, would develop, or at least be accused of carrying on, intimate relations with all three ladies.

That would lead to trouble later. But for the time being, the money flow kept everyone happy. Porter and Irving, who specialized in burglarizing silk, dry goods, and jewelry stores, found Leslie's assistance invaluable. Leslie, as C. G. Green, also helped Draper, alias A. D. Harper, plan the unprecedented $1.6 million Northampton Bank robbery that was pulled off in February 1876.

Then Leslie and Draper began focusing on an even larger job: one that originally had been someone else's idea, but which the two had since assumed responsibility for planning. Leslie bought a combination dial lock and brought it to his new residence at 861 Greene Avenue in Brooklyn, where he and Draper took it upstairs and began practicing on it. The lock, manufactured by Valentine & Butler, was a counterpart to the one on the vault door of the Manhattan Savings Institution.

◦━◡ ◡━◦

During the three years preceding the robbery, the cast of characters plotting it kept changing. Conspirators came and went, as some were jailed for other crimes or dropped out due to squabbles among the group members. Setbacks or mechanical failures were followed by long periods of inactivity. But the idea never died. Lured by the prospect of millions in loot and convinced that the bank, despite its formidable reputation, was in fact a "pudding," or soft target, the thieves kept coming back to planning the job.

The initial approach to Pat Shevlin occurred sometime in late 1875 or early 1876, after he took the night watchman job at the Manhattan Savings. A group of low-level mobsters—none of whom would participate in the eventual robbery—sounded him out on becoming an inside accomplice.

Shevlin did not discourage them. Discussions continued for a few months, after which he was sent to a barroom at Second Avenue and Tenth Street to meet a new, more talented group of burglars, including Jimmy Hope, Johnny Dobbs, and George Leslie. In time, Banjo Pete, Abe Coakley, and Worcester Sam would join the plotters as well. The infamous female thief and con woman Sophie Lyons, herself the wife of noted bank burglar Ned Lyons, was impressed with the group. She was "sure there was never before gathered together on one enterprise such a galaxy of talent."

Leslie was the chief, with Draper his partner in mapping overall strategy. Leslie studied the bank's architecture and determined how they would breach the vault and safes. Explosives were ruled out because the bank's large plate-glass windows, when shattered, would endanger the burglars and arouse the neighbors.

Jimmy Hope was put in charge of the interior safecracking work. He also served as the main liaison to Shevlin, telling him it would be easy to capture the bank's swag if he, Hope, were allowed inside to examine and work the locks. He showed Shevlin how to make a wax impression of the key to the bank's main entrance on Bleecker Street. It was Hope who promised Shevlin $250,000 for his cooperation.

Over a period of months, Shevlin let the intruders into the bank on several occasions, usually on Sunday mornings. (Large bank robberies invariably took place between Friday nights and Sunday mornings.) By experimenting with the Valentine & Butler lock, Leslie had decided the best way to breach the vault would be to drill a small hole just below the dial, then manipulate the tumblers with a thin steel wire.

The burglars' first attempt fell a little short. They did manage to open the vault, but once inside, they were confronted with combination-lock safes they couldn't open with the tools they had in the time they had. They decided to come back another night, so they closed the vault back up. But in trying to return the tumblers to their original locked positions, someone—Shevlin recalled it was Hope, though Walling said it was Leslie himself—was able to turn back only two of the three tumblers. Sophie

Lyons, in her sporadically accurate memoirs, blamed Hope because, she said, he lacked the mechanical skill and fine sense of touch that Leslie possessed.

The burglars puttied up the hole they had drilled so that the tampering would not be obvious from the outside. They knew, however, that because the tumblers were off, the bank officials would be unable to open the vault with the original combination the next time they tried and were likely to become suspicious.

One of the conspirators entered the bank the next morning to change a $100 bill and, staying to loiter awhile, was able to watch as bank officers tried in vain to open the vault door. He witnessed them send for a lock expert, who said the door would have to be removed and taken to his shop to repair. Remarkably, though, they did not seem to suspect a recent tampering.

On receiving their confederate's report, the conspirators decided to put things on hold. After eight or nine months passed, Shevlin let Hope and Dobbs in for another attempt. In the interim, the bank had fitted the vault door with a new lock of slightly different construction from the model Leslie had bought. As a result, Hope and Dobbs drilled their hole one-eighth of an inch too high for them to be able to move the tumblers.

Again they aborted the mission. By early 1878, frustrations and quarrels among the gang members developed, leading to another delay, even as the bank appeared unconcerned that anything nefarious was afoot.

One positive development for the conspirators was the recruitment of a New York City cop into their ranks. John Nugent was a former gambling "policy" writer (for the lottery or numbers game) who joined the police force in 1872. As a patrolman, he'd been suspected of participating in several burglaries and was charged at least once. He was introduced to Shevlin by some of the other plotters and agreed to serve as an outside watchman and mole for the gang. Nugent didn't tell Shevlin his name but represented himself as a headquarters detective of great influence who could keep tabs on what the police department knew.

The burglars were also fortunate in that money was not an issue for them. They were being financed by two of the most important players in New York's Gilded Age underworld—a pair of rival criminal fences who, between them, were long associated with virtually every member of the group.

CHAPTER SIX

QUEEN OF THE FENCES

I f putters-up such as George Leslie were the film directors of the robberies they carried out, then the producers were the fences, or receivers of stolen goods. Like theater owners or the promoters of mining
ventures, the fences were the financial backers who made robberies possible. They advanced money and expenses to the burglars and provided a
safe market for their ill-gotten gains. As Thomas Byrnes put it, fences
were the "root of the evil," because without them thieving would be too
risky and unprofitable.

The undisputed Queen of the Fences, and George Leslie's regular
backer, was a 250-plus-pound, mannish-looking Jewish immigrant
named Fredericka Mandelbaum, better known as "Mother" or "Marm."
One of the nineteenth century's most influential criminals, Mandelbaum
has been called the person who "first put crime in America on a syndicated basis."

She never stole a thing in her life. As Sophie Lyons, one of her pro-
tégées, wrote, Marm Mandelbaum "cracked no safes, she did not risk her
skin in house burglaries, her fat hand was never caught in anybody's

German-born Marm Mandelbaum, the acknowledged queen of criminal receivers, or fences. She took stolen loot off the hands of thieves, resold it for a hefty profit, and supplied financing for large-scale bank robberies.

pocket, no policeman's bullet was ever sent after her fleeing figure." Yet, as *The New York Times* observed in 1884, for the previous twenty years, Mandelbaum had been "the nucleus and centre of the whole organization of crime in New-York."

Her specialty was silk, but she dealt in anything—jewelry, cutlery, coins, clothing, commercial paper—that she considered good swag. She fenced for all the major burglars of the post–Civil War era, most often for George Leslie, Shang Draper, and the other Leslie gang members. She had a maternal fondness for Billy Porter and Johnny Irving, the Patchen Avenue duo she referred to as "my boys." (She called Porter "my most promising chick.")

Another of her favorites was fellow Jewish crook "Sheeny Mike" (Michael Kurtz), a regular member of Leslie's gang and, according to *The New York Times*, "probably the only first-class burglar of Hebrew birth born in this city." Kurtz, an expert safe blower, preferred robbing jewelry stores and silk merchants but would lend a helping hand with bank heists, especially if the job called for cutting through floors. He likely would have been involved in the Manhattan Savings heist had he not been in jail at the time.

Mother Mandelbaum also had a soft spot for female criminals, whom she mentored early in their careers. In addition to Sophie Lyons, her star pupils included the notorious jewel thief Black Lena Kleinschmidt and Old Mother Hubbard (Margaret Brown), an accomplished shoplifter and purse snatcher.* Mandelbaum made arrangements with counter clerks at the top New York department stores, such as Lord & Taylor and A. T. Stewart, to let her shoplifters carry off merchandise in exchange for a share of the profits. An early feminist entrepreneur, if a dishonest one, Mandelbaum found more to admire in women who thieved for a living than in those who only kept house.

Born in central Germany in 1825 to a family of itinerant Jewish peddlers, Mandelbaum came to America in 1850 with her husband, Wolf Israel (William) Mandelbaum, a small-time merchant she'd married two years earlier. Wolf ran a lager beer saloon where pickpockets reportedly thrived; possibly he preceded his wife in the fencing business. But he was a sickly man, not a strong presence, and melded into the background. Far surpassing him in business acumen, Marm became the main breadwinner for them and their four children.

During the 1850s and 1860s, Mandelbaum took advantage of the still relatively new and disorganized New York Police Department to expand her fencing operations. In those early years of booming population, the police put a priority on maintaining public safety and order and reducing violent crime. Meanwhile, so-called covert crimes committed by pickpockets, burglars, and sneak thieves became more common and inventive. Trafficking in stolen goods went almost unchecked, providing an opening for enterprising fences such as Marm Mandelbaum.

Typically, she paid thieves 10 percent to 20 percent of the wholesale price of merchandise, which she then sold to legitimate merchants for half or two-thirds of the regular wholesale price, producing a tidy profit. In time, she had customers—dressmakers, dealers, retailers—and selling agents throughout the United States and in Canada, Mexico, and Europe.

---

* The oft-repeated story that Mandelbaum opened an actual "Fagin" pickpocketing school for children on Grand Street is, however, apocryphal.

Over her career, she handled an estimated $10 million in pilfered loot, or $250 million in 2021 money. A robber baroness, she was as successful in her sphere as the Jay Goulds and Jim Fisks were in theirs. And at least within New York's immigrant community, she was more popular. Her enterprise made salable merchandise available to small retailers and street vendors at lower prices than what they would ordinarily have to pay. And as one study has observed, because her cohorts generally robbed the rich and their institutions, such as banks and luxury selling establishments, she "may have appeared to poor New Yorkers as a force pushing back against the profound wealth inequalities of the era."

A tough but fair negotiator, Mandelbaum paid thieves in cash and was true to her word. She dealt only with persons she knew and trusted, one at a time.

There was a good reason for her caution: she understood the strict rules of evidence that made fencing difficult to prosecute in the absence of independent corroborating witnesses (and the testimony of thieves and accomplices didn't count). If articles could be stripped of any unique identifiers, it was almost impossible to prove they were stolen. And even if a fence was found in possession of stolen property, the prosecution had to prove that he or she knew it was stolen. As a result, careful fences were rarely arrested, much less convicted.

As further protection, Mandelbaum paid off cops and politicians to leave her alone. She also provided bail money and legal representation to her thieving partners when they came under arrest. Walling said, only partly in jest, that she ran a "Bureau for the Prevention of Conviction."

To help run that bureau, Mandelbaum kept the era's two most successful and roguish criminal defense lawyers on a $5,000 annual retainer: the flashy, bejeweled, corpulent Big Bill Howe and his partner, the quiet, gnomish Abe Hummel, of the Howe & Hummel law firm (cable address LENIENT). Among their other clients were George Leslie and assorted hooligans and con artists, dive and brothel owners, abortionists, and dishonest Tammany officials.

Howe, the more flamboyant trial lawyer, could reduce witnesses and

juries to tears. By a shameless appeal to sympathy, for example, he se-
cured a verdict of manslaughter for Edward Unger, the man who had
confessed to the murder and mutilation of his roommate to Thomas
Byrnes. Hummel, more of a conference room attorney, maintained an
active theatrical practice in addition to his criminal defense work, repre-
senting entertainers such as P. T. Barnum, Lillian Russell, and Buffalo
Bill Cody. But Marm Mandelbaum was Howe & Hummel's most consistent and highest-paying client.

Mandelbaum operated her fencing business out of a pair of adjoining
buildings at the corner of Clinton and Rivington Streets on the Lower
East Side, in the Thirteenth Ward. It was part of Kleindeutschland (Little Germany), home to tens of thousands of German Jewish immigrants
who lived in tenements and worked as butchers, saloonkeepers, and small
tradesmen, often from their makeshift home "factories," or as pushcart
vendors on the narrow, dirty streets.

On the ground floor of 163 Rivington, a three-story framed structure
overlaid with brick, the Mandelbaums ran a dry goods store and haber-
dashery that served as a front. In separate rooms, Marm's children and
employees were kept busy at her real business. They removed tags, factory
numbers, and other identifying marks from stolen silks, furs, and clothing. They engraved over the monograms on watches, jewelry, and silverware, and melted down gold and silver. In other rooms, Marm's minions
packed crates of pilfered goods for shipment to customers and set up beds
for criminals who needed occasional shelter.

Thieves who came to dispose of their plunder entered through a secret
side door or the rear—never through the front entrance. Neighbors warned
Marm of any police nearby. She also had a trapdoor to let thieves escape
down through a hole in a basement wall into a tenement building she
owned next door. When necessary, she stashed hot lucre in a false chimney
that held a dumbwaiter. As her business expanded, she also stored stolen
goods in secret warehouses in Brooklyn and Passaic, New Jersey.

Angled around the corner at 79 Clinton Street, in a two-story wooden-
clapboard wing connected to 163 Rivington, was the Mandelbaum resi-

At her Lower East Side salon, 250-pound Marm Mandelbaum (seated far right) entertained members of New York's polite society, as well as common criminals who sought her protection from the law.

dence. It housed Victorian-style rooms, sumptuously decorated with the finest furniture, antiques, carpets, and silverware—all of it presumably stolen. Here, in Marm's salon, lawyers, judges, businessmen, police officers, and politicians mingled with common thieves and thugs, everyone worshipping at the feet of the gigantic woman in the ill-fitting ostrich-feathered bonnet.

Outwardly, she appeared coarse, even grotesque. Fleshy, with dark black eyes, heavy jowls, a protruding lower lip, and above average in height, Mandelbaum cut a Jabba the Hutt–like figure. But she was charming and socially adept—"a wonderful person; she changed character like a chameleon," George Walling recalled.

Fluent in English, if German-accented, she was a proper woman, a devoted mother, and attended synagogue regularly. Marm conducted her gatherings with Fifth Avenue propriety; guests were expected to get along and behave themselves—no stealing!—at least while they were there. "Piano Charley" Bullard, a concert-quality pianist and sometime partner of burglars Max Shinburn and Adam Worth, was a popular performer at her dinner parties. The finest wines and liquors, from her private cellar, were in abundance.

Inevitably, and perhaps at one of her parties, the debonair man-about-town George Leslie, late of Philadelphia, came to Mandelbaum's attention. He impressed her with his professionalism and sophisticated approach to bank robbery. He did his work, managed to avoid arrest, and had good relations with her New York darlings Shang Draper, Billy Porter, Johnny Irving, and Sheeny Mike Kurtz. Leslie became the head of her clique of silk-stealing and bank-robbing friends, brought her thousands in profits, and, according to Sophie Lyons, was her "pet and star."

By the time the Manhattan Savings job was in the planning, Mandelbaum (whose husband died in 1875) had expanded her operations to include financing bank robberies. They offered the prospect of sharing in a single, large haul of money and valuables as opposed to seriatim smaller transactions. Occasionally she would deal in stolen bonds, trading them or selling them back to the bank through a network of brokers willing to take the risk that the serial numbers could be matched.

George Walling said she supplied considerable money to the Manhattan Savings conspirators; other sources put Marm's contribution at a more modest $2,500 (about $60,000 in 2021 dollars), to purchase top-of-the-line burglar tools. Of course, that didn't include the amounts she paid regularly for the care and feeding of her minions, who were often in trouble with the law and low on funds due to blowing money on women, liquor, and gambling. She took a personal interest in the domestic lives of her yeggs and made sure they were gainfully "employed," both out of a genuine spirit of generosity and because it served her business interests.

The Manhattan Savings job was big enough that the gang also gave Mandelbaum's only serious fencing competitor, John D. Grady, a piece of the action. Grady, whose connections included Draper, Jimmy Hope, and Johnny Dobbs, conveniently had a small "diamond broker's" office at 645

Broadway, across from the Manhattan Savings Institution, that looked directly into the bank.

Grady's was a different business model from Mandelbaum's. He was a roving fence who carried his ready cash and loot—diamonds, watches, and jewelry—over his shoulder in a satchel as he made his daily rounds, pretending to be a peddler (hence his nickname, "Traveling Mike"). Grady boasted on several occasions that his satchel had property in it worth $125,000 to $150,000.

Grady's mobility gave him the advantage of being able to relieve pickpockets and other street thieves of their hot loot quickly and to pay them little for it. A short, thickset Irishman with a strong accent, he dressed shabbily and was not above snitching on small-time crooks to keep himself out of trouble. He frequented police headquarters and enjoyed the protection of higher-ups, although Walling and Byrnes snubbed him.

A bigger risk taker than Mandelbaum, Grady kept possession of stolen bank bonds and securities himself and tried to negotiate them for cash. He earned a reputation as a backer of first-class bank robbers as much as a receiver of stolen goods, and by one estimate advanced $10,000 to the Manhattan Savings plotters. He was particularly close with Jimmy Hope and Shang Draper, less so with Leslie.

According to a fictionalized dime detective novel written by Julian Hawthorne, son of the famous author Nathaniel, and supposedly based on Thomas Byrnes's secret diary, it was Traveling Mike Grady, not Mandelbaum, who provided the financing for the Manhattan Savings job. Sophie Lyons, whose memoirs contain heavy doses of embellishment, maintained the same thing: in her telling, Grady muscled Marm aside and cut her out of all financial investment in the heist.

That isn't likely. Mandelbaum was too powerful, and had too many close ties with Leslie and the other gang members, for her to have been barred from participating. It is possible, though, that the burglars' internal squabbles, which surfaced again in February 1878, led to a power struggle between Grady and Mandelbaum over future participation. For it was around that time that George Leslie—a Marm Mandelbaum man with fewer ties to Grady—began falling out with his compatriots.

Although tying up bank cashiers had never seemed to bother Leslie when the venture succeeded, the aborted Dexter bank robbery in February, which left a man dead, had greatly unnerved him. He had not entered the bank but had helped plan the heist and allegedly was seen, together with Draper, lurking outside at the time of the murder committed by Johnny Dobbs and Worcester Sam.

After the Dexter bank fiasco, an agitated Leslie accused his church-going wife, falsely, of infidelity, even as Leslie was himself openly consorting with Jennie Draper and other women. He was spotted walking in Brooklyn's Prospect Park with the comely Mrs. Draper, shopping with her at B. Altman's on Sixth Avenue, and buying her a camel's hair shawl at Marm Mandelbaum's (legitimate) dry goods store on Rivington Street. He'd also been suspected of intimacy with Billy Porter's beautiful wife, a New York schoolteacher, on an earlier trip to the Catskills, and with Johnny Irving's pretty sister, Babe, who, like Irving, was single.

Leslie's life turned reckless and dissolute. He began hanging out, uncharacteristically, in dive bars, where he got into violent quarrels with Porter, Irving, and Dobbs. They accused him of being "leaky" over the Dexter robbery and charged him with unfairness in dividing proceeds from various prior heists. He angrily denied their insinuations and offered to bet all comers that they weren't true. On at least two occasions, in Bowery saloons in May 1878, one or more of the crew of Dobbs, Irving, and Porter brandished pistols and threatened Leslie's life, while Draper, increasingly suspicious of his old friend, looked on.

Leslie became a wanderer, spending his nights with unknown women in Midtown Manhattan and Williamsburg, Brooklyn. He turned moody with his wife, who by now knew his true profession. At times he talked hopefully of going clean—perhaps opening a cigar shop—while at other times he spoke darkly of assassination plots, implying he had gotten into trouble with some criminal associates. The last time he saw his wife, at her mother's house in Philadelphia on May 10, he gave her a small amount of money he said might come in useful and told her where he had hidden some more.

On June 4, 1878, a mounted patrolman came upon the partially de-composed body of a man in a lonely wood near Yonkers, New York, at a place called Tramps' Rock. The dead man was well dressed, with a tweed coat, white shirt and collar, gold buttons, and silk necktie. He wore a styl-ish new hat and lay faceup, covered with brush and straw. A further trail of straw led from the body to the nearby roadside, causing police to suspect that the victim had been killed elsewhere and transported there by wagon.

A pearl-handled pistol was near the man's hand, which suggested suicide, but that was impossible: he'd been shot twice in the head from the rear, once behind each ear. Because none of his clothing, not even his shirt collar, showed any traces of blood, police figured he must have been naked in bed when murdered—possibly discovered in illicit relations with another man's wife. He'd been dead about a week, the police estimated.

Three days later the corpse, which had been kept on ice in a coffin at a local funeral parlor, remained unidentified. Marm Mandelbaum, though, had grown worried. Newspaper descriptions of the man matched George Leslie, who'd been missing for several days. She'd last seen him on May 27, Decoration Day (today, Memorial Day), in her store, when he bought the camel's hair shawl for Jennie Draper.

Some mysterious personal ads appeared on the front page of the *New York Herald* on June 2, 3, and 6, each addressed to "George": one from "Lizzie" (the name of Leslie's Chicago mistress); the other two from his "wife," imploring him to come home or at least say where he was. His real wife did not write them, and police suspected that the ads were placed by Jennie Draper. Mandelbaum, also a possible author, sent her trusted as-sistant Herman Stoude, who examined stolen goods at her warehouses, to the funeral home to inspect the body. He confirmed it was Leslie.*

---

* In *Gangs of New York*, Herbert Asbury writes mistakenly that Leslie took part in the Manhattan Savings robbery in October 1878 and continued committing other crimes until his death in 1884. Many writers since have perpetuated this same error.

Within days of his death, Leslie would be referred to—for the first time anywhere in print—as a notorious burglar and bank robber. Marm Mandelbaum was quoted as repeating, over and over, "Poor Shorge—he was such a nais man." She paid for his funeral at an Essex Street undertaker's shop, where she appeared visibly distraught. She also provided generous financial support to Leslie's widow, Molly, and spent much time consoling her.

After Leslie was identified, Johnny Dobbs and Worcester Sam, feeling renewed scrutiny of their roles in the Dexter bank murder, and now possibly Leslie's as well, went into hiding. Billy Porter and Johnny Irving were picked up for questioning about Leslie's murder and other crimes but were released for lack of evidence.

Two months later, in mid-August, Porter and Irving, along with Shang Draper, were arrested at the 152 Patchen Avenue mansion for a minor burglary. Draper was found hiding in a chicken shed in back of the house and refused to be photographed for a mug shot. The three of them were thrown into Brooklyn's Raymond Street Jail to await trial and were still there when the Manhattan Savings robbery took place.

Jennie Draper, who hadn't been present for the raid, fled to Cleveland, never to reunite with Shang. (A false rumor said she was found murdered in Staten Island a few months after Leslie's death.) The funds for her escape were provided by a close associate of Shang's who briefly harbored her at an office on Broadway. The benefactor then sent a curious letter to the New York police:

"Call off your dogs: the women you are pursuing are respectable."

It was signed by John D. Grady.

CHAPTER SEVEN

A STAR COP IS BORN

With George Leslie dead, Shang Draper in jail, and Marm Mandelbaum mournful and skittish, Jimmy Hope took over final planning of the Manhattan Savings job with Traveling Mike Grady's financial help. By that fall, Hope and his cohorts decided they'd had it with trying to manipulate combination locks. They would instead tie up the janitor, force the vault combination from him, and use the best of tools to break into the interior safes.

The men who took part in the actual burglary on the Sunday morning of October 27, 1878, were Jimmy Hope and his son Johnny, Banjo Pete Emerson, Abe Coakley, William Kelly, John Nugent, and a last-minute addition to the team identified by Shevlin only as Brooklyn Jimmy.* Some sources add Ed Goodie, a butcher cart thief who often served as a getaway driver and was frequently associated with Leslie, Mandelbaum,

---

* Possibly James Wilmont, alias "Mysterious Jimmy," named by Byrnes as a member of George Leslie's Brooklyn gang, and one of the burglars of the South Kensington bank.

and Grady. Pat Shevlin had agreed to be bound and gagged by the gang as a ruse if necessary, but, in the end, his presence was not required.

Using a wax impression key made by Hope (after the one made by Shevlin didn't work), the burglars got into the bank through the main Bleecker Street entrance, which led to the banking room and janitor Werckle's apartment. At two-fifteen in the morning, they went into a hallway above Werckle's apartment and waited there until daybreak.

Jimmy Hope and Billy Kelly assaulted Werckle at six o'clock and extracted the vault combination from him. Hope threatened to kill him if he refused or gave them the wrong number. The squarely built Kelly was left to guard Werckle and his family while Hope entered the vault and began attacking the safes. Kelly said later that the only one who gave them trouble was the "old woman," meaning Werckle's mother-in-law.

One of the burglars, either Coakley or Banjo Pete, helped them escape a close call when a beat cop walking past the bank noticed someone inside. The quick-thinking thief, pretending to be a janitor, began dusting a desk and nonchalantly nodded to the officer, who continued on his rounds.

The younger Hope and the latecomer Brooklyn Jimmy served as watchmen. It was Nugent who carried off the satchels of stolen loot, and perhaps Goodie who drove them away.

Of the $2.75 million hauled off, only $11,000 was in cash. About $2.5 million, or 90 percent, was in the form of nonnegotiable bonds registered in the name of the Manhattan Savings Institution and payable only to it. About $250,000 was in negotiable and coupon bonds payable to the bearer or on order, and as such were nearly the equivalent of cash.

The registered bonds, though, were worthless, in and of themselves, to anyone besides the bank. But that was no cause for despair: the robbers fully expected to be able to negotiate a return of them to the bank for some discounted amount of cash. And $250,000 in bearer and coupon bonds gave the burglars a liquid bundle of paper equivalent to $6.5 million in today's money.

The bank, meanwhile, was out the full $2.75 million. But despite its arguable negligence, it benefitted from what today would be called a government bailout of an institution "too big to fail." Congress and the New York State Legislature passed special legislation to issue Manhattan Savings replacement bonds and securities with new serial numbers, effectively reducing the bank's loss to the $11,000 in stolen cash. The robbers might still try to sell the original negotiable bonds, genuine on their face, to some unsuspecting person, but that would increase their risk of getting caught.

When Jimmy Hope learned of the bailout plan, he made each of the gang members contribute $600 from what they'd been paid as a first installment, ostensibly to hire a lawyer to go to Washington to lobby (or bribe) congressmen to vote against the legislation. Nothing came of the effort, and Hope likely just used the payments to line his own pockets and fund his escape to San Francisco. For Shevlin, the reduction of his already meager take from $1,600 to $1,000 so irked him that Byrnes easily put him in a mind to confess.

Although Byrnes effectively solved the case in the public's mind, obtaining convictions in those years was another matter. There were no telltale security camera tapes to review, no cell phone records to pore through, no fingerprints to find, much less feed into a computer database. To successfully put a robber behind bars, the cops had to either catch him (or her) red-handed, find a credible eyewitness or two who could positively identify the culprit, or obtain his or her confession. The human element was more important than technology.

A snitch's or accomplice's word might lead to an arrest, but rarely was that enough, by itself, to convict, since all criminals were viewed as liars. And that's assuming the thief could be found; as often as not, they went on the lam and remained hidden, at least until they were caught robbing again and were jailed for that crime or a prior one for which they'd served a partial sentence before breaking out.

That same pattern played itself out in the Manhattan Savings heist. In the end, only three of the conspirators were convicted: Patrick Shevlin, who pleaded guilty; Johnny Hope, fingered by witnesses who saw him misdirect the milkman; and Billy Kelly, based on Shevlin's unusually detailed testimony and the witnesses who'd seen Kelly lurking at the bank in the weeks before. Hope received a sentence of twenty years in Sing Sing; Kelly got ten. Despite Shevlin's and Byrnes's denials that he was promised leniency, and his pivotal role in the robbery, Shevlin spent little time in jail and was released sometime after testifying against Kelly in December 1879.

John Nugent made the mistake of attending Johnny Hope's trial, where he was recognized in court by Shevlin, who identified him in Byrnes's presence. Nugent went on trial and, to the surprise of nearly everyone, was acquitted. He was represented by the notoriously unethical William Howe and Abraham Hummel, and it was rumored that the jury had been bribed to reach its result.

Nugent was a free man, but his luck didn't hold. The police commissioners discharged him from the force, and in 1883 he was arrested in Hoboken, New Jersey, with two other men for assaulting a bank cashier in a robbery attempt aboard a train. Nugent fired a revolver at the pursuing train conductors before he was subdued. This time he wasn't represented by Howe & Hummel, and, after pleading guilty, he was sent to prison for ten years of hard labor.

Marm Mandelbaum was never arrested for the Manhattan Savings robbery. Neither was John Grady, who died of a heart attack two years later, in 1880, leaving Marm supreme among New York fences.

And what of the lead burglar of the Manhattan Savings job, Jimmy Hope? Disguising himself after the robbery for his exodus to San Francisco, Hope remained a fugitive in that city until 1881, when he was caught trying to rob a bank of $600,000. He was jailed in San Quentin Prison after California officials turned down Byrnes's request for extradition. Upon Hope's release in 1886, he was remanded to Byrnes's custody in New York and then sent to complete the final two years of an unexpired term for an upstate robbery.

Released from Auburn State Prison in New York in 1887, Hope was rearrested by Byrnes for the Manhattan Savings robbery. He had become the Jean Valjean to Byrnes's Inspector Javert. But for whatever reason— the passage of time, faded witness memories, or protection from friends in high places—Jimmy Hope was never brought to trial for the greatest of his heists.

In 1895 Byrnes reported that Old Man Hope had reformed and was living quietly on a farm in Connecticut. But ten years later, he was sus- pected of trying to pass $10,000 of the stolen Manhattan Savings bonds, almost none of which had ever been traced. From time to time over the years since 1878, small amounts of the bonds matching the original serial numbers had surfaced when some anonymous person tried to trade them, but bank officials believed most of the originals had been destroyed as worthless. When Hope died in June 1905, the secret of what happened to the stolen bonds died with him.

Although several of Hope's coconspirators likewise avoided prosecu- tion for their role in the great heist, they suffered retribution for other, less sensational, crimes.

After his arrest in Philadelphia in May 1879 for trying to sell some of the stolen Manhattan Savings bonds, Johnny Dobbs was indicted and held in the Tombs pending trial. He was discharged in February 1880, reportedly in exchange for his cooperation in providing information to Byrnes about the Manhattan Savings job. Smiling and chatty at his dis- charge hearing, Dobbs wasn't as happy when, a few months later, he was sent back to Connecticut State Prison to complete an unexpired term for a robbery committed in that state.*

Under pressure to make more arrests in the Manhattan Savings case, Byrnes nabbed Abe Coakley and Banjo Pete Emerson in April 1880 in Philadelphia. But the charges didn't stick, and both were released. Coak- ley later went to prison for eight years for pickpocketing a man of $545 on Grand Street.

---

* Released by Connecticut in 1881 for good behavior, Dobbs was captured in Massachusetts in 1884 for another bank robbery, convicted, and sentenced to ten years in Massachusetts State Prison. Discharged in 1892 for health reasons, he returned to New York and died that same year.

Banjo Pete was with John Nugent when they assaulted the bank cashier on a New Jersey train in Hoboken in 1883. Like Nugent, Pete received ten years in New Jersey's state prison for the crime. After his release, he returned to New York, married Jimmy Hope's daughter, and lived in the same house with Johnny Hope, who'd been released from Sing Sing in 1890 on a commutation for good behavior. The two of them—Johnny and Banjo Pete—lived out the rest of their days as upstanding citizens.

In June 1879, just before Johnny Hope's trial on the Manhattan Savings robbery began, Billy Porter and Johnny Irving escaped from Brooklyn's Raymond Street Jail, where they and Shang Draper had been kept since August 1878 after robbing a grain store of $600. Marm Mandelbaum temporarily secreted Porter and Irving in Passaic, New Jersey, where the flashily dressed pair walked about with the city's belles, spending money freely. But the two thieves were eventually recaptured and returned to prison.

Draper was extradited to Massachusetts to stand trial for the Northampton Bank robbery, along with Red Leary, who'd been recaptured by Pinkerton agents after his breakout from New York's Ludlow Street Jail. Before trial, bank officials offered Draper and Leary $100,000 if they would return $400,000 in bonds they had stolen. The burglars held out for $150,000, and the case went to trial.

The defendants were released when the prosecution witnesses—including the cashier who had been tied up and an accomplice and bank safe employee who had earlier turned state's evidence against some other burglars involved in the heist—suffered sudden memory loss. As one newspaper observed ruefully, Leary and Draper "went out of the courtroom in good spirits and departed for New York, where, it is reported, they held a reception on Saturday night, and were doubtless much honored and admired."

After his release, Draper quit bank robbing and opened a popular saloon at Sixth Avenue between Twenty-Eighth and Twenty-Ninth

Streets.* It was here, in 1883, that one of the most famous criminal epi-sodes of the entire Gilded Age occurred—one that put the Manhattan Savings robbery and, especially, the murder of George Leslie, back on the front pages five years after the fact.

From the very first, people suspected that Leslie had been, as Thomas Byrnes put it, "made away with by his pals." The prevailing theory was that jealousy over a woman—most likely, Shang Draper's wife, Jennie—had been the motive, and that Draper either pulled the trigger himself or had Porter or Irving do it. Another theory held that members of Leslie's gang—probably Johnny Dobbs and Worcester Sam—had offed him be-cause they were worried he would implicate them for the murder of trea-surer Barron in the Dexter Savings Bank robbery. It was also speculated that lingering bitterness over the division of spoils from past heists had motivated Leslie's murder.

The three theories were not mutually exclusive, and most observers believed that some combination of Draper, Dobbs, Porter, Irving, and Worcester Sam was responsible for the homicide. Police assumed that Leslie had been lured to his fate in Brooklyn by a note, probably from Jennie Draper, delivered to him at his regular hangout, Murphy's saloon at 354 Grand Street in Manhattan. He was shot in the back of the head, likely either at Porter's or Draper's Brooklyn abode, then driven by wagon to Yonkers. There a second bullet was put through his brain and his pistol placed near his hand in a feeble attempt to make it look like suicide. (Neither bullet matched the pistol.)

A local farmer remembered seeing near the murder site, around the time of Decoration Day, a horse-drawn wagon filled with straw that covered a bundle on the floor of the vehicle. It matched the description of the cart used often by Ed Goodie, a suspected getaway driver in the Manhattan Savings robbery. Other witnesses claimed to have seen Dobbs

---

* The address at the time was 466 Sixth Avenue; today it is 818–820, and the site of a different structure.

and Worcester Sam near Yonkers around the same time. But despite these disparate clues, no arrests were made.

One man who thought he knew what happened was John "Johnny the Mick" Walsh, head of a gang that was a rival to Porter's and Irving's Patchen Avenue outfit. A man of somewhat hideous appearance, with a massive forehead, Walsh had been a gambler, small-time politician, and liquor store owner before seeking greater riches through burglary. He was, in Byrnes's words, "pretty nearly the worst man in New York."

A history of bad blood between Walsh and Johnny Irving predated Leslie's murder. After Leslie's body was identified, Walsh sensed an opportunity to strike back at his nemesis. He went around New York speaking freely of Porter and Irving as the perpetrators and saying he could send them to the gallows if he wanted.

From the time Porter and Irving were both out of jail, in late summer 1883, they were gunning for Walsh, released from prison around the same time. On the night of October 16, 1883, they grabbed their revolvers and went looking for him.

At a quarter to two in the morning, Walsh was drinking with three underworld companions in Draper's Sixth Avenue saloon. With the legal closing hours past, the front door was locked and the curtains closely drawn. Behind the bar, mixing drinks, was Harry Hope, son of Jimmy and brother of Johnny and himself an ex-convict. Draper and Red Leary had gone next door to Kane's Restaurant for a late oyster supper.

As the four bar patrons were raising their glasses, a side door opened, and in burst Johnny Irving, a .38-caliber pistol in hand. Without a word, he fired at Walsh upon sight, grazing the lapel of his overcoat and shattering a mirror. Walsh, reaching for his gun, retreated behind an icebox alongside the bar and then into the billiards room in back, where Irving circled him. Then Porter came through the same side entrance to the barroom and ran into the billiards room to support his friend Irving.

None of the other men in the bar that night witnessed directly what happened in the back room, but they heard a barrage of gunshots. Minutes later, both Irving and Walsh were dead, splayed upon the floor at a right angle to each other, their feet nearly touching. Irving had a bullet in his brain and one in his right arm, while Walsh was shot in the left hand and fatally through the heart.

Porter was caught by police fleeing from the saloon with a revolver in his coat pocket. Three of the five chambers were freshly discharged, and the bullet that killed Walsh fit Porter's .32-caliber Smith & Wesson, not Irving's .38-caliber pistol. The police concluded that Porter had shot Walsh after Walsh gunned down Irving. "There is not the slightest doubt that Porter killed Walsh," said precinct captain Alexander S. Williams, who'd been awakened from bed and arrived shortly at the scene. "The bullets fit his pistol, he was seen on the spot, and the one shot that Irving fired at Walsh did not hit him."

Few people were distraught at the news of the killings. Informed of the affair at headquarters, Superintendent George Walling rubbed his hands in glee and exclaimed, "Glorious! Glorious!" Byrnes added that his only regret was that Porter was not among the victims.

Somehow Porter evaded conviction for the crime. Brought to trial thirty days later—speedy trials were the norm then—he was represented by Howe & Hummel, whose bills were paid by Marm Mandelbaum. Lawyer Howe sowed confusion with a theory that Walsh and Irving had simultaneously killed each other. It had all happened so fast, there were no eyewitnesses in the billiards room, and the testimony by those present was inconsistent.

At the not-guilty verdict, the gallery, filled with toughs, broke into applause. Porter beamed, thanked the jury, and vowed, as he left the courtroom, to lead an honest life thereafter. He did not.

⋆⇒◒◓⇐⋆

The Manhattan Savings Institution robbery and the murders associated with it were the central crimes in the careers of so many of the leading burglars of the age. The great bank heist was also a career-defining event for Captain Thomas Byrnes. Although the conviction rate was imperfect, this was, according to *The New York Times*, the first time that men who committed a bank robbery in New York City had actually been arrested.

At Byrnes's urging, the bank had refused to negotiate and hadn't paid the police department a cent except for travel fare for one detective. And of the burglars who couldn't be prosecuted for lack of evidence, many were convicted anyway for other crimes committed around the same time, rendering punishment for the Manhattan Savings job, in a sense, a moot point.

Byrnes's aggressive pursuit of the culprits was refreshing—a sign that the days of ransom and compromise were past. "He was the hottest customer I ever knew," wrote international jewel thief and safecracker Eddie Guerin in his memoirs. "The minute he had an idea you were crooked, he would keep his men after you until he had you inside."

Coupled with improvements in lock technology and greater attention paid by bank officials to security, Byrnes's unyielding policy of not paying ransom served to deter professional thieves from attempting anything remotely as brazen again, at least in New York. As one pair of crime historians would write in 1893, fifteen years later, "There has really been no great city bank robbery since the warning shock of the assault on the Manhattan Bank. . . . Our banks are now, with rare exceptions, excellently protected and guarded."

Moreover, in the aftermath of the Manhattan Savings case, the best bank burglars in the country—those aristocrats of crime—were either behind bars, in Europe, or dead. Less gifted burglars shifted to smaller and more vulnerable country banks and relied on cruder methods, such as dynamite and nitroglycerin, rather than mechanical ingenuity, to accomplish their goals.

The Manhattan Savings Institution heist was the high-water mark for American bank burglars in the nineteenth century. The nation's first golden age of bank robbery, which had begun after the Civil War, had come to a close. There would not be another until the 1930s, when the automobile and the tommy gun combined to support a succession of small-town and rural bank holdups by the likes of John Dillinger, Baby Face Nelson, and Bonnie and Clyde.

As a result of the Manhattan Savings case, Thomas Byrnes was on his way to becoming the best-known police detective in America. Before long, he would seize the opportunity to cement that title by making the detective bureau his own.

As for the man who'd masterminded the great heist, he achieved a notoriety in death that evaded him in life. And to this day, the murder of George Leslie, the King of the Bank Robbers, remains officially unsolved.

CHAPTER EIGHT

THE GREAT DETECTIVE

At the regular meeting of the New York Police Board on March 9, 1880, the commissioners made a surprising announcement: they voted to relieve Captain James Kealy of his position as head of the detective force and replaced him with Captain Thomas F. Byrnes, the star of the Manhattan Savings case.

For some time, the commissioners had been dissatisfied with the way the central detective bureau was run. A few men were performing the hard work of preventing crime and arresting criminals, while the rest did absolutely nothing. Some had not made an arrest in years. The detectives were reputed to be in collusion with the thieves and were in the habit of taking money from the proceeds of their crimes.

The commissioners thought a change in the bureau's head "would infuse more vim and vigor." And they saw Thomas Byrnes as someone to revitalize the force. Just recently, in January 1880, he and his right-hand man, Detective Edward Slevin, had hid behind a tree and wrestled two would-be burglars to the ground. Later that month, Byrnes broke up a gambling house on Bleecker Street, apprehending sixty patrons. He even had the temerity to arrest Harry Hill, whose Houston Street concert saloon was perhaps the most popular in New York, for selling liquor during performances.

The selection of Byrnes to head the detective force, reported *The New York Times*, was "in recognition of the energy and ability displayed by him in ferreting out and securing the arrest and conviction of the Manhattan Bank burglars and in other important cases in which he was remarkably successful." As a chronicler of the NYPD's early history would write a few years later, "This really marked the first serious and successful attempt to give New York City a Detective Department worthy of the name."

Byrnes, nominally a Democrat, was neither stridently pro- nor anti-Tammany. He would say later that he was "entirely free from and untrammeled by party obligations" and had never been a member of any political organization. But unlike some of his peers, he knew how to play the political game, which certainly didn't hurt his career progress.

Immediately upon assuming his new position, Byrnes made a politically deft move. Of course, Tammany Hall represented one power center that had to be assuaged. But there was another group that, in Gilded Age New York, had become increasingly important. They were the moneymen: the bankers, brokers, and merchants on Wall Street who were turning New York into the financial capital of the world.

To operate safely and profitably, though, they needed protection from the assorted bank sneak thieves, pickpockets, and forgers who frequented the Financial District. The best thieves found Wall Street to be fertile ground for their pillaging, and rarely a month passed without the disappearance of tin boxes containing money, bonds, securities, and other valuables. "Knavery was jubilant," a *Harper's Weekly* article observed. Thomas Byrnes promised to change all that.

As his first act, on the same day he took office, Byrnes established a detective substation on the second floor of 17 Wall Street. He staffed it with a half dozen of his best, most trusted men and linked it directly by telephone with the central office. Before this, when Wall Street businessmen were victimized by crime, they had to send for help to police headquarters at 300 Mulberry Street, nearly two miles away. They were generally unacquainted by sight with the plainclothesmen who walked the financial area, and thus didn't know where to find them when they were needed. For these reasons, most Wall Street men hired private detectives, who worked for a reward or fee, to guard against criminals.

Playing second fiddle to the Pinkertons of the world was unacceptable to Byrnes. "There is no reason why the men doing business in the great moneyed center of the chief city of this continent should not have at their disposal, without cost to them, the best detective talent to be found," he told the *New-York Tribune*. He was frankly appealing to businessmen downtown to give their detective business to him, not the Pinkerton Agency.

At the new substation, Byrnes stressed, his detectives would be on call at a moment's notice and could be anywhere in the Financial District within two or three minutes. For example, he explained, if bank officials suspected a check forger was surveying their premises, with a call to the substation they could have a detective at the bank before the forger even suspected he was under watch.

A day or two later, the president of the New York Stock Exchange, Brayton Ives, came to see Byrnes and asked him about his plans. Byrnes said he intended, if possible, to "protect those gentlemen from thieves," and added that he wanted to connect his substation by telephone to every bank and brokerage house in Lower Manhattan. Ives was so impressed that he convinced his Wall Street colleagues to give the police captain an office in the stock exchange itself to use as a substation, the expenses to be paid by them.

Byrnes's next move, which followed immediately, was even more dramatic. To great fanfare, he laid down his famous "dead line," an edict that known criminals venturing south of Fulton Street would be arrested on sight and shipped off to Blackwell's Island for a night in jail if they could not adequately explain their presence. Practically overnight, grateful businessmen could not help but notice the virtual elimination of thieves who had preyed on Wall Street for years.

Byrnes bragged that after he established the dead line, "not a penny, not a cent" went missing on Wall Street on account of professional thieves. That plenty of stock traders were themselves thieves who fleeced innocent investors was not Byrnes's concern.

Byrnes was making the world safe for plutocracy. But he wanted to do more: to turn New York's police detective bureau into another Scotland Yard—the fabled London police force—which boasted an elite secret service unit renowned for its covert operations. It wouldn't be easy; when he assumed command, Byrnes found the central detective office in a state of disorganization. Most of the detectives had been there for years and were lazy, incompetent, and worn out. The younger ones had no idea what was expected of them and would loll around in the morning until the roll was called.

Of the twenty-eight central office detectives stationed at Mulberry Street, Byrnes designated twenty-one of them as worthless and had them shipped back to patrol duty in the precincts. He replaced them with a new batch of men, many of them young and college educated, who had proven themselves honest, energetic, and competent as uniformed patrolmen.

In his effort to reorganize the detective force, Byrnes's hand was strengthened when, in April 1880, he was promoted to inspector to succeed the late John McDermott. Byrnes was now one of just four police inspectors, reporting directly to Superintendent Walling, while remaining head of the central detective squad.

With his additional clout, Byrnes was able to push a bill through the state legislature in 1882 reorganizing his force. He increased the number of headquarters detectives to forty, all handpicked by him, with the new rank of detective sergeant. Their pay was raised to $1,600 a year, equal to that of regular sergeants, and up from the $1,200 patrolman's salary they'd previously received. This elite group, dubbed the "forty immortals," would later come to include Arthur Carey.

The following year, the roughly sixty precinct detectives (two per precinct), were placed directly under Byrnes's control for the first time. Known as wardmen, these plainclothesmen were traditionally selected by the all-powerful precinct captains and were beholden to them. They mainly served as the captain's bagmen, or bribe collectors, and suffered little interference from the central office, the inspectors, or even the superintendent.

In theory, the wardmen were to use their incognito status to protect the public. But in reality, they were well known in their respective precincts by crooks and common citizens alike. They were constantly knocking on doors or meeting people in bars or at street corners to demand money for protection. With their covers thus blown, their effectiveness as undercover cops was virtually nil. "They can cope with a petty case of theft, assault, or swindling," *The New York Times* said of the wardmen, "but the moment a case of extraordinary importance comes into their hands, they content themselves with trusting to luck."

Under the reorganization promoted by Byrnes, all wardmen were transferred to the detective bureau at headquarters, placed under his command, and assigned by him to the precincts as needed. They would be rotated periodically so that every thief didn't know who they were. If any major crime occurred, they'd be expected to assist, without jealousy or interference, a detective sergeant from headquarters placed in charge of the case.

Byrnes's detective bureau became what NYPD police historians James Lardner and Thomas Reppetto have termed "a separate fiefdom," insulated from the corruption at the precinct level and largely independent of the police superintendent and even the civilian police board that ultimately controlled the department. George White, the celebrated bank robber, called it "a complete transformation of affairs."

In particular, White said that the "Bank Ring," a group of cops who let bank robbers off the hook in exchange for a percentage of their take, came to an end under Byrnes—which is one reason big bank robberies in New York dwindled to nothing after the Manhattan Savings heist. "Never in my days, when he was in charge of the Detective Bureau, did I have knowledge that he was other than honest," White said of Byrnes.

Byrnes also clamped down on cops who took a percentage of petty thieves' loot to leave them alone. White recounted a conversation he had once with a former member of the Bank Ring, who had taken a $100 bill from pickpocket Walter Brown rather than arrest him. "Within forty-eight hours, Byrnes called me in his office and said, 'Two days ago, you took a hundred from Brown, didn't you?'" the cop recalled. "I knew I was up against it. Well, he looked at me, and said, without roaring at me as he does sometimes, 'Turn that money in[to] the Pension Fund, and if anything like this happens again, I'll ask for your shield.'"

Byrnes thoroughly modernized the detective practice. He required each of his men to keep meticulous diaries of their interactions with criminals wherever they met them and had the information organized and filed. He kept statistics on the number of arrests, convictions, and years of sentencing of criminals apprehended by the bureau. And he made sure everyone knew when the stats improved.

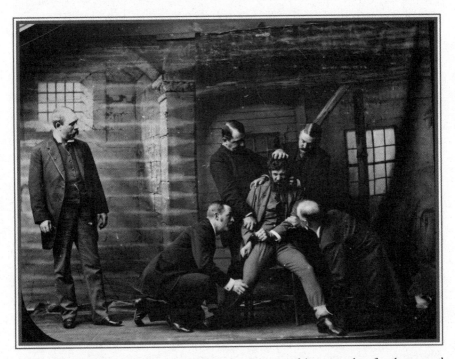

Thomas Byrnes (left) watches a criminal struggle to avoid his mug shot for the rogues' gallery.

Anyone arrested in the prior twenty-four hours was brought to 300 Mulberry Street for the "morning parade," a daily lineup that allowed detectives to view suspects up close. Byrnes also followed the practice of photographing each person arrested in the city, with the most wanted appearing in the famous rogues' gallery at police headquarters. The mug shots and accompanying rap sheets were also distributed to each of the city's thirty-some precincts and sent to police departments in other cities. The rogues' gallery was, for nineteenth-century American law enforcement, a tool akin to facial recognition systems in the twenty-first century.

Byrnes also coordinated with international authorities and, through photographs, helped derail a major European counterfeiting scheme a few months after his promotion to inspector. When some of the forgers were arrested in Florence and Milan, Italy, the American consul in Naples telegraphed Byrnes in New York, asking him if he could recognize any of the men in custody. Within forty-eight hours, the consul received the following cablegram:

YES, COLBERT IS "SHELL" HAMILTON; HARRY WILLIS IS GEORGE WILKES, AND JULIUS IS "PETE" BYRNES. ALL NOTORIOUS FORGERS AND COUNTERFEITERS ON A JOB IN ITALY.

BYRNES

As with the third degree, Byrnes's innovations, such as the rogues' gallery and daily lineup, were not new. But he expanded, systematized, and publicized them to such an extent that he has often been credited with inventing them.

After he was ensconced in office at central headquarters, Byrnes also took the opportunity to refine his third-degree psychological methods. He brought suspects into his solemn private office and showed them his "museum of crime" across the way. Likenesses of real-life burglars, shoplifters, pickpockets, and other assorted crooks stared out from the walls at visitors. The relics of celebrated cases filled glass-paneled cabinets that ran the width and height of the walls. Here, as Art Carey vividly recalled,

> were the tools of thieves, and the weapons of murderers, braces and bits, dark lanterns, lock picks, jimmies . . . skeleton keys, spurious gold bricks, and bunco men's lurid circulars for the gullible. There was a weird assortment of weapons—billies, pistols, daggers, slung shots, and vials—that had contained poisons and knockout drops. In the center of these were two black masks and a hangman's noose: both the accouterments of the public executioner which had actually been used.

Byrnes's museum housed the actual burglars' tools used in the Manhattan Savings robbery and the locks that Langdon Moore supposedly knew how to open by listening to them. Counterfeit railroad bonds, bogus tickets for the elevated train, and real opium and pipes in which to smoke it were on display as well. The point of this "shuddering horror," as *Harper's Magazine* put it, was to scare suspects into confessing by reminding them that punishment was inevitable.

Although he did not criticize him by name, Byrnes's boss, longtime police superintendent George Walling, was not a fan of what he considered Byrnes's "star chamber" tactics. But no one else seemed to know or care, perhaps because other cops could be even more brutal.

Alexander S. "Clubber" Williams, who had arrested Billy Porter for the murder of Johnny the Mick Walsh, was the paradigm. Second only to Byrnes in fame on the police force, and a year older, the Nova Scotia–born Williams gained his nickname for the deadly twenty-six-inch hardwood club he eagerly wielded against suspects. "There is more law in the end of a policeman's nightstick than a Supreme Court decision," the popular (and thoroughly corrupt) Williams is reputed to have said.

Williams established his reputation on his very first beat by tossing a

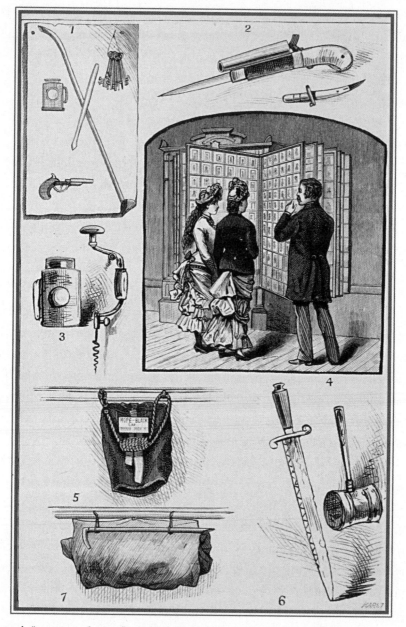

Byrnes's "museum of crime" across from his office, which displayed the actual burglar tools and murder weapons used in celebrated cases. Byrnes showed the items to suspects to convince them they were going to face punishment eventually and might as well confess. Recalcitrant crooks were subjected to the third degree. Also pictured is the famous rogues' gallery containing the photographs of known criminals.

Alexander "Clubber" Williams, so nicknamed because of his eagerness to use his deadly billy club on suspects. Thoroughly corrupt, Williams turned police bribe-taking into an art form.

pair of local toughs through a window. Or so it was claimed; tales of his early prowess are not always reliable. According to another possibly apocryphal story, he hung his watch on a lamppost at Thirty-Fifth Street and Third Avenue in the tough Gas House District, then, to prove to reporters how feared he was, he led them on a walk around the block and returned with them to find the watch still there. (A version of the same incident appears in Scorsese's film *Gangs of New York*.)

Like Byrnes, Williams had been a member of the Broadway Squad. He likewise rose quickly through the ranks and was promoted to captain in 1872, just six years after joining the force. By 1876, he was commanding the infamous Tenderloin, also known as Satan's Circus, a high-rent red-light district in the heart of Midtown Manhattan. Originally running from Twenty-Third Street to Forty-Second Street between Fifth and Seventh Avenues, the area today houses Madison Square Park, Macy's, the Empire State Building, and the New York Public Library.

A year later, Williams founded the Police Athletic Club, where he showed off his considerable boxing and wrestling skills. He also unofficially refereed boxing matches at the original Madison Square Garden, at Madison Avenue and Twenty-Sixth Street, jumping to center ring to prevent the likes of John L. Sullivan from going beyond legal sparring to illegally knocking out their bloodied opponents.

Unlike Byrnes, Williams's stardom derived less from cracking crimes than from cracking heads. Well above six feet tall, he was described as "almost a giant in stature, perfectly proportioned, with the bearing of a trained athlete." Possessed of great physical strength and a fighting spirit, Williams fearlessly took on the most dangerous criminals. He once reportedly held thirty-eight of them at gunpoint in a Broome Street saloon while another cop sought help.

Williams's aggression knew no bounds. He would be brought up on brutality charges 347 times in his career and fined or reprimanded more than 200 times, but he never had his badge taken away.

Byrnes could play rough, too. But apart from clubbing a group of demonstrators at a labor rally in Tompkins Square in July 1877, where he was hit in the hand by a brick, Byrnes was not known for personally resorting to deadly force. Instead, he placed a premium on intelligence gathering and criminal snitching. There was, he said frequently, no honor among thieves. To catch a thief, one had to know who they were, where they went, and how they operated. Byrnes said he spent two out of every twenty-four hours in the company of criminals brought before him as suspects or criminals—not because he enjoyed it, but because it gave him an education.

Byrnes had one of his greatest sleuthing triumphs with the arrest and conviction of Mike McGloin for the December 30, 1881, murder of French-born wine merchant Louis Hanier. At Hanier's saloon on West Twenty-Sixth Street, the proprietor was awakened from bed by the sound of nineteen-year-old McGloin and three confederates looting the bar downstairs. Hanier came down the stairs and was shot to death. ("Assassins!" he cried in French before dying almost instantly.) The murder of Hanier, a law-abiding father of seven, sparked outrage in the city's French community and commanded newspaper headlines for a month until Byrnes announced that he'd collared his man.

Mike McGloin, the nineteen-year-old gang member arrested by Thomas Byrnes for the murder of French wine merchant Louis Hanier.

McGloin was a brash young ruffian who'd been arrested at age twelve for tapping a beer till and later served time for larceny and assault. He led a gang of thieves, named for him, that operated a block from Hanier's bar. Although there were no clues or witnesses to the murder, Byrnes surmised that whoever shot Hanier, likely a poor street punk, might have been dumb enough to pawn the murder weapon rather than throw it away.

A search of area pawnshops led to one at Thirty-First Street and Ninth Avenue, where someone had hocked a revolver for a measly $2 the morning after the murder. It was traced to McGloin, who'd recently left it with a local bartender as security for a $1 loan, then retrieved it hours before Hanier was killed.

Byrnes recovered the fatal .32-caliber bullet and fit it inside McGloin's gun, but because ballistics forensics didn't allow for specific matching, the detective needed more. He had one of his men, Max Schmittberger, enter a saloon where McGloin was drinking with a fellow gang member. On Byrnes's orders, Schmittberger casually posted a $500 reward circular for Hanier's murderer directly over McGloin's head. After Schmittberger left, one of Byrnes's detectives who'd stayed behind overheard McGloin boast to his associate that he'd neither weakened nor turned white at the sight of the poster.

That was enough for Byrnes to raid the same saloon a few nights later, arrest McGloin and his companions, and bring them in for questioning. When confronted with the pawnshop and revolver evidence against him, McGloin broke down, saying he'd acted in self-defense because he thought Hanier was armed. (He wasn't.) Word of his arrest, McGloin told Byrnes, would break his aged mother's heart.

In a later version of the story, Byrnes is reported to have sat McGloin at a prison window where he could see his accomplices being led across the jail's courtyard and talking to officials, presumably turning state's evidence. "Squealed, both," Byrnes allegedly muttered, prompting McGloin to finally confess.

Defended unsuccessfully by Howe & Hummel, McGloin was convicted of first-degree murder after eleven minutes of jury deliberations and was sentenced to hang. (His pals received burglary sentences.) While being escorted by police to his death row cell, McGloin was greeted by other young toughs who rushed to shake his hand.

After all appeals failed, a remorseless, indifferent McGloin was hanged at the Tombs on the morning of March 8, 1883, following a final breakfast in which he asked for, and was given, an extra helping of pancakes. Before the gallows fell, he received a visit from his wailing mother and a woman he referred to as "his girl."

Defiant to the end, McGloin had previously been quoted as saying a gang member couldn't be considered tough "until he knocks his man out"—that is, kills him. The night before his execution, he reportedly invited Byrnes to attend his wake and "have a devil of a time."

Byrnes received the $500 reward out of a police fund. He donated it to Hanier's widow and orphans.

Byrnes was widely praised for bringing the Frenchman's murderer to justice. His work invited comparisons to Eugène François Vidocq, the famed head of the French detective force in the early 1800s. Himself a former convict, and considered the world's first true police detective, Vidocq employed a network of informants and followed the dictum that it takes a thief to catch a thief.

The rogues' gallery also continued to pay dividends. A few months after McGloin's hanging, Byrnes helped Belgian police officials identify two American burglars who were caught trying to rob a bank in the rural town of Verviers. The Belgians didn't know who exactly they had in custody until Byrnes told them they were Max Shinburn and Piano Charley Bullard, for whom police in the United States had been looking. Both men were sentenced to long terms in a Belgian prison in Liège.

Byrnes's crime-fighting reputation was further burnished in 1886 when more than two hundred pictures copied from the rogues' gallery were published in his landmark book *Professional Criminals of America*. Still in print today, it lists the vital statistics for each criminal, including any distinguishing marks such as tattoos or scars. Minibiographies describe the types of crimes they specialized in and any peculiar methodologies they practiced.

The earliest systematic attempt at crime prevention and control on a national scale, *Professional Criminals* became a working bible for law enforcement authorities across the country. Habitual criminals hated it because it publicized them to the world at large. Occasionally they struggled to avoid posing for a clear head shot until they were subdued and forced to sit still. Byrnes frequently pointed out when he considered a crook's picture to be "a good one." If a criminal turned his face away when photographed, as many of them did, Byrnes would note, as he did for Sheeny Mike Kurtz, that his picture was "a splendid one, although avoided."

Byrnes's book is full of lively observations:

"David Bliss, alias Doctor Bliss . . . has a hole on the right side of his forehead."

"Edward Dinkelman . . . dresses well, and is very quick in his movements."

He accompanied his analyses with various aphorisms, such as: the hotel thief strikes "when the unsuspecting prey fatigued by travel gives proof of his unconsciousness by deep, stertorous breathing"; "some of the most prominent forgers are chemists"; "the shoplifter is always a person of fair apparel, and she generally has a comfortable home."

Professional Criminals has little to say about the crimes of gambling, prostitution, and drug trafficking. Despite periodic raids he led or ordered, Byrnes tended to view these as both inevitable and under the protection of corrupt politicians and the lenient judges they appointed.

Nor does Byrnes's book deal with the topic of murder, as such. Most thieves did not carry guns in those days, and killings for purely business reasons were rare. As Art Carey would write many years later, Byrnes "did not regard slayers as professionals, and the thieves of that day, unlike the professional criminals of the present era, had not adopted murder as an incidental to robbery."

That day was coming. But in the meantime, Byrnes's focus was on property crimes and protecting the city's commercial class from habitual thievery. He knew where his bread was buttered. He shielded Jay Gould and other Wall Street men from various blackmailers and extortionists, and they rewarded him with investment advice and stock tips.

In one highly publicized case in 1881, Byrnes foiled a blackmail scheme against Gould by posting a slew of plainclothes detectives at post office stations from which a series of anonymous threatening letters were emanating. Byrnes inserted a personal ad in a daily newspaper that induced the blackmailer to write again, and they caught the culprit in the act of sending one too many missives. With a grateful Gould investing on his behalf—likely with the benefit of inside information—Byrnes quietly began accumulating a fortune in the form of securities and real estate.

Some years later, George Jay Gould, eldest heir to his father's fortune, was receiving threatening letters from an insane man and appealed to Byrnes for protection. Byrnes earned the tycoon's gratitude by summoning legendary Wild West gunfighter and former Dodge City sheriff Bat Masterson from Denver to serve as Gould's bodyguard. Byrnes explained that the job called for "a sure shot, a quick shot, and one who could be counted on not to hit the wrong person."

In addition to the richest Wall Street men, Byrnes sympathized with middle- and upper-class New Yorkers—perhaps a third of the city's population—whose increasing wealth made them inviting targets for hoodlums. Pickpocketing, the most common crime, was rampant, as gentlemen routinely kept their gold watches in vest pockets that were easy to pilfer from. And, in an age before credit cards, everyone carried wads of cash that merchants demanded as the sole source of payment. The celebrated pickpocket George Appo, an odd little half-Chinese, half-Irish fellow, could make $600 to $800 in a few days, when most working-men made less than that in a year.

When large public gatherings were expected in New York, such as the 1885 funeral of Ulysses S. Grant, Byrnes had all the city's known pick-pockets arrested in advance and held in jail. Out-of-town members of the light-fingered fraternity were taken into custody as soon as they stepped off their trains. Like his dead line, this caging practice was surely a viola-tion of due process. But to Byrnes, the ends justified the means, and habitual criminals had no rights a policeman was bound to respect.

Byrnes spent comparatively little time fretting about crime in the slums as long as it stayed there. And he was less concerned with the sad tales of out-of-town visitors who fell for Manhattan con artists' promises of easy money. "It's the fellow from the country that they take in, an' Byrnes never put up a bluff about tryin' to protect the countryman," ex-plained one reformed criminal, an anonymous, self-described former member of "Mother Mandelbaum's push." Byrnes, recalled this crook who had "squared it," was "in the Front Office to look after the people o' York, an' I'm one o' the old York thieves that thinks he did his job as well as it could be done."

A pessimist when it came to human nature, Byrnes thought most criminals were incapable of reform. "Once a thief, always a thief" was his frequent refrain. Nevertheless, he forged close relationships with many criminals, turning them into a friendly network of stool pigeons (informants). He tolerated their petty offenses so long as they served as snitches on more important crimes and coughed up their ill-gotten gains upon his request when the complaining victims were rich or famous.

After the journalist Lincoln Steffens told Byrnes his pay envelope had been stolen while he was riding a streetcar, Byrnes questioned him about the details, including which line he had taken home. "All right. I'll have it for you Monday morning," the detective promised. Byrnes, who knew which pickpockets were working the line, sent out the word that a friend of his had been robbed and that the money needed to be returned. Come Monday morning, Byrnes handed the envelope back to Steffens in the same condition as it had been when stolen.

Steffens knew, of course, that he got his money back only because Byrnes allowed small-time thieves to ply their trade. Normally skeptical of authority figures, Steffens was willing to overlook Byrnes's symbiotic relationship with at least some offenders. He also marveled at Byrnes's ability to switch between a courtly, polite-spoken man with reporters, public officials, and businessmen, and a tough, slangy, Irish street cop when trying to intimidate tougher criminals: for instance, "Ya bleeeedin' doooope ye" and "See youse in the *cawt*room." The more excited he was, the more pronounced his cockney accent and less grammatical his speech became.

Steffens's fellow muckraker Jacob Riis, author of *How the Other Half Lives*, the famous exposé of New York's slum housing conditions, likewise expressed qualified admiration. Byrnes was a czar, Riis wrote, "with all an autocrat's irresponsible powers." In Riis's view, Byrnes "was unscrupulous, he was for Byrnes—he was a policeman, in short, with all the failings of the trade. But he made the detective service great."

Under Byrnes, the NYPD's detective bureau came to rival in reputation Scotland Yard and the great detective departments of Paris and Vienna, Austria. Byrnes's detectives were far more respected than those in America's more "wide open" cities—notably Chicago, where the police department was relatively weak and indifferent to crime. To Byrnes, law-abiding New Yorkers deserved better police protection than one would receive in some western frontier town.

In time, modernizations such as fingerprinting and Art Carey's homicide bureau would further improve crime fighting. But there was a flip side. As policing in New York grew steadily more professional and sophisticated, so too did the city's criminals. The rogues in the gallery were not going to stand pat. Increasingly, they became more organized, commercial, violent—and deadly.

CHAPTER NINE

"TOO MUCH FOR OUR POLICE"

It was at night that the cry was heard: a musical, birdlike call meant to warn of the approach of the police. The sharp inflection rose almost to falsetto on the first syllable, falling to a low, drawn-out baritone on the second: *"Why-O! Why-O!"* It was the cry of the Whyo gang, the first in Gilded Age New York to make a business of crime.

To most people today, the phrase "gangs of New York" conjures images of the oddly dressed, street-battling rowdies in the 2002 Martin Scorsese film, set before and during the Civil War in the Five Points—the most degenerate of the city's overcrowded slums. Those early gangs, with colorful names such as the Dead Rabbits, the Plug Uglies, the Roach Guards, and the Bowery Boys, could certainly be violent, as evidenced by the Dead Rabbits Riot of July 4, 1857. But they were relatively hands-off when it came to ordinary New Yorkers. The gangs mostly beat up on one another when they felt their territory threatened by rivals. Their weapons of choice were clubs, fists, teeth, and brickbats, not guns or the deadly knives and axes seen in the movie.

Most gang members had day jobs as butchers, artisans, or laborers, and they banded together after hours around common ethnicity and lo-cale. Their goals were camaraderie and collective self-protection, not mayhem for money. Many became volunteer firefighters.

The Whyos were different.

Unlike their predecessors, the Whyos treated crime as a full-time occupation. They willingly preyed on everyday New Yorkers to make a buck. They thrived on the usual pickpocketing, petty thievery, and pimp-ing but also expanded their repertoire to include business crimes such as counterfeiting, extortion, and control of gambling houses. They employed violence, without the slightest hesitation, against citizens and cops alike. And their top brass carried pistols. They were, as one historian of Irish gangs has written, early racketeers, "a new breed of street-level capitalist criminal."

Exactly when they first emerged is unknown. Herbert Asbury main-tains that they came into existence in New York right after the Civil War, replacing the old gangs that had ruled the Five Points and that were dispersed shortly after war's end.

But that timeline is off by a decade or more. The first mention of the Whyos in any newspaper did not come until early 1884. The mid-1880s was their golden era, and remnants of the gang remained active until the early to mid-1890s.

Although their origins are obscure, their reputation was distinct. Op-erating out of the same Five Points neighborhood as the old gangs, the Whyos were considered the wickedest criminals up to their time. They dropped bricks on police officers from tenement rooftops and threw chairs at a saloon's shelf of liquor bottles if the bartender refused them free drinks. Among their main gathering spots was a Bowery saloon aptly known as the Morgue, named for the resemblance of the whiskey served there to embalming fluid, and perhaps for the many murders said to have been committed there.

The gang members lolled around by day and came out at night to rob. They would accost a lush—a drunken man lying asleep on the street. Or they'd target a slummer—a tourist or uptown society swell stumbling his way back to the elevated train after a night at Billy McGlory's Armory Hall, a haunt for harlots, brawlers, knockout-drop artists, and young men in drag speaking in high falsetto voices. If a policeman tried to arrest one of the Whyos, a swarm of others would descend upon the helpless officer, assault him, and wrest the prisoner away. The Whyos reveled in "doing up a cop."

The Whyos dwelt in the maze of backstreets around Mulberry Bend, among them Bottle Alley off Baxter Street, which Jacob Riis called the foulest spot in the city. It was common in the morning to find a fresh pistol bullet hole in the woodwork of the rickety tenement houses in Bottle Alley.

The crooked alleyways made it easy for gangs to set upon unsuspecting victims and then dart away to make their escape. One frequent

Bandit's Roost, an alley on Mulberry Street in the infamous Five Points slum neighborhood, was a frequent hideout for the cutthroat Whyo gang, the first in Gilded Age New York to make a business of crime.

underground passageway led from Bottle Alley to Bandit's Roost, another Whyo hideout at 57–59 Mulberry Street. Or, when chased by the police, gang members might run up to the tenement rooftop, jump the small gaps from building to building, descend through a skylight, and scamper down the stairs to the street to continue on their way.

Any serious loot was quickly placed with criminal fences. If a gang member needed to hide, there was always an empty tenement basement, scarcely high enough for a man to stand upright. Most of the Whyos were short, anyway: five foot four to five six was a common height, and a convenient one for a hooligan.

The Danish-born Riis, then a police reporter, experienced the Whyos' terrorism firsthand. One night he was turning a corner downtown in the small hours of the morning when he came upon a group of drunken roughs, members of the Whyo gang. Their leader had a long knife that he jabbed playfully into Riis's ribs, asking him what he thought of it. When Riis declined to play along, saying he thought it was two inches longer than the law allowed, the youth jabbed it in farther, just short of drawing blood, as the gang stood watching the silent struggle. "A human life was to them, in the mood they were in, worth as much as the dirt under their feet, no more," Riis recalled. Just then, Sixth Precinct captain John McCullagh emerged from around the corner with one of his detectives and scattered the ruffians, or else Riis might not have lived to write his groundbreaking book on the city's tenements.

Riis considered the Whyos "the worst cutthroats in the city," and a New York City guidebook said that "a more hopelessly vile and degraded set of miscreants probably never existed in a civilized community." Multiple contemporaneous newspaper references to the "notorious Whyo gang" confirm that this was the consensus view. But although the Whyos' reputation needs no embellishment, certain mythical stories about them have persisted through the years. The most exaggerated of them were originated by Herbert Asbury.

Asbury claimed that no one could be accepted into the Whyo gang until he had committed his first murder. According to Asbury, Mike

McGloin, the kid nailed by Thomas Byrnes for the Hanier murder, was an early Whyo, and after his statement that "a guy ain't tough until he has knocked his man out," the gang enshrined it as policy. Perhaps that fairly expressed their sentiment, but the notion that every Whyo was a murderer is fanciful. Moreover, although he was reportedly a hero of the Whyos, McGloin was never himself a member of the gang; instead, he headed a small gang in the West Twenties under his own name.

Another well-traveled Asbury tale has master thief "Dandy Johnny" Dolan inventing a copper eye gouger that the Whyos used in their fights with other gangs. But Johnny Dolan, who was hanged in 1876 for murdering a Greenwich Street brush maker, was never identified as a Whyo during his lifetime in the multiple newspaper stories about his career. Nor is there any account of him inventing, or even using, an eye gouger.

Yet another famous Asbury legend posits that a later Whyo, one Piker Ryan, had on him at the time of his arrest a list of crime tasks the gang would perform for hire. The escalating levels of violence commanded higher prices: a punch in the face for $2, a broken nose and jaw for $10, broken arms or legs for $19, a shot in the leg for $25, and $100 and up for "doing the big job"—in other words, murder.

This colorful tale has become the signature anecdote about the Whyo gang, recycled endlessly by internet bloggers and professional historians alike. But besides its inherent implausibility—why would a hoodlum put such an incriminating, easily memorized list in writing and keep it in his possession?—it is undermined by the evidence.

Asbury identified Piker Ryan as a well-known gangster and killer who flourished around 1900. But the Whyos were no longer in existence by that time. And the man whose rogues' gallery photo Asbury points to as "Piker Ryan" is someone else altogether: a little-known run-of-the-mill pickpocket named Patrick "English Paddy" Ryan who arrived in New York from England around 1893 at age thirty-seven. He was never associated with the Whyos and wasn't nicknamed "Piker."

During their heyday, the Whyos weren't the only gang in New York; in 1884 New York's *The Sun* identified some fifty others. "Every corner has its gang," Jacob Riis wrote, "not always on the best of terms with the rivals in the next block, but all with a common program: defiance of law and order, and with a common ambition: to get 'pinched,' i.e., arrested, so as to pose as heroes before their fellows."

The gangs maintained the tradition of evocative names: the Push Along Keep Moving Gang, the Never Sweats, the Sons of Leisure, the Merry Ramblers, the Forty Thieves. Others were named after their territory: the Stable Gang, near the Washington Street stables, and the Battle Row and Hell's Kitchen Gangs on the West Side. (Hell's Kitchen, now the name of an entire area in Midtown West, was then a literal address—551 West Thirty-Ninth Street, near Eleventh Avenue. Its entrance led up a staircase to a jumble of filthy little shanties.)

Most of the gangs had a dozen to thirty members, ages roughly fifteen to twenty-five, and stole for beer. "Rushing the growler" was a common ritual in those years, which involved sending women or children to the local tavern to fill a pail with beer to be brought back and consumed at home. The "growler" gangs topped up their pails, too, but without paying for them. They would steal them from women and children on the street, or from the ubiquitous saloons. They'd march inside a bar, tap a keg to fill their big can, and tell the saloonkeeper that if he didn't "hold his yawp," the entire gang would clean him out that night.

Some gangs specialized in certain types of loot. The Boodle Gang on the Lower West Side stole pigs off butcher carts, carved them up, and sold the pieces within the neighborhood at cut-rate prices. Other West Side gangs such as the Forty Thieves robbed from freight cars on the railroads along the Hudson River and fleeced the passengers.

The Short Tails, so named because they were younger and smaller, commonly pilfered rope from boats docked at the foot of Corlears Street on the East River. The Border Gang rowed out from nearby Gouverneur Slip to detain sloops, hold up their captains, and steal their money. Of the Push Alongs, who spent their evenings around Nineteenth Street and Sixth Avenue, one cop said, "Dey'll steal anything, a stove or de stockin's off your feet."

There were juvenile gangs and even female gangs, including one beer-drinking group of women who nightly occupied a house stoop on Sixteenth Street near Tenth Avenue. Led by Tidy Emma and Big Mag, they worked the growler and were just as likely as male gangs to rob some helpless person who fell into their hands. Women were also members of other gangs and occasionally served in the front lines in battles with the police. Partly this was "from sheer love of the 'fun,'" noted Jacob Riis, but mainly it was because "husbands, brothers, and sweethearts are in the fight to a man and need their help."

Many gangs pretended that they were social clubs and sold neighborhood citizens tickets to their annual picnics or balls. Although technically voluntary, anyone who didn't buy a ticket could expect a late-night visit from a gang member.

The younger rank-and-file gang members were often scruffy-looking, but their leaders were more presentable. Jim Caulfield, a boy pickpocket, remembered going with a friend to get a look at the criminal "celebrities" in the saloons. "A splendid sight one of these swell grafters was, as he stood before the bar or smoked his cigar on the corner," Caulfield recalled. "Well dressed, with clean linen collar and shirt, a diamond in his tie, an air of ease and leisure all about him, what a contrast he formed to the respectable hod-carrier or truckman or mechanic, with soiled clothes and no collar. And what a contrast was his dangerous life to that of the virtuous laborer."

Some of the gangs were just as capable of violence as the Whyos. The leader of the Kip's Bay Gang, which hung around Thirty-Seventh Street and First Avenue, killed a man with a billiard cue. His underlings threw two police officers into a water trough on East Thirty-Ninth Street and tossed another cop overboard at the pier. An Upper East Side gang stoned a roundsman to death in 1881. Few of the city's gang members had any compunction about shooting at pursuing cops.

From the decrepit, rat-infested tenement houses on South and Water Streets along the East River, gangs came out at night to victimize drunken sailors. If the seaman resisted too much, he'd be thrown into the water. The thieves were confident that if the drowned body was found, it would be assumed that the inebriated sailor had fallen overboard. Or maybe they'd dump him in the sewer beneath the infamous Gotham Court tenement on nearby Cherry Street, where the bodies of murdered men were sometimes found.

Even amid all this depravity, the Whyos stood out as the most important of all the gangs. For one thing, they were by far the largest, with an estimated 150 members in the Sixth Ward alone, which included the Five Points and the Bowery.* Absorbing many smaller street-corner groups, the Whyos expanded their influence beyond their own territory to all of Lower Manhattan and the city beyond. Crossing the water to Staten Island, for example, they got themselves jobs at an open-air amphitheater where shows with dancing girls were produced, the better to enable the gang to rob the spectators.

It's impossible to say how many total Whyos there were. Many purported members were merely copycats or pretenders. Because the Whyos operated generally in groups of three to seven, the press blamed them for almost any crime committed by roving bands of Irish lads. This, of course, only added to the gang's mystique.

More effectively than other gangs, the Whyos formed alliances with local politicians who, in exchange for votes and other favors, made charges against arrested gang members go away. One of their guardians was Thomas "Fatty" Walsh, a Sixth Ward alderman who ran a saloon on Mulberry Street. A former Five Points gang leader, Walsh had taken a bullet in the leg from a Bowery Boy during the July 1857 riots. Elected alderman in 1884, he routinely sprang Whyos from prison even when they were in for assaulting a police officer. When, on Election Day 1885, one Irish voter had the temerity to cast his ballot against Walsh, four Whyos beat him with an iron pipe and continued striking him all the

---

* At the time, ward and precinct numbers were the same, although in later years, as the city's population grew, the numbers changed and began to diverge.

way to police court even as the cops were escorting him there to give a statement.

The department's patrolmen found themselves outnumbered by the Whyos and other gangs. In 1884 *The Sun* decried what it called "gang rule in New York." That same year, the *New-York Tribune* lamented that the criminal groups were "apparently too much for our police authorities." In fact, a lot of cops were afraid of them. Some officers talked tough, saying the only way to deal with the gangs was, as one sergeant put it, to "club h[ell] out of them." But the gangs were apt to turn the tables by taking a policeman's club and using it on him, knocking him unconscious if they felt like it. As a result, there were parts of New York where no cop would go alone after dark.

The police were also frustrated by the unwillingness of politically appointed judges to hand out sentences that might have deterred the gangs. All it took was a whisper from a local Tammany man, and the court would dismiss the charges or administer a slap on the wrist. In one case, an Officer Nevins was beaten by several Whyos at Leonard and Mott Streets; one of them was arrested and sentenced to a month on Blackwell's Island (the prison for persons convicted of minor crimes) but never served time. In another typical episode, a police officer named Brady arrested two Whyos and was assaulted by nine other gang members who wrested his club from him. One of the Whyos received a $5 fine, while two others spent five days in the workhouse.

When an Officer McManus arrested Whyo member Timothy Sheehan on the charge of having sprung a disorderly female prisoner from police custody, the judge berated McManus in open court, said Sheehan was a respectable man, and discharged him. A Sixth Ward politician named Jimmy Oliver had gotten the judge's ear. As one cop lamented, "Any pothouse politician is able to get these fellows out by speaking to a justice, and we are sick and tired of doing anything about it."

The Whyos also inspired fear, or at least respect, within their local community. Citizens were afraid to testify against them, or even report them for arrest, lest they face the gang's retribution. Yet the Whyos were quasi-heroes in their neighborhoods. They weren't exactly Robin Hoods, because they stole for themselves, not for anyone else. But they were seen by at least some of the poorest New Yorkers as standing up to the rich and powerful.

Many "guns," as thieves were called, were considered no worse than the Gilded Age businessmen and politicians who grafted by "legitimate" means. "The business man is looking just as hard to make a pile as the professional gun is," said one habitual thief who later reformed, "and if it is his neighbor that he gets the best of, it makes no difference—business is business, and every man has got to take his chances. . . . Some of the most successful men commercially are noted for having done some very tricky things." The difference was that the hardened criminal ran the greater risk of significant time in jail, unless, like the Whyos, he enjoyed political protection.

For most kids from the slums, the risk of prison was worth it, anyway, since they had little to lose. "Not one out of ten thousand ever expects to amount to anything, or knows how to," explained the same former criminal. "If they're caught grafting, they think their life won't be any worse in the stir than on the street, and in winter not so bad, perhaps." As this reformed gun put it, young thieves learned that "they can make more by stealing than by shining shoes or selling newspapers, and they prowl around for chances." Thievery, he maintained, was "the one profession that as a ragamuffin I've got a fighting chance to win out in, and it amuses me to try my luck."

The goal was to spend a little, not a lot, of time in jail. And if a gang member did do his "bit" in prison, he was greeted with the applause of his cohorts when he finished his sentence, provided he hadn't squealed on them while in the pen. "They began to look up to me . . . because I was a fighter and had 'done time,'" recalled another ex-thief after being sprung.

Per the Whyos' special dialect, a month in jail was a "stone," a week was a "brick." They could simultaneously boast of their crime and insist, with a wink and a nod, that they'd never commit such a heinous act. "If I did dat, may I be as low as me mudder," was a favorite oath of denial. It

Irishman Danny Driscoll, leader of the Whyos, was considered "the toughest of the tough, the readiest with knife or revolver."

also served as a subtle reminder that their upbringing and impoverished circumstances were to blame for their lives of crime, a view that many social reformers shared.

Prison, for a Whyo and other hooligans, was a rite of passage on the way to gang leadership. The most feared and admired of the group's members was often the one who'd been most hardened by serving time. And the most hardened of them all was the Whyos' leader, Danny Driscoll.

⤙═◦═⤚

If Danny Driscoll was not the most depraved of New York's gang leaders in the Gilded Age, he was near the very top. Born in England to Irish immigrants around 1855, he grew up in the Five Points, where his mother, "Apple Mary," who lived on Baxter Street, ran a fruit stand in front of the nearby Tombs prison.

Driscoll became a child thief and at age fifteen was sent to Blackwell's Island for six months for picking pockets. In 1875 he was sentenced to eighteen months for stealing a man's watch, and a year later, in a three-cornered pistol fight, he shot two men in a saloon and was himself shot through the body. Hanging between life and death, he left his hospital bed to escape in a coach driven by friends, and when the other two men disappeared, the charges against him were dropped.

In and out of jail over the next few years, Driscoll was on his way to prison for a longer term in 1882 when he reportedly convinced a bum in the police van to change clothes and places with him. (The vagrant man had been sentenced to just ten days.) Driscoll got as far as paying the fine before the warden discovered the ruse and had him locked up again, though he didn't serve long.

In 1883, Driscoll shot a heavyset German sauerkraut peddler and his wife on Chrystie Street over some perceived slight. Chased down, arrested, and clubbed into submission by a cop, Driscoll was released, reportedly after the intercession of alderman Fatty Walsh.

Later that same year, Driscoll had a near-deadly scuffle with Patrick "Paddy" Green, a clerk at a lodging house at 2 Pell Street who'd ejected him a few days earlier for making a disturbance. Driscoll vowed to blow Green's brains out if he ever got a chance, and upon returning to the lodging house around five in the morning, he seized him by the throat. In the ensuing pistol fight, Driscoll wounded Green slightly in the face, then fell himself with a bullet to his cheek that passed into his throat. He was not charged.

In September 1884, after the female owner of a Chrystie Street bar refused Driscoll admittance to the upstairs rooms, and the bartender tried to throw him out, Driscoll shot the man in the leg. He commandeered a Second Avenue horsecar, seized the reins, lashed the whip, and drove off downtown at a frenzied pace, heedless of the cries of the conductor and frightened passengers. When a block of vehicles stopped his course, a little boy who'd run after him identified him to the police, whereupon Driscoll pistol-whipped the lad and broke his jaw. Arrested at the scene, Driscoll was locked up for the twenty-seventh time in his life and the twelfth time since January 1, 1884—surely some sort of record. Yet after this latest incident, he was again released with Walsh's help.

At the height of Driscoll's career, a newspaper reporter described him as "the toughest of the tough, the readiest with knife or revolver, the most reckless in threats against all who thwarted him, the steadiest in drink, the most industrious in thievery." He was, the paper averred, "the most venomous, worthless, sneaking, drunken, quarrelsome, and murderous reprobate known in the city."

Driscoll's thieving friend Jim Caulfield called him "one of the cleverest guns that ever came from the Sixth Ward," but said that "as a grafter, he had one great fault. He had a very quick temper. He was sensitive, and lacking in self-control. . . . He would shoot at a moment's notice." Burly and square-faced, Driscoll was of medium height, with wavy brown hair and a mustache in his later years. He wore an expression of bravado and moved with a swagger, a soft alpine hat rakishly cocked over one eye and ear "at the approved Bowery angle." Sticking close to his roots, he lived with his wife and young daughter at 11 Pell Street in the Five Points, in what the *New York World* called a "tumbledown, miserable little tenement."

Driscoll's body bore the markings of a criminal past that included forty to fifty affrays with guns, knives, and fists. He had an ugly scar on his chin, obtained in the 1883 pistol battle with Patrick Green. His friend Caulfield said that after that incident, Driscoll underwent four surgeries without anesthesia.

By the age of thirty, Driscoll had spent four terms in prison for a total of at least seven years, a quarter of his young life. All of the sentences were for larceny, not for any of the shootings and stabbings he had committed, so his jail time might easily have been double that but for the political protection he received. The day would come, though, when even Fatty Walsh would no longer bail out Danny Driscoll.

CHAPTER TEN

"FREDERICKA THE GREAT"

J ust as Danny Driscoll was being tossed into prison for the twenty-seventh time in his criminal career, Marm Mandelbaum was facing the real possibility of jail for the first time in hers.

On July 23, 1884, *The New York Times* ran a story under the headline "Mother Mandelbaum Trapped." She'd been the object of a sting operation carried out by the New York District Attorney's Office that caught her selling stolen silk to an undercover agent. But to the astonishment of New Yorkers, and the embarrassment of Inspector Thomas Byrnes, her arrest came without the involvement of a single New York cop.

Mandelbaum's edifice had begun to crumble a few months earlier when she lost a civil suit after her longtime associate, Sheeny Mike Kurtz, betrayed her. A Boston merchant sued her in New York State Civil Court, alleging that she had received and sold thousands of dollars' worth of silk and cashmere shawls stolen from his store in 1877 by Kurtz and two other robbers—one of them the since-deceased George Leslie.

Mandelbaum went to Boston to bail out Sheeny Mike. To avoid prosecution, he said to her, in front of the arresting officers, that she ought to give back the goods. When she asked what goods, he replied, the ones he had brought her. "Now, what do you think of that sucker, talking that way to me?" Mandelbaum said to another criminal colleague.

Kurtz was sentenced to jail in Massachusetts for twelve years for the crime but was pardoned by the governor and released three years into his term. He convinced prison physicians he was suffering from a mysterious, incurable disease. It turned out that he had deliberately ingested large quantities of soapsuds, which he discovered could make a person appear to be wasting away with consumption—the name then for tuberculosis. He also cut an incision in his body and rubbed into it a preparation that made pus flow, the better to make his case for a humanitarian discharge.

Just before his release, in a further bid for leniency, Kurtz signed an affidavit admitting to the Boston theft and stating that he had sold the stolen goods to Mandelbaum. Based on Kurtz's affidavit and the testimony of another turncoat—and with the benefit of a lower standard of proof than in a criminal trial—the merchant plaintiff won a civil judgment against Mandelbaum for $6,600. As the verdict was announced, the back of the courtroom was packed with thieves and burglars she had supported over the years. *The New York Times* observed that they "sat alongside nonprofessional citizens, looking as honest as anybody else."

The civil plaintiff in that suit had not sought any assistance from the New York police, who allegedly were in bed with Mother Marm. Adopting the same playbook, New York district attorney Peter Olney decided to pursue a criminal case against her, bypassing the police in favor of private detectives.

In early 1884 Gustave Frank of the Pinkerton National Detective Agency was sent undercover to infiltrate Mandelbaum's operation. A former dry goods seller, he boned up on the silk business by visiting buyers and auction houses. Then, disguised in scruffy clothing and under an alias, he presented himself to Mandelbaum as a customer looking to purchase silk at extremely cheap prices.

Suspicious at first, Mandelbaum became impressed with Frank's knowledge of the price and quality of silk and agreed to sell him a few yards. When nothing boomeranged on her, she sold him some more rolls and concluded what she'd suspected: that he was in the same crooked business that she was. She continued selling to him for several months—twelve thousand yards in total—and told him to resell them outside of New York. Meanwhile, Pinkerton agents surveilled her store from a rented office across the street and saw how diligently the neighborhood stood watch for her.

Unbeknownst to Mandelbaum, a few of the silks Frank ended up buying had recently been marked by the original dealers, at Olney's request, in a secret manner not easily discovered. Frank took the pieces to the dealers, who identified the merchandise as theirs and confirmed that it had recently been stolen.

Marm was finally caught, red-handed. She was placed under arrest, along with her longtime confidant Herman Stoude and her son, Julius, who worked in her store. Gustave Frank pretended to be arrested, too, but

In 1884 Marm Mandelbaum (shown center in this *Puck* magazine cartoon) was caught by private Pinkerton Agency detectives and charged with receiving stolen goods. After her arrest, District Attorney Peter Olney (left) accused the NYPD and Thomas Byrnes (right, in uniform) of having coddled her for many years.

when he revealed himself to her during the transport to police court and told her the best she could do would be to make a clean breast of it, she yelled and punched him in the face.

Mandelbaum's arrest begged the question as to how private Pinkerton agents had managed to accomplish in a few months what the New York Police Department and its detectives had failed to do in twenty-five years. To many, including the city's newspapers, the answer was obvious: the police were on the take. Known to every detective and judge in the city, Marm Mandelbaum had been under the law's protection for years, as if conducting a legitimate business.

"It was not imbecility but interest that prevented the making of a case against the woman," *The New York Times* editorialized. "Her intimacy with the detectives of the police force was only less close and confidential than her intimacy with the thieves." The whole episode, the paper concluded, was "an indictment of the police force."

District Attorney Olney did nothing to discourage such talk. His office further accused the police of laxity in enforcing the antigambling laws. One assistant district attorney claimed that the cops themselves could often be found playing at the gaming houses.

Logically, the charges reflected most directly on Superintendent Walling, who'd been the top man on the force since 1874. But they stung Thomas Byrnes, head of the detective bureau the previous four years, to an even greater degree. What could he say? The argument that it was just too hard to come up with enough evidence to convict a criminal fence (a mantra he would repeat two years later in his *Professional Criminals*) was no longer persuasive, given that the Pinkertons had done so without any difficulty.

Byrnes also claimed to have interviewed Mandelbaum, who told him she had given up the business. Of course, no one believed that Thomas Byrnes, the great detective, was naïve enough to take her word for it. He said her statement was consistent, though, with what others had told him. As further proof, he pointed to the fact that over several months working undercover, Gustave Frank was able to trace only a few pieces of stolen silk.

That was true enough: of the 12,000 yards he bought, Frank came up with only 160 yards of stolen merchandise, worth less than $200. It was a bit like nabbing a multimillion-dollar tax cheat for having falsified a few business lunches. But along with other pilfered items found in her home pursuant to a search warrant, it was enough to secure the district attorney an indictment of Mother Marm. Among the loot found was $4,000 worth of diamonds allegedly stolen from a Troy, New York, jewelry store in early 1884 by Sheeny Mike Kurtz and his partner Billy Porter. The robbery came just weeks after Porter, acquitted for the murder of Johnny the Mick in Shang Draper's saloon, had left the courtroom vowing to go straight.*

Lacking a convincing defense in the Mandelbaum matter, Byrnes went on the offensive. He accused Olney of trying to show up the police department out of jealousy, and he further suspected that the Pinkertons were eager to assist because the police had been taking away their business.

Byrnes added that Olney bore a personal grudge against him because, a few years earlier, Byrnes had refused to prostitute his position as police captain to get Olney elected in a state assembly primary race on the Tammany line over a rival Democratic faction. Olney reportedly said after that election that Byrnes was not enough of a politician for him and was not "a good Democrat in a tight place." In a sign of just how much of a political cipher Byrnes was, Olney denied the reported quote, saying he had always understood Byrnes to be a Republican. Political Byrnes certainly was, but not in any discernable party sense.

Byrnes also tried to turn the tables on Olney, saying that it was the

---

* Immediately after the Troy jewelry store robbery, Porter and Kurtz went to Europe and burglarized to great wealth. Upon their return to the United States in 1886, they were arrested and tried for the Troy robbery but acquitted for lack of evidence. Porter went back to Europe and resumed his life of crime, dying (it is thought) in Bordeaux, France, around 1892, after being convicted of a burglary there and while awaiting transport to a French penal colony off the coast of Australia.

  Kurtz opened a cigar store in New York City, bought a tobacco plantation and orange grove in Florida, and continued to be arrested for small-time thieving in New York and elsewhere. He died in New York in 1904 of consumption (tuberculosis), the illness he had once feigned to get out of jail.

district attorney's office, not the police force, that protected various gamblers, fences, and other criminals, and was masking its own corruption by accusing NYPD detectives of the same. An indignant Byrnes expressed confidence in his men, vouched for their integrity, and said that, all egotism aside, his reorganized detective bureau was "the greatest bulwark against crime in this or any other country."

The police inspector's best defense, though, was one he dared not make. As opposed to Byrnes's forty immortals in the central office, many of the precinct detectives—the wardmen who collected bribes for their captains—*were* corrupt and had been for years. That is partly why Byrnes had shaken up the detective bureau when he took over, bringing the precinct detectives directly under his authority. But just two years into that experiment, the precinct captains rebelled and insisted on restoring the old system under which they, not the detective bureau head, got to select and control their respective precinct detectives. Several of the captains had refused to have anything to do with Byrnes's central office detectives.

And so, in May 1884 the police commissioners bowed to pressure and allowed captains to pick and control their own wardmen once again. Byrnes could hardly afford to further alienate the powerful captains, and their detective lackeys, by failing to vigorously defend the department against corruption charges.

The war of words between Byrnes and the district attorney's office continued for a couple of weeks after Mandelbaum's arrest. But the public feud soon ended when both sides realized they were helping no one other than Mandelbaum and her crafty defense lawyers, Howe & Hummel. The controversy blew over without any lasting dent to Byrnes's reputation.

Byrnes may have secretly derived pleasure, though, from the denouement to the Mandelbaum case. On December 4, 1884, after months of delays, postponements, and wrangling over bail and the like, Mandelbaum was scheduled to appear in a New York court for trial on the charges of grand larceny and receiving stolen goods.

District Attorney Olney was there to try the case, along with three of his eager assistants. Private detectives Robert Pinkerton and Gustave

Frank were present, and sixteen of their colleagues sat in the gallery watching the panel of jurors. Fourteen prosecution witnesses were lined up to testify. At the defense table sat the inimitable, overstuffed figure of William Howe, resplendent as usual in diamonds and garishly attired, flanked by his dwarflike partner, Abe Hummel. The New York police, having been shut out of the case, were absent from the proceedings.

Three chairs sat empty, reserved for Mother Mandelbaum and her two codefendants: her son, Julius, and her assistant Herman Stoude. Around eleven o'clock, an assistant district attorney called out their names. No one answered. Twice more the prisoners' names were called, with the admonition that if they failed to show, their bail bonds would be forfeited. But they were nowhere to be found.

Everyone present smiled except for the judge, the prosecutors, and the Pinkerton agents. Howe and Hummel somehow managed to keep straight faces while insisting they had no idea where their clients were. Howe surmised that Mandelbaum had acted on impulse, following the theory that "absence of body is often better than presence of mind." Hummel was overheard murmuring, approvingly, "Fredericka the Great."

It turned out that she'd taken flight to Canada. Believing she was likely to be convicted, she set up an elaborate ruse to fool the Pinkerton detectives who'd been shadowing her day and night while she was out on bail. Mandelbaum dressed one of her stoutest maids in her own clothing and had her leave the house on Clinton Street, whereupon the imposter proceeded to lead the detectives on a wild-goose chase around the city. When the coast was clear, Marm hopped in a carriage that took her to a railroad station upstate, where she and her codefendants caught a train to Toronto. Briefly detained by Canadian authorities, she was let go because Canada lacked an extradition treaty with the United States at the time.

Before she escaped, Mandelbaum had arranged a series of transfers of the deeds to real estate that had been used as bail bonds for her and her accomplices. As a result, even though bail was forfeited, the properties were beyond the state's reach. This only added to the New York authorities' humiliation.

Mother Marm quietly lived out her years—another ten—in Hamilton, Ontario, near Niagara Falls, where she opened a dry goods store (whether legitimate or not is unclear). She reputedly was worth $500,000 ($13 million in 2021 dollars), an amount she had managed to secrete from the United States.

Mandelbaum returned one more time to New York, unmolested by the police, for the funeral of her daughter, who died prematurely of pneumonia in 1885. She immediately went back to Canada, never again to set foot in the Manhattan of her halcyon days. Still, she longed for New York. According to George Walling, who had always respected her for her pluck and skill, she would have gladly forfeited every penny of her wealth "in order to once more breathe freely the atmosphere of the Thirteenth Ward."

Mandelbaum may not have made it back all the way downtown, but she did make it to Broadway, at least in spirit. In September 1895, a year and a half after her death in Canada, of kidney disease, at age sixty-eight, the American Theatre at Forty-Second Street and Eighth Avenue debuted a melodrama titled *The Great Diamond Robbery*. In praising the opening night performance, *The New York Times* described one of the main characters, Frau (Mother) Rosenbaum, as "a receiver of stolen goods, of the Mother Mandelbaum type," who possessed "sufficient power to baffle justice." And during the curtain call, the most vigorous applause was reserved for the stocky, sixty-five-year-old Czech actress Francesca Janauschek, who played the German character recognized by everyone as Mother Marm. It seems the audience was clapping for both of them.

CHAPTER ELEVEN

"WIRED"

After the Mandelbaum case, Thomas Byrnes would again be accused of protecting a prominent New York City receiver of stolen goods. This time, though, Byrnes would outmaneuver his critics, nabbing the fence in one of the most celebrated bribery schemes of the nineteenth century. Rarely were the inspector's combined detective skills and political savvy on such display.

Henry Jaehne, a garrulous thirty-seven-year-old man of German parentage, was a four-term New York City alderman in 1886 and vice president of its board, the city's legislative body. Originally a Tammany Hall man, he switched his allegiance to a rival Democratic faction, the County Democracy, and was elected alderman on that slate in 1882. He headed a political club, the Henry W. Jaehne Coterie, which honored him at its 1885 annual picnic with a $1,000 diamond badge, a band rendition of the song "See, the Conquering Hero Comes," and a rousing chorus of "For He's a Jolly Good Fellow." Married and a father of four, Jaehne was a dashing, supremely confident politician who dressed faultlessly and sported a long, drawn-out mustache.

He was also a crook. A lifelong resident of the Eighth Ward (modern-day Soho), he ran a jewelry store on Broome Street where he received stolen silverware and instantly melted it down. He frequently did business with Marm Mandelbaum, who was described as "his guide, philosopher, and friend."

He was also a friend of Thomas Byrnes's and reportedly had long enjoyed Byrnes's protection, both because Jaehne had political influence and because he supplied Byrnes with valuable information about other thieves and thefts. According to *The New York Times*, Byrnes also helped Jaehne get reelected alderman in the fall of 1885, in a bitter contest with a Tammany foe, by making sure that Eighth Ward voters knew that Jaehne was the police department's favored candidate. Byrnes's men were said to have supplied vital assistance to Jaehne at the polling booths.

Byrnes's apparently preferential treatment of Jaehne was made public when, on March 12, 1886, Mrs. Schuyler Hamilton, the wife of Alexander Hamilton's great-grandson, surfaced an affidavit accusing Jaehne of fencing $1,100 of silverware stolen a year earlier from her home on West Thirty-Eighth Street. The thieves were a pair of Jaehne's cronies.

Gertrude Hamilton said that she had tried to persuade Byrnes to pursue the matter, but he brushed her off with the statement that Jaehne had sold his jewelry store to one of his clerks and that there was no evidence of Jaehne's involvement in the crime. The sale, though, was shown to be a sham transaction, and Mrs. Hamilton publicly accused Byrnes of trying to shift the blame from Jaehne to someone else. In due course, after unsuccessfully offering a police detective $100 to shut up Gertrude Hamilton, Jaehne paid her the value of the silverware while denying any guilt in the matter.

It looked like another Mandelbaum-type problem for Byrnes, and, indeed, the *Times* suggested that it was time for him to resign. And then, four days later, Byrnes dropped a bombshell: shortly before Mrs. Hamilton's allegations hit the newspapers, he had secretly arrested Jaehne on the charge of bribery. Jaehne was later charged with having accepted $20,000 to vote in favor of a Broadway railway franchise in August 1884.

Ever since that vote, rumors had swirled that Jaehne and his fellow aldermen had been paid off by an unscrupulous transportation magnate, Jacob Sharp, to grant him the right to build a horse railway along lower Broadway—that is, a smooth metal track in the middle of the street for cars pulled by horses. It was designed to replace the chaotic system of horse-drawn omnibuses (large, lumbering stagecoaches) that crowded Broadway below Fourteenth Street.

After years of opposition from merchants and property owners, Sharp finally obtained the franchise in 1884 when the board of aldermen voted to allow him to lay his lines and operate the horse railway. As it turned out, all but two of the twenty-four aldermen had accepted $20,000 bribes to approve Sharp's plan.

In early 1885, newly elected New York district attorney Randolph Martine, who had succeeded Peter Olney, Byrnes's nemesis in the Mandelbaum case, asked Byrnes to conduct a sting operation. Martine wanted the police inspector to try extracting a confession from his friend Jaehne. Byrnes agreed, and, over the next year, he met Jaehne from time to time in confidential sessions.

Byrnes found it easy to get Jaehne talking about the franchise vote, although the information came in fits and starts. In the familiar style he used on low-life criminals, Byrnes made Jaehne think he already knew all about the bribes. Byrnes made memoranda of his conversations and furnished progress reports to Martine.

The culmination of Byrnes's efforts came in the second week of March 1886. He summoned Jaehne for a more relaxed conversation at the detective's comfortable home at 59 West Ninth Street in Greenwich Village. When Jaehne arrived at the three-story brick town house around eight in the evening, he was ushered into the library, where he sat down with Byrnes at a table next to a door to the adjoining rear parlor. The sliding door separating the two rooms was left partially open. Concealed in darkness in the parlor were two of Byrnes's detective sergeants who were there to listen. They lay facedown on the floor, no more than six or seven feet away. Although no electronics were involved, the conversation, in effect, was wired.

As the *Times* reported, Byrnes "had so far wormed himself into Jaehne's confidence" that when he got him alone that night, he was able to obtain what he needed for an indictment. Jaehne admitted receiving $20,000 for his vote, provided details on who paid it and how, and implicated his fellow aldermen in the scheme.

When Jaehne left that night, Byrnes had his men tail him to make sure he didn't try to flee. The next morning, Jaehne was arrested. Byrnes admitted that, to gain Jaehne's confidence, he had once falsely promised to let him know if and when he was ever indicted, so that he might run away. Cross-examined by Jaehne's lawyer at trial, Byrnes was asked, "Did you believe that Jaehne was so silly as to give himself away to you?" Byrnes responded, "I did."

Based on Byrnes's testimony, corroborated by the two detectives in hiding, Jaehne was convicted of bribery in May 1886 and sentenced to nine years of hard labor in Sing Sing. There he joined fellow inmate Johnny Hope, one of the Manhattan Savings burglars Byrnes had put away. Like Hope and other prisoners with connections and means, Jaehne enjoyed special privileges, including short and easy work assignments and access to liquor and tobacco. Released after six years in jail, and sporting a new tailor-made suit, Jaehne returned to politics, switching his allegiance again back to Tammany Hall.

Jaehne's conviction led to prosecutions of twenty of his fellow aldermen, although only one of them ended up serving time in jail. Several fled to Canada, a few turned state's evidence, and ten others were indicted but never brought to trial. Sharp was convicted but had his verdict overturned on appeal and died before the new trial. In the meantime, a rival group headed by financiers Thomas Fortune Ryan and William Whitney had bought out Sharp and proceeded to monopolize the city's surface transit system by replacing horse-drawn cars with cable cars, as in San Francisco.

As with the Manhattan Savings robbery a decade earlier, the spotty conviction record in the "boodle aldermen" matter, as it came to be known, did nothing to dampen public recognition of Thomas Byrnes as the hero of the story. A few years later, calling his good work on the case "too well known to need repetition," the once-critical *New York Times* sang his praises. "Despite cajolery and threats, despite the most mighty and active political influence," the paper recounted, Byrnes "kept on with his work for justice, and it was entirely through the information gained by him that Alderman Jaehne was convicted and his colleagues in the board . . . were driven out of the country." Byrnes's previously lax treatment of Jaehne's fencing operations—and his equally unexplained failure to nab Marm Mandelbaum—were either forgiven or forgotten.

It is impossible to say whether Byrnes undertook his clandestine investigation of Jaehne's bribe taking out of a genuine desire to punish an elected official for betraying a public trust, or whether he acted out of self-interest, and opportunistically, to head off another Mandelbaum-style scandal. But no one appeared to care. After the boodle aldermen case, Thomas Byrnes was once again the most revered cop in America.

CHAPTER TWELVE

"EITHER THE WHYOS OR I MUST GO"

D anny Driscoll, leader of the Whyos, once boasted that he had seven bullets inside him from his various altercations. But it was a bullet he put in the stomach of his girlfriend, the prostitute and Whyo groupie Bridget "Beezie" Garrity, that finally undid him.

It happened on the night of June 25, 1886, a month after Henry Jaehne was convicted of bribery. Driscoll, then thirty-one, was out drinking with three friends, including Beezie, a spirited, beautiful young woman of nineteen. She reportedly had lived with Driscoll and his wife while plying her trade in the Five Points.

The site of the incident was a love hotel at 163 Hester Street, managed by thirty-five-year-old Englishman John McCarty, a former Whyo gang member who'd spent more than a dozen years in Sing Sing and other prisons. McCarty used the three-story lodging house, across the street from Billy McGlory's Armory Hall, to bilk customers with the help of a coterie of prostitutes, one of whom was Beezie Garrity (spelled "Bezie" or "Beezy" by some).

Driscoll and McCarty were sworn enemies, going back almost a year, to when the two had quarreled at the Hester Street house. McCarty threw out Driscoll and told him never to come back. Vowing revenge, Driscoll went to San Antonio, Texas, to escape arrest for another crime and ran a saloon there until he was slashed with a sword and nearly killed in a barroom scrape. Upon his return to New York in early June 1886, Driscoll immediately sought out McCarty, who again ejected him for disorderly conduct and fired two pistol shots at him—in self-defense, McCarty later maintained.

About a week later, at eight o'clock in the evening on June 25, Driscoll was drinking with his friend and fellow Whyo, junkman Owen "Owney" Bruen. They started home at midnight, from a saloon at 199 Worth Street, when they ran into Beezie and another girl and went back inside the bar with them.

After drinking there for three hours, the foursome wandered from one bar to another until four in the morning, when Driscoll decided he would settle things with McCarty. He hired a cab to take his group to 163 Hester Street, where Driscoll, knowing that McCarty would deny him admittance, sent the five-foot-three Beezie ahead to knock on the locked front parlor door. When McCarty opened it and let Beezie enter, Driscoll came forward to try to force his way in. McCarty slammed the door on him, but Driscoll managed to shove it open a crack.

What happened next is a matter of dispute. According to the officially accepted version, with some variations, it transpired as follows: Driscoll fired a bullet through the crack in the door, missing McCarty and hitting a wall opposite instead. McCarty reached for his revolver, and Beezie, described as the "gamiest and nerviest girl in the ward," grabbed and pulled on him, imploring him not to shoot. McCarty tore himself away, then ran into a rear room and jumped out a window.

By this time, with the front parlor door no longer blocked, Driscoll had burst in to chase his adversary. He saw a silhouette in the hallway leading to the back room and, thinking it was McCarty, fired and hit Beezie in the abdomen. "I'm shot!" she cried, crumpling to the floor.

When the police arrived and asked who her assailant was, the barely conscious girl said it was the man with the red whiskers, meaning McCarty, who wore a full red beard. McCarty, who had returned to the scene to clear himself, upon hearing her statement, immediately denied it. He gave himself up and showed the officers his revolver, which remained fully loaded with the barrel cold, proving that it hadn't been discharged. It was also a .32 caliber, inconsistent with the .38-caliber bullet that had flattened against the wall. (The bullet that killed Beezie was never found.)

Meanwhile, Driscoll had fled the lodging house and was chased by police, who fired their pistols at him. He ran to his house at 126 Baxter Street, two minutes away, then crossed a fire escape to enter a vacant room next door at 128 Baxter, where his mother had recently lived. Police found him there lying on the floor, feigning sleep, claiming he'd been in the same spot all night after getting drunk. He had no weapon on him, presumably having tossed it after accidentally shooting his mistress and leaving her in extremis.

Beezie Garrity, taken to St. Vincent's Hospital in Greenwich Village, lingered for almost twenty-four hours but died the next afternoon at five o'clock. Indicted for murder (McCarty was cleared by a coroner's jury), Driscoll went on trial in September 1886, represented by Howe & Hummel. It was one of the most celebrated murder trials of Gilded Age New York.

The prosecution advanced the official version, bolstered by testimony from neighborhood prostitute Carrie Wilson, who'd been at 163 Hester that night, that it was Driscoll who fired the fatal shot. A group of card players vouched that they saw McCarty jump out the window before Beezie was struck down. A police officer testified that he'd seen Driscoll's drinking party on the street an hour before the incident and that he overheard Beezie tell Driscoll, "If you shoot him, I will stick by you."

Driscoll changed his story at trial to admit he'd gone to 163 Hester Street that night, but he insisted he was unarmed and that it was McCarty who shot Beezie as soon as she got inside. Asked to confirm that Beezie lived with him, Driscoll denied it vehemently, saying his wife of eight years never would have stood for it. The district attorney's accusation was "as true as any lawyer can say" or "as true as you are speaking now," he shot back contemptuously on cross-examination. But he didn't dispute that he'd been almost daily in the girl's company in the month before her death.

Owney Bruen supported his friend Driscoll's account. "McCarty shot her. I seed it," the *Tribune* quoted him as testifying. Bruen denied that he or Driscoll were members of the Whyo gang; he had heard of the Whyos, he said, but had never attended any of their meetings. That left unexplained why the audience was filled with Whyos, described by the newspapers as misfits with low-crowned derbies, close-cropped hair, toothpick-pointed shoes, and, like their leader, bearing marks of violent personal encounters.

Defense lawyer Howe was confident that the conflicting testimony, not to mention the victim's identification of McCarty as her killer, was enough to create reasonable doubt and produce an acquittal. He attacked the credibility of the streetwalker Wilson and that of convicted felon McCarty; the latter, Howe argued, had plenty of time to change his pistol to the fully loaded one he handed to the police.

But another witness turned the tide against Driscoll. Beezie Garrity's mother, Mrs. Margaret Sullivan of 71 Mulberry Street in the Five Points, was brought forward by the prosecution. Elderly and feeble, she had to lean on a court officer as he escorted her to the witness box.

She testified that Beezie had refused to heed her warnings not to associate with the Whyos. Then Mrs. Sullivan spoke movingly of visiting her dying daughter at St. Vincent's. She related that as she entered the hospital room, Beezie turned her face toward her and said:

"Is that you, my mamma?" And I said yes. She asked for a drink of water, and the nurse said, "No," she could not get it; "she has been vomiting all morning." "Well," I said, "You might give her a piece of ice." So they got her a piece of ice. I says, "Bezie, I always thought when you would not do what I told you that you would come to this." She said, "Mamma, there is no use of you saying anything to me now, I am going to die." I says, "Bezie, what makes you think that? Many's a one got shot and they got better." "Yes," she says, "but not with such a ball as that was. . . . You have got to put two hands to that pistol to fire it." I says, "Bezie, who done that to you?" She says, "Danny Driscoll." . . . She died five or ten minutes to five. . . . I shut her eyes.

As *The Sun* reported, "There was not a dry eye visible in the courtroom" except for the cold, staring blue eyes of Driscoll. Lawyer Howe recognized the futility of trying to cross-examine the frail, bereaved mother and let her stand down with no questions.

The jury was out for only thirty minutes before returning a verdict of guilty on the count of first-degree murder. Though accidental, the crime was committed in the course of a felony and hence punishable by death. Driscoll was pale but expressionless as his wife, there with their three-year-old daughter, wept bitterly. Exiting the courtroom, Driscoll said he guessed that luck had not been with him.

In January 1888, after more than a year of unsuccessful appeals, Driscoll faced execution in the Tombs. Fatty Walsh, the Whyos' old protector, had become the prison warden by political appointment, giving Driscoll hope for escape. But when Walsh refused to help, Driscoll publicly accused him of denying him decent food and visitation rights and even went on a hunger strike briefly. Earlier, prison officials had found mortar and stones under Driscoll's bed, plus a pocketknife and screwdriver, evidence of an early-stage attempt to dig himself out. When caught, he said he didn't suppose anyone could blame him for trying to escape by any means he could.

Upon discovering another, more advanced escape operation later, Walsh foiled the plan by moving Driscoll to a different cell. "It came pretty near to being a fine job," Driscoll told one reporter. To another reporter he summoned to his cell, Driscoll expressed sorrow over the death of "poor Bezie." He insisted he was "not as black as I'm painted" and said he resented being "pictured as a monster who is ready to eat anybody who comes near me."

Otherwise, Driscoll accepted his fate stoically and philosophically. He composed a poem to the Catholic Sisters of Charity, took communion, and forgave his enemies, including Walsh, who declined to reciprocate the favor. He wrote final letters to his wife and friends, including Owney Bruen, who inherited Driscoll's brown derby in a symbolic transfer of leadership of the Whyos.

On January 23, 1888, the morning of his hanging, the dark-mustached Driscoll dressed in a black suit and starched white shirt and took a final breakfast of coffee and dry toast. He'd been sustained by cigars—thirteen in one day the week before.

The temperature on execution day was ten degrees above zero. As Mike McGloin had before him, Driscoll walked from his cell across the Bridge of Sighs, an outdoor footbridge in the prison courtyard over which condemned prisoners passed on their way to the gallows.

Police stood watch outside and on nearby rooftops to guard against any trouble from the Whyos. Specially invited citizens in silk top hats watched from above along with the cops. Newspaper reporters for Joseph Pulitzer's *World* posted themselves atop buildings as well, within view of the scaffold, poised to use flag signals to relay the word back to their office when the deed was done.

About thirty witnesses were present for the hanging, including social reformer and capital punishment critic Elbridge Gerry, anti-reformer and eager punisher Alexander "Clubber" Williams, ten or so newspaper reporters, and assorted sheriff's deputies and prison officials. When longtime Tombs hangman Joe Atkinson, who'd performed the execution of Mike McGloin five years earlier, stepped up to the gallows, Driscoll greeted him warmly and asked him to please make quick work of his task, which Atkinson promised to do.

As the black hood was pulled over his head, Driscoll was heard to ask

Jesus for mercy. Still, he maintained his innocence to the last. He died a hero and a martyr in the eyes of many of the impoverished working-class youths of the Five Points and the Whyo gang he had led.

Although Driscoll's execution had gone off without a snag, on the same day he was hanged, the *New York World* ran an article suggesting "a more civilized way" to execute people. Specifically, the paper urged the use of an electric chair, powered by the currents that had begun lighting New York's streets a few years earlier.

Driscoll proved to be one of the last persons executed in New York by hanging. The last man hanged in the Tombs, on December 5, 1889, was cop killer and Howe & Hummel client Harry Carlton, described by *The New York Times* as a member of the Whyo gang.

A day later, a German immigrant named John Greenwall, who killed a businessman while robbing his home in Bedford-Stuyvesant, Brooklyn, became the last man hanged anywhere in the state of New York. He went to the gallows in Brooklyn's Raymond Street Jail. Beginning in 1890, execution by the electric chair became the norm in New York until the state outlawed capital punishment a century later.

Owney Bruen would take over the Whyo gang, but he hadn't been Driscoll's first choice. When Driscoll was arrested in 1886, his friend Danny Lyons (no relation to Sophie) had assumed the Whyos' top spot. But in August 1887, while Driscoll sat on death row, the twenty-seven-year-old Lyons was gunned to death at a Five Points saloon on Worth Street, near the Tombs.

A drunken Lyons had been throwing bottles of mineral water at the bartender for refusing to serve him, on orders of owner Daniel Murphy, with whom Lyons had a history of bad blood. Murphy was also mad at Lyons for having recently bitten the tails off some kittens running around on the barroom floor.

When Murphy entered the bar from across the street, having heard the smashing glass, Lyons threw two bottles at his head, bloodying him with one of them. Murphy jumped behind the bar to grab his pistol and saw Lyons reach in his pocket for his. The sober Murphy was quicker on the draw and shot Lyons fatally through the head. A coroner's jury exonerated Murphy, calling it justifiable homicide.

In a quirk of history, in July 1887, a month before Danny Lyons was shot to death, a common thief by the name of Dan Lyons, with no connection to the Whyos, was convicted of murdering well-known wrestler Joseph Quinn in a fight over a woman. This Dan Lyons was placed in a cell at the Tombs next to Danny Driscoll, where the two became friends and cooperated on several unsuccessful escape efforts.

In August 1888 the Dan Lyons who shot Quinn was hanged for the murder. Beginning with Herbert Asbury, countless writers have confused him with Danny Lyons, the Whyo leader killed in the shootout at Daniel Murphy's bar in August 1887.

With the hanging of Danny Driscoll and the fatal shooting of Danny Lyons, leadership of the Whyos fell to twenty-two-year-old Owney Bruen. Having testified previously that he'd at least heard of the Whyos, Owney now claimed that there was no such gang—that it existed only in the minds of newspaper reporters. But the press continued referring to him as the successor to leaders Lyons and Driscoll.

Bruen's tenure was to be a short one. In September 1888 he was arrested for assaulting a grocer-pawnbroker named Hermann Bruns at 33 Park Street in the Five Points, next door to Owney's residence at 31 Park. (The street no longer exists.) Owney had pawned his revolver to Bruns for $3.50, and when Bruns refused to pay him the full agreed-upon amount, Owney hit him with the butt of his gun, struck him in the head with an iron weight, and shot at him over the counter, missing his body but piercing the man's coat.

Appearing in court later that month, Bruen was described as thickset and ugly-faced, with a bulldog expression and small, black, beady eyes. At trial he admitted he'd been angry and drunk but denied trying to shoot Bruns, claiming his gun had accidentally discharged. As Bruen explained it in his Lower East Side dialect, he'd borrowed money from the grocer "tousands of times," including on the gun itself. "He tuk a likin' to de revolver an' wanted to buy it," Bruen testified, "an' he did buy it for tree doll'rs an' a 'af, an' that night I asked 'im for dollar' 'n a 'af an' got it, an' wen I kem back for $2 he refused, an' we got to growlin' 'bout de bisness. I keduv shot him if I'd a wanted to."

Asked on cross-examination by District Attorney John R. Fellows, the prosecutor in the Driscoll case, what he did for a living, Bruen replied, "Junk." "Whereabouts do you work?" Fellows inquired. "'Long de East River."

"Is a revolver a necessary implement in collecting junk?"

"Naw."

"Have you a license for carrying a pistol?"

"Naw."

When questioned about his knowledge of the Whyos, Bruen said, "I don't know de meanin' of dat word. I've heard de perlice say such a thing existed."

Unimpressed, the jury quickly found Bruen guilty of assault in the first degree. He was sentenced to nine years in Sing Sing. The Whyos were now leaderless.

The deaths of Lyons and Driscoll and the imprisonment of Bruen, all taking place within little more than a year, did not mark the end of the Whyos. But it did put the gang on the path to extinction. Just before Bruen's arrest, the *New York World* ran a story under the headline "Weakening Wail of the Whyos," which credited Captain John McCullagh with driving the remnants of the "once vigorous" Whyo gang from the violent Sixth Precinct into the confines of the Eleventh. There Captain Edward Cassidy continued chasing after them and caused two of their members to be sent to prison for six months—"minor lights, but promising," the paper offered.

That represented quite a turnaround from just four years earlier, when the *Tribune* had declared the Whyos and other gangs "too much" for the police. In that same year, new captain McCullagh declared that "either the Whyos or I must go from this precinct." He launched a campaign to clean out the dives around Mulberry Bend frequented by the Whyos and other hoodlums.

Thirty-eight when appointed captain in 1883, the Ireland-born Mc-Cullagh was the nephew of another police captain, "Farmer John" H. McCullagh, who was celebrated for having broken up some earlier gangs, including Shang Draper's panel thief business in the early 1870s. The younger McCullagh, like his uncle, was a Republican and a man of greater education and means than most of his colleagues. (He had married well.) An accomplished equestrian, he was handsome and dashing in appearance, sporting a dark mustache of cavalry trim. A polite, agreeable manner, coupled with a strict attention to duty, marked him as a bit of a Boy Scout.

Serving notice that he was serious, young captain McCullagh arrested twelve Whyos inside a Mulberry Street bar in October 1884 after surrounding the establishment with ten police officers. The reason for the arrest was the gang's robbery of an Englishman at pistol point on Pell Street. Occasionally McCullagh went undercover himself to ferret out underworld crime, dressing as a tramp to disguise himself. He also broke up opium dens and gambling tables in Chinatown, especially the popular fan-tan game, where players bet on the number of beans left on the table by the croupier. Later, he would go on to serve as the first police chief of consolidated New York after its five boroughs were merged into a single city in 1898.

The anti-Whyo campaign was part of a broader effort by New York to liberate itself from gang rule. It was less a matter of improved policing techniques than an exercise of determination and political will on the part of the police and government officials.

It started with an attack on the city's dives, which George Walling called "the hotbeds of its crime." In 1886 Abram Hewitt, an anti-Tammany reform Democrat, was elected mayor on a pledge to crack down on immorality by closing the worst of the dives and cancan dance halls. Tammany had supported him as a compromise candidate to defeat the Republican, Theodore Roosevelt, and the progressive political economist and quasi-socialist Henry George, running on the United Labor Party ticket.

Among the resorts shuttered by Hewitt were the Haymarket in the Tenderloin, a prostitution mall masquerading as a legitimate, Moulin Rouge–style cabaret, and the American Mabille on Bleecker Street, a Parisian-style dance hall known for luring working-class girls from the shops and factories into a life of prostitution. Its proprietor was Theodore Allen, better known as "The. Allen" (with the distinctive period mark), a gambler, political organizer, and brother of several professional burglars. A former Dead Rabbit, Allen was a brawler who "when aroused, would think nothing of jamming the lighted cigar point into your face as the first move of conflict," and would end the fight by stomping on his adversary's face with the heel of his shoe.

The most important target, though, was Billy McGlory, whose Armory Hall was the scene of what the *New York World* called "the most immoral orgies." For years, it had been the favorite destination for uptown slummers who, it was said, needed two things if they wanted to visit the place: "a prize-fighter for a protector and a late start." McGlory was hounded by the police until he sold his hall to a furniture factory in 1889 and auctioned off all its contents.

The effects of these closings were not permanent. Hewitt's successor as mayor, Tammany man and liquor dealer Hugh Grant, initially committed to continue the policy of suppressing the worst dives. But many of them, usually represented by Howe & Hummel, were allowed to reopen or were replaced by others that were nearly as disreputable.

Still, the dive crackdowns gave the police a respite during which they were able to gather force against the gangs. In particular, the final closing of Armory Hall—under Grant's administration, not Hewitt's—made a significant dent in underworld violence around the Five Points and the Bowery. Coming a year after Owney Bruen's conviction, it helped hasten the Whyos' ultimate demise.

In 1891 *The Sun* declared that with the deaths of McGloin, Driscoll, and Lyons, and severe police crackdowns on the gangs, the days of the "toughs" were over. They were like curios, the paper said, that belonged in museums. "They have been cowed and whipped into better behavior, that's all there is to it," one cop was quoted as saying. "The present epoch doesn't take kindly to toughs and corner loafers, who are simply what might be called embryo toughs," he added. "It's too difficult nowadays to organize 'gangs,' and without a desperado like Driscoll or Danny Lyons or McGloin to lead it, toughs cannot flourish." The gangs continued to exist in weaker sway in some of the tenement districts along the riverfront, the officer said, but he added that "even these are being held in wholesome check."

By the time he was detailed to Goatville in the Bronx in 1891— allegedly for tolerating swindling games in his precinct, though he denied it—John McCullagh had made good on his vow to drive the Whyos from the "Bloody Sixth." The Whyos and other New York gangs had been turned into what *The Sun* called "feeble" reminders of their predecessors.

The police force had grown larger (from 2,900 in 1885 to 3,700 in 1892) and was better organized. Officers started tracking gang leaders and searching for any opportunity to send them to jail. When toughs came back from prison, the cops shadowed them constantly, looking for a chance to send them back. Lengthy time in the pen began convincing cocky hoods that it was better to follow a hardworking, law-abiding life than a habitually criminal one. For hoodlums, as well as the public, crime had become—at least for the time being—less romanticized.

The last nail in the Whyos' coffin was the demolition of Mulberry Bend, that maze of alleys and backstreets in the Five Points the gang had called its headquarters. Jacob Riis was convinced that not only the Whyos, whom he called "the worst of all the gangs," but also their ilk, could be destroyed by leveling the slums in which they lived and hid, and replacing them with parks and playgrounds. After much delay and wrangling, Mulberry Bend was finally torn down in 1895 and replaced, two years later, with Mulberry Bend Park (renamed Columbus Park by the growing Italian population in 1911, and now part of Chinatown).

Gradually the uptown parts of the city were built up with taller housing units that gave gang members less refuge than the tenements downtown, which increasingly were demolished. One newspaper even credited the influx of "peaceable foreigners from the south of Europe into the slums and rookeries and driving out the turbulent ones." That assessment would prove overly optimistic.

In any event, the trend was for the poorest New Yorkers to vacate their wretched Lower Manhattan tenements and move to better housing uptown, in new immigrant clusters, as soon as their economic circumstances allowed. Razing the downtown slums essentially forced these relocations and helped dissipate the worst of the gangs.

In 1896 the *New-York Tribune* declared that gang rule in New York "is at an end and has been fairly put down." There was "not a single gang worthy of the name from the Battery to Westchester."

Theodore Roosevelt, president of the Board of Police Commissioners, echoed the sentiment in an 1897 speech to a social reform club. He told the audience that toughs did not exist as they had before and that the Whyos and other gangs were no longer openly defiant.

After about 1895, and certainly by the end of the century, the press was referring to the Whyos in the past tense. Yet, as always in New York, new gangs would emerge to take the Whyos' place. In declaring the days of the gangs over, the newspapers were speaking too soon.

As for their legacy, the author of a recent biography of Howe & Hummel, their regular lawyers, asserts that the Whyos constituted "disorganized crime" because they were "unsystematic and crude." But it is better to think of them as transitional figures between the ragtag street brawlers of earlier times and the more business-oriented racketeers of the Prohibition era and later twentieth century. Loosely as they may have been structured, the Whyos bore some of the earmarks of organized crime: violence and intimidation, political connections, territorial expansion, and charismatic, if vulnerable, leadership. Like their later Mafia counterparts, the Whyos' leaders denied even the existence of their organization.

What the Whyos lacked was the kind of continuity that is best ensured by familial ties. They were the last of the dominant Irish gangs of Gilded Age New York, as organized crime increasingly came under the control of the newer immigrant classes: southern Italians and eastern European Jews. Indeed, the city's next two preeminent criminal gangs would come from those two groups.

After the Whyos' days had passed, Thomas Byrnes would be extolled for having brought about their demise, even though he'd had little to do directly with that outcome. (Neither Danny Driscoll nor the Whyos is even mentioned in his 1886 book.)* It was just one more building block in the growing legend surrounding the Great Detective.

* In an 1895 revised edition of his book, Byrnes did acknowledge the "notorious Whyo gang," but by that time, the Whyos were no longer active. Byrnes profiled several purported Whyo gang members, including Clops (or Slops) Connolly, Josh Hines, Dorsey Doyle, Bull Hurley, James "Fig" McGerald/Fitzgerald, Baboon Connolly, Michael Lloyd, and Googy Corcoran. With the exception of Fitzgerald and Corcoran, though, contemporaneous newspaper accounts do not identify any of these thieves as Whyos.

CHAPTER THIRTEEN

BETTER THAN SCOTLAND YARD

In a series of five-and-dime mystery novels published between 1887 and 1888, each purportedly based on Thomas Byrnes's diary and actual crimes he solved, author Julian Hawthorne extolled Byrnes as the greatest detective not only in New York but also all the world—an omniscient, endlessly resourceful cop who always got his man.

In these potboilers, wildly popular with the public if not the critics, who derided them as hackwork, Byrnes was also presented as an unassuming man simply doing his duty. His sole reward, he was quoted as saying in one of the novels, was "the success of my stratagems." He was America's Sherlock Holmes (who was first introduced to the reading public at this same time)—less eccentric, but just as brilliant.

Not everyone agreed.

In his 1887 memoirs, two years after being forced out as New York's police superintendent, George Walling took several veiled swipes at Byrnes, who had served under him for years both as a captain, as an inspector, and as chief of the detective bureau. Walling, himself a former head of the detective branch, scoffed at the public's belief that detectives had "supernatural powers" and were superlative beings blessed with a "wonderful brain." According to Walling, luck had more to do with solving crimes than did clues or what cops did with them.

Alluding to Byrnes even more pointedly, Walling disparaged what he called "quick-wittedness" in a detective. The "rapid generalizer," Walling wrote, tended to shape the facts to his theories rather than the other way around. "I have rather liked the hesitating man," Walling added, "the officer who doubted the correctness of his own theories."

Walling also wrote that New York's top detectives posed as successful thief catchers by taking credit for crimes they solved while keeping the public ignorant of all the ones that they didn't. Newspaper reporters, Walling added, helped maintain the façade. They deliberately exaggerated detectives' exploits because it sold papers and kept the journalists on the "in" with the detective corps. Because Byrnes was well known for cultivating friendly relations with the city's crime reporters, to whom he fed a steady diet of self-promoting stories, there is little doubt Walling was writing with Byrnes in mind.

The criminal defense duo of William Howe and Abraham Hummel, Byrnes's frequent nemeses, also sought to demythologize the alleged cleverness of the celebrated detective. Writing in 1886, the same year Byrnes's book on professional criminals was published, Howe and Hummel downplayed Byrnes's prowess, though they, too, declined to name him: "Ninety-nine out of a hundred cases are worked through the squeal of some thief, or ex-thief, who keeps posted on the doings of others of his class in the city," the authors wrote. "He knows some officer intimately; goes to him and tells him that the night before One-Thumbed Charley turned a trick on Church Street, and the stuff is 'planted' at such and such a place. Acting on this information, the officers visit the place indicated, and just sit around and wait till their man shows up. Lots of ability about that, isn't there?"

Walling, who was jealous of Byrnes's success, and Howe and Hummel, who viewed law enforcement as the enemy, were not exactly objective critics. But there is some validity to their criticisms. In forming his initial picture of a crime, Byrnes was sometimes too unwilling to depart from it. And it's true that when he won, he made sure everyone knew it; when he lost, the news was buried or dismissed as no big deal.

In 1888, for example, Byrnes doggedly investigated the fatal stabbing of Sicilian Antonio Flaccomio, a police informer in Little Italy, which may have been the first Mafia killing in New York City. (It was billed as the "Mafia" murder in the press.) With remarkable prescience, Byrnes described the Mafia as a secret society of Sicilians, fugitives from their native country, whose members were pledged to protect one another against officers of the law. "The members of this society are chiefly forgers, counterfeiters, and assassins," Byrnes was quoted as saying. "Murder with some of these men is simply a pastime." He accurately identified New Orleans and New York as their principal headquarters in America.

But after a jury failed to convict the man Byrnes arrested, he downplayed the verdict. Some sources quote him saying that as far as he was concerned, the Italians could all go kill one another. What appears to be the actual quote, though, garbled down the years, is far less callous: "They have their quarrels among themselves and . . . occasionally kill one another."

Byrnes declared that most Italian New Yorkers were law-abiding citizens, anyway, and not a danger to the public, citing as evidence that the rogues' gallery contained no portraits of Italian thieves. A year later, he emphasized that since the Flaccomio case, there had been no Italian murder in New York that seemed to be the work of an organized band of assassins, and that while the Mafia apparently was flourishing in New Orleans, it had kept quiet in New York.

Among successes, Byrnes was credited with sending a con man named Joseph Elzas, aka Joseph Lewis or Francis J. Alvany, better known as "Hungry Joe" Lewis, "King of the Bunco Men," up the river. In 1885, Lewis, whose previous victims included the Irish poet and playwright Oscar Wilde, went to Sing Sing for four years after Byrnes trapped and arrested him for swindling a wealthy English tourist. In 1888, Lewis went back to jail for another nine years after Byrnes nabbed him in New York for having conned a Baltimore businessman.

On his release in 1896, Lewis said he'd been framed by Byrnes, who held a grudge against him, and that if he could tell all he knew about the famous detective, "he, and not I, would today be serving time." Hungry Joe may have been blowing smoke at that point, but he was right that Byrnes could be an unforgiving man.

As for Howe and Hummel's observations, Byrnes did rely heavily—maybe too heavily—on stool pigeons. One ex-thief, while admitting that the squealer was an unavoidable necessity in ferreting out many crimes, opined that the "mouthpiece" (stool pigeon) system was flawed. "It tempts the honest officer to be lazy, it permits the dishonest officer to graft, and it involves payment to the mouthpiece in return for services rendered," he explained. "If the police were made to take their profession as seriously as the thieves take theirs, they would not have to fall back on the thief for aid when a puzzling crime came to their notice."*

But in the public's mind, Byrnes could do little wrong. He received mostly glowing press, even while some reporters viewed him with suspicion. He was never a Tammany stooge, which helped insulate him from the ire of reformers who saw the police department as corrupt. And whether he deserved the credit often given to him, New York was becoming a safer, less violent place heading into the 1890s than it was in 1880, when Byrnes took over the detective bureau.

In 1888, by a special act of the New York State Legislature, Byrnes was appointed to the newly created position of chief inspector, at a salary of $5,000 a year (up from $3,500). He became the number two man in the police department and remained head of the detective bureau.

Commenting on his promotion, *The New York Times* said that Byrnes's "management of the Detective Bureau has been brilliant, and his record as a 'thief catcher' is remarkable." *Harper's Weekly* ventured that he had "done more to disorganize organized crime than any other man who has ever been a police officer."

---

* In later years, the slang term "mouthpiece" came to refer more commonly to a criminal defense lawyer, especially one for gangsters, as in the 1932 Warner Brothers film *The Mouthpiece*.

In the same article, Byrnes asserted that his bureau did "far more" toward the prevention and detection of crime than either London's Scotland Yard or the fabled Parisian detective force. How did he know this? He said that many first-class American thieves went to England and France each year or so and came back with money to spend. This, even though the European authorities had certain advantages, he pointed out, that his men did not. For example, a French law required hotel owners to inform the police of the comings and goings of guests—their arrival dates, the number of persons in their party, and what luggage they carried. No such law would be tolerated in America, nor should it, Byrnes said.

He maintained further that in Europe, although "the authorities can hold suspected persons much better than we can," they "don't catch them as well." He omitted to mention that New York cops were permitted to arrest people on suspicion and even hold mere witnesses in a special house of detention, dubbed by one contemporary London publication as "a peculiar place for the innocent." By contrast, in London and elsewhere in Europe, as George Walling pointed out, the police "dare not lay a finger on a man unless he is engaged in the very act of violating the law." Walling nonetheless agreed with Byrnes that the New York City police force was the finest of its kind in the world, with fitter, better paid, and more vigilant men than the protectors of any other city.

Nevertheless, New York cops envied the exalted reputations of Scotland Yard and other foreign counterparts. Byrnes "was always very jealous" of Scotland Yard, recalled his friend, Assistant District Attorney Francis L. Wellman. And the rivalry burst into the open in the summer of 1888, when a series of brutal murders in London's East End, in the impoverished, Dickensian district known as Whitechapel, shocked the world while baffling the London police.

◆⇒ ⇐◆

To this day, no one knows for certain how many women were killed by the man who came to be known as Jack the Ripper. The historical consensus attributes five Whitechapel-area homicides, the "canonical five," to a single hand between August 31 and November 9, 1888.

More broadly, eleven unsolved Whitechapel murders, committed from April 3, 1888, to February 13, 1891, have variously been ascribed to the famous serial killer. Most, though not all, of the victims were prostitutes who had their throats slashed and their abdomens mutilated; in some cases, their disemboweled organs were taken away by the assailant.

With each new murder, the London populace was increasingly terrorized, and the police seemingly paralyzed. New York's newspapers eagerly joined the British press in mocking the apparent ineptitude of Scotland Yard. "The London police and detective force is probably the stupidest in the world," wrote *The New York Times* on September 9, 1888, the day after the fourth Whitechapel victim was discovered.

Two more female sex workers were sliced to death within minutes of each other on the night of September 30, 1888, prompting the *New-York Tribune* to accuse the London police of "incapacity and slothfulness." If such a series of nocturnal murders took place in New York, the *Tribune* ventured, Inspector Byrnes would have every house in the area searched and a cop stationed on every nearby block from curfew to breakfast time. "'Oh, for a transatlantic Inspector Byrnes!' might well be the cry of the panic-stricken multitude," wrote the *New York World*'s London correspondent.

Indeed, proud New York law enforcement officials, as well as the press, expressed the belief that if someone like Jack the Ripper, or even the Ripper himself, struck in their city, he would be caught in short order. Police Superintendent William Murray—Byrnes's fellow former Ellsworth Zouave—said that although he wished to cast no aspersions on the London force, he was confident that "no such crimes could continue under the system of the New York Police."

A New York City police court judge was more pointed in his criticism: "Seven such murders in succession would be impossible in this city. Inspector Byrnes would have had the man locked up long ago. All this simply goes to show us what a well-policed city we live in."

Prostitute Carrie Brown, also known as "Shakespeare" for her tendency to quote the English playwright when she was drunk, was the victim of a brutal 1891 murder that became known as New York's own "Jack the Ripper" case. Her naked, mutilated body was found in a run-down lodging house near the Brooklyn Bridge.

Byrnes joined the same chorus. The *World* quoted him as saying that a Ripper-style murderer in New York would be "run down in forty-eight hours." Interviewed in October 1888 by a London newspaper, Byrnes said he would have approached the Whitechapel investigation in a more direct manner than Scotland Yard had. "I should have gone right to work in a commonsense way and not believed in mere theories," he said, adding:

> With the great power of the London police, I should have manufactured victims for the murderer. I would have taken 50 female habitués of Whitechapel and covered the ground with them. Even if one fell a victim, I should get the murderer. Men un-uniformed should be

scattered over the district so nothing could escape them. The crimes are all of the same class, and I would have determined the class to which the murderer belonged. But—pshaw! What's the good of talking? The murderer would have been caught long ago.

Those words would threaten to boomerang on Byrnes when, three years later, it seemed that Jack the Ripper was possibly on the loose in New York.

⁕━━◉⊂━⁕

On the morning of April 24, 1891, an aging New York prostitute named Carrie Brown, known as "Shakespeare" for her tendency to quote the bard when she was drunk, was found naked and brutally disemboweled in the East River Hotel, a shabby lodging house at Catherine Slip and Water Street. It was a miserable, disease- and crime-ridden area in the shadow of the Brooklyn Bridge, full of dives and whorehouses catering to drunken sailors.

The victim had been strangled with her clothing first, then cut open with a four-inch table knife left lying on the floor next to the bed where she lay. Her right arm was twisted under her body, her left arm rested across her chest, and her legs were drawn up into a fetal position. An "X" was lightly carved on the back of her spine.

Notified by the hotel owner, the first responders were Captain Richard O'Connor and officers from the nearby Fourth Precinct station house on what was then Oak Street. Soon on the case were O'Connor's immediate boss, Divisional Inspector Clubber Williams, and Chief Inspector Thomas Byrnes, temporarily promoted to acting superintendent while Superintendent Murray was out of the city.

Byrnes took charge of the investigation at the Oak Street station house, where he began questioning witnesses. Meanwhile, detectives and crime reporters from across the city began converging on the scene on the top floor of the five-story East River Hotel.

The New York papers were already drawing comparisons to the Whitechapel murders and openly speculating that Jack the Ripper had crossed the Atlantic to claim new victims. "Is It Jack The Ripper?," the *Tribune* asked in a blaring headline, while *The Sun*, in an article headlined "Jack the Ripper's Mark," said that "an imitator of Jack the Ripper, if not Jack himself, butchered her."

The most important eyewitness Byrnes questioned was the assistant housekeeper on duty that night: Mary Miniter, the only person to have seen Carrie Brown at the hotel with her presumed killer. Brown had been drinking beer in the ground-floor saloon with a female friend around nine, and when the friend left with another girl a half hour later, the roughly sixty-year-old prostitute began telling Miniter about her life in a maudlin way. Her husband was a seaman who'd died many years earlier, and she had two daughters, one of whom was thirty-six. After her husband's death, Brown took up acting for a while, settled in New York, and turned to alcohol and prostitution. In and out of jail, she'd been released from Blackwell's Island just a few days before her murder.

Miniter said that after their conversation, Brown left the hotel and went to her home five minutes away, then returned shortly before eleven. She was now accompanied by a man about thirty-two years old, five feet eight inches tall, of slim build, with a heavy blond mustache to match his light hair. He dressed in a dark cutaway coat and wore a dented black derby. He was evidently a foreigner; Miniter thought he was German.

The couple wanted a room, and, for fifty cents, they were given the keys to room 31 on the top floor. The man gave his name as "C. Kniclo," and the hotel clerk listed them in the registry as "C. Kniclo and wife" to comply with the law. They asked for and were given a pail of mixed ale to take with them upstairs.

No one heard any screams from room 31 that night. Neither Miniter nor the hotel's night clerk saw Brown's companion leave, even though to exit the hotel through either of the two available doors, some hotel employee would have had to unlock the door for him. Police assumed that he escaped out the attic onto the roof and then down to the street, and blood reportedly was found on the attic opening. He apparently took the key to the room, as it was not there when the police arrived.

Between one and two in the morning, a man fitting the description provided by Mary Miniter showed up at the Glenmore Hotel, a cheap lodging house on Chatham Square, a few blocks from the murder scene. He asked for a room but had no money, and so he was turned away. The night clerk said the man's face, hands, and clothing were smeared with blood.

That he was the same man seen with Carrie Brown a few hours earlier seemed little in doubt. According to the Glenmore Hotel's night clerk, "The fellow spoke with a pronounced German accent . . . about five feet nine inches in height, light complexion, long nose, and light mustache. He . . . wore a shabby cutaway coat and a shabby old derby hat." It matched Mary Miniter's description of C. Kniclo to a tee.

For reasons that were never made clear, Byrnes lost interest in C. Kniclo. He later expressed his belief that the mysterious man who entered room 31 with Carrie Brown was simply a client who left after obtaining her services and had nothing to do with the murder.

More likely, Byrnes gave up on the lead because the man was nowhere to be found. Byrnes was under intense pressure to quickly arrest Carrie Brown's killer, especially given his previous boasts (which he now tried to back away from) that he'd have a Ripper-style murderer in custody in a couple of days in New York. But C. Kniclo had disappeared into the night, and Byrnes had no clue as to his whereabouts.

Consequently, Byrnes trained his attention on an entirely different pair of suspects. One of them he had in custody already. The other he was sure he could find. Curiously, they both went by the nickname of "Frenchy."

The man who became known as "Frenchy No. 1" was an Algerian Muslim by the name of Ameer Ben Ali, also known as George Frank. He was arrested as a material witness after police were told that he knew Carrie Brown. Ben Ali had recently met up with her at her lodging house at 49 Oliver Street and was seen drinking with her and another couple at a nearby saloon earlier on the day of the murder. More important, he had spent the night in room 33 of the East River Hotel, diagonally across from room 31.

Frenchy No. 1 was roughly forty years old, tall, thin, olive-skinned, and dark-haired. (He was thought to be Greek or Italian at first.) He obviously was not the light-haired, Germanic C. Kniclo, a fact that Mary Miniter confirmed when Ben Ali was shown to her at the station house. But he had a criminal record, a reputation as a physical abuser and robber of prostitutes, and a penchant for constantly changing his story.

When arrested, Ben Ali insisted he'd slept in Brooklyn the night of the murder, but later admitted he'd stayed in room 33, though he denied seeing Brown there or even knowing her.

He also gave conflicting statements about how he happened to have blood on his socks, shirt, and collar. He first ascribed it to a fight with another woman at a Long Island hotel on the night of the murder, then he said it was from a fight with an unknown man, and still later he maintained that the fight was with a woman in a basement somewhere in New York, though he couldn't say where. Ben Ali would prove to be his own worst enemy.

"Frenchy No. 2," a Moroccan named Arbie La Bruckman, was said to be a younger cousin of Frenchy No. 1, although the pair were apparently just close acquaintances. They were reportedly ruffians of the worst character who "were always in the company of the old hags who haunt the waterfront."

A New Jersey slaughterhouse worker, La Bruckman had black hair and a dark brown mustache and was strongly built and bullnecked (like Hercules, according to one description). Thus, he also failed to match the description of the slight, fair-complexioned German man provided by both Mary Miniter and the night clerk at the Glenmore Hotel.

Nonetheless, Byrnes announced at a late-night press conference on Saturday, April 25, forty-eight hours after the murder, that Frenchy No. 2 was the murderer of Carrie Brown and soon would be caught. Again,

Byrnes's reasoning is difficult to fathom. The only apparent link between Frenchy No. 2 and the murder was that he had been one of the foursome, along with Frenchy No. 1 and another woman, spotted drinking with Carrie Brown on the day of the murder. But unlike Frenchy No. 1, La Bruckman had not been seen at the East River Hotel that night.

Even more puzzling: Why would Byrnes publicly identify Frenchy No. 2 as the killer when he was still on the loose, with an opportunity to slip away? Reporters suspected that Byrnes was engaged in a ruse, either to throw off the real killer or to buy time with a public that was impatient for a quick capture.

Tracked down by police in Jersey City, New Jersey, a couple of days later, Frenchy No. 2 readily acknowledged that he was the man they were looking for: the "cousin" of Frenchy No. 1. He also made the amazing, self-incriminating statement that he'd previously been arrested and locked up in London on suspicion of being Jack the Ripper. As a cattleman-sailor, he made frequent transatlantic crossings and had arrived back in New York from London on April 10, two weeks before the murder.

But La Bruckman's claim to have been arrested for the Whitechapel murders was never corroborated and, in retrospect, seems to have been prompted by a bid for attention. More crucially, police ascertained that he had a solid alibi for the night of the murder: he was at his lodging house in New Jersey, as persons there verified. Combined with the fact that he didn't match the description of C. Kniclo, La Bruckman's alibi led to his quick release.

In fact, by the time La Bruckman was found, Byrnes was already publicly retracting his statement that Frenchy No. 2 was the killer. On April 27, less than two days after his nighttime press conference, Byrnes told reporters that he'd been misquoted and that he'd never said Frenchy No. 2 was the murderer or even that he had any evidence to prove it. At best, Frenchy No. 2 was a suspect, Byrnes "clarified." A day later, Byrnes said he did not believe that Frenchy No. 2 was the murderer.

Byrnes was engaged in pure misdirection at this point. Asked why he didn't release Frenchy No. 1, Byrnes replied, "How do you know I have not?"

"But have you?" he was asked.

"I refuse to answer."

"Well, what do you think of the murderer now?" he was asked.

"I have no theory for publication," the inspector responded. "I don't know anything more about the murder than you do."

All that the police seemed to be doing was performing a dragnet: arresting a string of light-complexioned men with long noses and yellow mustaches, then releasing them after questioning. While Byrnes had dozens of men scouring the dives and lodging houses of practically the entire Lower East Side, the city's newspapers were writing that the police were completely baffled and irritable ("Byrnes Quite Mystified," read one *New York Times* headline). Scotland Yard, reportedly excited to see Byrnes tested, could not have been unhappy to hear of his difficulties.

And then, on Thursday, April 30, six days after the murder, Byrnes announced that this time he really did have his man: Frenchy No. 1. In fact, it now appeared that Ameer Ben Ali had been the prime suspect all along, ever since his arrest and incarceration the previous Friday.

New information was leaked to the press that pointed circumstantially to Ben Ali as the murderer. Not only had he been arrested with blood on his clothing, which he'd failed to explain adequately, but police had also discovered a microscopic trail of blood on Friday the twenty-fourth, the first day of the investigation, leading from room 31, where Carrie Brown was slain, across the hall to room 33, where Ben Ali had spent the night.

Byrnes said they'd found bloodstains on both the outside and inside of the door to room 33, on the floor and a chair in the room, and on the bed and blankets. What's more, blood was found under Ben Ali's fingernails.

Detectives sent the fingernail blood, along with samples of the bloodstains, cut from pieces of wood and cloth with the aid of a magnifying glass, to Dr. Cyrus Edson, chief chemist for the New York City Board of Health. *The New York Times* reported that Edson and his colleagues determined that "the blood on the wood was human, and that there were traces of the same character under the fingernails."

Medical experts for the prosecution would later claim that the fingernail parings contained particles of partially digested food that "could not possibly have been obtained in any other way than during an operation on somebody's smaller intestine." To top it all off, the state's experts reported that these samples showed partially digested cheese, bread, and some form of cabbage—corresponding with Carrie Brown's last meal, a free lunch at the East River Hotel on the day of her death, consisting of cheese, bread, ham, and coleslaw.

Byrnes told the press that Ben Ali was a man of "wicked and unnatural habits" who, in addition to killing Carrie Brown, had probably robbed her of a few dollars after the man identified as C. Kniclo left her room on the night of the murder. Ben Ali was indicted and put on trial, where the district attorney described him as "a man, born in a valley in Algeria, an Arab by birth, of no education, imbued with all the spirit of the Mohammedan religion, and the fierce and ferocious habits of his native land . . . a man who is himself half savage . . . to whom human life is cheap."

Testifying in his own defense, Ben Ali did not help his cause with his contradictory testimony and tendency to make wild, excited outbursts. (At times he shouted out, "Allahu Akbar!"—"God is great!"—in Arabic.) Nor, despite competent lawyers appointed to represent Ben Ali pro bono, could the defense overcome the prosecution's array of high-priced experts. Mostly what they peddled was junk science; as they were forced to admit, it was not possible to say definitively that the blood was human rather than mammalian. The testimony purportedly tying the fingernail scrapings to Carrie Brown's last meal was a stretch at best; *The New York Times* called it "very slender and uncertain."

The defense argued that the blood on Ben Ali's clothing could be explained by his having had sex with a menstruating prostitute the night before the murder and that the mixture of blood and fecal matter under his fingernails might be the result of his unsanitary habits. There were no bloodstains on the doorknobs to either room 31 or 33, even though Ben Ali supposedly shuttled between the two rooms.

Captain O'Connor, the first cop on the scene, was unable to swear that on his initial visit he'd seen any of the blood evidence. The murder weapon—a bloody knife—was not convincingly traced to the defendant. The real killer, the defense maintained, was the mysterious man who'd accompanied Carrie Brown to room 31, then escaped and disappeared.

But the jury was unimpressed with the defense, and Ben Ali was convicted of second-degree murder and sentenced to life in prison. A conviction of first-degree murder would have meant the electric chair.

Although the *New York World* called it a victory for Byrnes, the inspector confessed to some disappointment with the verdict. He said that Ben Ali deserved to die but had escaped his just deserts. The jury, he said, apparently gave the defendant the benefit of the doubt by saying the murder was not premeditated but rather that Frenchy had demanded money from the victim and killed her in a fit of rage.

Asked if he thought Frenchy and Jack the Ripper were the same person, Byrnes said coyly he had documents showing that Ben Ali, after leaving Algiers, was in London at the time of some of the Whitechapel murders. But he said there had been no need to introduce the evidence at trial. "I do not say that he is the London ripper," Byrnes said, "but this has a tendency to indicate that he may be."

Most Ripperologists, as students of the London murders are known, would beg to differ. They emphasize that Jack the Ripper generally slit the throats of his victims—including each of the canonical five—before disemboweling them. The New York police originally noted the same fact in expressing their opinion that Carrie Brown's assailant was probably not the Ripper himself.

The police back then also pointed out, as have researchers since, that Shakespeare's killer butchered her in a clumsy, hacking manner that exhibited none of the precise surgical skill of the London murderer. The

Whitechapel killer did not strike in semipublic places, such as a lodging house, where many people were around. And unlike Carrie Brown's murderer, Jack the Ripper never left his knife at the scene of the crime. Finally, despite myths to the contrary, the Ripper did not mark his victims with an "X" or cross.

Following the verdict in Ben Ali's trial, the press remained skeptical that he was Carrie Brown's killer, much less Jack the Ripper. *The New York Times*, generally a Byrnes supporter, singled him out for criticism, editorializing that although he was "undoubtedly a keen and energetic officer," he had "more than once shown that success in catching and convicting somebody is more to him than the demands of exact justice. Even such a wretched specimen as the Algerian ought not to be sacrificed on insufficient evidence merely to demonstrate the infallibility of our detective system."

Eleven years later, after serving time in Sing Sing and a state mental hospital, Ameer Ben Ali was pardoned by New York governor Benjamin Odell, who cited the weakness of the prosecution's evidence at trial. Odell was heavily influenced by affidavits provided by Jacob Riis and other reporters who swore that they had arrived early at the murder scene and saw no blood in the hallway between rooms 31 and 33, nor any blood on the door to room 33, where Ben Ali had slept, or anywhere inside that room. Why these journalists never came forward at the time of trial was curious.

The journalists' affidavits suggested that the blood evidence may have been left inadvertently by the swarm of people—reporters and gawkers—who were allowed to roam the premises before they were sealed off. Today such unrestricted access would be considered a failure to preserve the integrity of the crime scene, tainting the investigation. Another possibility was that the blood samples were planted by the police. But unlike lawyers a century later for, say, O. J. Simpson, neither Ben Ali's defense team nor the press had the temerity to accuse Thomas Byrnes or his detectives of manufacturing evidence.

Upon Ben Ali's release from confinement in 1902, Byrnes was asked his opinion of the pardon. "The records show that I landed him . . . and what his personal record was. I haven't got time to go into the details of his career," was his curt response. He declined further comment, saying, "The governor can pardon whom he likes. It's nothing to me."

By that time, Byrnes was no longer a police officer and didn't care. But in 1891 his reputation as a crime solver mattered very much to him. And although he had his detractors, for the most part he was seen as the brilliant detective portrayed in Julian Hawthorne's dime novels. He may not have caught "New York's Jack the Ripper" in forty-eight hours, as promised previously, but he did it in less than a week, which sufficed to put his money where his mouth was. He had bested Scotland Yard.

Tammany Hall politician Timothy Sullivan (right), better known as "Big Tim" or the "Big Feller." Through his use of political patronage and gang muscle, he exercised virtually total control of jobs and vice below Fourteenth Street. He was dubbed "King of the Underworld" for his connections to gambling, prostitution, boxing, and other criminal activities. To his right are his half brother Larry Mulligan and half sister Margaret Hickey.

Few people at the time were willing to take Byrnes on publicly, but one who did was a then relatively obscure young state assemblyman and Lower East Side saloonkeeper named Timothy "Dry Dollar" Sullivan. He was better known later as "Big Tim" or the "Big Feller" for his six-foot-plus, 200-pound frame.

Like his mentor Fatty Walsh, Sullivan was a patron of the Whyos. They hung out at Sullivan's Chrystie Street dive in the Five Points, the neighborhood where he had grown up shining shoes and heading a gang of newspaper boys. Sullivan's close association with the Whyos got him elected a New York State assemblyman in 1886, the same year Danny Driscoll was convicted of murdering Beezie Garrity.

If Byrnes was the big Irish cop known for crime fighting, Sullivan was the big Irishman who enabled crime. He and Byrnes got into a major row in 1889 when Sullivan successfully opposed an assembly bill pushed by Byrnes to authorize the arrest of known criminals on sight—in effect, a codification and extension of Byrnes's dead line from Wall Street to the rest of the city.

Byrnes publicly blasted Sullivan as an associate of burglars, thieves, and murderers, and accused him of taking protection money from his "constant companion" Danny Driscoll and other gang members in exchange for helping them keep out of jail. Byrnes charged that Sullivan opposed the bill to keep cops out of his saloons, of which he owned several (though Sullivan himself did not drink).

The twenty-five-year-old Sullivan tearfully defended himself on the floor of the assembly, challenging Byrnes in a speech that Sullivan later said "made a man of me." It also brought him to the attention of Tammany's all-powerful boss, or grand sachem, Richard Croker, who'd gotten his start as a brawler and gang leader and was once tried for murder in a case that ended in a hung jury.

By 1892, Sullivan, now a Croker protégé, had sold off his saloons to pursue a steadier, more lucrative career as an ethically challenged politician. He soon gained virtually total control of patronage and graft below Fourteenth Street. He was labeled a philanthropist for the Christmas turkey dinners, Labor Day "chowders" (free boat excursions), and other charity he bestowed on his poor, multiethnic constituents. And in fairness, Tammany Hall did much good for thousands of underprivileged immigrants who lacked basic government and social services. One contemporary writer went so far as to call Sullivan "the Modern Robin Hood." But Big Tim was also dubbed "King of the Underworld" for his connections to gambling, prostitution, boxing (when it was illegal), and other criminal activities.

As a Tammany stalwart, Sullivan also relied on perennial election fraud, both in the form of hired "shoulder hitters" (gang muscle), and "repeaters." With Tammany's help in faking registrations or naturalization papers, noncitizen immigrants in the Five Points and similar enclaves were often made eligible to vote. But Sullivan saw no reason to limit them to one vote apiece. As he explained, "When they vote with their whiskers on, you take 'em to a barber and scrape off the chin-fringe. Then you vote 'em again with side lilacs and mustache. Then to the barber again, off comes the sides, and you vote 'em a third time with just a mustache. If that ain't enough, and the box can stand a few more ballots, clean off the mustache and vote 'em plain face. That makes every one of 'em good for four votes."

⋆⇒◯⇐⋆

As Big Tim climbed the ladder of politics and crime, Thomas Byrnes continued his meteoric rise in law enforcement. Nine months after the conviction of Ben Ali, he was elevated to police superintendent in New York, replacing the retiring, and ailing, William Murray. After nearly thirty years on the force, Byrnes was now the city's top cop.

Upon taking office, Byrnes declared that he was free from any party obligations and was not a member of any political organization. Consequently, he said, he would direct all his energy to protecting life and property and enforcing the laws without fear or favor, including those relating to prostitution, gambling, and Sunday liquor sales.

He was determined to maintain the prestige of the department and end any rumored corruption, and, to that end, he announced a sweeping police shake-up: all captains (with one exception) were immediately detailed to new precincts, and dozens of wardmen, their alleged bag collectors, were remanded to regular patrol duty. "A Cyclone Hit the Police," read a headline in *The New York Times*, which expressed confidence in Byrnes's purposes and promises, even while doubting that the shake-up would have any permanent effect. (At least one personnel move, little noted at the time, would prove significant: Patrolman Art Carey was transferred from the Second Precinct to the central office detective bureau, which Byrnes continued to keep a personal eye on as superintendent.)

To show that he meant business, on the first Sunday of his new tenure, Byrnes had his men arrest 120 saloonkeepers and bartenders for illegal sales. These were to be real arrests, he instructed his captains, with evidence that would hold up in court, not show arrests of the type so often made previously. He demanded detailed reports from his inspectors and captains of the existence of so-called vice in their districts and followed up with raids of 150 disorderly houses (brothels), closings of more than 200 gambling parlors, and hundreds more arrests for liquor law violations. His public standing never seemed higher.

But one evangelist from the pulpit wasn't buying it.

CHAPTER FOURTEEN

"EVERY CRIME HERE HAS ITS PRICE"

If playing leapfrog with naked prostitutes at Madam Hattie Adams's Midtown brothel was what it was going to take to prove that the NYPD was thoroughly corrupt, then the Reverend Doctor Charles Parkhurst was willing to make that sacrifice.

Hardly remembered today, Charles H. Parkhurst was among the most famous New Yorkers of the 1890s, perhaps the most schizophrenic decade in the city's history. It was still the Gilded Age, scorned for its excessive displays of wealth when so many lived in poverty. More nostalgically, it is remembered as the Gay Nineties, conjuring images of men in red-and-white-striped summer suits and boater hats and Casey dancing with the strawberry blonde while the band played on.

It was also the late Victorian era, when bourgeois morality sought to hold the fort against increasing sexual freedom and licentiousness. And it was the Progressive Era, during which crusading politicians, muckraking journalists, and civic and religious leaders sought to expose official corruption and reform the system.

Among the crusaders was the fifty-year-old Parkhurst, minister at the

The Reverend Charles H. Parkhurst, whose morality crusade in the 1890s led to the groundbreaking Lexow Committee investigation by the New York State Senate into police corruption in the city.

Madison Square Presbyterian Church. Originally from Massachusetts, he was a scholarly though zealous moralist, distinguished physically by a circle beard, little round spectacles, and a leonine mane of graying hair.

Parkhurst was elected in 1891 as president of the New York Society for the Prevention of Crime, a citizens' group dedicated to temperance and the eradication of the sources of crime and sin. With its own detective force, the SPC was ostensibly a supportive private arm of law enforcement. But Parkhurst increasingly came to view the police department, controlled as it was by Tammany Hall, as a group whose principal object was not to repress crime but to foster and profit from it.

Speaking to his wealthy flock in February 1892, Parkhurst boldly sermonized that the police were making millions in tribute paid by prostitutes and gamblers to allow them to continue in business, and by saloon-keepers to operate illegally on Sunday. Some of the most visible sinful establishments were just around the corner from Parkhurst's church at Madison Avenue and East Twenty-Fourth Street.

His church (which no longer stands)* was adjacent to the notorious Tenderloin district, the commercial and tourist center of New York. Home to a mélange of legitimate theaters and expensive restaurants, hotels, and shopping emporiums, it also featured high-class bordellos, gambling parlors, and concert saloons. (The Bowery, equally ablaze with light at night, remained the place for lowbrow entertainment.)

Parkhurst publicly excoriated the existing Tammany administration as "a lying, perjured, rum-soaked, and libidinous lot" of "polluted harpies." As for the police, Parkhurst did not dispute that they had helped reduce violent crimes against people and property. He would take no exception to a glowing *New York Times* article, titled "He Rules Through Fear," which claimed that Byrnes had virtually driven professional thieves and crooks from the city. But under the payoff system, Parkhurst maintained, the police did nothing to disturb so-called victimless crimes. "Every crime here has its price," he asserted.

When indignant city officials demanded proof of his incendiary charges, Parkhurst enlisted a worldly private detective and a clean-cut young parishioner and set off on a nocturnal slumming tour of Gotham's netherworld. It wasn't hard to find the dens of iniquity; they were everywhere.

An estimated thirty thousand to forty thousand prostitutes plied their trade daily on the city's streets or in bordellos. More than two thousand professional gamblers were known to the police, which didn't count the thousands of amateurs, both New Yorkers and visitors, who ventured through the doors of gaming houses. Roughly ten thousand city saloons regularly flouted the nightly one o'clock required closing time as well as the state's Sabbath and excise laws, which forbade selling alcohol on Sundays.

Most of the forbidden activity was heavily concentrated in the Tenderloin, the Lower East Side, and Greenwich Village. In the bawdy Eleventh Precinct, within the immediate vicinity of the Eldridge Street police

---

* It was demolished in 1909 to make way for the forty-eight-story Metropolitan Life Insurance Company Tower, the tallest building in the world until it was surpassed in 1913 by the Woolworth Building.

station, houses of prostitution or assignation stood literally side by side: at 6, 8, 10, 12, 14, and 16 Delancey Street; 21, 22, 23, 24, 28, 30, 32, and 33 Bayard Street; and 101, 102, 117, 119, 121, and 129 Canal Street.

In the Eleventh Precinct and elsewhere, illegal gambling establishments lined the streets, one after another: policy shops (for lottery and numbers games) and poolrooms (for offtrack betting, not to be confused with billiards parlors). Often, these places were hidden behind false fronts, such as candy or cigar stores or barbershops, but any sporting man with the password could get in.

To conduct their tour, Parkhurst's trio employed disguises, dressing as gauche out-of-towners with checkered pants and cheap ties. Over four nights, they found hundreds of examples of unmolested sex and sin. In a Chinatown opium den, a father, a mother, and their young son smoked a pipe together. At a Greenwich Village house of ill repute, a patrolman stood watch on the front steps while upstairs four French prostitutes danced a nude cancan.

"Show me something worse," the game Parkhurst kept telling his detective guide. Not far away, at the Golden Rule Pleasure Club, the reverend was indeed shocked to see heavily made-up men in drag speaking in high-pitched voices and calling each other female names. Meanwhile, Parkhurst sent out SPC investigators, who found 250 saloons selling liquor on a typical Sunday.

Although he admitted that he drank beer on their excursions, Parkhurst said he did not himself take part in the naked leapfrog game at Hattie Adams's place—it was the gentleman parishioner who danced with the prostitutes while the detective played the part of the frog. But that did not stop saloongoers from mocking the minister to the tune of the song "Ta-Ra-Ra-Boom-De-Ay":

Dr. Parkhurst on the floor
Playing leapfrog with a whore
Ta-ra-ra-Boom-de-ay,
Ta-ra-ra-Boom-de-ay.

Parkhurst's findings were detailed in a grand jury report alleging that the police collected $7 million to $10 million a year from lawbreakers to wink at violations. Parkhurst targeted Superintendent Thomas Byrnes and Inspector Alexander Williams for neglect of duty, or worse. An outraged Byrnes, who had a low regard for moral crusaders and "goo-goo" (good government) types, reacted angrily and engaged in a public war of words with the minister, even as he was making a show of raiding saloons, bordellos, and gambling houses in his first few months as police superintendent.

Byrnes maintained that Parkhurst's demand for total suppression was pie in the sky. Most gambling, Byrnes said, took place behind closed doors in obscure tenements and saloon back rooms and was difficult to discover.

As for prostitution, both Byrnes and Williams argued that it was better to confine the social evil to certain specific areas of town than to scatter ladies of the evening across the boulevards that respectable citizens trod. And Byrnes laid blame for nonenforcement of the excise laws on lenient judges who were in the pocket of Tammany politicians such as Big Tim Sullivan. Besides which, Byrnes added, ending Sunday drinking was unpopular with the masses.

Parkhurst and Byrnes continued trading ripostes through December 1892, with the pastor implying that the police superintendent was in league with criminals, and Byrnes responding that Parkhurst should stick to theology. Parkhurst had his SPC agents shadow police and city officials and mused aloud that he might need to "put a detective on Mr. Byrnes." Byrnes countered that SPC investigators, in their eagerness to collect evidence, were themselves blackmailing prostitutes and their madams.

Byrnes insisted that the police were doing the best they could to suppress illegality, citing statistics on the thousands of arrests of prostitutes and gamblers since he became superintendent. He maintained that New York was a cleaner, purer city than the foreign capitals where iniquity was deliberately licensed, adding mischievously that Parkhurst ought to know, as he had just spent the summer in Europe.

In January 1893 Byrnes sought to blunt some of Parkhurst's criticism by bringing formal charges against two of his inspectors, Clubber Williams and Thomas McAvoy, and three police captains, for failing to shutter several gambling houses and opium dens in their districts. Byrnes had gone behind his subordinates' backs by having some of his central office detectives raid the illegal establishments, disproving the officers' claims, in official reports they'd submitted to the superintendent, that no such places existed in their precincts.

At the police board hearing on the charges, Byrnes personally cross-examined Inspector Williams. Though they had been friends earlier in their careers, their relationship had turned increasingly uneasy as Clubber's reputation for corruption grew and Byrnes was promoted to superintendent, a job Williams had wanted for himself. As a precinct captain, before his promotion to inspector, Williams had fended off many previous charges of brutality and graft before the police board, including that he was in league with panel houses in the Eighth Precinct when Shang Draper's panel business flourished there in the early 1870s.

Transferred in 1876 from the low-rent Fourth Precinct to command of the Twenty-Ninth Precinct, in the heart of the Tenderloin, Williams was quoted as saying, "I have been living on rump steak in the Fourth Precinct; I will have some tenderloin now," thus coining the district's famous name. Although he would later say he had meant only that he would be residing in an area with higher-quality hotels and saloons, it was widely assumed he was referring to the more lucrative opportunities for graft available to police in Midtown, where he would serve as a captain for more than a decade.

Williams, a rock-solid Republican, had always managed to have all serious charges against him dismissed because the 2-to-2 party split among the police commissioners prevented a majority for conviction. As a result of his reputation for being ultra-tough on crime, he enjoyed the support of the Republican business establishment, including Elihu Root, a renowned lawyer (and future presidential cabinet member), who often defended him before the police board.

In Williams's last trial before the board as a captain, in 1887, in which he was represented by Root, the commissioners again divided 2 to 2. Inexplicably, after the charges were dismissed, Democratic commissioner John Voorhis, who had voted to convict Williams of conduct unbecoming an officer, turned around in the very same session to join the two Republicans in voting to promote Williams from captain to inspector.

In the 1893 police board trial, Williams, now an inspector, again beat the rap by feigning ignorance of the existence of any illegal establishments in his sprawling inspection district, covering almost the entire east side of town from the Battery to 110th Street. As he explained to Byrnes, he had to rely on the written reports from his captains, who attested that their precincts were squeaky clean. Besides, Williams testified, it was impossible to suppress all gambling in the city, a point Byrnes had made in responding to Parkhurst's charges and which the superintendent now had to concede.

The commissioners voted unanimously to dismiss all charges against Williams and Inspector McAvoy, who likewise pleaded ignorance, and let the three captains off with a censure and reprimand. "Not guilty, but don't do it again" is how *The Sun* characterized the outcome.

Parkhurst derided the trial as a farce and as further evidence that the system was rigged. He continued his public campaign, although the Panic of 1893 and the ensuing economic depression distracted attention from it. So did rising labor unrest, especially on the overcrowded Lower East Side, increasingly populated by Jewish immigrants from Russia and eastern Europe. Police crackdowns on striking and rioting workers positioned the NYPD, in the public mind, as a bulwark against the mounting threats of anarchism and socialism, rendering traditional "vice" a pale threat by comparison.

Superintendent Byrnes was a vocal critic of union activists, protesters, and radicals of all stripes, claiming them to be a greater menace than the criminals he'd spent his career subduing. They were particularly feared and vilified by the city's economic elite whose interests Byrnes protected.

Among Byrnes's new targets was the Russian Jewish anarchist Emma

Goldman, whom his detectives arrested in Philadelphia for allegedly in-
citing a riot at a Union Square rally in August 1893. Returning from his
summer country home along the Shrewsbury River in Red Bank, New
Jersey, Byrnes boasted that his surveillance methods, including the use of
undercover German-speaking detectives, had gotten the goods on Goldman when she switched from speaking in English to German, which
many of those in the audience spoke themselves, to mask her inflamma-
tory rhetoric.

After Goldman was convicted and sentenced to a year in prison on
Blackwell's Island, Byrnes reminded the press that it was his police department, not the do-gooder Parkhurst and his SPC agents, that protected the city from riot and bloodshed. For her part, Goldman claimed
that Byrnes had offered to free her if she agreed to inform from time to
time on Lower East Side radicals. Furious when she responded by calling
him a corrupt police chief, he raised a chair as if to strike her.

William "Big Bill" Devery, the notoriously corrupt cop whose wrongdoing as a
police captain was exposed by the Lexow Committee.

Another top cop who parlayed fears of anarchism into a public defense of his conduct was William S. Devery, captain of the Eleventh Precinct. Five foot ten and 250 pounds in his prime, with a fifty-inch waist, "Big Bill" was to become the third in the triumvirate of New York's most famous Gilded Age policemen, along with Byrnes and Clubber Williams.

A cigar-chomping product of the Irish East Side, where he was born above a saloon, and a close friend of Tammany boss Richard Croker, Devery was as shameless a political hack as could be found within the police force. Like Williams, the inspector to whom he reported, Devery viewed his position as virtually a license to steal. Told by his men that there was a lot of grafting going on in his precinct, he reputedly said, "If there's any graftin' to be done, I'll do it. Leave it to me."

When asked to admit to illegality under oath, though, his characteristic response was, "touchin' on an' appertainin' to that matter," either "I disremember" or "there's nothin' doin'." He advised cops to "keep your mouth shut when you're caught with the goods on you."

Loved by his fellow policemen, Devery was loathed by Reverend Parkhurst, who saw in him the worst evils of the corrupt system of protected illegality. In 1892 Devery had infuriated Parkhurst by framing Charles Gardner, the private detective who'd led Parkhurst on the nighttime tour. Gardner was charged with extorting money from a prostitution madam he'd been investigating for Parkhurst. Found guilty at trial, Gardner had his conviction ultimately overturned on legal grounds, but his reputation was ruined.

By 1893, when Devery assumed captaincy of the poverty- and crime-ridden Eleventh Precinct, he was in Parkhurst's cross hairs. The minister charged Devery with neglect of duty in allowing gambling and prostitution to flourish in the area, including at one disorderly house at 81 Eldridge Street, a block from the precinct station.

Variously dubbed "Jewtown" or "New Israel" for its high number of Russian and Polish Jewish immigrants, the Eleventh Precinct had replaced the Five Points as the most crowded slum in New York and perhaps the world. Its crime rate, by far the highest in the city, was double that of the Tenderloin, yet it was policed by only about two-thirds as many cops. And although the prostitution business wasn't as posh (street-walking Russian Jewish girls charged just fifty cents an hour), the volume of traffic and sheer concentration of brothels and gambling houses made the Eleventh just about as lucrative for grafting as Clubber Williams's famed district.

Devery chose to ignore the crime and attack the agitators. Playing off anti-Semitism and fears of radicalism, he didn't hesitate to bust heads in quashing riots and demonstrations by anarchists, socialists, and unemployed laborers, most of them Jewish. "Where Do Anarchists Riot?," *The New York Times* asked in a front-page headline, answering its own question: "Not in Capt. Devery's Precinct."

Effectively immunized from public censure, Devery was dismissive of the SPC's charges against him, and the police board chose not to credit any of them. Parkhurst scored a temporary coup in procuring a grand jury indictment against Devery in November 1893 for willful failure to close several disorderly houses run by convicted madams. But Big Bill was acquitted the following April in a trial attended by dozens of supportive bluecoats. Their cheers at the verdict made the building tremble and could be heard blocks away.

Parkhurst's crusade was running up against the spirit of the age, summarized succinctly by Tammany leader George Washington Plunkitt. Rationalizing having grown rich off what he called "honest graft" (for example, benefitting from inside information about upcoming public improvement projects), Plunkitt explained, "I seen my opportunities and I took 'em." It is hardly surprising that in such an atmosphere, when presented with more mundane grafting opportunities, many cops took them as well.

But Parkhurst also knew how to take his opportunities. Although police corruption had been around for decades, its origins predating Tammany's dominance, Parkhurst sought to tie it directly to the existing Tammany machine. After the Republicans regained control of the state legislature in the November 1893 elections, he persuaded the New York State Senate to open a public investigation into corruption within the NYPD and its Tammany connections.

Albany's Republican boss, Thomas Platt, had little interest in the doings of the NYPD. But he was eager to embarrass Tammany head Richard Croker, who'd recently been denying Republicans their small but customary share of the city's political spoils. Platt figured that an investigation by a committee chaired by his protégé Clarence Lexow of Nyack would probe just long and hard enough to force Croker to resume delivering patronage.

But Platt did not count on the vigilance of either Charles Parkhurst or the reverend's handpicked lawyer to lead the Lexow Committee's questioning: a stern, incorruptible Irish nationalist and quasi-revolutionary named John W. Goff. The forty-six-year-old Goff had once organized an American expedition to rescue a party of Irish rebels imprisoned in Australia by the British government. Though an Irishman, he was virulently opposed to Irish-dominated Tammany.

Consistent with Parkhurst's personal crusade, the Lexow Committee did not target gamblers, prostitutes, and excise law violators as such, but rather the system of police payoffs that allowed them to flourish. The committee also promised to look into allegations of widespread police brutality, election rigging, and the rumored purchase by cops of their appointments and promotions. The public was about to learn that, despite the NYPD's successes in advancing police methods and reducing the scourges of professional thievery and gang violence, there was a darker side to the development of the city's finest.

CHAPTER FIFTEEN

PAYING TRIBUTE

The Lexow Committee's hearings got under way in March 1894 in, of all places, a venue associated with Tammany corruption: the New York County Courthouse at 52 Chambers Street, commonly known as the Tweed Courthouse. Its costly construction, in the Italianate style, was a pretext for the bilking of millions of dollars by Tweed and his Tammany allies from the public coffers.*

In the first branch of the investigation, focusing on election fraud, the Lexow Committee identified numerous instances where it said the New York police acted essentially as agents of Tammany Hall in securing Democratic candidates the largest majorities possible. At the time, the Bureau of Elections was part of the NYPD, and the police oversaw polling places on Election Day. The committee found that police officers intimidated Republican voters or stood by while Tammany operatives did the same and aided or knowingly permitted illegal registration and repeat

---

* Still standing today as home to the New York City Department of Education, the Old New York County Courthouse is the second-oldest city government building in Manhattan, after city hall.

voting. In some cases, cops entered the voting booth to help men read and prepare their ballots and to instruct them on how to vote.

Some of the incidents bordered on the farcical. For example, a Republican election watcher told how one repeater forgot the name he was supposed to use because he was voting for the second or third time. In another case, the police stood by while about twenty-five Irishmen voted using "Hebrew names" they couldn't pronounce. And when some legitimate voters were turned away because repeaters had already voted using their names, precinct captain William Devery stood by laughing and talking with a Tammany chieftain.

Other incidents were not laughing matters. Big Tim Sullivan threatened one honest poll watcher, saying if he weren't running for senator himself, he'd "do so and so" to the complainant. During an Election Day meeting at the Eleventh Precinct's Eldridge Street station, Captain Devery warned his platoon that a lot of "silk stocking" people from uptown (that is to say, wealthy Republicans) were coming down to try to "bulldoze" the police into acting properly at the polling places. "If they open their mouths, stand them on their heads," Devery told his men.

Democrats on the committee downplayed the extent of irregularities and asserted that both parties engaged in them. In any event, because New Yorkers had already heard election fraud charges and countercharges exchanged by both sides for years, the committee's findings on this point produced surprisingly little public outrage.

The second, more eye-grabbing phase of the committee's inquiry addressed itself to police corruption and brutality. Committee lead counsel Goff, who had not participated in phase one, was aided by two young associate counsel who would attain later prominence. One was Frank Moss, a blue-blooded, reform-minded lawyer for Parkhurst's SPC (and nearly Parkhurst's equal as a moral scold). The other was the considerably less priggish William Travers Jerome, a former deputy assistant Manhattan district attorney who both smoked and drank but shared his colleagues' contempt for Tammany.

It was largely Goff's show. The cranky, prematurely white-bearded chief counsel resembled a cross between an Old Testament prophet and the later poster image of Uncle Sam. He mockingly browbeat witnesses he was convinced were lying or deliberately failing to recall. "Don't move your head like an automaton," he admonished one jail keeper. He accused a dissembling cop of having "made up your mind . . . to swear your way through this thing, haven't you?" Determined to get the truth, he admitted that he was willing to "plunge the knife in . . . and turn it around wherever I could."

At first, honest testimony was hard to come by. Witnesses, fearful of alienating the cops in their neighborhoods, steadfastly denied that they ever paid the police a cent in protection money. To avoid testifying, more than a hundred New York brothel madams formed a community of expatriates in Chicago pending completion of the committee's investigation. One of them, Matilda Hermann, the notorious owner of five Greenwich Village houses of ill fame, was given $1,700 by the police to flee the jurisdiction.

Police captain James K. Price, a former bagman for Clubber Williams, booked passage for Europe to skip the committee hearings. Price claimed he was leaving for health reasons, as did Tammany boss Richard Croker, who sailed for Europe in June 1894, just as the corruption phase of the investigation was heating up.

But gradually, under grants of immunity from prosecution, citizen witnesses commenced to tell how they were regularly shaken down by the police. The horror stories began with the prostitutes and their madams.

The going rate for bordello owners was a $500 initiation fee for the precinct captain and $25 to $50 a month thereafter, collected for him by his plainclothes wardman. Lena Cohen, a twenty-eight-year-old Houston Street madam from Germany, was brought out of the Tombs prison to confirm the practice. She testified that she had mortgaged her furniture to raise the $500 initiation fee, which the police characterized as a "permit." She told how a ward detective named Farrell collected $50 a month from her, at night in a saloon, all the while regularly seeing, and not paying, one of her girls. When she fell behind on her payments and declared she wanted to get out of the business, which would have ended their revenue stream, the police had her arrested. She was left in jail, penniless and $1,500 in debt.

Katie Schubert, a feisty, thirtysomething blond madam dressed stylishly in black, testified that she paid $2,900 in protection money over a two-and-a-half-year period to three Eleventh Precinct police captains: Cross, McLaughlin, and Devery. She was told to run the business quietly and there would be no trouble; true to their word, after she paid them what they wanted, they never raided her.

Other brothel owners told similar stories. Rhoda Sanford, a housekeeper turned brothel owner operating at 24 Bayard Street, handed her money in an envelope through an opening in her chain-link door. She understood it was for a "political organization." A reluctant witness, her face covered by a thick black veil, she was forced to admit that her account book, stolen from her home by an SPC detective, recorded a payment of "$500 for C," meaning the precinct captain.

When the cops felt they could, they upped the mandated payments. Austrian Karl Werner, one of six brothel operators on a single Delancey Street block, related how he received a nighttime visit from Captain Devery and his wardman Edward Glennon just three days after Devery became captain of the Eleventh Precinct. Devery, in plainclothes, said nothing about money other than to tell Werner to do whatever Glennon said. After a drink and a smoke, Devery left, and Werner never saw him again.

A couple of days later, in a private office at the station house, Glennon told Werner that the initiation fee had gone up from $500 to $600. "You must not think the money belongs to me," Glennon pointed out. He didn't say whose it was: nicknamed the "Sphinx," Glennon was a man of few words. Regardless, the payments were too rich for Werner, who closed after three months in business.

The prize for the most money paid went to brothel magnate Matilda Hermann. After voluntarily returning from hiding in Chicago, the heavyset, plume-hatted woman testified that she shelled out more than $30,000 in protection money (equivalent to $800,000 in 2021) to various police captains, wardmen, lawyers, and court officials in her seven years of operation.

Even the innocent faced trouble if they refused to play the game. The most woeful tale came from Russian immigrant widow Caela Urchitell, who related how she and her three children worked to scrape together $600 to buy a cigar store at 107 Orchard Street (next door to New York's current Tenement Museum). Then, on her first day in business, the police framed her on prostitution charges because she wouldn't cough up the usual bribe money.

Upon her release from jail, after paying a fine, she discovered that her children had been sent to an orphanage because she was a convicted prostitute. Associate committee counsel Frank Moss worked hard to secure their release, and, in a tearful scene, she and her children were reunited in the Lexow Committee hearing room. "While we have . . . listened to many harrowing stories upon this witness stand during our month's investigation, there is at least one silver lining to the black cloud," Goff announced as the children came forward and embraced their mother.

Streetwalking prostitutes, or "cruisers," operated on a different economic model. They paid a dollar a week for the privilege of bringing men into houses of ill repute. They would give their money to the house madam, who turned it over to the cops to ensure the girls' protection. Goff labeled the custom "a tax upon these unfortunate women in the street at night" and "the lowest form of oppression and corruption that possibly could be conceived by the human mind."

One such cruiser, a young African American woman from Wooster Street named Lucy Harriot, explained that the money that prostitutes and their accomplices stole from johns in panel houses was split with the cops. When the victim, often an out-of-towner, complained to the police, they'd advise him not to say anything for fear of being exposed for patronizing prostitutes, especially if the women were black. If he persisted, the cops would pretend to try to find the girl but report back that she'd gone to Europe or had otherwise disappeared. In fact, the police would demand the stolen money from the thieves, keep half for themselves, and allow the thieves and the house madam to divide the other half.

A similar partnership existed between the police and the city's liquor sellers. But saloonkeepers weren't treated with much more respect than prostitutes were.

Adolph Forst, who ran a "coffee saloon" on Houston Street, was arrested for allowing patrons to play cards and pool on Sunday (neither of which was illegal per se). When Forst said he could no longer afford the $10 payments required to stay open, he was told to put his pretty young wife in hock. Forst closed rather than suffer that indignity.

The most enthralling testimony by a liquor seller came from Harry Hill, the onetime owner of a legendary concert saloon at Crosby and Houston Streets where John L. Sullivan had boxed his first match in New York (illegally) in 1881. Himself a wrestler and boxer, the English-born Hill would tolerate no fighting or stealing in his establishment, though it was frequented by roughnecks and known criminals.

Wearing a straw hat and light suit, the nearly seventy-year-old Hill acknowledged upon taking the stand that, having run his popular joint for some thirty-four years starting in 1854, he was "about as well known in New York City as Broadway." Vowing not to implicate anyone who had ever done him a kindness, Hill testified that he'd made so much money over the years that he didn't mind paying a $500 initiation fee and a stray $50 bill now and then, which enabled him to keep his place open past one in the morning on weekdays and to sell alcohol on Sundays.

Hill never had much problem with the police, he said, until around 1886, when Captain Michael Murphy took command of the precinct. A Tammany man once connected to Boss Tweed, Murphy had been languishing in Goatville when Hill, a racetrack betting buddy, got him transferred to the more munificent downtown location.

But Murphy promptly betrayed his benefactor—doubling the initiation fee to $1,000 and continually "striking" Hill for hundreds more. Murphy even had the temerity to stop in every night and demand to drink Hill's most expensive imported wine—"Harry Hill's Own"—for which the captain never paid but merely shook the owner's hand. "I think I kind of hold the audience, don't I?" Hill boasted at that point in his testimony, and, when handed some ice water, he said it was "the first time I ever drank a glass of water in my life."

Hill had understood that his payments to Murphy and his wardman were supposed to go "around the corner" to police headquarters on Mulberry Street, but he began to fear that the money wasn't ending up with the right people. Murphy was so fond of the track that Hill thought some of the cash might "stick to his fingers." Through his lawyer, Hill was summoned to meet with Superintendent William Murray and Inspector Henry Steers, both old friends, who asked for details on how much and in what manner he'd been paying Murphy.

After Hill reluctantly "gave his guts away" on their promise of confidentiality, they turned on him, accused him of being a squealer, and pulled his theatrical license, forcing him to close. Having "gone back on the buttons" by refusing their demand for another $800 in protection money, he was hounded and denied a license when he tried reopening in Harlem and then in Brooklyn.

But it wasn't just high-class operators like Harry Hill who were repeatedly hit up by the police for tribute. At the low end of the economic totem pole, a parade of pushcart owners, fruit dealers, and shoe shiners—legitimate businessmen all—testified that they had to fork over a few bucks from time to time for the privilege of doing business.

On the Lower East Side, the mostly Jewish immigrant soda water sellers had to pay $5, labeled a "permit," to operate their stands. The money was pooled and collected by the soda water manufacturer, who passed it on to the police. Any seller who refused to pay had his apparatus disconnected, his faucets opened, and his syrup drained away.

Summing up this testimony, Goff noted sarcastically that despite using a microscope, the Lexow Committee had yet to find a business in the city that wasn't being extorted by the NYPD. As one member of the force would later comment, "Of course there are cops who have never taken a dollar; at least, I've heard about them, but I never saw one."

The police demanded protection payments from gamblers in much the same way they did from brothel owners, saloonkeepers, and street vendors. Perhaps the most popular illegal gambling game in the city was "policy," in which bettors laid down anywhere from a penny to $100 in hopes that their "gig" (a combination of three numbers, often selected by them based on dreams or omens) came up on the lottery wheel and paid off at 10 to 1.

Policy bettors included rich and poor men, women with babies, even schoolchildren—as well as cops, who often played for free. The lotteries were drawn somewhere in Kentucky and the results sold and telegraphed in cipher form to the backers of more than a thousand policy shops in New York. Known as policy kings, the backers paid the police $20 a month for the right to operate in certain exclusive territories assigned to them. Intruders were driven out or arrested by the police.

Poolrooms for offtrack betting on horses (also illegal then) flourished under police protection as well. The going rate was $200 to $300 a month. The collusive relationship between cops and politicians was virtually proven when Tammany's Boss Croker, reacting to public pressure—and practically at the snap of a finger—was able to have all the city's pool-rooms closed in 1893. (Unsurprisingly, they would later reopen.)

Given the prevalence of state-run lotteries and legalized offtrack betting in twenty-first-century America, the nineteenth-century reformers' obsession with shutting down policy shops and poolrooms seems quaint, if not wholly misguided, today. As New York City historian Mike Wallace has pointed out, "If reformers truly wanted to hit the grafters in their pocketbooks, then *de*criminalization might have been the better way to go."

The same cannot be said of the so-called green goods business, another class of crime the Lexow Committee found to illustrate the close and profitable collaboration between the police and lawbreakers. Unlike gambling, the green goods game was a pure swindle that provided its victims neither entertainment nor the possibility of winning. But it would furnish some of the most spellbinding testimony of the entire Lexow hearings.

CHAPTER SIXTEEN

-◇-▷═◁◇▷═◁-◇-

A WORLD STUFFED
WITH SAWDUST—
AND BLUE WITH PERJURY

Late in the morning on June 14, 1894, a curious little man—pale brown and yellowish of face, about five foot four, slightly built, and neatly dressed—stepped into a witness box in the Tweed Courthouse before a packed crowd of reporters and spectators attending that day's Lexow Committee hearings. He was thirty-six-year-old George Appo, one of the most accomplished and hardened criminals of Gilded Age New York and soon to become, by virtue of his testimony, a national celebrity.

Appo was the son of a Chinese immigrant father who was convicted of murder when George was three, and an Irish mother who abandoned him when he was six. A street urchin who never attended a day of school, Appo became a newsboy in the Five Points, then a world-class pickpocket and an opium addict. He was in and out of jail for pickpocketing from the age of sixteen, and served time in the Tombs, on Blackwell's Island, and at Sing Sing.

He bore the physical evidence of a tough life of crime: a dozen scars from various gun and knife wounds and a glass eye to replace the one he'd

George Appo, a one-eyed, half-Chinese, opium-addicted pickpocket who branched into New York's lucrative green goods business, involving the sale of bogus counterfeit notes to gullible out-of-towners. Appo's testimony about green goods methods of operation riveted the Lexow Committee hearings.

lost two years earlier when a suspicious intended victim shot him in the temple in a Poughkeepsie, New York, hotel room. But he was fashionably attired when he took the stand before the Lexow Committee, sporting a chain, watch, and diamond studs. He'd made plenty of money over the years, enough to pay the high-priced Howe & Hummel law firm to defend him when he got in trouble.

Appo had been subpoenaed to talk about the green goods business, having branched into it in his early thirties after completing the last of his prison terms for pickpocketing. Called the "sawdust game" in Byrnes's book on professional criminals, it involved the sale of purportedly counterfeit currency, or "green goods," to unsuspecting victims. And for sheer audacity and scale of operation, few if any con games in American history have topped it.

Almost everyone taken in by the green goods swindle hailed from outside New York City. After combing through city directories and Dun & Bradstreet–style reports, Manhattan operators sent out hundreds of thousands of circulars across the country to lure visitors. They would announce that they had, for example, $10,000 in fake currency manufactured with stolen government plates, which they were willing to sell at a heavy discount—say, for $1,000.

Gullible but greedy out-of-towners streamed to New York saloons and laid down their cash for an even greater stack of money dangled before them—which they believed to be counterfeit but which in fact was real. After leaving with the stash, they discovered that someone had substituted a package of worthless paper, salt, or sawdust for the stack they'd been shown.

Appo mesmerized the spectators with his colorful tales of the green goods business and the police complicity that sustained it. A self-described "good fellow," Appo said he was an involuntary witness and would not name names, a vow he mostly stuck to. But in a soft, high-pitched voice, he explained politely the elaborate, highly organized system and the cast of characters that went into making the green goods business perhaps the most lucrative of all the con operations.

The "backer," or bankroller, supplied the capital for the swindle: a stack of genuine money, $5,000 to $10,000, shown to the victim and described to him as counterfeit. The backer kept 50 percent of the gross revenues from the operation, out of which he paid the police hundreds monthly to guarantee protection of the gang.

The "writer" drafted the letters or circulars containing the offer and instructions to the victim on where to telegraph his reply (typically a fictitious address or a saloon connected to one of the operators). The circular's envelope included bogus newspaper clippings about a recent theft of government printing plates to make everything appear authentic. Other than by wink and nod, the writer rarely said he was in possession of counterfeit money. "My business is not exactly legitimate," one circular read, "but the Green Articles I deal in are safe and profitable to handle. The sizes are ones, twos, fives, and tens. Do you understand?" The writer received the other 50 percent of the gross, out of which he had to pay the rest of the accomplices their percentages or transaction fees.

The "steerer" (Appo's job) was sent to meet the victim at some hotel miles from the city—usually Poughkeepsie or nearby Fishkill, or Elizabeth, New Jersey—give him the password (for example, "speedy fortune") and escort him by train to Manhattan. The steerer then took the victim (known as the "come on" or "guy") to some saloon in the city, where he was told to wait. After informing his confederates that the come on was there, the steerer brought him to the turning joint, usually a bare storefront made to look like an office with a desk and furniture. The steerer received 5 percent of the swindle proceeds.

At the turning joint, the over-the-counter salesman, or "turner," did all the talking, showed the victim the $5,000 to $10,000 in good money described as counterfeit, and sold it to him on a discounted basis (as an example, $500 bought $5,000). The turner received $10 a transaction. The "old man," introduced to the victim as the turner's father (but really of no relation), just sat there silently, doing nothing, to lend an air of respectability to the affair. His fee was $5.

The turner boxed up the real money and put it on a shelf. While the victim was asked to sign a form, a false lid on the shelf was raised, briefly obscuring the box with the real currency. The "ringer," hidden behind a partition, then pulled off the switch, substituting an identical box with sawdust or a brick inside weighing about the same as $5,000 or $10,000. Or the box would contain worthless paper cut to the size of currency, with a real bill on top and bottom in case some suspicious victim (a "hard guy") took a peek inside. The ringer was paid $5 a victim.

The steerer then took the guy back to the train or ferry station, advising him not to open the box until he was safely out of the city. Cops and treasury detectives might be on the lookout, the steerer warned, and the crime of counterfeiting carried a sentence of ten to fifteen years.

The steerer and the victim were followed by a "tailer"—generally a big, strong, intimidating fellow. If, despite the steerer's warnings, the victim opened the box and discovered he'd been duped, then wanted to go back, the tailer would accost him. Pretending to be a cop of some type, the tailer scared the victim by telling him he was just as guilty as the crooks and that it was best to avoid the law, get back on the train, and go home. The tailer received $5 a victim for his efforts.

Telegraph operators and postal employees were in on the scam. For $50 a month, Western Union operators set aside the reply messages, addressed to where the victim had been instructed to telegraph them, and held them for pickup by agents of the gang. Postal workers were paid by the green goods men to work overtime stamping and mailing the circulars that flooded the country, sometimes as many as forty thousand a day.

The green goods game was enormously profitable for both the con men and the cops. Appo boasted that he once made $600 in a single day steering a series of victims. That was nothing, though, compared with the top backers, such as James McNally, for whom Appo admitted working. Known as "King" McNally, he averaged as much as $8,000 a day (about $235,000 in 2021).

McNally was a well-dressed sporting man who'd started out as a pimp before getting into the green goods business as a steerer. He also reputedly was an opium and later morphine addict. An ally of Tammany Hall, McNally developed close relationships with telegraph operators and US postal employees he paid off to help carry out his cons. By the late 1880s, he was the city's biggest green goods bankroller, employing a staff of eight to a dozen writers and paying the police $50 a month for each of them.

As with the backers of policy shops, the police gave green goods bankrollers exclusive territories in which to operate. If a victim pressed his complaint to police headquarters, the cops would threaten to arrest him if he didn't return home. McNally's bookkeeper, William Applegate, described for the committee how one unfortunate victim had been chased out of town as a counterfeiter. Chairman Lexow expressed surprise that anyone who'd been swindled out of so much money could be scared off that easily. "Well, a guy is a guy, and you can do almost anything with him," Applegate explained.

Informed by the victim of how much he had lost, the police would demand half of that amount from the swindlers. The relationship between the cops and green goods men was so cozy that when a precinct captain was transferred elsewhere, the backer would move his operations to the same neighborhood to continue the protection.

By any definition, this was organized crime on a nationwide basis, without parallel for its time. As Appo biographer Timothy Gilfoyle notes, "It required an extensive capital investment, high rates of return, a hierarchical and durable structure, the use of violence and corruption to achieve monopoly power, a range of talented operatives (some of whom saw themselves as professionals), and the patience to let the game play itself out over several weeks, if not months."

What interested the Lexow Committee most was the police department's role in the venture. Appo testified that although all the NYPD officers knew him to be a green goods steerer, they never arrested him, even when they saw him escorting a victim to or from the train station. He operated with impunity in New York City, the only place in the union, he said, where he had immunity from prosecution.

Part of the reason green goods operators enjoyed such free rein is that even though the city's top cops, such as Superintendents Walling and Byrnes, did not profit from the scam, they had little sympathy for country bumpkins willing to break the law to get rich quick. "Nine out of ten countrymen who are swindled by rogues in this city deserve to lose their money," Walling had said in 1883. Many were former Confederates looking for a way to hurt the government, which hardly endeared them to Union army veterans such as Byrnes.

Byrnes did order periodic arrests of green goods men, but his heart wasn't in it. The New York courts discharged the crooks anyway, typically on the grounds that the fraudsters hadn't actually trafficked in counterfeit currency, or that the victims had paid their money for an illegal purpose and hence weren't protected by the law. And in the case of King McNally, the gang was tipped off to a raid by one of Byrnes's own men. That allowed McNally's team to pack up shop and move to Jersey City, where they continued to flourish. As long as they were gone from New York, that was good enough for Byrnes.

George Appo concluded his memorable testimony with a flourish, though it was mostly an aside. He testified that he had often seen cops in the opium joints he frequented in Chinatown, smoking for free what others had to pay fifty cents or a dollar to imbibe.

Appo said the opium dens, usually laid out in some tenement back room, were left undisturbed by the police, even though white girls lived there as fallen women with Chinese men and smoked alongside them. Appo unabashedly admitted his own habit, what he called the "yen-yen," explaining that he could not "resist the fascinating temptation, the feeling, the inclination, to lay down."

Appo's appearance before the Lexow Committee was so entertaining that, six months later, he was hired to play himself in a Bowery theatrical reality show called *In the Tenderloin*. The five-part melodrama included one scene titled "Green Goods; or, A World Stuffed with Sawdust," set in a reproduction of a turning joint. Appo reenacted his role as a steerer and delivered several lines. His name and picture were plastered all over billboards in New York, and the sold-out show was taken to Broadway and then on the road. Gilded Age audiences were thrilled to see a real criminal on stage, and even cheered for him.

George Appo's Lexow Committee testimony effectively sounded the death knell for the green goods business in New York, which could not survive the light shone upon it. Driven from New York, King McNally moved his operations to Chicago in 1895, where he was arrested and convicted of postal violations, then was reduced to working as a waiter in a Coney Island restaurant after serving time in Illinois.

But Appo's cooperation also rendered him a marked man. Targeted as a squealer, he was hounded and harassed by his former fellow grafters and brutalized by the police, who framed him for assaulting a cop when it was the other way around. Declared criminally insane (though he wasn't), he spent three years in an upstate mental hospital before emerging a reformed man. He kicked the opium habit and, with the help of Frank Moss, who said he had always liked the little man, Appo became an undercover agent for the SPC, assisting in its investigation of opium dens and the increasingly prevalent cocaine. While employed by the SPC, he penned an autobiography that stands as one of the best of the genre of criminal memoirs. In the end, he was what he claimed to be: a good fellow.

⊷⇒◯⇐⊶

Committee counsel Goff used the police oppression of George Appo to segue to a broader inquiry into police brutality against the citizens of New York. A steady stream of victims appeared before the committee— as its final report would put it, "fresh from their punishment, covered with blood and bruises, and in some cases battered out of recognition."

Several were permanently disfigured. One Bleecker Street resident, Frank Angelo, showed up with a glass eye, having lost the original when he tried to break up a hallway fight between several neighbors and a cop named Zimmerman. Patrolman Zimmerman clubbed Angelo and broke his cornea, arrested him, and took him to the Jefferson Market police court. Angelo hired a lawyer, who told him he'd need to pay Zimmerman $25 to obtain a dismissal of the charges, which he did. Seeing Angelo's eye hanging from his socket, the judge dismissed him without asking any questions.

Similarly, Italian bootblack Frank Martine, who operated at Sixty-Seventh Street and Third Avenue, testified that he was struck and punched in the face when he complained to a pair of cops at the station house who wouldn't pay for the shoe shines he gave them. Cut and bleeding, he was arrested and taken to court, where the charges against him were dismissed. He brought his complaint directly to Superintendent Byrnes, who promised that the two officers would be punished. But when the case came to trial, Martine's lawyer, who was in league with the police, dropped the ball, and nothing ever came of it.

Thomas Lucas, a Lower East Side truckman with no criminal record, appeared before the committee with his head in bandages, a black eye, swollen lips, and the marks of twenty-seven stitches removed that morning. It was all the result of a clubbing he'd received two nights before. He'd fallen asleep on a friend's doorstep on Hudson Street, and, when he awoke to discover $4 missing from his vest pocket, he asked three nearby police officers if they knew who'd robbed him, implying that it might have been one of them. They mercilessly beat and clubbed him and arrested him on false charges of interfering with another officer's arrest. Even if guilty of that offense, Chairman Lexow stated, that in no way justified the brutal treatment Martine had received.

Goff noted that despite more than a hundred officers having been found guilty of assaulting citizens between 1891 and 1894, only one had been dismissed from the force, and most were let off with light fines. And many, if not most, cases led to complete acquittals. Too often the police commissioners in disciplinary hearings, or the courts in criminal trials, accepted the testimony of the accused cop and his brethren. The complainant usually had few if any corroborating witnesses (and certainly no cell phone camera or body-cam evidence), whereas numerous fellow officers showed up to support the defendant. It was easy for judges to reject the allegations of the victims, who were often either habitual criminals or citizens claiming they'd been falsely arrested. As Chairman Lexow noted ruefully, with regard to the frequent not-guilty verdicts in clubbing trials, "the air was blue with perjury."

To drive home these themes, Goff subpoenaed every cop convicted of clubbing in recent years to appear in uniform before the committee. A group of them were paraded to the stand, one by one, for a reading of the record against them. Red-faced from drinking, not shame, they all denied the allegations. *The New York Times* called it "a spectacle absolutely without parallel, as amazing as it was unique," and dubbed the hitherto unclassified body of men the "Clubbers' Brigade."

Among the most frequent offenders was Patrolman George Lair of the Eighth Precinct (now Soho), who'd been brought before the police commissioners twenty-four times on various charges. The most serious was when he assaulted a woman in a saloon at Thompson and Houston Streets. Claiming she was a prostitute, he threw her on the floor without provocation, put a finger in her mouth to tear her teeth out, then pointed a pistol at her, saying he had a good mind to put a bullet through her. For all of that, he was fined twenty days' pay, or $55, and kept his badge.

Respectable middle-class citizens were not immune from the policeman's billy club. Former newspaper police reporter Augustine Costello, author of a laudatory history of the NYPD, was nonetheless arrested and brutally beaten in a manufactured dispute over authorization of the book. Inspector Clubber Williams, who bore a grudge against Costello for prior articles written about his tolerating crime in the Tenderloin, falsely accused the author of continuing to claim official police endorsement of the book after the commissioners had withdrawn their backing of it.

Taking their cue from Williams, Captain William McLaughlin and two other cops beat Costello to a bloody, unrecognizable pulp with brass knuckles, to the point where he felt "more like a wild beast than a human being." After fainting in his overnight cell, Costello penned a note saying that if he were found dead the next morning, as he expected to be, he wanted it known that he'd been "murdered by Captain McLaughlin and his crowd." He recuperated but took no legal action because, as he put it, he saw no use in going to court with the devil in hell.

Commenting on the voluminous testimony concerning brutality, the Lexow Committee concluded: "The police formed a separate and highly privileged class, armed with the authority and the machinery for oppression and punishment, but practically free themselves from the operation of the criminal law." The committee's official report stated that "the harm thus done by engendering bitterness and hatred in the minds of multitudes of those people who look upon the police as the highest expression of governmental power, and their consequent inducement to phases of radicalism, thus forced upon them, cannot be estimated."

⊷⟹ ⟸⊷

By the fall of 1894, the Lexow Committee had amassed an impressive amount of evidence of police bribery, brutality, extortion of legitimate businesses, and other assorted misconduct. There had been rumors, always denied by the cop in question, that police officers routinely bought their positions and promotions, with the money going up the chain as high as the police commissioners themselves. Some disappointed applicants said they were told they had to pay $300 to $350 to obtain a patrolman's appointment, but that, after paying the money, they never received the promised job.

Based on bank records and other evidence, several testifying police officers were found to have borrowed exactly $300 just before obtaining their positions. But they, or their lenders, always put forth an innocent explanation for the loan, however implausible, and however strenuously Goff accused them, to their faces, of baldly lying. One cop testified that if he was foolish enough to give away $300 to get on the force, he would not be foolish enough to confess to it under oath.

For their part, the civilian police commissioners admitted that 85 percent to 90 percent of the appointments, promotions, and transfers they approved were on the recommendations of Tammany and other politicians, rather than strictly on merit. But they denied knowledge of any under-the-table payments by cops to secure their positions, and they especially denied having received any such payments themselves.

Preferring to appear clueless rather than malevolent, the commissioners—the ultimate heads of the police department—likewise denied knowing anything about bribes paid to cops, other than what they'd read in the newspapers. Rejecting the notion that they had any duty to personally investigate such rumors, the two influence-peddling Tammany commissioners, James J. Martin and John Sheehan, asserted that if the police department was guilty of corruption or neglect of duty in enforcing the laws, the fault lay with Superintendent Byrnes.

The closest the hearings had come to establishing any illicit pay-to-play arrangement for police appointments was testimony concerning a bizarre cheating scheme that resembled the college admissions scandal of 2019, in which prominent parents were revealed to have paid tens of thousands of dollars to rig their children's college admissions test scores. In the 1890s version, aspiring cops paid "tuition" to attend a so-called school that tutored them on how to pass the required civil service examination. In reality, the applicants were paying to have an impersonator take the test for them, or simply to have their scores altered by some clerk with influence in police headquarters.

In one vignette reminiscent of the college cheating scandal, police sergeant John Ryan asked the impersonator to score 100 for Ryan's son Danny, who was applying to the force for the second time. But Sergeant Ryan was told that anything above 75 would seem too suspicious because of how low Danny had scored on his first try. Regardless, a substitute took the test for him, and Danny received his appointment.

The scheme came to an end around early 1892, when Byrnes, then still an inspector, got wind of it. The story was recounted for the committee by a tall, loquacious Jewish tailor named Morris Jacobs, who spoke in an English cockney accent. Jacobs testified that beginning around 1890, he had paid a Tammany Hall man a total of $1,500 over two years in hopes of cheating his way onto the force. But Jacobs was strung along and finally denied an appointment because he'd once complained about a Tammany dive owner in his district.

Jacobs went to Byrnes, who asked him why he hadn't taken the civil service test himself—was it because he didn't think he would pass? The tailor answered no, that he'd been told this was the way it was done, and that even if he scored a perfect 100, it wouldn't matter because he needed to pay the right people to take care of everything. Byrnes had the ringleaders of the cheating scheme removed from the force, and the "School for Police," as the *Times* called it, closed its doors.

Two weeks after Jacobs's testimony in June 1894, the Lexow Committee went into summer recess, to resume in September. In the interim, the police commissioners felt compelled to put on disciplinary trial those cops who had been accused of the most egregious bribery offenses. At the trials held in central headquarters on Mulberry Street, Byrnes presented the formal charges while his friend Assistant DA Francis Wellman (the assistant prosecutor in the Carrie Brown murder case) prosecuted the accused cops. Many of the witnesses were the same ones who had previously leveled accusations before the Lexow Committee.

Fifteen police officers, including four high-ranking captains, were dismissed from the force. Among those receiving the axe were Captains Devery and Cross and Wardman Glennon (the Sphinx), all of whom had been implicated by prostitutes Katie Schubert and Rhoda Sanford for taking bribes.

Devery, acquitted previously on criminal charges of neglect of duty, refused to appear at the civil hearing, feigning illness. In reality, knowing he would lose his job, he preferred taking his chances on a successful court appeal for reinstatement. Tammany commissioner Sheehan, himself an alleged grafter, was the sole "no" vote to dismiss Devery and Cross, on the stated grounds that the two prostitutes were not to be believed.

On September 6, Captain John Stephenson was dismissed, by a vote of 4 to 0, for having extorted, through his wardman, four barrels of peaches and one barrel of apples in 1891 from a Duane Street fruit dealer for sidewalk protection. It seemed like penny ante stuff, but Stephenson's bullying was all the more insidious because the victim was a legitimate businessman, not an illegal gambler or brothel owner.

At the same session that Stephenson was canned, the Board of Police Commissioners voted to abolish the position of wardman. The testimony before the Lexow Committee had convincingly established that this plainclothes detective was little more than a bribe collector for the precinct captain. The commissioners gave Superintendent Byrnes authority to reassign all the current wardmen to regular uniformed patrol duty in other precincts.

Goff was now riding high. Speaking proudly at the Lexow Committee's October 16 session, he said the committee had broken through the brazen wall of bribery in the city that had never previously been so much as dented and that the public conscience was finally being aroused to the terrible evil that had been afflicting the people for years.

A new political star, Goff was proposed by reform groups as an uncompromising, anti-Tammany Fusion Party candidate for mayor in the citywide election to take place that November. The Fusion nomination for mayor (allowing the candidate to collect votes on multiple party lines) eventually went to an innocuous, blue-blooded Republican businessman, sixty-seven-year-old William L. Strong. Democrat Goff was chosen to run on the same ticket for the job of recorder, the top municipal judge in New York City and second only to the mayor in administrative rank.

On November 6 the Strong-Goff ticket swamped the Tammany forces, defeating Tammany's mayoral candidate, ex-mayor Hugh Grant, by nearly fifty thousand votes. (Incumbent Democratic mayor Thomas Gilroy, a Boss Croker puppet, did not seek reelection.) Reverend Parkhurst, who had worked tirelessly for the reform ticket, rejoiced that "The uprising of the voters has simply been a natural revolt against tyranny and misrule," adding, "God bless New York."

Boss Richard Croker, claiming to be out of politics, attributed the defeat to the tidal wave for reform created by the Lexow Committee exposés. New Yorkers couldn't stand the rotten police corruption, he acknowledged, but, he asserted, "They can't stand reform, either." The problem with reformers, he told *The New York Times*, was that "they stand up so straight in the endeavor to be straighter than others that sometimes they fall over backward." He predicted that Tammany would be back in power in the next election.

A further shock wave hit the police department on December 12, when a defiant ex-captain Stephenson, indicted by a grand jury for bribery after his dismissal from the force for extorting apples and peaches, was convicted and sentenced to three years and nine months in Sing Sing and fined $1,000. He was the first of the bribe-taking cops to be criminally convicted and the first New York City police captain sent to state prison.

Such a severe penalty for a relatively trivial offense did not augur well for the more than a dozen other dismissed officers who were then under indictment for taking much more substantial bribes. Pleased with the Stephenson verdict, Parkhurst attributed it to the change in atmosphere within the courts and in the public mind wrought by the Lexow Committee's disclosures.

By the date of Stephenson's conviction on December 12, the Lexow Committee had less than three weeks left to finish its work before the year-end deadline set by the legislature. The committee had already accomplished much, but Goff wanted more. He had plenty of testimony—more than he ever could have imagined—from both lawbreaking and lawful citizens alleging police corruption. After their initial period of hesitation, so many New Yorkers were coming forward with their tales of woe that many had to be turned away. But the tenacious lead counsel had yet to find a single cop who would admit under oath to collecting bribe money or paying for his position.

Goff was hoping that would change with the next scheduled witness: a fellow Irish nationalist with a sterling record for bravery and integrity.

CHAPTER SEVENTEEN

BUSTED

It was four in the afternoon on December 13, 1894, when fifty-five-year-old Bronx precinct captain Timothy J. Creeden, a handsome, polite, soldierly-looking man with white hair and a white mustache, took the stand in full uniform. By the solicitous manner in which the normally irascible John W. Goff began to question the witness, anyone present could tell that something unusual was coming.

Goff had Creeden recite the details of his commendable career, which somewhat paralleled that of Thomas Byrnes without attaining the same heights. Born in Ireland in 1839, Creeden emigrated with his family to New York in 1853, worked in a chandelier factory, became a volunteer firefighter (like Byrnes), and, also like Byrnes, enlisted in the Union army just after the fall of Fort Sumter. He saw action, as did Byrnes, at the First Battle of Bull Run, then went on to fight in twenty-two other engagements, including Antietam, Fredericksburg, Chancellorsville, and Gettysburg, finally earning a disability discharge for taking a ball in the shoulder at Bristoe Station, Virginia, in October 1863. He joined the NYPD as a patrolman in 1864, one year after Byrnes had, then worked his way up to roundsman, sergeant, and finally captain in 1892. His thirty-year record as a police officer was virtually unblemished.

After completing his review of Creeden's enviable record of service, Goff abruptly switched gears. "Now, Captain," Goff began, "I am sorry that my duty compels me to ask you, Captain, knowing you to be an honorable man as a soldier and a citizen, how much money did you pay to be made captain?"

Creeden was dumbstruck by the question. He hesitated for a long time, raising and lowering his hands on the arms of his chair several times, his eyes starting to well with tears, before he answered in a low voice: "I have not paid any money for my appointment." Both Goff and Chairman Lexow assured him that anything he said could not be used against him in a court or other proceeding and asked him again whether he had paid anything of value, directly or indirectly, to secure his position as captain.

Again Creeden hesitated but repeated his denial. He admitted to borrowing thousands of dollars around the time of his appointment from a group of backers that included theater owner Henry C. Miner and such dive owners as John McGurk, proprietor of the Bowery's infamous Suicide Hall. But Creeden had no knowledge, he said, of a $15,000 purse having been put together by his friends for the purpose of promoting him to captain.

Expressing surprise and disappointment at Creeden's attitude, an exasperated Goff said aloud that if there was one man in the police department he thought would tell the truth, it was him. After the captain left the stand, Goff called a series of witnesses and introduced checks, notes, and bank records establishing the existence of the $15,000 fund and its subscribers. But most of them said they merely understood the money to have been some sort of "testimonial" to, or wager on behalf of, Creeden, then a sergeant.

The next morning Goff recalled Creeden to the witness stand in front of a packed, tension-filled crowd. Having been tipped in advance that the captain wished to amend his testimony, Goff began by offering Creeden a chance to explain why he had hesitated so long before denying the previous day's questions about paying for his promotion. Creeden said that he had not wanted to implicate his friends and was willing to lie to protect them. But, after reflecting overnight with his wife and eight children, he had reconsidered. Goff then played upon their common Irish nationalist heritage, engaging him sympathetically with leading questions:

Q: In other words, you were determined to sacrifice yourself sooner than be called an informer—that is true?

A: That is true.

Q: That is your nature, Captain?

A: Yes, sir.

Q: And a distinguishing feature of your race?

A: With my family, particularly so. . . . Being revolutionists.

Q: Revolutionists in Ireland?

A: Yes, sir.

Q: So that the word *informer* carries with it a terrible significance there?

A: It does, sir.

Q: Hence you have hereditary dread of having that name applied to you?

A: Yes, sir.

Q: And it was that dread and terror that caused you to hesitate yesterday in giving your testimony?

A: Yes, sir.

The spectators listened anxiously as Creeden began to narrate how he had come to his captaincy. While testifying, he frequently mopped his brow with a handkerchief that he kept twisting in his hands. But the hesitancy from the prior day was gone.

Creeden explained that three or four times since 1887, he'd been eligible for promotion from sergeant and had passed the civil service exam, only to see men with lesser records and lower scores be promoted to captain ahead of him. Finally, he was told that to gain a captaincy, he'd need to pay for it—specifically, $12,000 to then police commissioner John Voorhis, leader of the New York County Democracy, Tammany Hall's rival Democratic faction.

With Creeden's blessing, his saloonkeeper friends assembled a $12,000 fund, only to find out that a rival applicant had also put up $12,000 for the same post. Now, Creeden was told, it was going to take an additional $3,000, or $15,000 in total (an astounding $425,000 in 2021), to gain the promotion. His friends dutifully ponied up the additional money, and, through intermediaries, the deal was sealed. It transpired later that two of the go-betweens, both political cronies of Voorhis's, initially split the $15,000 between themselves, with the understanding that the lion's share would eventually go to Voorhis—who hotly denied knowledge of any such transaction.

A snag developed when Creeden soon found out that instead of being promoted to captain of the Lower East Side's Eleventh Precinct, as he and his friends had been promised, he was slated to command the First Precinct, in the Financial District. As Big Bill Devery and others could attest to, the Eleventh Precinct was rich in the number and kinds of illegal joints and grafting opportunities that made it possible for a captain to recoup the money paid for his appointment and then some. As one police detective memoirist would explain later, "A man who paid a big sum for a boost up the line had to get his money back. How? Well, think it over."

By contrast, the First Precinct, long protected by Byrnes's dead line, was free of saloons and bordellos. Creeden and his backers considered reneging on the deal but were induced to go ahead with it on the tacit promise that Creeden would shortly be shifted to a more lucrative precinct. (And he was: to the Fifteenth in Greenwich Village, known as "the Little Tenderloin," an area inhabited today by New York University.)

Creeden said he fully understood the money he paid was a bribe intended for Voorhis. He finished by recalling that when he ran into Voorhis sometime later on the street, after the commissioner had left the police board to become a police court judge, Voorhis told him he'd heard a rumor that Creeden had paid for his position. If that was true, Voorhis said, then Creeden had been swindled. Creeden interpreted the judge's comment as just a bunch of dust thrown in his eyes in case the transaction ever came to light.

Creeden then stepped down and heard Goff express the unanimous view of the committee that he was to be commended for telling the truth and should suffer no adverse consequences on account of doing so.

"Creeden Confesses—First Captain to 'Squeal,'" read the next day's front-page headline in the *New-York Tribune*, which called Creeden's appearance "by far the most sensational and dramatic scene" of the hearings to date. Wild applause greeted the captain when he left the witness chair, and as he made his way to the exit, spectators slapped his back. All the senators on the committee, as well as Goff, came forward to shake his hand. Creeden was still being cheered as he passed out of the room, with Chairman Lexow's gavel vigorously pounding the bench for order. A contingent of uniformed cops who were present sat in stony silence and turned their heads away from the man they considered a turncoat.

The triumphant mood was interrupted later that same day when the committee was informed that, at Superintendent Byrnes's request, the police board had suspended Creeden for paying for his appointment and denying it under oath. An outraged Goff and Chairman Lexow demanded to hear immediately from Byrnes and Commissioner James Martin, head of the board, and both men were hauled before the committee to explain themselves.

Sheepish and apologetic, Byrnes and Martin said they hadn't been aware of the committee's strong desire that Creeden not be punished, and they agreed to revoke his suspension. A renewed round of cheers broke out from the spectators. Restored to the force, Creeden would serve as

Inspector (formerly Captain) Max Schmittberger, whose candid testimony about police corruption before the Lexow Committee earned him the wrath of his fellow NYPD officers and his reputation as a squealer.

captain for another ten years and, even in retirement, march in every annual police parade until the final year of his life in 1936, when he died at age ninety-six, the oldest living Civil War veteran in New York.

If Timothy Creeden's testimony was the first to rupture the blue wall of silence the NYPD had created to mask its corruption, the wall came tumbling down with the appearance of Captain Max Schmittberger. A twenty-year veteran of the force, the tall, handsome, German-born Schmittberger had been a member of the Broadway Squad and a longtime protégé of Clubber Williams in the Tenderloin district, eventually ascending to captain. He'd compiled a good record, winning several commendations for meritorious service. Schmittberger was the cop who, in

1882, posted the reward circular above Mike McGloin's head that led to McGloin's arrest for the murder of French wine merchant Louis Hanier.

At the time of his testimony, Schmittberger was under indictment for having previously accepted a $500 bribe from a French steamship company while heading the Steamboat Squad, which had jurisdiction over all the docks and piers on the Hudson and East Rivers. The custom was for patrolmen working the docks to receive $5 or $10 a week from the steamship lines for working overtime to help with passenger security and other miscellaneous tasks. The patrolmen then passed half of their extra compensation up to the police squad captain.

Schmittberger stood accused of having greedily demanded 100 percent of the compensation when he took over as captain of the squad instead of the usual half. He'd also been named by several merchants and brothel owners as one of the NYPD's regular bribe takers.

Testifying in exchange for immunity from prosecution, Schmittberger entered the witness box on December 21. The dark-mustached captain was dressed fashionably in plain clothes instead of his police uniform, a hint of what was to come. He showed signs of not having slept for days; just that morning, his wife had practically threatened to divorce him if, rather than tell all, he went to prison and left her and their eight children to starve or go on the street.

Schmittberger decided, as he told Goff, to make "a clean breast of everything I know." He reasoned, "The pillars of the church are falling and have fallen, and I feel in justice to my wife and my children that I should do this." A soft-spoken, publicity-shy man, he was about to become famous.

Speaking in a clear voice to a densely packed courtroom, Schmittberger confirmed the pay-to-play system that Creeden had described. The system weakened the force, he explained, because cops who bought their positions considered themselves independent and immune from any meaningful disciplinary action for clubbing or neglect of duty.

But it was Schmittberger's testimony about bribery collection that most rocked the hearing room. He said he had regularly collected bribes for Captain Williams in the Tenderloin district to protect disorderly houses and gamblers and saloonkeepers such as Shang Draper. That much was not news, except that Schmittberger had admitted it under oath. What was more startling was his account of how the payments went up the chain and how pervasive the practice was.

After he became a captain, Schmittberger continued demanding bribe money through his wardmen: $20 a month from policy shops, $200 a month from poolrooms, and $10, $25, or $50 from houses of ill fame, depending on the number of prostitutes. In some months, he received as much as $800 (more than $20,000 in 2021 dollars). He took 80 percent of the money and let his wardman keep 20 percent. Then he gave 20 percent of his own share, or $200 a month, to the inspector above him, who was Clubber Williams.

The custom was so deeply ingrained that the transaction required no explanation. Schmittberger simply handed Williams an envelope of cash in person at the station house or at headquarters and said, "Here is something for you." He had to pay off Williams, he said, because as inspector, Williams could order raids on gambling shops in the precinct, which would have ended the captain's revenue stream. Williams also could have preferred charges against his captain for failing to shut down the illegal establishments. Of course, Williams had no more interest in doing that than Schmittberger did.

So, with a wink and a nod, Schmittberger would falsely report to Williams that there were no gambling places or disorderly houses in the precinct, and Williams would dutifully certify the same thing in writing to Superintendent Byrnes. But there was no doubt, Schmittberger said, that Williams knew of the existence of such places in his precinct, as they were running openly and notoriously and couldn't have continued to operate without police protection.

Schmittberger followed the same collection practices when he was reassigned to the Leonard Street station and later the West Forty-Seventh Street station, both within the jurisdiction of Inspector Thomas McAvoy.

Schmittberger recalled that McAvoy, a religious man, said he didn't want any money that came from houses of prostitution, but some of it did, and he didn't turn it down.

In his four years as a police captain, Schmittberger had commanded six different precincts, and in every one of them, he found the custom of bribery collections regularly established from long before. Knowing that he'd struck gold, Goff asked Schmittberger pointedly:

> Q: Now, Captain . . . was it a matter of common understanding among the captains of the various precincts that they were to take advantage of any opportunity that presented itself to make money out of their respective precincts?
> A: Certainly.

Schmittberger did not hesitate to name names. In addition to Inspectors Williams and McAvoy, he implicated two fellow police captains, James K. Price and Frederick W. Martens, in wrongdoing—Price, for serving as Williams's regular bribe collector, and Martens, for putting up the customary $300 to become a roundsman, $1,600 for promotion to sergeant, and, finally, $14,000 to be made a captain.

Schmittberger also fingered Tammany police commissioners Martin and Sheehan in the web of corruption. The captain had made substantial political contributions to both men because he was told it was advisable to do so. Nonetheless, Martin had him moved from the Twenty-Seventh Precinct to the less desirable Fifth as punishment for having carried out, more aggressively than others, newly appointed superintendent Byrnes's orders to enforce the Sunday liquor laws.

Now Schmittberger would have his payback. He testified that when he sent one of his men to raid a house of ill fame kept by Sadie West at 234 West Fifty-First Street, based upon formal citizen complaints, Mrs. West told the arresting officer that she was a friend of Martin's and that he'd better not do anything until hearing from the commissioner.

Schmittberger testified that the next day, Martin ordered him to send the officer back to apologize to the woman and say he'd made a mistake. (Martin rather unconvincingly denied having done so.)

Similarly, Schmittberger told how Sheehan, widely known as a Tammany wire puller, sent word to him that he was not to disturb a gambling house at Forty-Second Street and Broadway run by a friend of one of Sheehan's political allies. When Schmittberger consulted the new superintendent, Byrnes, who had recently issued strict orders that no gambling houses were to be permitted anywhere, Byrnes responded, "Schmittberger, if you allow that gambling house to open, I will break you." Under the circumstances, Schmittberger had the place closed, explaining to a furious Sheehan that Byrnes "was very hot about it" and "wouldn't have it." As a result of Schmittberger's testimony, Sheehan's reputation as a civil servant was in ruins; both he and Martin would be removed from the board a year later when their terms expired.

Schmittberger had nothing bad to say about Byrnes, though. He called him "an honest and fair man" who wanted to do the right thing but was hampered by Tammany and other politicians. "I think this is the secret of the whole trouble," Schmittberger offered. Goff followed up:

Q: Outside of this one man that you exempt, can you say that
   outside of this one man, that the system itself is corrupt?
A: It is, to the core.

With that, Republican state senator Edmund O'Connor declared that the committee had all the facts that it needed to justify radical legislation to reform the NYPD. Goff agreed, saying, "I think if you had nothing but today's testimony, you would have quite enough."

Overnight, Schmittberger became a favorite of Parkhurst and other reformers. Lincoln Steffens made him the hero of an unpublished novel. But he was now a pariah among his fellow cops, who vilified him as a squealer. Schmittberger was hissed in the first annual police parade held after the Lexow hearings and later banished from it altogether for a time.

But, represented by Howe & Hummel, he avoided prosecution and stayed on the force.

Even more so than Creeden's, Captain Max Schmittberger's testimony had the greatest impact of any before the Lexow Committee. A *New-York Tribune* headline called it "The Crowning Exposures" of the senate investigation. But there were two final key witnesses the committee and the public were eager to hear from as the year drew to a close.

"I am so well known here in New York that car horses nod at me mornings." So boasted Alexander S. Williams, the man they called Clubber, shortly after taking the Lexow Committee witness stand on December 26, 1894. After the laughter in the room subsided, counsel John W. Goff chided Williams for his glib comment and said the witness was there to answer questions, not "crack jokes." But for three days of testimony, the snide remarks would continue passing back and forth between the two men in the most highly anticipated confrontation of the hearings, which had entered their final week.

The fifty-five-year-old Williams was resplendent in his handsome new full-dress uniform, featuring velvet cuffs, five gold stripes on his coat sleeves, and a solid gold shield on his breast, befitting his inspector's rank. He remained physically fit and distinguished-looking with his salt-and-pepper hair and carefully manicured mustache. He was bold, defiant, and combative throughout, at times flushing red with anger at Goff as if preparing to lunge at him. Repeatedly, when confronted with uncomfortable facts, he claimed a complete failure of recollection.

And he denied everything.

Williams denied taking bribe money from Max Schmittberger, whom he dismissed as a perjurer out to save his own skin. He denied knowledge of any disorderly or gambling houses in the precincts commanded by Schmittberger or other captains over whom Williams had authority, and said he accepted their written reports that there were no such places open.

As an inspector, he said, he had no duty to determine the facts on his own. "I rest on a report," he proclaimed, adding that he never personally submitted a report he knew to be false.

Williams implausibly denied taking a cent for bribery while captaining the Tenderloin or any other precinct. He admitted having known of some eighty-three houses of ill fame in Soho at one time, but said none of them had paid him anything. He had suppressed as many as he could, he claimed, though he couldn't identify even one of them by name or address. But he admitted he'd deliberately left some others alone. Asked why, by Goff, Williams responded, "Because they were kind of fashionable at the time."

An astonished Chairman Lexow interjected, "Don't you apprehend that that is rather an extraordinary answer to the question?" Williams said he couldn't answer it any other way, adding that it was impossible to wipe out all the disorderly establishments because they were constantly being raided when complaints were made, only to reopen a few days later. In any event, Williams saw no problem with letting them exist alongside schoolhouses, as long as they kept their windows shuttered.

Williams insisted he'd never stolen a single thing in his life, and anyone who claimed he did was a liar. Goff then confronted him with charges that Superintendent George Walling had brought against him in 1874 for having taken expensive silk stockings, pocket handkerchiefs, and slippers, plus a pistol and a gold-headed cane, from the keeper of a disreputable house downtown. Williams said he didn't even remember the case. Although he'd been brought up on trial before the police board at least eighteen times, the records in many others had been lost, and this was one of them.

Still, Goff was incredulous that Williams claimed not to recall such a specific, vivid accusation as stealing belongings from a brothel madam. "Have you any moral sense at all . . . Anything left of shame?" Goff inquired. "Yes," was Williams's curt response.

In another spirited exchange, Goff referred in passing to "dives" and "slums." Williams denied knowing what those things even were. He said he'd heard the terms before but didn't know what they meant. Goff was left almost speechless, while Williams remained unmoved.

Despite his reputation as the "champion clubber" of the police force, which he acknowledged, Williams also denied using excessive force against any citizen. "Did you ever club any man?" Goff demanded to know. "Yes, certainly I did," Williams answered, but "never one respectable man in my life." That failed to satisfy Goff:

Q: What right have you to determine who is respectable?
A: Those people go around looking for a fight, and they are pretty liable to get it.
Q: In fact, you have been charged with more clubbing than any policeman?
A: Yes.
Q: And you rather glory in it?
A: No, I do not.

Williams admitted that once, as a plainclothesman on duty on Vesey Street downtown, he'd grabbed a citizen by the throat and thrown him into the street, even though the man hadn't laid a hand on him. The victim deserved it, Williams maintained, because he'd taken Williams for a "come on," stopped him on the street, and was planning to try to swindle him. Goff shot back:

Q: I haven't any doubt that there is nothing under the sun that is outrageous and unlawful that you would not do.
A: That is your opinion.
Q: And the opinion of this city.
A: It is not.
Q: I don't want to get into a personal altercation with you.
A: You better not, either.

Goff wanted to know how, earning only a police officer's salary for many years, Williams had become so rich: in addition to a residence on East Tenth Street, near Astor Place, Williams owned a seventeen-room mansion, a fifty-three-foot yacht, and a boathouse on the waterfront in Cos Cob, Connecticut. He claimed that before he joined the NYPD as a patrolman in 1866, he'd built up a net worth of $15,000 to $20,000 running dockyards in Shanghai, China, and Hong Kong and speculating in Japanese real estate. He had no records to back that figure up, though, explaining that he'd kept the money in a since-deceased friend's private safe because he didn't trust thieves not to steal it from a bank. But few people doubted that, one way or another, the bulk of Williams's wealth had come from his years of police grafting.

Throughout the testimony, Goff accused Williams of being either incompetent or corrupt; Williams responded smugly that he was neither. As the questioning drew to a close, Goff gave the witness one final chance to come clean:

Q: You mean to say that in the face of this mountain of evidence
  against you both as a neglectful man and as a corrupt man
  that you are in a position to say everyone has lied about you?
A: Yes, sir.

The New York Times reported that Williams gave off "the air of a man unconquered." When he finished his testimony on December 28, he was congratulated by about forty friends who crowded around him, shook his hand, and patted him on the shoulder when they were tall enough to reach his six-foot-plus height. He happily received their adulation with a self-satisfied smile.

The reviews from the critics were less favorable. The *Times* referred to his "brazen bluff of forgetfulness," while the *Tribune* expressed confidence that "nobody believes Williams's denials." The *Tribune* editorial page called Williams "the boldest, most impudent, and most shameless man who has occupied a witness chair in many years," adding that he was a "bully and braggart who does not know what truth is."

On December 29, 1894, one day after Williams completed his testimony, the Lexow Committee would hold its last hearing session. Its final witness would be the only man on the police force more famous than Clubber Williams.

⊷≒◉═≒⊷

It was almost five o'clock on Saturday, December 29, and the committee members, facing a December 31 deadline, announced that they intended to finish all remaining witness testimony that evening. They weren't going to meet on Sunday, and they weren't able to reconvene on Monday, New Year's Eve, either. Because the investigation had tarnished not just Tammany but also some Republican politicians and high-ranking Republican cops, the Albany legislature was not inclined to renew the committee's mandate. It was now or never for completing its work.

Unfortunately, Superintendent Byrnes had yet to testify, and Chief Counsel Goff was still only halfway through his examination of Inspector William McLaughlin, head of the detective bureau. McLaughlin had recently come under fire for allegedly, while he was a captain, taking $500 in protection money from prostitute Katie Schubert, and for beating police reporter Augustine Costello to within an inch of his life. McLaughlin adamantly denied both charges under oath and disputed other allegations of personal grafting. (Like Williams, McLaughlin had become rich while serving on the force.)

Desperate to get to Byrnes, who was waiting in an adjoining anteroom, Goff cut short his examination of McLaughlin and called out Byrnes's name to take the stand. He would be the 678th, and last, witness to testify.

There was a stir in the room, then silence, as Byrnes made his way to the witness chair, where he would testify for the next four hours. He wore a dark coat and tie over a crisp white wing-collar shirt, his hair thinner and his walrus mustache considerably lighter at age fifty-two than when he'd joined the force, at twenty-one, in the middle of the Civil War.

Some committee members had merely wanted to solicit Byrnes's expert opinion on how best to reform the administration of the police department. But Reverend Parkhurst insisted publicly that Byrnes, as the personification of the NYPD, be treated like any other witness, "without any display of gentleness" on the committee's part.

After taking Byrnes through his thirty-one-year career, Goff launched into the subject of the superintendent's finances. The ensuing testimony was startling: Byrnes revealed a net worth of $350,000, or $10 million in 2021 dollars. More than 80 percent of it was in real estate: his Manhattan residence at 17 West Fifty-Eighth Street worth $40,000, a property at Forty-Sixth Street and Fifth Avenue valued at $165,000, another at Fourteenth Street and Seventh Avenue worth $60,000, a three-acre summer home near Red Bank, New Jersey, for which he'd paid $25,000 five years earlier, and a recently purchased $2,500 Long Island property. He'd placed these properties, all of which he owned free and clear of debt, in his wife's name to insulate them from lawsuits—a ploy that would not work today.

Byrnes testified frankly and without hesitation about his wealth. He said that almost all of it came from profits on stock investments made by Wall Street men on his behalf. Jay Gould had wanted to reward Byrnes for defeating the 1881 blackmail scheme against him, which the financier did by taking $10,000 of Byrnes's money and magically turning it into $185,000. After Gould's death, his son George made another $43,000 for Byrnes in the market.

Similarly, Cornelius Vanderbilt had been impressed with Byrnes's handling of the 1872 case in which the Commodore's brother-in-law had shot one of Byrnes's detectives, who then sued his assailant and won a settlement. The Commodore invested $2,000 of Byrnes's money and produced a threefold increase, to $6,000, in a matter of months.

Byrnes made none of the investment decisions himself. He'd never bought a stock on his own in his whole life, he said, where he didn't lose everything he put up. He admitted readily that all of his good fortune in the stock market had resulted from the care and good judgment of influential friends and that it was only by virtue of his official position that he'd obtained those opportunities. But he insisted that in protecting his benefactors, he had simply been doing his duty and that he'd done it well.

Most important, Byrnes maintained, none of his wealth had come from collecting bribe money from gamblers, brothel madams, saloonkeepers, or fellow police officers. "I defy any man in the police department that wears a uniform today . . . or any man outside of the police department, to point his finger at me and ever say he ever gave me a dollar in his life in a dishonest way," he testified proudly.

But, Goff wanted to know, what of the widespread corruption within the police force? What accounted for it, what had Byrnes known about it, and what steps had he taken to end it? Here the superintendent was less surefooted. At times he appeared to downplay the problems, saying that while there were a few bad apples, the vast majority of patrolmen were honest public servants. There was nothing on earth they wouldn't do to protect the people of New York if commanded properly by captains who set a good example, he maintained.

Yet Byrnes also acknowledged that the department was "honeycombed with abuses." The men, he said, were completely demoralized by the pay-to-play system that placed money and politics above merit in matters of appointment and promotion. As long as that system prevailed, he said, "You cannot make a good department of it."

Local politicians, Byrnes went on, were "a curse to this department and always have been." They used their influence with the police commissioners to secure transfers of honest cops out of their precincts—those who had been doing what Byrnes had ordered them to do, such as enforcing the excise laws. Meanwhile, politically connected judges refused to punish violators, rendering the liquor laws "simply a farce."

Byrnes said the sources of abuse had grown steadily for thirty years, and nothing would rectify it without some radical legislation. In particular, he thought the police superintendent should be given the absolute power of reassignment and discipline, including decision-making power in the trials of the all-powerful captains.

Too often, he said, the police commissioners had overridden his decisions and recommendations. For example, he had asked them to change the rules to hold inspectors responsible for violations of the vice laws in their districts. But the commissioners declined.

The department had to be reorganized in both systems and personnel, he believed, to make it almost a physical impossibility for corruption of the kind unearthed by the Lexow Committee to creep into the uniformed force. The present system, Byrnes avowed, was wrong, "It is all wrong."

As for his prior knowledge of corrupt acts and his efforts to stop them, Byrnes was rambling, defensive, and at times less than convincing. He appeared to vouch for the accuracy of the reports he received regularly from captains and inspectors as to the existence or nonexistence of gambling and disorderly houses in their respective jurisdictions, even though it was well established by that point that such reports were routinely falsified.

He cited statistics on the number of arrests his men had made and took most of the credit for having driven bordello owners "from pillar to post" until they were forced out of business. (He gave some of the credit to Parkhurst, even though, as Byrnes put it, "He is just pounding me every time he gets a chance.") But when Byrnes asserted that the only illegal proprietors who paid protection money to the police were those who were raided and eventually shut down, Goff had to correct him. "You are mistaken," the chief counsel told him. "As a matter of fact, the principal witnesses to that blackmail have been women who were undisturbed in their houses for years."

Asked whether it had ever come to his attention that wardmen collected bribe money from gamblers and the keepers of disorderly houses, then passed the money up the chain to captains and inspectors, Byrnes said, "No, sir; not in the way you put it." "In what way, then?" was the obvious follow-up question, but Goff didn't ask it. Despite Parkhurst's admonition not to be overly deferential, Goff wasn't interrogating Byrnes as mercilessly as he had many other witnesses.

Goff did ask Byrnes about Schmittberger's admission to having extracted bribery money from lawbreakers in every precinct he ever captained and then paying a portion of it to the inspector in that district. Had Byrnes ever heard of that? "No, sir," he answered. "If these things are true," Byrnes continued, then over time, the captains and inspectors would come to collude to such a degree that "it would be very difficult for the superintendent of police, providing he was an honest man, to know it; they will tell thieves about it; they won't tell an honest man." Byrnes was saying that, being an honest man himself—and Schmittberger had already testified that he was—he had no knowledge of the pervasive custom of bribe collection. Goff did not press him further on the point.

As his testimony drew to a close, the hour now nearing nine o'clock on a Saturday night, two days from the new year, Byrnes turned melancholy. Fighting an uphill battle, he said, he had tried his best to use the police department for the public good but had continually found himself buffeted between forces on both sides. On one side were the police commissioners, who, for political reasons, hampered his every attempt to enforce the laws uniformly. On the other side was the Reverend Parkhurst, "taking a smash at me once in a while."

Byrnes had thought about quitting, he said, and would have done so except that he felt he owed a duty to the people of New York. Besides, he did not want to be seen as having been forced out of office. Then one day, about six weeks before his current testimony, when he was walking up Broadway, he saw a poster with the phrase "A man without a country." Gazing at it, he said to himself, "This fits my case exactly; I was a man without a party."

And so, after thinking it over, he decided to send a letter to Mayor-elect Strong, which he did on December 13. This being the last night of the Lexow Committee investigation, Byrnes said he wanted to make public the contents of the letter, which he dramatically handed up to Goff.

Neither Goff nor those in attendance had any forewarning of what was coming. But as Goff began reading the letter aloud, the stunning news became clear: after nearly thirty-two years on the force, Superintendent Thomas Byrnes, the most celebrated cop in America, had tendered his resignation.

CHAPTER EIGHTEEN

-‹-⟨══⟩◦ ◦⟨══⟩-›-

ONE ROUGH RIDER

Thomas Byrnes didn't really want to resign as head of the NYPD. But Theodore Roosevelt, who soon became the new president of the Board of Police Commissioners, wasn't going to let the superintendent change his mind.

Nearly five months after dropping his bombshell at the close of the Lexow Committee hearings, Byrnes was still in his job, which had been retitled from superintendent to chief of police. Mayor Strong had taken no action on Byrnes's resignation letter and reportedly asked him to stay on, perhaps because the mayor's Wall Street friends favored Byrnes's retention as well.

Strong's dithering on Byrnes was in sharp contrast to the total house-cleaning the mayor had performed on the police board. In the wake of the Lexow revelations, Strong replaced all four former commissioners and appointed four new members to the board, which by a recently passed law, and no longer only by custom, had to be bipartisan.

The Reform Board, as it became known, included two Republicans—Roosevelt and Frederick Grant (son of the late former president)—and a

Theodore Roosevelt, brought in to reform the NYPD in 1895 after the Lexow Committee revelations, shown here in his position as president of the Board of Police Commissioners. His cluttered desk and paper-littered floor reflect his energetic approach to the job. His friend Jacob Riis, the muckraking journalist, said, "I don't care who the other commissioners are, TR is enough."

pair of independent, non-Tammany Democratic lawyers: West Point graduate and ex–army officer Avery Andrews, and Andrew Parker, a former assistant district attorney since involved in private practice. Roosevelt accepted the position only after being satisfied that his associates on the board were decent, reform-minded men. Jacob Riis, whose exposé on the slums had turned him and Roosevelt into friends, did not think it mattered. "I don't care who the other commissioners are," he said. "TR is enough."

The new commissioners quickly elected Roosevelt as board president, traditionally more of an honorary position. First among equals in title, Roosevelt had statutory powers no greater than those of the other three members. But legal niceties would not impede the energetic, thirty-six-year-old former state assemblyman from New York City's Silk Stocking district. A Harvard graduate, author-historian, and Dakota cowboy, he was fresh off a stint on the US Civil Service Commission in Washington, D.C., where he had proved to be a veritable bull in a china shop. There he had vigorously demanded enforcement of the civil service laws over the reigning spoils system, furthering his reputation as a maverick. Roosevelt would do likewise on the police board, arrogating power to himself as, in effect, the executive and operational head of the police department.

It was the same type of czarist role Byrnes envisioned for himself. He wanted to stay on as chief with enhanced powers that would make him independent of the police board. The Albany legislature passed a bill granting him such powers, but Roosevelt persuaded Mayor Strong to veto it under statutory power the mayor had been granted.

Byrnes's time on the Lexow stand had damaged his public standing. "Though no personal corruption was established, the spell was broken," the historian Arthur M. Schlesinger wrote later. If not corrupt, Byrnes was, in Roosevelt's view, a relic of an outdated era. It was time for the onetime innovator to go.

"I think I shall move against Byrnes at once," Roosevelt wrote, twelve days after being sworn in to his new office, in a postscript to his friend Massachusetts senator Henry Cabot Lodge. "I thoroughly distrust him and cannot do any thorough work while he remains. It will be a very hard fight, and I have no idea how it will come out."

Within a week, Byrnes was gone, as was Clubber Williams, whose scalp Roosevelt had also sought. Seeing the handwriting on the wall, both men took "voluntary" retirement, with the legally mandated pension of half pay for life ($3,000 a year for Byrnes, $1,750 for Williams).

Calling Byrnes "the greatest thief taker this city has ever known," *The New York Times* said that he retired "with all the honors of war." But it was widely understood that the new police board, and Roosevelt in particular, had pressured him to quit. "It was absolutely necessary that Byrnes should go," Roosevelt told his friend Seth Low, president of Columbia College. "In the detective force he will be missed, but as chief of police, his loss will not be felt in the least."

The newspapers recalled Byrnes's greatest triumphs: the solving of the Manhattan Savings Institution robbery, the arrest and conviction of murderer McGloin, the nabbing of Jay Gould's blackmailer, and the clever eliciting of a confession by Unger, who had butchered his roommate. The Whyos and other violent gangs that had menaced the citizenry were broken up on Byrnes's watch, leaving New York City, in the opinion of the *Times*, "the safest in proportion to its inhabitants in the world."

After handing in his resignation at police headquarters, Byrnes walked into the detective bureau office, where some of the older men had tears in their eyes as they bade him farewell. Speaking for reporters, Jacob Riis wrote:

> There was not one of us all who had known him long who did not
> regret it, though I, for one, had to own the necessity of it; for Byrnes
> stood for the old days that were bad. . . . He was the very opposite
> of Roosevelt—quite without moral purpose or the comprehension of
> it, yet with a streak of kindness in him that sometimes put preaching
> to shame. . . . I believed that, untrammeled, Byrnes might have been
> a mighty engine for good, and it was with sorrow I saw him go. He
> left no one behind him fit to wear his shoes.

Upon leaving 300 Mulberry for the last time as a police officer, Byrnes joined his family at his New Jersey country home. He declined all comment to the newspapers.

Williams did not go so quietly. Boasting that no grand jury had indicted him for his alleged corruption, he could not resist taking a parting shot at Captain Max Schmittberger, the cop who'd squealed. "There was a man who threw mud at me while he was before the Lexow Committee," Williams told reporters. "He is thinking now of going to Carlsbad [a spa town in the Bohemia region of present-day Czechoslovakia] to take mud baths for his health. He ought to. I mean that Schmittberger."

"I am getting the Police Department under control," Roosevelt wrote to his sister Bamie a few days later. "I forced Byrnes and Williams out, and now hold undisputed sway." He found his new job "absorbingly interesting," adding that he'd never worked harder in his life than in the previous four weeks. But he was just getting going. Indeed, he was about to put a greater stamp on the NYPD than anyone since the legendary pair of cops whose departures he had arranged for.

⋆⊷≡◉⊜⊷⋆

Theodore Roosevelt was a dynamo in the job from the start. On his first day in office, he bounded up the steps of the aging headquarters building at 300 Mulberry, yelled, "Hello, Jake!" to Riis when he saw him, then waved the rest of the reporters to follow. Lincoln Steffens, introduced to Roosevelt for the first time that day, by Riis, recalled the new head commissioner blurting out a barrage of questions: "Where are our offices? Where is the board room? What do we do first?"

Roosevelt cut a peculiar but indelible figure: a massive square head; a bull neck; pince-nez eyeglasses; a full mustache; an aristocratic, raspy voice; and, most noticeable of all, oversized, gleaming white teeth. Awaiting his daily arrival at Mulberry Street became a ritual for the newspaper reporters whose admiration he cultivated. As Roosevelt biographer Edmund Morris describes it, "About 8:30, he would come around the corner of Bleecker Street, walking with a springy tread, goggling his spectacles enthusiastically at everything around, about, and behind him. There was a rapid increase in pace as he drew near Police Headquarters, followed by a flying ascent of the front steps."

Well that he should hurry. The nearly four-thousand-man force Roosevelt inherited was demoralized by the Lexow investigation disclosures and lacked a command structure. Nearly half the thirty-seven precincts were without captains due to indictments, suspensions, and semi-forced retirements. Only one of the four inspector positions was filled. The force was three hundred officers short of full strength.

Byrnes's successor, Acting Chief Peter Conlin, a suave and shrewd career professional, was little more than a caretaker who blew with the prevailing political winds. (Although Conlin was basically honest,

Roosevelt would later call him "a coward and feeble scamp.") The rank and file knew that the old system was flawed, but the way forward was unclear.

Except to Roosevelt. By his own admission, he knew nothing about police management, but he knew what he wanted. His goal was to professionalize, modernize, systematize, and depoliticize the police department. He would also demand honesty and integrity on the part of its members and strict enforcement of the law. His mission, though ambitious, was in keeping with the search for efficiency, order, and morality that characterized the Progressive Era.

Roosevelt's first public statement as board president was emphatic and to the point. "The public may rest assured that so far as I am concerned, there will be no politics in the department," he declared. "All appointments and promotions will be made for merit only, and without regard to political or religious considerations."

To that end, new applicants were forbidden even to allude to their political affiliations or religious beliefs. Cops had to resign from, and could no longer join or contribute money to, any political club or association. The rule virtually decimated Tammany's Pequod Club, whose many cop members, including the disgraced Captain Devery, put the squeeze on businessmen to buy tickets to the club's social outings.*

The examination process was also stripped of politics. Although the NYPD nominally had been subject to the civil service rules since 1884, test scores played little role in the selection process. Henceforth, the police board decided, appointments were to be made in the precise order candidates placed in the competitive examinations. The days of paying $300 for an appointment were over.

Physical and medical standards for admission were tightened, includ-

---

*Current NYPD regulations prohibit members from joining a political club only within the precinct to which they are assigned, or soliciting, collecting, or receiving money for any political fund, club, or association, with no prohibition on personal contributions. A blanket ban on all such activities arguably would be unconstitutional.

ing a revised upper age limit of thirty for new patrolmen and a onetime pass-fail test for various athletic exercises. (In the past, applicants who failed could reapply in six months.) Background investigations into a man's moral character were conducted in earnest for the first time, and Roosevelt personally vetoed anyone who had ever worked in the liquor business. Cornelius Willemse, later a celebrated detective, was refused an appointment by Roosevelt because he'd manned the lunch counter at a Bowery hotel where liquor was sold.

The written civil service tests became tougher, too, as evidenced by the following sample question:

> The total number of arrests made in the City of New York during the year 1893 was 86,484. If for every 9 men arrested, 2 women and 1 child were also arrested, how many men, how many women, and how many children were arrested in New York City in that year? Give work in full.*

Roosevelt also eliminated a section of the test that required applicants to identify and locate New York City landmarks, public buildings, and neighborhoods, because it discriminated against out-of-towners. He had broader subjects substituted—basic United States geography, history, and government—although he was startled to find test-takers flubbing simple questions such as "Who assassinated Abraham Lincoln?" ("Thomas Jefferson" was one response), and "Name five New England states" (answers included Ireland, Wales, Cork, and Africa).

Roosevelt deliberately expanded recruiting efforts upstate to attract more American-born officers to the department. The effort was a success: In the first eighteen months of his tenure as commissioner, about 1,500 new police officers were appointed to the force, more than in the previous six years combined. And 80 percent of them were native born, including

---

* The answer—64,863 men, 14,414 women, and 7,207 children—derives from the algebraic equation 9x + 2x + 1x = 86,484, in which x equals 7,207.

ninety-four of the last one hundred appointed, significantly "American-izing" a police force that in 1895, when Roosevelt became commissioner, was more than 50 percent foreign born.

The upstate American boys, who "besieged the department in droves for the first time," as Detective Willemse recalled later, tended to be Protestant, better educated—and Republican. Derided by some old-timers as "goo-goos," the recruits nonetheless reduced the amount of cronyism and improved the overall quality of the force.

When it came to promotions, as opposed to initial appointments, Roosevelt placed a man's record and any special qualities above all other considerations. A case in point was Italian-born Giuseppe (Joseph) Petrosino, a tailor's son who came to America at age twelve, became a shoe shiner, street cleaner, and garbage hauler, and then joined the uniformed police force in 1883.

In July 1895, on Roosevelt's recommendation, Petrosino was elevated from patrolman to detective. The new commissioner was looking for an Italian to police the Italian immigrant population, the fastest growing in the city. The number of Italian Americans living in New York, less than a thousand in 1850, would mushroom to a quarter million in 1900—mainly poorer, illiterate peasants from southern Italy carrying an average of $17 when they arrived at Ellis Island. About three-fourths of them male, they congregated around Mulberry, Prince, and Elizabeth Streets on the Lower East Side, and a second Italian settlement in East Harlem centered around East 108th Street.

Roosevelt found his man in the thirty-five-year-old Petrosino, a native of Padula in Italy's Salerno province south of Naples. A year later, after Petrosino had made ninety-eight arrests, captured two accused murderers, and recovered $2,500 in stolen property, he was promoted, with Roosevelt's blessing, to detective sergeant, making him the highest-ranking Italian police officer in the nation.

Roosevelt was undeterred by the fact that Petrosino was a protégé of Clubber Williams, having patrolled a Tenderloin beat for many years when Williams ruled that district. Nor was Roosevelt bothered by

Mulberry Street in Little Italy, 1900. By the end of the nineteenth century, the once predominantly Irish Lower East Side was giving way to immigrant peasants from southern Italy and Jewish immigrants from Russia and eastern Europe.

Petrosino's five-foot-three height—a full five inches below the new minimum for applicants set by the Reform Board.

In one of the few early battles he lost as commissioner, Roosevelt, himself five foot eight, opposed the board's decision to raise the minimum a half inch, up from five foot seven and a half. Roosevelt held the view that short, stocky men were more efficient than taller ones. In any event, because Williams had obtained a waiver of the height requirement for Petrosino when he originally joined the force, the Italian was unaffected by the change—though he did wear lifts in his shoes to increase his stature.* The pudgy but muscular detective befriended his new

---

* Police departments began phasing out minimum height requirements in the 1970s. The NYPD now requires only that a candidate's height and weight be proportionate.

benefactor Roosevelt and would go on to one of the NYPD's most illustrious careers.

Presaging his famous ode to "the man in the arena," Roosevelt emphasized the soldierly qualities of bravery, daring, and meritorious conduct in the field. With great fanfare, he held more than a hundred public ceremonies at police headquarters to award medals and honors to especially heroic officers. The honorable mentions, as they were called, had typically saved someone from drowning or from a burning building, stopped a runaway team of horses, or arrested a violent lawbreaker under exceptional circumstances.

These morale-boosting displays helped make up for the absence of the popular annual police parade, which the Reform Board canceled, on Roosevelt's motion, as one of its first acts. No official explanation was offered other than the board thought it best, but Roosevelt was more candid in private. "We will parade when we need not be ashamed to show ourselves," he told Jacob Riis, referencing the taint of the Lexow investigation.

Perhaps the most audacious of Roosevelt's personnel decisions was his hiring, on his fourth day in office, of a female private secretary. Seventeen-year-old Minnie Gertrude Kelly of 160 East Eighty-First Street, a family friend of the Roosevelts', became the first woman employed by the police department in an administrative capacity. Previous female hires were jail matrons or housekeepers.

At the time, Roosevelt justified the move as a cost-cutting measure: as a typist and stenographer, she would be paid $1,700 to do the job of two men who had previously earned a combined $2,900 to perform the same tasks. Later the same year, Roosevelt insisted that another woman hired as a temporary stenographer for the police civil service board receive the same weekly wage as the regular male stenographer, who was ill, because "he [TR] believed a woman should be paid the same as a man if she did the work."

Minnie Kelly's hiring caused quite a stir. Described by the press as small and attractive, she showed up for duty in a tight-waisted black dress. A newspaper sketch portrayed a bespectacled, librarian-ish young woman typing at a desk, her short black hair pulled into a bun. Just above was an illustration showing a group of uniformed officers combing their hair in a mirror and shining their shoes. "She has arrived at Police Head-quarters, and the 'Finest' primp up a little in consequence," read the caption. She married an NYPD officer in 1899 and left the department in early 1901.

Minnie Kelly would show up again a century later as the inspiration for a character in Caleb Carr's 1994 novel *The Alienist* (set in 1896) and was played by Dakota Fanning in a 2018 television series of the same title. Her character was also based in part on the NYPD's first female detective, Isabella Goodwin, though Mrs. Goodwin's appointment to that position would not come until 1912.

⊷═◯═⊷

At two-thirty on the morning of June 7, 1895, five days after telling his sister that he'd never worked harder than in the previous month, Com-missioner Theodore Roosevelt began an even more grueling regimen. Accompanied by Jacob Riis, he embarked on the first of a series of in-trepid nocturnal inspections to see for himself how police officers were performing their nightly patrol duties. He discovered quickly that they weren't.

After a late dinner at the Union League Club at Fifth Avenue and Thirty-Ninth Street, Roosevelt and Riis set out on a tour of the Twenty-First Precinct, which ran from Forty-Second to Twenty-Seventh Streets east of Fourth (now Park) Avenue. Though a lifelong New Yorker, Roo-sevelt was unfamiliar with the city by night, so he brought a map with him, along with a list of ten posts where he knew patrolmen should be present.

Over the next three hours, while wandering down Third Avenue, then back up Second, the incognito pair found only one cop who was

231

Roosevelt's well-publicized "midnight rambles" revealed many police officers missing from their posts, neglecting duty, or asleep on the job. This cartoon from the time shows terrified cops cowering at night under the approach of a jack-o'-lantern drawn to resemble Roosevelt.

performing his work faithfully. The rest were either lounging lazily, talking to one another when they were supposed to be patrolling alone, sleeping, or missing altogether.

A few who were gossiping among themselves in front of a liquor store, not recognizing their new head commissioner, told him to mind his own business and threatened to arrest him after he asked why they weren't at their posts. When Roosevelt revealed who he was, they quickly scampered away.

One loudly snoring patrolman, sitting asleep on an overturned bucket in the middle of the sidewalk, resented being aroused from his slumber. Introducing himself, Roosevelt sternly told Officer Elbert Robertson to report to headquarters the next morning.

The same fate awaited Patrolman Thomas Connors, who objected to being interrupted in his conversation with a petticoated female streetwalker by someone he took to be a meddlesome citizen. "Officer, is this the way you attend to your duty?" Roosevelt inquired after watching them chat for ten minutes, to which Connors replied that the busybody had better run along or else he'd club him.

When Roosevelt refused to budge, Connors asked his companion, "Shall I fan [club] him, Mame?" and she responded laughingly, "Fan him hard." At last identifying himself, Roosevelt said Connors would do no such thing and ordered him to be at 300 Mulberry at nine-thirty the next morning. After some further meanderings, Roosevelt and Riis arrived at headquarters themselves, sleepless, at a quarter to seven.

"Roosevelt as Roundsman" read the headline in the next day's *Tribune*, while the *Times* titled its story "Police Caught Napping." The *World* weighed in by observing that Roosevelt "saw policemen as citizens see them, not as they usually appear at police headquarters on their best behavior."

A week later, Roosevelt was back out after midnight again, this time with fellow commissioner Andrews and journalist Richard Harding Davis. After a steak-and-salad supper at Mike Lyons's all-night Bowery restaurant, they turned up several absent or loitering patrolmen, prompting Roosevelt to vow to have them and their respective roundsmen brought up on charges. By the time of his press statement, it was six o'clock and daylight.

On yet another of these jaunts, near the East Sixty-Seventh Street station house, Roosevelt's party searched Patrolman William Rath's post four times in vain for any sign of him. They finally stumbled upon him standing at a bar on Third Avenue, feasting on a large bowl of oysters.

"What the ____ is it to you?" Rath retorted when Roosevelt asked him why he was there instead of covering his beat. (The newspapers deleted the expletive.) "I'm Commissioner Roosevelt," came the reply, but the impudent officer refused to believe it until the bartender rushed forward and said excitedly, "Shut up, Bill, it's his nibs, sure! Don't you see his teeth and glasses?" A chastened Rath obeyed Roosevelt's command to return to his post at once; he would plead guilty to misconduct charges and resign from the force a few months later.

Roosevelt's legendary late-night prowls were enormously popular with the public. He was caricatured in graffiti on the walls of police stations, by peddlers passing off dentures and eyeglasses as his likeness, and in numerous editorial cartoons. Sketches typically showed terrified cops cowering at night under the approach of a grinning face consisting of little more than spectacles and huge bright teeth—in one case, a scary jack-o'-lantern drawn to resemble Roosevelt.

"These midnight rambles are great fun," Roosevelt wrote his sister Bamie on June 16 from Sagamore Hill, his home in Oyster Bay on Long Island. (He returned there on weekends from his place in the city, Bamie's town house at East Sixty-Second Street and Madison Avenue.) The excursions were tiring, he admitted: each of them meant his going forty hours straight without sleep. But he felt he was "toning up" the force and, at the same time, receiving a valuable education into how the other half lived. He saw the horrors of tenement life and heard the babel of languages—Italian, German, Yiddish, Russian, and Chinese—that changed from precinct to precinct and even from block to block. "My whole work brings me in contact with every class of people in New York, as no other work possibly could," he told Bamie, "and I get a glimpse of the real life of the swarming millions."

Roosevelt "wanted certain information, and he wanted it at first hand, and, as usual, he got it," is how Commissioner Avery Andrews explained Roosevelt's nocturnal rambles. Andrews, though a Democrat, was proving to be Roosevelt's greatest—and as it would turn out, only—ally on the four-person police board.

⊷⊨⊨⊷

As important to Roosevelt as ferreting out miscreants in the police department was punishing them strictly and impartially. In the past, penalties for transgressions such as drunkenness, insubordination, and even grafting had been light—typically a few days of docked pay. Under Roosevelt, who presided at the weekly misconduct trials and dominated the questioning, the police board more than doubled the amount of fines and dramatically increased the number of dismissals—from eleven in 1893, to eighty-eight in 1895, and ninety-eight two years later.

No longer was political pull an accused officer's ace in the hole. As

Roosevelt announced, "Corrupt or inefficient men, no matter what friends they have or what influence, must go." Roundsmen with a record of looking the other way were reassigned to patrol duty and replaced by a new group of officers—true "shooflies," in police nomenclature—who were to report violations without fear of the delinquents' political connections.

Similarly, the Reform Board made clear that it had the backs of police officers who arrested men of influence who violated the law. An early test case came on the night of Sunday, June 23, 1895, when rookie cop Edward Bourke, patrolling in plain clothes, raided a Bowery saloon run by Mike "King" Callahan, an ex-assemblyman and Tammany favorite. Callahan had been arrested and released many times before for assaulting police officers, and once beat a murder rap. His popular tavern, at 12 Chatham Square, was also a hangout for the last remnants of the Whyo gang.

When Bourke boldly announced he was closing down the place, Callahan punched him and rolled with him onto the sawdust-covered bar floor, whereupon the bouncer and regular patrons began stomping on the officer's face. But the young cop drew his revolver and, brandishing it along with his billy club, held the crowd at bay while he whistled for assistance.

Smacked in the face again by Callahan when he took him outside, Bourke smashed the bar owner twice on the head with his revolver, then arrested him with the help of an arriving patrolman. Callahan alleged that Bourke clubbed him all the way to the Elizabeth Street station house.

When Callahan appeared in police court the next morning for arraignment, he was backed by the usual phalanx of politicians and friends there to testify on his behalf, while Bourke was left to fend for himself. As Roosevelt recalled later, it was said that the police could not touch Callahan because he had pull. Indeed, Roosevelt averred, twelve months earlier, the presiding judge would have rebuked the cop and let the lawbreaker go.

But this time, word arrived at the courthouse that Roosevelt was invested in the case, fully supported the young police officer, and was on his way to the hearing to be there in person. After some hesitation, Judge John Voorhis—the same man who, as a police commissioner, had demanded $15,000 to make Timothy Creeden a captain—signed off on charging Callahan with violating the excise laws and assaulting a police officer.

An elated Roosevelt called Bourke in to congratulate him and promised to promote him to roundsman at the first opportunity. "Bourke, you have begun well," Roosevelt told the handsome twenty-eight-year-old officer as he shook his hand. "Remember always that the board is behind you."

Bourke became a Roosevelt protégé and was ostracized by Tammany for his friendship with him. Years later, after retiring as a police captain, the man nicknamed "Fearless Ed" for his many daring raids on saloons and gambling houses served proudly as superintendent of the late president's New York City birthplace museum at 28 East Twentieth Street. He would always refer to himself as "a Roosevelt cop."

Confrontations such as Bourke's with Callahan, and a fatal attack on an undercover police officer by a street thug in September 1895, led Roosevelt to overturn one of the reforms instituted by Thomas Byrnes when he was superintendent: the elimination of the policeman's lethal nightstick. In place of the twenty-six-inch baton made of heavy locust wood, which could crack skulls on contact, Byrnes had his men carry a lighter, fourteen-inch billy club. Tucked inside a special pants pocket, it was to be drawn only in an emergency, such as a riot, or in self-defense, and was not to be twirled or brandished gratuitously in a threatening manner. In summoning for help, cops were to use a whistle rather than rapping the pavement with their stick.

Byrnes, always keenly aware of what Scotland Yard was doing, took note that the London police had done away with clubs. But although reformers welcomed his initiative, it had not been a popular move with the rank and file. The Reform Board, at Roosevelt's urging, summarily reversed the anti-clubbing policy. "The nightsticks are in, and they will stay," Roosevelt declared, adding, "They ought never to have been taken away."

Roosevelt insisted that the police force treat respectable, law-abiding citizens with courtesy, and he vowed that cops who used their clubs without provocation on the innocent would be severely disciplined. But he had no sympathy for violent criminals. "I do not want a policeman to draw his club unless he needs it," he said, but "when he does require it, I want him to have the most efficient club there is." His attitude reflected his view of the police force as a quasi-military organization at war with crime, as well as his later saying that one should "speak softly and carry a big stick." Most of the public had little objection to applying that maxim to hardened criminals.

It did seem that whatever Byrnes had done before, Roosevelt wanted to undo. If Byrnes abolished the nightstick, Roosevelt was going to bring it back. Byrnes had gotten the local plainclothes wardmen eliminated because they were habitual bribe collectors in their precincts; Roosevelt restored the position with a renewed focus on undercover work.

Byrnes's detective bureau had always made catching professional crooks its number one priority; Roosevelt redirected the emphasis toward ferreting out prostitution. This ran the risk, which sometimes materialized, that some big diamond robbery would prompt criticism that the Reform Board was neglecting dangerous thieves. The new direction was also controversial, because undercover detectives, posing as clients, routinely offered money to entrap female prostitutes, in effect, manufacturing a crime. The press had great fun citing expense vouchers by which plainclothesmen sought reimbursement for paying women to undress in front of them, or for buying them expensive wine at the higher-class brothels.

Roosevelt acknowledged that such methods were distasteful, but he defended them as the only effective way to gather evidence. He also pointed to a doubling of convictions for prostitution in his first year in office. Besides, the police board decreed that under no circumstances was an officer to engage in sexual intercourse with a prostitute or watch her strip down beyond what was necessary to establish her illicit intent. To what extent undercover cops adhered to these commands cannot be known, for they had a fair amount of discretion, and what happened in the Tenderloin tended to stay in the Tenderloin.

Roosevelt also targeted for extinction the extensive network of stool pigeons that Byrnes had employed. The new head commissioner considered it morally objectionable to let some lawbreakers off the hook, or even to go easy on them, simply because they ratted out their fellow crooks on other crimes. Why the ends justified the means in combating prostitution but not professional thievery, he never quite explained.

In any event (and as anyone who has ever seen a 1930s Warner Brothers gangster movie knows), stool pigeons never went away. Commissioner Andrew Parker, who would become Roosevelt's nemesis on the board, said it would be foolish to dispense with them altogether, although he agreed they should not receive total immunity for their crimes. Instead, the police would continue to pay them small sums—five dollars, or fifty cents for a meal—for the information they provided. A few years later, writer Josiah Flynt, a onetime tramp who became a prolific chronicler of the criminal underworld, confirmed that the "mouthpiece system" was indeed alive and well in New York.

At the same time the Reform Board was considering limiting the use of stool pigeons, the NYPD expanded its evidence-gathering operations into wiretapping of telephones—perhaps regarding it as an alternative to snitches. Little is known about this early practice, as it didn't come to light until a 1916 legislative investigation revealed that Mayor John Purroy Mitchel had recently instructed Police Commissioner Arthur Woods to intercept the phone conversations of Catholic priests suspected of charity fraud. Woods created a special six-man squad that operated out of an undisclosed location on Church Street. They used the wiretaps only to develop leads, not for evidence to be testified to in court, thereby maintaining the program's secrecy.

The 1895 origins of the practice were mentioned only in passing in

1916. No records of it were kept, and the details were not made public. But a 1938 *New Yorker* article maintained that the surveillance operations got their start when a former telephone worker who had joined the NYPD suggested that the authorities listen in on criminals' phone calls. Mayor Strong reportedly authorized the taps, which went on secretly for years with the informal cooperation of the New York Telephone Company despite a state law punishing wiretapping as a felony.

More recently, *The New York Times* has suggested that the electronic surveillance that began in 1895 in New York had earned the NYPD the title of "the father of official government wiretapping." Given how important electronic eavesdropping has become for law enforcement in the twenty-first century (just watch any episode of HBO's crime series *The Wire*), that designation is weighty indeed.

Did Byrnes, who was still the NYPD superintendent until late May 1895, know about it? Did Roosevelt? If they did, neither of them ever said so. But given their closeness to Mayor Strong, it is hard to believe that they were kept completely in the dark.

Although he had no direct hand in it, Roosevelt's reign as commissioner also saw the end of Byrnes's famous dead line. In October 1895 a career criminal named Henry Murphy wandered down to Pine and William Streets in the Financial District and was promptly arrested for loafing there, despite a lack of evidence that he was contemplating any crime. The police court judge let him go. "The law knows no district in which habitual criminals or suspected men are forbidden to go," explained Magistrate John O. Mott. "I have read of the 'dead line' in the newspapers and have heard it talked about . . . but so far as my rulings in court go, none exists." Acting Police Chief Conlin went so far as to declare, "There never was any 'dead line'. . . . It is absurd to say that no man who ever stole anything shall set foot below Liberty Street."

Under Roosevelt's leadership, the police board also oversaw a host of scientific and technological advances to improve the department's crime-fighting capacity beyond that of the Byrnes era.

When Roosevelt became commissioner in 1895, the telegraph was still the basic link between police headquarters and the various precincts. The telephone communication system between headquarters and Wall Street that Byrnes established hadn't been greatly expanded over the years. During Roosevelt's tenure, telephone call boxes were installed on the streets, and the entire telephone network was upgraded to connect many more of the precincts to police headquarters and with one another.

Byrnes had popularized the rogues' gallery of mug shots; the Reform Board amplified it with the Bertillon system of identification, named after the French police officer who pioneered the method in the 1880s. The theory was that no two individuals shared the same anthropometric measurements, such as arm and ear length, skull size, and height while seated. A criminal's measurements were meticulously recorded and kept on file on index cards, to be used against him the next time he was arrested to prove he was a repeat offender and deserved a stiff sentence.

Commissioners Andrews and Roosevelt prevailed in forcing the implementation of the system over the objections of others who thought the old rogues' gallery worked fine, including their fellow commissioner Parker and Police Chief Conlin. Bertillon advocates pointed out that crooks could change their appearance, making photographs of limited utility. Mug shots weren't dispensed with; instead, Roosevelt had an in-house photography studio and darkroom built at police headquarters. (Previously, crooks were escorted to a public studio for their mug shots.)

But the Bertillon system had its limitations. Taking body measurements required a great deal of expertise, as well as painstaking effort, to be done accurately. The minutest of mistakes could render the recordings worthless. And the system was useless in identifying unknown perpetrators. A victim or witness could hardly tell the police the number of millimeters between a mugger's elbow and hand, but they might identify the assailant from a photograph.

From its formal adoption by the NYPD in early 1897, the Bertillon system remained in place for the next fifteen years. It would yield to fingerprinting, which offered foolproof identification, was much less time-consuming, and gave promise of catching unknown culprits. But the

Among Roosevelt's best-known innovations as police commissioner was creation of the bicycle squad, shown in this 1899 photograph. Charged with arresting reckless, speeding bicyclers ("scorchers"), it was the predecessor of the NYPD's Traffic Enforcement Department.

Bertillon system represented a modest advancement in law enforcement technology—and it certainly sounded modern and scientific. For Roosevelt, that was good enough at the time. Tellingly, though, in his 1913 autobiography, in which he touted a number of the police department's innovations under his stewardship, he made no mention of the by-then-obsolete Bertillon system.

By contrast, Roosevelt was forever proud of the department's most visible modernization during his tenure as police commissioner: the bicycle squad. Created in December 1895, it was the first unit of its kind anywhere in the world. Although initially skeptical of the idea, which originated with Commissioner Andrews (himself a bicycle enthusiast), Roosevelt soon embraced it and agreed to a trial program. The first four men were selected from sixty applicants and were assigned to posts on the busiest sections of the Western Boulevard, a north-south avenue (now part of Broadway) that ran from Fifty-Ninth Street to 155th Street.

At the time, there were no traffic rules or traffic cops, and the bicycle craze was filling the streets with swarms of speeding cyclists known as "scorchers." The experimental squad arrested scorchers and reckless or drunken drivers, directed congested traffic, and ran down and caught thieves and pickpockets. Often, they would pull up alongside a team of runaway horses traveling at full speed, somehow managing to jump into the wagon to slow it down or arrest the driver. "Any feat of daring which could be accomplished on the wheel, they were certain to accomplish," Roosevelt wrote in his autobiography.

When the annual police parade was resumed in 1896, the new bicycle squad at the head of the column was the most novel and talked-about feature. Within its first year, the squad grew to twenty-nine men and was responsible for 1,366 arrests; later, it would number a hundred two-wheelers, including the record-breaking cycling athlete Charles Minthorn "Mile-a-Minute" Murphy, and would have its own station house and uniforms. When the automobile entered New York's streets, the bicycle squad assumed responsibility for arresting speeding motorists, effectively serving as the predecessor of the NYPD's Traffic Enforcement Department of today.

Roosevelt could also boast of establishing a pistol range, a precursor of the modern police academy. The training school, set up in the basement of a recently built armory at Ninety-Fourth Street and Park Avenue, was run by a bona fide revolver champion, William E. Petty, especially promoted from roundsman to acting sergeant. Twice he'd been forced to fire at criminals who resisted arrest, and, in each case, he hit his man in the arm or leg to stymie him, without endangering the crook's life.

Most NYPD cops at the time, by contrast, were dreadfully poor shots. They carried a variety of cheap, unreliable handguns and rarely kept them loaded or cleaned. Some had never fired or even holstered a gun. The immediate spur to launching the firearms school was an incident wherein two officers held down a mad dog while another, aiming to kill it, instead shot a girl in the leg as she passed on the other side of the street.

At the opening of the pistol school in December 1895, the police made what *The Sun* called "a remarkably bad showing." Firing .38-caliber revolvers at military targets only ten yards away, the officers' average score was only 17 out of a possible 75 (a score of 45 was necessary to qualify as pistol ready). Two men scored only 2 points out of 75, and two others carded complete goose eggs: 0 for 75. One man shot off a gas burner many feet from the target.

In time, however, "the marksmanship of the force was wonderfully improved," Roosevelt recalled in his memoirs. Officers learned how to handle and care for their guns; the Colt .32-caliber revolver became the standard issue, and every man was required to purchase and carry it. (NYPD cops had to pay for their own firearms in those years.) Men began qualifying as teams of "marksmen" (scoring 65 out of 75 at fifteen yards) or "sharpshooters" (70 of 75 at twenty yards). Chief Conlin called the pistol training "an incalculable value to the force."

Roosevelt considered among his most important reforms one that had little to do, strictly speaking, with police work: eliminating the so-called tramp lodging houses. For years, by law, the police department was required to give shelter to all homeless vagrants, an obligation the department fulfilled by allowing hundreds of what Roosevelt termed "the shiftless or vicious" to sleep in the various precinct stations.

The "drunken, dirty, oftentimes diseased wretches," as Chief Conlin called them, were huddled like cattle in the unventilated, poorly lit station house basements, where they slept on wooden planks without receiving food, baths, or clothes. They contaminated the air breathed by the patrolmen on reserve who were sleeping upstairs, Conlin told the police board, and they were "a traceable source of sickness among the officers and men." Besides which, their constant coming and going prevented the cops from getting a good night's sleep.

Influenced as well by Jacob Riis, who deplored the police lodging houses, Roosevelt successfully moved the Reform Board to shut them down and to redirect the occupants to city shelters. These well-intentioned charitable establishments, however, were overwhelmed by the sheer numbers of homeless. As a result, many tramps who had previously slept in police stations were arrested for vagrancy and tossed in jail. But at least they were no longer annoying the hundreds of cops on reserve who continued to sleep at the station houses in conditions so grim that, as Detective Cornelius Willemse memorably wrote, no jail keeper would tolerate them.

⋆⇌ ⇋⋆

Had Roosevelt's record as police commissioner ended there, he would today be considered among the most popular and successful municipal officials in the history of New York City. But a quixotic and ultimately disastrous morality campaign would undo much of the goodwill he established with his other reforms.

CHAPTER NINETEEN

"TO HELL WITH REFORM"

The police were going "After the Saloon Men," declared the head-line in the June 11, 1895, *New York Times*. The paper was reacting to a meeting Commissioner Roosevelt held at police headquarters the day before. He had summoned the precinct commanders to his office to instruct them to keep every one of the city's twelve thousand to fifteen thousand saloons closed from midnight Saturday to midnight Sunday, in conformity with the excise law, or else face charges themselves.

Speaking loudly to the roomful of captains and sergeants, Roosevelt told them that even if they thought it was a bad law—and Roosevelt himself, a light drinker but no prohibitionist, considered it too strict—they were to enforce it to the letter. "I do not deal with public sentiment," he announced later to reporters, anticipating the backlash that was sure to come, "I deal with the law."

Prior attempts by Byrnes and others to apply the excise laws had been partial and temporary; this was to be total war. At the time, Roosevelt had the full support of the other police commissioners and of Mayor Strong. Chief Conlin was on board as well.

On June 16, 1895, the first Sunday after Roosevelt's announcement, New York's finest began descending upon startled saloonkeepers across the city to shutter them. A second round of raids went down the following Sunday. Noting that June 23 was the nearest approach yet to a really dry Sunday, *The Sun* reported that "the drought that settled on the town at midnight extended from the southern boundary of Harlem to Battery Park." One wayfarer from upstate, where Sundays were typically dry, remarked, "Well, I'll be hanged if this town isn't worse than Schenectady."

Throughout the summer of 1895, as the weather got hotter and New Yorkers thirstier, the Sundays became drier, with saloon closings approaching 100 percent. Many sweltering New Yorkers left the city on ferry excursions to the wetter climes of Coney Island and New Jersey. One Manhattan hotelier said that even if he'd kept his bar open on Sunday, he wouldn't have sold anything because "all the drinking men have gone out of town."

Protests came, most vociferously from the city's German population, with its old-world custom of festive beer garden outings on Sunday afternoons. Tenement-dwelling Irish Catholics, who sought respite in the saloons on their only day off following a long week of sweaty labor, were fuming as well. Meanwhile, as Roosevelt's critics pointed out, his wealthy Protestant friends were able to enjoy Sunday champagne in the Union League Club and similar private enclaves, where liquor could be served legally.

Roosevelt's uncompromising crackdown on saloons won him plaudits from temperance advocates, church groups, and other reformers, especially those from upstate and west of the Hudson. And early on, he earned grudging respect even from some urban poor people and German American groups for his honest enforcement of the law. Roosevelt argued to them that strict enforcement of an overly strict law was the best means of ensuring its eventual repeal—perverse logic to those who preferred an illegal drink today to the possibility of a legal one tomorrow.

As July turned to August and then to early fall, Roosevelt's massively unpopular excise law campaign began to collapse. His fellow commissioners weakened in their support, and with city elections looming in November, Republican politicians, including Mayor Strong, urged him to let up. But he would not budge even a particle, Roosevelt vowed.

Roosevelt's unbending stance cost his party dearly in that November's elections. Tammany Hall's municipal slate was elected in a landslide, with 80 percent of the German American vote, normally Republican, turning Democratic. Even Republican Clubber Williams, certainly no reformer or friend of Roosevelt's, was defeated by the Tammany wave in his run for state senate from his old police inspection district on the East Side.

The outcome left Roosevelt crestfallen and politically wounded, perhaps fatally. He would not drop his excise campaign, but his reform efforts were now concentrated on improving the police force internally.

The Republicans in Albany, who had fared well in the statewide elections, tried to come to the rescue by enacting a new liquor law that took effect in April 1896. It raised the tax on saloons and fines for excise violations in hopes of driving the lowest of them out of business. It also mandated open curtains on Sundays, so that the police could see inside.

Under the Raines Law, named for the bill's sponsor, hotels with at least ten furnished bedrooms were permitted to sell alcohol on Sunday to their guests, provided the liquor was served together with a meal in the hotel dining room or in the private guest rooms. The question was: What is a "meal"? Clever hotel operators typically sold patrons alcohol and gave them a small snack as a "free lunch." Judges hostile to the excise law liberally interpreted a meal to be as little as a pretzel accompanying seventeen beers, or a single untouched sandwich kept on display to do meal duty for countless rounds of drinks. Sometimes the "sandwich" was just a brick in between two slices of stale bread.

Commenting on the scam, Roosevelt said, "If I ask for a beer, and a cracker and cheese is thrust at me, that is a 'fake' lunch—not a meal." But

Chief Conlin's police generally took the position that a sandwich, at least, constituted a meal. "A man may be hungry enough to eat a side of beef or a sandwich," Conlin commented, but "he must be the judge of his own appetite."*

Contrary to what most histories state, the hotel meal exemption was not new with the Raines Law but had been on the books since at least 1893. Likewise, under both the old and new laws, restaurants and saloons with only a liquor license, not a hotel license, could not sell alcohol on Sundays, with a meal or not.

What changed, dramatically, was not the law but the enforcement of it. Before the Raines Law, most restaurants and bars still sold alcohol on Sundays, and until Roosevelt became commissioner, cops usually looked the other way if paid a bribe. With Roosevelt's crackdown, though, liquor sellers went searching for legal loopholes. And when the 1896 Raines Law reaffirmed the hotel meal exemption, they seized on it.

Bar and restaurant owners suddenly rushed to convert their establishments into "hotels" so that they could sell booze with token meals. They carved up their places into ten or more "guest rooms," separated by nothing more than thin partitions and curtains. To recoup their remodeling costs, and adding moral insult to injury, they then rented out the shoddily constructed cubicles to prostitutes and unmarried couples.

Hundreds of such "Raines Law hotels," as they were dubbed, sprung up overnight. A law intended to cut down on the number of saloons had led not only to more Sunday drinking but also to more prostitution. In the words of New York City historian Mike Wallace, Roosevelt had indirectly "managed to engineer a quantum leap forward in the city's quotient of sin."

---

* A similar issue arose during the 2020 coronavirus pandemic, when New York governor Andrew Cuomo banned the sale of alcohol to bar and restaurant customers who did not also buy food. "Bars and restaurants offering outdoor dining must serve something closer to a meal with any alcohol," Cuomo was quoted as saying. "A proprietor serving a bag of potato chips with a couple of beers would be in violation." *The New York Times*, July 16, 2020.

In addition to the blowback he faced on his excise crusade, Roosevelt was beset with police board infighting. Throughout 1896 and into early 1897, his relationship with Democratic commissioner Parker deteriorated steadily. Congenial at first, Parker came to resent Roosevelt's imperiousness and usurpation of power. ("Thinks he's the whole board," Parker sneered privately to Lincoln Steffens.) As time went on, the two commissioners were no longer on speaking terms.

In truth, Roosevelt *was* imperious, usually because he was impatient to get things done. In a typical instance, the board was running behind in a meeting when TR grabbed a large bundle of papers and said, "These all relate to civil service matters. With the board's permission, I will decide them all. Even if I decide some of them wrong, that will be better than taking up the board's time with them."

Parker increasingly used his power as a single commissioner to block promotions, which required a unanimous vote of all four board members (or three plus the recommendation of the chief of police). Roosevelt was especially enraged when Parker repeatedly held up the promotion of Republican John McCullagh from acting inspector to full inspector. McCullagh, the swashbuckling young former captain who'd rescued Jacob Riis from the Whyos' clutches, then drove the gang out of the Sixth Ward, was exactly the kind of courageous, incorruptible cop Roosevelt championed. Parker also persuaded Chief Conlin to withhold his approval of McCullagh.

When Parker forged an alliance with the weak, pliable Grant—Roosevelt's fellow Republican on the board—the resulting 2-to-2 deadlock paralyzed the board on promotions and other significant business. (Democrat Andrews remained solidly in Roosevelt's camp.) Parker took to skipping board meetings, bothering to show up only to veto some Roosevelt recommendation.

The impasse confirmed Roosevelt's view that the law requiring a bipartisan police board was a grievous mistake. Like Parkhurst and other reformers, Roosevelt had advocated a single commissioner to head the police department, believing that centralized executive control under a professional civil servant was the only way to prevent political horse-trading. But the Albany Republicans under Thomas Platt wanted a split board to ensure equal representation for their party. "A more foolish or vicious law was never enacted by any legislative body," Roosevelt bemoaned.

Politically weakened by the Sunday liquor law fiasco, chafing under the restrictions of the four-person board, and practically disowned by his own state party head, Boss Platt, Roosevelt resigned his police commissionership in April 1897 and was succeeded as police board president by Frank Moss, the former Lexow Committee associate counsel. TR left to become assistant secretary to the navy under President William McKinley, a move that Roosevelt's antagonist Parker mocked as a "glorious retreat."

A year later, when the battleship USS *Maine* exploded in Cuba's Havana Harbor—thought to be the work of Spanish terrorists—the United States declared war on Spain, and Roosevelt quit his secretary position to form the First US Volunteer Cavalry Regiment, better known as the Rough Riders. His victorious charge up San Juan Hill propelled him to the governorship of New York in 1899; the vice presidency under McKinley two years later; the presidency following McKinley's assassination just six months into his second term; and, finally, to Mount Rushmore. But it was the fame he gained in his two years as president of New York's police board that started him along that path to glory.

◄◦═◍ ◖═◦►

If Theodore Roosevelt's record as head police commissioner was a mixed one, so, too, was the legacy of the Lexow Committee investigation that had led to his appointment. Most notably, the disciplinary and criminal cases against the police officers implicated in the Lexow investigation totally collapsed. Habitual bribe takers such as Captains Cross and Devery and Wardman Glennon (the Sphinx) were reinstated to their positions with back pay. The reason given most often by judges was that the cops' accusers, generally prostitutes, were not worthy of belief absent corroboration.

Likewise, virtually all of the criminal indictments and convictions were either eventually quashed or overturned, including those of Inspector McLaughlin, who'd been accused of bribery by brothel madam Katie Schubert, and of Captain Stephenson, who'd been convicted for extorting peaches and apples from a fruit dealer. Big Bill Devery, indicted four times and repeatedly under administrative charge, beat every rap. Against Roosevelt's orders, Chief Conlin even allowed Devery to march in the 1896 police parade (resumed after the prior year's cancelation). Swaggering along with a defiant look, Devery was repeatedly, and loudly, cheered by the crowd.

When Roosevelt left the police board in 1897, not one of the two dozen police officers criminally charged as a result of the Lexow hearings, including ten captains, was in jail, and every man dismissed from the force had been restored with back pay. Lexow historian Daniel Czitrom acknowledges that "from the strictly legal perspective of punishing police officers found guilty of criminal behavior, the Lexow Committee's impact was, in the short term, nil."

Furthermore, while the Lexow investigation had confirmed that many NYPD cops were on the take, it produced little if any evidence that the cops shared with Tammany politicians any of the huge chunks of money they extorted from prostitutes, saloonkeepers, and gamblers. The department's bribery system was more entrepreneurial than political and was designed to line its members' own pockets. Like Clubber Williams, a fair number of precinct captains and inspectors—the principal bribe takers—were Republicans. Grafting was mostly the product of a long-standing job culture. In that respect, Reverend Parkhurst fell short of his goal to tie police corruption inexorably to Democratic Tammany Hall.

⋅─◉ ◎─⋅

In the fall of 1897, the city was again facing municipal elections, this time to select a mayor and others to govern the new City of Greater New York, which came into existence on January 1, 1898, after referendum voters approved the charter consolidation of the boroughs of Manhattan, the Bronx, Brooklyn, Queens, and Staten Island. Overnight, the city's square mileage went from 60 to 360 and its population from about 2 million to 3.4 million, making it second in the world only to London. Brooklyn, the nation's third-largest city, was now part of New York.

Meanwhile, eighteen separate police departments in the consolidated area, many of them small village departments in Queens, merged into a single police force of 6,400 patrolmen and 7,500 total staff.* More than two-thirds of the force was from the old Police Department of the City of New York.

Consolidation also brought the first African American into the ranks of the NYPD: a formerly enslaved, proud, quiet, forty-two-year-old North Carolinian named Moses Cobb. He had joined the Brooklyn force in 1892 after scoring second in the civil service exam. Cobb would serve another twenty years in Brooklyn and inspire his wife's brother, Samuel Battle, to join the NYPD in 1911 as the first black man hired directly by the department.

In 1898, though, neither racial diversity nor reforming the NYPD was uppermost in the minds of New York voters. To the contrary, "reform" had become a dirty word to many citizens, to whom it meant simply that they couldn't buy a drink on Sunday. Boss Croker, who'd sailed back to New York from England in September on what the press called his "Return from Elba," handpicked Tammany's mayoral candidate, little-known Judge Robert Van Wyck, who ran on a slogan of "To Hell with Reform."

When Van Wyck and the Tammany ticket were swept into office, validating Croker's prediction from three years earlier, jubilant Tammany

---

* By comparison, the NYPD today has approximately 36,000 uniformed officers and 19,000 civilian employees to police a city of 8.5 million, for a ratio of roughly 6 to 1,000 in 2021 versus 2 to 1,000 at the turn of the century. Whether the current size will be reduced in response to calls to "defund," or repurpose, the police remains to be seen.

workers jammed Broadway to chant, "Well, well, well, reform has gone to hell!" In front of Tammany headquarters on Fourteenth Street (dubbed the Wigwam as part of the society's adoption of Native American nomenclature), Democrats voiced the same refrain as they waved upright broomsticks, the traditional symbol of a sweep.

At Croker's bidding, Mayor Van Wyck installed a new Tammany-controlled police board and forced the retirement of Police Chief John

THE BIG CHIEF'S FAIRY GODMOTHER
Mr. Devery tells "where he got it"

William Devery is lampooned in this 1902 *Harper's Weekly* cartoon for his silence concerning his ill-gotten gains from illegal gambling, which he controlled from his position as police chief. He was totally unfit for that position, wrote journalist Lincoln Steffens, "but as a character, as a work of art, he was a masterpiece."

McCullagh, who had succeeded Conlin the previous year. In his short time in office as the first police chief of consolidated New York, McCullagh had managed to alienate Tammany—and Big Tim Sullivan in particular—with his gambling raids. In a move that outraged Parkhurst and other good-government types, Van Wyck promptly replaced McCullagh with . . . Big Bill Devery.

In the annual police parade that spring, Devery rode proudly atop his horse, leading more than four thousand bluecoats from the Battery up Broadway. This time, on Devery's orders, Max Schmittberger was banished from the festivities altogether. It was as symbolic an end to the Lexow-inspired reform movement as could be imagined.

With Devery in charge, prostitutes, lawbreaking saloonkeepers, and gamblers—especially gamblers, for Devery, in league with Sullivan and horse racing sportsman Frank Farrell, was one of them—were back in business. He wore his graft on his sleeve and cared little for discipline. He once fined one of his reckless gun-toting officers, not for shooting at someone in the streets but for "not hittin' nobody."

Often absent from headquarters for days while on a drinking binge, Devery ran the department mostly out of a saloon at Twenty-Eighth Street and Ninth Avenue, where he could be found conducting "business" every night from nine to about three. His constituents were Tammany, his rank and file cops, and—most of all—Bill Devery. He was totally unfit to be a chief of police, thought Lincoln Steffens, "but as a character, as a work of art, he was a masterpiece."

⊶⇒◉⇐⊷

If the impact of the Lexow investigation was less than what anti-Tammany reformers had hoped for, it nonetheless accomplished something valuable. Everyone had assumed that the police were corrupt; Lexow established the goal in the public mind that they *shouldn't* be. Honesty, competence, and efficiency in policing became the new ideal. And for decades afterward, the NYPD continued to be well populated by a generation of honest patrolmen who, like Eddie Bourke, had gotten their start between the reform years of 1895 and 1897. They would forever regard themselves as "Roosevelt men."

Lexow's aspirational values were also touchstones for highly publicized twentieth-century investigations into police misconduct that were launched roughly every twenty years. Probably the most famous of them was the 1970s corruption investigation spawned by whistle-blower Frank Serpico, a spiritual successor to both Reverend Parkhurst and Captains Creeden and Schmittberger. (More recent inquiries have focused on the issue of police brutality and discrimination against African Americans.)

In addition, the Lexow investigation laid the groundwork for changes that would come along a little later. In 1901 New York's governor signed legislation replacing the police board and the office of police chief with a single police commissioner appointed by the mayor—the model that Parkhurst and Roosevelt had favored. It has been in place ever since. (Recent commissioners familiar to New Yorkers include Bernard Kerik, Raymond Kelly, and Bill Bratton.)

The same bill ended the police department's long-standing supervisory responsibility for elections, a reform that Parkhurst and others had unsuccessfully pressed for in 1895. A new position—state superintendent of elections—was filled by former police chief John McCullagh. The man who appointed McCullagh to the election job and who pushed through the new single commissionership bill was none other than Theodore Roosevelt. It was one of his last acts as governor before becoming vice president of the United States.

The new legislation, in part designed to remove Devery from power, left the corpulent chief out of a job temporarily. But Boss Croker wasn't about to let the police department be run by an independent man. Croker's stooge, Mayor Van Wyck, appointed ex-army colonel Michael C. Murphy (no relation to the corrupt former NYPD captain) as New York City's first police commissioner. Murphy, in turn, promptly named Devery as his first deputy, delegating to him de facto command of the department. Lexow or no, Tammany remained firmly in control of the NYPD.

One other man particularly affected by the Lexow experience was Detective Arthur Carey. After Byrnes was forced to retire, his protégé Carey was demoted to patrolman and sent to Goatville. But in 1897, after solving the Guldensuppe "headless torso" case, he was back in the central detective bureau.

From that point on, Art Carey would remain a murder man.

CHAPTER TWENTY

THE MAN IN THE STRAW HAT

Art Carey's family never doubted he would become a policeman. His father, who came from Ireland to America as a young boy, joined the force in New York, left it to go into business, but rejoined it shortly after Arthur was born, never to leave it again. It was too much of a lure for an Irishman who wanted to try his hand at governing, seeing as how, back in the old country, the Irish were the governed rather than the governors.

As a toddler, his sister recalled, Art donned navy-blue shorts, the color of his father's uniform, and stood in front of his family's home in Lower Manhattan, swinging a miniature policeman's billy club. At age seven, he began accompanying his father to the Chambers Street station along the Hudson River, where pirates and wharf rats roamed the docks.

Young Art Carey's first impressions at the precinct house were of the stylish beards that nearly every blue-coated patrolman wore and the side-whiskers sported by the higher-ups. But he became even more taken with the detectives in civilian clothes; enigmatic figures who stood aloof from the uniformed men. The plainclothesmen would briskly search the thieves they brought in while peppering them with questions. The detectives spoke their own special language: honest men were "citizens," an arrest was a "collar," a pickpocket a "dip," a stolen purse a "leather."

Carey heard the plainclothesmen telling colorful tales about some of the same professional criminals that his later mentor, Thomas Byrnes, would confront. Most of them were members of George Leslie's robbery gang: Shang Draper, Sheeny Mike Kurtz, Jimmy Hope, Banjo Pete Emerson, and Marm Mandelbaum. Carey also learned that the detectives routinely and bravely infiltrated the most sordid dives "where a man was supposed to take his life in his hands whenever he entered": places such as Billy McGlory's and McGurk's Suicide Hall. To Art Carey, the detectives he so admired "seemed to be privileged above all men; to be able to wander about in ordinary clothes with the magic power to haul men in." Their world was "mysterious and fascinating to me."

Homicides were relatively infrequent in those days, but Carey eagerly soaked up any talk of the most lurid murders, past and present, when, after school, he hurried down to Chambers Street to watch and listen. He especially longed to become one of the lawmen who tracked down killers.

As soon as he could, Carey took the civil service exam for patrolmen and passed. On March 1, 1889, as he recalled, he "hotfooted it to police headquarters to be sworn in. It was like going after something that by right of inheritance is yours."

Later, as a homicide detective, Carey seldom took vacations and existed on little sleep. Unlike the stereotypical Irishman of his day, he didn't drink. At his home in the Bronx, he had his family (including two future NYPD detectives), his dog, his pipe, and his books on poisons, weapons, and wounds. But he was most comfortable on the murder hunt, and, a year after the Guldensuppe case, he was at work on two of the most sensational murder cases of the nineteenth century.

⊷⇒◉⇐⊷

At nine-thirty on the morning of August 16, 1898, a chambermaid rapped furiously at the door to room 84 of the Grand Hotel at Broadway and Thirty-First Street, a popular Tenderloin gathering place for sporting and theatrical figures. (It still stands today as a landmarked building.)

After no one answered her repeated knocks, the maid pushed open the unlocked door and found the body of a comely young woman splayed on the floor, face turned sideways, fully clothed. Her head lay in a pool of blood. She'd been bludgeoned with a lead pipe to the skull, her neck was broken, and one of her earlobes was torn by the violent removal of an earring. Her clothing was undisturbed, the bed linens fresh and unmussed. On a table in the center of the room stood an empty champagne bottle and two glasses.

On the day she was killed, the fashionably attired woman, wearing a large hat, had checked in alone and was seen having lunch at the hotel, for which she paid a dollar using a ten-dollar bill and left a ten-cent tip. She exited the hotel and returned between five and six with an unidentified man in his early thirties. On the slender side, with sharp features, he wore a dark blue suit and a black bow tie, and had a dark mustache. Everyone recalled that he sported a white straw hat.

Shortly after six o'clock that Monday evening, the couple went up to room 84, on the fourth floor, having ordered a bottle of French champagne, which was brought up to their room with two glasses. The man in the straw hat gave the bellboy $2 for the $1.75 bottle and told him to keep the change.

The man and woman left the hotel together about seven and returned around midnight to retire. The night elevator boy told the police he saw a man sneaking down the marble staircase and hastily exiting the hotel shortly after two in the morning, although the lad had given little thought to it at the time.

The autopsy performed on-site put the time of death at about one in the morning. No one at the hotel had heard a struggle. Eight dollars and ninety cents—the dead woman's change from lunch—was still on her person. But the diamond earrings and diamond-and-ruby ring the hotel clerk had noticed on her earlier were missing, along with thousands of dollars' worth of other jewelry she typically kept in a small leather bag tucked inside her corset.

The head of the detective bureau, and Art Carey's boss, was a trusted Byrnes favorite: George "Chesty" McClusky. A dapper man of gracious manners and shrewd intelligence, McClusky looked like a Wall Street broker and made his unofficial headquarters at Delmonico's. He was given his nickname by Big Bill Devery, who considered him too much of a haughty aristocrat to be effective.

McClusky summoned Detective Carey to room 84, where he found his boss, the coroner's physician, and several other cops viewing the body. Chief Devery made an appearance as well. One of the lead investigators was Tenderloin captain James K. Price, the combative former Clubber Williams protégé who'd been indicted for bribery and suspended from the force as a result of the Lexow investigation, only to be reinstated after the indictment was dismissed.

Among those present at the crime scene, Carey noticed that the seventeen-inch lead pipe lying beside the corpse was deliberately bent at one end to form a handle and was thickly bound with bicycle tire tape at the other. An iron rod had been inserted inside the pipe to fortify it. An obviously homemade weapon, it told Carey immediately that the murder was premeditated.

From a windowsill and wastebasket in room 84, the police recovered torn scraps of a doctor's prescription form for Phillips' Milk of Magnesia, which when pieced together bore the words "E. Maxwell and wife, Grand Hotel." These matched the names "E. Maxwell and wife, Brooklyn," which the victim had used in signing the hotel register before meeting the man in the straw hat.

The most curious item recovered, though, was a check tucked into the dead woman's corset, which fell out during the autopsy. It was made payable to "Emma Reynolds" in the amount of $13,000. Dated August 15, 1898, the previous day, it was drawn on the Garfield National Bank, signed by a "Dudley Gideon," and endorsed on the back by "S. J. Kennedy."

Papers in a pocketbook found on the mantelpiece identified the dead woman not as Mrs. E. Maxwell of Brooklyn but as Mrs. E. C. Reynolds

Twenty-one-year-old Emeline "Dolly" Reynolds, who was found brutally murdered in room 84 of Manhattan's Grand Hotel in 1898. The sensational homicide case was one of many investigated by NYPD detective Art Carey.

of 370 West Fifty-Eighth Street, just off Columbus Circle. The woman's African American housekeeper was brought down to view the body. She identified the victim as twenty-one-year-old Emeline "Dolly" Reynolds, the daughter of prosperous Westchester County parents.

Dolly was petite, round-faced, and had an attractive figure. Two years earlier, she had moved into the city to pursue a stage career, biding her time by selling encyclopedias on commission to wealthy bankers and brokers. Something of a penny pincher, she fared well as a salesperson and was particularly adroit at winning the favor of her male customers.

One of them, a Georgia-born stockbroker named Maurice B. Mendham, paid her rent and for her singing lessons, lived with her virtually as man and wife, and passed himself off as "Mr. Reynolds" to make her appear respectable to the other tenants. But, in fact, Dolly was single. She and Mendham were rumored to have quarreled recently over his demand that she return some expensive jewelry he'd given her, though he would later deny it in court. The sole piece of jewelry found on her at her death was a gold necklace and locket with a picture of Mendham inside.

Mendham was an obvious suspect. But the portly forty-two-year-old sugar daddy was not the younger man in the straw hat who'd accompanied Dolly to room 84, for the police determined that Mendham was in Long Branch, New Jersey, at the time of the murder.

Dr. Samuel J. Kennedy, a
Staten Island dentist, the
accused murderer of Dolly
Reynolds.

On Tuesday afternoon, a cashier at the Garfield National Bank at Sixth Avenue and Twenty-Third Street informed detectives that the bank had no account with a Dudley Gideon, who was apparently fictitious, which made the check worthless. But the bank did have a depositor, S. J. Kennedy, who maintained a small balance. He was Samuel J. Kennedy, a reputable, married, thirty-two-year-old Staten Island dentist with a practice on West Twenty-Second Street in Manhattan. With his wife and child, he shared a house with his parents in New Dorp, on Staten Island's East Shore, where he was a popular member of the Sea View Tennis and Social Club.

Meanwhile, police had brought Dolly Reynolds's mother from Mount Vernon, an inner suburb of New York, to the Nineteenth Precinct station house in the Tenderloin for questioning. According to Mrs. Cristina Reynolds, her daughter had told her recently that while treating her for a toothache, Dr. Kennedy tipped off Dolly to a horse racing betting scheme that guaranteed winnings of up to 50-to-1 odds. It worked because the jockey had an "electric saddle" to spur the horse. Or, according to another version, because hoodlums intercepted wire reports of the race results and held them back from the poolroom until they could wager on the winner (as in the 1973 movie *The Sting*, starring Paul Newman and Robert Redford as a pair of con men).

Mrs. Reynolds said that Dolly withdrew $500 from her bank in Mount Vernon to make the bet, gave Kennedy the money on Sunday, August 14, and was to meet him at six o'clock in the evening on Monday the fifteenth to collect on a race he said would net her $4,000. He told her to bring a handbag to carry away the $4,000, or the $500 he promised to return if the race didn't pay off. The satchel Dolly brought with her was discovered on the floor at the crime scene, slashed open by someone who'd taken whatever money and valuables were inside.

Carey arrested Kennedy at his Manhattan dental office at three-thirty on the afternoon of August 16, just five hours after the discovery of Dolly Reynolds's body. Initially, Kennedy said he didn't know an Emma C. Reynolds or a Dolly Reynolds. When Carey reminded him that she was a patient of his and told him where she lived, the dentist replied, "Oh, is that the person you mean?" He admitted to being her regular dentist and that he had treated her in his office on Thursday or Friday of the previous week. But he said his relationship with her was purely professional, not social. He denied ever placing any bets for her. After first saying he didn't recall being in the Grand Hotel on the night in question, he insisted later that he'd never set foot in the place.

The mysterious $13,000 check made payable to Dolly Reynolds, endorsed on the back by Samuel Kennedy, and found on her bludgeoned body. She supposedly had gone to the Grand Hotel to meet Dr. Kennedy and collect her winnings from a horse racing betting scheme.

Kennedy further denied that the endorsement signature on the back of the check was his, even though a bank clerk said the handwriting matched the dentist's signature on file with the Garfield National. At Kennedy's later trial, several handwriting experts would testify that the check endorsement by S. J. Kennedy—in fact, the entire check—was written by the same hand that wrote "E. Maxwell and wife, Grand Hotel" on the prescription form found in tatters.

Identical prescription forms for "Phillips' Milk of Magnesia, 12 oz.," available only to doctors, dentists, and druggists, were found on a pad in Dr. Kennedy's office when police searched it. They also found a checkbook, of a type no longer used by the Garfield National, but corresponding exactly to the style of check found on Dolly Reynolds.

From a lineup at the Tenderloin precinct station, Kennedy was positively identified by five hotel employees—including the bellboy who'd delivered them champagne in their room—as the man in the straw hat who'd accompanied Dolly Reynolds the night of the murder. One glitch: they all described the man's mustache as dark or even "very" dark, while Kennedy's was lighter.

At the police station, Kennedy ran into Mendham, one of his longtime patients, who had originally introduced the dentist to Dolly and paid her dental bills. Kennedy understood that she was Mendham's mistress. "You've gotten me into a hell of a lot of trouble!" Kennedy shouted at him.

The prime suspect gave conflicting accounts of his whereabouts on the night of the murder. At first, Kennedy drew a complete blank, saying he couldn't remember where he'd been or what he'd been doing. Then he remembered attending Proctor's Theatre on West Twenty-Third Street, but he couldn't recall the name of the play, nor a single thing about it, because he slept through it. He explained that he was tired and drowsy from having stopped off for a couple of drinks after work and surmised that he must have inhaled fumes from a sedative drug named chloral hydrate—which he used in his practice and also took himself for insomnia—when a bottle of it broke on his office floor on Monday.

The dentist said he slept all the way on the cable car from Twenty-Third Street to the Battery and during the entire ferry ride to Staten Island. Because he was too late to catch a trolley or train home from the St. George ferry terminal when he arrived, he walked six miles to get home, about a two-hour hike through mud and muck.

Kennedy did have one witness who claimed to have seen him at the ferry house at Battery Park a little after midnight, before the boat left for Staten Island. She said she saw him again later, asleep on the ferry. Another alibi witness said he was walking with Kennedy on Sixth Avenue around the time the dentist was supposedly having dinner with Dolly. Kennedy's parents also naturally vouched for their son's innocence.

In strip-searching Kennedy, Carey spotted a blue-black smear on his underwear; a chemist later identified it as lead, consistent with that on the lead pipe found in room 84. In Kennedy's basement workshop on Staten Island, Carey found a small piece of lead pipe of the same type as the murder weapon and a section of iron rod an expert later testified fit exactly inside the bludgeon. A vise in the dentist's cellar that Carey retrieved also had serrations on the clamp that, the state's expert testified, corresponded with marks on the weapon.

There was still the matter of the straw hat, which police hadn't found. Kennedy said he didn't own one, and, when arrested, he was wearing a black felt fedora. At Kennedy's office, Carey spotted a new plaid bicycle cap in a closet, and when he picked it up, he found that it bore the label of Smith, Gray & Co., a store at Broadway and Thirty-First Street, next to the Grand Hotel. Carey went there and found a salesman in the hat department who said he'd sold a straw hat on Monday, the day of the murder, to a man matching Kennedy's description, as well as the bicycle cap found in the dentist's office. When shown Kennedy as part of a lineup, the store clerk picked him out as the man to whom he'd sold the two hats.

Carey was sure that Kennedy was Dolly's killer, as was McClusky, but the police needed to find a motive. Carey pegged Dolly for a gold digger who'd greedily jumped at the prospect of a sure bet. He theorized that

Kennedy arranged to meet Dolly for the "payoff," but, in fact, there was to be none because the whole horse racing scam was made up. According to the theory, Dolly was just one of the "lambs" that Kennedy, a feeder for a group of confidence men, was tasked with separating from their money.

Carey surmised that Kennedy wrote out the words "E. Maxwell and wife, Grand Hotel" on the prescription form so that Dolly would know where to go and under what name to register. The prosecutors believed that he gave her the check to satisfy her, then killed her before she figured out that both the check and the betting scheme were bogus. He took her earrings and ring to make it look like a robbery, emptied the contents of her pocketbook and satchel, then fled without finding the incriminating check, which was hidden in her corset.

The theory had some problems, though: If the planned betting payoff was $4,000, why was the check for $13,000? Assuming that Kennedy gave Dolly the check on the day it was dated—August 15, the day of the murder—then he must have created the murder weapon before he even had a motive to kill her. Why would he buy a straw hat, just hours before the murder, that could connect him to the crime—even going so far as to chat up the hat clerk by telling him that he was a dentist in that area, as the clerk testified? And why would he go down the stairs, where he might be spotted by a night watchman, rather than exiting via the fire escape just outside the window?

Nonetheless, in March 1899 the jury took less than three hours to render a guilty verdict, and Dr. Kennedy was sentenced to die in the electric chair that May in Sing Sing. Score one for Art Carey and the NYPD.

But their victory was temporary. In November 1900 the New York Court of Appeals, the state's highest court, granted Kennedy a new trial on the grounds that critical hearsay evidence was improperly admitted at trial. It consisted of testimony by Captain Price about statements hotel employees made to him identifying Kennedy as the man in the straw hat.

At the second trial, in February 1901, the same hotel witnesses and others who originally identified Kennedy repeated their testimony. But the judge cut the heart out of the prosecution's case by refusing to allow its handwriting experts to testify that Kennedy's signature on the check matched that on the torn prescription form. He reasoned that because neither specimen was admitted or proved to be in Kennedy's hand, the comparison was irrelevant.

In addition, the prosecution expert who had previously testified that the iron rod found in Kennedy's basement fit perfectly inside the murder weapon now contradicted himself and said they were not, in fact, a match. The defense also procured an affidavit by a Staten Island plumber accusing Carey and another detective of having manufactured evidence concerning the lead pipe. Carey ridiculed the charge, and the plumber retracted it under oath, but the damage was done.

With the state's case severely weakened, the jury voted 11 to 1 to acquit but couldn't break the deadlock. Kennedy, who had appeared remarkably unperturbed throughout both trials, was disappointed at the lack of a total acquittal.

At the third trial, which began in May 1901, new defense witnesses and theories emerged to further cast doubt on Kennedy's guilt. Some of the hotel employees who'd been so sure of their identification of him three years earlier were now equivocating. Although the state's handwriting experts were allowed to testify, the defense had its own experts who opined that none of Kennedy's alleged writing was a match. In addition, a Garfield National Bank cashier teller testified that he could not say one way or the other whether the endorsement on the back of the check was Kennedy's signature.

Maurice Mendham testified for the first time, and his evasiveness about the extent of his relationship with Dolly Reynolds fed the defense's insinuation that he was somehow behind the murder. The implication was that Mendham, or someone acting for him, had deliberately framed Kennedy, forged his endorsement on the check, and impersonated him in buying the straw hat, all as part of an elaborate plot to obtain the return of Dolly's jewelry.

Oddly, it came out at trial that all her missing jewelry, other than her stolen earrings and ring, had turned up in her apartment about a week after the murder when her housekeeper found it behind a sugar bowl in the pantry. Dolly's jewelry was in the small leather bag she normally wore about her waist. How it got there, or whether it was in the pantry all along and the police simply missed it in their original search, was never established. But it left a big question mark.

Perhaps most damaging of all to the prosecution, the proprietor of the Grand Hotel testified that there had been another robbery on the night of the murder, on the same floor as room 84, that had been reported to police. The hotel owner allowed as how a burglar could have entered any room on the floor through the window via the fire escape. This new testimony lent support to the alternative defense theory that the murder was not the premeditated work of a refined, educated man such as Dr. Kennedy, but rather a chance killing by a brutal mugger carrying a typical thug's weapon.

As at the first two trials, Kennedy did not testify.

Outside the courtroom, large crowds sympathetic to Kennedy shouted, "Let him loose!" and "Let him go!" When the jury hung again, with eight to four in favor of acquittal, the court declared another mistrial. The state elected not to pursue the case and dropped its indictment.

Released from death row in the Tombs, Dr. Samuel J. Kennedy returned a hero to Staten Island, where two thousand residents celebrated his arrival with displays of electric lights, Chinese lanterns, and fireworks. He resumed his dental practice and lived quietly in New Dorp, dying at age eighty-one in August 1948, almost fifty years to the day after the murder of his patient Dolly Reynolds.

No one was ever convicted of the murder, which remains officially unsolved. Overlooked by most of those who write about the case is the fact that, if Dr. Kennedy was truly innocent of the crime and knew nothing about it, then Dolly must have made up the story about his guaranteeing her a betting payoff. But why? Either that, or someone she trusted, and who knew she knew Kennedy—Mendham, perhaps, or the mysterious "E. Maxwell"—fed her the phony story to lure her to the hotel.

"Who did kill Dolly Reynolds?" Art Carey asked in his memoirs. He had to admit that he didn't have the answer. But he observed that because Dolly was a shrewd businesswoman who craved wealth, "If anyone owed her money and did not pay on demand, or attempted to swindle her, Dolly would have made life pretty miserable for that person."

Writing thirty years after the case, Carey pictured Dolly in room 84 that August night, having "a sip of champagne, perhaps to toast her dream of wealth so suddenly come true." Carey was sure she would not have tucked away a worthless check in her bosom, knowing it to be such. "What happened after that, no one, I fear, will ever know," he concluded. "It remains one of those unfinished spots that appear in so many murder pictures." In an age before modern forensics, many such pictures remained incomplete.

CHAPTER TWENTY-ONE

◆➤━━◉ ◉━━◆◆

THE POSTMAN RANG TWICE

A rt Carey was much more certain of the guilt of Roland Molineux. This sensational homicide case, which began just as New Yorkers were gearing up for Dr. Samuel Kennedy's second trial, was even closer to Carey's heart, as it was his from the start.

On Christmas Eve 1898, Harry Cornish, the athletic director of New York's posh Knickerbocker Athletic Club (KAC), received a package in the club's mailbox addressed to him from an anonymous sender. Inside the package was a Tiffany & Co. jewelry box, in the iconic robin's-egg-blue color, containing a bottle of Emerson's Bromo-Seltzer and a silver holder in the shape of a small candlestick. Accompanying these articles was a small embossed Tiffany's envelope of the kind used for enclosing cards sent with gifts, but there was no card in the envelope.

Cornish figured that the sender forgot to include the card, or else it was a joke Christmas gift from a club member—a suggestion that he might need some of the popular headache and heartburn remedy for an anticipated spate of holiday drinking. Or perhaps the sender was a secret lady admirer: rakish and divorced, on the grounds of adultery, the thirty-five-year-old Cornish was a hopeless womanizer and frequenter of Tenderloin district bordellos.

Mailed from the general post office on December 23, the package had no return address. Oddly, the club's handwritten address on the manila wrapping paper, which Cornish saved, misspelled it as Madison Avenue and "Fourty"-Fifth Street instead of the correct *Forty*-Fifth.

Three days later, Cornish attended the theater with his distantly related aunt and landlady, the widowed Katherine Adams, and her grown daughter Florence. Afterward they had a late supper and wine at an Upper West Side café near the apartment they shared at Columbus Avenue and West Eighty-Sixth Street.

A bit hungover the next morning, the sixty-two-year-old Mrs. Adams asked Cornish for a dose of the Bromo-Seltzer, then swallowed a heaping teaspoonful of the bitter-tasting powder mixed with a half glass of water. She immediately began convulsing and retching, collapsed unconscious, and, within minutes, was dead. Cornish, who became violently ill himself after sampling the tonic, was saved by doctors.

The autopsy by the coroner's physician concluded that the Bromo-Seltzer had been laced with potassium cyanide, a deadly poison. Mrs. Adams was the unintended victim of a premeditated murder by mail.

Cornish, an accomplished amateur sportsman, and track-and-field and college football coach, professed mystery at who might want to do away with him. The press speculated that the killer was a jealous woman—perhaps Cornish's ex-wife or even his live-in cousin Florence, then separated from her husband. A woman, it was said, was more likely to prefer assassination from afar to a direct attack.

Consulted for his opinion by William Randolph Hearst's *New York Journal*, Julian Hawthorne, author of the admiring books about Thomas Byrnes, weighed in with his view: "Since women naturally shrink from deeds of physical violence," he speculated, "it is only to be expected that they should avail themselves of so refinedly diabolic a means as poisons afford. They don't like blood—unless they are Spanish ladies at a bull fight—and they are incompetent to struggling with daggers and defending themselves with firearms."

But Art Carey, to whom detective bureau chief Chesty McClusky assigned the case, had other ideas.

Carey took the bottle of Bromo-Seltzer to New York University professor Rudolph Witthaus, the nation's foremost toxicologist, with whom Carey had worked on the Guldensuppe and Dr. Buchanan murder cases. Dr. Witthaus determined that the deadly ingredient in the bottle had not been potassium cyanide but instead cyanide of mercury, a much rarer though equally toxic compound. Witthaus later examined Mrs. Adams's digestive organs and confirmed that cyanide of mercury caused her death.

Cyanide of potassium, though poisonous, was readily available in most drugstores and was used in many commercial applications, such as wet-plate photography. But mercuric cyanide, commonly used as an antiseptic gargle up to the Civil War, was no longer stocked by most druggists. It was seldom prescribed even by physicians because it was considered too dangerous. Few people, outside of chemical workers, had much access to it anymore. That would help narrow the focus of Carey's investigation.

In the meantime, the detective caught a break: when New York's newspapers ran front-page photos of the mailing label on the poison package anonymously sent to Cornish, a secretary of the Knickerbocker Athletic Club recognized the handwriting from some correspondence he had on file. The penmanship matched that of a former club member who had repeatedly clashed with Cornish in the past.

The club member was thirty-one-year-old Roland Molineux, a handsome amateur boxer and national gymnast champion. The previous year, Molineux had complained that Cornish had committed some petty violations of club rules and allegedly mismanaged the club restaurant and baths. In March 1898, after KAC officers refused his demand that they fire Cornish as their athletic director, Molineux resigned and switched his membership to another club.

Roland Molineux, a national gymnast champion, was accused of two separate murders by poison sent through the mail in 1898. Art Carey was the lead investigator in the case, which featured a heavy dosage of sex, a love triangle, a femme fatale, and jealousy and hatred among friends and enemies, all culminating in the "trial of the century."

The angry letters Molineux had written the KAC secretary not only appeared to match the handwriting on the poison package label but also, glaringly, had misspelled the word "Forty" as "Fourty" in the same way. That alone made Molineux an obvious suspect in the minds of Carey and his boss McClusky. But there was much more to come.

Molineux's father was a decorated Union Civil War general from Brooklyn who, following the war, operated a large paint manufacturing company in Bayonne, New Jersey. Roland learned the paint and chemicals business while working in his father's factory and studied chemistry for two years in school.

In 1893 Roland was hired as superintendent and chief chemist for the Morris Herrmann Company in Newark, which made colored dyes for paint. His well-equipped laboratory contained mercury, arsenic, and

The incriminating label on the package of poisoned Bromo-Seltzer sent to Molineux's enemy Harry Cornish at the Knickerbocker Athletic Club, allegedly in Molineux's handwriting, with the address misspelled as "Fourty"-Fifth Street.

other chemicals from which various poisons, including cyanide of mercury, could be produced. He kept an apartment in the factory building and, until he resigned, a room in the KAC in Manhattan. At the athletic club, he continued to practice the skills that had made him the national amateur horizontal-bar champion in 1885 and several times since.

Molineux cut an impressive physical figure: muscular and trim, with a finely waxed, upturned mustache, and always impeccably dressed. He bore himself with an aristocratic demeanor that struck many as snobbish. Unlike the pugilistic and uncouth Harry Cornish, a man's man who was well liked by his fellow club members, the suave, dandyish Molineux, though admired for his gymnastic prowess, was not especially popular with them. He was too supercilious, often flitting in and out of conversations he interrupted freely.

With Molineux in his cross hairs, Carey went about trying to trace the silver Bromo-Seltzer holder to its source. He saw that at the bottom of the holder the letter "L" was stamped into a small curved crescent, with the word "Sterling" above it and the number 814 below. He ascertained that the "L" and crescent were the logo for Lebkuecher & Company, silverware manufacturers in Newark (814 being their catalog number).

Carey took the item to the silverware factory, where the company's president, Frank Lebkuecher, confirmed that his firm had made the article. He explained that it wasn't a receptacle for a bottle, Bromo-Seltzer or otherwise; instead, it was a match or cigarette holder with a silver ashtray base.

Questioned further as to where his factory might have distributed the items, Lebkuecher gave Carey a list of numerous jewelry stores across the country, including three local outlets. Based on the style of the price sticker that had been partially scraped off, Carey traced the match holder to a Newark store, C. J. Hartdegen jewelers.

A holiday salesclerk there recalled selling the item on December 21 to a gentlemanly, debonair man in his early thirties who was looking for a Bromo-Seltzer bottle holder. She persuaded him that the silver match holder would work just as nicely. (In actuality, the fatal Bromo-Seltzer bottle was a chemist's bottle to which an Emerson's Bromo-Seltzer label was attached. The real bottle would have been too large for the holder.)

Carey took note that the C. J. Hartdegen jewelry store was only a mile from the Morris Herrmann dye manufacturers in Newark, where Roland Molineux worked as a chemist, blending dry colors for paint. The pieces all seemed to fit.

There was one problem: the Hartdegen jewelry store clerk could not identify Molineux as the purchaser. She recalled a man with a reddish Vandyke beard, whereas Molineux sported only a dark mustache and no beard. But Carey wasn't ready to give up on his prime suspect. He figured that either the salesclerk was mistaken or Molineux had donned a red wig and fake whiskers. Carey was soon heartened to find a Newark police detective who said he had seen and spoken with Molineux near the jewelry store on December 21, having recognized the man from his amateur boxing days.

Although most of the evidence pointed to Molineux, his suspected motive for killing Cornish—disputes over minor club matters—seemed weak. Then came another break: it turned out that another antagonist of Molineux's, one who offered a clearer motive for Molineux to do away with him, had recently died under strikingly similar and suspicious circumstances.

Thirty-two-year-old stockbroker Henry Barnet was also a member of the Knickerbocker Athletic Club, where he occupied the room next to Molineux's. Known as Barney, the convivial Barnet had once been one of Roland Molineux's warmest personal friends. That ended when Molineux's love interest, a young aspiring singer named Blanche Chesebrough, whom Molineux had introduced to Barnet at the Metropolitan Opera House, fell for Barnet instead. On Thanksgiving Day 1897, Blanche spurned Molineux's marriage proposal because she was in love with Barney.

Twenty-three at the time, Blanche was statuesque and stylish, with an almost regal bearing. She was free-spirited, loved dinners and champagne at Delmonico's and the Waldorf-Astoria, and dreamed of studying opera abroad in Paris.

Over the next year, she went back and forth between the two men. Molineux was richer, handsomer, and a better prospect for providing her the lavish lifestyle she fancied. Barnet was a storyteller and a flirt and the more entertaining of the two. Though quite plump, and physically unprepossessing, he had an animal magnetism that Molineux lacked. And in the trysts that he and Blanche conducted behind Roland's back, Barney more adroitly satisfied her admittedly growing passion for sex. For all his athleticism, Molineux, nicknamed Mollie, had an effeminate streak that left Blanche cold. Even after she finally broke things off with Barnet in September 1898 and secretly agreed in principle to marry Molineux, Roland remained intensely jealous of Barney.

On October 28, 1898, Barnet collapsed in his room at the KAC and started convulsing and vomiting. Barnet told his doctors he thought the cause of his trouble was a dose of Kutnow's Powder, a popular effervescent stomach remedy made from mineral salts that competed with

Bromo-Seltzer. Barnet said he'd taken the Kutnow's after receiving an anonymous free sample in the mail. But the principal treating doctor diagnosed his affliction as a case of diphtheria, a common throat infection in those days that could lead to further complications.

Barnet remained in agony for almost two weeks as his condition worsened. He died on November 10, officially ruled due to a diphtheria-induced heart attack. Before he died, Blanche Chesebrough sent him flowers and a get-well letter asking him to let her prove her sincerity and not to be angry with her anymore, phrases she was never adequately able to explain.

A few days after Barney's death, Blanche finally accepted Molineux's marriage proposal, and they were wed on November 29, 1898—nineteen days after Barnet's death and twenty-five days before Katherine Adams drank the fatal poison intended for Roland's other bête noire, Harry Cornish.

Now Carey delved into the details of Henry Barnet's death. The Kutnow's Powder, found on a table next to the victim's bed, was analyzed by Dr. Witthaus, who determined it had been laced with cyanide of mercury, the same poison that killed Katherine Adams.

After Barnet's body was exhumed, Witthaus discovered cyanide of mercury in his organs. But because Barnet, shortly before he died, had taken calomel, a common diphtheria treatment containing mercury, there was some question as to whether the tainted Kutnow's Powder had caused his death. Nonetheless, several medical experts, including Dr. Henry Loomis, who performed the autopsy, concurred that Barnet had indeed died from mercuric cyanide poisoning, just as Katherine Adams had.

Carey, suspecting that Molineux had sent Barnet the Kutnow's Powder, visited Kutnow Brothers' offices at 13 Astor Place, where he and company clerks sat for countless hours scouring its files. Among the hundred thousand letters they looked through, a female bookkeeper finally located a handwritten letter she thought matched the poisoned package handwriting Carey had shown her. It was written on fancy robin's-egg-blue notepaper, embossed at the top with a distinctive crest of three interlocking silver crescents in the shape of a fleur-de-lis. It had arrived at the Kutnow offices on December 22 and read: "Please send me a sample of Salts to 1620 Broadway" and was signed, "H. Cornish."

Carey showed the note to Cornish, who said it wasn't his signature.

Next, the detective went to 1620 Broadway, near West Forty-Ninth Street. There he found Joseph Koch, who ran a small-time commercial advertising agency and printing business and owned a mail drop at the same location. Private letter boxes were common then, before the post office began leasing them. Koch told Carey that a man had rented the letter box under Cornish's name on December 21, 1898, the day before Kutnow Brothers received "Cornish's" request for a sample.

When Carey brought Cornish down to 1620 Broadway, Koch confirmed that he was not the man. Nor was Molineux the box renter, Koch said. But he would testify later that the week before, Molineux, whom he knew from prior business dealings, had shown up at his office and inquired about renting the private letter box for a friend—presumably the man who, as H. Cornish, showed up on December 21 and rented the box. His identity, like that of the red-bearded man who bought the silver holder, would forever remain unknown.

Koch supplied Carey with the contents of the mailbox the unidentified man had rented from him but not yet picked up. One was a sample of Kutnow's Powder that "H. Cornish" had requested. Another was a letter and sample box of Calthos capsules, a purported cure for "male debility"—that is, impotence—a forerunner of modern-day Viagra. Advertised as Professor Julian Laborde's Wonderful French Preparation That Restores Lost Manhood, Calthos was later determined to be worthless, its main ingredient being yellow phosphorous, itself a form of toxin.

The Calthos came from the Von Mohl Company of Cincinnati, a patent medicine mail-order firm. At the request of the police, Von Mohl sent Detective Chief McClusky the letter from "H. Cornish" requesting the samples. It appeared to be in the same handwriting as the mailing label on the fateful package received by Cornish on December 24. The letter was also written on the same type of peculiar eggshell-blue, embossed notepaper with three interlaced silver crescents that Carey had obtained from the Kutnow Brothers' files.

What became known as the "Cornish" mailbox seemed to tie the seeker of Kutnow's Powder and a male impotence cure to the poisoner of Harry Cornish, or Henry Barnet, or both. But a second mail drop box drew the net even tighter. The first clue to its existence came from enterprising reporters at the *New York Herald*, who, like Hearst's *Journal* and Pulitzer's *World*, were doggedly pursuing the case alongside—and at times a step ahead of—the police, a fact the papers relentlessly touted and often exaggerated.

From the Von Mohl Company's files in Cincinnati, the *Herald* obtained another telltale letter requesting a sample of its popular pink Calthos pills. But this one, though in handwriting that matched the letter request from "H. Cornish," was from a different sender. The name on the letter was "H. C. Barnet."

"H. C. Barnet" listed a return address of 257 West Forty-Second Street, which turned out to be a small advertising agency near Longacre Square (what is now Times Square) run by one Nicholas Heckmann. Like Joseph Koch, Heckmann also offered a private letter box rental service. When Carey went there, Heckmann told him that on May 27, 1898—five months before Barnet fell ill—he'd rented box 217 to a man identifying himself as "Mr. H. C. Barnet." Heckmann described him as slim, handsome, and athletic, with a handlebar mustache and the air of a gentleman—a description that matched Molineux, not Barnet.

Heckmann had seen "Mr. Barnet" picking up his mail about twenty times over the next few weeks. The man who called himself Barnet came regularly for a while, about every other day, then suddenly stopped calling for his mail between mid-June and August, a period corresponding with Roland Molineux's summer trip to Europe.

Heckmann never saw "H. C. Barnet" again, although small packages and letters continued arriving at his box that fall and into January 1899.

Heckmann would later positively identify Roland Molineux in court as the man who had rented box 217 under the name H. C. Barnet and showed up fifteen to twenty times to claim his mail.

The contents of the "Barnet" mailbox, as it was called, were similar to those found in the "Cornish" letter box. According to Heckmann, one package was marked "Kutnow Powders" and another one "Von Mohl" (Calthos). The rest of the letters concerned various marriage guidebooks, sex manuals, and purported impotence remedies.

The most significant correspondence was between "H. C. Barnet" and the Marston Remedy Company at 19 Park Place in downtown Manhattan. At the end of May 1898, just after renting the "Barnet" mailbox, "Barnet" had requested Marston's marriage guide and a month's supply of the impotence remedy it advertised. He received back a blank self-diagnosis form consisting of sixty-three detailed questions he needed to fill out and return, along with $5 and a urine sample, for the appropriate remedy to be sent to him.

The press was daily mocking the police for not solving the crime and for following clues developed by reporters. But Carey, whose visit to the Kutnow Brothers' office had kicked off the entire sequence of mailbox evidence, was quietly nailing down the last of those clues. He visited the Marston Company's office and obtained "Barnet's" completed questionnaire. The author gave his age as thirty-one—the same as Molineux's at the time—and his chest and waist measurements as thirty-seven and thirty-two inches, respectively, both of which corresponded exactly with those of Molineux. The real Barnet, by contrast, was a year older and had a forty-inch chest and an even larger waist.

The author of the questionnaire also stated that he was single and contemplating marriage, that he had once suffered from gonorrhea, and that there was a history of consumption in his family. Carey ascertained that Molineux's maternal grandmother had died of consumption.

Additional damning evidence came in the form of the so-called Burns letter, a note received by Dr. James Burns, a Manhattan physician. Dr. Burns had a side business selling an ointment called Marvelous Indian

Giant Salve, touted as a guaranteed cure for male "atrophy" (impotence) made from an ancient Mohawk tribe mix of buffalo fat, tree bark, and special herbs.

The handwritten note was later turned over to the police by an alert file clerk who'd been following the case in the newspapers. The note requested that Dr. Burns send the writer a sample box of the magic elixir for twenty-five cents. It was written on the same style of elegant light blue stationery with the fleur-de-lis, tri-crescent imprint that "H. Cornish" had used in two of his medicine requests. The return address was 6 Jersey Street in Newark, the location of the Morris Herrmann dye factory where Roland Molineux worked. And it was signed, not by any alias, but by Roland Molineux himself.

Art Carey further bolstered the circumstantial case when he interviewed Mary Melando, Molineux's housekeeper in his living quarters above the Morris Herrmann Company laboratory. Mamie, as she went by, had worked in the paint factory of General Molineux, Roland's father, where she was seduced, at age thirteen, by twenty-one-year-old Roland. Five years later, she followed Molineux to Morris Herrmann, where he installed her as a forewoman and personal maid while continuing their dalliances. She remained loyal to him, even after he dismissed her from her job when he began courting Blanche Chesebrough. Mamie offered information to the police only very reluctantly and was later tricked by Carey into entering New York so that she could be subpoenaed for trial.

She was honest enough, though, to supply Carey with what he was looking for when he interviewed her. He showed her the robin's-egg-blue stationery with the silver crescents used by "H. Cornish" to request samples of Kutnow's Powder and impotence remedies and by Molineux to obtain an atrophy cure under his own name. She said that in the fall of 1898, she had found six sheets of the identical notepaper in a cabinet drawer in Roland's apartment. Because she liked the classy stationery so much, she took three sheets for herself and left three for Molineux.

Carey also ascertained that the fatal Bromo-Seltzer package had been mailed from the general post office at City Hall Park between four and five o'clock on the afternoon of December 23, 1898. From three to about six that same afternoon, Molineux was at Morris Herrmann's Manhattan office at 255 Pearl Street, a mere ten minutes' walk away. Addressed to Cornish, the package arrived at the Knickerbocker Athletic Club on West Forty-Fifth Street on the morning of December 24.

It remained for everything to be tied together, which is where the handwriting experts came in. McClusky and Carey assembled all the various papers believed to be in Molineux's handwriting or known to have been written by him and laid them before William Kinsley, the nation's leading handwriting expert.

The Molineux materials Kinsley examined included the mailing label on the Bromo-Seltzer package sent to Cornish, the various notes and letters from "H. Cornish" and "H. C. Barnet," and the Burns letter requesting the Native American balm, which Molineux admitted was written by him. Kinsley declared that one man—Molineux—had written them all. Thirteen other handwriting experts backed up his conclusion.

Kinsley next matched the Molineux documents to handwriting samples Molineux voluntarily supplied to the police at their request. In the presence of the district attorney and his own lawyers, Molineux was asked to write whatever Kinsley, who was at the same table, dictated. Molineux confidently wrote various words, sentences, and numbers Kinsley had selected carefully from the other handwriting specimens the police had collected.

One of the things Molineux was asked to write was the address of the Knickerbocker Athletic Club. He spelled it "Fourty"-Fifth Street instead of *Forty*-Fifth—the same mistake made by the anonymous sender of the poisoned Bromo-Seltzer to Harry Cornish. From the police standpoint, it was case closed.

⊷▱◖▱⊷

Indicted in early 1899 for the murder of Katherine Adams, Molineux was imprisoned in the Tombs pending trial. Although the police and prosecutors believed that Molineux had murdered Henry Barnet as well, that alleged crime was not charged in the indictment. Since Barnet had taken calomel for his supposed diphtheria, the cause of his death was ambiguous.

Still, the prosecutors believed the poisoning of Barnet was highly relevant, as it gave Molineux the confidence to carry out a similar act of revenge upon his enemy Harry Cornish. Evidently Molineux decided at the last minute to eschew the use of poisoned Kutnow's Powder, which had killed Barnet, in favor of spiked Bromo-Seltzer in the guise of a Christmas present intended for Cornish.

Molineux went on trial in November 1899 in the Court of General Sessions, one of the courts that heard criminal cases in New York County. The presiding judge was well known to the public: John W. Goff, the cantankerous former chief counsel to the Lexow Committee. Goff, not someone any defendant would want against him, was convinced of Molineux's guilt, as evidenced by his consistent rulings in favor of the prosecution.

The trial would run nearly three months, the longest and most expensive murder trial in New York's history up to that time. It was also, in the opinion of many, the most sensational. It featured a heavy dosage of sex, a love triangle, a femme fatale, jealousy and hatred among friends and enemies, and, of course, poison. Blanche Chesebrough—Mrs. Molineux—attended, playing the role of the sorrowful wife, and General Molineux, the defendant's venerated father, sat by his son's side throughout. A true media circus, it might have been dubbed the trial of the century, except that it technically spanned two centuries, having started in the waning days of the nineteenth and ended early in the twentieth.

Convinced he would be acquitted, Molineux affected an air of nonchalance, almost boredom, throughout the trial, sometimes playing tic-tac-toe. His lawyers chose not to put him on the stand, nor any other defense witnesses, preferring to argue that the state had not proved its case.

It was a strategic mistake. On February 11, 1900, after eight hours of deliberation, the all-male jury of twelve found Roland Molineux guilty of the premeditated first-degree murder of Katherine Adams. Goff sentenced him to die in six weeks by the electric chair in Sing Sing, where he was sent to await his fate.

Molineux took the cell next to an equally famous convicted murderer sitting on death row: Dr. Samuel Kennedy. When Kennedy's conviction was overturned nine months later in favor of a new trial, Molineux, whose own case was on appeal, was the first to congratulate him. Six other death row inmates quickly joined the chorus of cheers.

Having already spent a year in the Tombs, Molineux sat on death row in Sing Sing for twenty long months as he awaited the appeals court's ruling. While in prison, he wrote a book called *The Room with the Little Door* about his experiences in Sing Sing. A visiting prison chaplain who remembered him from the Tombs described Molineux as a courteous gentleman who "received me with his usual blandness."

Finally, in October 1901 the state's highest court reversed Molineux's conviction. By a 4-to-3 margin, the appeals court ruled that Goff had improperly allowed testimony and prosecution argument in the Adams murder trial concerning Molineux's alleged poisoning of Henry Barnet.

The landmark decision established what would become known as the "Molineux rule." The court of appeals held that, with a few exceptions, the prosecution must limit its presentation of evidence to the crime charged in the indictment, not some prior crime or other bad acts of the defendant. Designed to avoid unfairly prejudicing the accused based on past conduct having nothing to do with the crime at issue, the Molineux rule remains a bedrock principle of both state and federal criminal procedure to this day. New York lawyers still move for a "Molineux hearing" to prevent a jury from hearing about a defendant's "prior bad acts."*

No longer on death row, Molineux was returned to the Tombs to

---

* Three of the appeals court judges thought that proof of Barnet's poisoning should have been allowed. They reasoned that it was relevant to establishing a modus operandi very similar to that involved in the Adams poisoning. Depending on the degree of similarity, modus operandi can be allowed today as an exception to the Molineux rule.

await his second trial. The rebuilt Tombs featured an overhead, enclosed Bridge of Sighs, ornately modeled on its namesake in Venice, Italy, connecting the prison with the criminal court building so that defendants could be shuttled back and forth without stepping outdoors. The old Bridge of Sighs, over which condemned prisoners walked to the gallows, had ceased serving that purpose when New York stopped hanging convicted murderers in the Tombs prison yard in favor of electrocution in Sing Sing.*

Roland Molineux would spend another year in the Tombs awaiting his second trial, which began in October 1902, more than three and a half years after his original arrest and imprisonment. This time he would take the stand in his own defense.

---

* The 1902 version of the Tombs was torn down in the 1940s. The colloquial Tombs appellation still attaches to the present-day Manhattan Detention Complex at 125 White Street, roughly in the same location. It consists of a jail and court facilities connected by an overhead enclosed bridgeway evoking somewhat the Bridge of Sighs, though no longer generally referred to by that name.

CHAPTER TWENTY-TWO

"HOW STRANGE IS PUBLIC OPINION"

During the time Roland Molineux sat in jail, much had changed in the world outside his prison walls. The century had turned, President McKinley had been assassinated, and President Theodore Roosevelt was planning to build the Panama Canal.

New York City had a new mayor, Columbia University president Seth Low, elected in November 1901 on a Fusion reform ticket that benefitted from another public revolt against Tammany outrages. Under Police Chief Devery and Boss Croker, New York had been as open to grafters as at any time since the years immediately preceding the Lexow investigation. Police corruption was about as bad, too, though now it was more centralized and focused on the profitable business of high-stakes gambling, under the control of a syndicate run by Devery, Big Tim Sullivan, and poolroom king Frank Farrell.

Devery was further tarnished by his shameful handling of the Tenderloin race riot in August 1900, one of the worst in the city's history. As mobs of Irishmen randomly beat hundreds of African American citizens, ostensibly in retaliation for a black man's having stabbed a white undercover cop to death, several hundred of Devery's men either stood by idly or intervened on behalf of the mob. The cops mercilessly clubbed the black Tenderloin residents, most of them recent migrants from the South. The *New York Herald* called it a "police riot," and reform groups placed the blame squarely on Devery and the Tammany-dominated police force.

Mayor Low fulfilled his campaign pledge to oust Devery and the figurehead police commissioner, Michael C. Murphy. Even Tammany was too embarrassed by Devery to protect him any longer. The following year, running for mayor as an independent, Devery received less than 1 percent of the vote, despite promising to give the people what they wanted: "beer and ham sandwiches." He retired from official public life and partnered with Farrell to buy the Baltimore Orioles American League baseball club, which they moved to New York and named the Highlanders in time for the 1903 season. The team would be renamed the Yankees in 1913 and sold by Devery and Farrell to Colonel Jacob Ruppert in 1915 after a string of losing seasons.

The 1901 election ended the sixteen-year reign of Boss Croker, who stepped down as Tammany's chieftain and sailed to Europe, this time for good, to raise horses on his castle estate in Dublin, Ireland. He was succeeded by a new, more enlightened grand sachem, a former saloonkeeper known as "Silent Charlie" Murphy. But it was the Big Feller, Tim Sullivan, who continued to wield the real power below Fourteenth Street, operating from his headquarters at the Occidental Hotel at the corner of Bowery and Broome Street.

The 1901 Fusion slate also brought in a new district attorney, political maverick William Travers Jerome, who assumed supervisory responsibility for the Molineux case. A first cousin of Lady Randolph (Jennie) Churchill, Winston's mother, Jerome had been the associate counsel, along with Frank Moss, in the Lexow Committee investigation. He went on to a minor judgeship in New York City but found a way to use the position to achieve celebrity. Casting off his judicial robes, Jerome personally led raids of gambling joints and high-end brothels. Wielding an axe and holding warrants for the arrest of John Does, he would smash his way into betting parlors, jump up on a gaming table, declare court in session, pull out a Bible to swear the witnesses, and administer justice right then and there.

In contrast to the low-key, colorless Seth Low atop the Fusion ticket, Jerome waged a spirited campaign in which he lambasted Tammany, Devery, and Croker by name at every turn in the fiercest of language. He vowed to bring to justice "that little bunch of criminals—yes, criminals; I say it advisedly—who for four long years have held our City of New York in their grasp." Cries of "the Second Teddy!" greeted candidate Jerome at his campaign stops. Zipping around the city by automobile to make speeches, he attracted an enthusiastic following of idealistic young men, including up-and-coming novelist Upton Sinclair.

In mock eulogies delivered at a huge victory rally on election night, Mark Twain told the giddy crowd that the hated Van Wyck, Devery, and Croker were no more and that Tammany itself was dead. It was a delicious riposte to those who had chanted "Reform has gone to hell!" along Broadway four years earlier.

Upon taking the district attorney's office in 1902, Jerome continued the raids he'd begun as a judge, earning the special enmity of Big Tim Sullivan. During the campaign, Sullivan had sneered that "Jerome lives on highballs and cigarettes," indulgences that Big Tim himself avoided. Jerome also had a young mistress, though Big Tim didn't know it.

Jerome, who had considered Theodore Roosevelt's excise campaign a case of good intentions gone astray, shrugged off Sullivan's jibe. "I have never found that my own thirst stopped at twelve o'clock on Saturday night and began again at five o'clock on Monday morning," he said. "I have always found that I was just about as thirsty on Sunday as on any other day."

Among the best-known gambling establishments Jerome shuttered was Shang Draper's opulent Tenderloin casino at 6–8 West Twenty-Eighth Street, which Draper had opened in the 1890s to replace the saloon where Johnny Irving and Mick the Walsh had met their deaths in

1883.* Jerome's invasion, conducted the night after Molineux's second trial got under way, recovered $800,000 taken from Draper's safe as his customers scampered out the back. Driven from business, Shang retired to Hot Springs, Arkansas, where he would die in 1913, thirty-five years after the Manhattan Savings robbery he planned with George Leslie, the man he may have murdered.

Jerome had a flair for public relations. On the night of December 1, 1902, his axe men crashed Richard Canfield's legendary casino at 5 East Forty-Fourth Street, a palatial, luxuriously furnished town house described by the *Times* as "the most magnificent gambling house in the United States." It was next door to Delmonico's, whose restaurant patrons came outside in their evening clothes and overcoats to watch Jerome follow a group of policemen up a ladder and climb through a shattered window into the elegant gaming rooms.

No gambling was in progress, Canfield having been tipped off in advance. But the lawmen started chopping up the luxurious interior anyway. Closeted away from the mahogany paneling, Chippendale furniture, Chinese porcelains, and paintings by Canfield's friend James Whistler, they found a treasure trove of gambling paraphernalia: roulette wheels, poker tables, and ivory chips, "each bearing on both sides," the *Times* reported, "the three interlaced crescents like that on the stationery of the Molineux case." It was a reference that required no explanation to the paper's readers.

His marquee establishment torn up and padlocked, Canfield fled the city, repairing to run his upstate gambling resort in Saratoga Springs before finally closing it in 1907. Once "the best known and wealthiest individual gambler in the world," in the words of the *Times*, Canfield would lose most of his fortune in the Panic of 1907 and be forced to sell his Whistler collection. He would die of a fractured skull in 1914 after stumbling on the steps of the Fourteenth Street subway station.

---

* Unlike Draper's original Sixth Avenue saloon, the casino building at 6–8 West Twenty-Eighth Street still stands.

On the same night that Jerome crashed Canfield's Manhattan casino in December 1902, a play titled *The Great Poison Mystery* opened in a theater in Jersey City. Its barely disguised characters needed no introduction to the audience: Robert Milando, the young head of a chemicals company and death row prisoner in Sing Sing facing a second trial; his father, General Milando; Robert's sweetheart, Blanche Marlboro; his enemy, Harrison Cornwall, athletic director of the Metropolitan Sporting Club; and Cornwall's aunt, Mrs. Adamson, who dies from drinking a headache remedy laced with cyanide of mercury. To wild applause, the accused Milando is pronounced innocent by the jury, and the villainous Cornwall is exposed as the true killer.

It was an absurdly melodramatic production—a "ridiculous paraphrase" of the actual case, the *Brooklyn Daily Eagle* reviewer called it—that never made it to Broadway. But while bad art, it had accurately imitated life. For three weeks earlier, Roland Molineux, the most famous convicted murderer in America still in jail, was acquitted in his second trial for murder.

The long passage of time between Molineux's first and second trials had proved to his advantage. For one thing, there was a new judge: in place of John W. Goff was John S. Lambert, who was more sympathetic to the defense and kept things moving along briskly. Some key prosecution witnesses had died or, in the case of Mary Melando, avoided the jurisdiction and couldn't be subpoenaed. New surprise alibi witnesses for Molineux came out of the woodwork four years after the murders with stories that were as questionable as they were belated, but they introduced an element of doubt.

The defense put on its own handwriting expert, David Carvalho, to rebut the state's experts' specimen comparisons. Like prosecution expert Daniel Ames, the highly credentialed Carvalho had been a defense expert in the famous 1899 treason case in France against Captain Alfred Dreyfus, in which handwriting evidence had played a major role. The defense also pointed the finger at Cornish as the real poisoner of his aunt. And Roland Molineux, who took the stand in his own defense this time, held up ably during his cross-examination.

Complicating life for the prosecution was the fact that all references to Henry Barnet's poisoning were kept from the jury. That rendered irrelevant both the letter box evidence to prove a common scheme and the evidence of Molineux's jealousy of Barnet over Blanche Chesebrough. She neither testified nor showed up at the second trial.

The jury needed only thirteen minutes of deliberation to return its verdict of not guilty. Among those who watched the joyful defendant and his father leave the courtroom in triumph was District Attorney Jerome, who made the pro forma motion to discharge the prisoner from the Tombs.

"Justice prevails. I am a happy man," Molineux declared to cheering onlookers outside, while his father issued a statement that read, "The strife is over, the battle won, and Might has lost, but Right has won."

Their joy would not last long.

＊⇒◎⇐＊

A week after Roland's acquittal, Blanche Chesebrough Molineux filed for a divorce in Sioux Falls, South Dakota, the quickie-divorce capital of America at the time. Her act especially dumbfounded General Molineux, who had worked hard to make her appear loyal to his son throughout the long ordeal. It seems in retrospect that she had been estranged from Roland the moment he first entered the Tombs.

Blanche married her divorce lawyer, Wallace Scott, and signed to become a singer, under the name of Blanche Molineux Scott, at Proctor's on Twenty-Third Street, the same theater where Dr. Samuel Kennedy claimed to have slept through a performance the night of Dolly Reynolds's murder. When General Molineux threatened suit to restrain her from using the Molineux name, Blanche abandoned the vaudeville effort and went back out west. She and Scott divorced, reconciled, divorced, and reconciled again before his death in an auto accident in 1930, after which she settled in New York. She lived her last years as an eccentric old woman, heavily made up and garishly dressed, dying in poverty, and obscurity, in 1954 at the age of eighty.

With his book on prison life published in 1903, Roland Molineux turned to further writing. In 1907, for the *New York Herald*, he covered the next "Trial of the Century," concerning the murder of socialite architect Stanford White by multimillionaire Harry Kendall Thaw. The case required no police work, as the mentally disturbed Thaw had shot White from two feet away in full view of hundreds of spectators at the rooftop restaurant of Madison Square Garden. Thaw held the gun aloft over White's fallen body and shouted, "He ruined my wife!" (or possibly "life"), a reference to White's prior sexual relationship, when he was forty-seven, with sixteen-year-old chorus girl Evelyn Nesbit, who had since married Thaw. As district attorney, William Travers Jerome handled both the first trial of Thaw, which produced a hung jury, and the second, in which Thaw was found not guilty by reason of insanity.

In 1913 Molineux authored a play, *The Man Inside*, a fictional, heavily didactic work centered on the theme of penal reform, a cause that had become dear to his heart. It was produced by famed impresario David Belasco but garnered negative reviews during its brief Broadway run. However, Roland's theatrical foray did yield some fruit: he married his much younger theatrical agent the same year.

Roland's behavior became increasingly erratic, though. The following year, he suffered a nervous breakdown and was sent to a sanitarium in Babylon, Long Island. After escaping from there, half clad underneath a bathrobe, he ran down the main street, shrieking incoherently and knocking down everyone in his path until subdued and thrown in jail. "Alienists" (the name then for psychologists) pronounced him insane.

Roland Molineux died on November 2, 1917, at age fifty-one, a result, according to the autopsy, of paresis, or damage to the brain brought on by untreated syphilis. A degenerative disease, it had driven him to madness and perhaps, almost twenty years earlier, to murder.

Did Molineux mail the fatal poison that killed Katherine Adams, a stranger to him, and to Henry Barnet, his onetime close friend? Close students of the case have divided on the question over the years.

As for Art Carey, he wrote in his memoirs in 1930 that he preferred not to express an opinion, saying it would avail nothing so many years later. But between the lines, he seemed to indicate his true feelings. "Many New Yorkers who remember the trials of Molineux still consider him innocent," Carey wrote. "How strange is public opinion, sometimes."

CHAPTER TWENTY-THREE

RETURN OF THE GANGS

"They shot up the town in regular Wild West style," said one of Inspector Max Schmittberger's detectives who witnessed the scene at Rivington and Allen Streets on the hot summer night of September 15, 1903.

At about two in the morning, a pair of rival gangs squared off in a ferocious gunfight under the arch of the Second Avenue elevated train. As terrified residents and business owners barred their doors and pedestrians ducked for cover, more than fifty gangsters rained a fusillade of bullets upon one another. Shots ricocheted off the iron railway pillars and shattered tenement and storefront windows. The melee left one man dead, another dying, and others seriously wounded before reserves from three police stations were able to chase off the antagonists and make arrests.

The Battle of Rivington Street, as it became known, was between the two most powerful gangs in New York: an Italian outfit known as the Paul Kelly Association, and the Eastman gang, which was predominantly Jewish. They were led, respectively, by the dapper Paul Kelly and the

Edward "Monk" Eastman, leader of the most feared Jewish street gang in New York just after the turn of the century. He turned extortion into a business and sent his men out each day, "just like mechanics goin' to work."

thuggish Monk Eastman. Kelly and Eastman were the most feared hoodlums in the city since Danny Driscoll, the last great Irish gang leader of Gilded Age New York.

The pair's ascendancy coincided with the mass migration of southern Italians and eastern European Jews to New York that began in the 1890s and had accelerated since. With it came a resumption of violent gang activity that the NYPD had subdued, at least temporarily, when it drove the Whyos out of existence in the early to mid-1890s. Some Irish gangs were still around or continued to form over the next decade, among them the West Side's Gophers and Hudson Dusters, and the East Side's Gas House Gang and Car Barn Gang. But Jews and Italians now took pride of place in New York's underworld.

Paul Kelly, despite his Irish-sounding name, was born Paolo Antonio Vaccarelli in New York City in 1876 to parents from Potenza in southern Italy. And Eastman, widely assumed to be Jewish, or perhaps Irish, because he often went by the alias William Delaney, was apparently of

The Italian Paul Kelly (real name Paul Vaccarelli), Eastman's rival gang leader, was closer to most people's concept of an urbane, pin-striped twentieth-century gangster.

English ancestry. He was born Edward Eastman in Lower Manhattan in 1873, to a New Hampshire–born, respectable wallpaper hanger and his Anglo-Saxon wife.*

Following his parents' divorce when he was a boy, Monk lived for a time with his mother and grandfather on East Seventy-Fifth Street in Manhattan, then in Brooklyn, before making his way back to the Lower East Side. It was from the tenements there that most of Monk's eventual gang members would come—young German, Russian, and Polish Jews, nearly all of them under age twenty-five.

From around the turn of the century, Kelly and Eastman vied for dominance of the area along the Bowery below Fourteenth Street.

---

* Herbert Asbury and other writers contend that Eastman was born Edward Osterman in the Williamsburg section of Brooklyn to a Jewish restaurant owner. Eastman, who was wont to mask his identity, listed himself in the 1900 census as having been born in New York City in 1876 to German-born parents.

Monk's gang patrolled down to about present-day Chinatown and east to the river, while Kelly's Italian crew held sway farther to the north and west. Both outfits trafficked in the same illegal activities—gambling, prostitution, and thievery—so their proximity on the Lower East Side brought them into competition for local rackets.

The Battle of Rivington Street had begun on September 15 at nine-thirty at night in Livingston's saloon at First Avenue and East First Street just above Houston Street. As the fighting moved south, the word went out for both gangs to send in reinforcements. The scuffling spread two lengthy blocks west to the Bowery and finally, almost five hours later, another few long blocks south and east to the corner of Rivington and Allen Streets. The immediate catalyst for the gunfight under the Allen Street railway arch was a dispute over the spoils of the card game stuss, or "Jewish faro," at a nearby joint, which Eastman claimed for himself.

Despite their rivalry, the two enemy gangs shared the same political patron, Big Tim Sullivan, for whom they provided Election Day muscle and repeater votes in return for his keeping them out of jail. Whenever an Eastman or Kelly found himself arrested, Big Tim would have bail money and a Tammany-appointed lawyer on hand in court to secure a quick release. If the case went forward, a corrupt or malleable judge could usually be prevailed upon to lessen any punishment.

Although Irish through and through, Big Tim harbored few ethno-religious prejudices. He'd don a yarmulke if the occasion called for it, and he later pushed the bill to make Columbus Day a state holiday in New York to celebrate Italian heritage.

He could also count. With the Irish percentage of the city's population declining, Sullivan welcomed Jews and Italian immigrants into his Tammany melting pot as fast as they could come. And he used mob leaders Kelly and Eastman to keep them there. Election days were when rival gangs ceased their warfare and worked together toward a common goal.

The two gangs' chieftains were studies in contrast. Monk Eastman, an ex-saloon bouncer (or sheriff, as they were called), looked like a villain out of a *Dick Tracy* cartoon. He was short and squat (five foot six, 167 pounds) and thick-necked, with a bullet-shaped head, cauliflower ears, a face full of knife scars, and a broken, pug-shaped nose. Two upper teeth were capped in gold, and a lower one was missing. Although he dressed expensively, his suits were ill-fitting, and his perennially unkempt hair was topped by a derby several sizes too small. He spoke in the stereotypical New York dialect: "Toity-toid" Street, "Toid" Avenue, and "dems," "dese," and "dose."

Some thought he'd been nicknamed Monk because he looked like a chimpanzee. But others maintain it was because he climbed like one. He displayed great agility in scaling the sides of buildings, swinging like an ape through windows in upper stories to carry out burglaries.

An eager brawler, Eastman relished leading his men into club-wielding, ear-biting fights. Early in his career, he'd regularly worn brass knuckles as a bouncer at the New Irving Dance Hall at Broome and Norfolk Streets, and was said to have cut a notch in those metal weapons every time he battered an unruly customer. Legend holds that one night he waylaid a man who was minding his own business while quietly drinking at the bar. Eastman explained that he "had forty-nine nicks in me stick, an' I wanted to make it an even fifty." But he drew the line at bludgeoning women. "I only give her a little poke, just enough to put a shanty on her glimmer [give her a black eye], but I always takes off me knucks first," he was quoted as saying, at least according to yarn spinner Herbert Asbury.

In time, Eastman became adept with a revolver and was quick to use it. Once, in 1901, he practiced by shooting out the windows of Public School No. 110, across the street from a Broome Street pet store he operated as a front for his illegal operations. He stopped after the headmistress ran out and scolded him for scaring and endangering the children inside, including a couple of his own. "Yer all right," Eastman told her, she recalled later to *The New York Times*. "Yer a good sport f'r not callin' th' cops."

Eastman could take a bullet or two as well. That same year, 1901, he was shot—fatally, it was thought—by the Donovan brothers, saloon-keeper enemies who decided to strike first before Monk could move against them. Monk had been drinking in Assemblyman Charles "Silver Dollar" Smith's saloon at 64 Essex Street (so named because its floor was inlaid with real silver dollars), where he'd worked as a bouncer before graduating to the New Irving. "Peggy" (or "Piggy") Donovan entered the saloon and opened fire without warning, missing Monk but wounding another bar patron.

Monk ran into the street, pursued by the two Donovans, who shouted, "Stop, thief!" As Eastman stated later, "Two men grabbed me, thinking I was a thief. 'Peggy' Donovan reached me first. He pulled his revolver, pressed it against my stomach and fired into my abdomen. I fell to the sidewalk. Then the other brother [James] shot me behind the ear as I lay on the walk."

Monk crawled his way to Gouverneur Hospital, nearly a mile away on Water Street. Told by doctors he was going to die, he named his killers. Much to the surprise of everyone, including readers of *The New York Times*, which had pronounced him dead, Monk survived. True to the gangland code, he retracted his earlier deathbed statement and refused to provide evidence against his attackers, instead vowing to obtain his private revenge.

For all his toughness, Monk did have a soft spot—for small animals and birds ("boids," as he pronounced it). He listed himself as a "bird salesman" in the 1900 census, and, according to one oft-repeated, if unsubstantiated, story, he became so attached to the hundreds of cats and pigeons he kept at his Broome Street shop that he refused to sell any of them.

Eastman also set up another front: a bicycle rental store that supplied wheels for his gang members. (A modern writer has dubbed it "the prototype for Citi Bike," the public bicycle-sharing system in New York.) One of Monk's cohorts, a Fagin-like figure named Simon Erenstoft, who went by "Crazy Butch," headed Eastman's Squab Wheelmen. They were named in honor of Monk's favorite bird. Butch was known to ride his bike into people, knock them over, and start an argument while associates picked their pockets.

In contrast to the brutish Monk Eastman, Paul Kelly was more in line with most people's concept of an urbane, pin-striped twentieth-century gangster. Despite being only five foot two or three, with a slightly flattened nose from early years as a lightweight boxer, he was a charming, silk-bow-tied, carefully coiffed figure who kept his nails manicured and his hair well oiled and flattened. He donned flashy jewelry—whether his own or pilfered from others—and wore patent leather shoes. He also spoke multiple languages and enjoyed classical music and literature.

According to one relatively contemporaneous story, a married couple, accompanied by a central office police detective, went slumming downtown in search of the famous gangster Paul Kelly. They entered Mike Lyons's Bowery restaurant, where they were squeezed into a table with some seedy-looking diners. The woman turned to the more elegant tablemate seated to her left and began engaging in conversation with him. He was "a dark, sallow little man" who spoke in low, quiet tones, alternating among Italian, French, and English with the other patrons. When the three visitors were back in the street, the woman expressed astonishment that a man of such grace and culture should be found in such crude surroundings. "Surely, he doesn't belong there," she said. "Who is he?"

"Who is he?" repeated the central office detective. "I thought your hubby wised you up. That's Paul Kelly."

That Kelly was stylish doesn't mean he wasn't a tough. He proved it on Democratic primary election day in September 1901, in the contest for the Second Assembly District (the old Fourth Ward along the East River). Kelly's repeaters and shoulder hitters beat up the would-be voters for Tammany old-timer Paddy Divver, delivering the victory instead to Big Tim Sullivan's man, upstart Tom Foley (later mentor to future New York governor Al Smith and for whom Foley Square in Lower Manhattan is named).

Three months later, Sullivan repaid the favor when Kelly was charged with first-degree assault for beating and robbing a man of a watch and chain. Given his record of two prior assaults, the offense carried a ten- to twenty-year sentence, but Sullivan's boys got the police to reduce it to third-degree assault, for which Recorder John Goff was constrained to sentence Kelly to nine months in jail upon his conviction. Calling the result "shameful," a disgusted Goff barked at Kelly, "They tried in every way in their power to shield you."

A skilled amateur boxer and wrestler from the time he was a teenager, Kelly assumed his Irish name because it led to greater bookings as a semiprofessional. (It would be hard to call any boxer a "professional" in those days because the sport remained illegal.) Even after his career turned to professional gangsterism, he liked to fight "just to keep in trainin'." He was arrested several times both for hosting and participating in illegal prizefights, including one, in 1901, in which he reportedly knocked three men down in a half hour.

Kelly could whip men far greater in size, as in 1903, when the twenty-seven-year-old bantamweight Italian bested a six-foot, 230-pound East-man man. The Eastmans' Jack Shimsky had insulted Kelly, calling him a "runt" upon running into him in a Bowery saloon. Challenges issued and accepted, the pair stripped to the waist and donned skintight gloves for a bout in the saloon's basement, with beer kegs marking the corners of the makeshift ring.

Onlookers from both gangs wagered a total of $1,800 on the refereed match, which ended when Kelly knocked Shimsky to the floor in the third round. After his seconds carried him from the ring, Shimsky approached Kelly and said, "You've done me square, an' I want to shake. What'll you have?" And then a Kelly drank with an Eastman, marking a cease-fire between the two gangs.

When it came to gang warfare not governed by the Marquess of Queensberry rules, Kelly preferred directing operations from his headquarters, originally a dingy dive located at 190 Mulberry Street. Fittingly, a huge portrait of Big Tim Sullivan hung above the bar there. Kelly had a bodyguard as well—"Eat 'Em Up" Jack McManus, formerly the bouncer at McGurk's Suicide Hall.

Kelly was happily married for eight years before he was widowed in 1908, then long happily married again. By contrast, Eastman's two wives seem to have taken a backseat to the many ladies of the evening he squired about town. Both his wives may have been streetwalkers themselves before he married them, and it's not clear he ever legally divorced the first one, whom he married in 1896.

Although Kelly was the suaver and more sophisticated of the two gang leaders, it was the loutish, unpolished Monk Eastman who was the greater innovator and trailblazer in the development of organized crime in New York. "Kelly stood second in importance to Eastman," the *New-York Tribune* opined retrospectively.

Eastman rose in the underworld through the ranks of existing networks of gangs, gradually at first. Over time, he muscled aside some of his rivals and formed alliances with others. "I was in wrong from a kid," he would say later. "I was an ordinary kind of East Side boy, and I got in with a gang. Then I got an ambition to be leader of the gang, and I fought my way to the top."

At the outset of his career, while serving as a saloon bouncer, Eastman was a garden-variety thief, with some minor run-ins with the law in the early 1890s. His first serious arrest came in 1898, when he was caught carrying burglars' tools. Giving his name as William Murray, he was sent to prison on Blackwell's Island for three months. He'd be apprehended many more times over the next five years—more than a hundred, by one estimate—but never convicted of a crime. The *World* called him not only the most notorious but also "certainly the most immune thug in New York, if not in America."

Eastman recruited his gang members first from among his assistants at the New Irving Dance Hall, then from the Lower East Side tenements. He began managing a group of young Jewish pickpockets and branched out into the more lucrative "cadet" business—that is, pimping and procuring women to ply their trade as prostitutes. He also began exerting his influence over gambling operations, especially the popular stuss, from which he derived a regular take.

But it occurred to Eastman that he could greatly supplement his direct revenue streams by extorting the profits of others. He targeted both legitimate businesses (pushcart peddlers, stores, and restaurants) and illegal ones (gambling houses and brothels). An effective protection racket, he came to realize, required only two things: a willingness to intimidate and threaten people with physical harm and enough muscle and manpower to back up the bravado. Violence ruled, and gang size mattered.

And so, Eastman set about to grow his legion of thugs by enlisting them from anywhere he could find them. By the turn of the century, he was commanding a paramilitary army of thieves, pickpockets, prostitutes, head crackers, and leg breakers on the Lower East Side. Herbert Asbury put their strength at twelve hundred, likely an exaggeration. (He ascribed similar numbers to Kelly's gang.) A more realistic estimate would place the total number of regulars for both gangs at a few hundred at any given time, swelling to five hundred or more on Election Day, when repeaters were in high demand.

Still, by all accounts, the Eastman gang was more powerful than any of its predecessors. As his biographer Neil Hanson has observed, "Monk's gang was less a single entity, like one of the old Irish gangs, than a series of separate but interlinked organizations." He could augment his forces by calling up all his affiliates and his juvenile gangs, known as the Junior Eastmans. He even used women as gun-toting auxiliaries; one of them, fifteen-year-old Driga "Bridget" Colonna, "could be seen flourishing a revolver and joining in the furious rushes of the gang with all the abandon of a young brigand."

One of Monk's enforcers was Max Zweifach, a trigger-happy lieutenant who once shot a man dead over a card game. Zweifach, who went by the name "Kid Twist," would walk into a gambling joint and demand $50, promising to "shoot up your [expletive] place" if the proprietor refused. When the money was coughed up, he'd say, "I'll see you again in about a month."

As the Lexow investigation had revealed, the New York police also routinely extorted money from both permitted and illicit businesses. But what the cops offered was protection from the *law*. Monk Eastman was offering something different: protection from *crime*—namely, his own.

Eastman was surely not the first criminal to make money from extortion, but he took it to a degree that was unprecedented. This was large-scale organized crime, and Monk was New York's first true big-time racketeer. And while he may not have looked like a businessman, he acted like one. He sent his men out each day, "just like mechanics goin' to work," one gangster recalled. He also reputedly required his deputies to file written reports of the criminal jobs they'd been hired to perform. Although he led by brute force and fear, he had, *The New York Times* conceded, "a crude instinct for leadership and enough talent for organization to maintain a 'gang' of lesser ruffians."

One of the first gangsters to see the profit potential in labor disputes, Eastman provided muscle to whoever hired him—whether management seeking to bust the heads of picketing union workers, or unions wanting to do the same to strikebreaking scabs. His fee was $7.50 a day, or $10 for Monk to do the job himself.

According to a 1903 *New York World* article, the Eastmans, as well as Kelly's gang, also maintained a written price list for crimes they were willing to commit for hire:

For an ordinary punching	**$5**
For an ordinary punching and a razor cut to the face	**$15**
For a beating with brass knuckles	**$30**
For a beating that will send a victim to the hospital	**$50**
For a stabbing	**$75**
For a murder	**$100**

This story echoes Herbert Asbury's essentially debunked tale crediting the Whyos with keeping a similar price list. The later anecdote might be an urban legend as well. But whether there was a formal price list, "doing up" a man for cash was indeed part of Eastman's business model. He accepted commissions from individuals and organizations to inflict violence on their enemies or to forcefully collect debts they were owed. One who used his services was a young card game operator and loan shark artist named Arnold Rothstein, who went on to become the nation's leading gambler and the fixer of the 1919 World Series, in which eight members of the American League champion Chicago White Sox threw the series to the opposing Cincinnati Reds, forever branding the losers as the "Black Sox."

In October 1903 two Eastman gang members were charged with accepting $300 from a wealthy woman either to disfigure her dentist husband, from whom she was separated, by throwing acid in his face or to do away with him altogether. The plot was foiled when a rival gang, whom the woman had originally approached for the job before she hired the Eastmans, warned the man.

On another occasion, several of Monk's goons were hired to attack two members of an Orchard Street Jewish congregation at the behest of a rival faction that was disputing the election of synagogue officers. The thugs allegedly quoted a cut-rate price of $15 for killing and $10 for maiming with brass knuckles and iron bars. The victims were knocked unconscious, cut in the face, and one of them was left almost without one of his eyes before the culprits escaped.

The most fabled of Eastman's commission jobs, though, was one he chose to carry out himself. Many sources have quoted him as saying, "I like to beat up a guy once in a while. It keeps me hand in." The quote is probably fanciful, but the sentiment was real. This particular hands-on engagement would be his most notorious brush with the law, and it came closer to sending him up the river, for a long time, than anything he'd done previously.

◂┈═◉ ◉═┈▸

CHAPTER TWENTY-FOUR

SKATING

David Lamar—or Lewis, or Levy, or Simon Wolf, or Isaac Frankenstein, or any other of the many pseudonyms he used—was better known as "the Wolf of Wall Street." He was a "plunger": someone who shorted (bet against) stocks while creating false rumors of trouble for the targeted corporations to drive down their share prices so that he could turn a hefty selling profit.

In the summer of 1903, the fraudster Lamar hired Eastman to beat up a coachman who had disobeyed Mrs. Lamar's order to fetch her runaway dog. Just as the coachman was about to give his evidence against Lamar in a New Jersey police court on an assault charge, and was having his shoes shined for the occasion, he was set upon by Eastman and one of Monk's thugs. They busted the man in the jaw, knocked out some teeth, cut his face, and left him unconscious and all but dead. Arrested by detectives in New York, Monk told them they'd better watch themselves. He "cut some ice in this town," he said, and had "made" half the big politicians in New York.

Extradited to New Jersey for trial, Monk seemed to be headed for conviction this time. The victim had quickly identified him and his co-hort from photographs in the rogues' gallery, then picked them out of a lineup. Lamar admitted hiring Eastman, but claimed it was merely to guard his wife and home, an assertion nobody believed.

Disregarding the overwhelming evidence of guilt, the jury acquitted Lamar, Eastman, and the other Eastman ruffian. Aware of rumors that they'd been bought, the jurors beat a hasty retreat from the courthouse and were hooted by the spectators. For their part, Monk Eastman and his accomplice professed surprise when informed of the verdict by a prison official, telling him he must be joking.

The acquittal came a month after the Battle of Rivington Street, which took place while Eastman was out on bail in the Lamar case. Characteristically, Eastman, who'd carried a revolver into the Rivington Street affray, skated that time as well. He was arrested on suspicion of shooting twenty-seven-year-old Paul Kelly Association member Michael Donovan, who died that night. The police speculated that Monk had finally gotten revenge for his near-fatal shooting in April 1901 by the Donovan brothers, thought to be relatives of the slain man.

Represented as usual by Tammany lawyers, Eastman was discharged the next morning for lack of evidence. Monk maintained he'd just been passing by, unarmed, when he heard the shooting start. The other mortally wounded Kelly man, before dying, said he'd been shot not by any Eastman but by an NYPD officer, who was later cleared on the grounds that he acted in self-defense.

Of the roughly twenty thugs who were apprehended following the Rivington Street shootout, only one ended up going to jail. He was a Monk lieutenant named George "Lolly" Meyers, who'd robbed an Allen Street saloonkeeper at gunpoint and shot another man in the cheek. Because—and probably only because—the presiding judge in his criminal case was John W. Goff, the sentence was a harsh one: fourteen years of hard labor in state prison.

Almost all popular histories describe the Battle of Rivington Street as the culmination of a bloody Hatfields and McCoys–style feud between the Eastmans and Kellys that had been raging a year or more. Kelly, in turn, is invariably described as having been the head of the Five Points gang, or Five Pointers, named for the famous slum neighborhood that so many prior rowdies had made their dominion.

But some more recent crime historians persuasively contend that Paul Kelly was never a member, let alone the leader of the Five Points gang, a multiethnic if mostly Italian collection of hoodlums whose membership and leadership were constantly in flux. Cofounded by boxing manager and saloonkeeper Jack Sirocco and boxer and future politician Giovanni "Jimmy Kelly" DeSalvio, the Five Pointers, like Paul Kelly's gang, were connected with Tammany Hall.

Business-oriented gangsters frequently switched sides in those days, and keeping track of the latest shifts in membership and loyalties wasn't easy. Gang members didn't wear name tags, and they were prone to giving out misinformation. In some cases, the newspapers or even the police got gang leaders or members mixed up, and subsequent writers have compounded the errors. It's possible that Paul Kelly and his association were allied with the Five Pointers at some juncture, but, for the most part, they were entirely separate, and by 1905, they clearly were rival groups.

Geography provides further clues to indicate that Paul Kelly wasn't a Five Pointer. Kelly was not from the Five Points, never lived there, and never made his headquarters in that neighborhood. His association typically hung out farther uptown on the Lower East Side, its headquarters always moving north: from 190 Mulberry Street in 1901, to 24 Stanton Street by mid-1903, and, finally, by 1905, to a pair of interconnected buildings at 57 and 59 Great Jones Street. There Kelly ran his misleadingly named New Brighton Athletic Club—in reality, a seedy saloon and dance hall—and the adjacent Little Naples Café, christened in honor of his gang's mostly Neapolitan makeup. (The two structures, however decrepit, still stand today.) Kelly's association also had a branch at 111th Street and Second Avenue in the Little Italy section of East Harlem.

Unlike Kelly's gang, the Five Pointers did operate out of the old Five Points area, with headquarters, in 1902, at 126 White Street and, by

1905, at a piano dive bar at 12 Pell Street in Chinatown called the Pelham. Its unfortunate nickname, Nigger Mike's, was for the saloon's dark-complexioned Russian Jewish owner, gangster Mike Salter (sometimes spelled "Saulter").

Gang histories commonly state that Salter's Pelham Chinatown saloon marked the lower boundary of disputed turf between the Eastmans on the one hand and Paul Kelly's gang on the other. It's not clear whether that is fact or legend, and the Kelly Association's involvement in that dispute, if any, is uncertain. But in either event, the Pelham, a popular slumming place for rich and famous uptowners, provides us with an appropriate entry point for a trip to Chinatown and a brief detour from the Kelly-Eastman rivalry.

⋯⇌ ⇋⋯

At the turn of the century in New York, Chinatown was a regular stop for sightseers who were led on paid tours by a Pelham regular, the pseudophilosopher and vaudevillian sage Chuck Connors. An Irish ex-boxer and Tammany hack, Connors liked to show slummers fake opium dens filled with white women and Chinese men posing as addicts.

Irving Berlin also worked at Salter's café as a singing waiter and wrote his first song there. He recalled later that he "never mingled with the real tough people, so-called gorillas," but kept strictly to business—although among his jobs was picking up heavy laxatives from a nearby drugstore that Salter used to spike the drinks of disfavored customers.

Curiously, despite their proximity to Chinatown, neither the Eastmans nor the Bowery's Italian gangs tried to horn in on the lucrative gambling, opium, and prostitution operations run by Chinatown's indigenous criminal organizations, known as tongs. A sort of Chinese Mafia with some benevolent attributes, the highly organized tongs independently controlled their own grafting and delivery of local social services. They handed over a portion of their enforced tribute to crooked cops or to Tammany politicians, particularly Big Tim Sullivan, as necessary, for protection. The so-called mayor of Chinatown, bearded Tom Lee—who was Asian, not white—was himself a Tammany-connected politician who got himself named a New York County deputy sheriff.

The long-running battles between Lee's On Leong Tong and the rival Hip Sings, a tong led by the young upstart Mock Duck, were no less bitter or vicious than those between the Jewish and Italian gangs. The two leaders each had a price on the other's head, and some murderous exchanges between their groups took place at a sharp bend on Doyers Street. It was known as the Bloody Angle, for the perfect ambushing spots it offered to hired shooters and hatchet men. Miraculously, both Tom Lee and Mock Duck survived repeated attempts on their lives, aided by the chain-mail shirts they took to wearing.

But the tong wars involved exclusively Asians killing Asians, and the tongs never sought influence in New York beyond their small Chinatown enclave, then consisting of little more than Mott and Pell Streets and Doyers in between. As a result, the tongs attracted less police and public attention than the Jewish and Italian gangsters did.

While Tammany used the tongs to turn out Chinese registered voters on Election Day, there weren't many of them. Police intervention in Chinatown's affairs was generally limited to periodic raids on gambling houses—fan-tan was the game of choice—in furtherance of the cops' never-ending efforts to collect bribes. The tong wars would rage on and off for the remainder of the decade before ending in a truce.

⋅→⋙ ⋘←⋅

For all the stories about a supposed long-running war between the Kelly and Eastman gangs, there is no evidence that the two leaders were mortal enemies before the Battle of Rivington Street. Most of Monk Eastman's pitched, bloody encounters that predated the Rivington Street gunfight were with the Five Pointers, not with the Paul Kelly Association, which wasn't even mentioned in the newspaper accounts of the clashes.

The Eastmans also regularly fought with and eventually defeated the Yakey Yakes, an old Irish gang from around Water and Cherry Streets that was in steep decline. Throughout 1902 and into 1903, it seemed as if Monk's minions were involved in almost nightly shootings with one group or another.

Tammany leaders such as Big Tim Sullivan and Alderman Tom Foley didn't like what they were seeing. Tammany already had a reputation for coddling criminals, and this open gang warfare threatened to further tarnish the society's image. Following a series of particularly bloody encounters between the Eastmans and Five Pointers in 1902, Foley brokered a cease-fire. If they continued to behave like fighting Kentucky mountaineers, he told them, then Tammany would withdraw its political protection. The respective representatives gave their word that they would "never more be bad."

The promise was not to be fulfilled. By the following July 4, the two factions were all chummy, celebrating together on a chowder excursion to New Dorp, Staten Island. But when six hundred of the revelers arrived back in New York by ferry at midnight, they marched up Broadway behind a big brass band and fired their revolvers in the air on the way to Mulberry Bend Park. A small contingent of fifteen police officers tried to restore order, but the unruly gangsters overpowered them, and the officers were able to make only two arrests.

Ten weeks later, the Battle of Rivington Street provoked public outrage. Occasional shootouts between Lower East Side gangsters were one thing, and Chinatown tong wars didn't much concern the average New Yorker. But now, with the Rivington Street affair, ordinary citizens had been caught in the cross fire. Tammany had to do something. Foley negotiated another truce, this time between the city's two premier gang leaders, Monk Eastman and Paul Kelly.

They met face-to-face in the Palm, Monk's Chrystie Street headquarters, where peace was declared. Foley organized a ball in his district at which Monk and Kelly made a public show of their settlement while gang members and their prostitutes whooped it up. "Each gang danced with the best girls of the other, and everybody shook hands," *The Sun* would recall later.

Another group fed up with gang warfare was the NYPD. The police commissioner was retired general Francis V. Greene, a West Point graduate and Spanish-American War hero. His appointment by Mayor Seth Low in December 1902 had the blessing of their mutual friend, now president, Theodore Roosevelt, who was just coming off his successful mediation of the anthracite coal strike that threatened a nationwide coal shortage that winter.

But the commissioner was not interested in compromise. The day after the Battle of Rivington Street, emerging from a conference with Inspector Max Schmittberger, Greene declared, "There will be no more of that kind of lawlessness, if I can help it. There is entirely too much of it." Voicing the police department's frustration, Schmittberger said of the gangs, "We have arrested them time and time again, but the magistrates let them go." Greene unleashed Schmittberger to crack down on the Lower East Side mobsters.

Just before midnight on September 19, 1903, four nights after the Rivington Street gun blaze, Schmittberger led twenty-five plainclothesmen in what *The New York Times* called "a spectacular raid" on a gathering of the Paul Kelly Association at its 24 Stanton Street headquarters. Proceeding without warrants, the police appeared at the club's doorsteps, when a detective who'd been working the Lower East Side opened the front door and entered. Several of the association members, recognizing the man, threw chairs at him and made a rush for him, but they were met by Schmittberger and his men, who poured into the room. The gang members then bolted toward the windows, only to find them guarded by police. The gangmen surged back against Schmittberger's policemen and, as the *Times* put it euphemistically, "were treated with scant courtesy."

At that point, Schmittberger jumped on a table and shouted, "This meeting is adjourned, and it is the last meeting you'll ever hold here! The Paul Kelly Association is dead from now on!" Three of the gangsters who were caught trying to conceal pistols were arrested, and the others, told to vacate the premises, were pummeled as they exited. Schmittberger confiscated some papers and had his men trash the place, breaking chairs and wrecking the rest of the contents. "You cannot deal too severely with that class of men," the inspector said afterward. "We will attend to the other gangs in a similar way."

Two nights later, Schmittberger took about two dozen men on a raid of the Eastman gang's haunts around the Bowery. Disguised as motormen, butchers, and street sweepers (some of them wearing false beards and mustaches), detectives arrested seventeen Eastmans and one member of the Five Points gang on various charges, including carrying concealed weapons, possession of knockout drops, or, when nothing better could be pinned on them, vagrancy. After that, Schmittberger and eight of his men shadowed Monk everywhere he went. Schmittberger declared that Monk's reign of terror was at an end. "I don't expect to have much more trouble with Eastman," he told the press.

Eastman continued to be hounded by the cops even as he kept avoiding conviction. In December 1903 he was arrested, along with eight of his followers, for smoking opium in a house on Avenue A on the Lower East Side. Acting on a tip from an informant, detectives went to the house at one in the morning and, using the password the tipster gave them ("smoke up"), pushed through the door when someone inside opened it for them. The cops found nine men lying down amid pipes and bowls of opium. They recognized one of the smokers as Eastman, who gave his name as William Smith, a printer.

Monk was let go, but the following week was arrested again, together with seven of his associates, this time on suspicion of pickpocketing spectators at a Madison Square Garden bicycle race. Plainclothes detectives, ordered by Inspector McClusky to apprehend any known thieves on sight, spotted Monk and took him and his men into custody "on general principles," proving that the spirit of McClusky's mentor, Thomas Byrnes, still lived. The Sun referred to the police action, somewhat facetiously, as "Eastman's weekly arrest."

But the police court judge discharged the prisoners because no incriminating evidence was found in their possession, and they couldn't lawfully be detained simply for being present in a public place. "We can arrest Eastman at any time, but we can't convict him," said McClusky, who'd been promoted to inspector in 1903 and made head of the detective bureau. McClusky said he doubted Eastman could be convicted even if he were seen sticking a knife into his victim on Broadway in broad daylight, sworn to by a score of reputable witnesses.

Three weeks later, on January 1, 1904, another judge released Monk and six of his gang members after they were arrested for venturing below the dead line on New Year's Eve, allegedly to pick the pockets of a crowd that had gathered to listen to the Trinity Church chimes. (Byrnes's dead line, which Chief Peter Conlin had pronounced a dead letter in 1895, apparently retained some life.) Monk and his pals left the court mumbling curses under their breaths and threatening the police. "I say it's getting to be a pretty pass when a citizen, an innocent citizen, can't walk the streets of New York without getting pinched," Eastman told reporters.

Monk claimed the police had even detained him the week before to prevent him from attending his mother's funeral in Brooklyn. "Like a good, dutiful son, I starts to go to her funeral. I ain't in the doorway before a copper comes up to me and says, 'I want you, "Monk."' He let me go to me mother's funeral? Not on your life. Pinched me right there, and the funeral went off without the 'Monk.' What did they do with me? Let me go after they had made me miss my mother's funeral." The veracity of his accusation is questionable, given that Monk had buried his mother the day before Thanksgiving, a full month earlier. In any event, after finishing his speech, Eastman and his gang friends made for their haunt on Forsyth Street to begin celebrating the new year. "They ain't got nothin' on me," he crowed. "Bet your life they ain't."

But the walls were closing in on the Monk. He was "forced by the police to retire from more active operations," the *New York World* reported. His gang laid low, turning its attention to training a new crop of Junior Eastmans in thievery. The gangsters recruited kids from Lower East Side public schools to attend "Fagin kindergartens," as the *Tribune* called them, where they could learn the tricks of the pickpocketing trade before promotion to bolder lines of criminal work. To prevent members of the Fagin gangs from tainting their classmates, the principal of one school segregated them in a class by themselves.

"It's simply a side play of the Monk's gang," explained one police officer. "These thieves and murderers have been driven to cover by the police, and now they are seeking to live and make profit by teaching these boys to steal for them." A young thief's reward was typically a trip to the theater on Saturday afternoon to see the melodramatic stage heroes and villains, a small price Monk's men paid for the money and jewelry their artful dodgers pilfered.

Notwithstanding that the Eastmans were relatively quiescent following the Battle of Rivington Street, writers have generally contended that Monk's gang and the Paul Kelly Association resumed their hostilities to the point where Tammany again had to intervene to avert bloodshed. According to the traditional story, a Kelly man named Ford (sometimes given as Fordin) got into a vicious barroom brawl with an Eastman named Hurst, broke Hurst's nose and bit off one of his ears. Monk told Paul Kelly that if he didn't sufficiently punish the miscreant Ford, the Eastmans would "wipe up de earth with youse guys."

After discussing matters as they faced each other across the table, with big cigars in their mouths and pistols in hand, Kelly and Eastman agreed to settle their differences via a boxing match between the two of them. On a cold winter night, the two principals—each accompanied by fifty armed bodyguards—repaired to a barn in the farthest reaches of the Bronx. As Herbert Asbury writes:

Because of his early experience in the professional prize ring, Kelly possessed superior science, but it was offset by Eastman's weight and greater ferocity. They fought for two hours without either gaining an advantage, and, at length, after they had collapsed and lay one across the other still trying feebly to strike, their followers loaded them into carriages and hauled them to the East Side and the Five Points. The bout was pronounced a draw, and as soon as they had recovered from their wounds, the gang chieftains marshaled their resources and prepared for war to the finish, despite the protests of the politicians.

As irresistible as the story is, it never happened. There *was* a prizefight in late December 1903, in a remote section of the Bronx, attended by a couple hundred members of the Monk Eastman and Paul Kelly gangs. As recorded by *The Sun*, the fight did take place inside an old barn, on the deserted Berkeley Oval, an outdoor athletic field at University Avenue and West 179th Street. But the bout wasn't between Monk Eastman and Paul Kelly, neither of whom was reported as even being there that night. Instead, a bantamweight named George Betts, a self-promoter having no affiliation with either gang, squared off against one Kid Mullins (or Mullens) of Philadelphia.

The fight, refereed by Eastman gang member Phil Furst (possibly Hurst), lasted two rounds, not two hours, when a battered Mullins quit the ring. There were no reports that the gangmen in attendance were armed, nor was there any fighting between the Eastmans and Kellys, who returned to the city, happy if weary, after two in the morning.

In another twist on the story, Kelly recalled in a 1908 interview with the *New York Herald* that about eight years earlier, he and Monk agreed to settle a bitter dispute between the Eastmans' Hurst and the Kelly Association's Fordin by having those two antagonists fight in a barn—not in the Bronx but in College Point, a somewhat isolated neighborhood in northern Queens. Kelly refereed and declared his man Fordin the winner after Hurst refused to continue. Eastman reluctantly had to concede that Kelly was right.

Over the years, that fight morphed into a bout between the two gang chieftains themselves in a Bronx barn and was confused with the actual fight there in 1903 between different parties. The Fordin-Hurst boxing match, which Kelly placed around 1900, was "the nearest Eastman's crowd ever came to fighting us, crowd against crowd," he told the *Herald* in 1908. In the same interview, he described Monk Eastman as "a soft, easygoing fellow," who had "a gang of cowardly loafers around him."

Given the Battle of Rivington Street in September 1903, Kelly's claim that his gang never fought Eastman's was false. But the frequent contention that the two gangs remained at war after that battle is equally inaccurate. There are no contemporary newspaper accounts of any confrontations between the Kellys and Eastmans after the Rivington Street shootout. Police Commissioner Greene's vow to end gang warfare was, at least for the time being, carried out.

But if the two gangs did harbor any notions of fighting again, such thoughts turned moot in the early morning hours of February 2, 1904. That's when the authorities finally got Monk Eastman.

CHAPTER TWENTY-FIVE

UP THE RIVER

The most fateful night of Monk Eastman's life to date began with his feasting on roast pig and downing pints of beer in a Bowery saloon. Starting around nine o'clock in the evening on February 1, 1904, he was partying with several of his gang members at McDermott's, a gin mill at Bowery and Stanton Street, where the owner was hosting a celebration of the establishment's recent opening. After a couple of hours there, Eastman and several of his pals decided to head uptown to the Tenderloin, so they climbed aboard the Third Avenue streetcar and transferred at Forty-Second Street.

Monk's gang had rarely ventured so far north in previous years, but for the past month, Inspector McClusky noted, they'd been spending much time there because "a certain woman whom Monk admired grew ambitious to shine in Broadway society." It was also reported that there were slimmer pickings downtown for thieves lately, so Monk's men had begun seeking out wealthy swells patronizing Tenderloin establishments in the wee hours. Monk and his companions would find one such mark on this night.

About two-thirty on the bitterly cold night, a drunken youth stumbled out of Jack's Restaurant on Sixth Avenue and began making his way down to Forty-Second Street, where he turned west. Just then, Monk and his buddies came out of Sig Cohen's saloon at Forty-Second and Sixth, where they'd continued downing beers while listening to men singing around the piano bar upstairs. Monk would say later that he had "twenty glasses of lager" in him by that time, though he claimed not to have been drunk.

Most of Monk's friends were just engaging in horseplay as they emerged from Sig's saloon, but Monk and one of his cohorts, Christopher Wallace, took notice of the well-dressed, intoxicated young man staggering in the direction of Broadway and decided to follow him. He stopped a few feet down the block, pulled out a fat, green roll of bills, and began to count them. Monk and Wallace then leapt from the shadows and set upon their prey, intending to relieve him of the wad of cash. Little did Monk and his accomplice know that the youth, and now they, were being watched closely.

It turned out that the wayward youth was being shadowed by two private detectives of the Pinkerton Agency, who'd been hired by the boy's father to keep him under surveillance during his debauches. When Detective George Bryan stepped forward and hollered to the assailants to stop, Wallace took off running down Forty-Second Street toward Broadway.

Bryan gave chase, jumping over the outstretched foot of Eastman, who tried to trip him. Several shots were fired by persons and from directions unknown. Bryan caught up with Wallace halfway down the block in front of Lewis & Conger, a home furnishing store at 130 West Forty-Second Street, where first Eastman and then Bryan's detective partner, John Rogers, arrived in short order.

Rogers, who was unarmed, saw his fellow detective Bryan holding Wallace in front of him as a human shield and turning him from left to right to avoid Eastman, who was brandishing a revolver and shifting back and forth trying to obtain a better shooting angle. "Let him go, you goddamned son of a bitch, or I will kill you!" Eastman shouted. From a crouching position eight or ten feet away, Eastman fired two shots at Bryan without result. He then moved to the other side of the detective, who twisted his prisoner around to protect himself, and fired two more shots. These, too, missed Bryan but crashed the glass in Lewis & Conger's window.

At that point, Bryan let go of Wallace with his right hand while keeping hold of him with his left, pulled out his revolver and placed it under Wallace's armpit to return fire. Eastman, out of ammunition, threw his weapon at Bryan's head. Bryan ducked as the gun went crashing into Lewis & Conger's window and fell inside the store, where it was later retrieved by police as evidence.

Eastman and Wallace, who had broken free, started running west but were met by several policemen who had heard the shooting, including plainclothes detective John Healy—at two hundred pounds, one of the huskiest men on the force. Healy and his fellow NYPD officers clubbed both robbers with their nightsticks and felled them.

The cops took Eastman and Wallace to the West Forty-Seventh Street station house, kicking and punching Monk along the way. The pair were arraigned the next day and later indicted, Eastman on charges of felonious assault and attempted first-degree murder, and Wallace for attempted larceny. Monk's arrest was one of about six hundred homicide arrests in New York City that year, double the number of reported homicides in the city in 2019 (though far less than the roughly two thousand recorded in most years from the 1970s to the 1990s).

Confident as always, Eastman gave his name as William Delaney, "newspaper speculator," and provided a false address. At trial, he would say he was Edward Eastman, pigeon dealer.

Monk claimed he had been minding his own business at the crime scene when he heard gunshots and took off running, fearing that, given his reputation, he'd be blamed for any mishaps. He saw Detective Bryan scuffling with Wallace—over what, he didn't know—but Monk denied that he had gotten anywhere near Bryan, denied firing any shots at the detective, and denied even being armed at the time. He expected to be discharged, or at least bailed, as usual.

The first sign that things might be different this time was when Judge John W. Goff set Monk's bail at a staggering $15,000, and no one from Tammany would post it. Friends later raised a defense fund to bail him out, but Tammany's willingness to protect him, despite his value at election time, had seemingly diminished.

In part, this was because Tammany, having warned Monk to behave himself, had grown tired of his antics. Tammany had returned to power in 1904 after the reelection defeat of Fusionist mayor Seth Low by Democrat George McClellan Jr., son of the Civil War general. To replace Frederick Greene as police commissioner, McClellan tabbed William McAdoo, a former New Jersey Democratic congressman and the assistant navy secretary immediately before Theodore Roosevelt.*

While McClellan and McAdoo, both Protestants, were not reformers in the Parkhurst mold, neither were they as closely tethered to the Irish Tammany machine as earlier Democratic officials had been. District Attorney Jerome, who was eying a New York governor's run on the Democratic ticket, praised both McClellan and McAdoo for being "sincere in their efforts . . . to disassociate Tammany from any connection to these criminal classes."

McAdoo, like Jerome, was strongly anticorruption and committed to cracking down on gambling, prostitution, and Sunday drinking. An innovator, he formed a traffic bureau with accompanying regulations and ordered his men to check automobile registry numbers to catch drivers who provided false identification when arrested for accidents or speeding violations. He sent Detective Sergeant Joseph Faurot to study fingerprinting at London's Scotland Yard. McAdoo also laid the cornerstone

---

* He was no relation to William Gibbs McAdoo, the treasury secretary under President Woodrow Wilson, with whom he is often confused.

for a new police headquarters at 240 Centre Street, a grand, elegant, granite-walled fortress that would replace the aging structure at 300 Mulberry Street a few blocks south.*

The blue-blooded McAdoo had a low opinion of Lower East Side immigrants, especially Jews and Italians, who were moving into the crowded, squalid tenements the Irish were vacating as soon as they could afford to move uptown. The new immigrant classes were "utterly un-American in appearance, habits, traditions, and history," McAdoo wrote, and their "barbarous customs were in evidence everywhere."

McAdoo had a similarly prejudiced opinion of African Americans, at least what he called "the Tenderloin type of Negro," a "flashy-bejeweled loafer, gambler, and, in many instances, general criminal." He did, however, show greater solicitude for the protests by African American leaders of police brutality than prior police officials had evidenced. Following the "Battle of San Juan Hill," a race riot on the Upper West Side in July 1905 in which many black residents were beaten, and one killed, by the police, McAdoo pledged to "carefully guard against the unwarranted arrest of colored people under any hue and cry." He also transferred the allegedly racist captain who had been in command during the incident.

Monk Eastman, whom Ron Arons, author of *The Jews of Sing Sing*, has called "the first true *Jewish gangster* in New York," clearly was not McAdoo's kind of guy (even if Monk wasn't Jewish). "This fellow has been running with a free hand too long," McAdoo said of Monk after his arrest for shooting at Bryan. In office barely a month, the new police commissioner said his men needed to build "as strong a case against him as we can."

Another factor may have influenced the authorities' determination to finally make the charges against Monk stick. It had to do with the identity of Monk's intended robbery victim—the prodigal son of a prominent man.

---

* Known as the Police Building, the Baroque revival–style palace served as NYPD headquarters from late 1909 to 1973. Today it houses luxury apartments.

No newspaper at the time of Eastman's arrest identified the youth in print; the police, the Pinkerton Agency, and city officials all refused to reveal his name. At Eastman's trial in April 1904, the victim never appeared, leading the defense to charge that no such "drunken youth" existed—that he was invented by the police as part of a conspiracy to put Monk behind bars.

The prosecution identified him only as the "son of a man distinguished in public life in the United States." Prosecutors argued further that because the youth was so intoxicated on the night in question, his testimony would have been worthless anyway. But the defense insisted that it was entitled to know his name, and Judge Goff, who this time ran a fairly evenhanded trial, agreed.

"Whetmore," testified Detective Rogers of the Pinkerton Agency, though he wasn't sure of the spelling and didn't know the youth's first name. It was actually spelled "Wetmore," without an "h," District Attorney Jerome, who knew who the individual was, told the press afterward.

For more than a hundred years, neither the wayward youth nor his father was identified in any public writing. Then in 2008, a book on New York Jewish gangsters named the father as "C. W. Wetmore . . . a captain of industry—the former president of LaClede Gas Light Company," a Saint Louis corporation.

Although Charles Wilson Wetmore was indeed a successful private businessman who lived in New York, he didn't quite fit the prosecution's description of Wetmore senior as "a man distinguished in *public life* in the United States." More important, both Wetmore and his wife were childless.

But there was another Wetmore who did fit the description: US senator and former Rhode Island governor George Peabody Wetmore, who owned a château in Newport, Rhode Island, and a Fifth Avenue home in New York. A Republican, Senator Wetmore was a confidante and reliable supporter of President Theodore Roosevelt. He also had a twenty-one-year-old bachelor son who maintained a New York residence in February

1904. Rogers Pickman Derby Keteltas Wetmore, an unreconstructed, reckless playboy, was almost certainly the youth attacked by Monk Eastman.

Because Wetmore's father was a US senator who was close to the former police commissioner, now President Roosevelt, the law enforcement authorities in New York had good reason to handle the case both diligently and by the book. For the politically ambitious district attorney Jerome, and the brand-new police commissioner McAdoo, allowing Eastman to walk free once again was not an option. Tammany's usual string pulling was of no use: this time it would be just Monk Eastman against the facts of the case.

After a three-day trial, Eastman was convicted on April 14, following a little over two hours of jury deliberation. It was a compromise verdict. Through the first two ballots, the jurors voted 11 to 1 for guilt on the count of attempted murder, which would have carried a sentence of twenty-five years. But on the third ballot, a stubborn holdout caused them to settle for a finding of first-degree assault, with a maximum ten-year prison term.

Although some newspapers reported that Monk reacted to the verdict without emotion, a *New York Times* reporter caught the convicted man turning white. He seemed stunned, his jaw dropping before he regained his equanimity. Later, Eastman said he'd done a lot of favors for big men but supposed that this time he was in "too deep."

Eastman's lawyer appealed to Recorder John W. Goff for clemency, asserting that Monk was in poor health from a life of crime. "Me stomach is all shot away, I'm held together by bandages," Monk declared, alluding to his near-fatal 1901 shooting by the Donovan brothers.

But Judge Goff was unmoved and gave Eastman the maximum ten years in Sing Sing, with the possibility of parole in six and a half years. Upon hearing his sentence, Monk threw up his hands and said, "This is me finish." Though only thirty years old, he was sure he wouldn't survive his prison term.

Monk asked for a few days in the Tombs to wind up his affairs; he said he had some pigeons setting and he wanted to see how their eggs hatched out. "As soon as me boids are off the nest, I won't make no kick against starting up to serve my term," he told the press.

The papers suggested he was trying to buy time for his gang to set up an escape along the train route to Sing Sing. But if so, the plot never materialized. A crowd of five thousand, including gang members but mostly curious onlookers, saw him off at the railroad station, where, hands manacled, he waved with a grin. After boarding, he buried his face in a newspaper.

The press and public officials predicted that Monk's conviction and sentence would spell the end of the gangs of New York. A certain amount of gloating and revisionist history marked many of the comments by Inspector George McClusky. "Monk Eastman was not dangerous," claimed the man Devery had dubbed "Chesty." Eastman "had one good punch, and if he caught a man alone and had enough of his own crowd with him, he had the nerve to give that punch and put the man out. The other members of the gang were more cowardly, even, than Monk and stuck to him only because they were afraid of him. Nobody is more relieved at getting rid of Eastman than his own companions."

Like several others quoted in the papers, McClusky insisted that by the time Monk was eventually released from prison, his old haunts, and the gangs, would be things of the past. "There will be no more gangs, for the class that has produced them has been eliminated from the East Side," McClusky said.

Echoing that sentiment was Chief Inspector Moses Cortright, a longtime veteran of the force. "There is no Five Points in these days," he told *The Sun*. "There is no particular locality, no block or street corner, that can be pointed out and described as the worst place in New York or as a hangout of a desperate gang of thugs." Business, as much as anything else, had accomplished this, he said, citing tremendous growth in the number of retail shops that were taking the place of the slums.

A neighborhood settlement-house worker agreed, adding that entrepreneurial young men were increasingly trying to go into business for themselves and had less interest in the criminal life. "Monk Eastman was an anomaly, one of the last survivals of a state of savagery that now has no practical existence in New York," this individual said. "Seven years from now, when Monk Eastman leaves prison, the East Side will be a model community."

The optimists received a further boost when, the following year, Paul Kelly and his association were driven from the gang business.

With Monk Eastman sidelined, the Kelly Association took up fighting with the rival Five Points gang of Jack Sirocco and Jimmy Kelly (Giovanni DeSalvio). If the Five Pointers had ever overlapped with Paul Kelly's gang, they were now bitter foes.

One casualty of the conflict was "Eat 'Em Up" Jack McManus, Paul Kelly's enforcer and, by many accounts, the toughest brute in New York. In May 1905 McManus allegedly shot a Five Points honcho named Chick Tricker in the leg after Tricker insulted one of Kelly's showgirls inside the club. The following evening, McManus was walking along the Bowery, accompanied by fellow Kelly Association tough John Cucco, aka Kid Griffo, when an assassin crept up from behind and bashed in McManus's skull with a lead pipe concealed in a newspaper. McManus was taken to Bellevue Hospital and pronounced dead.

Griffo was originally held by police but was later released. According to the conventional story told by Herbert Asbury and others, the actual killer was a thug named Sardinia Frank, allegedly hired by Tricker to obtain revenge.

No one was ever formally charged with McManus's murder, and neither the assailant nor the motive has ever been satisfactorily established. Curiously, a contemporaneous *New York Times* article identified McManus as most recently employed as the bouncer at Five Pointer Jimmy Kelly's Fourteenth Street resort, the Folly, not Paul Kelly's headquarters on Great Jones Street. Kid Griffo, the article reported, was the bouncer at Paul Kelly's complex; the two fellow Italians had been bare-knuckle sparring partners in the past.

The *World* later reported a rumor that McManus had been done in by the Paul Kelly Association because he'd somehow turned on his old boss. Further confusing matters, Eat 'Em Up was buried by the Kelly Association, not the Five Pointers to whom he had reportedly gravitated.

Flash-forward six months to November 1905, when the Five Pointers' coleader Jack Sirocco was shot in the arm outside Paul Kelly's joint on Great Jones Street, supposedly in a dispute over the spoils of Election Day work. A couple of days later, around midnight on November 22, three gun-toting Five Pointers stormed the Kelly Association's upstairs meeting room, intending to kill Kelly.

The hit squad was led by James T. "Biff" Ellison, a hot-tempered thug who'd been convicted three years earlier for viciously beating a cop in a Fourteenth Street saloon. Ellison, who dressed like a prosperous-looking Wall Street broker, was known as the former owner of Paresis Hall, an infamous gay and transvestite bar on the Bowery that was later featured in *The Alienist* book and television series.

On the night in question, Ellison took a shot at Kelly but missed, instead hitting Kelly's bartender/bodyguard, a young Italian who went by the Irish name of Harrington. He died instantly when struck through the left breast. The motive for the attack is unclear. Most assumed it was in retaliation for the recent wounding of Sirocco, but another version held that Ellison was seeking to avenge the death of his friend McManus, for which he blamed the Paul Kelly gang.

A half hour after the fracas, a police officer from the Mercer Street station noticed that Kelly's Little Naples Café, normally brightly lit and full of dance hall music at that hour, was dark and deserted. Upon entering the upstairs meeting room, he saw chairs and tables overturned, revolvers and papers strewn upon the floor, and bullet holes in the walls. Downstairs, he found a pair of legs protruding from a bathroom under a swinging door; they were attached to the lifeless body of Harrington, presumed to have been killed upstairs then dragged to the first-floor saloon below. Above the bar near him was a picture of Big Tim Sullivan.

After several days of searching for Paul Kelly, the police found him relaxing at a cousin's home at East Ninety-Sixth Street and Park Avenue, calmly smoking a cigar, having just finished giving some interviews to the press. Dressed as if ready to go out, he claimed he was about to head downtown to give himself up. There being no evidence tying him to the shooting of Harrington, he was never charged with anything, though few doubted that he had tried to return fire upon the hitmen.

According to most accounts, someone turned the meeting room lights out as soon as the shooting started, after which bullets flew back and forth in the dark. The traditional story that Kelly suffered three gunshot wounds is erroneous, but he was at least grazed in the side, as evidenced by the white waistcoat he gave to the police. It had a bullet hole through it and showed powder stains.

It wasn't until six years later that the authorities caught up with the fugitive Biff Ellison and put him on trial. He was convicted of first-degree manslaughter and given eight to twenty years in Sing Sing.

The November 22, 1905, fracas marked the end of Paul Kelly's reign as a New York gang leader. His New Brighton and Little Naples were closed by order of Commissioner McAdoo, who declared, "We are going to drive Kelly's and all the lesser gangs out of existence."*

Kelly made it easy for the authorities. He moved uptown to the Little Italy section of East Harlem, became a union organizer, president of the Scow Trimmers Union, whose members sifted garbage loaded onto barges for disposal, and vice president of the International Longshoremen's Association. He used his positions to initiate strikes and harass strikebreakers as well as to negotiate settlements. He legally changed his name back to Paul Vaccarelli and expressed his desire to live in peace as a respected labor official.

----

* That Kelly disbanded his Paul Kelly Association in 1905 refutes the many accounts claiming that Al Capone and Lucky Luciano were early members of his gang. Capone and Luciano were only six and eight years old, respectively, in 1905.

◆⇒◉⇐◆

The confident forecasts of the demise of the gangs that followed Monk Eastman's 1904 conviction and Paul Kelly's 1905 exodus would, like similar predictions before them, prove premature. Gang warfare on the Lower East Side continued as violently as ever, if not more so. And while control of graft and turf remained the central objects of the leaders who succeeded Eastman and Kelly, the gangs became more sharply divided along ethno-religious lines—specifically, Jew versus Italian.

After Monk Eastman went away to Sing Sing in early 1904, coleadership of his gang fell to two of his most pugilistic lieutenants: twenty-year-old Kid Twist (the Austrian Jew Max Zweifach), and the Irish American Richie "Kid" Fitzpatrick, an older (thirty-two) Eastman gang veteran and former schoolmate of Monk's. Although "Fitzpatrick" sounds suspiciously like a pseudonym, since almost all of Eastman's gang members were Jewish, census records establish that Fitzpatrick was his name and that his father was from Ireland.

The Kid Twist–Richie Fitzpatrick partnership was a contentious one, as each felt he deserved the sole top spot. Both men had reputations as remorseless killers. On November 1, 1904, ostensibly to discuss their power-sharing arrangement, Twist invited Fitzpatrick to a peace conference in a saloon at 77 Sheriff Street in the shadow of the recently completed Williamsburg Bridge. (The street no longer exists.)

Exactly what happened next remains unclear, but the net result was that Fitzpatrick, sensing a setup, bolted the meeting and went out onto the street, where a gunman, presumably one of Twist's henchmen, shot him dead through the heart. A Twist ally named Harris Stahl, aka Kid Dahl, was fingered—or by some accounts volunteered to take the rap—but was acquitted at the direction of a judge who saw insufficient evidence that he was the actual triggerman. Meanwhile, Kid Twist took over as undisputed head of the Jewish Eastman gang, vowing that "no wop and no mick" would ever rule the Lower East Side of New York.

Twist refined and expanded upon Monk Eastman's strong-arm gang methods. He developed his own brand of celery tonic, a mixture of syrup and carbonated water popular in the Jewish community (still available today as Dr. Brown's Cel-Ray Soda), and distributed it to small shopkeepers at an inflated price. Any store owner who refused to buy the Twist brand had his business smashed to pieces and his life threatened.

According to investigative journalist Alfred Henry Lewis, writing a few years after the fact, Twist pressured a gambler named Charles Greenwich, known as the Bottler, into giving up 50 percent of the take from a stuss game he ran on Suffolk Street. The half interest went to Harris Stahl, a reward that Twist decided was appropriate for the man who'd offed Richie Fitzpatrick, or at least had willingly stood trial for it.

Twist soon demanded 100 percent from Greenwich, an associate of the Italian Five Points gang, which would effectively force him out of business. When the Bottler balked, Twist ruthlessly had him rubbed out. Some reports said the killer was Stahl, while others hold that it was Twist's friend and housemate Sam Tietch, a former professional wrestler and circus sideshow strongman who went by the name Vach "Cyclone" Lewis. No one was ever prosecuted for the crime.

Twist's reign was cut short when, on the evening of May 14, 1908, he and Cyclone Lewis were taking an after-dinner stroll on the Coney Island boardwalk with two female companions. The foursome was accosted by Louis "Louie the Lump" Poggi (or Pioggi), a nineteen-year-old Italian hoodlum nicknamed for his squat, heavyset build. Poggi was supposedly jealous that one of the two women, his former live-in girlfriend and music hall singer Carril "Carrie" Terry, who was married to an actor, had left the Lump for the likewise married Kid Twist.

Poggi fired repeatedly, plugging Lewis with six bullets and Twist with a single shot behind his right ear. The two men staggered down the boardwalk and collapsed at the barroom entrance to a large hotel, both of them dying before an ambulance could get there. Carrie Terry, who'd been hit in the shoulder but wasn't seriously wounded, was taken to the hospital, where, upon regaining consciousness, she identified her ex-boyfriend Poggi as the assailant.

Both Alfred Henry Lewis and Herbert Asbury asserted that Poggi did not act alone or out of jealousy but rather carried out a calculated mob hit in conjunction with a dozen or more fellow Italian gangsters. The motive, they claimed, was either to avenge the death of the Bottler or, more broadly, to complete the breakup of the rival Jewish Eastman gang. No evidence was ever adduced to support their conspiracy theories.

Poggi, the sole person accused of the crime, claimed predictably that he'd acted in self-defense. He got off relatively easy for a double homicide, pleading guilty to manslaughter and receiving a year in prison in Elmira, New York. Lewis, a former prosecutor turned creative writer whose stories Asbury tended to embellish upon, quoted Poggi as saying he could do that amount of time "standin' on me head."

The Coney Island incident further inflamed tensions between the Jewish and Italian gangs. A few days afterward, a group of Eastmans invaded the Gotham Theatre in East Harlem seeking revenge for their leader Kid Twist's death. "Is there a dago in this here place?" one Eastman wanted to know. "We want to kill somebody." The police broke up the commotion before any blood could be shed.

And so it would go over the next several years, as Jewish and Italian gangs continued to vie for control of the lucrative extortion and racketeering markets in downtown New York. The Five Points gang was led by Jack Sirocco and Chick Tricker, who took over much of Paul Kelly's Lower East Side operations after he left for East Harlem.

When the Five Pointers weren't fighting Monk Eastman's successors, they were fending off incursions by Giovanni DeSalvio's Jimmy Kelly gang, a rival Italian faction that had split off from the Sirocco-Tricker group after Paul Kelly's retirement. The politically connected saloonkeeper DeSalvio enjoyed strong Tammany and police support. He also employed Kid Twist's slayer, Louie the Lump Poggi, who had been associated with the Five Points gang, as one of his chief gunmen.

In late 1910 control of the old Eastman gang passed to Zelig Lefkowitz, better known as "Big Jack" Zelig. Unusually tall for a gangster at five foot eleven, and given to fits of rage, he had begun his criminal career

Big Jack Zelig, the Jewish gangster who succeeded to the head
of Monk Eastman's old gang.

as a pickpocket under the tutelage of Eastman disciple "Crazy Butch" Erenstoft, who was shot to death in 1906 by a Five Points member, or possibly by Kid Twist, in a dispute over a girl.

Zelig was also boyhood friends with Kid Twist, and after Twist's murder in 1908, he moved up the Eastman gang ladder. He anointed himself head, at age twenty-two, after he knocked out three murderous thugs—including the late Richie Fitzpatrick's younger brother—in the Chatham Club, a shabby dive on Doyers Street in Chinatown where gangsters, Tammany politicians, and the colorful raconteur Chuck Connors regularly hung out.

After assuming the helm of downtown's Jewish underworld, Zelig carried on a bitter, violent war with the Sirocco-Tricker Italian gang. Following the same business model pioneered by Monk Eastman and built upon by Kid Twist—extortion, gambling, and prostitution—Zelig was mainly motivated, like his predecessors, by financial considerations. But he was fiercely proud of his Jewish heritage and took a special interest in protecting residents of the Jewish quarter from encroachments by Italians looking to extort Jewish shopkeepers or enlist Jewish girls as prostitutes.

For this, he was revered by his people. Zelig "made it possible for the Jews not to get tossed around," recalled one admirer.

In the same vein as Monk Eastman, Zelig was no detached, hands-off commander. He fatally shot one Five Points gang member he understood was hired to assassinate him and took a bullet himself in the neck from a Five Points gunman, somehow managing to survive.

The fighting between Jews and Italians had degenerated into a free-for-all. "Kid Twist died, but the gang spirit lived," reported *Munsey's* magazine. "During 1909 and 1910, the trade in revolvers increased, and conditions on the East Side grew steadily worse."

⋯⇒ ⇐⋯

While the NYPD war on street gangs was going back and forth over the first decade of the new century, another, very different criminal element was making its influence felt in New York. Its members were overwhelmingly Sicilian, unlike the Italians of earlier New York gangs, such as Paul Kelly's, who tended to be Neapolitan.

The Sicilians didn't form themselves into street gangs, and their leaders didn't flaunt themselves in public. Continuing a trend in organized crime that began in the 1890s, they shifted their attention from more visible "vice" (commercial sex, gambling, and saloon and dance hall culture) to extorting retail and other business establishments and conducting large-scale counterfeiting operations in secret.

At least at first, and throughout the Gilded Age, the Sicilians avoided costly, bloody wars with rival Neapolitan factions. (Those would come later.) Sicilian gang members were more like covert bands of criminals who preferred preying upon their own people. They acquired ominous-sounding nicknames: "the Ox," "the Wolf," or "the Clutch Hand."

They relied on cunning as much as brute force—not that they didn't resort to violence. Explosives, once used by thieves to rob banks, now became a tool for demanding money directly from the well-to-do. Murders were carried out not with pistols on street corners, or in a barroom

333

full of witnesses, but in private with stilettos, the victims then displayed in public for all the world to see.

The Sicilian underworld was so mysterious that most New York cops had no idea how to come to grips with it. Or they had no interest in preventing what they considered a bunch of savage aliens from devouring themselves. As a result, it was going to take a fellow Italian to confront the organization that some people referred to as the Mafia or La Cosa Nostra, and others grouped under the sinister label the Black Hand.

CHAPTER TWENTY-SIX

"SEND FOR THE DAGO!"

At five-thirty on the rainy morning of April 14, 1903, scrubwoman Frances Connors was on her way to work, intending to stop off at a bakery along the way to buy some rolls. As she passed in front of a small lumber factory on East Eleventh Street just off Avenue D, she spotted a large wooden barrel on the sidewalk, some clothing sticking out of it.

When she went to retrieve the fabric for herself and peered down the barrel, she shrieked: crammed inside was a still-warm, doubled-over body. The dead man's throat was slit from ear to ear, and his head hung by a thread from his neck, which bore more than a dozen knife wounds.

A blood-soaked white linen collar found inside the barrel was inscribed with the initials "M.U.R.L." Not a scrap of paper, though, gave any clues to identify the olive-complexioned, middle-aged man.

Inspector George McClusky, in charge of the investigation, wanted two specific detectives on the case. One was Art Carey, who had identified (correctly, in McCluskey's opinion) both Dr. Samuel Kennedy and Roland Molineux as the killers in their respective sensational murder cases. Most recently, Carey had played a key role in another celebrated

NYPD detective Joseph "Joe" Petrosino. As head of the department's Italian Squad, he battled the early Mafia as well as Black Hand extortionists who terrorized fellow Italians. A master of disguise and surveillance, Petrosino maintained a mental file of hundreds of Italian criminals, his own itinerant rogues' gallery.

homicide case by unmasking the murderer of eighty-four-year-old Texas millionaire William Marsh Rice, whose estate went on to establish Rice University in Houston.

Rice, who had moved to New York from Texas, was found dead in his apartment on Madison Avenue where he lived alone with his valet. Carey's investigation concluded that Rice's lawyer, one Albert Patrick, had forged the old man's will, named himself as the inheritor of the bulk of the estate, then enlisted the valet to kill Rice with chloroform as the old man slept. (Yes, the butler did it.) Patrick, the lawyer, was convicted in 1902 and sentenced to be electrocuted at Sing Sing.*

---

* After six years on death row, Patrick had his sentence commuted to life in prison. Then in 1912 New York's governor issued a full pardon based on doubts about the medical evidence.

The other detective McClusky assigned to work with Carey on the Barrel Murder case, as it came to be called, was a man dubbed the "Italian Sherlock Holmes."

⋄⇒◌⇐⋄

In the years since Police Commissioner Theodore Roosevelt had promoted him to detective in 1895, Joseph Petrosino had forged a reputation as the resident Italian expert in the central office. As *The Sun* noted, Italy's jails were filled with criminals Petrosino had caught in the United States and sent back home.

Virtually alone among his detective colleagues, Petrosino understood the Italian immigrant community and spoke their language. He mastered all the regional dialects, including those of Naples, Sicily, and his native Salerno province in the Campania region. He knew that police bluster and threats of arrest were of no avail in ferreting out Italian-on-Italian crimes because of his native countrymen's attitude of "fix it myself." The uncooperative victims' lips were sealed by their fear of reprisal and the code of silence, or omertà.

Even to be seen talking to a cop put one in danger. Besides, many Italian immigrants didn't speak English, they distrusted the predominantly Irish police force, and they were reluctant to place themselves in the hands of the American justice system. Widely viewed as dirty and dangerous, the Italians stuck to themselves in their Lower East Side or East Harlem ghettos and, according to the popular trope, were continually sticking knives in one another.

Short, heavyset, and moonfaced, Petrosino frequently embedded himself in colonies of New York's Italian American community, discarding his customary dark suit and black derby for clever disguises. It was the only way to secure sensitive information. He might take a job as a laborer for several weeks, or pose as a blind beggar, a city bureaucrat, an organ grinder, a bearded Orthodox Jew, or a black-robed Catholic priest.

He had a network of informants, including both lowlifes and members of the professional classes: doctors, bankers, lawyers, and musicians.

Early in his career, Petrosino had served as an informant for Clubber Williams, earning the enmity and distrust of his own people as well as a series of death threats. The accusations and frightening letters got so bad that he was forced to move out of downtown's Little Italy into an Irish neighborhood. Yet others of his countrymen took pride in a fellow Italian's having attained a position of such importance in the nation's largest city.

Petrosino maintained a mental file of hundreds of Italian criminals, his own itinerant rogues' gallery. He never forgot a face, as he demonstrated vividly twice in 1903 by nabbing felons he recognized from the fleeting contact he'd had with them many years before.

In the first case, he collared a swindler he remembered arresting for forgery in 1889—fourteen years earlier. In the second, he was climbing an interior apartment staircase to see some friends when, through an open doorway, he spotted a familiar-looking man sitting at a table. From a mug shot photo he'd seen in 1899, Petrosino recognized the man as Frank Sineni, a barber wanted by the Chicago police for murdering a man with a razor. When Sineni gave Petrosino a false name, the detective promptly arrested him and dragged him to police headquarters, where, confronted with his photograph, Sineni confessed to the crime.

In his rise through the ranks, Petrosino had enjoyed other notable successes. In 1893, while still just a patrolman, he broke up an insurance fraud ring whose Italian members faked their own deaths, buried someone else, and collected on the policies.

In 1898 his detective work cleared a young Italian named Angelo Carbone of a murder charge for which the youth had been swiftly convicted. Less than two weeks before Carbone was scheduled to die by the electric chair in Sing Sing, Petrosino tracked down an alternative suspect, sixty-two-year-old Salvatore Ciaramello, Carbone's cousin. The detective had been following his quarry for nearly a month before finally tracing him to a house outside Baltimore, where friends and relatives were hiding him.

After placing the premises under surveillance, Petrosino gained entrance by donning a fake beard and posing as a health inspector who said he'd heard there was smallpox inside. When Ciaramello gave his name as "Fioni," Petrosino corrected him, kicked away an axe standing against the wall nearby, and grabbed his target by the neck. The startled Ciaramello confessed to killing the victim during an argument outside a Leonard Street bar and produced the knife he'd used to do it.

Petrosino telegraphed 300 Mulberry Street to say he'd arrested Ciaramello and obtained a full confession. When Carbone, sitting in his death row cell, was handed an English-language telegram that, translated for him, stated his cousin had confessed to the crime, he burst into tears and cried out that he was saved. Detective bureau chief McClusky called it a remarkable case, as it was the first time an Italian in America had confessed to a murder, and one of the rare instances in which an Italian New York criminal had escaped the city and was later captured, despite being shielded by allies.

In mid-1900 Petrosino was assigned to infiltrate a nest of Italian anarchists living in Paterson, New Jersey. One of their number, Gaetano Bresci, had recently traveled to Italy and assassinated King Umberto I, the politically conservative monarch, on July 29, 1900. The United States was under pressure by the Italian government to investigate whether Bresci had any accomplices.

Petrosino took a job at a construction site in Paterson and spent three months among the local anarchists, pretending to be one of them and learning as much as he could about their activities and intentions. One startling revelation: the revolutionary group was planning more assassinations of world leaders, including President William McKinley.

Petrosino relayed his findings to the authorities in Washington—by some accounts, in person to McKinley and Vice President Roosevelt in the White House, though that seems doubtful. He cautioned that the president should avoid going into large public assemblies. But no one took the warnings seriously, and Petrosino returned to New York.

A few months later, on September 6, 1901, while shaking hands at the Pan-American Exposition in Buffalo, New York, President McKinley was fatally shot by twenty-eight-year-old anarchist Leon Czolgosz. A Michigan-born son of Polish American parents, Czolgosz was inspired by the assassination of Italy's king.

Although Petrosino reportedly wept when he heard the news of McKinley's shooting, he was described by colleagues as taciturn, unsmiling, and rarely one to laugh aloud, hardly the stereotypical emotional Italian. At the time of the Barrel Murder case in 1903, he was a forty-two-year-old bachelor, married to his work. "There's so much sudden death in this business. A man hasn't the right to bring a woman into it," he was once quoted as saying.

But though he possessed only a sixth-grade education, Petrosino was well versed in the arts and music, which he could discuss entertainingly in private. He played the violin and loved the opera, particularly Verdi. Yet it was as a catcher of Italian criminals that he was known, so much so that for almost any major crime involving Italians, the call went out: "Send for the dago!"

And thus it was that Joe Petrosino was teamed with Art Carey to get to the bottom of the Barrel Murder case.

At first glance, they were an unlikely pair. Carey was patient, analytical, and enjoyed plumbing the psychology of both victim and perpetrator, as he did in his most famous cases. What was it, he pondered, that drew Dolly Reynolds to that fatal rendezvous in the Grand Hotel? Why did Roland Molineux send Kutnow's Powder to Henry Barnet, but Bromo-Seltzer to Harry Cornish? Carey accepted judicial setbacks philosophically: if a jury didn't think Dr. Samuel Kennedy was guilty, who was he to disagree? He bristled at the very notion that he might plant evidence. He liked the chess game, played by the rules, and worked within the system.

Joe Petrosino was frustrated to no end whenever courts freed men he'd captured. He shared the view of Carey's mentor Thomas Byrnes, that dangerous criminals had no rights worth respecting and were fair game for the third degree. "The gangsters who had had dealings with him bore marks of 'interrogation' for months," wrote Petrosino's biographer, the Italian journalist Arrigo Petacco. "Especially when he realized that the evidence in his hands would not be sufficient grounds for an indictment or a deportation, he never boggled at attacking them physically. 'This way you'll remember who Petrosino is,' he would remind them after he had finished beating them."

Carey held the normal prejudices of a middle-aged Irish cop, often stereotyping other ethnic groups, minorities, and recent foreign immigrants. But he bore them no personal animosity. His memoirs stressed that murderers came in all shapes, sizes, races, ethnicities, sexes, levels of intelligence, and socioeconomic backgrounds. He'd worked too many murder cases over the years—more than ten thousand by one estimate—to think otherwise. He also held his Italian partner Petrosino in high regard (though he misspelled his name as "Petrosini," a mistake the newspapers often made as well).

Compared with Carey, Petrosino took things more personally. He carried an understandable chip on his shoulder from the second-class treatment he'd received early in his career, when he was virtually the only Italian on the police force and was disliked, insulted, or simply ignored by his Irish colleagues. It had taken him ten years to win his first promotion, from patrolman to roundsman. In a rare sideswipe against the much-venerated Petrosino, historian Humbert Nelli, himself an Italian American who has written extensively on Italian crime in America, posits that the delay in Petrosino's progress was "in part because of prejudice against Italians, in part because he was not noted for an incisive or probing mind."

A probably apocryphal quote attributed to Petrosino by his biographer Petacco nonetheless captured his sentiment: "Do you know what my compatriots say when they talk about America?" Petrosino asked then police commissioner McAdoo, who was complaining that the Italians didn't trust the police department. "They say: 'An Italian discovered it, and the Jews and the Irish run it.' Try giving the Italians a little power, too, and maybe there will be some change."

History does not record what Petrosino thought about his partner Art Carey. But they would make a good team on the Barrel Murder case.

Carey, arriving early at the scene in front of Mallet & Handle's lumber works on East Eleventh Street, began developing a picture of the crime. The corpse was draped in a cloth overcoat. The man's cuffs, collar, and handkerchiefs—one of them a woman's, and highly perfumed—as well as the victim's clean, soft, manicured hands, indicated he was someone of means and not a manual laborer. His pockets also contained a small crucifix and a silver watch chain that was missing the watch.

The dark-mustached, curly-haired man looked Mediterranean, and a torn fragment of a letter found on him, written in Italian in a woman's hand, confirmed his nationality. Carey further guessed that the victim was Sicilian because of his pierced ears, then a mark of a native of Sicily.

Petrosino, summoned from police headquarters, translated the Italian words from the torn letter as "Come quickly" and "it is most urgent," which suggested the victim had been lured to his doom. Carey assumed that because the man's left hand and right leg protruded from the barrel, he was killed by some secret society, such as the Mafia, that wanted to make sure the body was discovered so that it might serve as a warning to others.

At the bottom of the barrel, Carey found a thick layer of sawdust put there to prevent blood from seeping out. The sawdust had been trampled upon and contained Italian cigar butts and red onion skins; Carey concluded it had come from the floor of an Italian restaurant. The autopsy would reveal the contents of the man's stomach: just before his death, he had eaten spaghetti, salad, beans, beets, and potatoes, which Petrosino described to Carey as a typical Sicilian meal.

The barrel also contained sugar, which Carey took to be evidence that it belonged to some candy or pastry shop. On the outside of the drum near the bottom was the most promising clue: the stenciled marks "W & T" and "G.223."

The main sugar refineries that supplied the city's grocery and eating establishments were on the Long Island side of the East River. Carey went from manufacturer to manufacturer along the waterfront until he found one who identified the barrel as his and explained the stencil markings. "W & T" were the initials of the Wallace & Thompson grocers at 365 Washington Street in Manhattan, and "G.223" was the shipping lot number.

At Wallace & Thompson, employees confirmed that they'd received six barrels of sugar in the 223 lot, but they could not recall and had no records of where they had shipped the barrels. "Have you got any Italian customers?" Carey inquired. "Only one," a clerk replied. "Pietro Inzerillo, who has a pastry shop in Elizabeth Street."

Accompanied by Petrosino, Carey went to Inzerillo's Café Pasticceria at 226 Elizabeth Street, a sort of bakery, candy store, and lunchroom combined. In the basement there, the two detectives spotted a sugar barrel identical to the one in which the murdered man's body was found stuffed and bearing the same "W & T" and "G.223" stencil marks.

Questioned by Carey and Petrosino, the graying, middle-aged Inzerillo was by turns mum and unconvincing. First, he denied that the barrel containing the victim could have come from his place; then he claimed he'd sold several of the "W & T" barrels a couple of weeks earlier to three or four men who came around, none of whom he could identify or even describe. He insisted he'd never been arrested and, without prompting, said he didn't know what the Mafia was. Shown a picture of the murdered man, he swore he didn't recognize him.

As it turned out, the Café Pasticceria was one of three regular gathering spots, each within a block or so from the others, for a gang of Sicilian counterfeiters of which Inzerillo was a member. On the very night of the Barrel Murder, they were being shadowed by agents of the US Secret Service, whose primary mission in those years was to combat the widespread counterfeiting that followed the Civil War. Then part of the Department of the Treasury (where it remained until 2003, when it was placed under the Department of Homeland Security), the Secret Service devoted many more of its resources to catching counterfeiters than it did to protecting the president, a task it was first given after the 1901 assassination of President McKinley.

Working in conjunction with Joe Petrosino, and aided by informants, the New York bureau of the Secret Service had been pursuing the Sicilian counterfeiting gang since the turn of the century. A number of its members had been arrested for passing bad bills, and several had been convicted, including a group of Sicilians nabbed in Yonkers as recently as January 1903.

The Sicilian band was also suspected of having carried out the July 1902 murder of Brooklyn grocer Giuseppe Catania, a Mafia counterfeiter who talked too much when he was drunk. Catania had his throat slit and his naked body stuffed in a potato sack that was found among the bushes in Bay Ridge, Brooklyn. The Sicilians, the authorities said, had "as little compunction about murdering a man as they would have about killing a dog."

Giuseppe Morello, known as "the Clutch Hand" for the deformity he displayed in this mug shot around 1900. Morello's Sicilian counterfeiting gang is today referred to as the "First Family" of New York's Mafia.

No one was ever charged with Catania's murder. But Joe Petrosino was convinced, as were detective head McClusky and William J. Flynn, chief of the Secret Service's New York bureau, that the grisly killing—and the eerily similar Barrel Murder—were committed at the behest of the same man.

⋯⇒○⇐⋯

Giuseppe Morello was a slight thirty-five-year-old former cattle thief from the Sicilian town of Corleone. He had fled to America in 1892 after being arrested in his native land for counterfeiting, a crime for which he was convicted in absentia by a Sicilian court. He also was accused of shooting a Sicilian security guard chief and plotting the killing of a woman who'd witnessed the murder and was prepared to testify against him in court. Several other murders in Sicily have been attributed to him, though none proven.

More cold-blooded than any prior New York gang leader, Morello also *looked* more menacing. Danny Driscoll was a cocky, smirking Irish kid, Monk Eastman almost a comic book figure, and Paul Kelly a silky-smooth gangster. Morello dressed like a stereotypical poor Italian laborer or peasant, with a thick, droopy black mustache and stubble beard to match his dark, tousled hair. But rather than bleakness, his stony face, combined with jet-black eyes that seemed to pierce right through anyone who stood before him, marked him as utterly callous.

Frightening above all was his signature feature: a deformed right arm, barely half the normal length, with a lobster claw of a hand that was missing all but the little finger. In a photograph from the time, he displays the hideous-looking paw across his chest, not burying it Napoleon-style inside his vest but instead holding it aloft proudly, propped up by a white string necklace. It gave him his nickname "Clutch" or "the Clutch Hand."

Stepson of Bernardo Terranova, a Corleone Mafia member, Morello settled briefly in New York in 1892. He was followed shortly by the arrival at Ellis Island of his wife and baby, his mother and stepfather, and

his Terranova half siblings. The Panic of 1893 and its dire economic effects drove them south to Louisiana, where they worked the sugar planta-
tions, then to Texas, where they picked cotton and contracted malaria. In
1897 they returned to New York, where Morello failed at several small,
legitimate businesses for a couple of years before resuming life as a counterfeiter.

From a printing press in an apartment in East Harlem, Morello and
a few associates turned out crude $5 bills that they sold for $2 to Irish
"queer pushers" (as in "queer as a three-dollar bill"). When Morello
learned that his widowed Irish maid, Margaret "Mollie" Callahan, stumbled upon the plates in mid-1899, she mysteriously disappeared and was
later presumed dead.

After Mollie's boyfriend Jack Gleason, one of Morello's minor gang
members, was arrested in Queens in June 1900 with some other confederates, he fingered Morello to the Secret Service. Morello was charged
with counterfeiting, along with several associates, including a woman
named Margaret Callahan (which suggests that she was alive, after all).

Morello had none of the incriminating phony notes on him at the
time of his arrest and was released for lack of evidence, as was Callahan.
But three of his Irish queer pushers and one of his Sicilian associates were
sent to prison—the Sicilian for six years.

After his close call with the law, Morello purged his gang of Irishmen
and established an all-Sicilian enterprise. He came to head what is now
referred to as the First Family of New York's Mafia, the Morello-
Terranova family. It would evolve into the Mafia organization taken over
by Lucky Luciano and led later by Frank Costello. Subsequently it became the Genovese crime family, the oldest and largest of the "Five
Families" of New York. As a result, the Sicilian counterfeiting ring led by
Giuseppe Morello beginning in turn-of-the-century Manhattan is widely
acknowledged today as providing "a continuous link in New York's organized crime history."

By 1902, Morello was running a saloon at 8 Prince Street that fronted as a headquarters for his gang members, now roughly thirty in number. Tucked behind it was a dark, dingy spaghetti kitchen that smelled of garlic and worse. His inner circle congregating there were all related to him by blood or marriage or were trusted men from Corleone. Those he didn't know personally came from other Sicilian towns, invariably recommended by Corleone mafiosi. Morello disdained the earlier gangland practice of recruiting any willing punk from off the streets.

Finding a trustworthy spouse was no less important. In 1903 Morello married a spirited girl about sixteen years his junior, brought from Sicily to replace the wife he'd lost to death, likely from malaria, five years earlier. Lina Morello (née Nicolina Salemi) would have the distinction of becoming perhaps the first bona fide Mafia wife in America. Fully aware of her husband's mob activities, she would render loyal support to him for the rest of their lives together. Once, during a Secret Service raid, she hid her husband's incriminating correspondence by swooping her baby daughter into her arms and stuffing a half dozen letters inside the child's diaper.

The saloon at 8 Prince Street and an ostensible wine importing business across the street at 9 Prince were owned by twenty-six-year-old Ignazio Lupo, who became Morello's brother-in-law in 1903 by marrying one of his half sisters. Known as Lupo the Wolf, he was second in importance only to Morello in the counterfeiting ring. Lupo would become known as the businessman of the organization.

Unlike Morello, who grew up poor in a small town, Lupo was a big-city kid from the Sicilian capital, Palermo, and the product of a prosperous family. He dressed fashionably in tailored clothes, had a round, clean-shaven face, and affected a flashy presence. By contrast, Morello was a hairy, foxlike lurker who wore plain worker's garments to avoid drawing attention to himself. "They say I am the chief of the Mafia," he would later tell Petrosino. "Look at me and see if I could be one."

But the two Sicilians' outward differences obscured their fundamentally similar, heartless tendencies. Like Morello, Lupo was a fugitive from justice in his native land, having killed a man in a fight in Palermo in 1898, when he was twenty-one, before fleeing to America. Lupo was also the last person seen with Giuseppe Catania, the Brooklyn grocer found in a potato sack in 1902, and was arrested for that murder, though never formally charged.

Volatile and violent, Lupo "only needed to touch you to give you the feeling that you had been poisoned," recalled the Secret Service's Flynn. Art Carey wrote that when the names of Morello and Lupo were mentioned in the presence of the residents of Little Italy, "they crossed themselves and frequently appealed to parish priests for protection."

Starting around 1901, Lupo opened a series of grocery stores in New York and a wholesale business he used to extort small independent grocers. If they didn't pay the extravagant prices he charged for the wine, cheese, lemons, and olive oil he imported in large quantities from Italy, they'd find their stores, or even their homes, bombed.

Lupo's thriving retail groceries, the highest in quality in Little Italy, attracted wealthy customers the Morello gang could target for blackmail. Morello also plucked prospective victims from the local gossip he picked up at a barbershop and cobbler he owned in the West Fifties, along with similar legitimate businesses he acquired with money laundered from the gang's illegal activities. Flynn estimated Morello's and Lupo's war chest at around $200,000.

Morello's acquisitiveness knew few bounds. He made it a habit to walk into a shop, inquire of the owner in a friendly manner as to the prosperity of his business and the health and well-being of him and his family, then lay down an obviously counterfeit bill and ask for silver in return. Shopkeepers learned not to put up any resistance but instead to comply with gratitude. They knew what was in store for them if they refused. Morello was "utterly cruel when it came to decreeing death," Flynn declared, though it's not clear whether the Clutch Hand ever committed murder with his own hands after leaving Italy. "He didn't have to; he had men to do it for him," the Secret Service chief said.

To broaden their reach, Morello and Lupo formed a real estate company in which they sold shares of stock to their fellow countrymen, using the proceeds to construct and sell rows of tenement houses to Italian immigrants in lightly settled areas of the Upper Bronx. They named it the Ignatz Florio Co-operative Association, in honor of a well-known Sicilian businessman with Mafia ties but no actual connection to the real estate venture.

Despite the scrutiny it was under from the police and Secret Service, the Morello gang also continued its counterfeiting operations. Rather than print the fake currency from plates in New York City, the members found it safer to have the notes manufactured in Italy and then smuggled into the United States. The counterfeits were typically hidden inside olive oil cans that attracted little attention from customs agents when off-loaded onto Manhattan's piers.

The Morello gang partnered for a time with a group headed by Stella Frauto, a woman the Secret Service considered one of the best and most persistent counterfeiters in the country. (She specialized in bogus coins.) The alliance came to an end in May 1902 when, based on an anonymous tip Petrosino received, Frauto and several of her associates were arrested in Hackensack, New Jersey, and later sentenced to prison terms.

One of those rounded up, but who escaped conviction based on an alibi, was a mysterious Palermo-area native named Vito Cascioferro. A leftist mafioso with ties to the anarchists suspected of plotting King Umberto's murder, Cascioferro served three years in prison for kidnapping a young baroness socialite, then came to America in September 1901 to escape harassment by the Italian authorities.

Shortly before arriving in New York, Cascioferro was invited by a Brooklyn friend to "eat a plate of macaroni together" with a Sicilian assemblage that included Giuseppe Morello. For the next two and a half years, Cascioferro would serve as an informal adviser to Morello, teaching him in the ways of the Sicilian Mafia. Morello's group stood on its own, though, not as a formal branch of the native Italian organization.

During the first two weeks of April 1903, as William Flynn's Secret Service agents kept up a daily watch of the Morello gang's movements in

Little Italy, Cascioferro was often seen with Morello and others coming in and out of the gang's three rendezvous spots: the saloon at 8 Prince Street, the pastry shop at 226 Elizabeth Street, and a butcher shop at 16 Stanton Street run by Morello lieutenant Vito Laduca. Clearly, the Sicilians were up to no good.

Indeed, they had murder on their minds.

CHAPTER TWENTY-SEVEN

THE NEWCOMER

On the afternoon of April 13, 1903, the day after Easter, Flynn's Secret Service agents started seeing what they described as unusual activity in and around the Morello gang's usual hangouts. Around two o'clock, a wagon pulled up in front of the butcher shop at 16 Stanton Street and dropped off a man the agents identified as "Italian #11" and dubbed the Newcomer because they had not previously seen him.

The Newcomer spoke to a couple of men, remounted the wagon, and drove off. Later that afternoon, he reappeared inside the butcher shop with Morello and Cascioferro, who had been spotted earlier at the pastry shop at 226 Elizabeth Street talking earnestly with each other.

Inside the butcher shop, Morello and Cascioferro, along with a couple of other Italians, took the Newcomer to the rear of the store and talked with him for about ten minutes. At one point, the Newcomer was off by himself in front of the butcher shop, appearing nervous, while the others held an animated discussion in back. After a time, one of the men tacked a curtain over the front-door window. Morello and Cascioferro then left to return to 226 Elizabeth Street.

Over the next few hours, various Italians were seen shuttling back and forth between Vito Laduca's butcher shop, Inzerillo's pastry shop, and Morello's establishment at 8 Prince Street. Exactly where the Newcomer was last seen is unclear. Some reports said he was still inside the butcher shop at 16 Stanton Street when the agents discontinued their surveillance around nine at night. Other sources say he was last spotted leaving the butcher shop arm in arm with Morello and another gang member as they escorted him in the direction of Morello's Prince Street saloon-restaurant. Years later, Art Carey would write that at the end of the evening, a Secret Service operative watched the Newcomer walk from the pastry shop to Morello's saloon just around the corner and enter it without coming back out. When the lights inside were turned off, the operative ended his watch and went home.

Regardless, one fact became clear: the Newcomer and the man found in the barrel the next morning were one and the same. After a photograph of the dead man appeared in the *New York World* on the evening of April 14, Flynn sent his agents to the city morgue to confirm their suspicions that he was the same man they'd seen milling around the Morello gang's various headquarters the night before. After viewing the corpse, they identified it as "a stranger designated as #11 [who] mixed with Morello et al. last evening."

The identity of the dead man remained a mystery. His Bertillon measurements were taken but did not match any on file. But because he'd been seen with Morello and his band the night of the murder, the authorities had enough basis to round up the gang on suspicion of being involved with or knowing something about the crime.

On the evening of April 15 and into the following day, thirteen of the gang's members were arrested near their usual haunts—a "murderous-looking crew," *The Sun* called them. They included the Clutch Hand; his partner, Lupo the Wolf; and his bodyguard and enforcer, twenty-four-year-old Tomasso "Thomas" Petto (real name, Luciano Perrino). Petto was known as "Il Bove" ("the Ox") for his hulking physique and oafish demeanor.

Nearly all those apprehended were heavily armed with fully loaded .45-caliber revolvers, deadly daggers, or both. Morello and Petto the Ox, ambushed by four NYPD detectives at the corner of Bowery and Delancey Street around eight-thirty, made moves to pull out their weapons but were subdued before they could inflict any harm. Morello, knocked off his feet, recovered from his bewilderment to find another pair of hands slipping handcuffs on his good and bad arms. The Ox staggered back, then lunged forward—only to take a fist between the eyes that bashed him nearly unconscious.

Several others arrested that night tried to put up a fight but submitted when the police threw them to the sidewalk and placed pistols at their heads. Lupo the Wolf was taken at midnight at his home on West Fortieth Street, where he claimed to be ill and bedridden. Pietro Inzerillo put up no resistance when arrested at his Elizabeth Street pastry shop; he was soon bailed out by Big Tim Sullivan, then a US congressman as well as a Tammany leader, proving that the Sicilians were not without their own political pull.

The one person the authorities sought to arrest but couldn't find was Vito Cascioferro, who'd been seen with the Newcomer and Morello the night of the murder. They looked for him at his apartment and regular stomping grounds for days after April 13. It turned out that he had left for New Orleans just after the Barrel Murder, then returned to Sicily, where he became one of the most powerful leaders of the Sicilian Mafia. He reputedly bore a grudge against Joe Petrosino, whose photograph he kept in his wallet.

Searches of Morello's and Lupo's apartments and headquarters, as well as the absent Cascioferro's residence, turned up no contraband. But the authorities did find reams of correspondence, written in Italian, with Mafia branches in New Orleans and other large cities. Cigars taken from Morello's and Petto's pockets were of the same shape and brand as those found in the pockets of the victim. In Morello's apartment, the police located linen collars marked "M.U.R.L.," identical to the ones found inside the barrel. Carey visited Morello's restaurant at 8 Prince Street and scooped up sawdust containing onion skins and cigar butts matching the mixture in the barrel.

The New York police, including Detective Chief McClusky and Inspector Max Schmittberger, in whose district the murder occurred, were described as jubilant. The Secret Service's Flynn said he was certain that Morello's Mafia group had murdered not only the man in the barrel but also grocer Catania the year before. The *New-York Tribune* pronounced the Morello gang "the most desperate and bloodthirsty criminals that have lurked in the shadows of the Italian quarter of the East Side."

The police assumed that the Barrel Murder victim had gotten himself crosswise with Morello and was killed out of revenge or to silence him. Still, no one knew who the man was, and the Sicilians claimed not to recognize him. They would admit nothing. Morello, taken by Art Carey to the morgue, where he was shown the dead man's body, shook his head. "Poora feller . . . I no know him," the Clutch Hand avowed quietly in broken English.

A break came when an anonymous letter addressed to Petrosino showed up at police headquarters three days after the arrests. It asserted that the dead man was a counterfeiter from Buffalo who'd come to New York looking for money from the Morello gang. A prisoner in Sing Sing named Giuseppe Di Priemo "can tell you all," the anonymous letter writer promised.

After conferring with Flynn, McClusky learned that Di Priemo was one of the Sicilian members of Morello's gang arrested in Yonkers by the Secret Service earlier that year and convicted of counterfeiting by a federal court. Di Priemo had adamantly refused to cooperate and had recently begun serving a four-year sentence in Sing Sing. McClusky tasked Petrosino with traveling thirty miles upstate to the infamous state prison overlooking the Hudson River and getting something out of his fellow Italian.

Uncommunicative at first, Di Priemo sprang to attention when Petrosino showed him a photograph of the barrel victim. "That is my brother-in-law, Benedetto Madonia. What is the matter with him?" the prisoner asked. Told by Petrosino that his brother-in-law was dead, Di Priemo reportedly fainted. After recovering, he would provide little information beyond the fact that Madonia, a stonemason from Palermo, now lived in Buffalo. Petrosino could extract nothing concerning the Mafia or Morello's gang from him.

But back in New York, among the documents taken from Morello's apartment at 178 Chrystie Street was an angry letter to him from Madonia expressing a desire to exit the gang due to dissatisfaction with his treatment. Madonia's name and Buffalo address were also found on the leaf of a book in Morello's room. The notation, in the Clutch Hand's scrawl, was written in red ink.

Interviews by Petrosino of Madonia's wife and stepson in Buffalo, both of whom confirmed Di Priemo's identification, plus detective work by Carey and his colleagues in New York, helped piece together the victim's movements in the days leading up to the murder. Madonia had been a road agent for Morello's counterfeiting group, traveling routes between Buffalo, Pittsburgh, and Chicago frequented by counterfeiters. When his brother-in-law Di Priemo was arrested in Yonkers, along with other Morello gang members, for passing bad bills, Madonia helped raise a defense fund for him. But Morello appropriated the money and left Di Priemo to take the fall for the crime. Madonia's letter to Morello had complained bitterly of the Clutch Hand's indifference to Di Priemo's fate.

Over the Easter weekend, before his murder on Monday night, Madonia came to New York to demand from the Morello gang the money they had stolen from Di Priemo as well as Di Priemo's share of the counterfeiting profits. When Morello denied the request, Madonia threatened to expose the gang. That, and the hard feelings already existing between him and Morello, made Madonia a target for assassination. It was Madonia's wife, fearing for his safety, who had sent him the urgent telegram to return at once to Buffalo.

Before leaving Buffalo for New York, Petrosino told the press that "as sure as you live," Madonia's murderer was "among the batch we arrested." But while it seemed clear enough that the Morello gang bore collective guilt for the crime, fastening it on any specific individual would prove difficult absent some physical evidence linking him directly to the murder.

Such evidence would come from the pocket of Petto the Ox. Upon his arrest, the police took from him a $1 pawn ticket for a watch, pledged to David Fry's Capital Loan Company, a pawnbroking shop at 276 Bowery.

Although the watch chain on Madonia when he was found in the barrel was missing the watch, Mrs. Madonia had described it to Petrosino as a large, expensive gold timepiece. Police therefore initially assumed that the watch pawned to Fry's for a mere dollar was Petto's, not Madonia's.

But Madonia's stepson, Salvatore, told Petrosino that the watch his father ended up taking on his trip to New York was a different one, made of cheap tin and bearing several scratches and a distinctive engraving of a locomotive. It was worth no more than $4 or $5, about what might fetch a $1 loan from a pawnbroker.

After Petrosino telegraphed the watch's description to police headquarters in New York, Carey and his frequent detective partner James McCafferty, who'd worked with him on the Molineux case, went to Fry's pawnshop to retrieve it. Coincidentally, Fry's was located directly across the street from the Kugler & Wollens hardware store at 277 Bowery, where, six years earlier, Carey had developed the first clues to the Guldensuppe murder. This visit would also prove productive.

A clerk in the shop produced the watch, which had a locomotive stamped on the case. It perfectly matched the description given by Madonia's stepson, who was brought to New York and immediately identified it as the watch in question.

The watch had been pawned on Tuesday, the day Madonia's body was found inside the barrel, obviously after he'd been murdered. Whether out of petty greed or sheer dim-wittedness, Petto had ripped the watch from its chain and, instead of tossing it, pawned it for a measly dollar. It was the same type of mistake that ended up sending young Mike McGloin

Lead investigators Joe Petrosino (left) and Art Carey (right) escort Morello gang member Thomas "the Ox" Petto (center) to the Tombs prison after his arrest for the 1903 Barrel Murder, allegedly ordered by the Clutch Hand. The victim, a Sicilian member of Morello's counterfeiting gang, was found stuffed inside a sugar barrel, his throat slit from ear to ear and his head hanging by a thread from his neck.

to the gallows twenty years earlier, after Thomas Byrnes figured that the murderer of French wine merchant Louis Hanier might have pawned the revolver used to kill him rather than throw it away. Crime may have become more sophisticated over the years, but criminals were not always any smarter.

With the watch and pawn ticket, the authorities now had their first concrete evidence connecting a Morello gang member to the murder of Madonia. Inspector McClusky went so far as to declare the case solved. Detective Sergeant McCafferty said the police had enough evidence to send Petto to the electric chair. As for Petto, while he did not deny that the pawn ticket was his, he claimed, unconvincingly, that it had been given to him by his friend "John" (whose last name he didn't know), because John feared losing it.

On May 1, 1903, an inquest jury was impaneled. It was "obtained by the coroner with considerable difficulty because of alleged fear of the Mafia's vengeance," *The New York Times* reported. After a week of testimony, the coroner's jury found that Madonia was killed by some person or persons unknown. The jury called for the detention of Petto and six other Sicilians as accessories to the crime, including leader Morello, butcher Laduca, and confectioner Inzerillo.

Petto was subsequently indicted for the murder. But the case against the Morello gang began to collapse. Three key witnesses—Madonia's wife, his stepson, and his brother-in-law Di Priemo—all retreated from the statements they originally gave to Petrosino and others. Shown the watch they had positively identified as Madonia's, Mrs. Madonia and son Salvatore now said they weren't so sure it was the one Madonia was wearing at the time of his death. That testimony considerably weakened the one tangible link tying Petto to the murder.

Di Priemo then testified that Petto was his very good friend and surely would not have killed his brother-in-law. And Inzerillo, who had shown signs of being willing to turn state's evidence, suddenly clammed up, refusing even to admit to the presence of sugar barrels found in his pastry shop.

Art Carey had an explanation for the changes of heart. When the witnesses began to be questioned, "There was a shuffling of feet and hissing in the court room, which was filled with swarthy-faced men. One of these jumped up and put his fingers to his lips." It was a reminder of the omertà code of silence. Understandably, none of the state's witnesses wanted to end up in a barrel with their own throats slit.

One by one over the next several months, on the district attorney's recommendation, the seven Sicilians were released for lack of evidence, including, finally, Petto himself in January 1904. Plenty of finger-pointing went around. The coroner's physician accused District Attorney

William Travers Jerome of incompetence and called for his resignation. The Secret Service's Flynn blamed the NYPD's McClusky for arresting the original suspects prematurely and then locking them up together, giving them a chance to coordinate their stories.

McClusky expressed great disappointment but had no criticism for anyone. "I was in hopes that one of the suspects would squeal, but all kept their mouths shut," he told the press. "I am thoroughly convinced that every one of the men we had in custody knew all about the murder. The fate of Madonia, who had not even been a squealer, was enough to keep them silent."

Although the case was technically unsolved, Joe Petrosino and Art Carey had done all they could to bring the killers to justice. Accordingly, they suffered no loss of reputation. Carey continued his work as a murder man and was elevated to lieutenant two years later, to captain in 1907, and then, in 1908, was made the head of the NYPD's Homicide Squad, the first organization of its kind in the world. Among other innovations, he had his men demonstrate the effects of gunshot wounds by firing bullets into the shaved heads of dead hogs.

Joe Petrosino, meanwhile, was tasked with confronting a new criminal threat coming out of the Italian quarter. Loosely related to the Mafia and the Morello gang, but distinct in Petrosino's mind, its hand was not clutch but black. And to most of New York's Italian immigrants, it was even more menacing.

CHAPTER TWENTY-EIGHT

THE BLACK HAND

The first reported target of the Mano Nera, or Black Hand, in New York turned out to be one of the luckier ones.

On August 3, 1903, with stories of the Barrel Murder still circulating in the daily press, a prosperous Brooklyn contractor named Nicola Cappiello received the following letter, written in Italian:

> *If you don't meet us at Seventy-second Street and Thirteenth Avenue, Brooklyn, to-morrow afternoon, your house will be dynamited and you and your family killed. The same fate awaits you in the event of your betraying our purposes to the police.*
>
> *La Mano Nera*

The letter was embellished with black crosses and skulls and crossbones.

Two days later, after ignoring the demand, Cappiello received another letter:

You did not meet us as ordered in our first letter. If you still refuse to accede to our terms, but wish to preserve the lives of your family, you can do so by sacrificing your own life. Walk in Sixteenth Street, near Seventh Avenue, between the hours of four and five tonight.

Beware of Mano Nera

Again Cappiello declined to go along. Several days later, some close friends came to his house to say that the "Black Hand" society for which they were serving as intermediaries wanted $10,000 to spare his life but would likely accept $1,000 to go away. Cappiello reluctantly paid the $1,000, but a few days later, the same men were back to demand another $3,000.

Convinced that the threats would never end, Cappiello went to the police. With the benefit of confessions obtained by his nephew, the blackmailers—several of them prior hires of Cappiello's—were arrested and later convicted. Still, Cappiello's family continued to live, as his wife put it, "in constant expectation of death."

The method of Black Hand extortion followed a predictable pattern. It would begin with a letter or note mailed to a male head of household demanding a sum of money and threatening severe consequences if he failed to respond: death to him or his family, kidnapping of his children, or a bombing of his home or business. One letter to a Brooklyn woman, sent while her husband was away, read, "Dear Madame, unless you put an envelope with $500 in it on your front steps some night before Monday morning, we will take one of your children and kill it. We mean bizness. The Black Hand."

Typically, the threatening note was illustrated with hands drawn in black ink, daggers dripping with blood in red ink, or a coffin, and instructed the recipient when and where to deliver the cash. Victims were admonished not to notify the police, and, unlike Nicola Cappiello, most did not. Those who paid invariably faced escalating demands in subsequent letters and were bled dry of their resources until they turned in desperation to the authorities, were killed, or fled the city.

Although the poor were occasionally targeted, most Black Hand victims were wealthy or moderately prosperous Italian immigrants who had established themselves as businessmen or professionals in the New World. As such, they could be assumed to have accumulated a considerable bank account ripe for plucking.

According to Joe Petrosino, the perpetrators were usually wanted for similar crimes in Italy. They came to America figuring there was greater freedom of movement in this country, less draconian treatment of wrongdoers, and an opportunity to blend in with a limitless supply of compliant victims in the heavily Italian quarters.

It didn't take much to break into the Black Hand business—just some paper, a pen, and ink—although more serious Black Handers backed up their threats with a stiletto or bomb. Explosive devices ranged from simple "pumpkin bombs"—wrapped paper bags filled with powder that did no more than fill a room with odiferous smoke—to olive oil cans containing nails and other shrapnel; to fireworks strung together in so-called dago bologna chain links; and, most destructive of all, dynamite sticks stolen from the construction sites of the subway system being built mostly by Italian laborers.

The term "Black Hand" was not new in 1903: it had been applied before to opponents of the Spanish Inquisition, to the southern Italian secret societies of the 1750s, and by the Spanish government and religious establishment to a group of anarchists in rural Spain in the late 1800s who championed the poor and downtrodden. In 1885 *The New York Times* also reported on an unsuccessful libel suit brought by a German American New Yorker against a journalist who had called him "a member of the death-dealing secret society, the Black Hand of Berlin."

To Joe Petrosino, the phenomenon wasn't new either. As early as 1901, he became aware of a series of extortion and blackmail gangs operating in the Italian colonies of New York. "Scores of Italian murderers are lurking in the lower part of the city and plying their trade of Black

Hand extortion," he wrote in his diary that year. "Unless checked at once, they will so extend their operations that the police will be sorely tried in running them down."

Yet the crimes received little official attention until the Cappiello case in August 1903, the first one in New York to be publicly attributed to the Black Hand. The Mafia "is not unknown in this country, nor in New York, where it has perpetrated many murders," the *New York World* asserted, "but this is the first time that the 'Black Hand' has been seen here. The latter has but one purpose—extortion. The alternative is death."

Ironically, it had taken the April 1903 Barrel Murder case, which did not even involve extortion or blackmail, to crystallize New Yorkers' interest in Italian American crime. In time, the "Black Hand" became the preferred term for practically every Italian-on-Italian crime committed in New York, supplanting the word "Mafia."

Some observers, however, mixed the two. The Secret Service's Flynn, for example, regularly (and inaccurately) referred to the early New York Mafia, and Morello's group in particular, as the Black Hand. Echoing the thought, in February 1904 the Third Avenue Theatre billed its latest thriller, *The Black Hand*, as "a Mafia melodrama" about a powerful and evil secret society.

But unlike the Mafia, with its structure and hierarchy bound by family ties, the Black Hand was more of a modus operandi or methodology than an actual organization. Joe Petrosino, one of the few who understood this, declared emphatically, "There is no big central organization of criminals called the 'Black Hand.'"

Rather, Black Handers were small groups of criminals, or even individuals working alone, with no connection to one another. They did not coordinate with Italian Black Hand groups in other American cities, or with the Sicilian Mafia or its counterpart, the Neapolitan camorra. Thus, while mafiosi such as the Morello counterfeiting gang sometimes employed Black Hand extortion methods, most Black Hand racketeers were not members of the Mafia.

Lupo the Wolf, Morello's partner in crime, illustrated the point.

Although a counterfeiter, he dabbled in Black Hand activities, having been accused in the kidnapping of the fourteen-year-old son of an Italian banker who had helped set up the Lupo-Morello real estate venture. Lupo was later arrested for allegedly shaking down an Elizabeth Street wine importer to the tune of $10,000 but was released when the merchant failed to appear at a hearing to testify.

On the flip side, Lupo claimed that his well-publicized wealth as a successful mafioso made him a target of Black Handers, who preyed upon the criminal as well as law-abiding classes. He asserted that, over the years, he paid more than $10,000 to various extortion artists. Lupo viewed the payments as the cost of doing business that any prominent New York Italian must accept.

That the Black Hand was distinct from the Mafia didn't make it any less dreaded. Petrosino was constantly urging his superiors to take the Black Hand more seriously, lest it expand to English-speaking victims. For a time, police department colleagues told him he was an alarmist— that the Black Hand was a myth invented by tabloid newspapers. But while he agreed that the notion of an all-powerful, central Black Hand society was indeed a myth, Petrosino insisted that the threat was real. Certainly Ciro Poggioreale, whose storefront at 252 Elizabeth Street was blown up in July 1904 for refusing to deliver $2,000 to the Black Hand, though he survived, would have concurred. Many other Italian New Yorkers could have attested to the Black Hand's existence had they not been murdered or disappeared after receiving Mano Nera letters.

By the summer of 1904, a year after the Cappiello case, New York was on the verge of a full-fledged Black Hand panic. The leader of New York's Italian Chamber of Commerce complained of an "epidemic of kidnapping and blackmail" that had prevailed in the city for the previous several months.

The most galvanizing incident was the abduction of eight-year-old Antonio Mannino, who was lured from a Brooklyn candy store on August 9 by a discharged former employee of the boy's father, Vincenzo Mannino, a wealthy contractor. The ex-employee, a teenager named Angelo Cucozza, had offered little Antonio, who spoke both Italian and English, fifty cents if he'd come with him into Manhattan to serve as an interpreter. After buying some candy and soda water for his playmates with a shining fifty-cent piece, Antonio went outside to meet Cucozza, who said to him, "Come along, Tony; it is time we were off."

The pair was seen disappearing into the night, and it was presumed that Cucozza delivered the boy to a group of Black Handers who demanded $50,000 in ransom from Antonio's father. If the money wasn't paid, the boy would be "slowly cut to pieces," a letter warned. A Brooklyn police captain on the case received letters with crosses and dagger saying, "Stop chasing us, or you will be killed."

Shortly after the kidnapping, the police apprehended Angelo Cucozza, who admitted he'd been paid $2 by the Black Handers to get young Tony into Manhattan. Cucozza led the cops on a wild-goose chase to places he thought the boy might be being held, but he refused to reveal the names of the kidnappers. "I would rather go to the chair than give away the man who stole the boy. I might as well, for they would kill me anyway," Cucozza told the authorities.

For ten days, New Yorkers held their breaths as little Tony's whereabouts and well-being remained unknown. Police fruitlessly followed various tips and alleged sightings of the boy throughout the New York–New Jersey area. Then, just after midnight on August 19, Tony turned up mysteriously, spotted by a relative on the street, two blocks from his Brooklyn house. He'd been let go by the kidnappers, then made his way home.

Petrosino, who had discouraged Tony's father from paying any ransom, was convinced that Vincenzo Mannino, having lost confidence in the police, had given the kidnappers $500 to get his son back. (It wasn't unusual for Black Handers to settle for far less than the original demand.) The boy told the authorities he'd been treated well while kept in a little room in the rear of an East Harlem tenement by a stout man, a thin man, a woman, and a baby called Judy (or Juda). But when three suspects from East 106th Street matching the adults' descriptions were brought before him, young Tony stammered and gave conflicting stories, ultimately failing to positively identify them. The police believed the boy's father had schooled him not to answer in a way that might incriminate the captors.

The Mannino kidnapping case, it turned out, had connections to the Barrel Murder case of the previous year. Vincenzo Mannino, Antonio's father, had contributed to the defense fund of the suspects. Nonetheless, because he had money, the Black Handers decided to abduct his only child. The suspected ringleader of the kidnappers, though he was released after arrest, was Vito Laduca, the butcher whose 16 Stanton Street shop was among the last places where Benedetto Madonia was seen the night of his murder. Laduca the counterfeiter was moonlighting as a Black Hander, proving that Morello's Mafia and the Black Hand, while separate, did overlap to some extent.

The summer of 1904 was overcome with what became known as "Black Hand Fever." Black Handers set a Brooklyn candy store on fire, suffocating its owner to death. A wealthy Bronx contractor's wife was taken from him for more than a week before he paid a pair of Italians to have her returned. Her main abductor was later released when, likely out of fear, the wife testified that she'd left of her own free will because she liked the man.

The wives of prosperous Italian businessmen began spiriting their children away to the countryside to keep them safe from kidnappers. One prominent banker sent his children to a remote part of upstate New York to be guarded by detectives.

But the Black Hand would not be confined. On August 28 Joseph Graffi was stabbed to death in a New Rochelle tenement because, police believed, he'd refused to pay tribute to the Black Hand. Two days later, the Black Hand was reported to have turned up in Greenwich, Connecticut, where prosperous Italian families were taking to arming themselves with pistols. Many Italians began having themselves sworn in as deputy sheriffs so they could carry firearms and shoot any Black Hand outlaw they could find. Some patrolled in front of their homes with shotguns; others hired bodyguards or bought Saint Bernard watchdogs.

Many Black Handers were simply copycats, while others were fakes. In one case, a thirteen-year-old boy from White Plains, New York, wrote a letter to a businessman demanding $1,000 under a threat of death. Upon his arrest, the boy claimed that three Italians threatened to kill his father if he didn't write the letter, but the police said he made up the story.

Then in October 1904, when a false rumor flew that the Black Hand was planning to dynamite Public School No. 172 on East 108th Street, five hundred panicked parents stormed the front doors demanding that the two thousand pupils inside be released. "It has come to pass that a little matter has kindled a great fire," the *Brooklyn Daily Eagle* editorialized. "There is need of detective work by someone, and speedily."

Petrosino didn't disagree. Despite the occasional pranks and unfounded rumors, he considered the problem to be greater than the public generally believed. For every one of the dozen or so Italians who walked into his office each day to show him Black Hand letters and ask for protection, dozens if not hundreds more cases went unreported.

Most parents of kidnapped children quietly paid to get them back. Petrosino practically pleaded for victims of Black Hand crimes to promptly go to the police and not to give in to the extortionists' demands. But most of his countrymen had no faith in the non-Italian cops or were too afraid to go to them.

Petrosino and others advocated a solution: to gain the trust and confidence of law-abiding Italians, create a special unit of Italian detectives to work directly with the Italian community, as Petrosino had been doing virtually alone the past several years. Italian Americans were not cowardly by nature, Petrosino maintained, but they lacked concerted action. "The trouble is that everyone is waiting for everyone else to act first," he explained. "If they would form a Vigilance League that would drive into the hands of the police Italian malefactors, they would be as safe as anyone else."

Police Commissioner William McAdoo resisted the idea. He thought that because the Italians wouldn't ask for help, they weren't worthy of any special treatment. Although he paid lip service to the notion that most Italians were decent, honest, and hardworking, McAdoo said that police work would not produce the desired results unless it was "followed up by a moral movement on the part of the better class of Italians." Besides, an all-Italian police unit would alienate the Irish cops who would be ineligible to serve on it. Although enlightened and innovative in other police matters, McAdoo turned down Petrosino's repeated lobbying efforts over several months in 1904.

But the terror inspired by the sheer number of unnerving incidents, real and imagined, finally forced McAdoo's hand. In September 1904 he announced the creation of a small bureau of five Italian-speaking detectives, to be chosen and headed by Petrosino, charged with wiping out Black Hand outrages. It would become known as the Italian Squad.

Of the approximately eight thousand NYPD officers in 1904, only seventeen spoke Italian. From this group, Petrosino, a sort of Italian Elliot Ness, selected five trusted, incorruptible associates. They included Maurice Bonnoil, a French-descended veteran of the central detective bureau who grew up on the Lower East Side and spoke fluent Sicilian. Among the Italians on the squad was one Hugh Cassidy, who, according to legend, chose his last name in honor of the western outlaw Butch Cassidy. More likely it was an Americanization of his given name (said to be Ugo Cassidi).*

It was unrealistic, though, to think that six detectives could adequately police a New York City Italian population of nearly a half million, especially since, in Petrosino's estimate, ten thousand Italian criminals infested the city. And the NYPD didn't make things any easier for the "mysterious six," as they were dubbed. They were given no office space in the headquarters building at 300 Mulberry Street, so they drifted from

---

* New Yorkers were fascinated with Wild West gunfighters. When Bat Masterson, a transplanted Manhattanite and sports journalist, was named a deputy US marshal in early 1905 by President Theodore Roosevelt, *The Sun* declared that the Mafia and Black Hand had better watch out. So far as history records, Masterson never lifted a finger against either of them.

one temporary meeting spot to another for a while, including Petrosino's own apartment.

At one point, Petrosino and his men took up headquarters in a rented room at 176 Waverly Place, a quiet side street in Greenwich Village, where they posted a sign as a real estate business and disguised themselves as laborers. Suspicious neighbors complained to the precinct police, who assumed that the Italians congregating there were a criminal band.

One night in 1905, while Petrosino and his men were off chasing real criminals, Captain John O'Brien and his men from the Charles Street station broke into the Waverly Place room, tore it up, and confiscated a bunch of papers written in Italian. O'Brien asked headquarters for an Italian Squad member to translate them but was told he'd need to wait because all the Italian detectives were out of town.

For three days, the cops waited for the Italians to return, and when Petrosino showed up at Waverly Place, O'Brien drew his gun and tried to arrest him. After learning he'd nearly handcuffed an esteemed fellow police officer, a chastened O'Brien was transferred to Greenpoint in Brooklyn. Petrosino and his little unit, now homeless, found new quarters.

Despite the resentment of their peers and the obstacles they faced, the Italian Squad scored some notable successes. In one case, Petrosino apprehended a Black Hander who'd been persecuting Cerino Nizzari, a baker, for six months. In September 1905 the extortionist broke into Nizzari's bakery at 98 Bayard Street and fired a shot that missed him but resulted in the death of his grandchild. While trying to distract the shooter, Nizzari's daughter dropped her baby, who was burned to death by a pot of boiling water knocked over in the fracas.

Assigned to the case, Petrosino arrested the assailant within hours of Nizzari's complaint. While testifying, the defiant defendant said, "I'll go to jail, but he [Nizzari] will pay the penalty. My friends will look after him, all right." But Nizzari continued running his bakery, dying of natural causes ten years later.

In February 1906 Petrosino and an associate arrested three Lower East Side Italians for dynamiting the storefront of a Brooklyn

saloonkeeper while he, his wife, and seven children slept upstairs, un-
hurt. Just two days later, Petrosino scored another coup with an ingenious
plan to nab a Bleecker Street man who was expected to show up that day
at Petro Miano's nearby butcher shop to collect part of the money he'd
been demanding from him.

Petrosino had four of his detectives hide in the huge meat freezer, into
which he drilled four peepholes, one for each sleuth. While Petrosino
kept watch outside, the four detectives stood shivering inside the freezer
for several hours, waiting for the blackmailer to arrive. Miano's wife
slipped them hot coffee and steak from time to time to keep them warm
while the men "prayed that they might not become as a young calf that
hung beside them frozen stiff," *The Sun* reported in a story headlined
"Four Detectives on Ice."

In due course, the Black Hander, one Giacohino Napoli, arrived and
accepted an envelope containing $10 in marked bills. The four detectives
pounced on him, and Petrosino rushed in to apply the coup de grâce—
gripping Napoli's shoulder "with a hand of iron," *The Sun* reported (and
probably much more). Black Hand letters were found on Napoli and on
his two fellow gang members, whom Petrosino arrested the next day
based on clues developed from Napoli's arrest.

With each new arrest of a Black Hand criminal—and his squad made
hundreds of them—the Petrosino legend grew. So did the size of his
squad. In 1905, McAdoo granted him a few additional detectives, and in
1906, McAdoo's successor as police commissioner, Theodore Bingham,
an autocratic, one-legged former army general, added a couple dozen
more. They included a unit in Brooklyn under Detective Sergeant Antonio Vachris, who would later succeed Petrosino as head of the squad.

The Italian Squad's colorful exploits made great press fodder. When,
in early 1907, Petrosino and three of his trusted men quietly entered a
saloon and pounced on five Black Handers lined up against the bar, an
irreverent young American was heard to exclaim outside, "Gee. Dey've
pinched some more guys wid black hands! It's a wonder dem dagoes
wouldn't wash their mitts once a month!"

Four decades later, Edward Radin, perhaps the leading American criminologist of his generation, recalled Petrosino's career admiringly. "His exploits were recounted and embellished in countless coffeehouses and wineshops," Radin wrote. "Small children tagged at his heels as he strode through crowded streets, his dark, restless eyes studying the faces of everyone he passed."

In extolling Petrosino, however, Radin helped perpetuate at least one myth that appears in practically every book and article on Petrosino written since. Radin claimed that Petrosino trapped the writer of a Black Hand letter who was trying to extort money from opera star Enrico Caruso. The story has grown tentacles over the years, to the point where Petrosino supposedly begged Caruso not to pay the blackmailers, then donned a cape and suit to impersonate the singer and met with the letter writers at an agreed location, where the detective overpowered and arrested them.

In 1910 Caruso did, in fact, receive Black Hand letters in New York demanding $15,000, which he refused to pay. And the NYPD did trap and catch the culprits at a remote spot in Brooklyn, using a dummy package. But Petrosino played no role whatsoever in planning or executing the sting operation.

The Caruso story was not the only exaggeration of Petrosino's accomplishments. In fact, for all the touting of the Italian Squad, it was proving to be no match for the Black Hand. Crimes attributed to Black Handers continued to increase, with 424 Black Hand cases and 44 bombings reported in New York in 1908. The 33 Black Hand offenses that made their way into the pages of New York's newspapers that year were just the tip of the iceberg. "When one remembers that for every case of extortion reported to the police there are probably 250 of which nothing is said, the size of the cloud which the Black Hand has thrown over New York becomes appalling," declared *Cosmopolitan* magazine in an article titled "The Black Hand Scourge."

The conviction rate remained low—only around 15 percent of arrests resulted in guilty verdicts—and sentences were light, averaging about a year for extortionists and bomb throwers. Many victims, moreover, remained unidentified. "It is by no means uncommon to find the headless bodies of Italians floating in the river or hidden away in boxcars or in the swamps on the edge of the city," *Cosmopolitan* observed.

Everyone expressed outrage at the situation. Writing in September 1908, a journalist for *Everybody's Magazine* labeled the existence and growth of the Black Hand "a demoralizing disgrace to our system for maintaining public order." The decentralized nature of the so-called society contributed to its elusiveness, the writer added. "It is little wonder that the American police have not been able to make much headway against so indefinite an organization."

That same year, impassioned speakers for Italian American groups protested against the opprobrium attached to members of their nationality. Italian opinion leaders belittled the importance or even the existence of the Black Hand, the *New-York Tribune* reported, "at the same time denouncing the police for their inefficiency in failing to stamp it out if it really existed."

At an overflow mass meeting attended by more than a thousand Italians at 178 Park Row, the Italian Vigilance Protection Association was organized in light of the perceived inadequacy of police protection. An Italian newspaper editor who was elected to head the organization advised any members who sustained property losses due to bomb explosions to sue the city for damages.

Some Italian New Yorkers, such as Francesco Spinella, whose tenements on East Eleventh Street were bombed repeatedly by Black Handers, claimed that the Irish police force refused to protect them unless they paid for the privilege. "Are we not dagoes?" Spinella rhetorically asked. "They [the police] leave us alone unless they, too, can blackmail us."

The combative police commissioner Bingham, a self-styled opponent of graft who had promised to "raise hell" in the office, strenuously denied that charge. But Bingham, a blue blood like his predecessor, McAdoo, took a dim view of immigrants generally. In a controversial 1908 article in the *North American Review*, he claimed that 50 percent of the city's criminals were "Russian Hebrews." But the "Italian malefactor," he asserted, was "by far the greater menace to law and order," part of a "riffraff of desperate scoundrels, ex-convicts, and jailbirds of the camorra and Mafia, such as has never before afflicted a civilized country in time of peace." Under a storm of protest, he retracted his charge against Jews, saying he'd been given inaccurate statistics, but he did not withdraw his condemnation of the Italian race.

In all events, it remained clear to everyone that forty Italian Squad detectives were far too few to handle the overwhelming number of Black Hand cases. "The employment of Irish policemen in Rome would be an analogous circumstance, since there are more Italians in New York than in the capital of Italy," the former president of the United Italian Society complained in April 1908. Bingham acknowledged the problem but insisted that young Italian men preferred going into business to entering public service. Besides which, he said, few Italian newcomers would be able to pass the police civil service exam.

Bingham had no criticism of Petrosino, whom he considered one of the NYPD's best men. "Petrosino has done good work, but the situation has become too great for him and his little squad to handle," Bingham contended. "And they are all known, which partly destroys their usefulness." The first thing an Italian criminal did off the boat at Ellis Island, the commissioner said, was to acquaint himself with the appearance of Petrosino and the other Italian detectives. "Fresh *parsley* for sale! See the beautiful *parsley*!" vegetable peddlers took to shouting loudly in Italian as a warning that Petrosino, whose name sounded like the Sicilian word for parsley (*petrosello*), was near. As the *Tribune* put it in July 1908, Mayor McClellan could more easily walk the streets of New York without being recognized than could Petrosino's Italian Squad.

The tough-on-crime Bingham proposed creating a new secret police force of ten or so picked men, known and answerable only to him, that he rather implausibly claimed could crush the Black Hand in no time.

But Big Tim Sullivan and his aldermen, widely suspected of being in league with New York's underworld, refused to appropriate funds for the operation, calling it dangerous and undemocratic. Undaunted by "crooked politicians," Bingham privately raised a $30,000 fund from an anonymous group of Italian merchants and wealthy New Yorkers. (Andrew Carnegie and John D. Rockefeller were mentioned as possible contributors.) The money was for a fifteen-man covert operation, reportedly to be headed by Petrosino.

Bingham contemplated a mission to send the Black Handers back to whence they came. The consensus of American-born New Yorkers, and even some Italian American leaders, was that simply too many bad men from Sicily, Naples, and other parts of southern Italy were pouring into the United States as a result of lax immigration laws. And if it was impossible to keep out the criminals, the only solution was to deport them.

It was a view that Petrosino shared. "The United States has become the dumping ground for all the criminals and banditti of Italy, Sicily, Sardinia, and Calabria," he lamented. He had no desire to make it more difficult for those of his honest countrymen seeking better lives in America to reach its shores. But he advocated a stricter inspection at ports of embarkation to prevent Italian fugitives from justice from entering the country. For example, he wanted to forbid admission to anyone without a proper passport, signed by the US consul, certifying that they had a clean record back home.

Petrosino also urged taking advantage of a new US immigration law, passed by Congress in 1907, that gave authorities the power to deport any immigrant residing in the United States for less than three years who'd been convicted of a crime in his native country. "I have already got a long list of names of men with records of crimes committed in Italy," Petrosino said. He also personally made a trip to Ellis Island to scour for additional incriminating information.

But securing evidence sufficient to satisfy the immigration authorities who would hear deportation cases meant obtaining records from Italy. Specifically, US law enforcement officers needed copies of Italian penal certificates—rap sheets—verifying the criminal's history of arrests and convictions in that country. The quickest way of gathering such information would be to send someone directly to Italy. And to Bingham, there was only one man for the job.

⟿⟾

In early February 1909 Joe Petrosino was nowhere to be found in New York, prompting rumors that he was in Italy to study the Black Hand and its methods. Bingham first denied it, then admitted that Petrosino might be on the ocean, bound for Europe, because he had "lots of money and a roving commission, and might be almost anywhere." But most observers thought he couldn't be far from Greater New York, and one insider scoffed at the notion that the Italian Sherlock Holmes had gone to his native country. "He may be in Italy," the man said, "but I'll bet my next month's check that it is Little Italy where 'Joe' is, and I wouldn't be surprised if he was working [Italian] Harlem streets with a hand organ and a 'monk' at that."

It wasn't just New York's newspaper readers who were curious to learn of Petrosino's whereabouts. Up on East 138th Street, a printer named Antonio Comito became privy to a conversation between two mafiosi about Petrosino's rumored trip to Italy. Comito, who'd been forcibly recruited by Giuseppe Morello's counterfeiting gang to manufacture fake $5 Canadian and $2 American notes, was summoned to a meeting in a tenement built by the Ignazio Florio Co-operative Association, the real estate company formed by Morello and Lupo the Wolf some years earlier.

The Florio Association was now teetering on bankruptcy, a victim of the Panic of 1907 and Petrosino's relentless efforts to expose it as a sham business that bilked hapless Italian investors of hundreds of thousands of dollars. Petrosino, who had a special dislike of Lupo, impounded $50,000 worth of his consigned goods from a New Jersey pier and chased him from New York City, sending him off with a severe beating.

Morello had gone so far as to threaten Petrosino with a libel suit for damaging his and Lupo's commercial reputation. It was the collapse of their real estate venture and Lupo's grocery business that had prompted the pair to resume the counterfeiting operations they had lain off after evading prosecution for the Barrel Murder five years earlier.

After being ushered into the meeting room by a man named Antonio Cecala, Comito was introduced to a black-eyed, dark-mustached man who, because of the deference Cecala paid him, was obviously the head of the group. What immediately caught Comito's attention was the leader's deformed, shriveled hand. Comito was face-to-face with the Clutch Hand himself.

After quizzing Comito about counterfeiting niceties, Morello had a cryptic conversation with Cecala about an unnamed member of the gang, referred to as "the Calabrian," who'd been given a traveling assignment. In a subsequent confession, Comito recalled the following conversation:

> CECALA: Tell me something, Piddu [a nickname for Morello].
>   Have you arranged for the fare for the Calabrian?
> MORELLO: I have not arranged for it yet.
> CECALA: Why not?
> MORELLO: It is not sure that this low detective will go. . . . For
>   it is a secret thing and not even known to many of the police
>   as yet.
> CECALA: Damn detective. He guards his own hide without
>   calculating how many he has ruined.

About a week later, at a lonely farmhouse upstate in Highland, New York, now the relocated center of the actual counterfeiting operations, Comito was present again to hear several of the gang members speaking as they ate and drank merrily over a big Italian meal. They included Lupo the Wolf, Cecala, a man named Cina, and an older man known as Uncle Vincent.

> LUPO: You know all the news that I bear, except that it is said
>   Petrosino has gone to Italy.

VINCENT: If he went to Italy, he will be killed.

CINA: If it could only be done successfully.

LUPO: He has ruined many. . . . But I can tell you that I have given the Calabrian his fare.

CECALA: You have done well. Let us drink to our health, and to hell with that *carogna* [scum; lowlife].*

The rumors were true. On February 9, 1909, a couple of days before his Mafia enemies' feast in Highland, Joe Petrosino had set sail for Italy in what would be his first return to his native land in thirty-five years.

---

* The literal translation is "dead, putrid animal carcass," but according to Flynn, the word was used among Sicilian mafiosi to designate anyone who brings harm to any gang of criminals.

CHAPTER TWENTY-NINE

ENDINGS

The forty-eight-year-old Petrosino, now a lieutenant, had mixed feelings about going. A lifelong workaholic bachelor, he'd been married in December 1907, had a ten-week-old baby girl, and was starting to enjoy domestic life at their Lafayette Street apartment.

His friends warned him that Sicily would be hostile territory for a Mafia-busting American cop, even an Italian one. He was at once unafraid yet philosophical about the danger, having said often, to the effect, "Some day they will get me." But he answered the summons to duty and set sail for Italy, alone, on his secret mission, posing as a Jewish businessman under an assumed name.

Traveling first-class on the *Duca di Genova*, Petrosino was carrying hundreds of criminals' names while packing a .38-caliber Smith & Wesson revolver. After a stormy passage, he disembarked in Genoa and arrived in Rome on February 21, where he marveled at his first sight of St. Peter's Basilica and the Sistine Chapel.

In Rome he met with Italian government and police officials before heading south by train for a quick visit to his hometown of Padula. From there, he took the train to Naples, where he caught a mail boat for Palermo. Arriving there on February 28, he checked into the Hôtel de France, off the city square Piazza Marina, and registered under another false name, this one Italian.

From the moment he stepped off the boat in Palermo, Petrosino's cover was blown already, his presence known to anyone who was interested. As early as February 5, two weeks before the headline-hungry Commissioner Bingham blabbed to the press that his star detective might be Europe bound, an Italian language newspaper in New York, *L'Araldo Italiano*, had printed details of his itinerary and the purpose of his mission. On February 20 the European edition of the *New York Herald* published a story, apparently based on leaks from Bingham's office, that Petrosino had gone to Sicily in search of records that could be used to deport New York's Italian criminals.

Newspapermen and some fellow passengers recognized Petrosino, and in Rome, he noticed he was being followed by a man he'd seen before in New York but couldn't quite place. Upon being discovered, the man quickly ran off and went to a post office, where Petrosino, trailing, watched him head for the telegraph window. Petrosino learned that the man had sent a telegram to Noto, in southern Sicily, but its contents could not be ascertained. From that point forward, Petrosino always had the feeling he was under surveillance in Italy.

After so many years in America, Petrosino seemed out of his element in his native country. His legendary photographic memory had failed him when it came to the stranger he'd caught following him. He confessed to his wife in a letter that he didn't really like Italy and felt lonely and disoriented there.

The Italian authorities were polite but weren't going out of their way to be helpful. Petrosino gathered plenty of penal certificates but suspected that others had been altered to delete mention of crimes for persons heading to America. In fact, though Petrosino didn't know it, for 500 lire, any Italian seeking entry to the United States could bribe an Italian government official to issue him or her a clean certificate.

Petrosino turned down an offer of a bodyguard from Palermo's police chief, whom he didn't totally trust, preferring to rely on his own protective coterie of friends and informants. They managed to provide him access to judicial sources that only persons in high places could have known about.

The Sicilian police, in turn, kept up their own watch over Petrosino, who was visiting what they called "the most dangerous underworld" spots in Palermo and holding nightly conferences with mysterious unidentified individuals. The local police chief complained in a report to a superior that Petrosino was taking unnecessary risks—meeting with public officials when he didn't need to and talking too much with employees of the Café Oreto, near his hotel, where he took his nightly meals. Incautiously, he opened a bank account in his own name and had his mail directed there. He traveled Palermo's streets unarmed.

It all seemed so uncharacteristic of Petrosino, who, back in New York, had lately been in the habit of having a colleague trail him at night because he was such a target. It was that sort of behavior that caused New York mafiosi to curse Petrosino for guarding his own hide while making life so difficult for them.

Early in the evening on March 12, back at his hotel, Petrosino went over his notebook of Italian candidates for deportation. He added to it a name and description: "Vito Cascioferro . . . dreaded criminal." Cascioferro was by then the undisputed head of the Sicilian Mafia, but what prompted the particular note is unclear, since he was living near Palermo, having fled the United States just after the Barrel Murder in 1903. Did the detective somehow know that Cascioferro, whose arrest for counterfeiting in 1902 was based on Petrosino's tip to the Secret Service, had vowed revenge upon him?

Around seven-thirty, after a rainstorm ended, Petrosino set off for dinner. He made the one-minute walk from his hotel across the Piazza Marina square to the Café Oreto. He took his usual precaution of seating himself with his back to the wall so that no assailant could come upon him from behind. He then ordered his favorite Sicilian meal of pasta with tomato sauce, fish, fried potatoes, cheese, and wine.

As he was eating the cheese course, two unidentified men entered the restaurant, came up to greet him, and remained standing as they spoke to him for a few minutes. He waved them off as if to indicate he'd see them a little later, then after they left, he paid the bill and walked out into the dark, deserted square, weakly illuminated by yellowish gaslights.

Petrosino did not head directly for his hotel but instead walked to the ornate iron fence that enclosed the Garibaldi Garden in the middle of the square. One bystander saw him—a sailor from off a ship docked at the nearby marina, who was waiting at the tram terminal a hundred feet away.

Some accounts say Petrosino seemed to be looking to rendezvous with someone—perhaps the two men from the restaurant, or another informant. According to the sailor, two men crept up behind Petrosino and fired four shots, three of which hit him. One shot pierced his lungs, another went through his throat, while the last shot struck the side of his face, apparently as he spun around to confront his attackers. He grabbed hold of the iron gate as he fell.

After the sailor saw the two assailants flee into the darkness, he ran to the scene. He found Petrosino lying dead, a revolver alongside him and his derby hat a few feet away. It turned out that the gun wasn't his but had been left behind by the killers, contradicting initial reports that Petrosino had returned fire. His own pistol, unloaded, was found back in his hotel room.

Inside Petrosino's pockets were some money and checks, lists of criminals' names, including the recent addition of Cascioferro, and letters and memoranda concerning upcoming meetings and to-do items. Police also found a picture postcard addressed to his wife but as yet unsent; it read, "A kiss for you and my little girl, who has spent three months far from her daddy."

Petrosino's murder made the front page of every major New York newspaper. Reaction ranged from shock to sorrow to anger. "Oh, my poor Joe!" his wife shrieked when she received the news before collapsing. Cries of *"E morto, il povero Petrosino!"* ("He's dead, poor Petrosino!") were heard at the doorsteps of tenements in Little Italy. Italian newspapers across the country hailed him as a hero of his people.

Naturally the Mafia and/or Black Hand were assumed to be behind the killing. The American press and public officials, and even *La Tribuna*, a Roman newspaper, blamed the Palermo police for their alleged indifference to Petrosino's safety and their apparent cluelessness as to his murderers' identity. Some placed responsibility on loose immigration laws or the character of the Italian people themselves. A defensive Bingham sought to downplay his indiscretion in allowing Petrosino's trip to become public, but it was a factor in his dismissal as police commissioner four months later.

The 1909 funeral of Joe Petrosino, the "Italian Sherlock Holmes," drew thousands of fellow NYPD officers and citizen mourners. Former president Theodore Roosevelt said of his friend: "Petrosino was a great and good man. I knew him for years. He did not know fear."

Petrosino's body was brought back to New York for a funeral at old St. Patrick's Cathedral between Mulberry and Mott Streets, where he'd been married less than two years earlier. (It was later the site of the baptism scene in the film *The Godfather*.) More than two hundred thousand New Yorkers lined the streets and filled balconies and windows along the funeral procession from the church to Calvary Cemetery in Woodside, Queens, for burial with honors.

To the sound of muffled drums and the tolling bells, more than a thousand of the 3,200 NYPD officers who attended the funeral, most of them Irish, marched behind the horse-drawn hearse. They were led by Chief Inspector Max Schmittberger on a bay steed. A police band played "Nearer, My God, to Thee" and *Requiem* by Petrosino's favorite, Verdi. Flags flew at half-mast, including those atop city government buildings, all of which were closed by order of the mayor, as well as at such bastions of old-line Protestantism as the Waldorf Astoria and the Union Club.

"If Petrosino had died a President or an Emperor, no deeper or truer show of feeling could have been manifested," *The New York Times* offered. Former president Theodore Roosevelt said of his friend: "Petrosino was a great and good man. I knew him for years. He did not know fear . . . I regret most sincerely the death of such a man as 'Joe' Petrosino."

Art Carey, the detective's ex-partner, wrote that Petrosino's "most tragic" death had "robbed the New York Police Department of one of its bravest men." Big Tim Sullivan sponsored a state senate bill to grant Petrosino's widow a $2,000 pension, her honest husband having died with little money to his name, unlike crooked cops such as Petrosino's original mentor, Clubber Williams.

Petrosino's killers were never brought to justice. Several Mafia types, including Cascioferro, were arrested and questioned by the Italian authorities, but there was no hard evidence to hold any of them.

Although the case remains officially unsolved, the consensus of those who have studied it is that Petrosino's murder was plotted by Morello and Lupo and carried out under the supervision of Cascioferro. That conclusion is bolstered not only by Antonio Comito's confession but also by anonymous letters someone in New York, seemingly possessed of inside information, sent to the Italian police immediately after news of Petrosino's murder surfaced. The letters asserted that the killing was ordered by Morello, Lupo, and their associates, including Morello's Terranova half brothers and Inzerillo, the pastry shop owner.

The Morello group allegedly sent a pair of assassins to Sicily and then turned the job over to Cascioferro for execution. The motive was some combination of revenge for the past and preventing future trouble Petrosino might cause. Comito recalled further that when news that Petrosino was dead arrived at the upstate New York farmhouse where the Morello gang printed its counterfeits, everyone was elated. Of the murder, Lupo told the group, "The way it was done, it could never fail."

Among ten or so individuals variously suspected of having pulled the trigger, the ones mentioned most often are Morello gang members Carlo Costantino (one of the men arrested in the Barrel Murder case) and his "construction business" partner in New York, Antonino Passananti. The two of them had sailed for Sicily from New York the day after Petrosino left the United States. They met with Cascioferro days before the assassination and were seen together on a bench in the Piazza Marina just hours before Petrosino's murder. A cryptic telegram found in Costantino's pocket, from Morello, read, "Why cut his whiskers off?"

Cascioferro had an alibi for the night in question, supplied by an Italian politician who said the Mafia don had been staying with him in a town fifty miles south of Palermo. Many years later, while imprisoned by Benito Mussolini's Fascists, Cascioferro supposedly bragged that he himself was the gunman. While that confession is of doubtful validity, there is little question that Cascioferro was involved in the murder.

Joe Petrosino was the first, and remains to this day the only, New York policeman killed on foreign soil in the line of duty. His positive legacy includes a number of innovations in law enforcement techniques, from the use of undercover disguises, to infiltration of criminal groups, to the study of bomb components and tracking down of bomb makers—the forerunner of the Bomb Squad, which he is credited with founding.

As an NYPD cop, he cooperated with other federal agencies, including the Secret Service and US immigration authorities, as well as with foreign police, in a manner now commonplace. As one historian of prominent Italian Americans writes, "Today, a century after Petrosino made his final, tragic journey across the Atlantic Ocean, New York detectives are stationed around the world to combat international crime and terrorism."

Petrosino is the subject of several biographical films, including *Black Hand* (1950), starring Gene Kelly as a character based loosely on the Italian detective, and *Pay or Die!* (1960), starring Ernest Borgnine. A 1972 Italian television miniseries and a 1973 Italian crime film (with American character actor Lionel Stander as Petrosino) featured him as well. As of this writing, Petrosino reportedly is also slated to be played by Leonardo DiCaprio in another Hollywood biopic under development.

In 1987 the name of a small triangular park in Little Italy was changed from Kenmare Square to Petrosino Square in his honor. (The original name was conferred by Big Tim Sullivan in 1911 in memory of the village in Ireland from which his mother emigrated.) The concrete park fell into disrepair, but in 2009, a hundred years after Petrosino's death, the City of New York reopened and rededicated an expanded Lieutenant Petrosino Square that included trees, benches, a paved pedestrian walkway, and space for public art exhibitions. A bronze relief portrait of Petrosino was added in 2014.

The park is a three-minute walk north of the police headquarters that replaced 300 Mulberry Street in December 1909, nine months after the lieutenant's murder. Fittingly, the new building included rooms for the redesignated Italian bureau first headed by Petrosino, as well as the homicide bureau first led by Art Carey.

The new headquarters also featured a revamped lineup room where prisoners were paraded daily, with special bright lights that allowed detectives to view the suspects without being seen themselves. A gymnasium with an elevated running track, a 130-foot pistol range, a school for instruction, and an entire first floor for the detective bureau were additional improvements. Finally, on the top floor was a state-of-the-art rogues' gallery.

The daily lineup, detective bureau, and rogues' gallery were, of course, made famous by perhaps the NYPD's greatest innovator and most influential leader. And six months after the department's headquarters moved from 300 Mulberry to 240 Centre Street, as the Gilded Age came to a close, he, too, would be gone.

⊷⊜⊜⊶

After his forced retirement as police superintendent in 1895, Thomas Byrnes largely avoided the limelight. He took a job as general manager of the burglary department of a Wall Street insurance company in 1896 and, two years later, opened a private detective agency at John Street and Broadway, offering "high-class service" to lawyers, bankers, corporations, and individuals. (In *The Alienist* novel and television series, both set in 1896, then private detective Byrnes appears as a rather sinister figure who counsels the likes of robber baron J. P. Morgan.) In retirement, Byrnes continued dabbling in Manhattan real estate and monitoring his investments. Yachting and driving horse trotters were his favorite hobbies.

Although he consulted with New York's mayors on police department matters from time to time and at least once was mentioned as a potential candidate for police commissioner, Byrnes never returned to the NYPD. But that didn't stop him from voicing strong opinions about its operation. In a 1908 interview, with crime in the city again on the rise, Byrnes declared that although the police force was sound from the ground up, it was inefficient due to "the incompetent head [Bingham] and incompetent deputies, who know nothing at all of the character of the work they are to supervise."

Earlier commissioners, he maintained, were worse than incompetent—they were dangerous. Of the first five commissioners to that time, including Bingham, none had come up through the NYPD ranks; four were former army generals or colonels, while the other, McAdoo, was a lawyer. But "neither West Point nor the law school gives a man the training that qualifies him to command the police department," Byrnes insisted. Blaming politics, he observed that an elected mayor appointed the police commissioner, who was either selected or accepted by the party leader irrespective of merit.

What the force needed instead, Byrnes said, was "a strong man who thoroughly understands police business." It was a description that Byrnes knew fit himself. And in the long run, it became the prevailing criteria: since the mid-1980s, every New York City police commissioner has had a solid law enforcement background, usually including specific NYPD experience. (The commissioner in 2021, Dermot F. Shea, mimicked Byrnes's background: the son of Irish immigrants, he previously served as chief of detectives.)

The *Harper's Weekly* reporter who conducted the 1908 interview of Byrnes found him at his New Jersey summer home, which featured a tree-filled lawn and a sprawling, large-windowed porch overlooking the Shrewsbury River. Inside, the rambling house was strewn with toys for the youngest of his five grandchildren.

Of Byrnes himself, the journalist wrote that "all the old power seems to be there." Graying but still muscular, his eyes alert as ever, he stood "straight and well poised, still moves with all the old precision, vigor, and balance."

But not long after that, Byrnes began suffering from an ailment that turned out to be stomach cancer. He died on May 7, 1910, at age sixty-eight, in his Manhattan home at 318 West Seventy-Seventh Street. He was survived by his wife and five daughters, three of whom were married. After a funeral attended by many old-timers of the police department, including nearly all the former notables still living, he was buried at Calvary Cemetery, where he joined Joe Petrosino in eternal rest.

Ex-inspector William McLaughlin, one of Byrnes's early right-hand men (he aided him in nabbing the Manhattan Savings Institution robbers), called Byrnes "the greatest policeman New York ever had." In its front-page obituary, *The New York Times* said: "For fifteen years or more, 'In Tom Byrnes's day' has been the standard way of introducing the best of Police Department yarns. When Byrnes ruled the department with a mailed fist, he made the Detective Bureau famous."

He was, the *Times* commented, the "last important figure connected with the reorganization of the New York force over the undisciplined body which had come up from the days when New York was a grown-up village to a modern system adequate to the needs of one of the greatest cities in the world." The NYPD itself had grown from about three thousand officers in 1886, when Byrnes published his landmark *Professional Criminals* book, to more than ten thousand in 1910.

In many ways, Byrnes had become a figure of the past, of Old New York, with crime fighting having passed him by. "Of the many complex problems due to the mixed races that flocked to New York in recent years, the chiefs in Byrnes's day knew little or nothing," the *Times* said eight days after his death in an article headlined "New Police Methods Supersede the Old." When Byrnes was at the height of his fame, the *Times* pointed out, the Irish were to a large extent the only foreign element he encountered. He never had to deal with the influx of Jewish, Italian, and Sicilian gangsters who began terrorizing the Lower East Side underworld around the turn of the century, or the tongs who dominated Chinatown.

The types of adversaries Byrnes typically faced—the high-society bank robber George Leslie, the charming criminal fence Marm Mandelbaum, the clever pickpocket and green goods man George Appo—seemed quaint compared with the vicious, gun-carrying mobsters of later years. And the deductive, pavement-pounding methods of detection he employed and imparted to protégés such as Art Carey were beginning to be replaced by fingerprinting and other forensic analysis.

In 1911 NYPD lieutenant Joseph Faurot's expert testimony would produce the first criminal conviction in the United States based solely on fingerprint evidence. Had fingerprinting or accurate blood typing been available in Byrnes's day, he might have quickly identified New York's Jack the Ripper, just as Art Carey might have easily solved the murder of Dolly Reynolds or the Roland Molineux case.

And yet, as the subhead to the *Times*'s "New Police Methods" story conceded, "The Work Inaugurated by the Late Inspector Thomas Byrnes Was the Foundation of the Present System." New departments such as the traffic squad, the health squad, and the Italian bureau were merely branches of the general structure he had put in place with the reorganized detective bureau. And detective work, even with scientific advances, still required much legwork, intelligence gathering, and cultivation of informants— tactics that Byrnes pioneered.

A decade after Byrnes's death, Prohibition would usher in another period of turbulent change in crime and law enforcement in New York City and elsewhere. But by the close of the Gilded Age, the underpinnings were in place. It had been roughly thirty years from that Sunday morning in 1878 when the cigar-chomping Captain Thomas Byrnes arrived at Bleecker Street and Broadway to take charge of the Manhattan Savings robbery investigation, to the day of his death in 1910, by which time the Mafia had firmly established itself in New York. And those eventful years had indeed seen the birth of modern policing and organized crime in Gilded Age New York.

Cops

After losing his state senate bid in 1895, **Alexander "Clubber" Williams**, the ex-czar of the Tenderloin, and the man who gave the district its name, went into the insurance business and made even more money. To the end of his life, he maintained defiantly that there wasn't a single person he ever clubbed who didn't deserve it. He died in 1917, at age seventy-seven, at his West Ninety-Fifth Street home.

That same year marked the passing of sixty-six-year-old **Max Schmittberger**, who had named names, notably including that of Williams, in the Lexow Committee hearings. Schmittberger survived his squealer reputation and served on the force another twenty-three years, rising eventually to chief inspector, the highest rank an NYPD officer could then attain. According to some, Schmittberger returned to bribe taking later in his career, but the charges were never proven.

Williams and Schmittberger were followed in death by **Big Bill Devery**, who succumbed to apoplexy at age sixty-five in June 1919. He died six months before the mediocre New York Yankees team he once owned acquired Babe Ruth's contract from the Boston Red Sox and went on to become the most successful professional sports franchise of all time.

After the firing of Police Commissioner Bingham in 1909, a police shake-up the following year led to **Art Carey**'s being reassigned from head of the Homicide Squad back to precinct duty. Four years later,

Carey was back as the head of the squad, reappointed by new commissioner and former journalist Arthur Woods, a reformer and modernizer who brought a scientific and sociological approach to law enforcement. The Harvard-educated Woods advocated community policing, better police training and discipline, and applying the latest innovations in criminology, including a psychopathic laboratory to study murder and sex crimes. Carey was his favorite commander.

Carey continued to head the Homicide Squad until December 1928, when yet another departmental reorganization forced his retirement at age sixty-three on a captain's pension despite his having attained the position of deputy inspector. Citing statistics showing that the twenty men under Carey's command had made only two arrests in 228 homicide cases reported to them that year, Police Commissioner Grover Whalen, an appointee of New York's flamboyant Roaring Twenties mayor Jimmy Walker, abolished the central homicide squad. In its place, he established in each of the five boroughs separate homicide squads accountable directly to deputy inspectors. (The NYPD homicide teams remain organized by borough today.)

Whalen also blamed Carey, among others on the force, for failing to solve the murder of the notorious gambler Arnold Rothstein, who, in 1928, was shot in a card game in room 349 of the Park Central Hotel, at West Fifty-Sixth Street and Seventh Avenue. Carey procured sufficient evidence leading to the indictment of Rothstein's gambling buddy George McManus, but the case was later dismissed and was never solved.

Two years after his retirement, Carey published his autobiography, *Memoirs of a Murder Man*, which became one of the classic texts on crime in late Gilded Age New York. He died on December 13, 1952, at age eighty-seven, at his Bronx residence, survived by his wife and seven children, including two sons who were NYPD detectives at the time of his death.

CROOKS

Despite escaping prosecution for their presumed involvement in the 1903 Barrel Murder case and the 1909 hit job on Joe Petrosino,

Giuseppe (the "Clutch Hand") Morello and his gang ended up faring none too well.

Thomas (the "Ox") Petto, in whose pocket the victim Benedetto Madonia's pawn ticket was found, moved to Pennsylvania after being released from jail for the murder. In October 1905 the twenty-six-year-old Petto was gunned down outside his home near Wilkes-Barre, felled by five rifle shots that left gaping holes in his chest. The assassin was never found.

Various theories hold that Petto was killed either by relatives of Madonia seeking revenge or on orders of Morello himself. Perhaps the Clutch Hand was angry that the Ox had stupidly pawned Madonia's watch and kept the ticket, putting the other gang members in jeopardy. Or else Morello figured that Petto knew too much.

Morello and his partner **Lupo the Wolf** and several cohorts were arrested for counterfeiting by the Secret Service in late 1909 and, based largely on printer Antonio Comito's testimony, were convicted by a federal jury in February 1910, despite death threats to the judge and government witnesses during the trial. Morello and Lupo begged for mercy as they were sentenced, respectively, to twenty-five and thirty years' hard labor.

After Morello's imprisonment, his youngest half brother, Nick Terranova, took over operation of the gang but was killed by Brooklyn camorra gunmen in 1916. Released from prison in 1920, Morello became a lieutenant to Joe "the Boss" Masseria, who profitably ran the Morello-Terranova crime family during Prohibition. But Morello was murdered by rival mafiosi in 1930, when he was sixty-three, followed by the murder of Masseria a year later, orchestrated by Lucky Luciano and other Mafia leaders.

Lupo, also released from prison in 1920, avoided a Mafia death sentence but was kept from power. Despite being suspected of various additional murders, he was paroled and pardoned conditionally to allow him to travel outside the country. In 1936, following fresh extortion charges in the United States, he was sent back to federal prison to serve the remainder of his 1910 counterfeiting sentence. Released in 1947, he died of natural causes three weeks later at the age of sixty-nine. He and Giuseppe Morello were both buried in Calvary Cemetery, not far from Joe Petrosino, the man they had ordered killed.

The **Black Hand** continued striking fear into New Yorkers for several years after Joe Petrosino's murder. (In an early scene in the film *The Godfather Part II*, set in 1917, the white-suited Don Fanucci is portrayed as a Black Hander.) Its decline began around 1915, and after World War I and Prohibition, it went into eclipse. Among the factors leading to its extinction: a severe police crackdown initiated by Commissioner Arthur Woods; the more lucrative opportunities that bootlegging offered hoodlums; a federal mail fraud statute that criminalized extortionate letters; and stricter immigration laws that reduced both the number of potential victims and perpetrators.

Although **Paul Vaccarelli (aka Paul Kelly)** maintained ties with the criminal underworld after his gang was broken up in 1905, his effort to rebrand himself as an honest labor-union leader was largely successful. When he died at age fifty-nine in April 1936, his *New York Times* obituary described him as a "dock strike conciliator" and, remarkably, made no mention of his criminal past. The *Times* noted merely that Vaccarelli, under the name Paul Kelly, had once held "considerable political power on the Lower East Side through his friendship with Big Tim Sullivan."

Monk Eastman was not as lucky. He was released from Sing Sing in 1909 after serving half his term for the 1904 Wetmore incident. Finding his old gang scattered and his leadership services no longer desired, he resumed a life of petty crime. In 1912 he was convicted of running an opium den and spent eight months in jail on Blackwell's Island, and in 1915 he was sent to prison in far upstate New York for stealing silverware and jewelry worth $10,000 in an Albany burglary.

Released in 1917, Eastman vowed to go straight. He joined the army and served valorously in World War I in the 106th Infantry Regiment of the Twenty-Seventh Division in France, earning an "excellent" service record. Wounded and gassed at the Battle of Vierstraat Ridge on the

Hindenburg Line in 1918, he escaped from his hospital bed in his pajamas, which he exchanged for a roughly fitting uniform he found in a salvage dump before making his return to the firing lines. In May 1919 New York governor Al Smith restored Eastman to the citizenship he had lost upon his previous felony convictions.

But the glow of heroism was short-lived. Shortly after four o'clock on Christmas night, December 26, 1920, Eastman was gunned down, gangster style, in front of the subway entrance on the south side of East Fourteenth Street, just off Union Square. He had five bullets in him from a cheap .32-caliber pistol, one of which fatally pierced his heart. He'd been shot at point-blank range, his hands raised to shield himself.

Because $144 was found in Monk's pocket, and his watch and chain were still on him, the motive for the killing wasn't robbery. Police speculated that it followed a quarrel over the gains of illegal rum traffic in which Eastman was reputedly engaged. A week later, a former Prohibition agent with a criminal record admitted shooting Eastman, claiming he'd acted in self-defense.

Given a military funeral in Brooklyn, Eastman was dressed in a private's uniform and placed inside a flag-draped coffin. After being laid to rest, he was honored with a rifle salute and the playing of taps. Only forty-seven years old, he was, in the *New York Herald*'s view, seventy-four in experience. Calling him "one of the toughest, most picturesque, cruelest gangsters that America has developed," the paper added that "wherever the story of the Lower East Side is told in book or tongue, his renown has spread. He died as he had lived—violently."

Big Tim Sullivan, the political patron of both Eastman and Kelly, suffered a nervous breakdown in 1912 and was committed to a mental institution. He would die a year later, run over by a freight train after slipping away from his confinement. He was fifty-one.

Curiously, for someone so closely associated with the criminal underworld, Big Tim's final legacy was a gun control measure, the first of its kind, that he pushed through the New York State Legislature in 1911. Known as the Sullivan Act, and still on the books today in New York, it made it a felony to carry a concealed weapon without a permit and required gun dealers to ask for proof of same before selling a firearm.

Sullivan insisted he had a sincere desire to cut down on the alarming rise in gun violence in the city, which was giving the law-abiding citizens of the Lower East Side a bad name. But others suspected his motive was to enable Tammany to direct selective police prosecution of any gangsters who strayed from the Tammany fold. Cops used the law so frequently to plant guns on hoodlums that crime bosses took to sewing up their coat and suit pockets and having their bodyguards or molls carry their revolvers.

The year 1912 also saw the end of the short but eventful reign of twenty-four-year-old **Jack Zelig**, who had succeeded to the Eastman gang's throne just two years earlier. Zelig's demise came in October 1912 when, riding the Second Avenue trolley past East Thirteenth Street, he was shot in the back of the head by a small-time pimp named "Red Phil" Davidson.

Davidson claimed Zelig had been threatening him, but that explanation has failed to convince many crime historians. It is likely no coincidence that Zelig was scheduled to testify the following day in the sensational trial of police lieutenant Charles Becker, accused of plotting the murder of gambler Herman Rosenthal, who had been blabbing to the press and DA's office about the protection money he was paying Becker.

Rosenthal was gunned down as he left the Hotel Metropole café near Times Square around two o'clock in the morning on July 16, 1912. He'd been summoned by an unidentified man who entered the café and said, "Can you come outside a minute, Herman?"

Witnesses identified Rosenthal's killers as four of Zelig's Jewish gangster associates, who, it transpired, had been hired by other gamblers affiliated with Becker to perform the deed. The gambler plotters, given immunity, testified that Becker, for whom they collected graft, had ordered the murder to shut up Rosenthal. The four accused gunmen were convicted at trial and later executed at Sing Sing.

The Becker-Rosenthal case, presided over initially by Judge John W.

Goff, would ultimately send forty-five-year-old Charley Becker to the electric chair in 1915. He was the first—and, to date, last—NYPD cop to receive the death penalty, although many writers down the years have questioned his guilt. Mentioned in F. Scott Fitzgerald's 1925 novel, *The Great Gatsby*, the case was both a coda to the story of crime and punishment in Gilded Age New York and a foreshadowing of what was to come during Prohibition and in later decades. It featured elements of illegal gambling, police corruption, detective sleuthing, hired gunmen, and cold-blooded, gangster-style murder.

And one other thing, nearly unprecedented at the time: the use of an automobile as a getaway car. As Herman Rosenthal was being called outside the Metropole, a gray Packard came to a halt thirty yards away on the other side of the street, the motor idling. While the chauffeur waited in the car, several dark-suited figures threw open the passenger doors and walked to the hotel entrance where the gambler was gunned down. At the first sound of shots, the car made a U-turn in the street to collect its passengers. And when Rosenthal's killers jumped onto the Packard's running boards as it sped away, then ducked inside the car, it was clear that one era had given way to another.

ACKNOWLEDGMENTS

My special thanks to my editor at Dutton, Brent Howard, and to my longtime agent, Jim Donovan, and his colleague Melissa Shultz, for their vision, encouragement, and guidance on this project from the start and throughout.

Many thanks, as well, to the Dutton/Penguin Random House production and editorial team, including senior production editor LeeAnn Pemberton, interior designer Kristin del Rosario, copyeditor Philip Bashe, editorial assistants Cassidy Sachs and Grace Layer, and production manager Bill Peabody.

Several crime and police historians read the manuscript and provided valuable insights, comments, and suggestions. Tom Hunt has an encyclopedic knowledge of Gilded Age and early-twentieth-century crime (the Mafia in particular) and frequently steered me in a more accurate direction. Bernie Whalen, a veteran NYPD lieutenant and author of a comprehensive book about the NYPD's first fifty years (from 1898), was especially helpful on police matters.

Tim Gilfoyle, perhaps the nation's leading expert on late-nineteenth-century urban underworld subcultures and the commercialization of sex, had numerous useful comments and suggestions. So did author and prolific myth buster Jerry Kuntz, a particularly great source on early Gilded Age crime. His annotated comments on Thomas Byrnes's *Professional*

Criminals of America and Herbert Asbury's *The Gangs of New York* were frequent, valuable references.

Daniel Czitrom, whose book on the Lexow investigation set the standard for that subject, provided many helpful suggestions for fitting the narrative into a larger sociopolitical context.

Authors Bob Pigott and Beverly Enwall, both of them fine writers, read the entire manuscript and provided numerous editorial suggestions that always improved the flow. Bob had many NYC-history-based comments, especially about city buildings and landmarks, while Beverly was able to provide a non–New Yorker's perspective on things.

Dave Larkin improved the manuscript in countless ways with comments large and small. As usual, my former Willkie Farr & Gallagher law partner and cliché expunger Larry Kamin took his sharp editing pen to the entire manuscript. Former Willkie Farr colleague and historian Hal Kennedy also provided great assistance, as did Kyler Culver, a friend and true scholar.

All errors, of course, remain mine alone.

Thank you to Chris Erichsen for his excellent maps; that's twice now.

Also thanks to the Oller and Sutton families for their help and encouragement.

I am grateful to the following libraries/archives/institutions: Detroit Public Library; Dickinson State University (Theodore Roosevelt Digital Library); Harvard College Library (Theodore Roosevelt Collection); John Jay College of Criminal Justice, Lloyd Sealy Library (Ellen Belcher); Library of Congress (Photographs and Manuscript Division); Museum of the City of New York; National Archives (College Park, Md.); New York City Municipal Archives; New York Public Library (Main Branch, Photographs, and Lincoln Center for the Performing Arts); Preservation Society of Newport County; and Redwood Library and Athenaeum, Newport, R.I.

ABBREVIATIONS

Books

Byrnes (1886) Thomas Byrnes, *Professional Criminals of America,* with introductions by Arthur M. Schlesinger Jr., and S. J. Perelman (1886; repr., New York: Chelsea House, 1969).

Byrnes (1895) Thomas Byrnes, *Professional Criminals of America*, rev. ed. (New York: G. W. Dillingham, 1895).

Carey Arthur A. Carey, *Memoirs of a Murder Man*, in collaboration with Howard McLellan (Garden City, N.Y.: Doubleday, 1930).

Walling George W. Walling, *Recollections of a New York Chief of Police* (New York: Caxton, 1887).

Newspapers

Herald *New York Herald*
NYT *New York Times*
Sun *The Sun* (New York)
Tribune *New-York Tribune*
World *New York Evening World*
WAPO *Washington Post*

Legislative Materials

Lexow Hearings New York State Senate, *Report and Proceedings of the Senate Committee Appointed to Investigate the Police Department of the City of New York*, 5 vols. (Albany, N.Y.: James B. Lyon, 1895).

Census, marriage, and birth and death index citations are taken from Ancestry.com. Unless indicated otherwise, *Trow's New York City Directory* for a given year (published annually by John F. Trow and affiliated companies) is cited in short form as, for instance, *Trow's for 1853–'54* (where the place and date of publication are New York, 1853). Where string citations of related newspaper articles appear, the year is cited only once, at the end, for each separate newspaper and year (example: *NYT,* July 1, 4, 5, 1882, November 1, December 9, 1883; *Tribune,* July 2, 5, 1882). For the *World*, particular editions are indicated in parentheses (for example, "last," "6 o'clock"). Short-form citations appearing in the notes can be cross-referenced to the bibliography. Page numbers in the notes correspond with the page in text where the cited or quoted passage begins, regardless of where it ends.

PROLOGUE: FORMING THE PICTURE

1 The torso was found . . . electric chair in Sing Sing: The account of the Guldensuppe case and Carey's background are drawn from Arthur A. Carey, *Memoirs of a Murder Man*, in collaboration with Howard McLellan (Garden City, N.Y.: Doubleday, 1930), 1–3, 16, 28, 48–51 (quotations, 49–50); Paul Collins, *The Murder of the Century: The Gilded Age Crime That Scandalized a City and Sparked the Tabloid War*s (New York: Broadway Paperbacks, 2011); Cait Murphy, *Scoundrels in Law: The Trials of Howe & Hummel, Lawyers to the Gangsters, Cops, Starlets, and Rakes Who Made the Gilded Age* (New York: Smithsonian Books/HarperCollins, 2010), 88–94; *NYT*, July 20, 1895 (Carey transfer), June 27, 28, 29, July 1, 5, 9, 12, November 10, 11, 13, 1897, December 14, 1952 (Carey obituary); *New York Journal and Advertiser*, June 28, 29, 30, July 1, 2, 3, 4, 7, 1897; *Tribune*, June 28, November 10, 1897; *Sun*, June 29, July 8, 1897; *Herald*, June 26, 27, 28, July 1, 4, November 8, 1897; *New Haven (Conn.) Register*, November 9, 1897.

For a description of the Bowery in 1897, see Helen Campbell, *Darkness and Daylight; or, Lights and Shadows of New York Life*, with additional material by Thomas W. Knox and Thomas Byrnes (1892; repr., Hartford, Conn.: Hartford Publishing Company, 1897), 211–14, 225, 422, 605.

See also Cornelius W. Willemse, *A Cop Remembers* (New York: Dutton, 1933), 35 (Bowery in 1888).

McGurk's Suicide Hall and bouncer Jack McManus are described in *Sun*, June 8, October 11, 1899; Luc Sante, *Low Life: Lures and Snares of Old New York* (New York: Farrar, Straus and Giroux, 1991), 119–20; Stephen Paul DeVillo, *The Bowery: The Strange History of New York's Oldest Street* (New York: Skyhorse, 2017), 128–30; Patrick Downey, *Gangster City: The History of the New York Underworld, 1900–1935* (Fort Lee, N.J.: Barricade Books, 2004), 11–12; Alfred Henry Lewis, *The Apaches of New York* (Chicago: M. A. Donohue, 1912), 18 ("with his teeth"); *Tribune*, May 27, 1905; *World*, November 28, 1905 (evening) (caveman look).

6 **"there is no one obvious clue . . . executives at headquarters":** Carey, 51.

6 **won him a transfer back . . . first homicide squad:** Carey, 55; *NYT*, December 14, 1952.

6 **Bertillon system . . . hardly reliable:** Richard Zacks, *Island of Vice: Theodore Roosevelt's Quest to Clean Up Sin-Loving New York* (New York: Anchor Books, 2012), 340–45; Ben Macintyre, *The Napoleon of Crime: The Life and Times of Adam Worth, Master Thief* (1997; repr., New York: Broadway Paperbacks, 2011), 174–75; Bernard J. Whalen, Philip Messing, and Robert Mladinich, *Undisclosed Files of the Police: Cases from the Archives of the NYPD from 1831 to the Present* (New York: Black Dog & Leventhal, 2016), 42, 45; Keith Inman and Norah Rudin, *Principles and Practice of Criminalistics: The Profession of Forensic Science* (Boca Raton, Fla.: CRC Press, 2000), 29–31.

6 **Medical examiners could detect poison . . . Buchanan poisoned:** Carey, 38–44; Paul Collins, *Murder of the Century*, 76–78.

6 **Witthaus implicated Martin Thorn . . . blood on the washboard:** *Brooklyn Daily Eagle*, August 23, 1897; Murphy, *Scoundrels in Law*, 89; Paul Collins, *Murder of the Century*, 119–20.

6 **forensic science could not . . . around 1900:** Inman and Rudin, *Criminalistics*, 32.

7 **tried first to develop a picture of what had probably happened:** Carey, 19–27.

7 **He had guessed correctly . . . a deserted wood:** *NYT*, June 28, 1897; Paul Collins, *Murder of the Century*, 23, 280n12.

7 **"Here's the picture . . . I want you to get":** Carey, 30.

8 **The Gilded Age . . . economic pie:** Esther Crain, *The Gilded Age in New York, 1870–1910* (New York: Black Dog & Leventhal, 2016); Alan Axelrod, *The Gilded Age, 1876–1912: Overture to the American Century* (New York: Sterling, 2017); "Our Robber Barons," editorial, *NYT*, May 28, 1882. See also T. J. English, *Paddy Whacked: The Untold Story of the Irish American Gangster* (2005; repr., New York: HarperCollins, 2006), 35, for a comparison of Gilded Age gangsters with the robber barons. For New York City racial/ethnic makeup, see Campbell Gibson and Kay Jung, "Historical Census Statistics on Population Totals by Race, 1790 to 1990, and by Hispanic Origin, 1970 to 1990, for Large Cities and Other Urban Places in the United States" (working paper POP-WP076, US Census Bureau online, Washington, D.C., February 2005), n.p., table 33: *"New York—Race and Hispanic Origin for Selected Large Cities and Other Places: Earliest Census to 1990,"* https://www.census.gov/population/www/documentation/twps0076/NYtab.pdf.

10 **"New York's Finest":** *NYT*, July 15, 1889, May 4, 2017.

CHAPTER 1: MAKING A NAME

11 **Police captain Thomas F. Byrnes . . . four years in state prison:** *NYT*, October 22, November 19, December 2, 1871, January 7, 8, May 25, June 25, 27, 28, July 2, 3, 4, 6, 16, October 16, December 25, 1872, January 3, 5, 7, October 17, 30, 1873; *Herald*, November 25, 1871, January 6, 7, 8, June 28, 29, July 2, 3, 4, 9, 16, December

25, 1872, January 7, 1873; H. W. Brands, *The Murder of Jim Fisk for the Love of Josie Mansfield* (New York: Anchor Books, 2011); Lisa Steele, "Ballistics," in *Science for Lawyers*, ed. Eric York Drogin (Chicago: American Bar Association, 2008), 1–3, https://apps.americanbar.org/abastore/products/books/abstracts/5450051chap1_abs.pdf; George W. Walling, *Recollections of a New York Chief of Police* (New York: Caxton, 1887), 159 (Fisk), 394–98 (Tombs); Augustine E. Costello, *Our Police Protectors: History of the New York Police from the Earliest Period to the Present Time*, 2nd ed. (New York: self-pub., 1885), 356 (Fifteenth Precinct). That McCadden, not Byrnes, was the officer who had Fisk identify Stokes at the hotel is clarified in the July 2, 1872, editions of both *The New York Times* and the *New York Herald* and the December 25, 1872, *Herald*. The misidentification of Byrnes stems from the January 7, 1872, *Herald*. See also Robert Pigott, *New York's Legal Landmarks: A Guide to Legal Edifices, Institutions, Lore, History and Curiosities on the City's Streets*, 2nd ed. (New York: Attorney Street Editions, 2018), 65–66 (Tombs).

17 **William Henderson . . . Crawford was produced:** *NYT*, May 25, 26, 1872; Costello, *Our Police Protectors*, 410. See also T. J. Stiles, *The First Tycoon: The Epic Life of Cornelius Vanderbilt* (New York: Knopf, 2009), 528.

18 **Byrnes arrested Paul Lowe . . . obtained his confession:** *NYT*, May 27, 28, 1872; *Washington (D.C.) Evening Star*, May 27, 1872; *Herald*, June 23, 1872; Costello, *Our Police Protectors*, 410 (misspelled as Paul "Law").

18 **Van Tine silk . . . got Byrnes's name right:** *Herald*, June 30, July 1, 1872; James Lardner and Thomas A. Reppetto, *NYPD: A City and Its Police* (New York: Henry Holt, 2000), 73.

CHAPTER 2: A COP IS BORN

19 **born on June 15, 1842 . . . became a volunteer firefighter:** Biographical information about Byrnes's birth and family is taken from the following: New York, Emigrant Savings Bank Records, 1850–1883, for Thomas Byrnes, Test Records 1867 (Ancestry.com) ("Thomas Byrnes, 409 Greenwich St., policeman, b. 1842, County Wicklow, single, parents dec[eased]? Wm. [Byrnes] and Rose Doyle"); New York, Emigrant Savings Bank Records, 1850–1883, for Thomas Byrnes, Test Records 1865 (Ancestry.com) (1845 arrival on the *Yorkshire*); 1855 New York State Census, New York City, Ward 5, Election Dist. 2 (William Burns, family and neighbors); 1860 US Census, New York, N.Y., Ward 5, Dist. 1 (same); *Trow's for 1853–'54* (James Hardy, laborer, and Patrick Madagan, laborer, both at 30 Jay); *Trow's for 1856–'57* (William Burns, porter, James Hardy, laborer, and Joseph Ward, laborer, all at 30 Jay); *Trow's for 1860–'61* (William Burns, laborer, Francis Falk, shoes, Cornelius Gorman, porter, and Francis Hanlon, carman, all at 10 Caroline); William Perris, *Maps of the City of New-York*, 3rd ed. (New York: n.p., 1857), plate 17, "Map Bounded by West Street, Laight Street . . . Hubert Street," reprinted in Lionel Pincus and Princess Firyal Map Division, the New York Public Library Digital Collections online, accessed December 8, 2020, https://digitalcollections.nypl.org/items/5e66b3e8-d5d6

-d471-e040-e00a180654d7; *NYT,* April 14, 1892, May 28, 1895, May 8, 1910
(Byrnes obituary); *Tribune,* May 28, 1895; *National Cyclopaedia of American Biography*
(New York: James T. White, 1910), vol. 14, supp. 1, 308.

    In addition to bank records, the 1845 immigration date is confirmed by the 1855
New York census, which lists William and Rose Burns and their three sons, all born
in Ireland, as having lived in New York for ten years, and the three Burns girls,
ages nine, seven, and three, each born in New York, as having lived there since birth.
The fictionalized information about Byrnes's childhood years appears in J. North
Conway, *The Big Policeman: The Rise and Fall of Thomas Byrnes, America's First, Most
Ruthless, and Greatest Detective* (Guilford, Conn.: Lyons Press, 2010), 36–47 (quotation, 46).

    For multifamily housing conditions in mid-nineteenth-century New York, see
NYT, March 14, 1856; Edwin G. Burrows and Mike Wallace, *Gotham: A History of
New York City to 1898* (New York: Oxford University Press, 1999), 746–48; Tyler
Anbinder, *City of Dreams: The 400-Year Epic History of Immigrant New York* (Boston:
Houghton Mifflin, 2016), 151–58; Frank Moss, *The American Metropolis: From Knick-
erbocker Days to the Present Time* (New York: P. F. Collier, 1897), 3:108–10 (Gotham
Court); Tyler Anbinder, *Five Points: The Nineteenth-Century New York City Neighbor-
hood That Invented Tap Dance, Stole Elections, and Became the World's Most Notorious
Slum* (New York: Free Press, 2001), 72–77, 91–97; Ric Burns and James Sanders,
New York: An Illustrated History, with Lisa Ades (New York: Knopf, 1999), 79 (Croton water).

    For the volunteer fire companies, see Burrows and Wallace, *Gotham,* 491, 634,
754, 823; Adam Goodheart, *1861: The Civil War Awakening* (New York: Knopf,
2011), 211–13; Augustine E. Costello, *Our Firemen: A History of the New York Fire
Departments, Volunteer and Paid* (New York: self-pub., 1887), 171–74; Anbinder, *Five
Points,* 183–85.

22 Byrnes and his oldest brother . . . came to enlist: Costello, *Our Firemen,* 503, 594;
Annual Report of the Adjutant-General of the State of New York for the Year 1862 (Albany, N.Y.: C. Van Benthuysen, 1862), 191, 401; *NYT,* August 21, 1861, April 14,
1892, May 28, 1895; *Third Annual Report of the Bureau of Military Record of the State
of New York* (Albany, N.Y.: C. Wendell, 1866), 105–6.

22 Ellsworth's Zouaves . . . first Union officer killed: Goodheart, *1861,* 274, 281–85,
288; Robin Smith, *American Civil War Zouaves* (1996; repr., London: Osprey, 1998),
56–58.

22 Edward Byrnes, the elected head of Ellsworth's Company B: *Annual Report of the
Adjutant-General of the State of New York for the Year 1862,* 401; see https://catalog.loc
.gov/vwebv/holdingsInfo?searchId=11884&recCount=25&recPointer=5&bibId
=9161714; *Third Annual Report of the Bureau of Military Record,* 106–7.

22 First Battle of Bull Run . . . suffered more casualties: Goodheart, *1861,* 290; *Third
Annual Report of the Bureau of Military Record,* 107–8.

23 Byrnes admitted . . . as fast as anybody: William Inglis, "Celebrities at Home:
Thomas F. Byrnes, Former Chief of the New York Police," *Harper's Weekly,* November 14, 1908, 11.

NOTES

23 The demoralized Zouaves . . . mustered out of service: *Third Annual Report of the Bureau of Military Record*, 108–9; Goodheart, *1861*, 378.

23 Hudson Hose Company . . . 304 Washington Street: Costello, *Our Firemen*, 528; *NYT*, April 14, 1892, May 28, 1895. Hose Company No. 21 was located at the foot of Duane Street in the mid-1850s but by 1859 had moved to 304 Washington Street. Costello, *Our Firemen*, 131, 629; New York City Register, 5, in *Trow's for 1859–'60*; George W. Sheldon, *The Story of the Volunteer Fire Department of the City of New York* (New York: Harper & Brothers, 1882), 358.

23 "scrimmages" . . . prompting Byrnes to confess: Costello, *Our Firemen*, 528.

23 December 10, 1863 . . . Fifteenth Precinct: Costello, *Our Police Protectors*, 404–5; *NYT*, December 9, 1888, December 10, 1893. Some sources state that Byrnes began as a patrolman in the Third Precinct (see, for example, *NYT*, April 14, 1892, May 28, 1895), but Byrnes himself testified that it was the Fifteenth. Costello, *Our Police Protectors*, 405.

23 a coveted job . . . pay was good: Costello, *Our Police Protectors*, 212, 215, 218, 236, 296–97, 306; Lardner and Reppetto, *NYPD*, 59; Thomas A. Reppetto, *American Police: The Blue Parade, 1845–1945* (1978; repr., New York: Enigma, 2010), 43; James F. Richardson, *The New York Police: Colonial Times to 1901* (New York: Oxford University Press, 1970), 66, 171–73; Willemse, *A Cop Remembers*, 71, 74–75 ("on reserve" conditions and hours); Crain, *Gilded Age*, 208 (same); Edward Young, chief of the Bureau of Statistics, US Treasury Dept., *Special Report on Immigration* (Washington, D.C.: US Government Printing Office, 1871), ix, 213, 219–20 (wage statistics); Burrows and Wallace, *Gotham*, 970 (middle-class wages); Anbinder, *Five Points*, 112 (labor statistics).

24 a checkered . . . Wood's Municipal Police: Lardner and Reppetto, *NYPD*, 3, 16–17, 23, 31–32, 36–38; Reppetto, *American Police*, 43–45; Burrows and Wallace, *Gotham*, 635–38; Richardson, *New York Police*, 17–24, 49–55, 64–65, 90, 105; Costello, *Our Police Protectors*, 144 (London comparison); Larry K. Hartsfield, *The American Response to Professional Crime, 1870–1917* (Westport, Conn.: Greenwood Press, 1985), 42–43 (reward system); Sante, *Low Life*, 237–38; Anbinder, *Five Points*, 278–79 (two-thirds Irish); Burns and Sanders, *New York*, 90 (Irish population); Walling, 54; *Sun*, July 8, 1888 (comparison of old and current police force); *NYT*, May 14, 1865 (same).

Claims of being the first full-time paid police force in America have been advanced on behalf of Boston (1838), New Orleans (1809), and Charleston, South Carolina (1822), although the southern cities' forces were more in the nature of slave patrols. See Roger Lane, *Policing the City: Boston, 1822–1885* (Cambridge, Mass.: Harvard University Press, 1967), 35–38; Edward L. Ayers, *Vengeance & Justice: Crime and Punishment in the 19th-Century American South* (New York: Oxford University Press, 1984), 83.

26 "Bill the Butcher" . . . Poole's killer: Walling, 49–51; English, *Paddy Whacked*, 24–25; Lardner and Reppetto, *NYPD*, 37; Richardson, *New York Police*, 73; Anbinder, *Five Points*, 275.

26 Matters came to a head . . . Wood finally acquiesced: Walling, 54–61; J. T. Headley, *The Great Riots of New York, 1712 to 1873* (New York: E. B. Treat, 1873), 129–31;

Richardson, *New York Police*, 96–108; Costello, *Our Police Protectors*, 137–42; Reppetto and Lardner, *NYPD*, 38–40; Burrows and Wallace, *Gotham*, 838–39; *NYT*, July 24, 1874 (Walling).

28 During the confusion . . . failed to keep the city safe: Conflicting reports on the Dead Rabbits Riot are nearly impossible to reconcile. Primary and secondary accounts may be found in *NYT*, July 6, 7, 1857; *Herald*, July 6, 7, 8, 1857; Costello, *Our Police Protectors*, 142; Headley, *Great Riots*, 131–34; Herbert Asbury, *The Gangs of New York: An Informal History of the Underworld* (1928; repr., New York: Vintage Books, 2008), 101–6; Burrows and Wallace, *Gotham*, 839–40; Anbinder, *Five Points*, 280–92; Sante, *Low Life*, 202–4; English, *Paddy Whacked*, 27–28 and n6; Richardson, *New York Police*, 109–10.

29 another riot six years later . . . came in for high praise: *NYT*, July 14, 15, 16, 17 (Paddy McCaffrey), 1863; Costello, *Our Police Protectors*, 160–200; Walling, 78–86; Burns and Sanders, *New York*, 119–27; Headley, *Great Riots*, 145–57 (quotations, 155–56); Richardson, *New York Police*, 135–39, 142; Lardner and Reppetto, *NYPD*, 43–49. For absorption/reinstatements of Municipals, see *NYT*, January 11, June 22, 26, 1858, April 8, September 24, 1859, February 18, March 10, 1860, November 22, 1861.

31 It is possible . . . broke up for good: *Third Annual Report of the Bureau of Military Record*, 109; Goodheart, *1861*, 378; *NYT*, July 15, 1863; see also Walling, 82.

31 he did not engage . . . Byrnes is also supposed: Conway, *Big Policeman*, 56–59, 62–63. The man who rescued Kennedy was local resident John Eagan. Headley, *Great Riots*, 156; Costello, *Our Police Protectors*, 167.

31 Soon after being assigned . . . Third Precinct: *NYT*, December 9, 1888.

31 160 Chambers Street . . . 328 Greenwich Street: *Trow's for 1864–'65* (Thomas Byrnes, police); New York City Register, 4, in ibid. (precinct house).

31 parents . . . died around this time: William Burns does not appear in city directories after 1863, nor do he or his wife appear in the 1870 US Census. Bank records suggest that they were deceased by 1867. New York, Emigrant Savings Bank Records, 1850–1883 for Thomas Byrnes, Test Records 1867 (Ancestry.com).

31 In October 1868 . . . on July 1, 1870: *NYT*, December 9, 1888, December 10, 1893; *Tribune*, May 28, 1895; Costello, *Our Police Protectors*, 404–5; Lardner and Reppetto, *NYPD*, 73.

32 thirty-some captains . . . their respective precincts: Richardson, *New York Police*, 98, 164, 225; Walling, 380, 577; Costello, *Our Police Protectors*, 261, 266–69, 277, 285; Jay Stuart Berman, *Police Administration and Progressive Reform: Theodore Roosevelt as Police Commissioner of New York* (Westport, Conn.: Greenwood Press, 1987), 62.

32 In 1870 . . . patronage was dispensed: Daniel Czitrom, *New York Exposed: The Gilded Age Police Scandal That Launched the Progressive Era* (New York: Oxford University Press, 2016), 33–34; Lardner and Reppetto, *NYPD*, 52–53; Reppetto, *American Police*, 49; Costello, *Our Police Protectors*, 137–38, 239–40; Richardson, *New York Police*, 162–64, 214–17, 224; *Lexow Hearings*, 1:53–54, 421–22, 446–47, 2:1424, 2305 (commissioner powers and practices); Avery D. Andrews, "Theodore Roosevelt as Police Commissioner," *New-York Historical Society Quarterly* 42, no. 2 (April 1958): 130 (commissioners subservient to parties). For a good overview of the police department around 1870, see James D. McCabe Jr., *Lights and Shadows of New York Life; or, The Sights and Sensations of the Great City* (Philadelphia: National Publishing, 1872), 171–85. See also *NYT,* December 18, 30, 1873, January 1, 1874 (annexed Westchester towns).

33 Byrnes began his captaincy . . . nearer the East River: Costello, *Our Police Protectors,* 337–39 (Twenty-First), 380–81 (Twenty-Third), 404; *NYT,* April 24, 1880, December 9, 1888, May 8, 1910; *Lexow Hearings,* 5:5709.

33 Orangemen . . . Slaughter on Eighth Avenue: *NYT,* July 13, 1871, December 9, 1888; *Tribune,* July 13, 1871; Headley, *Great Riots,* 293–305; Walling, 158; Burrows and Wallace, *Gotham,* 1003–8; Costello, *Our Police Protectors,* 124, 244–48; *Frank Leslie's Illustrated Newspaper,* May 22, 1880, 195; Brands, *Murder of Jim Fisk,* 48–58.

34 "The Police . . . law-and-order-loving citizens": *NYT,* July 13, 1871.

34 "To defend . . . stood it nobly": Headley, *Great Riots,* 306.

34 1874 . . . Broadway Squad: Costello, *Our Police Protectors,* 266, 361, 405; McCabe, *Lights and Shadows,* 177–78; *Lexow Hearings,* 5:5709; *Herald,* January 11, June 2, December 3, 1874, February 10, 1876; Burrows and Wallace, *Gotham,* 945–46 (Ladies' Mile). Contrary to the December 9, 1888, *New York Times,* Byrnes never captained the Fourteenth Precinct.

34 "well proportioned . . . young and pretty": *Harper's Weekly,* March 9, 1872, 189.

34 in 1875 he married . . . all daughters: *National Cyclopaedia,* 308; *Tribune,* May 8, 1910; *NYT,* May 8, 1910; 1870 US Census, New York, N.Y., Ward 8, Election Dist. 12 (Lyman Jennings and Ophelia Jennings); *Trow's for 1867–'68* (Lyman Jennings, bartender, 119 Varick); *Trow's for 1873–'74* (Lyman Jennings, liquors, 119 Varick, and Thomas Byrnes, police, 109 Greenwich); *Trow's for 1876–'77* (Thomas Byrnes, police, 110 Greenwich); 1880 US Census, New York, N.Y., Enumeration District (hereafter, Enum. Dist.), 174 (William Byrnes and Ophelia Byrnes, 59 West Ninth Street). The 1880 census mistakenly lists the ages of Byrnes and his wife as thirty-three and twenty-three, respectively. Those were their ages at the time of their marriage.

34 In 1876 . . . but passed over: *NYT,* December 16, 1876; *Herald,* February 19, March 8, 21, April 15, July 19, 27, 1877, April 12, 1878; *Tribune,* July 18, 1878.

CHAPTER 3: HEIST OF THE CENTURY

36 October 27, 1878 . . . had some names in mind: *NYT,* October 28 (quotation), 29, 1878, February 12, June 2, 13, October 6, 1879; *Herald,* October 28, 1878; *Sun,* December 17, 1879; *Tribune,* April 30, 1880; Walling, 265–66; Sophie Lyons, *Why Crime Does Not Pay* (New York: J. S. Ogilvie, 1913), 151, 156, 163 (bank construction); Carey, 28 (Byrnes's clothing); 1880 US Census, New York, N.Y., Enum. Dist. 15, Ward 17, Election Dist. 24 (Louis Wer[c]kle, 38 Rivington St.).

38 Professional criminals . . . money was stored: Byrnes (1886), 1 (quotation), 7–43, 55, 162 (butcher cart business); McCabe, *Lights and Shadows*, 522–39; Edward Crapsey, *The Nether Side of New York; or, The Vice, Crime and Poverty of the Great Metropolis* (New York: Sheldon, 1872), 14–23; Costello, *Our Police Protectors*, 343; Walling, 321; Maximilian Schoenbein, *King of Burglars: The Heist Stories of Max Shinburn*, ed. with a foreword by Jerry Kuntz (Warwick, N.Y.: Wickham House, 2018), 118; Benjamin P. Eldridge and William B. Watts, *Our Rival the Rascal: A Faithful Portrayal of the Conflict between the Criminals of This Age and the Defenders of Society—The Police* (Boston: Pemberton, 1897), 187–90 (bunco).

39 "The professional bank burglar . . . in high degree": Byrnes (1886), 2.

39 Jesse James . . . ex-Confederates: The best exposition of this theme is in T. J. Stiles, *Jesse James: The Last Rebel of the Civil War* (New York: Knopf, 2002).

40 Many professional bank burglars . . . shied from using violence: Eldridge and Watts, *Our Rival*, 42–44; Byrnes (1886), 54; Hartsfield, *American Response*, 30; Schoenbein, *King of Burglars*, 115; Kuntz, foreword to Schoenbein, *King of Burglars*, ix; Macintyre, *Napoleon of Crime*, 24–25; Walling, 236, 321.

40 "Instead of the clumsy . . . 'neat job' behind him": Allan Pinkerton, *The Bankers, Their Vaults, and the Burglars* (Chicago: self-pub., Fergus, 1873), 3.

40 "probably the most expert . . . in the country": Byrnes (1886), 310.

40 A debonair . . . a castle: Byrnes (1886), 252–53; Kuntz, foreword to Schoenbein, *King of Burglars*, vii, ix; Schoenbein, *King of Burglars*, 45, 105, 132–34; Asbury, *Gangs of New York*, 196; Eldridge and Watts, *Our Rival*, 45, 51; *NYT*, April 8, 1883, June 30, 1895.

40 a talented jailbreaker . . . a Canadian bank: Schoenbein, chaps. 4, 10 in *King of Burglars*; George M. White (alias George Bliss), *From Boniface to Bank Burglar; or, The Price of Persecution* (Bellows Falls, Vt.: self-pub., Truax, 1905), 247–65; *NYT*, April 8, 1883, June 30, 1895.

40 His specialty . . . nitroglycerin: Byrnes (1886), 253; George M. White, *From Boniface*, 211; Schoenbein, *King of Burglars*, 31–32, 46, 50–51, 84–85, 98, 118, 182, 196; William A. Pinkerton, "Safe Burglary: Its Beginning and Progress," *National Police Journal* 6, no. 5 (August 1920): 10–11; Allan Pinkerton, *Bankers, Vaults*, 6–7; *Decatur (Ill.) Daily Republican*, June 26, 1888.

41 After the Civil War . . . prove it wrong: William Pinkerton, "Safe Burglary," 10–11, 31, 33; Eldridge and Watts, *Our Rival*, 36–41, 395–400; Schoenbein, *King of Burglars*, 98–99, 102–3, 108–12.

41 combination lock . . . listening to the clicks: William Pinkerton, "Safe Burglary," 31, 33; David Erroll and John Erroll, *American Genius: Nineteenth-Century Bank Locks and Time Locks* (New York: Quantuck Lane Press, 2006), 95, 127, 355–56; *NYT*, June 30, 1895 (Shinburn); Eldridge and Watts, *Our Rival*, 45 (Shinburn); Hartsfield, *American Response*, 17, 26 (Moore); Richard Wheatley, "The New York Police Department," *Harper's New Monthly Magazine*, March 1887, 514 (Moore); Lyons, *Why Crime Does Not Pay*, 57 (Shinburn). One source calls the image of the "stethoscope-wearing safecracker" likely fictional. Erroll and Erroll, *American*

Genius, 118. Moore himself is coy on the subject. Langdon W. Moore, *His Own Story of His Eventful Life* (Boston: self-pub., 1893), 67, 456–57.

41 numbers 0 to 100 . . . lock got trickier: William Pinkerton, "Safe Burglary," 33.

41 George White . . . "little joker": Schoenbein, *King of Burglars*, 43–44 and Kuntz, foreword to same, xi; Eldridge and Watts, *Our Rival*, 51–52; William Pinkerton, "Safe Burglary," 31, 33; George M. White, *From Boniface*, 203–5, 234–35, 243; Byrnes (1886), 4; Allan Pinkerton, *Criminal Reminiscences and Detective Sketches* (New York: G. W. Dillingham, 1878), 125–26. See also Allan Pinkerton, *Bankers, Vaults*, 6 (apparent reference to Shinburn).

42 scored several coups . . . carry out bank robberies: Allan Pinkerton, *Criminal Reminiscences*, 126; George M. White, *From Boniface*, 205, 272–73.

42 While planning . . . altered its locks: George M. White, *From Boniface*, 234–35, 337–40, 414.

42 White bought a facsimile . . . remained a mystery: *NYT*, June 29, July 1, 1869; Walling, 249; Allan Pinkerton, *Criminal Reminiscences*, 135–36; George M. White, *From Boniface*, 205, 217, 229, 234–42.

43 another common tactic . . . cut through the ceiling: Byrnes (1886), 5, 140; George M. White, *From Boniface*, 322–33; Walling, 249–52; Allan Pinkerton, *Criminal Reminiscences*, 136; *NYT*, June 29, 1869; Eldridge and Watts, *Our Rival*, 42, 60; Allan Pinkerton, *Bankers, Vaults*, 7–10.

43 $800,000 to $1.2 million . . . crooked New York cops: George M. White, *From Boniface*, 301–16, 333–36, 341–44; Walling, 247–55; Eldridge and Watts, *Our Rival*, 43, 47, 52; Byrnes (1886), 139–40, 253, 337; *NYT*, June 29, 30, 1869, June 30, 1895; Allan Pinkerton, *Criminal Reminiscences*, 135–36; Lyons, *Why Crime Does Not Pay*, 57–58. The identities of all the burglars involved, and the amount stolen, have never definitively been established. See Sante, *Low Life*, 208–9; *NYT*, March 17, 1907.

43 By the early 1870s . . . forced into bankruptcy: Allan Pinkerton, *Bankers, Vaults*, 6; William Pinkerton, "Safe Burglary," 10–11; Moore, *His Own Story*, 506–7; Byrnes (1886), 3–4; Lyons, *Why Crime Does Not Pay*, 152–54, 159; George M. White, *From Boniface*, 89–490; *NYT*, June 30, 1895.

43 "All at sea" and "completely outwitted": *NYT*, October 29, 31, 1878.

43 impunity . . . severe blow: "The Big Bank Burglary," *NYT*, October 31, 1878.

43 Bank officials were bracing . . . Byrnes agreed: *NYT*, October 31, 1878 (editorial), October 6, 1879; Josiah Flynt, *The World of Graft* (New York: McClure, Phillips, 1901), 93–95; George M. White, *From Boniface*, 301–3, 309–18; Schoenbein, *King of Burglars*, 95, 113, 121–22; Murphy, *Scoundrels in Law*, 112; Crapsey, *Nether Side*, 51 (quotations). See also *NYT*, February 17, 1876 (Northampton Bank robbery).

44 Shinburn was living . . . in Europe: *NYT*, April 8, 1883, June 30, 1895; Allan Pinkerton, *Criminal Reminiscences*, 121; Byrnes (1886), 253; Schoenbein, *King of Burglars*, 194.

44 White was in jail . . . Barre Bank: George M. White, *From Boniface*, 207–10; Byrnes (1886), 254; Eldridge and Watts, *Our Rival*, 52–53.

44 Langdon Moore . . . would have nothing to do with: Byrnes (1886), 84–86; Moore, *His Own Story*, 204, 497–510; Hartsfield, *American Response*, 30.

44 William Sharkey . . . disguised as a woman: *NYT*, November 20, 21, 1873; Walling, 251–52, 292–96; Costello, *Our Police Protectors*, 362; Byrnes (1886), 146 (Shinburn connection). Walling asserts that Sharkey was involved in planning the Ocean National Bank robbery with Shinburn and White.

44 put a tail . . . ringleaders: *NYT*, February 12, June 2, October 6, 1879; *Herald*, June 3, 1879.

44 The first arrest . . . "Red" Leary and John McCarthy: *NYT*, December 14, 1878.

44 Along with his wife . . . standing joke: *NYT*, June 27, 1875 ("The Rogues' Gallery: Sketches of Prominent Criminals"); Byrnes (1886), 206; Eldridge and Watts, *Our Rival*, 56, 68.

45 Northampton, Massachusetts, bank robbery . . . gave them the combinations: Eldridge and Watts, *Our Rival*, 43; *NYT*, January 29, 1876, December 14, 1878; *Sun*, March 9, 1879; Walling, 241–43; *The Greatest Burglary on Record: Robbery of the Northampton National Bank* (Northampton, Mass: Steam Press of Gazette, 1876), 1–24; "The Northampton National Bank Heist, the Biggest in U.S. History," New England Historical Society online, last modified 2020, http://www.newenglandhis toricalsociety.com/northampton-national-bank-heist-biggest-u-s-history/; David Freeland, *Automats, Taxi Dances, and Vaudeville: Excavating Manhattan's Lost Places of Leisure* (New York: NYU Press, 2009), 111; Erroll and Erroll, *American Genius*, 25.

45 After the robbery . . . $400 Yale time lock: *Greatest Burglary*, advertisement following p. 24. See also Erroll and Erroll, *American Genius*, 26, 143, 162–64, 357.

45 Byrnes had no real evidence . . . Red's prison bathroom: *NYT*, December 14, 1878, October 6, 1879; *Sun*, May 9, 1879; Walling, 302–5; Edward Van Every, *Sins of New York as "Exposed" by the Police Gazette* (New York: F. A. Stokes, 1930), 237; Greg Young and Tom Meyers, "The Legend of Bank Robber 'Red' Leary, His Wife Kate, and the Greatest Jail Break in Lower East Side History," *The Bowery Boys: New York City History*, last modified June 20, 2012, http://www.boweryboyshistory.com/2012/06/legend-of-bank-robber-red-leary-his.html.

45 not actually Leary . . . Jimmy Hope: *NYT*, February 12, 1879; *Sun*, June 2, 1879.

45 "Old Man Hope" . . . died the next day: Byrnes (1886), 82–83, 133 (Dexter), 311; *NYT*, February 12, 1879 (Dexter), August 24, 1889, June 3, 1905 (South Kensington); Walling, 244–47 (Dexter), 272 (South Kensington); Lyons, *Why Crime Does Not Pay*, 166 (Jimmy Hope), 177–80 (South Kensington); *Portland (Maine) Daily Press*, February 23, 25, 26, 27, March 22, 1878 (Dexter); *Sun*, March 9, 1879 (South Kensington and Dexter); Allan Pinkerton, *Professional Thieves and the Detective: Containing Numerous Detective Sketches Collected from Private Records* (New York: G. W. Carleton, 1883), 161–69 (South Kensington and Dexter). See also Jerry Kuntz, "#20 James Hope," *Professional Criminals of America—REVISED: Revised Biographies Based on NYPD Chief Thomas Byrnes' 1886 book, 'Professional Criminals of America'"* (blog), May 24, 2018, https://criminalsrevised.blog/2018/05/24/20-james -hope/.

47 Hope could not be found . . . closely linked to Hope: *Herald*, June 3, 1879; *NYT*, February 12, 1879, July 6, September 29, 1881, August 24, 1889; Byrnes (1886), 83.

47 A further clue . . . Abe Coakley: *Herald*, June 3, 1879; *Sun*, March 9, 1879; *NYT*, April 30, 1880; Byrnes (1886), 83; Walling, 246.

47 "Every time . . . they want me, too": *NYT*, February 12, 1879.

47 Two witnesses identified . . . younger Hope arrested: *NYT*, February 12, 1879; Walling, 268. See also *NYT*, June 14, 1879; *People of the State of New York v. John Hope*, Court of General Sessions, City and County of New York, trial transcript at 54–56 (testimony of Edward Gilgar), 93–96 (testimony of Annie Sample), reprinted in *Supreme Court, General Term, John Hope Against The People of the State of New York, Error Book* (New York, 1879), https://books.google.com/books?id=pXQkHnfh SiUC&pg=RA24-PP1#v=onepage&q=john%20hope&f=false (hereafter, *People v. John Hope*, Trial Tr.).

47 Johnny Dobbs . . . was arrested: *Herald*, May 7, 1879; *NYT*, May 7, 1879; Byrnes (1886), 133.

47 Raised in the Fourth Ward . . . "a first-class workman": Byrnes (1886), 132–33 (quotation); *Herald*, May 7, 1879; *Sun*, May 7, 1879; *NYT*, May 7, 1879, March 7, 1884; *Trow's for 1861–'62* (John Kerrigan, dining, 283 Water); Kuntz, "#64 Michael Kerrigan," *Professional Criminals—REVISED* (blog), June 15, 2018, https://criminal srevised.blog/2018/06/15/64-michael-kerrigan/.

47 He was part of the gang . . . left him to die: Byrnes (1886), 133, 277; *Herald*, May 7, 1879; *Sun*, March 9, May 7, 1879; *NYT*, May 7, 1879; Walling, 246, 272; Lyons, *Why Crime Does Not Pay*, 177.

48 Byrnes went to Philadelphia . . . slept on a sofa: *Sun*, May 7, 1879; *Herald*, May 7, 1879; *NYT*, May 7, 1879; Byrnes (1886), 132.

48 Byrnes smiled slyly . . . original Sunday morning: *Herald*, May 7, 1879.

48 "The more of them . . . better it will be for me": *Sun*, May 7, 1879.

48 Banjo Pete Emerson . . . joined a minstrel company: Byrnes (1886), 81; *NYT*, April 30, 1880, July 29, 1883; Kuntz, "#90 Peter Ellis," *Professional Criminals—REVISED* (blog), September 8, 2018, https://criminalsrevised.blog/2018/09/08/90-peter-ellis/.

48 "Worcester Sam" Perris . . . was wanted for the murder: Byrnes (1886), 133, 276 (quotation), 311; Walling, 246; *Sun*, March 9, 1879; *NYT*, April 30, 1880; Lyons, *Why Crime Does Not Pay*, 177; Kuntz, "#199 Samuel Perris," *Professional Criminals—REVISED* (blog), July 22, 2018, https://criminalsrevised.blog/2018/07/22/199 -samuel-perris/.

48 Thomas "Shang" Draper . . . friend and accomplice: *Sun*, March 9, 1879, December 7, 1913; *Tribune*, August 13, 1878; Walling, 242.

48 Born in Ireland . . . same line of work: 1850 US Census, Kings County, Brooklyn, N.Y., Ward 2 (John Draper, laborer, Thomas Draper, age seven); *Tribune*, August 13, 15, 1878; *Sun*, March 9, 1879 (father a cotton broker); *Augusta* [Ga.] *Chronicle*, June 8, 1879 (respected parents); *Boston Herald*, February 25, 1912 (disowned by wealthy parents). Early biographical information about Draper is hard to come by, but records confirm that his father, John Draper, originally a laborer in Brooklyn, became a cotton broker and that his brother, William, joined the family business. See *Trow's for 1867–'68* (John Draper & Son, cotton); 1875 New York State Census, Kings County, Brooklyn City, Ward 10, Election Dist. 4 (John Draper and William Draper, cotton brokers).

In his otherwise helpful discussion of Shang Draper's background, David Freeland states that Draper's father, William Draper, died when Shang and his brother Henry were children and that their widowed mother, Elizabeth, lost the family house at foreclosure, forcing Shang and Henry to live on their own. Freeland, *Automats*, 110. But Shang's father was named John, not William, and he was still living as of 1880. John's wife was not named Elizabeth (she is variously listed in census records as Frances, Fanny, or Esther). Shang's brother was William, not Henry, and both were living with John and Frances Draper in 1860. See 1860 US Census, Kings County, Brooklyn, N.Y., Ward 6, Dist. 3 (John Draper, cotton broker).

49 prostitution cons . . . gambling kingpin: McCabe, *Lights and Shadows*, 593 (panel thieving); Freeland, *Automats*, 107–12; *New-York Commercial Advertiser*, July 22, 1875; *Tribune*, August 13, 15, 1878; *NYT*, August 13, October 31, 1878 (king of the panel thieves); August 10, 1879; *Sun*, March 9, 1879 (Jennie Mooney, Draper's wife), December 7, 1913; *Washington (D.C.) Times*, February 10, 1907 (Northampton robbery); *Boston Herald*, February 25, 1912 (same); Sante, *Low Life*, 185–86 (panel houses); Costello, *Our Police Protectors*, 334 (shutdown of panel houses); Byrnes (1886), 117 (description of Draper under alias A. D. Harper); Allan Pinkerton, *Professional Thieves*, 180 (Mrs. Draper); *Herald*, October 2, 1883 (Jennie Mooney, wife of Shang Draper); 1870 US Census, New York, N.Y., Ward 15, Dist. 2 (Thomas and Jennie Draper).

Jennie Draper, whose maiden name was Mooney, had previously married a panel thief, Billy English, who was sentenced to many years at Sing Sing. She then became Draper's companion, "availed herself of her legal rights," and married Shang. *Sun*, March 9, 1879; see also *Herald*, October 2, 1883; *NYT*, October 17, 1883. *The New York Times* referred to her as Draper's "reputed" wife. *NYT*, October 4, 1880. It may be that she never formally divorced Billy English and instead became Draper's common-law wife or mistress.

CHAPTER 4: THE THIRD DEGREE

51 Pat Shevlin was not . . . Shevlin testified later: *NYT*, June 2, 17, 1879; *Sun*, June 2, 17, 1879; Lyons, *Why Crime Does Not Pay*, 166–69; Walling, 266–68; *People v. John Hope*, Trial Tr. 122, 172–77 (Shevlin testimony); *Herald*, December 18, 1879; *Sun*, December 18, 1879.

52 Byrnes did not invent . . . New York Police Department: Reppetto, *American Police*, 55; Timothy J. Gilfoyle, *A Pickpocket's Tale: The Underworld of Nineteenth-Century New York* (New York: W. W. Norton, 2007), 251–52; *NYT*, October 6, 1901 ("Third Degree in Police Parlance"); Costello, *Our Police Protectors*, 410; *Tribune*, October 6, 1905.

52 pitiless tactics . . . "a little wholesome 'slugging' ": Reppetto, *American Police*, 55; Arthur M. Schlesinger Jr., "The Business of Crime," introduction to Byrnes (1886), xvii–xviii; Jacob A. Riis, *The Making of an American* (New York: Macmillan, 1901), 341 (quotation), 342; Harold C. Syrett, ed., *The Gentleman and the Tiger: The Autobiography of George B. McClellan, Jr.* (Philadelphia: Lippincott, 1956), 298–99.

52 "But all the crying . . . fair sex": Campbell, *Darkness and Daylight*, 523.

52 psychological warfare . . . broke down and confessed: Riis, *Making of an American*, 341–42; *NYT*, January 31, 1887, October 6, 1901; Inglis, "Celebrities at Home," 11; Schlesinger, "Business of Crime," xviii.

53 "It is not remorse . . . mental strain": *NYT*, May 15, 1910.

53 "It was simply the work . . . forcing him to tell it": Inglis, "Celebrities at Home," 11.

53 "I don't expect . . . a little persuasion?": Jack Finney, *Time and Again* (1970; repr., New York: Simon & Schuster, 1995), 274.

53 "His very manner . . . the average crook": "Tom Byrnes, the Chief," *Collier's*, May 21, 1910, 13.

53 chatting casually . . . unnerve his man: *NYT*, May 8, 15, 1910; Lardner and Reppetto, *NYPD*, 85.

54 "a man who would . . . get you he would": Lincoln Steffens, *The Autobiography of Lincoln Steffens*, vol. 1 (New York: Harcourt, Brace, 1931), 201.

54 got Pat Shevlin . . . impressing upon him: *NYT*, June 2, 1879.

54 offered him immunity . . . Shevlin denied it later: *People v. John Hope*, Trial Tr. 177–78 (Shevlin testimony).

54 bit of mockery . . . a full confession: Lyons, *Why Crime Does Not Pay*, 169–71; Lardner and Reppetto, *NYPD*, 78–79; *People v. John Hope*, Trial Tr. 162 (Shevlin testimony).

54 police manuals . . . to confess: *Miranda v. Arizona*, 384 U.S. 436, 448–55 (1966).

54 "to display an air . . . dismissed and discouraged": *Miranda*, 384 U.S. at 450.

54 "involuntary" . . . allowed the confession: See, generally, *Bram v. United States*, 168 U.S. 532 (1897); Wesley MacNeil Oliver, "The Neglected History of Criminal Procedure, 1850–1940," *Rutgers Law Review* 62, no. 2 (2010): 447, 455, 461, 464, 483–93.

CHAPTER 5: KING OF THE BANK ROBBERS

56 King of the Bank Robbers: Van Every, *Sins of New York*, 234; Asbury, *Gangs of New York*, 185. See also *Augusta (Ga.) Chronicle*, June 8, 1879 ("king of the New York bank thieves"); *NYT*, November 6, 1879 ("the prince of safebreakers").

57 no evidence . . . little joker: The claim that Leslie invented and used the little joker appears most prominently in J. North Conway, *King of Heists: The Sensational Bank Robbery of 1878 That Shocked America* (Guilford, Conn.: Lyons Press, 2009), a book described by its author as "fictional realism." Ibid., xiii.

57 a big-picture man . . . every nook and corner: Walling, 262–63, 269–70; *Sun*, March 9, 1879; Allan Pinkerton, *Professional Thieves*, 176; Van Every, *Sins of New York*, 236–37; *NYT*, March 7, 1875 (putters-up).

57 According to author Herbert Asbury . . . critiqued their performance: Asbury, *Gangs of New York*, 187–88.

57 Walling estimated that 80 percent: Walling, 278.

58 Ocean National Bank . . . nothing to do with: Asbury, among others, credits Leslie with the Ocean National heist. But George White's lengthy account of the robbery makes no mention of Leslie. Neither Byrnes, Walling, nor Allan Pinkerton connected Leslie to the Ocean National. Furthermore, Leslie did not take up residence in New York City until 1874, five years after the robbery.

58 Virtually all . . . posthumously: Despite an extensive search of nineteenth-century newspapers, I was unable to find a single article published during Leslie's lifetime unequivocally connecting him to any robbery. Philadelphia's *The Daily Age* of October 24, 1865, reported the arrest in that city of "a young man giving the name of George Leslie" on the charge of being a boardinghouse thief, but whether this is the same George Leslie is not known.

The richest source of biographical information on Leslie comes from *The Sun* of March 9, 1879, written less than a year after his death and based, in part, on an interview with his widow. The lengthy article does, however, exaggerate the number of criminals with whom he associated. For example, there is no evidence that he ever collaborated with Max Shinburn or George White, neither of whose memoirs mentions Leslie.

58 He was born . . . Civil War bounty jumper: 1870 US Census, Philadelphia, Ward 5, Dist. 15, 2nd Enum. (George H. Howard, age thirty); Walling, 269–70; Allan Pinkerton, *Professional Thieves*, 172–73; Van Every, *Sins of New York*, 236; *Sun*, March 9, 1879; *Springfield (Mass.) Republican*, July 18, 1878. The Find a Grave website entry for Leslie states that he was born in Cincinnati in 1842. "George Leonidas Leslie," Find a Grave, last modified January 2, 2007.

58 group of bushwhackers . . . Saint Louis: *NYT*, June 17, 1878; *Sun*, March 9, 1879; Allan Pinkerton, *Professional Thieves*, 172.

59 did some counterfeiting . . . balked at the prospect: Allan Pinkerton, *Professional Thieves*, 173, 182.

59 "Red-headed Lizzie" . . . end of his days: *NYT*, June 10, 17, 1878.

59 "was a great favorite . . . his favoritism": *Bulletin* (San Francisco), September 15, 1886, quoting *New-York Commercial Advertiser*.

59 five foot eight . . . handsome: *NYT*, June 5, 1878; Walling, 270–71; Byrnes (1886), 54 ("a fine-looking man"), 117 (description of C. G. Green, Leslie's alias); *Cleveland Plain Dealer*, August 3, 1913 ("Handsome George").

59 came east to Philadelphia . . . protected from arrest: Allan Pinkerton, *Professional Thieves*, 173–74; 1870 US Census, Philadelphia, Ward 5, Dist. 15, 2nd Enum. (Mary E. Couth [*sic*, Coath], George H. Howard, and Mary H. Co[a]th); Walling, 271–72; *Sun*, March 9, 1879; *Bulletin* (San Francisco), September 15, 1886 ("His address"); *The Philadelphia Inquirer*, June 8, 1878 (Blue Shirts); Kenneth W. Milano, chap. 3 in *Hidden History of Kensington and Fishtown* (Charleston, S.C.: History Press, 2010) (Blue Shirts); Lardner and Reppetto, *NYPD*, 76 (Taggart). See also *Gopsill's*

Philadelphia City Directory, 1882 (Philadelphia: James Gopsill), 919 (Mary H. Leslie, wid[ow] George). Further as to mother and daughter, see 1880 US Census, Philadelphia, Enum. Dist. 67 (Mary E. Co[a]th, age forty-five, Mary H. Leslie, widow, age twenty-four). Molly's grave site lists her birth year as 1857, which would have made her only thirteen in 1870. "Mary Henrietta 'Molly' Coath Leslie," Find a Grave, last modified June 15, 2010.

60 May 1870 . . . failed to appear for trial: *NYT*, June 17, 1878; Allan Pinkerton, *Professional Thieves*, 174–75; Walling, 271; *Sun*, March 9, 1879.

60 next few years . . . more thefts: Walling, 269, 273; *Sun*, March 9, 1879; *The Philadelphia Inquirer*, June 8, 1878; *Chicago Tribune*, February 14, September 16, 1874, February 15, 19, 1877 (robbery of First National Bank of Quincy, Illinois); Byrnes (1886), 115–17 (same); *Tribune*, August 15, 1878 (Quincy bank with Draper).

60 Apparently, his doings . . . settling with detectives: *The Philadelphia Inquirer*, June 8, 1878; *NYT*, June 17, 1878.

60 had a falling-out . . . coonhound: *Sun*, March 9, 1879; Walling, 272–73; Pinkerton, *Professional Thieves*, 175–76; Geo. T. Lain, *Lain's Brooklyn City and Business Directory for the Year Ending May 1st, 1876* (Brooklyn: Lain, 1875) (George L. Howard, 478 Fulton).

60 He socialized . . . Sam Devere: Kuntz, "#90 Peter Ellis," *Professional Criminals— REVISED* (blog); *Sun*, March 9, 1879; Lain, *Lain's for the Year Ending May 1st, 1876* (Samuel Devere, actor, 478 Fulton).

61 "nothing vulgar . . . nor conversation": *Sun*, March 9, 1879.

61 silk robberies . . . take this precaution: *Sun*, March 9, 1879; Byrnes (1886), 44–45; Walling, 280; Lyons, *Why Crime Does Not Pay*, 198; McCabe, *Lights and Shadows*, 541–42.

61 continued to study . . . Jennie Draper: *Sun*, March 9, 1879, October 17, 1883 (Porter and Irving); *Tribune*, August 13, 15, 1878; Byrnes (1886), 143–45 (Porter and Irving), 152–53 (Leslie gang); *Augusta (Ga.) Chronicle*, June 8, 1879; Walling, 274–75, 299; Van Every, *Sins of New York*, 236; *NYT*, August 10, October 22, November 6, 1879, April 30, 1880 (Leslie gang); October 17, 1883 (Porter and Irving), June 23, 1888 (Porter); Allan Pinkerton, *Professional Thieves*, 176–77, 180–81; Kuntz, "#74 William O'Brien," *Professional Criminals—REVISED* (blog), November 29, 2018, https://criminalsrevised.blog/2018/11/29/74-william-obrien/. Johnny Irving is sometimes confused with an older burglar named John T. Irving, who once famously confessed to a murder in San Francisco he did not commit so that he could get a free ride back to New York. Kuntz, "#86 John T. Irving," *Professional Criminals— REVISED* (blog), September 3, 2018, https://criminalsrevised.blog/2018/09/03 /86-john-t-irving/; *NYT*, March 7, 1884. The August 13, 1878, *Herald* article erroneously conflates the two Irvings.

62 specialized in burglarizing silk . . . Northampton Bank robbery: Walling, 241–43 (Northampton); *Sun*, March 9, 1879; Byrnes (1886), 144; Allan Pinkerton, *Professional Thieves*, 183; *NYT*, August 10, October 22, November 6, 1879, June 23, 1888.

62 Leslie bought a combination . . . counterpart: *NYT,* October 6, 1879; Walling, 273; *Sun,* March 9, 1879. See also Lyons, *Why Crime Does Not Pay,* 152.

62 a "pudding": Walling, 262; Murphy, *Scoundrels in Law,* 115–16.

62 initial approach . . . frustrations and quarrels: *NYT,* June 2, October 6, 1879; *Sun,* March 9, June 2, 1879; *Cleveland Leader,* June 2, 1879; *Tribune,* June 24, 1879; Walling, 261–64; Van Every, *Sins of New York,* 235–37; Lyons, *Why Crime Does Not Pay,* 150 ("galaxy of talent"), 154 (blamed Hope), 159; George M. White, *From Boniface,* 492 (apparently describing Hope's second attempt); *People v. John Hope,* Trial Tr. 131–38, 157–62 (Shevlin testimony); *Herald,* December 18, 1879 (additional Shevlin testimony).

Shevlin mentioned another conspirator, "Tall George," with a scar on his face, as a frequent presence during the planning discussions. (George Leslie had a scarred face, but, at five foot eight, he could not have been considered tall; see *NYT,* June 5, 1878.) Shevlin recalled this man's name as George Howard, but said he was not the same person as George Leslie, who also was involved. It seems likely that Shevlin conflated the two last names and that the man he remembered as Tall George was someone other than Leslie. Possibly he was George Mason, a tall burglar with a long scar on his cheek, identified by Byrnes as having been involved with Jimmy Hope in an early but unsuccessful attempt on the Manhattan Savings. Byrnes (1886), 89, 91; *NYT,* June 2, 1879. In testifying at the subsequent trial of William Kelly, Shevlin said he let George Howard inside the bank to inspect the vault; here he seems clearly to be referring to Leslie. *Herald,* December 18, 1879; *Sun,* December 18, 1879.

64 John Nugent . . . headquarters detective: *NYT,* June 14, 15, 24, October 6, 1879, July 29, 1883; *Tribune,* June 24, 1879; *Sun,* June 15, 1879, January 14, 1880. See also Lyons, *Why Crime Does Not Pay,* 155–56.

CHAPTER 6: QUEEN OF THE FENCES

66 "root of the evil": Byrnes (1886), 44. See also Lyons, *Why Crime Does Not Pay,* 186–87; McCabe, *Lights and Shadows,* 540–42; Walling, 279; Crapsey, *Nether Side,* 83.

66 "first put crime . . . syndicated basis": Macintyre, *Napoleon of Crime,* 27, quoting Carl Sifakis, *The Encyclopedia of American Crime,* 2nd ed. (New York: Smithpark, 1992), 470.

66 "cracked no safes . . . her fleeing figure": Lyons, *Why Crime Does Not Pay,* 187–88.

67 "the nucleus . . . of crime in New-York": "Crime and the Police," editorial, *NYT,* July 24, 1884.

67 specialty was silk, but she dealt in anything: Walling, 291; *NYT,* July 24, 1884; *Sun,* March 9, 1879; Van Every, *Sins of New York,* 242.

67 all the major burglars . . . "my boys": *Sun,* March 9, 1879, July 23, 1884; *NYT,* August 13, 1879; Walling, 286; Murphy, *Scoundrels in Law,* 128–29; Macintyre, *Napoleon of Crime,* 28–35; *Herald,* July 24, 1879 ("my boys").

67 "my most promising chick": Kuntz, "#74 William O'Brien," *Professional Criminals—REVISED* (blog), quoting *The Boston Globe.*

NOTES

67 "Sheeny Mike" . . . jail at the time: *NYT,* April 29, 1876 (quotation), July 20, 1882, January 24, 1884; Byrnes (1886), 152–54; Kuntz, "#80 Michael Kurtz," *Professional Criminals—REVISED* (blog), September 28, 2018, https://criminalsrevised.blog /2018/09/28/80-michael-kurtz/; *Sun,* March 9, 1879, May 26, 1905; *Herald,* July 24, 1879.

67 female criminals . . . only kept house: Karen Abbott, "The Life and Crimes of 'Old Mother' Mandelbaum," *Smithsonian online,* last modified September 6, 2011, https:// www.smithsonianmag.com/history/the-life-and-crimes-of-old-mother -eamandelbaum-71693582/#oM4il7K847kzEDoU.99; Rona Holub, "Fredericka Mandelbaum (1825–1894)," in *Immigrant Entrepreneurship: German-American Business Biographies, 1720 to the Present,* vol. 2, *The Emergence of an Industrial Nation, 1840–1893,* ed. William J. Hausman (Washington, D.C., German Historical Institute, October 15, 2013), http://www.immigrantentrepreneurship.org/entry.php?rec= 160; Van Every, *Sins of New York,* 244. See also Byrnes (1886), 194, 197–98, 206.

68 Born in central Germany . . . estimated $10 million: Holub, "Fredericka Mandelbaum"; Walling, 280–82; Lyons, *Why Crime Does Not Pay,* 188–91; Murphy, *Scoundrels in Law,* 130–31; Gilfoyle, *Pickpocket's Tale,* 150–52; Van Every, *Sins of New York,* 240, 242; Crapsey, *Nether Side,* 11–12 (covert crime), 91 (fences). See also "Fredericka Henriette Auguste 'Marm' *Wiesener* Mandelbaum,"Find a Grave, last modified May 27, 2014; 1870 US Census, New York, N.Y., Ward 13, Election Dist. 10, 2nd Enum. (Wolf Mandelbaum and family, 163 Rivington); 1860 US Census, New York, N.Y., Ward 17, Dist. 7 (Wolf and Henriette Mandelbaum); *Trow's for 1867–'68* (Wolf Mandelbaum, dry goods, 163 Rivington).

One source from 1872 claims, contrary to most other accounts, that Wolf Mandelbaum was a lawyer, a "man of brains," and himself an accomplished receiver of stolen goods. Crapsey, *Nether Side,* 87–88.

69 "may have appeared . . . inequalities of the era": Holub, "Fredericka Mandelbaum," text after n102.

69 A tough but fair . . . when they came under arrest: *NYT,* March 7, 1875, July 24, 1884; Holub, "Fredericka Mandelbaum"; Walling, 280–81, 285–86; Gilfoyle, *Pickpocket's Tale,* 151; Van Every, *Sins of New York,* 242; Crapsey, *Nether Side,* 91 (legal obstacles); Murphy, *Scoundrels in Law,* 130–31.

69 "Bureau for the Prevention of Conviction": Walling, 281.

69 $5,000 annual retainer . . . Buffalo Bill Cody: Walling, 281; Van Every, *Sins of New York,* 242; Murphy, *Scoundrels in Law,* xv–xvi, xviii–xix, 130, 295n60; Richard H. Underwood, *Gaslight Lawyers: Criminal Trials and Exploits in Gilded Age New York* (Lexington, Ky.: Shadelandhouse Modern Press, 2017), xvii–xix (Howe & Hummel), 12–16 (Unger case); *NYT,* July 26, 1884 (Howe & Hummel).

70 a pair of adjoining buildings . . . Marm's salon: Walling, 283, 284 (illustration), 285, 290 (illustration), 291; *NYT,* July 24, 1884; *Sun,* March 9, 1879, July 23, 1884; Holub, "Fredericka Mandelbaum," text at n34, 68, 83–85; Lyons, *Why Crime Does Not Pay,* 191–92, 196–99; Van Every, *Sins of New York,* 240–41; Murphy, *Scoundrels in Law,* 127; Macintyre, *Napoleon of Crime,* 29. Descriptions of the building complex in the above sources are inconsistent, but the balance of evidence points to 163 Rivington, the taller structure, as the location of the dry goods store and fencing business, and 79 Clinton as the residence. See also *Trow's for 1870–'71* (Wolf Mandelbaum, fancygoods, 163 Rivington, h[ome] 79 Clinton). The configuration can be seen on the 1857–1862 Perris fire insurance map of New York, plate 26. https://digitalcollec tions.nypl.org/items/510d47e0-bf4f-a3d9-e040-e00a18064a99.

71 **Outwardly, she appeared . . . Fifth Avenue propriety:** *NYT,* January 24, July 24, 26, 29, 1884; *Sun,* March 9, 1879, July 23, 1884; Walling, 281 ("a wonderful person"), 291; Lyons, *Why Crime Does Not Pay,* 188; Holub, "Fredericka Mandelbaum."

72 **"Piano Charley" . . . popular performer:** Macintyre, *Napoleon of Crime,* 35, 175–76; Eldridge and Watts, *Our Rival,* 49–50, 53–54 (Bullard); Byrnes (1886), 326–27 (same).

72 **Leslie became . . . head of her clique:** Walling, 269; *Sun,* March 9, 1879; *NYT,* August 13, 1879.

72 **"pet and star":** Lyons, *Why Crime Does Not Pay,* 199.

72 **By the time . . . Occasionally she would deal:** "Wolf Israel 'William' Mandelbaum," Find a Grave, last modified May 27, 2014; Walling, 291; Macintyre, *Napoleon of Crime,* 30; Murphy, *Scoundrels in Law,* 129, 295n59; Lardner and Reppetto, *NYPD,* 77.

72 **she supplied considerable money . . . more modest $2,500:** Walling, 262; Holub, "Fredericka Mandelbaum," text at n53; *NYT,* April 28, 1889.

72 **John D. Grady . . . advanced $10,000:** *NYT,* October 4, 1880; *Memphis Daily Appeal,* October 9, 1880; Walling, 262; Crapsey, *Nether Side,* 84–85 ("Traveling Mike"); *Sun,* March 9, 1879.

73 **According to a fictionalized . . . it was Traveling Mike Grady:** Julian Hawthorne, *The Great Bank Robbery, from the Diary of Inspector Byrnes* (New York: Cassell, 1887), 129, 175–79.

73 **Grady muscled . . . cut her out:** Lyons, *Why Crime Does Not Pay,* 188, 199, 201–3.

74 **greatly unnerved him . . . accused his churchgoing wife:** *Sun,* March 9, 1879; Walling, 274; *NYT,* April 30, 1880.

74 **openly consorting . . . sister, Babe:** *Sun,* March 9, 1879; *NYT,* June 17, 1878; Walling, 274–75; Van Every, *Sins of New York,* 236; Allan Pinkerton, *Professional Thieves,* 180–81. Some sources refer to Irving's sister, Babe, as Shang Draper's mistress, but they appear to confuse her with Jennie (Mooney) Draper.

74 **He began hanging out . . . last time he saw his wife:** *Sun,* March 9, 1879; Walling, 274–75; Allan Pinkerton, *Professional Thieves,* 183.

75 **On June 4, 1878 . . . confirmed it was Leslie:** *NYT,* June 5, 7, 10, 17, 1878; *Sun,* March 9, 1879; Walling, 268–69.

76 **Leslie would be referred to . . . notorious burglar:** *NYT,* June 7, 1878; *The Philadelphia Inquirer,* June 8, 1878.

76 **"Poor Shorge . . . nais man":** *Sun,* March 9, 1879.

76 **paid for his funeral . . . support to Leslie's widow:** *Sun,* March 9, 1879; *NYT,* June 10, 1878; Walling, 278.

76 After Leslie was identified . . . Raymond Street Jail: *Sun*, March 9, 1879, October 17, 1883 (Porter and Irving); Walling, 278; *NYT,* June 17, 1878, June 2 (Porter and Irving), July 11 (Draper), October 6, 22, November 6, 1879 (Porter and Irving), June 23, 1888 (Porter); *Tribune*, August 13, 31, 1878; *Augusta (Ga.) Chronicle*, June 8, 1879; *Herald*, September 27, 28, 1878 (Draper), July 24, December 18, 1879 (Porter). Draper does not appear in any extant rogues' gallery photograph or in Byrnes's *Professional Criminals*. The only surviving image of him—an etching of unconfirmed authenticity—was made when he was sixty-three, a few years before his death. See *Washington (D.C.) Times*, February 10, 1907.

76 Jennie Draper . . . A false rumor: *Herald*, October 1, 1878; *Sun*, March 9, 1879, October 4, 1880.

76 The funds . . . John D. Grady: *Sun*, March 9, 1879; *NYT,* October 4, 1880.

CHAPTER 7: A STAR COP IS BORN

77 Jimmy Hope took over . . . would instead tie up: Walling, 264; *People v. John Hope*, Trial Tr. 180 (Shevlin testimony); *NYT*, June 17, October 6, 1879.

77 The men who took part . . . Goodie who drove them: *People v. John Hope*, Trial Tr. 124–40, 146–57, 179–80 (Shevlin testimony); Walling, 263, 267 (Nugent), 286, 475 (Goodie); *Tribune*, April 30, 1880; *NYT,* October 28, 29, 1878, June 2, 13, 17, 18, 24, December 18, 1879, March 17, 1907 (Coakley); Byrnes (1886), 153 (Wilmont), 163 (Coakley), 189–90 (Goodie); *Sun*, March 9 (Wilmont), June 14, 15 (Nugent), December 17, 18, 1879; *Brooklyn Daily Eagle*, March 10, 1879 (Wilmont); *Herald*, December 18, 1879; Lardner and Reppetto, *NYPD*, 78 (Coakley); Lyons, *Why Crime Does Not Pay*, 160–63 (Goodie and Banjo Pete).

78 Of the $2.75 million . . . from $1,600 to $1,000: Byrnes (1886), 81–82; *NYT,* June 2, December 18, 1879, June 14, 1896, April 16, 1901; *Sun*, June 2, December 18, 19, 1879; *Herald*, December 18, 1879; Lyons, *Why Crime Does Not Pay*, 167, 171. After contributing the $600, Shevlin received another $400, making his net take about $1,400.

79 only three . . . were convicted: *People v. John Hope*, Trial Tr. *passim; NYT,* June 2, 6, 15, 17, 18, 22, December 18, 19, 20, 1879; *Sun*, June 2, 17, December 18, 19, 20, 1879; *Herald*, December 18, 19, 1879; *Tribune*, March 15, 1880 ("Detectives in Wall St."). John Hope served nine years of his prison term before his sentence was commuted by the governor of New York for good behavior. *NYT,* October 23, 1890. A newspaper columnist later claimed that Hope was pardoned on Byrnes's admission to the governor that young Hope was innocent, and that Byrnes had arrested him only to try to pressure his father, Jimmy, into coming forward. Kuntz, "#19 John Hope," *Professional Criminals—REVISED* (blog), May 25, 2018, https://criminalsrevised.blog/2018/05/25/19-john-hope/. I have found no substantiation for that contention.

80 Nugent made the mistake . . . bribed to reach its result: *NYT,* June 14, 15, 1879; *Sun*, January 18, 1880; Walling, 268; Murphy, *Scoundrels in Law*, 121–23.

80 **The police commissioners . . . ten years of hard labor:** *Sun*, January 25, 1880, July 29, 31, 1883; *Tribune*, January 25, 1880; Walling, 268, 531–34; Murphy, *Scoundrels in Law*, 123. Nugent received back pay from the date he was arrested by Byrnes in June 1879 to the date he was dismissed from the force. *People ex. rel. Nugent v. Board of Police Commissioners*, 114 N.Y. 245 (1889).

80 **Grady, who died of a heart attack:** *NYT*, October 4, 1880; *Memphis Daily Appeal*, October 9, 1880.

80 **Disguising himself . . . died with him:** *Sun*, December 18, 1879; *NYT*, July 6, September 29, 1881, December 17, 1886, June 3, 1887, August 24, 1889, October 23, 1890, January 15, 1896, April 16, 1901, February 9, June 3, 5, 1905; *St. Paul (Minn.) Daily Globe*, November 12, 1881; Byrnes (1886), 82–83; Byrnes (1895), 53; Eldridge and Watts, *Our Rival*, 55.

81 **Dobbs was indicted . . . Connecticut State Prison:** *NYT*, February 6, 7, 1880, March 7, 1884; *Sun*, February 6, 1880, June 10, 1884; Kuntz, "#64 Michael Kerrigan," *Professional Criminals—REVISED* (blog).

81 **Byrnes nabbed . . . upstanding citizens:** *Tribune*, April 30, 1880; *NYT*, April 30, 1880, July 29, 31, 1883, August 31, 1899; Kuntz, "#90 Peter Ellis," *Professional Criminals—REVISED* (blog); Eldridge and Watts, *Our Rival*, 55–56.

82 **Porter and Johnny Irving escaped . . . returned to prison:** *Tribune*, August 13, 1878; *NYT*, June 2, August 10, October 22, November 6, 8, 1879, October 17, 1883, July 24, 1884 (Mandelbaum), June 23, 1888; *Sun*, June 2, 1879; *Augusta (Ga.) Chronicle*, June 8, 1879; *Herald*, July 24, 1879.

82 **Draper was extradited . . . sudden memory loss:** *NYT*, August 10, October 22, November 6, 1879; Freeland, *Automats*, 112; Walling, 243–44; *Portland (Maine) Daily Press*, February 11, 1881; *Washington (D.C.) Evening Star*, March 19, 1881; *National Republican* (Washington, D.C.), March 19, 1881.

82 **"went out . . . honored and admired":** *New Haven (Conn.) Morning Journal and Courier*, March 23, 1881.

83 **"made away with by his pals":** Byrnes (1886), 54.

83 **The prevailing theory . . . no arrests were made:** *NYT*, June 7, 17, 1878, August 10, October 6, 22, November 6, 1879, April 30, October 4, 1880; *Sun*, March 9, May 7, June 2, 1879; *Springfield (Mass.) Republican*, July 18, 1878; *Herald*, October 1, 1878, October 2, 1883; *Brooklyn Daily Eagle*, March 10, 1879; *Augusta (Ga.) Chronicle*, June 8, 1879; Walling, 274–78; Allan Pinkerton, *Professional Thieves*, 170–71, 183–84.

84 **"Johnny the Mick" . . . Porter had shot Walsh:** *NYT*, October 17, 19, 1883; *Brooklyn Daily Eagle*, October 16, 1883 ("worst man"); *Sun*, October 17, 1883; Walling, 399–402; Freeland, *Automats*, 109–10.

85 **"There is not the slightest doubt . . . did not hit him":** *Sun*, October 17, 1883.

85 **"Glorious! Glorious!" . . . his only regret:** *Brooklyn Daily Eagle*, October 16, 1883.

85 **Porter evaded conviction . . . vowed, as he left:** *NYT*, October 25, November 17, 20, 21, 1883, July 24, 1884 (Mandelbaum).

85 **the first time . . . travel fare:** *NYT*, June 6, 1879.

86 "He was the hottest customer . . . until he had you inside": Eddie Guerin, *Crime: The Autobiography of a Crook* (London: J. Murray, 1928), 60.

86 "There has really been no . . . protected and guarded": Eldridge and Watts, *Our Rival*, 62. See also Erroll and Erroll, *American Genius*, 32–35, 143, 239, 297.

86 Less gifted burglars . . . to accomplish their goals: Eldridge and Watts, *Our Rival*, 50. See also Hartsfield, *Professional Response*, 72.

CHAPTER 8: THE GREAT DETECTIVE

88 At the regular meeting . . . "would infuse more vim and vigor": *NYT*, March 10, 1880 (quotation), April 14, 1892.

88 hid behind a tree . . . liquor during performances: *Tribune*, January 4 (burglars), 22 (Hill), 27 (gambling house), 1880.

89 "in recognition . . . remarkably successful": *NYT*, March 10, 1880.

89 "This really marked . . . worthy of the name": Costello, *Our Police Protectors*, 402.

89 Byrnes, nominally a Democrat: *NYT*, September 23, 1878, April 23, 1880.

89 "entirely free . . . party obligations": *NYT*, April 14, 1892.

89 assorted bank sneak thieves . . . other valuables: Costello, *Our Police Protectors*, 405, 409; *NYT*, April 14, 1892.

89 "Knavery was jubilant": Wheatley, "New York Police Department," 511.

89 established a detective substation . . . Wall Street men hired private detectives: *Tribune*, March 15, 1880, May 28, 1895; Costello, *Our Police Protectors*, 405; *Sun*, March 14, 1880; *NYT*, March 14, 1880, April 14, 1892, May 28, 1895.

90 "There is no reason . . . talent to be found": *Tribune*, March 15, 1880.

90 Brayton Ives . . . paid by them: Costello, *Our Police Protectors*, 405 ("protect those gentlemen"), 407, 409; Wheatley, "New York Police Department," 511.

90 Byrnes's next move . . . "dead line": Schlesinger, "Business of Crime," xvi; Wheatley, "New York Police Department," 511; Lardner and Reppetto, *NYPD*, 82; *NYT*, May 28, 31, 1895, May 8, 1910; Carey, 34–35. The boundaries were Fulton Street on the north, Greenwich Street on the west, down to the Battery, and across to the East River. Costello, *Our Police Protectors*, 409.

91 Byrnes bragged . . . "not a penny, not a cent": Wheatley, "New York Police Department," 511 (quotation); Byrnes (1886), 7.

91 state of disorganization . . . new batch of men: Costello, *Our Police Protectors*, 405, 407, 409; Wheatley, "New York Police Department," 511; William E. Fales and George W. Curtis, "Chief Inspector Thomas Byrnes," *Harper's Weekly*, February 9, 1889, 111–12; Carey, 30–31; *NYT*, April 14, 1892, May 8, 1910; Burns and Sanders, *New York*, 198.

91 promoted to inspector . . . "forty immortals": *NYT*, April 23, 24, 1880, May 26, 1882, December 9, 1888, May 8, 1910; Carey, 17 (quotation); Costello, *Our Police Protectors*, 287.

91 sixty precinct detectives . . . without jealousy or interference: Czitrom, *New York Exposed*, 39; Reppetto, *American Police*, 55; Lardner and Reppetto, *NYPD*, 85–86;

Richardson, *New York Police*, 208–9, 211; *NYT,* July 9, 1882 ("They can cope"); *Sun,* May 10, 1884; *Lexow Hearings,* 1:45–46, 471–73, 4:3671, 5:5323, 5340.

92 **"a separate fiefdom":** Lardner and Reppetto, *NYPD,* 83.

92 **"a complete transformation of affairs":** George M. White, *From Boniface,* 317.

92 **"Bank Ring" . . . came to an end:** White, 317.

92 **"Never in my . . . other than honest":** White, 317–18.

93 **"Within forty-eight hours . . . 'ask for your shield'":** White, 317.

93 **Byrnes thoroughly modernized . . . rap sheets were also distributed:** Czitrom, *New York Exposed,* 40; Wheatley, "New York Police Department," 514–15; Carey, 30, 35; Lardner and Reppetto, *NYPD,* 81; *NYT,* October 13, 1901 (record department), May 8, 1910; *Tribune,* January 10, 1892.

94 **"YES, COLBERT . . . BYRNES":** De Francias Folsom, ed., *Our Police: A History of the Baltimore Force from the First Watchman to the Latest Appointee* (Baltimore: n.p., 1888), 505–7. See also Byrnes (1886), 304.

94 **Byrnes's innovations . . . were not new:** *NYT,* May 14, 1865, November 20, 1873, June 27, 1875 (all for rogues' gallery); Lardner, *American Police,* 55 (rogues' gallery, lineups); Costello, *Our Police Protectors,* 410.

94 **"museum of crime" . . . real opium and pipes:** Carey, 29 (quotation); Wheatley, "New York Police Department," 514–15; Walling, 187–91.

95 **"shuddering horror":** Wheatley, "New York Police Department," 514.

95 **Walling . . . "star chamber" tactics:** Walling, 590.

95 **Alexander S. "Clubber" Williams . . . never had his badge taken:** Costello, *Our Police Protectors,* 364–68; Czitrom, *New York Exposed,* 19, 47–58, 326–27n18; Mike Dash, *Satan's Circus: Murder, Vice, Police Corruption, and New York's Trial of the Century* (2007; repr., New York: Three Rivers, 2008), 50; Sante, *Low Life,* 247; Paul Moses, *An Unlikely Union: The Love-Hate Story of New York's Irish and Italians* (New York: NYU Press, 2015), 119 (pair of toughs and watch on lamppost); James W. Shepp and Daniel B. Shepp, *Shepp's New York Illustrated: Scene and Story in the Metropolis of the Western World* (Chicago: Globe Bible, 1894), 414 ("almost a giant"); *NYT,* August 7, 1883 (boxing match), December 18, 1884 (same), May 25, 1895 (career).

98 **clubbing a group . . . Tompkins Square:** *NYT,* July 26, 1877; Lardner and Reppetto, *NYPD,* 57–58.

98 **intelligence gathering . . . gave him an education:** Costello, *Our Police Protectors,* 416–17; Carey, 35; Czitrom, *New York Exposed,* 40; *NYT,* May 13, 1884; *Tribune,* May 8, 1910 (two hours).

98 **conviction of Mike McGloin . . . "devil of a time":** *NYT,* December 31, 1881 (murder), February 2 (McGloin's arrest), 3, 7, 10, March 2 ("until he knocks"), 3, 4, 7, 23 (pals), June 19 (McGloin Gang), October 28, November 7, 1882 (appeals), March 9 (final meal), 10 (execution), 1883; *Tribune,* February 2, March 2, 1882; *Sun,* September 8, 1884 (McGloin Gang); 1880 US Census, New York, N.Y., Enum. Dist. 351 (Michael McGloin, age seventeen, 252 W. 28th St.); Riis, *Making of an American,* 342 ("devil of a time"), 343 ("Squealed, both"); Byrnes (1886), 372–373; Murphy, *Scoundrels in Law,* 52–53, 57–59; Czitrom, *New York Exposed,* 44–45.

100 Byrnes received . . . donated it: *NYT,* February 7, 1882.

100 Vidocq . . . catch a thief: Reppetto, *American Police,* 30; *NYT,* December 10, 1893 (comparison), March 31, 1935 (Vidocq).

101 Byrnes helped Belgian police . . . prison in Liège: Macintyre, *Napoleon of Crime,* 176–78; Byrnes (1886), 255–56; Eldridge and Watts, *Our Rival,* 49–50; *NYT,* June 30, 1895.

101 *Professional Criminals* . . . "a good one": Byrnes (1886), 53 and *passim;* Walling, 193; Carey, 18.

101 "a splendid one, although avoided": Byrnes (1886), 154.

101 "David Bliss . . . Dinkelman": Byrnes, 59, 63.

102 "when the unsuspecting . . . a comfortable home": Byrnes, 13, 19, 31.

102 "did not regard slayers . . . incidental to robbery": Carey, 18.

102 they rewarded him . . . real estate: *NYT,* November 14, 15, 1881 (Gould); *Lexow Hearings,* 5:5710–14, 5720–26. See also Maury Klein, *The Life and Legend of Jay Gould* (Baltimore: Johns Hopkins University Press, 1986), 217.

102 George Jay Gould . . . "the wrong person": Robert K. DeArment, *Bat Masterson: The Man and the Legend* (1979; repr., Norman: University of Oklahoma Press, 1989), 345. See also *NYT,* February 7, 1905; *Tribune,* March 29, 1905.

103 middle- and upper-class . . . a third: Burrows and Wallace, *Gotham,* 726, 966.

103 Pickpocketing . . . George Appo: Gilfoyle, *Pickpocket's Tale,* 65, 67.

103 large public gatherings . . . arrested in advance: Byrnes (1886), 34; Gilfoyle, *Pickpocket's Tale,* 61, 250; *NYT,* April 22, 1889. George Walling claims to have initiated the practice. Walling, 196, 219.

103 "It's the fellow . . . as well as it could be done": Flynt, *World of Graft,* 94–95.

103 A pessimist . . . "always a thief": "Current Topics," *Albany Law Journal* 40 (July 13, 1889): 21.

103 forged close relationships . . . served as snitches: Costello, *Our Police Protectors,* 416; Schlesinger, "Business of Crime," xvii; Zacks, *Island of Vice,* 34, 203; Dash, *Satan's Circus,* 50.

104 Lincoln Steffens . . . in the same condition: Steffens, *Autobiography,* 1:222.

104 He also marveled . . . cockney accent: Steffens, *Autobiography,* 1:210, 218–19. See also M. R. Werner, *It Happened in New York* (New York: Coward-McCann, 1957), 111 (accent).

104 "with all an autocrat's . . . made the detective service great": Riis, *Making of an American,* 339–40.

104 Chicago . . . weak and indifferent: Reppetto, *American Police,* 192–97; Flynt, *World of Graft,* 16–19, 32.

CHAPTER 9: "TOO MUCH FOR OUR POLICE"

106 It was at night . . . "Why-O!": *NYT,* January 6, 1884; *World,* January 23, 1888 (extra); *Herald,* December 27, 1891; *Tribune,* February 16, 1896. One source asserts that the

Whyos derived their name from a Gaelic phrase meaning "noble few." English, *Paddy Whacked*, 18.

106 they were relatively hands-off . . . volunteer firefighters: Burrows and Wallace, *Gotham*, 634; Mike Wallace, *Greater Gotham: A History of New York City from 1898 to 1919* (New York: Oxford University Press, 2017), 583–84; Anbinder, *Five Points*, 283–89 (Dead Rabbits Riot); Ted Chamberlain, "Gangs of New York: Fact vs. Fiction," *National Geographic online*, last modified March 23, 2003, https://news.nation algeographic.com/news/2003/03/oscars-gangs-of-new-york/; Dash, *Satan's Circus*, 159–60; *Sun*, July 20, 1919.

107 full-time occupation . . . carried pistols: Dash, *Satan's Circus*, 160; Wallace, *Greater Gotham*, 584; English, *Paddy Whacked*, 33–34; Gilfoyle, *Pickpocket's Tale*, 180–81, 190–91; DeVillo, *The Bowery*, 113; Anthony M. DeStefano, *Gangland New York: The Places and Faces of Mob History* (Guilford, Conn.: Lyons Press, 2015), 10–12; *Sun*, September 28, October 10, 1884; *Herald*, December 27, 1891.

107 "a new breed . . . capitalist criminal": English, *Paddy Whacked*, 34.

107 Asbury maintains . . . after the Civil War: Asbury, *Gangs of New York*, 206.

107 first mention . . . early 1884: *Herald*, February 1, 1884.

107 They dropped bricks . . . tenement basement: *Herald*, February 1, 1884, December 27, 1891; *Sun*, September 15, October 6, 20, 1884, January 29, 1888, August 13, 1895 ("doing up a cop"), July 10, 1898; *Tribune*, February 16, 1896; *World*, January 23, 1888 (extra) (alleys), April 17, 1889 (Daniel Sullivan); Timothy J. Gilfoyle, *City of Eros: New York City, Prostitution, and the Commercialization of Sex, 1790–1920* (1992; repr., New York: W. W. Norton, 1994), 229 (Billy McGlory's); Jacob A. Riis, *A Ten Years' War: An Account of the Battle with the Slum in New York* (Boston: Houghton, Mifflin, 1900), 201–2 (Bottle Alley); Anbinder, *Five Points*, 357–61 (Mulberry Bend); Neil Hanson, *The Heroic Gangster: The Story of Monk Eastman, from the Streets of New York to the Battlefields of Europe and Back* (New York: Skyhorse, 2013), 64 (rooftop escapes).

109 a common height: Byrnes (1895), 303–4, 307, 309, 314.

109 Riis . . . McCullagh emerged: Riis, *Making of an American*, 239–40 (quotation).

109 "the worst cutthroats in the city": Riis, *Making of an American*, 240.

109 "a more hopelessly . . . civilized community": Shepp and Shepp, *Shepp's New York City Illustrated*, 204.

109 "notorious Whyo gang": See, for instance, *Herald*, February 1, 1884; *Sun*, September 18, 1884; Byrnes (1895), 335 (Hurley). See also *Sun*, September 15, 1884 ("great gang of murderers . . . largest gang"); *World*, January 23, 1888 (3 o'clock) ("more than one hundred thieves, cut-throats and scoundrels").

109 Asbury claimed . . . "knocked his man out": Asbury, *Gangs of New York*, 211.

110 reportedly a hero . . . under his own name: *Tribune*, September 28, 1886; *Sun*, September 8, 1884, October 1, 1886.

110 "Dandy Johnny" Dolan . . . eye gouger: Asbury, *Gangs of New York*, 212–13.

110 never identified as a Whyo . . . Nor is there any account: See, for example, *Herald*, October 9, 10, 11, 27, 28, 1875; *NYT*, October 28, 1875, April 10, 1876 (Dolan's history). See also Walling, 402–4; Jerry Kuntz, "Dandy Johnny in the News," *Asbury's The Gangs of New York—Annotated: Re-Examinations of the Classic Sketch of Nineteenth-Century Underworld Life*, last modified December 12, 2019, https://gangsannotated.blog/2019/12/12/dandy-johnny-in-the-news/.

110 Piker Ryan . . . "doing the big job": Asbury, *Gangs of New York*, 211; *Sun*, July 20, 1919.

110 Asbury identified Piker Ryan . . . flourished around 1900: *Sun*, July 20, 1919. Asbury's source appears to have been a 1908 *New York Herald* article that called Ryan "a present-day metropolitan thug." See *Idaho Statesman* (Boise), April 5, 1908, reprinting *Herald* article and publishing photo of alleged price list. The author of the article, magazine writer Broughton Brandenburg, has been described as a "serial fraudster." Tony O'Connell, "Brandenburg, Broughton," *Atlantipedia*, February 9, 2015, http://atlantipedia.ie/samples/brandenburg-broughton-n/.

A 1909 newspaper article also implied that Ryan's alleged price list was then of relatively recent vintage. *New York Evening Post*, October 23, 1909.

110 Whyos were no longer in existence: Sources differ on exactly when, during the 1890s, the Whyos ceased to exist, but all agree they were no longer active by century's end. See, for instance, *World*, December 27, 1893 (6 o'clock), May 16, 1895; *Sun*, July 20, 1893, March 17, 1897, July 10, 1898; *Tribune*, November 4, 1900; *NYT*, May 28, 1895; Dash, *Satan's Circus*, 160 (around 1895); Shepp and Shepp, *Shepp's New York City Illustrated*, 204 ("a thing of the past" in 1894); Sante, *Low Life*, 217 (early 1890s).

110 rogues' gallery photo . . . Patrick "English Paddy" Ryan: Asbury, *Gangs of New York*, 209; Byrnes (1895), 296. The photograph of Patrick Ryan, which appears in Byrnes's 1895 book following page 298, is of the same man Asbury identifies as Piker Ryan.

110 weren't the only gang . . . some fifty others: *Sun*, September 8, 15, 1884.

110 "Every corner . . . before their fellows": Jacob A. Riis, *How the Other Half Lives: Studies Among the Tenements of New York* (New York: Charles Scribner's Sons, 1890), 217.

111 evocative names . . . steal their money: *Sun*, September 8, 15, 1884; *Tribune*, February 16, 1896.

111 "Dey'll steal anything . . . off your feet": *Sun*, September 8, 1884.

112 female gangs . . . members of other gangs: *Sun*, September 8, 1884, July 10, 1898.

112 "from sheer love . . . need their help": Riis, *Other Half*, 225.

112 Many gangs pretended . . . late-night visit: Riis, *Other Half*, 230–32.

112 "A splendid sight . . . virtuous laborer": Hutchins Hapgood, ed., *The Autobiography of a Thief* (New York: Fox, Duffield, 1903), 27–28. Jim Caulfield, a reformed thief, is the book's narrator.

112 just as capable . . . fallen overboard: *Sun*, September 15, 1884.

113 Gotham Court . . . bodies of murdered men: Moss, *American Metropolis*, 3:108–10.

113 Whyos stood out . . . formed alliances: *Sun*, September 8, 15, 18, October 6, 1884, August 16, 1887 (Staten Island); *Herald*, February 1, 13, 1884, December 27, 1891; *Tribune*, February 16, 1896 (the "most famous" gang); *World*, January 23, 1888;

Sante, *Low Life*, 214; Murphy, *Scoundrels in Law*, 51–52; Gilfoyle, *Pickpocket's Tale*, 179–81, 190–91.

113 **"Fatty" Walsh . . . routinely sprang Whyos:** Anbinder, *Five Points*, 269–72, 287; *Sun*, October 6, 1884; Gilfoyle, *Pickpocket's Tale*, 188.

113 **Election Day 1885 . . . continued striking him:** *NYT*, November 4, 1885; *Herald*, November 4, 1885.

114 **found themselves outnumbered . . . "gang rule in New York":** *Sun*, September 8 ("gang rule"), October 6, 1884.

114 **"apparently too much for our police authorities":** *Tribune*, October 28, 1884.

114 **cops were afraid . . . after dark:** *Sun*, September 8 ("club h[ell]"), October 6, 1884; *World*, December 27, 1893; *Tribune*, February 16, 1896; Gilfoyle, *Pickpocket's Tale*, 186.

114 **police were also frustrated . . . five days in the workhouse:** *Sun*, October 6, 1884.

114 **Officer McManus . . . judge's ear:** *Sun*, September 18, October 10, 1884.

114 **"Any pothouse politician . . . tired of doing anything about it":** *Sun*, September 8, 1884.

114 **Whyos also inspired fear . . . quasi-heroes:** *Sun*, September 15, 1884; George Benson, letter to the editor, *World*, August 1, 1889 (2 o'clock), December 27, 1893 (6 o'clock); *Tribune*, February 16, 1896; Gilfoyle, *Pickpocket's Tale*, 186, 194–95.

115 **"The business man . . . very tricky things":** Flynt, *World of Graft*, 208–209.

115 **"Not one out of . . . try my luck":** Flynt, 168–70.

115 **he was greeted . . . when he finished:** *Sun*, September 8, 1884; Riis, *Other Half*, 232–33; Gilfoyle, *Pickpocket's Tale*, 189.

115 **"They began . . . 'done time'":** Hapgood, *Autobiography of a Thief*, 50.

115 **"stone" . . . "as me mudder":** *Sun*, August 17, 1887.

116 **Danny Driscoll . . . released with Walsh's help:** *World*, January 23, 1888 (extra and last) (criminal career); *Sun*, September 28, 1884 (Chrystie Street bar incident, twenty-seventh lockup), January 24, 1888; *Tribune*, November 21, 1883 (shot by Patrick Green), June 27, 1886 ("Apple Mary"), February 16, 1896 (criminal career); *Herald*, December 27, 1891 (career); Gilfoyle, *Pickpocket's Tale*, 178–80; Murphy, *Scoundrels in Law*, 59–61; *People of the State of New York Against Daniel Driscoll*, Case on Appeal (New York, 1886), trial transcript at 121–22, 144–48 (criminal record), reprinted in https://books.google.com/books?id=opXbBzEKaHkC&printsec=frontcover#v=onepage&q&f=false (hereafter, *People v. Driscoll*, Trial Tr.); Municipal Archives, New York City, "D. A. Cases, Court of General Sessions, New York County, Grand Jury Indictments 1879–1893, Daniel Driscoll, 07/08/86, Murder, 1st Degree, Folder 2209, Box 225" (hereafter, Driscoll Indictment File), 730–31 (1884 Chrystie Street incident).

It is possible that the two Chrystie Street shooting incidents, one in 1883 and the other in 1884, are the same. In 1883, Driscoll was described as a member of the Border Gang, which further supports the view that the Whyos did not emerge as a named gang until 1884. *Tribune*, May 28, 1883.

118 **"the toughest of the tough . . . known in the city":** Quoted in Gilfoyle, *Pickpocket's Tale*, 178, and in Murphy, *Scoundrels in Law*, 60.

118 "one of the cleverest guns . . . moment's notice": Hapgood, *Autobiography of a Thief*, 279–80.

118 Burly and square-faced . . . "miserable little tenement": *Sun*, October 1, 1886; *World*, January 23, 1888 (extra) ("tenement"); Gilfoyle, *Pickpocket's Tale*, 178; Willemse, *A Cop Remembers*, 43 ("Bowery angle").

118 Driscoll's body . . . ugly scar: *World*, January 23, 1888 (extra); *People v. Driscoll*, Trial Tr. 133.

118 four surgeries without anesthesia: Hapgood, *Autobiography of a Thief*, 280.

118 four terms in prison . . . for larceny: *Sun*, September 30, 1886; Gilfoyle, *Pickpocket's Tale*, 179–80.

CHAPTER 10: "FREDERICKA THE GREAT"

119 she lost a civil suit . . . "as honest as anybody else": *NYT*, January 24, 1884 (quotations); *Sun*, January 24, 1884; *Tribune*, May 26, 1905 (Kurtz feigned illness); Lyons, *Why Crime Does Not Pay*, 78–82 (same); Byrnes (1886), 153 (same).

120 Olney decided to pursue . . . punched him in the face: *NYT*, July 23, 24, 1884; *Sun*, July 23, 25, 1884.

122 "It was not imbecility . . . indictment of the police force": "Crime and the Police," editorial, *NYT*, July 24, 1884. See also "Police Detective Methods," editorial, *NYT*, July 29, 1884.

122 His office further accused . . . gaming houses: *NYT*, August 8, 1884.

122 claimed to have interviewed Mandelbaum . . . a few pieces of stolen silk: *NYT*, August 3, 1884.

123 of the 12,000 yards . . . 160 yards: *NYT*, July 23, 1884.

123 Among the loot found was $4,000 worth of diamonds: *Sun*, July 23, 1884, May 26, 1905; *NYT*, July 24, December 10, 1884, March 21, 22, June 26, 1886; Byrnes (1886), 145, 154.

123n Porter and Kurtz went to Europe . . . died in New York in 1904: *NYT*, January 21, 1886, January 23, 1888; Byrnes (1895), 77, 80; Kuntz, "#74 William O'Brien," *Professional Criminals—REVISED* (blog); *Sun*, May 26, 1905; *Tribune*, May 26, 1905.

123 Byrnes went on the offensive . . . masking its own corruption: *NYT*, August 3 (not "a good Democrat"), 5 (Olney response), 1884; Gilfoyle, *Pickpocket's Tale*, 388n17 (citing *Lexow Hearings*, 5:5671–72) (Pinkertons).

124 "the greatest bulwark . . . any other country": *NYT*, July 29, 1884.

124 precinct captains rebelled . . . select and control their own: *Sun*, May 10, 11, 1884; Reppetto, *American Police*, 55; Richardson, *New York Police*, 211–12; Lardner and Reppetto, *NYPD*, 85–86; *Lexow Hearings*, 1:45–46, 471–73, 4:3671, 5:5323, 5340.

124 The war of words . . . soon ended: *NYT*, July 27, 29, August 3, 5, 8, 1884; Murphy, *Scoundrels in Law*, 137.

124 On December 4, 1884 . . . "Fredericka the Great": *Herald*, December 5, 1884. See also *NYT*, December 5, 1884.

125 taken flight to Canada . . . beyond the state's reach: *NYT,* December 5, 6, 7, 9, 10, 13, 1884, February 27, 1894; *Herald,* October 10, 1886; Murphy, *Scoundrels in Law,* 141–43.

126 quietly lived out her years . . . returned one more time: *NYT,* November 12, 1885, February 27, 1894; *World,* February 26, 1894; Walling, 289.

126 "in order to once more . . . Thirteenth Ward": Walling, 289.

126 In September 1895 . . . Francesca Janauschek: *NYT,* September 5, 1895 (quotations); Gerald Bordman, ed., *The Oxford Companion to American Theatre,* 2nd ed. (New York: Oxford University Press, 1992), 378.

CHAPTER 11: "WIRED"

127 Henry Jaehne . . . at the polling booths: *NYT,* August 27, 1885 (picnic), March 26, May 16, 22, 1886; *Herald,* March 24, 1886 ("his guide"); *Albuquerque Morning Democrat,* March 28, 1886; *Boston Evening Transcript,* March 22, 1886; *World,* October 15, 1892.

128 Mrs. Schuyler Hamilton . . . Jaehne paid her: *NYT,* March 13, 14 ("Crime and Politics," editorial), 1886; *Tribune,* March 13, 14, 1886.

128 *Times* suggested . . . resign: "Crime and Politics," editorial, *NYT,* March 14, 1886.

128 Byrnes dropped a bombshell . . . arrested Jaehne: *NYT,* March 19, 20, 1886; *Tribune,* March 19, 1886.

129 Jacob Sharp . . . accepted $20,000 bribes: *Sun,* July 31, August 1, 6, 8, 1884; *Tribune,* August 6, September 1, 1884; *NYT,* March 4, 24, May 17, 1885, March 19, May 9, 1886; *World,* October 15, 1892; James Blaine Walker, *Fifty Years of Rapid Transit, 1864–1917* (New York: Law Printing, 1918), 4–8, 46; Robert T. Swaine, *The Cravath Firm and Its Predecessors, 1819–1947,* vol. 1, *The Predecessor Firms, 1819–1906* (1946; repr., Clark, N.J.: Lawbook Exchange, 2012), 404–12; Philip C. Jessup, *Elihu Root,* vol. 1, *1845–1909* (New York: Dodd, Mead, 1938), 146–53; Gustavus Myers, *The History of Tammany Hall,* 2nd ed. (New York: Boni and Liveright, 1917), 263–65; Burrows and Wallace, *Gotham,* 1057–58; James Nevius, "The Elevated Era," *Curbed New York,* last modified June 27, 2018, https://ny.curbed.com/2018/6/27/17507424 /new-york-city-elevated-train-history-transportation.

129 a sting operation . . . Byrnes admitted: *NYT,* March 19 (quotation), 23, May 15, 1886; *Insurance Maps of the City of New York,* vol. 3 (New York: Sanborn-Perris Map, 1895), plate 54, available at New York Public Library Digital Collections, accessed December 27, 2020, https://digitalcollections.nypl.org/items/98041e7e-a691-76a2 -e040-e00a180605a3 (59 West Ninth).

130 "Did you believe?" . . . "I did": *NYT,* May 15, 1886.

130 Jaehne was convicted . . . Sharp was convicted: *NYT,* May 15, 16, 21, 1886; Swaine, *Cravath Firm,* 1:412; Myers, *History of Tammany Hall,* 263–65; *World,* October 15, 1892, October 15, 1894; Gilfoyle, *Pickpocket's Tale,* 131, 166–67 (special privileges); *Sun,* November 26, December 20, 1886 (same); Burrows and Wallace, *Gotham,* 1057–58.

131 "too well known . . . out of the country": *NYT,* April 14, 1892.

NOTES

CHAPTER 12: "EITHER THE WHYOS OR I MUST GO"

132 seven bullets inside him: *Tribune,* January 21, 1888.

132 night of June 25, 1886 . . . died the next day at five o'clock: *Tribune,* June 27, July 2, September 29, 30, 1886; *NYT,* June 27, 28, July 2, September 29, 30, 1886; *Sun,* June 28, September 29, 30, 1886, January 24, 1888 ("gamiest and nerviest girl"); *World,* January 23, 1888 (extra); *People v. Driscoll,* 107 N.Y. 414 (1887); Gilfoyle, *Pickpocket's Tale,* 181–83; *People v. Driscoll,* Trial Tr. 7–151; Driscoll Indictment File, 704–7 (police officer John Mulholland testimony), 714–15 (ages of Driscoll, Garrity), 833 (126 Baxter), 840 (126, 128 Baxter), 853–54 (McCarty age and account). McCarty's name was often spelled "McCarthy" in news articles, but he signed it "McCarty." Driscoll Indictment File, 854; Gilfoyle, *Pickpocket's Tale,* 398n12.

134 prostitute Carrie Wilson . . . time to change his pistol: *Tribune,* September 29, 30 ("I seed it"), October 1, 1886; *NYT,* September 29, 30, October 1, 1886; *Sun,* September 29, 30, 1886; *World,* January 23, 1888 (extra); Murphy, *Scoundrels in Law,* 65; *People v. Driscoll,* Trial Tr. 7–28, 101–3 (Carrie Wilson), 71 ("stick by you"), 105–15 (Bruen supported Driscoll; denial of Whyo membership or meetings at 111–12), 127 (Driscoll ran to 128 Baxter), 137 ("as true as"), 138–39 (in the girl's company); Gilfoyle, *Pickpocket's Tale,* 191 (denials of Whyo membership). The *Tribune's* September 30, 1886, article erroneously reported that Bruen admitted attending Whyo meetings.

135 Mrs. Margaret Sullivan . . . her warnings: *People v. Driscoll,* Trial Tr. 90–95; *Sun,* September 30, 1886; *NYT,* September 30, 1886; *Tribune,* September 30, 1886; *World,* January 23, 1888 (extra).

135 "'Is that you, my mamma?' . . . I shut her eyes": *People v. Driscoll,* Trial Tr. 92, 95; *Sun,* September 30, 1886. See also *NYT,* September 30, 1886; *Tribune,* September 30, 1886; Driscoll Indictment File, 717, 724–25.

136 "There was not . . . in the courtroom": *Sun,* September 30, 1886.

136 The jury was out . . . luck had not been with him: *Sun,* October 1, 1886; *NYT,* October 1, 1886; *Tribune,* October 1, 1886.

136 Driscoll faced execution . . . ask Jesus for mercy: *World,* September 29, 1886 (first escape attempt), January 10, 17, 18, 19, 20, 21, 23, 1888 (last days and execution); *NYT,* September 29 (first escape attempt), October 9 (sentencing), 1886, January 21 (complaints), 23 (last day), 24 (temperature), 1888; *Sun,* October 9 (sentencing), December 20 (Walsh appointment), 1886, February 11 ("not as black"), November 30 (final appeal), December 3 (second escape attempt), 1887, January 18, 23, 24, 1888 (last days and execution); Murphy, *Scoundrels in Law,* 67, 68 ("came pretty near"), 70–71; *People v. Driscoll,* 107 N.Y. 414 (1887); Gilfoyle, *Pickpocket's Tale,* 192–94 (hero and martyr). The Bridge of Sighs is described in Crain, *Gilded Age,* 222, and Esther Crain, "The 'Bridge of Sighs' over a Downtown Prison," *Ephemeral New York* (blog), January 4, 2012, https://ephemeralnewyork.wordpress.com/2012/01/04/the-bridge-of-sighs-over-a-downtown-prison.

138 "a more civilized way" . . . electric chair: *World,* January 23, 1888 (extra). See also *World,* January 24, 1888 (extra) (more humane way).

138 Harry Carlton . . . John Greenwall: *NYT,* October 31, 1888 (Carlton), December 6, 2009 (Greenwall); Murphy, *Scoundrels in Law,* 72–74, 77–78.

138 Danny Lyons . . . justifiable homicide: *Sun,* August 14, 15, 16, 17, 1887; *Tribune,* August 14, 1887; *NYT,* August 14, 1887.

139 In a quirk of history . . . writers have confused: *Sun,* August 14, 15, 16, September 22, 30, 1887; Gilfoyle, *Pickpocket's Tale,* 397n1 (pointing out confusion); Robert Wilhelm, "Murder Among the Whyos, Part 2," *Murder by Gaslight* (blog), March 4, 2017, http://www.murderbygaslight.com/2017/03/murder-among-whyos-part-2.html; Asbury, *Gangs of New York,* 212 (citing wrong Danny Lyons as Whyo leader).

139 twenty-two-year-old Owney Bruen . . . successor to leaders Lyons and Driscoll: *Sun,* August 15 (no such gang), 16, 17, 1887; February 27, April 13, September 19, 1888; *World,* September 17, 1888 (last); *NYT,* September 22, 1888; *Tribune,* September 19, 1888.

139 In September 1888 . . . piercing the man's coat: *Sun,* September 18, 19, 1888; *World,* September 17, 1888 (last); *NYT,* September 22, 1888; *Tribune,* September 19, 1888.

139 thickset . . . accidentally discharged: *World,* September 17, 1888 (last); *Sun,* September 19, 1888; *Tribune,* September 19, 1888.

139 "tousands of times . . . such a thing existed": *Sun,* September 19, 1888.

140 guilty of assault . . . nine years in Sing Sing: *Sun,* September 19, 1888; *NYT,* September 22, 1888; *Tribune,* September 22, 1888.

140 "Weakening Wail" . . . "but promising": *World,* July 10, 1888 (baseball extra).

140 "either the Whyos or I . . . this precinct": *Tribune,* February 16, 1896.

141 McCullagh was the nephew . . . attention to duty: Costello, *Our Police Protectors,* 318–19, 333–34; *Sun,* January 25, 1891, August 26, 1897; *NYT,* March 7, 1893, September 19, 1897, January 4, 1917; *Tribune,* November 4, 1900.

141 McCullagh arrested twelve . . . broke up opium dens: *Sun,* October 10, 1884, January 25, 1891, August 26, 1897.

141 "the hotbeds of its crime": Walling, 479.

141 Abram Hewitt . . . worst of the dives: Sante, *Low Life,* 115–16; Lardner and Reppetto, *NYPD,* 92–93; Walling, 496; Everett P. Wheeler, "Tammany Hall," *Outlook,* September 13, 1913, 76–77; Gilfoyle, *City of Eros,* 194–96.

142 Haymarket . . . cabaret: Gilfoyle, *Pickpocket's Tale,* 118–20; Sante, *Low Life,* 114–15; Greg Young and Tom Meyers, *The Bowery Boys: Adventures in Old New York—An Unconventional Exploration of Manhattan's Historic Neighborhoods, Secret Spots and Colorful Characters* (Berkeley, Calif.: Ulysses Press, 2016), 312–13.

142 American Mabille . . . "The. Allen": Walling, 488–89; Gilfoyle, *City of Eros,* 228–29; Van Every, *Sins of New York,* 206–7 (quotation); *Tribune,* September 18, 1878; *World,* March 19, 1892 ("wickedest man in New York"); Byrnes (1886), 236.

142 Armory Hall . . . auctioned off: Gilfoyle, *City of Eros,* 229, 232; Gilfoyle, *Pickpocket's Tale,* 114–17; Mark Caldwell, *New York Night: The Mystique and Its History* (New York: Scribner, 2005), 194–95; Sante, *Low Life,* 111–12, 115, 189–90; William Howe and Abraham Hummel, *Danger! A True History of a Great City's Wiles and Temptations* (Buffalo, N.Y.: Courier Company, 1886), 220 ("prize-fighter . . . late start"); *World*, June 8, 1888 ("orgies"), June 3, 1889 (baseball extra) (McGlory sold); *Sun*, July 18, 1891; *Tribune*, January 25, 1889 (hounded).

142 **Grant, initially committed . . . final closing of Armory Hall:** *Sun*, January 29, 1888; *World*, January 25, 26, June 3, 1889.

142 **days of the "toughs" . . . "wholesome check":** *Sun*, March 29, 1891.

143 **detailed to Goatville . . . swindling games:** *Sun*, January 24, 25, 1891.

143 **"feeble" reminders . . . time in the pen:** "The Man with a Pull and the New Order," editorial, *Sun*, July 8, 1888 (quotation); *Tribune*, February 16, 1896; *Report of the Police Department of the City of New York for the Year Ending December 31, 1895* (New York: Martin B. Brown, 1897) (hereafter, *1895 Annual Police Report*), 5 (growth of police force).

143 **demolition of Mulberry Bend . . . Mulberry Bend Park:** Riis, *Ten Years' War*, 8, 169–73, 176 ("worst of all the gangs"), 177–79, 184–88, 201–3; Burrows and Wallace, *Gotham*, 1198–99; Anbinder, *Five Points*, 426–33.

143 **uptown parts . . . "the turbulent ones":** *Tribune*, February 16, 1896.

144 **gang rule in New York "is at an end . . . to Westchester":** *Tribune*, February 16, 1896.

144 **Theodore Roosevelt . . . gangs were no longer openly defiant:** *Sun*, March 17, 1897.

144 **After about 1895 . . . past tense:** *World*, May 16, 1895; *Tribune*, November 4, 1900; *Sun*, July 10, 1898, August 19, 1900; *NYT*, May 28, 1895; Shepp and Shepp, *Shepp's New York City Illustrated*, 204.

144 **"disorganized crime" . . . "unsystematic and crude":** Murphy, *Scoundrels in Law*, 59.

144 **Like their later . . . denied even the existence:** Gilfoyle, *Pickpocket's Tale*, 191.

145 **Byrnes would be extolled . . . their demise:** *NYT*, May 28, 1895. See also Crain, *Gilded Age*, 219.

145n **1895 revised edition . . . Whyo gang members:** Byrnes (1895), 261, 291, 297, 303, 304, 307, 309, 314, 335; *Herald*, December 27, 1891 (Corcoran, Fitzgerald). Thieves John "Red Rocks" Farrell and Hoggy Walsh are sometimes identified as Whyos, but Byrnes did not include them as members of the gang. *Sun*, September 21, 1884 (Farrell); *Herald*, December 27, 1891 (Walsh); *Tribune*, February 16, 1896 (Walsh). See also Asbury, *Gangs of New York*, 210.

CHAPTER 13: BETTER THAN SCOTLAND YARD

146 **five-and-dime mystery novels . . . greatest detective:** Hawthorne, *Great Bank Robbery*, 70; Julian Hawthorne, *An American Penman, from the Diary of Inspector Byrnes* (New York: Cassell, 1887); Julian Hawthorne, *A Tragic Mystery, from the Diary of Inspector Byrnes* (New York: Cassell, 1888); Julian Hawthorne, *Section 558; or, The Fatal Letter, from the Diary of Inspector Byrnes* (New York: Cassell, 1888); Julian Hawthorne, *Another's Crime* (New York: Cassell, 1888). See also Gary Scharnhorst, *Julian Hawthorne: The Life of a Prodigal Son* (Urbana: University of Illinois Press, 2014), 123–24; LeRoy Lad Panek, *Probable Cause: Crime Fiction in America* (Bowling Green, Ohio: Bowling Green State University Popular Press, 1990), 36–37.

146 **"the success of my stratagems":** Hawthorne, *Section 558*, 245.

147 "supernatural powers" . . . "wonderful brain": Walling, 517.

147 luck . . . solving crimes: Walling, 518, 590.

147 "quick-wittedness" . . . "his own theories": Walling, 518.

147 top detectives posed . . . "in" with the detective corps: Walling, 590.

147 "Ninety-nine . . . isn't there?": Howe and Hummel, *Danger!*, 192–93.

148 stabbing of Sicilian . . . could all go kill one another: See *NYT*, October 22, 1888, March 27, 1889 ("Mafia" murder), May 22, 1893; *World*, March 28, April 23, 27, 1889; Thomas Reppetto, *American Mafia: A History of Its Rise to Power* (New York: Henry Holt, 2004), 22–24; Mike Dash, *The First Family: Terror, Extortion, Revenge, Murder and the Birth of the American Mafia* (New York: Random House, 2009), 83–87.

148 "They have their quarrels . . . kill one another": "Romances of the Day No. III: Organized Assassination," *Illustrated American* 4, no. 38 (November 8, 1890): 328.

148 Byrnes declared that most . . . no portraits: Dash, *First Family*, 86–87.

148 since the Flaccomio case . . . quiet in New York: "Romances of the Day," 328.

148 "Hungry Joe" . . . Baltimore businessman: Byrnes (1886), 167–68; Byrnes (1895), 86; Kuntz, "#95 Joseph Lewis," *Professional Criminals—REVISED* (blog), November 27, 2018, https://criminalsrevised.blog/2018/11/27/95-joseph-lewis/; *NYT*, May 22, 23, 1885, December 8, 21, 1888, May 3, 1896.

149 "he, and not I . . . serving time": *NYT*, May 3, 1896.

149 "It tempts . . . services rendered": Flynt, *World of Graft*, 128.

149 "If the police . . . their notice": Flynt, 126.

149 credit often given . . . safer, less violent: Czitrom, *New York Exposed*, 20, 31.

149 In 1888, by a special act . . . number two man: *NYT*, April 19, December 9, 1888; Lardner and Reppetto, *NYPD*, 83.

149 "management of the Detective Bureau . . . remarkable": *NYT*, December 9, 1888.

149 "done more to disorganize" . . . "don't catch them as well": Fales and Curtis, "Chief Inspector Thomas Byrnes," 111–12.

150 "a peculiar place for the innocent": Charles Williams, "The New York Police," *Contemporary Review* 53 (January–June 1888): 225.

150 "dare not lay a finger . . . violating the law": Walling, 194.

150 "was always very jealous": Francis L. Wellman, *Luck and Opportunity: Recollections* (New York: Macmillan, 1938), 80.

151 "incapacity and slothfulness": *Tribune*, October 4, 1888.

151 "'Oh, for a transatlantic' . . . panic-stricken multitude": *World*, October 2, 1888 (last).

151 proud New York . . . caught in short order: Underwood, *Gaslight Lawyers*, 38–39; *NYT*, November 10, 1888, July 18, 1889 ("London's Weak Police," editorial).

151 "no such crimes . . . New York Police": *Sun*, November 10, 1888.

151 "Seven such murders . . . city we live in": *Herald*, October 3, 1888.

152 "run down in forty-eight hours": *World*, April 25, 1891. See also *NYT*, April 25, 1891.

152 "I should have gone . . . caught long ago": *London Sun*, October 4, 1888, quoted in Wolf Vanderlin, "The New York Affair, Part II," *Casebook: Jack the Ripper,* accessed December 27, 2020, https://www.casebook.org/dissertations/rn-nya2.html, reprinted from *Ripper Notes: The American Journal for Ripper Studies*, no. 17 (January 2004). See also *Nottingham (UK) Evening Post*, October 5, 1888 (same quotation).

153 **prostitute named Carrie Brown . . . the attic opening:** *NYT*, April 25, 1891; *Tribune*, April 25, 1891 ("Is It Jack?"); *Sun*, April 25, 1891 ("Jack the Ripper's Mark"). See also *Sun*, April 27, 1891 (Carrie Brown background); *NYT*, April 26, 1891 (same). For my account of the murder, police investigation, and criminal trial, I have also drawn from the excellent discussions in Vanderlin, "New York Affair, Part II"; Wolf Vanderlin, "The New York Affair, Part Three," *Ripper Notes*, no. 19 (July 2004): 8–57; and Underwood, *Gaslight Lawyers*, 37–80.

155 **"The fellow spoke . . . derby hat":** *NYT*, April 26, 1891.

155 **(now tried to back away from):** *Sun*, April 25, 1891; *Tribune*, May 1, 1891.

155 **"Frenchy No. 1" . . . couldn't say where:** *World*, April 30, July 1 (5 o'clock special), 1891; *NYT*, May 1, 3, 1891; *Sun*, May 1, 1891; Vanderlin, "New York Affair, Part Three," 9–11; Underwood, *Gaslight Lawyers*, 43–44.

156 **"Frenchy No. 2" . . . failed to match:** *NYT*, April 26, 1891 ("old hags"); *World*, April 29, 1891; Vanderlin, "New York Affair, Part Three," 32–46.

156 **late-night press conference . . . Reporters suspected:** *NYT*, April 26, 27, 1891; *World*, April 27, 1891 (last).

157 **Tracked down . . . quick release:** *NYT*, May 1, 1891; *Tribune*, May 1, 1891; Vanderlin, "New York Affair, Part Three," 32–45.

157 **he'd been misquoted . . . No. 2 was a suspect:** *NYT*, April 28, 1891; *World*, April 28, 1891 (last).

157 **day later . . . did not believe:** *NYT*, April 29, 1891.

158 **"How do you know" . . . "than you do":** *NYT*, April 29, 1891.

158 **performing a dragnet . . . baffled and irritable:** *NYT*, April 27, 1891; *World*, April 27, 1891 (last).

158 **"Byrnes Quite Mystified":** *NYT*, April 29, 1891.

158 **Scotland Yard, reportedly excited to see Byrnes tested:** *Sun*, April 25, 1891.

158 **did have his man . . . under Ben Ali's fingernails:** *World*, April 30, May 5 (2 o'clock), 13 (5 o'clock special), 1891; *NYT*, May 1, 1891; *Sun*, May 1, 1891.

159 **"the blood on the wood . . . under the fingernails":** *NYT*, May 1, 1891.

159 **"could not possibly . . . smaller intestine":** Wellman, *Luck and Opportunity*, 79; *NYT*, July 2, 1891.

159 **partially digested . . . Brown's last meal:** Wellman, *Luck and Opportunity*, 78–79; *Sun*, June 30, 1891.

159 **"wicked and unnatural habits":** *World*, May 1, 1891 (2 o'clock).

159 **"a man . . . life is cheap":** Underwood, *Gaslight Lawyers*, 71, quoting trial transcript.

159 **Testifying . . . stretch at best:** *Sun*, July 1, 2, 3, 1891; *NYT*, July 1, 2, 3, 4, 1891; Underwood, *Gaslight Lawyers*, 56, 60–65; Vanderlin, "New York Affair, Part Three," 15–19. See also *World*, May 14, 1891 (2 o'clock) (blood evidence).

159 **"very slender and uncertain":** *NYT*, July 5, 1891.

NOTES

159 The defense argued . . . not convincingly traced: Underwood, *Gaslight Lawyers*, 49 (O'Connor), 53 (knife), 59 (menstruating prostitute, unsanitary habits, real killer), 61, 68, 76 (no blood on doorknobs); Vanderlin, "New York Affair, Part Three," 21 (knife). See also *Sun*, June 30, 1891 (O'Connor); *World*, May 12, 1891 (last) (knife).

160 Ben Ali was convicted: *Sun*, July 4, 1891; *NYT*, July 4, 1891.

160 victory for Byrnes . . . disappointment: *World*, July 4, 1891 (2 o'clock); *Sun*, July 4, 1891.

160 "I do not say . . . he may be": *Sun*, July 4, 1891.

160 Ripperologists . . . did not mark: Vanderlin, "New York Affair, Part Three," 52; Trevor Marriott, chap. 17 in *Jack the Ripper: The 21st Century Investigation* (London: John Blake, 2007); Larry Barbee, "An Investigation into the Carrie Brown Murder," *Casebook: Jack the Ripper*, accessed December 27, 2020, https://www.casebook.org /dissertations/dst-carrieb.html; *Sun*, April 25, 1891 (throat not slit); *NYT*, April 26, 1891 (clumsy hacking). For the argument that Arbie La Bruckman, "Frenchy No. 2," may have been both Jack the Ripper and Carrie Brown's killer, see Michael Conlon, "The Carrie Brown Murder Case: New Revelations," *Ripperologist*, no. 46 (May 2003), reprinted in *Casebook: Jack the Ripper*, accessed December 27, 2020, https:// www.casebook.org/dissertations/rip-carriebrown.html.

In a comprehensive study of the case, an English historian offers the theory that a different Jack the Ripper suspect, George Chapman, may have committed the Whitechapel murders and the Carrie Brown murder, although that author concedes that no direct evidence links Chapman to any of the killings and that, at best, he is the "least unlikely" of the many suspects. Philip Sugden, chap. 22 in *The Complete History of Jack the Ripper* (1994; repr., London: Robinson, 1998). Compare Vanderlin, "New York Affair, Part Three," 22–26 (doubting Chapman's guilt).

161 "undoubtedly a keen . . . our detective system": *NYT*, July 5, 1891.

161 Ben Ali was pardoned . . . saw no blood: *Tribune*, April 17, 1902; *NYT*, April 17, 1902; *Sun*, April 17, 1902; Underwood, *Gaslight Lawyers*, 75–78.

162 "The records show . . . nothing to me": *NYT*, April 17, 1902.

163 Timothy "Dry Dollar" Sullivan . . . gang of newspaper boys: The best modern sources for Sullivan's background and career are Richard F. Welch, *King of the Bowery: Big Tim Sullivan, Tammany Hall, and New York City from the Gilded Age to the Progressive Era* (2008; repr., Albany: State University of New York Press, 2010); Daniel Czitrom, "Underworlds and Underdogs: Big Tim Sullivan and Metropolitan Politics in New York, 1889–1913," *Journal of American History* 78, no. 2 (September 1991): 536–58; and Alice Sparberg Alexiou, chap. 10 in *Devil's Mile: The Rich, Gritty History of the Bowery* (New York: St. Martin's Press, 2018). For a good overview by a Sullivan contemporary, see Oliver Simmons, "Passing of the Sullivan Dynasty," *Munsey's* 50, no. 3 (December 1913): 407–16.

163 Whyos got him elected: Simmons, "Sullivan Dynasty," 409; Welch, *King of the Bowery*, 37.

163 He and Byrnes . . . "made a man of me": Czitrom, "Underworlds and Underdogs," 536–37, 540 (did not drink), 541 ("made a man"); *NYT*, April 17, 1889 ("constant

438

companion"); Welch, *King of the Bowery*, 37–39; George Kibbe Turner, "Tammany's Control of New York by Professional Criminals: A Study of a New Period of Decadence in the Popular Government of Great Cities," *McClure's* 33, no. 2 (June 1909): 117–18 (dispute with Byrnes); Lardner and Reppetto, *NYPD*, 120–21; Gilfoyle, *Pickpocket's Tale*, 252 (assembly bill).

163 **Croker . . . tried for murder:** Alfred Connable and Edward Silberfarb, *Tigers of Tammany: Nine Men Who Ran New York* (New York: Holt, Rinehart, 1967), 201–2; English, *Paddy Whacked*, 106; *NYT*, April 30, 1922 (Croker obituary).

164 **"the Modern Robin Hood":** Alfred Henry Lewis, "The Modern Robin Hood," *Cosmopolitan*, June 1905, 186–92.

164 **"King of the Underworld":** Czitrom, "Underworlds and Underdogs," 547 (quotation), 548–51; see also Dash, *Satan's Circus*, 81–84.

164 **election fraud:** Turner, "Tammany's Control," 117–27; Anbinder, *Five Points*, 322–27; Anbinder, *City of Dreams*, 266–70; Welch, *King of the Bowery*, 48–49. See also *NYT*, February 15, 1871, October 21, 1891 ("Making Citizens," editorial), February 5, 1896.

164 **"When they vote . . . good for four votes":** Alvin F. Harlow, *Old Bowery Days: The Chronicles of a Famous Street* (New York: D. Appleton, 1931), 504–5.

164 **elevated to police superintendent . . . Murray:** *NYT*, April 13, 14, 1892.

164 **Byrnes declared . . . without fear or favor:** *NYT*, April 14, 1892.

165 **maintain the prestige . . . sweeping police shake-up:** *NYT*, April 15, 20, 1892. See also *Lexow Hearings*, 4:3924–26, 5:5347, 5729.

165 **"A Cyclone Hit the Police":** *NYT*, April 20, 1892.

165 **expressed confidence . . . while doubting:** *NYT*, April 24, 1892.

165 **Carey was transferred . . . detective bureau:** *NYT*, May 25, 1892; Carey, 28.

165 **on the first Sunday . . . not show arrests:** *Sun*, April 25, 1892; *NYT*, April 25, 1892; Czitrom, *New York Exposed*, 89; *Lexow Hearings*, 5:5354.

165 **He demanded . . . hundreds more arrests:** *Tribune*, May 25, 1892; *NYT*, May 25, 1892; Czitrom, *New York Exposed*, 88.

CHAPTER 14: "EVERY CRIME HERE HAS ITS PRICE"

166 **Charles H. Parkhurst was among . . . boldly sermonized:** Jay Stuart Berman, "The Taming of the Tiger: The Lexow Committee Investigation of Tammany Hall and the Police Department of the City of New York," *Police Studies: The International Review of Police Development* 3, no. 4 (Winter 1981): 55–57; Czitrom, *New York Exposed*, 1–2, 9–10; Charles H. Parkhurst, *Our Fight with Tammany* (New York: Charles Scribner's Sons, 1895), 2–13; Werner, *It Happened*, 36–38.

168 **"a lying, perjured . . . polluted harpies":** Parkhurst, *Our Fight*, 10.

168 **"He Rules Through Fear":** *NYT*, December 10, 1893.

168 **"Every crime here has its price":** Parkhurst, *Our Fight*, 13.

168 **Parkhurst enlisted . . . unpopular with the masses:** *NYT*, April 14, May 25, 1892; *Tribune*, May 25, 1892; Werner, *It Happened*, 40–51; Czitrom, *New York Exposed*,

10–20 (quotation, 14), 21 (song), 30–32; Zacks, *Island of Vice*, 3, 11–23; Richard Zacks, "Teddy Roosevelt's Battle with the Deeply Depraved New York of Yore," MetroFocus.org, last modified March 5, 2012, https://www.thirteen.org/metrofocus /2012/03/teddy-roosevelts-battle-with-the-deeply-depraved-new-york-of-yore/; Campbell, *Darkness and Daylight*, 209–12; Connable and Silberfarb, *Tigers of Tammany*, 211–12; *Lexow Hearings*, 2:1484–85, 1544–45, 1835–37 (addresses), 2012–16, 2406–21, 3:3174–77, 3250–59 (gambling places); Wallace, *Greater Gotham*, 616–18 (policy shops and poolrooms); Albert Fried, *The Rise and Fall of the Jewish Gangster in America* (1980; repr., New York: Columbia University Press, 1993), 21 (poolrooms). For descriptions of the Tenderloin, see Czitrom, *New York Exposed*, 5; Costello, *Our Police Protectors*, 367–69; Dash, *Satan's Circus*, 5. The Tenderloin later expanded west to at least Eighth Avenue and north to Fifty-Seventh Street.

170 **continued trading ripostes . . . summer in Europe:** *NYT*, December 7, 8 (quotations), 9, 1892.

171 **In January 1893 . . . Byrnes personally cross-examined:** *NYT*, January 17, 1893; *Tribune*, January 17, 1893; *World*, January 16, 1893 (2 o'clock and last).

171 **their relationship . . . Williams had wanted for himself:** Murphy, *Scoundrels in Law*, 184–85.

171 **Williams had fended off . . . from captain to inspector:** Czitrom, *New York Exposed*, 50–59; *Lexow Hearings*, 3:2832–33 (promotion), 5:5490–92, 5498–99 (panel house charges), 5569 (tenderloin quote), 5570 (higher quality); Marilynn S. Johnson, *Street Justice: A History of Police Violence in New York City* (Boston: Beacon Press, 2003), 42–44.

172 **again beat the rap . . . censure and reprimand:** *NYT*, January 17, 1893; *Tribune*, January 17, 1893; *World*, January 16, 1893 (2 o'clock and last); Czitrom, *New York Exposed*, 110–11; *Lexow Hearings*, 5:5739–40.

172 **"Not guilty, but don't do it again":** *Sun*, January 17, 1893.

172 **Parkhurst derided . . . anarchism and socialism:** Czitrom, *New York Exposed*, 112, 116–20.

172 **Byrnes was a vocal critic . . . radicals:** Czitrom, *New York Exposed*, 121–23. See also Thomas Byrnes, "The Menace of 'Coxeyism': Character and Methods of the Men," *North American Review* 158, no. 451 (June 1894): 696–701; Thomas Byrnes, "How to Protect a City from Crime," *North American Review* 159, no. 452 (July 1894): 100–107.

172 **Emma Goldman . . . Byrnes reminded the press:** Czitrom, *New York Exposed*, 121–24.

173 **Goldman claimed . . . he raised a chair:** Emma Goldman, *Living My Life*, vol. 1 (New York: Knopf, 1931), 125–27.

174 **William S. Devery . . . "goods on you":** *NYT*, June 2, 1899 (weight); Zacks, *Island of Vice*, 23 (waist); Brian J. Rizzo, "A Lexow Effect? Daniel J. Czitrom's *New York Exposed*," *Gotham: A Blog for Scholars of New York City History*, July 21, 2017, https://www .gothamcenter.org/blog/a-lexow-effect-daniel-czitroms-new-york-exposed ("If there's any graftin'"); Robert C. Kennedy, "On This Day, September 6, 1902: The Big Chief's Fairy Godmother," *HarpWeek*, September 6, 2001, http://movies2.nytimes.com

/learning/general/onthisday/harp/0906.html ("I disremember"); Oliver E. Allen, *The Tiger: The Rise and Fall of Tammany Hall* (Reading, Mass.: Addison-Wesley, 1993), 148 ("nothin' doin'"); Bill Lamb, "Bill Devery," *Society for American Baseball Research online*, accessed March 18, 2020, https://sabr.org/bioproj/person/500ba2d3#sdendnote6sym. See also *Cleveland Leader*, July 27, 1902 ("touchin on"); *World*, June 21, 1919 (final) (same); *NYT*, September 13, 1901 ("keep your mouth shut").

174 loathed by Reverend Parkhurst . . . 81 Eldridge Street: Czitrom, *New York Exposed*, 106–7, 115–16, 127; Zacks, *Island of Vice*, 29–31, 34–38, 40; Reppetto, *American Police*, 63 (Gardner); *NYT*, November 21, 1893 (Gardner conviction overturned).

174 "Jewtown" . . . about as lucrative: Zacks, *Island of Vice*, 3, 38, 40 ("Jewtown," citing Jacob Riis), 41; Moss, *American Metropolis*, 3:154–62 ("New Israel"); Czitrom, *New York Exposed*, 115–16; Fried, *Rise and Fall*, 7–10 (Jewish prostitutes and fifty cents); *1895 Annual Police Report*, 6, 22 (officers and arrests by precinct).

175 Playing off anti-Semitism . . . most of them Jewish: Czitrom, *New York Exposed*, 119–22.

175 "Where Do Anarchists Riot?" . . . "Not in Capt. Devery's Precinct": *NYT*, August 24, 1893.

175 Devery was dismissive . . . heard blocks away: Czitrom, *New York Exposed*, 122, 125, 127, 159–61; *Tribune*, August 24, 1893; *World*, November 29, 30 (both 2 o'clock), 1893 (indictment); Zacks, *Island of Vice*, 45–49; *Sun*, April 10, 1894 (verdict).

175 "I seen . . . and I took 'em": George Washington Plunkitt, *Plunkitt of Tammany Hall* (New York: McClure, Phillips, 1905), 4.

176 he persuaded . . . John W. Goff: Connable and Silberfarb, *Tigers of Tammany*, 212–13; Berman, "Taming of the Tiger," 59–60; Lardner and Reppetto, *NYPD*, 102–3; Murphy, *Scoundrels in Law*, 178 (Goff); Czitrom, *New York Exposed*, 144–45, 170–71, 229 (Goff); Dash, *Satan's Circus*, 63–64 (Goff).

CHAPTER 15: PAYING TRIBUTE

177 Tweed Courthouse: Pigott, *New York's Legal Landmarks*, 45–46.

177 election fraud . . . stood by laughing: Czitrom, *New York Exposed*, 55, 154–55; Berman, "Taming of the Tiger," 61–62; *Lexow Hearings*, 1:15–17, 182–86 (police in booths), 216–17 (looked at ceiling), 262–63, 275–77 (voters turned away, Devery laughing), 302–5 ("Hebrew names").

178 Big Tim Sullivan threatened . . . "do so and so": *Lexow Hearings*, 1:191–93.

178 "silk stocking" people . . . "stand them on their heads": *Lexow Hearings*, 1:202–8.

178 Democrats . . . both parties engaged: *Lexow Hearings*, 1:62–67. See also *NYT*, April 5 (bipartisan police bill debate), 16 ("Purpose of the Investigation," editorial), 1894. As has been argued, nineteenth-century claims of voter fraud were often used to mask voter suppression. Czitrom, *New York Exposed*, 73–77, 95–101, 300.

178 Moss . . . Jerome: Czitrom, *New York Exposed*, 170–71; Mary Cummings, *Saving Sin City: William Travers Jerome, Stanford White, and the Original Crime of the Century* (New York: Pegasus, 2018), 42–47, 62–63, 124.

179 "Don't move . . . automaton": *Lexow Hearings*, 3:3305.

179 "made up your mind . . . haven't you?": *Lexow Hearings*, 4:4087.

179 "plunge the knife . . . wherever I could": *Lexow Hearings*, 5:5303.

179 Witnesses . . . denied: See, for instance, *Lexow Hearings*, 1:32–33, 2:1342–43, 1568, 1575, 1585, 1591–95, 1678, 1725, 2122.

179 brothel madams formed . . . in Chicago: *Lexow Hearings*, 4:3640–41, 4194, 4211–12.

179 Matilda Hermann . . . given $1,700: *Lexow Hearings*, 1:28, 4:4185–87; *World*, November 2, 1894 (last); *NYT*, November 3, 1894. Some sources appear to confuse Hermann with the fat, bewhiskered "French Madame," Eliza Porret, who ran a Tenderloin district brothel. See Jerry Kuntz, "The Many French Madames," *Asbury's The Gangs of New York—Annotated,* last modified May 22, 2020, https://gangsannotated.blog/2020/05/22/the-many-french-madames/.

179 Price . . . booked passage: *World*, March 13, 1894 (6 o'clock); *NYT*, April 1, 1894, July 12, 1913; *Tribune*, April 14, 1894; *Lexow Hearings*, 1:460–473, 579–88, 4:3882–86, 5:5322–23, 5342–43. Later suspended from the force and indicted for bribery, Price was eventually reinstated after his indictment was dismissed. *NYT*, October 29, 1895, November 28, 1897.

179 Croker . . . sailed for Europe: *NYT*, June 10, 1894.

179 $500 initiation fee . . . $50 a month thereafter: *Lexow Hearings*, 1:33–34, 954–60, 989, 2:1536–37, 1554; Czitrom, *New York Exposed*, 175–76; *World*, June 1, 1894 (last).

179 Lena Cohen . . . $1,500 in debt: *Lexow Hearings*, 1:1247–48, 2:1249–60; *NYT*, June 7, 1894; Werner, *It Happened*, 69.

180 Katie Schubert . . . never raided her: *Lexow Hearings*, 1:1122–31; *NYT*, June 5, 1894. See also *NYT*, August 16, 1894.

180 Rhoda Sanford . . . "$500 for C": *Lexow Hearings*, 1:983–1010; *World*, June 1, 1894 (sporting extra); Werner, *It Happened*, 69.

180 Austrian Karl Werner . . . closed after three months: *Lexow Hearings*, 2:1484–93 (Glennon quotation, 1489); *Tribune*, June 14, 1894; Zacks, *Island of Vice*, 28, 42 ("Sphinx").

180 Hermann . . . $30,000: *Lexow Hearings*, 1:28, 4:4166; *NYT*, November 3, 1894; *Tribune*, November 3, 1894.

181 Caela Urchitell . . . reunited: *Lexow Hearings*, 3:2733–38, 2960–67, 3364–65, 4:3639–40; *Sun*, October 4, 1894; *NYT*, October 20, 1894; Czitrom, *New York Exposed*, 220–22.

181 "While we have . . . black cloud": *Lexow Hearings*, 4:3640.

181 Streetwalking prostitutes . . . dollar a week: *Lexow Hearings*, 4:3614–17, 3621.

181 "a tax . . . human mind": *Lexow Hearings*, 4:3616.

181 Lucy Harriot . . . divide the other half: *Lexow Hearings*, 4:3617–23; *World*, October 19, 1894 (sporting extra).

182 A similar partnership . . . liquor sellers: *Lexow Hearings*, 1:1239–46, 2:1326–34, 1349–51, 1477–78, 3:3003–5.

182 Adolph Forst . . . closed rather than suffer: *Lexow Hearings*, 3:3012–14; *Sun*, October 4, 1894. See also *Lexow Hearings*, 2:1349–53 (Serapio Arteaga testimony),

1679–1714, 1737–62, 5:5345–49 (Czech liquor dealers); *World*, June 8, 1894 (6 o'clock); *NYT*, June 13, 16, 1894.

182 Harry Hill . . . John L. Sullivan: Sante, *Low Life*, 109–10, 115; *NYT*, August 28, 1896 (Hill obituary).

182 "about as well known . . . as Broadway": *Lexow Hearings*, 2:1927; *NYT*, June 21, 1894.

182 didn't mind paying . . . "water in my life": *Lexow Hearings*, 2:1927–33 (Hill quotations); *World*, June 20, 1894 (6 o'clock). See also *NYT*, September 23, 1878 (Murphy).

183 Hill had understood . . . denied a license: *Lexow Hearings*, 2:1933–37 ("around the corner," "stick to his fingers"), 1938 ("gave his guts away"), 1939–43 ("buttons"), 1944–50; *World*, June 20, 1894 (6 o'clock); *NYT*, June 21, 1894. See also *Sun*, March 12, 14, April 5, September 30, 1887.

183 pushcart owners . . . a few bucks: See, for example, *Lexow Hearings*, 2:2007–11 (William Mayston testimony), 2154–56 (Francisco Scholastico testimony), 2281–84 (Carlos Capalita testimony). See also ibid., 2:1991–2007, 2095–102, 2134–49 (sidewalk operators); *NYT*, June 23, 27, 28, 30, 1894.

183 soda water sellers . . . syrup drained away: *Lexow Hearings*, 3:3403–21, 3478–82; *NYT*, October 18, 19, 1894.

183 Goff noted sarcastically . . . had yet to find a business: *Lexow Hearings*, 3:3404.

184 "Of course there are cops . . . I never saw one": Willemse, *A Cop Remembers*, 105.

184 "policy" . . . exclusive territories: *Lexow Hearings*, 1:36–37, 3:3130–78 (Vincent Majewski testimony); 3235–64 (J. Lawrence Carney testimony); 5:5341, 5362, 5405 (Schmittberger testimony); Sante, *Low Life*, 154–56 (explanation of game); Werner, *It Happened*, 87–89; Wallace, *Greater Gotham*, 616.

184 Poolrooms . . . closed in 1893: *Lexow Hearings*, 1:19, 37, 4:3839 (Croker), 5:5347, 5357 (Schmittberger testimony), 5744–46 (Byrnes testimony); Wallace, *Greater Gotham*, 617–20; *Sun*, December 17, 1893 (Croker).

184 "If reformers . . . better way to go": Wallace, *Greater Gotham*, 618.

CHAPTER 16: A WORLD STUFFED WITH SAWDUST—AND BLUE WITH PERJURY

186 curious little man . . . diamond studs: *Sun*, June 15, 1894; *NYT*, March 31, April 27, 1882, February 13, March 20, 29, 1893, June 15, 1894; *Lexow Hearings*, 2:1622–24, 1639–41; Gilfoyle, *Pickpocket's Tale*, xiii–xv, 3–24, 146–47, 226–46, 273, 317–18, and *passim*.

187 green goods business . . . sawdust for the stack: *Lexow Hearings*, 1:37–39; Byrnes (1886), 47–49, 191; *NYT*, November 27, 1887, October 19, 1890; Walling, 126–27; Gilfoyle, chap. 15 in *Pickpocket's Tale*.

188 "good fellow" . . . would not name names: Gilfoyle, *Pickpocket's Tale*, xv, 223 (quotation), 245–46; *Lexow Hearings*, 2:1621, 1631–33.

188 "backer" . . . would move his operations: *Lexow Hearings*, 2:1621–64 (Appo testimony); *NYT*, June 15, 1894; *Sun*, June 15, 1894; *World*, June 14, 1894 (6 o'clock) (all

Appo testimony); *Tribune*, June 3, 1883 ("My business"); *Lexow Hearings*, 3:2539–45, 2563–67, 2569–71, 2573–41 (all Applegate testimony) ("a guy" quotation, 2593); *NYT*, May 9 (Western Union), September 11 (Applegate), 1894; *Tribune*, September 12, 1894 (Applegate); *Lexow Hearings*, 3:2545–63 (circulars), 2567–69 (telegraphs), 2808–14 (post office); W. T. Stead, *Satan's Invisible World Displayed; or, Despairing Democracy: A Study of Greater New York* (London: Mowbray House, 1898), 108–16; Gilfoyle, chap. 15 in *Pickpocket's Tale;* ibid. 244–46; Werner, *It Happened*, 73–75; Czitrom, *New York Exposed*, 181–84 (Appo), 219–20 (Applegate and McNally).

191 "It required . . . if not months": Gilfoyle, *Pickpocket's Tale*, 221.

191 Appo testified . . . had immunity: *Lexow Hearings*, 2:1634–35, 1645–46.

191 green goods operators enjoyed . . . continued to flourish: Gilfoyle, *Pickpocket's Tale*, 212–15, 218–21; *Tribune*, June 3, 1883 (Walling quotation); *Lexow Hearings*, 3:2579–80 (Byrnes ordered arrests); *NYT*, December 2, 3, 1887, May 7, 1893; Flynt, *World of Graft*, 94–95.

192 seen cops in the opium joints . . . "to lay down": *Lexow Hearings*, 2:1661–64.

192 Appo's appearance . . . In the Tenderloin: Gilfoyle, *Pickpocket's Tale*, 260–70.

192 McNally moved . . . a waiter: *NYT*, March 17, 1907; Gilfoyle, *Pickpocket's Tale*, 303–4.

192 marked man . . . autobiography: Gilfoyle, chaps. 19–21 in *Pickpocket's Tale*.

193 oppression of George Appo to segue: *Lexow Hearings*, 3:2836–61 (Thomas Coleman testimony); *NYT*, October 3, 1894; Gilfoyle, *Pickpocket's Tale*, 257–58.

193 "fresh from their punishment . . . battered out of recognition": *Lexow Hearings*, 1:31.

193 Frank Angelo . . . judge dismissed him: *Lexow Hearings*, 4:4465–69; *NYT*, December 6, 1894.

193 Frank Martine . . . nothing ever came of it: *Lexow Hearings*, 4:3575–79; *NYT*, October 20, 1894.

193 Thomas Lucas . . . in no way justified: *Lexow Hearings*, 3:2874–79; *NYT*, October 3, 1894.

194 Goff noted . . . light fines: *Lexow Hearings*, 1:30–31, 3:2825–26; see also ibid., 3:3277 (Moss statement), 5:4660–61; *NYT*, October 3, 1894.

194 "the air was blue with perjury": *Lexow Hearings*, 3:3439.

194 subpoenaed every cop . . . "Clubbers' Brigade": *Lexow Hearings*, 1:30–31, 3:2825–27, 2836–912; *NYT*, October 3, 1894 (quotations); Czitrom, *New York Exposed*, 226–28; Johnson, *Street Justice*, 50–55; Werner, *It Happened*, 85.

194 Patrolman George Lair . . . kept his badge: *Lexow Hearings*, 3:2898–901; *NYT*, October 3, 1894; Werner, *It Happened*, 86.

195 Augustine Costello . . . devil in hell: *Lexow Hearings*, 4:4518–31 (Costello testimony) (quotations, 4526, 4528), 4531–32 (William Jenkins testimony), 5:4654–57 (Abraham Hummel testimony); 4657–62 (Charles Duffy testimony); 4662–68 (Michael Stanley testimony), 4668–78 (Costello testimony); *NYT*, December 6, 7, 1894; Czitrom, *New York Exposed*, 258–60.

195 "The police formed . . . cannot be estimated": *Lexow Hearings*, 1:30–31.

195 rumors . . . never received the promised job: *Lexow Hearings*, 1:47, 2:2267–71 (John Ott testimony); 2298–311 (Charles Miller testimony). See also ibid., 1:943–50 (Arthur Dennett testimony).

196 Based on bank records . . . baldly lying: *Lexow Hearings*, 1:47 (Goff), 870–82, 888–904 (Patrick Shea testimony), 904–8 (John Roth testimony), 908–12 (John Hogan testimony), 4:4077–79 (Moses Huntoon testimony), 4079–90 (Harvey Corey testimony), 5:4704–30, 4857–58 (Etienne Bayer testimony).

196 One cop . . . would not be foolish enough: *Lexow Hearings*, 1:899–900 (Shea testimony).

196 police commissioners admitted . . . fault lay with Superintendent Byrnes: *Lexow Hearings*, 1:438, 446–47, 479–514, 532–35 (Martin testimony), 599–600 (Commissioner John McClave testimony), 643–64 (Gideon Granger testimony), 4:3681–4044 (Sheehan testimony); Czitrom, *New York Exposed*, 158–59 (Martin), 171–73 (McClave), 243–44 (Sheehan); Werner, *It Happened*, 66 (McClave). See also *NYT*, April 1, 7, 8, 1894, March 20, 1909 (Martin), May 22, 23, 24, 25, June 7 (McClave, Granger), October 26, 27, 31, November 1 (Sheehan), 1894; *Sun*, October 30, 1894 (Sheehan).

196 bizarre cheating scheme . . . closed its doors: *Lexow Hearings*, 2:1365–79, 1403–36 (Jacobs testimony); 1379–87 (George Barmstroff testimony), 1460–76 (Charles Clark testimony); *Sun*, June 9, 13, 1894; *NYT*, June 9, 13 ("School for Police"), 1894. For the 2019 college admissions scandal, see, for instance, *NYT*, March 12, 13, 2019; *Hartford (Conn.) Courant*, March 14, 2019.

197 Byrnes presented . . . sole "no" vote: *NYT*, July 9, 17, August 16, 21, 31, September 1, 1894; Czitrom, *New York Exposed*, 214–15; *Lexow Hearings*, 4:3876–77 (Sheehan).

198 Stephenson was dismissed . . . Byrnes authority to reassign: *NYT*, September 5, 7, 1894.

198 October 16 session . . . finally being aroused: *Lexow Hearings*, 3:3290.

198 Goff was proposed . . . Strong-Goff ticket swamped: *NYT*, October 6, November 7, 1894; Czitrom, *New York Exposed*, 228–29, 248–49.

199 "The uprising . . . God bless New York": *NYT*, November 7, 1894.

199 Croker . . . "They can't stand reform, either": Steffens, *Autobiography*, 1:256.

199 "they stand up so straight . . . fall over backward": *NYT*, November 12, 1894.

199 He predicted . . . in the next election: Steffens, *Autobiography*, 1:256.

199 ex-captain Stephenson . . . Parkhurst attributed it: *NYT*, November 17, December 13, 14 (Parkhurst), 20, 27, 1894; *World*, December 13, 1894 (night).

CHAPTER 17: BUSTED

201 Timothy J. Creeden . . . virtually unblemished: 1900 US Census, New York, N.Y., Enum. Dist. 421 (Timothy J. Creeden); *Lexow Hearings*, 5:4919–23; *NYT*, December 14, 1894, June 19, 1936 (Creeden obituary); *Sun*, December 14, 1894.

202 "Now, Captain . . . pay to be made captain?": *Lexow Hearings*, 5:4923.

202 Creeden was dumbstruck . . . an exasperated Goff: *Sun*, December 14, 1894; *NYT*, December 14, 1894; *World*, December 13, 1894 (night); *Lexow Hearings*, 5:4923–31.

202 Goff called a series of witnesses . . . "testimonial": *Lexow Hearings*, 5:4931–63; *World*, December 13, 1894 (night); *NYT*, December 14, 1894; *Sun*, December 14, 1894.

202 Goff recalled Creeden . . . no adverse consequences: *World*, December 14, 1894 (2 o'clock and night); *NYT*, December 15, 1894; *Sun*, December 15, 1894; *Tribune*, December 15, 30 (Voorhis denial), 1894; *Lexow Hearings*, 5:4966–82 (Creeden testimony) (quotations, 4967–68), 4982 (Goff statement), 4982–5011, 5013–24, 5047–64 (John Reppenhagen testimony), 5253–56 (William Mooney testimony); Lardner and Reppetto, *NYPD*, 65; Willemse, *A Cop Remembers*, 162 ("think it over"); Werner, *It Happened*, 101–5 ("Little Tenderloin").

205 "Creeden Confesses" . . . "dramatic scene": *Tribune*, December 15, 1894.

205 Wild applause . . . renewed round of cheers: *Tribune*, December 15, 1894; *World*, December 14, 1894 (night); *NYT*, December 15, 19, 1894; *Sun*, December 15, 1894; *Lexow Hearings*, 5:5024–29 (Martin testimony), 5030–37 (Byrnes testimony); Czitrom, *New York Exposed*, 263.

205 Creeden would serve . . . oldest living: *NYT*, June 19, 1936.

206 appearance of Captain Max Schmittberger . . . didn't turn it down: Costello, *Our Police Protectors*, 364 (Schmittberger background); *NYT*, February 2, 1882 (McGloin arrest), December 9, 1890 (promotion to captain), October 10, 12, 16, 17, 28, November 13, 17, December 19, 20 (all Steamboat Squad custom and indictment), 22 (Lexow Committee testimony), 1894, March 14, 1909 (career), November 1, 1917 (obituary); *Sun*, December 22, 1894; *Tribune*, December 22, 1894; *Herald*, December 21, 1894 (wife); *Lexow Hearings*, 2:1984–91 (Steamboat Squad), 3:2512 (gratuities a felony), 3040–90, 3185–95, 5:5065–127, 5160–62, 5176–84 (all Steamboat Squad), 5311–84 (Schmittberger testimony) ("Here is something," 5350, "clean breast . . . pillars," 5381–82); Stead, *Satan's Invisible World*, 79–85; Czitrom, *New York Exposed*, 265–68; Zacks, *Island of Vice*, 60–62; Lardner and Reppetto, *NYPD*, 65, 103–4.

209 "Now, Captain" . . . "Certainly": *Lexow Hearings*, 5:5337.

209 James K. Price and Frederick W. Martens . . . $14,000: *Lexow Hearings*, 5:5322–23, 5342–43 (Price), 5378–80 (Martens); *Tribune*, December 22, 1894; *NYT*, December 22, 1894.

209 Martin and Sheehan . . . not to disturb: *NYT*, April 25, 1892 (excise arrests), December 22, 1894; *Tribune*, December 22, 23, 1894; *Lexow Hearings*, 5:5354–57, 5362–65 (Martin), 5365–69 (Sheehan), 5617 (Martin denial).

210 "Schmittberger, if you allow . . . wouldn't have it": *Lexow Hearings*, 5:5366–67.

210 "an honest and fair man" . . . "to the core": *Lexow Hearings*, 5:5383.

210 O'Connor declared . . . "would have quite enough": *Lexow Hearings*, 5:5385.

210 favorite of Parkhurst . . . avoided prosecution: Czitrom, *New York Exposed*, 311; Murphy, *Scoundrels in Law*, 182–83; Zacks, *Island of Vice*, 277; Lardner and Reppetto, *NYPD*, 111–12, 117–18; Reppetto, *American Police*, 66, 68.

211 "The Crowning Exposures": *Tribune*, December 22, 1894.

211 "I am so well known" . . . "crack jokes": *Lexow Hearings*, 5:5448.

211 Williams was resplendent . . . solid gold shield: *Sun*, December 27, 1894; Werner, *It Happened*, 108.

NOTES

211 flushing red: *NYT,* December 28, 1894.

211 Williams denied . . . "Yes, sir": Williams's complete testimony appears at *Lexow Hearings,* 5:5431–55 (December 26), 5456–500, 5511–26 (December 27), 5532–78 (December 28). Extensive, almost verbatim coverage appeared in the December 27, 28, and 29 editions of *The New York Times,* the *Tribune,* the *World,* and *The Sun.* Quotations in the text appear in *Lexow Hearings,* 5:5453–55 ("rest on a report"), 5459 ("any moral sense?"), 5466–67 ("kind of fashionable . . . extraordinary answer"), 5484–87 ("champion clubber . . . You better not, either"), 5496–97 ("Did you ever club . . . No, I do not"), 5548–49, 5561–62 ("dives" and "slums"), 5574 ("You mean to say . . . Yes, sir"). See also Czitrom, *New York Exposed,* 269–72.

214 "the air . . . unconquered": *NYT,* December 28, 1894.

214 When he finished . . . self-satisfied smile: *NYT,* December 29, 30, 1894.

214 "brazen bluff of forgetfulness": *NYT,* December 30, 1894.

214 "nobody believes . . . what truth is": *Tribune,* December 29, 1894.

215 almost five o'clock . . . Byrnes made his way: *World,* December 29, 1894 (night); *NYT,* December 30, 1894; *Sun,* December 30, 1894; *Lexow Hearings,* 5:5639–709 (McLaughlin testimony); Lardner and Reppetto, *NYPD,* 105.

216 "without any display of gentleness": *NYT,* December 21, 1894; Berman, "Taming of the Tiger," 63.

216 After taking Byrnes . . . dramatically handed up: Byrnes's testimony appears in *Lexow Hearings,* 5:5709–58, with complete coverage in the December 30, 1894, editions of *The New York Times,* the *Tribune,* *The Sun,* and the *World.* Quotations in the text appear in *Lexow Hearings,* 5:5728 ("he is just pounding me"), 5729 ("from pillar to post"), 5731 ("You are mistaken"), 5732–33 ("No, sir . . . won't tell an honest man"); 5740 ("I defy any man"), 5741–42 ("honeycombed with abuses"), 5743 ("You cannot make . . . a curse"), 5744 ("simply a farce"), 5755 ("taking a smash . . . man without a party"), 5757 ("It is all wrong").

220 Goff began reading . . . tendered his resignation: *Lexow Hearings,* 5:5755–56; *NYT,* December 30, 1894; *Sun,* December 30, 1894.

CHAPTER 18: ONE ROUGH RIDER

221 Byrnes didn't really want . . . asked him to stay on: *NYT,* May 25, 1895; Czitrom, *New York Exposed,* 287; Zacks, *Island of Vice,* 84, 91; Lardner and Reppetto, *NYPD,* 111.

221 Strong replaced all four . . . reform-minded men: *NYT,* April 25, May 1, 4, 7, 1895; Berman, *Police Administration,* 36–46; Zacks, *Island of Vice,* 68; Czitrom, *New York Exposed,* 281–85.

222 "I don't care . . . TR is enough": Steffens, *Autobiography,* 1:257.

222 commissioners quickly elected Roosevelt . . . head of the police department: Berman, *Police Administration,* 46, 53–56; Edmund Morris, *The Rise of Theodore Roosevelt* (1979; repr., New York: Random House, 2010), 402–36 (Civil Service Commission), 497 (election as board president); Andrews, "Roosevelt as Police Commissioner," 119.

223 czarist role Byrnes envisioned . . . independent of the police board: Czitrom, *New York Exposed*, 287; Berman, *Police Administration*, 52.

223 legislature passed . . . Roosevelt persuaded Mayor Strong: Zacks, *Island of Vice*, 74–75.

223 "Though no personal corruption . . . spell was broken": Schlesinger, "Business of Crime," xxiii.

223 "I think I shall move . . . how it will come out": TR to Henry Cabot Lodge, May 18, 1895, in *The Letters of Theodore Roosevelt: The Years of Preparation, 1868–1898*, ed. Elting E. Morison, vol. 1 (Cambridge, Mass.: Harvard University Press, 1951), 458.

223 Byrnes was gone . . . declined all comment: *NYT*, May 25 (Williams), 28 (Byrnes and quotations), 1895; *World*, May 27, 1895 (night); *Tribune*, May 28, 1895; *Sun*, May 28, 1895; TR to Seth Low, May 29, 1895, in Morison, *Letters of Roosevelt*, 1:459 ("It was absolutely . . . will not be felt"); Riis, *Making of an American*, 339–40, 343 ("There was not . . . his shoes").

224 "There was a man . . . I mean that Schmittberger": *Herald*, May 25, 1895.

224 "I am getting . . . absorbingly interesting": TR to Anna Roosevelt, June 2, 1895, in Morison, *Letters of Roosevelt*, 1:459.

225 "Hello, Jake! . . . What do we do first?": Steffens, *Autobiography*, 1:257.

225 "About 8:30 . . . front steps": Morris, *Rise of Roosevelt*, 505. See also *NYT*, July 21, 1895.

225 demoralized . . . Peter Conlin: *NYT*, March 20 (indictments), May 26, 28, December 7, 1895; *Report of the Police Department of the City of New York for the Year Ending December 31, 1896* (New York: Martin B. Brown, 1897) (hereafter, *1896 Annual Police Report*), 5–6; Zacks, *Island of Vice*, 69–71, 85, 93; Lardner and Reppetto, *NYPD*, 111 (Conlin); TR to Avery D. Andrews, August 25, 1897, Theodore Roosevelt Digital Library, Dickinson State University, https://www.theodorerooseveltcenter.org/Research/Digital-Library/Record?libID=o278939 ("coward and feeble scamp").

226 knew nothing about police management: *Herald*, July 14, 1895.

226 His goal . . . Progressive Era: Theodore Roosevelt, *An Autobiography* (New York: Macmillan, 1913), 193–94; Berman, *Police Administration*, xiv–xvi, 59–60, 93–97; Reppetto, *American Police*, 65. See also Robert W. Wiebe, *The Search for Order, 1877–1920* (New York: Macmillan, 1967).

226 "The public may rest . . . religious considerations": Berman, *Police Administration*, 47, quoting Avery D. Andrews, "Citizen in Action: The Story of T. R. as Police Commissioner," Theodore Roosevelt Collection, Harvard College Library, Cambridge, Massachusetts, 32.

226 applicants were forbidden . . . where liquor was sold: Berman, *Police Administration*, 67–74; Zacks, *Island of Vice*, 73, 76–77, 86–87; *NYT*, May 14, 1895 (political clubs); *1896 Annual Police Report*, 85–96; Police Department of the City of New York, "Patrol Guide: Public Contact—Prohibited Conduct," Procedure No. 203–10, January 31, 2017, https://www1.nyc.gov/assets/nypd/downloads/pdf/public_information/public-pguide1.pdf; *Lexow Hearings*, 5:5319–21 (Pequod Club); Willemse, *A Cop Remembers*, 49–52, 65–66.

227 **"The total number . . . Give work in full":** Berman, *Police Administration*, 72, citing *1896 Annual Police Report*, 100.

227 **Roosevelt also eliminated a section . . . "Name five New England states":** Berman, *Police Administration*, 72–73. See also Aida D. Donald, *Lion in the White House: A Life of Theodore Roosevelt* (New York: Basic Books, 2007), 71.

227 **expanded recruiting efforts upstate . . . improved the overall quality:** Berman, *Police Administration*, 76; Reppetto, *American Police*, 65, 67; Richardson, *New York Police*, 259–60; Willemse, *Cop Remembers*, 82 ("besieged the Department"); Lardner and Reppetto, *NYPD*, 114–15.

228 **When it came to promotions . . . a man's record:** Roosevelt, *Autobiography*, 193–95; Berman, *Police Administration*, 61.

228 **Petrosino, a tailors's son . . . obtained a waiver:** New York, Passenger and Crew Lists for Guiseppe [Giuseppe] Petrosino, arrival November 28, 1872, on *Denmark*, M237, Roll 369 (Ancestry.com); *NYT*, July 20, 1895, March 14, 1909, March 12, 1944; *Tribune*, August 5, 1896 (made detective sergeant); *WAPO*, June 28, 1914 (general background); Stephan Talty, *The Black Hand: The Epic War Between a Brilliant Detective and the Deadliest Secret Society in American History* (2017; repr., Boston: Mariner Books, 2018), 7, 10–16; Moses, *Unlikely Union*, 119, 124; Lardner and Reppetto, *NYPD*, 128; *1895 Annual Police Report*, 45 (Italian immigrant arrivals); Andrew Paul Mele, *The Italian Squad: How the NYPD Took Down the Black Hand Extortion Racket* (Jefferson, N.C.: McFarland, 2020), 9 (Italian peasants carrying $17); Burrows and Wallace, *Gotham*, 1122 (Italian population); David Critchley, *The Origin of Organized Crime in America: The New York City Mafia, 1891–1931* (New York: Routledge, 2009), 15–16 (Italian sections); *NYT*, May 16, 1895 (TR opposed increasing height minimum); Donald, *Lion in the White House*, 66 (TR height).

229n **NYPD now requires . . . proportionate:** *NYT*, July 23, 1973, October 6, 1981.

230 **soldierly qualities . . . honorable mentions:** Berman, *Police Administration*, 60–61; Roosevelt, *Autobiography*, 195–97; *1895 Annual Police Report*, 11; Zacks, *Island of Vice*, 78.

230 **police parade . . . canceled:** *NYT*, May 14, 1895.

230 **"We will parade . . . show ourselves":** Jacob Riis, *Theodore Roosevelt the Citizen* (New York: Macmillan, 1912), 131.

230 **Minnie Gertrude Kelly . . . black dress:** *NYT*, May 10 (Minnie Kelly, misspelled "Vinie"), December 14 ("a woman should be paid"), 1895; *World*, May 9 (6 o'clock), 10 (night), 1895; Morris, *Rise of Roosevelt*, 852n44 (family friend); Berman, *Police Administration*, 77; Zacks, *Island of Vice*, 73–74. Her age of seventeen is confirmed by the entries for Minnie Reiffert in the New York State Censuses for 1905 and 1915 and the 1910 US Census.

231 **"She has arrived . . . in consequence":** *World*, May 10, 1895 (night).

231 **She married . . . officer:** Minnie Kelly married NYPD roundsman, later sergeant, Franklin Reiffert in October 1899 and by October 1901 had a one-month-old boy. Minnie Kelly Reiffert to TR, October 3, 1901 (Theodore Roosevelt Papers, Library of Congress Manuscript Division); *Tribune*, August 8, 1900 (roundsman Franklin A.

Reiffert), February 26, 1901 (Kelly no longer with department); *NYT,* December 23, 1902 (Sergeant Reiffert), August 29, 1903 (same).

231 **At two-thirty on the morning of . . . "best behavior":** Coverage appears, with minor variations, in the *World* of June 7, 1895 (night) ("saw policemen"), and the June 8 editions of *The New York Times* ("Police Caught Napping"), the *Tribune* ("Roosevelt as Roundsman"), and *The Sun.* See also *Brooklyn Daily Eagle,* June 7, 1895; Riis, *Making of an American,* 330–32; Andrews, "Roosevelt as Police Commissioner," 119–20; Morris, *Rise of Roosevelt,* 508–9; Zacks, *Island of Vice,* 94–98.

233 **A week later . . . resign from the force:** *NYT,* June 15, 1895; *Sun,* June 15, November 16 (Rath resigned), 1895; *Herald,* June 16, 23, 1895; *Cleveland Plain Dealer,* June 24, 1895; *Tribune,* July 12, 1895 (Rath pleaded guilty); Morris, *Rise of Roosevelt,* 509–11; Andrews, "Roosevelt as Police Commissioner," 120 ("Shut up, Bill").

233 **He was caricatured . . . huge bright teeth:** Morris, *Rise of Roosevelt,* 510–11; Donald, *Lion in the White House,* 66–68; Doris Kearns Goodwin, *The Bully Pulpit: Theodore Roosevelt, William Howard Taft, and the Golden Age of Journalism* (New York: Simon & Schuster, 2013), 208–9. See also Andrews, "Roosevelt as Police Commissioner," 123; Zacks, *Island of Vice,* 98.

234 **"These midnight rambles . . . swarming millions":** TR to Anna Roosevelt, June 16, 1895, in Morison, *Letters of Roosevelt,* 1:462–63. See also Morris, *Rise of Roosevelt,* 512; Andrews, "Roosevelt as Police Commissioner," 121–23 ("toning up"); *NYT,* March 1, 1998 (Sagamore Hill, Bamie's town house); Donald, *Lion in the White House,* 68 (same).

234 **"wanted certain information . . . he got it":** Andrews, "Roosevelt as Police Commissioner," 123.

234 **As important to Roosevelt . . . ninety-eight two years later:** Andrews, "Roosevelt as Police Commissioner," 126; Berman, *Police Administration,* 81–83; *1896 Annual Police Report,* 7; Zacks, *Island of Vice,* 162.

235 **"Corrupt or inefficient men . . . must go":** *NYT,* July 12, 1895.

235 **Roundsmen . . . were to report violations:** Berman, *Police Administration,* 80–81; Richardson, *New York Police,* 260; Reppetto, *American Police,* 163 (shoofly).

235 **Edward Bourke . . . "board is behind you":** *NYT,* June 24, 26 (quotations), July 12, 1895; *Sun,* June 24, 25, 26, 1895; *World,* June 23, 1895 (night); Roosevelt, *Autobiography,* 211–13; Morris, *Rise of Roosevelt,* 514–15; Zacks, *Island of Vice,* 112–14; Warren Sloat, *A Battle for the Soul of New York: Tammany Hall, Police Corruption, Vice, and Reverend Charles Parkhurst's Crusade Against Them, 1892–1895* (New York: Cooper Square Press, 2002), 172 (Callahan).

236 **"Fearless Ed" . . . "a Roosevelt cop":** *NYT,* July 4, 1919 (ostracized), January 8, 1922 (Roosevelt Police Dinner), January 24, 1945 (Bourke obituary and quotations). A photograph of Bourke and a description of his friendship with Roosevelt appear in Roosevelt, *Autobiography,* 211–13.

236 **Confrontations such as Bourke's . . . hardened criminals:** *NYT,* October 7, 29, 1892 (Byrnes initiative), December 10, 1893, September 24 ("most efficient club"), October 2 ("nightsticks are in"), 1895; *Lexow Hearings,* 5:5749–50; Czitrom, *New York Exposed,* 100; Roosevelt, *Autobiography,* 198 (no sympathy for criminals); Zacks,

Island of Vice, 163–64; Johnson, *Street Justice*, 88–91; Lardner and Reppetto, *NYPD*, 62, 147; Berman, *Police Administration*, 60 (military analogy); Oliver, "Neglected History," 478 (public attitude).

237 Roosevelt restored the position . . . information they provided: Zacks, *Island of Vice*, 202–8, 220–21, 270–73; Czitrom, *New York Exposed*, 292; Richardson, *New York Police*, 254–55; Berman, *Police Administration*, 64–66, 100–105; *NYT*, May 29 (stool pigeons), September 12 (same), December 31 (diamond robberies and stool pigeons), 1895, January 2, 1896 (wardmen); *World*, July 25, 1895 (night) (stool pigeons); Lardner and Reppetto, *NYPD*, 114 (same).

238 "mouthpiece system" . . . alive and well: Flynt, *World of Graft*, 125–47.

238 wiretapping . . . a felony: Oliver, "Neglected History," 466; Wesley MacNeil Oliver, "Wiretapping and the Apex of Police Discretion," Widener Center School of Law Research Paper series no. 10–14, April 22, 2010, available at https://ssrn.com/abstract=1594282; Meyer Berger, "A Reporter at Large," *New Yorker*, June 18, 1938; *NYT*, April 16, May 4, 6, 1916; *Minutes and Testimony of the Joint Legislative Committee Appointed to Investigate the Public Service Commissions* (Albany, N.Y.: J. B. Lyon, 1916), 4:1187–204 (John Swayze testimony), 5:98–122 (Arthur Woods testimony), 192–202 (Frank Lord testimony), 351–64, 368–94 (George Yunge testimony).

239 "the father . . . wiretapping": Michael Pollak, "A Short History of Wiretapping," *NYT*, February 28, 2015.

239 dead line . . . "below Liberty Street": *NYT*, October 22, 1895.

240 telephone call boxes . . . connect many more: Berman, *Police Administration*, 87–88; Richardson, *New York Police*, 169–70, 263; *1895 Annual Police Report*, 48–53; *1896 Annual Police Report*, 14.

240 Bertillon system . . . yield to fingerprinting: Zacks, *Island of Vice*, 340–45; Berman, *Police Administration*, 84–86; *1896 Annual Police Report*, 13–14; Raymond B. Fosdick, "Passing of the Bertillon System of Identification," *Journal of the American Institute of Criminal Law and Criminology* 6, no. 3 (May 1915–March 1916): 363–69.

241 Created in December 1895 . . . serving as the predecessor: *1896 Annual Police Report*, 15–16, 20, 24–25; Andrews, "Roosevelt as Police Commissioner," 137–41; Roosevelt, *Autobiography*, 201–3; Berman, *Police Administration*, 88–89; Zacks, *Island of Vice*, 219; *Tribune*, June 2, 1896; "History of Traffic," CWA Local 1182 online, accessed December 28, 2020, https://local1182.org/about-us/history-of-traffic.

242 pistol range . . . "value to the force": *NYT*, November 1, 1895 (immediate spur); *Sun*, December 31, 1895 ("remarkably bad"); Roosevelt, *Autobiography*, 198 ("wonderfully improved"); *1896 Annual Police Report*, 20 ("incalculable value"), 72–73 (marksmen and sharpshooters); Zacks, *Island of Vice*, 219–20; Berman, *Police Administration*, 89; Lardner and Reppetto, *NYPD*, 115.

243 tramp lodging houses . . . no longer annoying: Roosevelt, *Autobiography*, 218; *1896 Annual Police Report*, 12 ("shiftless and vicious"), 53 ("drunken . . . source of sickness"); Riis, *Making of an American*, 254–59; Zacks, *Island of Vice*, 215–19; Berman, *Police Administration*, 91–92; Lardner and Reppetto, *NYPD*, 115.

CHAPTER 19: "TO HELL WITH REFORM"

245 "After the Saloon Men" . . . enforce it to the letter: *NYT,* June 11, 1895 (headline); *Sun,* June 11, 1895; Berman, *Police Administration,* 107–8; Morris, *Rise of Roosevelt,* 513–16.

245 "I do not deal . . . I deal with the law": Quoted in Zacks, *Island of Vice,* 109; Berman, *Police Administration,* 108–9.

246 On June 16, 1895 . . . "worse than Schenectady": *Sun,* June 17 ("the drought"), 24 ("Schenectady"), 1895; *NYT,* June 17, 24, 1895.

246 Throughout the summer . . . he would not budge: *NYT,* June 30, July 2, 3, 7, 8 ("all the drinking men") 10, August 4, 11, 19, 25, September 7, 1895; Zacks, *Island of Vice,* 133–41, 151–54; Morris, *Rise of Roosevelt,* 517–27; Berman, *Police Administration,* 109–13.

247 November's elections . . . politically wounded: Zacks, *Island of Vice,* 169–85; Morris, *Rise of Roosevelt,* 530–32.

247 new liquor law . . . "his own appetite": *NYT,* July 2, 7 ("'fake' lunch"), 1895, March 30, April 5, May 4, 1896; *Tribune,* April 21, 1896 ("his own appetite"); Richardson, *New York Police,* 253; Zacks, *Island of Vice,* 120–21, 244–46.

248 hotel meal exemption . . . since at least 1893: *Laws of the State of New York, Passed at the One Hundred and Sixteenth Session of the Legislature, Begun January Third, 1893, and Ended April Twentieth, 1893, in the City of Albany,* vol. 1 (Albany, N.Y.: n.p., 1893), 1047, 1054–55, chap. 480, secs. 19 (1) (2), 32 (1) (6). See also *NYT,* July 7, 8, 9, 10, 1895; *Tribune,* April 13, 1896.

248 rushed to convert . . . "Raines Law hotels": *Sun,* April 15, 23, July 10, August 6, December 2, 1896; *Tribune,* April 13, 20, 21, 1896; *NYT,* August 25, 1896; Berman, *Police Administration,* 115; Zacks, *Island of Vice,* 256–62; Richardson, *New York Police,* 253; Committee of Fifteen, *The Social Evil: With Special Reference to the Conditions Existing in the City of New York* (New York: G. P. Putnam's, 1902), 159–68.

248 "managed to engineer . . . quotient of sin": Burrows and Wallace, *Gotham,* 1203.

249 police board infighting . . . skipping board meetings: Berman, *Police Administration,* 55, 116–18; Zacks, *Island of Vice,* 221–26, 228–30, 242–43, 246–52, 267–70, 289–93; Morris, *Rise of Roosevelt,* 540–45, 548–49, 554–57; Richardson, *New York Police,* 256–59; Steffens, *Autobiography,* 1:258 ("Thinks he's the whole Board"); Andrews, "Roosevelt as Police Commissioner," 120 ("I will decide").

250 "A more foolish . . . any legislative body": Theodore Roosevelt, *Works: American Ideals* (New York: P. F. Collier & Son, 1897), 209–10. See also Roosevelt, *Autobiography,* 189; Berman, *Police Administration,* 35–36, 54–55; Morris, *Rise of Roosevelt,* 559–60; Reppetto, *American Police,* 65; Czitrom, *New York Exposed,* 278–80, 283–84, 291.

250 "glorious retreat": *World,* April 9, 1897.

250 disciplinary and criminal cases . . . restored with back pay: Czitrom, *New York Exposed,* 280, 289, 293–94; Zacks, *Island of Vice,* 77–78, 275–78, 338, 350–51 (Devery); Lamb, "Bill Devery"; Roosevelt, *Autobiography,* 189–90; *NYT,* March 16, 27 (Cross), October 29, 30 (indictment dismissals), December 31, 1895, January 4, 1898,

December 26, 1925 (all Stephenson), October 14, 1933 (McLaughlin); *Tribune*, June 2, 1896 (parade); Lardner and Reppetto, *NYPD*, 117–18 (parade).

251 "from the strictly . . . nil": Czitrom, *New York Exposed*, 293.

251 little if any evidence . . . Republicans: Czitrom, *New York Exposed*, 299.

252 consolidated . . . 6,400 patrolmen: Crain, *Gilded Age*, 293–95; Bernard Whalen and Jon Whalen, *The NYPD's First Fifty Years: Politicians, Police Commissioners, and Patrolmen* (Lincoln, Neb.: Potomac Books, 2014), 1, 3, 229–30; Wallace, *Greater Gotham*, 53–55; *Report of the Police Department of the City of New York for the Year Ending December 31, 1898* (New York: Martin B. Brown, 1899), 7–17.

252 Moses Cobb . . . Samuel Battle: Lardner and Reppetto, *NYPD*, 139–41; New York City Police Department, "Pioneering NYPD Officer Moses Cobb Honored in Brooklyn," *NYPD News*, last modified February 28, 2018, http://nypdnews.com /2018/02/pioneering-nypd-officer-moses-cobb-honored-brooklyn/; Jane Phillips, "Kinston's Moses Led Way for African-Americans in the NYPD," *Neuse News*, last modified August 18, 2018, https://www.neusenews.com/index/2018/8/16/jane -phillips-moses-led-the-way-for-his-people.

252 "reform" had become . . . "has gone to hell!": Connable and Silberfarb, *Tigers of Tammany*, 215–18; Welch, *King of the Bowery*, 55–56.

254 Van Wyck promptly replaced . . . Big Bill Devery: Richardson, *New York Police*, 268–70; Welch, *King of the Bowery*, 56; *NYT*, March 9, May 18, 22, 25, 1898, January 4, 1917 (all McCullagh); Lardner and Reppetto, *NYPD*, 121; Zacks, *Island of Vice*, 358; Whalen and Whalen, *First Fifty Years*, 7–8.

254 Devery rode proudly . . . Schmittberger was banished: *NYT*, June 2, 1898; Reppetto, *American Police*, 68; Lardner and Reppetto, *NYPD*, 121.

254 With Devery in charge . . . back in business: Zacks, *Island of Vice*, 360–61; Welch, *King of the Bowery*, 57; Reppetto, *American Police*, 69; Richardson, *New York Police*, 270–72; Whalen and Whalen, *First Fifty Years*, 9–11, 15.

254 "not hittin' nobody": Lardner and Reppetto, *NYPD*, 123. See also Whalen and Whalen, *First Fifty Years*, 14.

254 Devery ran the department . . . out of a saloon: Lardner and Reppetto, *NYPD*, 122.

254 "but as a character . . . a masterpiece": Steffens, *Autobiography*, 1:330.

255 "Roosevelt men": Reppetto, *American Police*, 68.

255 In 1901 . . . Theodore Roosevelt: Whalen and Whalen, *First Fifty Years*, 12–13; Richardson, *New York Police*, 273–75; Czitrom, *New York Exposed*, 291, 301; Lardner and Reppetto, *NYPD*, 122.

255 Michael C. Murphy . . . named Devery: Richardson, *New York Police*, 279–82; Lardner and Reppetto, *NYPD*, 123; Whalen and Whalen, *First Fifty Years*, 13–14; Connable and Silberfarb, *Tigers of Tammany*, 224; *NYT*, February 23, 1901.

256 Arthur Carey . . . back in the central detective bureau: Carey, 55.

CHAPTER 20: THE MAN IN THE STRAW HAT

257 Art Carey's family . . . books on poisons: Carey, xv (at home), 1–15 (background and quotations), 140 (no vacations), 310 (didn't drink).

NOTES

258 August 16, 1898 . . . Dr. Kennedy was sentenced: The account of the Dolly Reynolds murder through the first trial of Dr. Samuel Kennedy is drawn from the following: *NYT*, August 17 ("You've gotten me"), 18, 19, 20, 21, 1898, March 25, 28, 30, 31, April 1, 1899, October 5, 1900; *Sun*, August 17, 18, 19, 20, 21, 1898; *Tribune*, March 29, 1899; *People v. Kennedy*, 164 N.Y. 449, 58 N. E. 652 (1900); Carey, 54–64; *People of the State of New York v. Samuel J. Kennedy*, Trial # 261, May 6, 1901, third trial transcript, John Jay College of Criminal Justice, Lloyd Sealy Library, Criminal Trial Transcripts of New York County Collection (hereafter, *People v. Kennedy*, Third Trial Tr.); Patricia M. Salmon, *Staten Island Slayings: Murderers and Mysteries of the Forgotten Borough* (Charleston, S.C.: History Press, 2014), 71–81; Underwood, *Gaslight Lawyers*, 127–32; Marjorie Mears, "Who Killed Dolly Reynolds?," *Illustrated Detective Magazine* 4, no. 3 (September 1931). A slightly fictionalized account by an American mystery novelist, nonetheless useful because it sticks largely to the facts, appears in Bayard Kendrick, "The Dolly Reynolds Case," in *New York Murders*, ed. Ted Collins (New York: Duell, Sloan and Pearce, 1944), 85–108.

Kennedy's age of thirty-two is established by the 1900 US Census, Ossining Township, N.Y. (Sing Sing State Prison), Enum. Dist. 107. For Mendham, see "Maurice B. Mendham," Find a Grave, last modified April 25, 2015; 1870 US Census, Augusta, Ga., Ward 3 (Maurice B. Mendheim).

For McClusky, see Carey, 45–46; *NYT*, August 31, 1897, November 7, 1908, December 18, 1912 (obituary); Lardner and Reppetto, *NYPD*, 87, 123.

266 In November 1900 . . . fireworks: *People v. Kennedy*, 164 N.Y. 449, 58 N. E. 652; *NYT*, November 21, 23, 1900, February 5, 12, 13, 14, 15, 16, 17, 19, 23, May 15, 16, June 14, 16, 17, 19, 1901; *Sun*, June 14, 15, 16 ("Let him loose!"), 17, 1901; *World*, February 7, 11, 14, June 7 (cashier), 1901 (night); *Tribune*, February 15, 21, 1901; *People v. Kennedy*, Third Trial Tr. (cashier Douglas's testimony at 2371–409); Underwood, *Gaslight Lawyers*, 132–37; Salmon, *Staten Island Slayings*, 82–96; Carey, 62–63; Kendrick, "Dolly Reynolds Case," 96–108.

268 resumed his dental practice . . . August 1948: *NYT*, August 26, 1948.
269 "Who did kill . . . so many murder pictures": Carey, 63–64.

CHAPTER 21: THE POSTMAN RANG TWICE

270 Roland Molineux . . . the same mistake: The best summaries of the Molineux case are found in *People v. Molineux*, 168 N.Y. 264, 61 N.E. 286 (1901); Carey, 69–95; Jim Fisher, "Document Examination: The Molineux Case," *Jim Fisher—The Official Website*, last modified January 7, 2008, http://jimfisher.edinboro.edu/forensics/mol1.html; Randolph N. Jonakait, "*People v. Molineux* and Other Crime Evidence: One Hundred Years and Counting," *American Journal of Criminal Law* 30, no. 1 (Fall 2002): 1–43; and the chronology and introduction in Samuel Klaus, ed., *The Molineux Case* (London: George Routledge, 1929), ix–x, 3–43. See also the summary of evidence provided by Recorder John W. Goff at Molineux's first trial, appearing in *People of the State of New York, Respondents, Against Roland B. Molineux, Appellant,*

Court of Appeals, State of New York, Case on Appeal (New York: Martin B. Brown, 1901 (hereafter, *People v. Molineux*, Appeal), 3:2703–26.

An engaging full-length account is Harold Schechter, *The Devil's Gentleman: Privilege, Poison, and the Trial That Ushered in the Twentieth Century* (New York: Ballantine Books, 2007). Schechter bases his book in part on Blanche (Chesebrough) Molineux Scott's unpublished memoirs. So does, to a much greater extent, Jane Pejsa, *The Molineux Affair* (1983; repr., New York: St. Martin's Press, 1987).

For a discussion of cyanide and its use in the Molineux case, see Deborah Blum, *The Poisoner's Handbook: Murder and the Birth of Forensic Medicine in Jazz Age New York* (2010; repr., New York: Penguin, 2011), 55–62; Schechter, *Devil's Gentleman*, 162–63; Klaus, *Molineux Case*, 266–74 (Witthaus testimony). See also *NYT*, January 6, 1900 (Molineux's laboratory).

For images of many of the key documents and handwriting facsimiles at issue in the case, see the photo insert in Klaus, *Molineux Case*, and Daniel T. Ames, *Ames on Forgery: Its Detection and Illustration* (New York: Ames-Rollinson, 1900), 216–36.

For newspaper stories up to the point of Molineux's indictment, see, for instance, *NYT*, December 29, 30, 31, 1898, January 1, 3, 5, 6, 7, 8, 9, 10, 11, 26, February 3, 9, 10, 11, 22 (Blanche), 28 (Molineux arrest), March 2 (indictment), 1899; *New York Journal*, December 27, 28, 29, 30 (Hawthorne quotation), 31, 1898, January 1, 2, 4, 6, 9, 10, 23, 26, 27, 1899.

Additional helpful citations from the first trial transcript are at *People v. Molineux*, Appeal, 2:1493–504 (Marston), 3:2299–319 (Marston), 2649–50 (Pearl Street office), 4:2823–26 (blue notepaper), 2902–4 (Koch), 2915–21 (Melando), 2929–30, 2938–40 (medicine requests and responses), 3124–26 (Melando). See also the following excerpts of testimony in Klaus, *Molineux Case*: 89–106 (Melando), 188–90 (Gray of Kutnow Brothers), 190–92 (Evans of Dr. Burns), 198, 255, 272 (Carey), 212–14 (Farrell of Newark police), 286–301 (Koch), 301–312 (Heckmann), 312–13 (Hamill of Marston), 314 (Edmund Barnet, brother of Henry).

For Calthos, see, for example, *San Francisco Call*, October 29, 1899 (advertisement), and I. F. Kebler, "Nostrums and Fraudulent Methods of Exploitation: Lost Manhood Restorers and Nervous Debility Cures," *Journal of American Medical Association* 47, no. 20 (November 17, 1906): 1624 (worthless yellow phosphorous).

Some sources erroneously list the date of Blanche Chesebrough's marriage to Roland Molineux as November 19, 1898. The wedding was on November 29, 1898, as confirmed by the *Brooklyn Daily Eagle*, November 30, 1898, and New York, N.Y., Extracted Marriage Index, Blanche Chesebrough, November 29, 1898, certif. no. 18320. See also *People v. Molineux*, Appeal, 3:2705 (Goff summary).

282 Indicted . . . "Molineux rule": *People v. Molineux*, 168 N.Y. 264; Klaus, *Molineux Case*, 19–34; Schechter, chaps. 53–81 in *Devil's Gentleman*; Ames, *Ames on Forgery*, 216–36; Jonakait, "Other Crime Evidence"; Fisher, "Document Examination," 2–4; Carey, 93; *NYT*, March 2 (indictment), December 5, 6, 8, 9, 13, 14, 16, 29, 30, 1899, January 5, 6, 13, 23, February 7 (all trial reports), 11 (guilty verdict), November 21 (congratulated Kennedy), 1900, June 18, 20 (appeals argument), October 16 (appeals

NOTES

court decision), 1901; John Josiah Munro, *The New York Tombs, Inside and Out!* (Brooklyn, N.Y.: self pub., 1909), 281 ("he received me"); Underwood, *Gaslight Lawyers*, 161 (Molineux rule).

284 returned to the Tombs . . . Bridge of Sighs: *NYT*, October 18, December 7, 1901, October 14, 1902; Pigott, *New York's Legal Landmarks*, 65–69; Crain, *Gilded Age*, 222; Crain, "The 'Bridge of Sighs' over a Downtown Prison."

CHAPTER 22: "HOW STRANGE IS PUBLIC OPINION"

286 Seth Low . . . about as bad: *NYT*, November 6, 1901, February 11, 1926 (Farrell); Lardner and Reppetto, *NYPD*, 123; Reppetto, *American Police*, 71; Flynt, *World of Graft*, 34–56; Richardson, *New York Police*, 281–83.

286 Tenderloin race riot . . . "police riot": Lardner and Reppetto, *NYPD*, 138–39; Johnson, *Street Justice*, 57–69; Wallace, *Greater Gotham*, 805–7; Will Mack, "The New York City Race Riot (1900)," BlackPast.org, last modified November 22, 2017, https://www.blackpast.org/african-american-history/1900-new-york-city-race-riot-1900.

287 Mayor Low fulfilled . . . pledge to oust: *NYT*, October 10, 1901, January 1, 2, 1902; Whalen and Whalen, *First Fifty Years*, 15–16.

287 "beer and ham sandwiches": *Tribune*, August 4, 1903.

287 Highlanders . . . renamed the Yankees: Lamb, "Bill Devery."

287 Boss Croker . . . Murphy: Welch, *King of the Bowery*, 59, 68–75; Connable and Silberfarb, *Tigers of Tammany*, 222, 226–38; *NYT*, May 2, 1903 (Croker), April 30, 1922 (Croker obituary); *Tribune*, September 19, 1901 (Sullivan); Lewis, "Modern Robin Hood," 190–91 (Sullivan and Murphy).

287 William Travers Jerome . . . enthusiastic following: Cummings, *Saving Sin City*, 3–10, 59–63; Reppetto, *American Police*, 72–73; Welch, *King of the Bowery*, 60–62; *NYT*, October 22 ("Second Teddy"), 23 ("that little bunch"), 1901.

288 In mock eulogies . . . Mark Twain told: *NYT*, November 7, 1901.

288 "Jerome lives on" . . . "any other day": Richard O'Connor, *Courtroom Warrior: The Combative Career of William Travers Jerome* (Boston: Little, Brown, 1963), 80. See also Cummings, *Saving Sin City*, 47 (Roosevelt's excise campaign), 124–25 (mistress); Reppetto, *American Police*, 72–73.

288 Shang Draper's . . . would die in 1913: *NYT*, October 15, 16, 1902; Freeland, *Automats*, 115–27; *Sun*, December 7, 1913 (obituary).

289 his axe men crashed . . . "stationery of the Molineux case": *NYT*, December 2 (quotations), 3, 1902. See also O'Connor, *Courtroom Warrior*, 99–109.

289 Canfield fled . . . fractured skull: *NYT*, December 12, 1914; Cummings, *Saving Sin City*, 282. See generally Alexander Gardiner, *Canfield: The True Story of the Greatest Gambler* (Garden City, N.Y.: Doubleday, 1930).

290 *The Great Poison Mystery* . . . "ridiculous paraphrase": *NYT*, December 2, 1902; *Brooklyn Daily Eagle*, December 9, 1902 (quotation); Schechter, *Devil's Gentleman*, 433–34.

290 three weeks earlier . . . acquitted: *World*, November 11, 1902 (night); *NYT*, November 12, 1902.

290 John S. Lambert . . . rendered irrelevant: Schechter, *Devil's Gentleman*, 406–20; Jonakait, "Other Crime Evidence," 24–25; Klaus, *Molineux Case*, 34–40; Fisher, "Document Examination," 3–4 (Carvalho and second trial), 4; *Los Angeles Times*, January 30, 1898 (Ames and Dreyfus case); Ames, *Ames on Forgery*, 237–41 (same).

291 The jury needed only thirteen minutes: *NYT*, November 12, 1902.

291 "Justice prevails . . . Right has won": *World*, November 11, 1902 (night).

291 Blanche Chesebrough Molineux . . . at the age of eighty: *NYT*, November 18, 1902; Schechter, *Devil's Gentleman*, 446–47; Pejsa, *Molineux Affair*, 234–39; Klaus, *Molineux Case*, 40–41.

292 In 1907 . . . he covered: O'Connor, *Courtroom Warrior*, 209; *Oregonian* (Portland), February 10, 1907.

292 "Trial of the Century" . . . by reason of insanity: The Thaw-White-Nesbit case has been chronicled in numerous books and articles. In addition to full accounts in Cummings, *Saving Sin City*, and O'Connor, *Courtroom Warrior* (both from Jerome's standpoint), see, for example, Paula Uruburu, *American Eve: Evelyn Nesbit, Stanford White, the Birth of the "It" Girl and the Crime of the Century* (New York: Riverhead, 2008), and Simon Baatz, *The Girl on the Velvet Swing: Sex, Murder, and Madness at the Dawn of the Twentieth Century* (New York: Mulholland, 2018).

292 The Man Inside . . . untreated syphilis: *NYT*, November 8 (marriage), 12 (play), 1913, September 7, 1914 (Babylon spree); *World*, September 7, 1914 (final night) (same), November 2, 1917 (final) (obituary); *Tribune*, November 3, 1917 (obituary); Schechter, *Devil's Gentleman*, 439–42; Klaus, *Molineux Case*, 41–43.

293 Close students . . . divided: Fisher, "Document Examination" (collecting sources). In *Devil's Gentleman*, the most recent full-length book on the case, Harold Schechter expresses the opinion that the jury in Molineux's first trial rendered the correct verdict (guilty). Ibid., 450. This author would agree.

293 As for Art Carey . . . preferred not to express: Carey, 94–95.

293 "Many New Yorkers . . . public opinion, sometimes": Carey, 95.

CHAPTER 23: RETURN OF THE GANGS

294 "They shot up . . . Wild West style": *NYT*, September 17, 1903.

294 At about two in the morning . . . make arrests: *World*, September 16, 1903 (night); *Brooklyn Daily Eagle*, September 16, 1903; *Tribune*, September 17, 1903; *NYT*, September 17, 1903; *Sun*, April 12, 1904 (two died).

295 Some Irish gangs . . . continued to form: Lardner and Reppetto, *NYPD*, 126; Wallace, *Greater Gotham*, 584; English, *Paddy Whacked*, 35, 111, 115–19 (Gas House Gang, Gophers, Hudson Dusters); *NYT*, May 10 (Car Barn Gang), December 26, 1910 (Gophers), January 22, 1912 (Gophers), September 17, 1913 (Hudson Dusters), December 26, 1926 (Car Barn Gang); *World*, March 13, 1912 (final) (Dusters); *Sun*, July 30, 1912 (Dusters). Herbert Asbury and others place the Gophers' and Hudson

Dusters' origins in the 1890s, but those estimates are early by about fifteen years. See also Jerry Kuntz, "The Devolution of the Hudson Dusters," *Asbury's The Gangs of New York—Annotated*, last modified December 6, 2019, https://gangsan notated.blog/2019/12/06/the-devolution-of-the-hudson-dusters/.

295 Paul Kelly . . . southern Italy: *NYT*, April 15, 1936 (obituary); "Paul 'Paul Kelly' Vaccarelli, Find a Grave, last modified August 15, 1999; 1920 US Census, Bronx, N.Y., Assembly Dist. 6, Enum. Dist. 347 (Paul A. Vaccarelli); *World*, November 28, 1905 (evening); Critchley, *Origin*, 19.

296 Edward Eastman . . . eventual gang members: Hanson, *Heroic Gangster*, 13–18, 40, 43; Asbury, *Gangs of New York*, 256 (Osterman); 1900 US Census, New York, N.Y., Enum. Dist. 240 (Edward Eastman, 101 East 1st St.); 1880 US Census, New York, N.Y., Enum. Dist. 610 (George Parker, Mary Eastman, Edward Eastman); New York, N.Y., Extracted Death Index, Edward Eastman, December 26, 1920, certif. no. 33332; Ron Arons, *The Jews of Sing Sing: Gotham Gangsters and Gonuvim* (Fort Lee, N.J.: Barricade Books, 2008), 33–34, 52–54.

296 Kelly and Eastman vied . . . competition for local rackets: Hanson, *Heroic Gangster*, 31, 77; Turner, "Tammany's Control," 122–24; Wallace, *Greater Gotham*, 583–84; *Idaho Statesman* (Boise), April 5, 1908; *World*, November 28, 1905 (evening); *Sun*, August 3, 1919.

297 The Battle of Rivington Street . . . card game stuss: *World*, September 16, 1903 (night); *Tribune*, September 17, 1903; *NYT*, September 17, 1903; Hanson, *Heroic Gangster*, 96. For a description of stuss (Yiddish for "joke" or "nonsense"), see Fried, *Rise and Fall*, 20–21.

297 Big Tim Sullivan . . . used mob leaders: Welch, *King of the Bowery*, 48–49; Hanson, *Heroic Gangster*, 55–60; Czitrom, "Underworlds and Underdogs," 546; Turner, "Tammany's Control," 122–24; *Sun*, October 28, 1901; *Tribune*, April 26, 1903, December 27, 1920, January 2, 1921; Steven P. Erie, *Rainbow's End: Irish-Americans and the Dilemmas of Urban Machine Politics, 1840–1985* (Oakland: University of California Press, 1990), 103 (yarmulke).

297 Monk Eastman . . . swinging like an ape: Hanson, *Heroic Gangster*, 41–42, 74; Sing Sing Prison Register for Edward Eastman, April 22, 1904, no. 54863, New York State Archives, Albany, N.Y., Record Group B0143 (Ancestry.com) (height, weight, scars, teeth); *Sun*, March 15, 1903 (monkey), August 3, 1919 (unkempt hair); *Brooklyn Daily Eagle*, December 27, 1920 (agility).

298 "had forty-nine nicks . . . an even fifty": Asbury, *Gangs of New York*, xx.

298 "I only give her . . . takes off me knucks first": Asbury, 257.

298 adept with a revolver and was quick to use it: *World*, December 22, 1902 (night); Turner, "Tammany's Control," 122.

298 "Yer all right . . . f'r not callin' th' cops": *NYT*, May 29, 1910.

298 he was shot . . . Monk survived: *NYT*, April 14, 15 (quotations), 1901; *Sun*, May 11, 1903.

299 he retracted . . . private revenge: *Sun*, May 11, 1903; *Tribune*, December 27, 1920; *NYT*, September 9, 1923.

299 soft spot . . . refused to sell any: Hanson, *Heroic Gangster*, 15–16, 41; Asbury, *Gangs of New York*, 255–56; Lewis, *Apaches of New York*, 211–12.

299 bicycle rental store . . . "Crazy Butch": *NYT*, July 1, 1904 (Erenstoft); Hanson, *Heroic Gangster*, 46–47; *Sun*, October 27, 1912; Lewis, *Apaches of New York*, 211–16; Anna Merlan, "The Prototype for Citi Bike Was Invented by Monk Eastman, a Pigeon-Loving Gangster from Williamsburg," *Village Voice*, November 27, 2013.

299 Kelly was more in line . . . "That's Paul Kelly": *Sun*, October 11, 1903; Hanson, *Heroic Gangster*, 73–74; Asbury, *Gangs of New York*, 253–55; Lewis, *Apaches of New York*, 259–61 (quotations).

300 Democratic primary election . . . upstart Tom Foley: Turner, "Tammany's Control," 124; Welch, *King of the Bowery*, 67; Connable and Silberfarb, *Tigers of Tammany*, 225; *Tribune*, September 17, 19, 1901.

301 "shameful" . . . "to shield you": *NYT*, December 7, 1901.

301 amateur boxer and wrestler . . . "just to keep in trainin'": *Sun*, July 24, 1901 (quotation); *World*, May 14, 1903 (7th home) (wrestling match); *Idaho Statesman* (Boise), April 5, 1908 (name change); Eric Ferrara, *Manhattan Mafia Guide: Hits, Homes & Headquarters* (Charleston, S.C.: History Press, 2011), 75–76.

301 arrested . . . knocked three men down: *World*, September 24, 1901 (night) (knocked three men down). See also *Sun*, July 24, 1901 (arrested); *NYT*, July 24, 1901 (same), February 9, 1903 (police raid).

301 Kelly could whip . . . "What'll you have?": *Sun*, October 3, 1903.

301 headquarters . . . Jack McManus: *Tribune*, November 2, 1901 (190 Mulberry Street); *Sun*, October 11, 1903 (portrait); *World*, November 28, 1905 (evening) (McManus); *Saint John (NB) Daily Sun*, June 3, 1905 (McManus); Turner, "Tammany's Control," 125 (McManus).

301 Kelly was happily married . . . again: *Tribune*, February 23, 1908; *NYT*, April 5, 1936; "Paul 'Paul Kelly' Vaccarelli," Find a Grave.

301 Eastman's two wives: Hanson, *Heroic Gangster*, 11–12, 40–41, 75, 114, 120, 130, 136–37; 1900 US Census, New York, N.Y., Enum. Dist. 240 (Edward Eastman and Margaret Eastman, m. 1896); Arons, *Jews of Sing Sing*, 52; New York, N.Y., Extracted Marriage Index, Edward Eastman, February 8, 1911, certif. no. 4106.

302 "Kelly stood second": *Tribune*, December 27, 1920. See also *Tribune*, April 26, 1903 (Eastman enjoyed "primacy in the world of thugs").

302 Eastman rose . . . alliances with others: Hanson, *Heroic Gangster*, 39–40.

302 "I was in wrong . . . my way to the top": *World*, April 19, 1904 (11 o'clock).

302 At the outset . . . extorting the profits: Hanson, *Heroic Gangster*, 27–31, 39–45, 50–51; *People of the State of New York v. William Delaney, Alias Monk Eastman*, Court of General Sessions of the Peace in and for the County of New York, trial transcript, http://www.crimeinnyc.org/sites/default/files/transcript-pdf-original/421.pdf (hereafter, *People v. Delaney*, Trial Tr.), 260, 270–71 (early arrests); *World*, December 11, 1903 (night) (hundred arrests), April 12, 1904 (11 o'clock) ("most immune thug"); *Sun*, December 12, 1903; Turner, "Tammany's Control," 122–23; Harlow, *Old Bowery Days*, 501–5; *Tribune*, April 26, 1903.

303 Asbury put their strength . . . A more realistic estimate: Asbury, *Gangs of New York*, 234. Eastman's biographer adopts the twelve hundred number and states that Monk could draw on a private army of nearly two thousand in the field at times. Hanson, *Heroic Gangster*, 45–47. Some writers have put forth similar numbers, claims that Mike Wallace considers "dubious." Wallace, *Greater Gotham*, 584. A contemporaneous newspaper article, reporting on a wrestling match between Paul Kelly and one Joe Bernstein, stated that "the 'Monk' Eastman crowd, the Paul Kelly Association—some 500 strong—and the Ike Bernstein 'Guerillas'" would be in attendance. *World*, May 14, 1903 (7th home). See also Turner, "Tammany's Control," 123–24 (Eastman could produce four hundred to five hundred repeaters, and Kelly a thousand in cases of emergency).

303 "Monk's gang was less . . . interlinked organizations": Hanson, *Heroic Gangster*, 46.

303 Junior Eastmans: Hanson, 47; *NYT*, October 5, 1903.

303 "could be seen flourishing . . . young brigand": *NYT*, September 27, 1903; *Kansas City Star*, October 2, 1903 (quotation).

303 "Kid Twist" . . . "in about a month": Rose Keefe, *The Starker: Big Jack Zelig, the Becker-Rosenthal Case, and the Advent of the Jewish Gangster* (Nashville: Cumberland House, 2008), 56–57, 61, 77–78; *Tribune*, August 18, 1903; *World*, August 18, 1903 (night); *NYT*, June 9, 1912 (quotation).

304 "just like mechanics goin' to work": Turner, "Tammany's Control," 122.

304 required his deputies . . . strikebreaking scabs: Hanson, *Heroic Gangster*, 42–43, 46–48, 51; *NYT*, April 16, 1904 ("crude instinct"), May 13, 1915; Turner, "Tammany's Control," 123; *Tribune*, April 26, 1903; Fried, *Rise and Fall*, 26–29.

304 $7.50 a day, or $10 for Monk: *NYT*, May 13, 1915.

304 written price list . . . "For a murder $100": *World*, October 23, 1902 (night).

305 He accepted commissions . . . Arnold Rothstein: Hanson, *Heroic Gangster*, 48; Turner, "Tammany's Control," 123; *World*, April 12, 1904 (11 o'clock) (hired out for assaults); *NYT*, April 15, 1904 (hiring out), June 9, 1912 (doing up); *Herald*, December 27, 1920 (commissions); David Pietrusza, *Rothstein: The Life, Times, and Murder of the Criminal Genius Who Fixed the 1919 World Series* (New York: Carroll & Graf, 2003), xv, 32.

305 charged with accepting $300 . . . warned the man: *NYT*, October 22, 1903.

305 Monk's goons were hired . . . culprits escaped: *Tribune*, April 2, 1904; *Sun*, April 2, 3, 1904.

305 "I like to beat up . . . keeps me hand in": Asbury, *Gangs of New York*, 258.

CHAPTER 24: SKATING

306 David Lamar . . . "plunger": *NYT*, May 5, 1909, October 28, 1923, January 14, 16, 1934; *World*, May 1, 1916.

306 Lamar hired Eastman . . . all but dead: *World*, July 29, 30, 31, 1903 (night eds.); *Sun*, July 29, 30, 31, August 3, 1903; *Tribune*, August 1, 2, 4, 7, 8, 1903; *NYT*, July 30, August 2, 1903.

306 Extradited to New Jersey . . . must be joking: *Tribune*, August 4, 18, 1903; *NYT*, August 18, October 17, 1903; *World*, September 1, October 13, 14, 15 (night eds.), 16 (sporting), 1903; *Sun*, August 7, 18, October 13, 16, 17, 18, 1903; Turner, "Tammany's Control," 123 ("cut some ice"); Hanson, *Heroic Gangster*, 82–94.

307 skated that time . . . fourteen years: *NYT*, September 17, 18, 21, October 17, 1903; *World*, September 16, 17, November 5, 1903 (night eds.); *Sun*, September 17, 21, 1903, April 12, 1904; *Tribune*, September 17, 1903.

308 Kelly was never a member . . . entirely separate: Ferrara, *Manhattan Mafia Guide*, 74–83; Bill Feather, "The Mustache Pete's [NYC]: Influential Italian Gangsters [pre Cosa Nostra]," *Mafia Membership Charts*, last modified October 3, 2015, http://mafi amembershipcharts.blogspot.com/search?updated-max=2015-10-14T13:18:00 -07:00&max-results=7; Brewster Adams, "The Street Gang as a Factor in Politics," *Outlook*, August 22, 1903, 987–88 (Five Points Social Club). In most newspaper accounts at the time, the Paul Kelly Association and the Five Points gang were identified as separate organizations. Occasionally, though, they were described as overlapping. For example, on April 16, 1903, the *World* reported that "until recently the Five Points and the Kellys were deadly enemies, but they have now amalgamated and their power is vastly increased."

308 by 1905 . . . rival groups: *NYT*, May 27, 1905; *Saint John (NB) Daily Sun*, June 3, 1905. See also *Idaho Statesman* (Boise), April 5, 1908; *NYT*, June 9, 1912.

308 Kelly was not from the Five Points . . . East Harlem: Ferrara, *Manhattan Mafia Guide*, 77, 80; *Tribune*, November 2, 1901 (190 Mulberry Street); *NYT*, February 9 (same), September 20 (24 Stanton Street), 1903; *World*, November 28, 1905 (evening) (Great Jones Street); Maggie Locker, "57 Great Jones Street," *Locker-Polding Index*, last modified February 3, 2018, http://lockerpoldingindex.com/home/2018/2/3 /57-great-jones-street; *Tribune*, July 9, 1903 (Little Italy), November 30, 1905 (Great Jones Street); *Sun*, November 27, 1905 (East 111th Street).

308 Five Pointers did operate . . . 126 White Street: *NYT*, October 12, 1902. See also *Sun*, March 15, 1903 (Five Points Social Club at White Street).

309 the Pelham . . . disfavored customers: *NYT*, May 27, 1905; "Mike Salter's Pelham Café: Birthplace of Irving Berlin," *Infamous New York: A Gangland Tour of New York City's Most Infamous Crime Scenes*, last modified August 12, 2013, https://infamous newyork.com/2013/08/12/mike-salters-pelham-cafe-birthplace-of-irving-berlin/ (Connors and Berlin); Stephen Birmingham, *"The Rest of Us": The Rise of America's East European Jews* (1984; repr., Syracuse, N.Y.: Syracuse University Press, 1999), 184 (Salter and Berlin); James Kaplan, *Irving Berlin: New York Genius* (New Haven, Conn.: Yale University Press, 2019), 16 (laxatives), 17 ("never mingled"), 18–21 (first song); *Tribune*, December 16, 1922 (Salter obituary); *Herald*, December 18, 1922 (same); Bruce Edward Hall, *Tea That Burns: A Family Memoir of Chinatown* (New York: Free Press, 1998), 122–24 (Connors); DeVillo, *The Bowery*, 123, 156–58 (Connors); Sante, *Low Life*, 125–29 (Connors).

309 tongs . . . fan-tan: Jeffrey Scott McIllwain, *Organizing Crime in Chinatown: Race and Racketeering in New York City, 1890–1910* (Jefferson, N.C.: McFarland, 2004),

105–25 (tongs), 166–72 (Doyers Street); Hall, chap. 6 in *Tea That Burns* (tong wars); Sante, *Low Life*, 143–45, 226–29; Wallace, *Greater Gotham*, 595, 648n5; *NYT*, August 7, 8, 13, 1905; *Tribune*, August 8, 13, 1905; *World*, November 4, 1904, March 18, August 29, 1905 (evening eds.); *Sun*, March 19, August 8, 22, 29, 30, 1905. For the best recent discussion of the tong wars, see Scott D. Seligman, *Tong Wars: The Untold Story of Vice, Money, and Murder in New York's Chinatown* (New York: Viking, 2016). One historian argues that the turn-of-the-century On Leong Tong and Hip Sing Tong (sometimes given as Hep Sing Tong) were arguably far ahead of the Eastmans and Five Pointers/Kellys in "organizational development, criminal sophistication, and breadth and depth of criminal networks." McIllwain, *Organizing Crime*, 186.

310 Most of Monk Eastman's . . . not with the Paul Kelly Association: *NYT*, September 30, October 5, 6, 12, 1902; *Sun*, October 12, 1902, March 15, August 3, 1903; Ferrara, *Manhattan Mafia Guide*, 77, 80.

310 defeated the Yakey Yakes . . . nightly shootings: *Tribune*, April 26, 1903; Hanson, *Heroic Gangster*, 78–79. See also *NYT*, March 9, 1903; *Sun*, March 15, 1903.

311 Foley brokered a cease-fire . . . "never more be bad": *NYT*, October 12, 1902 (quotation); *Sun*, October 12, 1902, March 15, 1903.

311 the following July 4 . . . only two arrests: *NYT*, July 6, 1903; *Tribune*, July 6, 1903. Both the *Times* and the *Tribune* reported that the Fourth of July celebrants were members of the Five Points gang, "known as the Paradise Social Club." But in its September 23 night edition, the *World* described the Paradise Social Club as being "made up mostly of members of the Eastman gang and similar coteries and women of equal notoriety." Complicating matters, the July 9 *Tribune* identified the "Paul Kelly Social Club" in East Harlem as "a branch of the Paradise Social Club of Five Points." It seems most likely that the six hundred returning picnickers on July 4 were a conglomeration of various gangs and social clubs.

311 "Each gang danced . . . everybody shook hands": *Sun*, June 20, 1909 (quotation); Hanson, *Heroic Gangster*, 99.

312 Francis V. Greene . . . had the blessing: *Baltimore American*, December 4, 1902.

312 "There will be no more . . . too much of it": *NYT*, September 18, 1903.

312 "We have arrested them . . . magistrates let them go": *NYT*, September 17, 1903.

312 "a spectacular raid" . . . "other gangs in a similar way": *NYT*, September 20, 1903 (quotations); *Tribune*, September 20, 1903.

313 a raid of the Eastman gang's haunts . . . vagrancy: *NYT*, September 22, 1903; *Tribune*, September 22, 1903.

313 shadowed Monk everywhere . . . "trouble with Eastman": Hanson, *Heroic Gangster*, 93, quoting *Herald*, October 17, 1903.

313 In December 1903 . . . William Smith, a printer: *Sun*, December 7, 1903.

313 pickpocketing spectators . . . "on general principles": *World*, December 11, 1903 (night).

313 "Eastman's weekly arrest": *Sun*, December 12, 1903.

313 judge discharged . . . public place: *World*, December 11, 1903 (night).

313 **"We can arrest ... can't convict him":** *World*, April 12, 1904 (11 o'clock). See also *NYT*, March 14, 1903, December 18, 1912 (McClusky).

314 **January 1, 1904 ... "miss my mother's funeral":** *World*, January 1, 1904 (night).

314 **Monk had buried ... day before Thanksgiving:** *People v. Delaney*, Trial Tr. 255–56; Arons, *Jews of Sing Sing*, 53.

314 **celebrating the new year ... "Bet your life they ain't":** *World*, January 1, 1904 (night).

314 **"forced by the police ... active operations":** *World*, January 20, 1904 (night).

314 **new crop of Junior Eastmans ... "Fagin kindergartens":** *Tribune*, January 31, 1904.

315 **"It's simply a side play ... steal for them":** *World*, January 20, 1904 (night).

315 **a Kelly man named Ford ... "protests of the politicians":** The earliest version of the story appears in *The New York Times* of June 9, 1912, and a later version in the *Times* of September 9, 1923. The quotations are from Asbury, *Gangs of New York*, 264–65. See also Hanson, *Heroic Gangster*, 105–8; Jorge Luis Borges, *A Universal History of Infamy*, Norman Thomas di Giovanni, trans. (1935; repr., Hammondsworth, Middlesex, UK: Penguin Books, 1975), 58–59. Compare *Tribune*, January 2, 1921 (gang leaders fought to a draw in saloon and declared a truce).

316 **There *was* a prizefight ... happy if weary:** *Sun*, December 30, 1903. For the Berkeley Oval and its location, see *The World Almanac and Encyclopedia 1903* (New York: Press, 1902), 493; *NYT*, May 27, 1922.

316 **Kelly recalled ... "cowardly loafers around him":** *Idaho Statesman* (Boise), April 5, 1908, reprinting *Herald* story.

CHAPTER 25: UP THE RIVER

318 **feasting on roast pig ... pair were arraigned:** *People v. Delaney*, Trial Tr. 6–13 (prosecution opening), 29–62 (Bryan testimony), 63–80 (Rogers testimony), 80–84 (Ryan testimony), 85–91 (police officer Charles Baxter testimony), 91–95 (police officer John O'Brien testimony), 95–103 (Healy testimony), 111–114 (Sheehan testimony), 114–15 (police officer Charles Terhune testimony), 145–49 (defense opening), 248, 256, 272 (Eastman testimony) (roast pig, clubbed on way, "twenty glasses"); *World*, February 2 (evening), 5 (night), 1904; *Sun*, February 3, 4 ("a certain woman"), 5, 1904; *NYT*, February 3, 1904.

320 **one of about six hundred ... 1970s to the 1990s:** *Report of the Police Department of the City of New York for the Year Ending December 31, 1904* (New York: Martin B. Brown, 1906), 46, 58; *New York Daily News*, December 31, 2019 (315 homicides in 2019); Andrew Karmen, *New York Murder Mystery: The True Story Behind the Crime Crash of the 1990s* (New York: NYU Press, 2000), 16–17 (historical city murder statistics).

320 **William Delaney, "newspaper speculator" ... denied even being armed:** *Sun*, February 3, 1904; *People v. Delaney*, Trial Tr. 250–55, 260–68, 272–85.

321 **$15,000 ... defense fund:** *Sun*, March 30, 1904; *World*, April 12, 1904 (11 o'clock). Some sources give the bail amount as $7,500.

321 McClellan . . . study fingerprinting: Whalen and Whalen, *First Fifty Years*, 30–31, 35–38, 41–44, 56 (McClellan and McAdoo); Connable and Silberfarb, *Tigers of Tammany*, 240–41 (same); *Sun*, March 30, 1904 ("sincere in their efforts"); Charles DeMotte, *Bat, Ball & Bible: Baseball and Sunday Observance in New York* (Dulles, Va.: Potomac, 2013), 76 (McAdoo); *NYT*, July 20, 1905 (automobile violations), June 8, 1930 (McAdoo obituary); Lardner and Reppetto, *NYPD*, 152, 221 (traffic bureau, fingerprinting); William McAdoo, *Guarding a Great City* (New York: Harper & Brothers, 1906), 243–50 (traffic bureau); Wallace, *Greater Gotham*, 596–97 (fingerprinting).

322 "utterly un-American . . . in evidence everywhere": McAdoo, *Guarding a Great City*, 158.

322 "the Tenderloin type of negro . . . general criminal": McAdoo, 93.

322 "carefully guard against . . . hue and cry": *NYT*, July 20, 1905.

322 transferred . . . racist captain: *NYT*, July 25, 1905. See also Johnson, *Street Justice*, 80–83.

322 "the first true *Jewish gangster* in New York": Arons, *Jews of Sing Sing*, 33 (emphasis in original).

322 "This fellow has been running . . . as we can": *Sun*, February 5, 1904.

323 victim never appeared . . . a conspiracy: *World*, April 13, 1904 (11 o'clock); *People v. Delaney*, Trial Tr. 147.

323 "son of a man . . . public life in the United States": *People v. Delaney*, Trial Tr. 8.

323 so intoxicated . . . worthless anyway: *People v. Delaney*, Trial Tr. 77.

323 "Whetmore" . . . without an "h": *People v. Delaney*, Trial Tr. 79; *Sun*, April 20, 1904 (Jerome); *Tribune*, April 13, 20, 1904.

323 "C. W. Wetmore . . . LaClede Gas Light Company": Arons, *Jews of Sing Sing*, 43; *Gould's St. Louis Directory for 1904* (St. Louis: Gould Directory, 1904), 2196 (Charles W. Wetmore); *NYT*, May 28, 1903.

323 Charles Wilson Wetmore . . . childless: "Charles Wilson Wetmore," Find a Grave, last modified December 6, 2016. Wetmore's wife was the former Elizabeth Bisland, an author best known for losing to Nellie Bly in their race around the world in 1889. "Elizabeth Bisland Wetmore," Find a Grave, last modified June 5, 2013. See also *NYT*, June 3, 1919 (Charles obituary), January 9, 1929 (Elizabeth obituary); *Electrical World*, June 14, 1919, 129 (Charles obituary); *National Savings and Trust Company v. Sarolea*, 269 F. Supp. 4 (D.D.C. 1967) (Elizabeth's will).

323 George Peabody Wetmore . . . President Theodore Roosevelt: *Washington (D.C.) Evening Star*, September 12, 1921 (obituary); "George Peabody Wetmore," Find a Grave, last modified November 23, 2002; Holly Collins, "A Study of Chateau Sur Mer, Part I: The Wetmore Family and Domestic Life at Chateau Sur Mer," research report, Preservation Society of Newport County, June 14, 2000, 13–27, https://www.newportmansions.org/documents/a_study_of_chateau_sur_mer_report_i_the_wetmore_family_and_their_domestics.pdf (hereafter, "Wetmore Family"); "Wetmore Family Papers (RLC.Ms.546), Biographical Note," accessed December 29, 2020, *RIAMCO (Rhode Island Archival and Manuscript Collections Online)*, Redwood

Library and Athenaeum, Newport, R.I., https://www.riamco.org/render?eadid=US
-RNR-ms546&view=biography. For Wetmore's relationship with Roosevelt, see, for
instance, TR to Wetmore, November 15, December 30, 1901, January 8, August 2,
1902, November 14, 1904, June 24, 1905; Wetmore to TR, January 4, 1906 (all in
Theodore Roosevelt Papers, Library of Congress Manuscript Division); William
Kloss and Diane K. Skvarla, *United States Senate Catalogue of Fine Art* (Washington,
D.C.: Government Printing Office, 2002), 320 (Wetmore and bust of Roosevelt);
George Peabody College for Teachers: Its Evolution and Present Status (Nashville: George
Peabody College for Teachers, 1912), 150–52 (Wetmore and Roosevelt as cotrust-
ees); *Washington (D.C.) Evening Star*, January 22, February 5, 1904, November 10,
1905 (Wetmore family at White House social events).

324 Rogers Pickman Derby Keteltas Wetmore . . . reckless playboy: "Rogers Pickman
Derby Keteltas Wetmore," Find a Grave, last modified February 27, 2018. Born in the
Hotel Bristol in Paris in 1882, he skipped college and fancied horses and women.
Shortly after the Eastman incident, he was arrested for speeding and failed to appear
for a court hearing. In 1907 he was charged with hitting a female pedestrian with his
automobile in Washington, D.C., and then fleeing the scene of the accident. The following year, he would come to blows with, and reportedly be challenged to a duel by,
a onetime friend over a woman. Wetmore claimed to feel so threatened at the time that
he sought, and was given, a full police guard by detectives at his hotel, quite possibly
because he recalled how similar protection had saved him in 1904. His antagonist's
father, the mayor of Philadelphia, told the newspapers that the threat was "just a fancy
of young Wetmore's brain." Rogers Wetmore would die suddenly in 1917, at age
thirty-five, of an undisclosed cause. See Holly Collins, "Wetmore Family," 15, 45; *St.
Louis Republic*, August 18, 1904 (home in New York); *Washington (D.C.) Evening Star*,
March 25, 1904 (speeding), August 15, 1907 (leaving the scene); November 25 (police
guard), 26 ("fancy of . . . brain"), 1908, April 28, 1917 (obituary), September 12, 1921
(horseman); *Tribune*, November 26, 1908 (police guard and dueling).

There is one alternative candidate: Rogers Wetmore had an older brother, William Shepard Keteltas Wetmore, who adopted an independent lifestyle and lived
with an actor friend on Staten Island. But at age twenty-eight in 1904, he would be
hard to describe as a "youth" or "boy." Besides, he was the responsible rather than
dissolute sort. A Yale University graduate and secretary of the Hongkong and Shanghai Bank in New York (now known as HSBC), he was "well known in New York
society" and on Mrs. Caroline Schermerhorn Astor's list for "the new One Hundred."
In 1902 he served as Special Envoy Whitelaw Reid's secretary as part of a delegation
sent by President Roosevelt to attend the coronation of King Edward VII of Great
Britain. "William Shepard Keteltas Wetmore," Find a Grave, last modified February
27, 2018; Holly Collins, "Wetmore Family," 15, 45; *Tribune*, April 2, 1915 (actor
friend); *Bizbee (Ariz.) Daily Review*, March 6 ("well known" . . . "new One Hundred"), 12 (secretary to Reid), 1902; *NYT*, January 31, 1925 (obituary).

324 Eastman was convicted . . . seemed stunned: *Tribune*, April 13, 14, 15, 1904; *Sun*,
April 13, 14, 15, 1904; *World*, April 14, 1904 (night); *NYT*, April 15, 1904.

324 **"too deep"**: *World*, April 19, 1904 (11 o'clock).

324 **Eastman's lawyer . . . face in a newspaper**: *World*, April 19 (11 o'clock) ("Me stomach . . . me finish"), 22 (final results) ("me boids"), 1904; *NYT*, April 20, 1904 (Goff); *Sun*, April 20, 23 (face in newspaper), 1904.

325 **"Monk Eastman was not dangerous" . . . "will be a model community"**: *Sun*, April 24, 1904.

326 **Jack McManus . . . buried by the Kelly Association**: *NYT*, May 27, 1905. See also *World*, May 26, November 28, 1905 (evening eds.); *Sun*, May 30, 1905; *Tribune*, May 27, 1905; *Saint John (NB) Daily Sun*, June 3, 1905; Lewis, *Apaches of New York*, 18; Asbury, *Gangs of New York*, 241–42 (Sardinia Frank). According to the *New York Times* story, the same night McManus was killed, a man concealed in a doorway stabbed Five Points leader Jimmy Kelly in the back with a stiletto, sending Kelly to the hospital. Some subsequent writers have confused the two Kellys, stating that it was Paul Kelly who was stabbed. For Paul Kelly and Cucco (Kid Griffo) as previous sparring partners, see *Sun*, July 24, 1901; *NYT*, July 24, 1901.

327 **November 1905 . . . fugitive Biff Ellison**: *Sun*, November 23, 24, 1905, August 3, 1919 (Paresis Hall); *NYT*, November 24, December 2, 1905, June 9 (Ellison conviction), 1911; *World*, November 28, 1905 (evening); *Tribune*, December 2, 1905; Lewis, *Apaches of New York*, 251–59, 261–71; Ferrara, *Manhattan Mafia Guide*, 83–84; Jonathan Katz, *Gay American History: Lesbians and Gay Men in the U.S.A.* (New York: Crowell, 1976), 46–47 (Paresis Hall); Will Kohler, "The Alienist: The Real History Paresis Hall, 'Fairy Sexual Degenerate' Hangout," *Back2Stonewall*, last modified January 24, 2018, http://www.back2stonewall.com/2018/01/paresis-hall.html.

328 **"We are going to drive . . . out of existence"**: *World*, November 28, 1905 (evening). See also Locker, "57 Great Jones Street."

328 **He moved uptown . . . respected labor official**: Ferrara, *Manhattan Mafia Guide*, 84–88; Hanson, *Heroic Gangster*, 127–28; *NYT*, April 5, 1936 (Kelly obituary).

329 **twenty-year-old Kid Twist . . . undisputed head**: *NYT*, November 2, 1904, March 1, 1905; *Sun*, November 2, 1904; *World*, November 2, 1904 (evening); Keefe, *Starker*, 78–79 (Fitzpatrick's father); Lewis, *Apaches of New York*, 53–54; Fried, *Rise and Fall*, 29–30; Charles E. Van Loan, "Disarming New York," *Munsey's* 46, no. 5 (February 1912): 689–90; "Max 'Kid Twist' Zweifach," Find a Grave, last modified June 9, 2012; 1880 US Census, New York, N.Y., Enum. Dist. 143 (Richard Fitzpatrick); 1900 US Census, New York, N.Y., Enum. Dist. 284 (Richard Fitzpatrick).

329 **"no wop and no mick"**: Fried, *Rise and Fall*, 30, quoting Joel Slonim, "The Jewish Gangster," *Reflex* 3 (July 1928): 38.

330 **his own brand of celery tonic . . . life threatened**: Turner, "Tammany's Control," 123; Lewis, *Apaches of New York*, 123–24; Fried, *Rise and Fall*, 30.

330 **Twist pressured a gambler . . . had him rubbed out**: Lewis, *Apaches of New York*, 51–62 (Cyclone Lewis the killer); *NYT*, June 3, 1907 (Stahl the suspected killer); Keefe, *Starker*, 87–88, 300n3 (note to chap. 5) (noting Stahl-Lewis conflict); *Perth Amboy (N.J.) Evening News*, December 4, 1904 (Cyclone Lewis as wrestler); "Sam 'Cyclone Louis' Tietch," Find a Grave, last modified October 18, 2012.

330 Twist's reign . . . "standin' on me head": *NYT*, May 15 (Coney Island), October 6 (Poggi plea), 1908, February 15, 1912 (Poggi sentence); *Sun*, May 15, 22, 1908, August 3, 1919 (Asbury); *World*, October 5, 1908 (final results); 1920 US Census, New York, N.Y., Assembly Dist. 5, Enum. Dist. 405 (Carril M. Terry); New York, N.Y., Extracted Marriage Index, Sarah Birnbaum/Max Zweifoch [Max Zweifach], June 25, 1904, certif. no. 13530; Keefe, *Starker*, 89–92; Robert Grey Reynolds Jr., *Louis Pioggi: New York City Gang Leader* (self-pub., Smashwords, 2017); "Louis 'Louis the Lump' Pioggi," Find a Grave, last modified July 8, 2009; Lewis, *Apaches of New York*, 62–67 (quotation); DeStefano, *Gangland New York*, 31–32; Asbury, *Gangs of New York*, 271–73, quoting Lewis.

331 "Is there a dago . . . kill somebody": *Tribune*, May 19, 1908.

331 Jack Sirocco and Chick Tricker . . . Jimmy Kelly gang: Ferrara, *Manhattan Mafia Guide*, 76–78, 84; Feather, "Mustache Pete's"; *NYT*, November 8, 1908, June 9, 1911, February 15, June 6, 7, 9, 1912, December 13, 1913; *Sun*, July 28, 1912; *Tribune*, June 7, 23, 1912; Keefe, *Starker*, 179.

331 Poggi . . . chief gunmen: *NYT*, November 8, 1908, February 15, June 6, 7, 9, 1912, *Sun*, April 4, 1912; *Tribune*, June 23, 1912.

331 "Big Jack" Zelig . . . took a bullet himself: Keefe, *Starker*, 15, 49, 55–60, 93, 105–10, 118 ("made it possible"), 120, 126–30, 141–49; Feather, "Mustache Pete's"; *Tribune*, June 7, 23, 1912; *Sun*, May 15, 1908 (Crazy Butch death), July 28, 1912; Lewis, *Apaches of New York*, 220–21 (Crazy Butch death); Fried, *Rise and Fall*, 31–32; DeStefano, *Gangland New York*, 32–33; Wallace, *Greater Gotham*, 587–88 (Zelig); Jerry Kuntz, "Crazy Butch, the Darby Kid, and Harry the Soldier," *Asbury's The Gangs of New York—Annotated*, last modified January 4, 2020, https://gangsannotated .blog/2020/01/04/crazy-butch-the-darby-kid-and-harry-the-soldier/ (Crazy Butch death).

333 "Kid Twist died . . . grew steadily worse": Van Loan, "Disarming New York," 690.

333 at first . . . avoided costly, bloody wars: Dash, *First Family*, 251–53.

CHAPTER 26: "SEND FOR THE DAGO!"

335 Frances Connors . . . Not a scrap: *World*, April 14 (night), 15 (7th home), 1903; *NYT*, April 15, 1903; *Sun*, April 15, 16 ("M.U.R.L."), 1903; *Tribune*, April 15, 1903; Carey, 113–14; William J. Flynn, *The Barrel Mystery* (New York: James A. McCann, 1919), 1–7. Some sources claim that the victim's genitals had been removed and stuffed inside his mouth, but no such report appeared in newspapers at the time.

336 William Marsh Rice . . . Albert Patrick: Carey, 96–110; *NYT*, September 28, 1900; Martin L. Friedland, *The Death of Old Man Rice: A True Story of Criminal Justice in America* (New York: NYU Press, 1996), 35, 47–48, 55.

337 "Italian Sherlock Holmes": Talty, *Black Hand*, xiv.

337 Italy's jails . . . sent back home: *Sun*, August 7, 1901.

337 mastered all the regional dialects . . . Campania: Talty, *Black Hand*, 13; *NYT*, March 12, 1944.

337 police bluster ... "fix it myself": *Tribune*, June 21, 1898 (quotation); *WAPO*, June 28, July 12, 1914; *NYT*, March 12, 1944.

337 frequently embedded ... mental file: Talty, *Black Hand*, xiv, 11–13, 16–17, 21; Arrigo Petacco, *Joe Petrosino*, trans. Charles Lam Markmann (1972; repr., New York: Macmillan, 1974), 36–40; Lardner and Reppetto, *NYPD*, 128 (informer); Mele, *Italian Squad*, 13 (same); *Sun*, November 6, 1906 (disguised as laborer); *World*, March 13, 1909 (final results) (disguises); *NYT*, March 12, 1944.

338 collared a swindler ... fourteen years earlier: *Tribune*, May 22, 1903.

338 he spotted ... Sineni confessed: *Tribune*, August 17, 1903; *NYT*, August 17, 1903.

338 In 1893 ... insurance fraud ring: Frank Marshall White, "New York's Secret Police," *Harper's Weekly*, March 9, 1907, 350; *WAPO*, June 28, 1914.

338 cleared a young Italian ... he was saved: *NYT*, December 29, 1897, January 27, 28, 1898, March 12, 1909; *Tribune*, January 28, 1898; Talty, *Black Hand*, 19–22. It took months for Carbone to be released, during which time he went insane, as did Ciaramello during his incarceration. Thomas Hunt, "'Keep Him Away! He's Coming to Take Me to the *Chair*!,'" *Informer online*, November 2018, 12–22, https://drive.google.com/file/d/1Fr4_Nupz7_a—0cwSDmv8CDQIzDwCM4j/view?usp=sharing.

339 McClusky ... a remarkable case: *NYT*, January 28, 1898.

339 In mid-1900 ... Czolgosz was inspired: *Tribune*, August 6, 21, 1900; *Sun*, August 6, 1900; *NYT*, March 14, 1909, March 12, 1944; *WAPO*, June 28, 1914; *World*, March 13, 1909 (final results). Some sources contend that Roosevelt suggested Petrosino for the mission. Talty, *Black Hand*, 72–75. There is no documentation of this.

340 reportedly wept ... McKinley's shooting: *WAPO*, June 28, 1914; *NYT*, March 14, 1909.

340 taciturn ... rarely one to laugh: *NYT*, March 12, 1944; Arthur Train, *Courts and Criminals* (New York: McKinlay, Stone & Mackenzie, 1912), 109. See also *World*, March 13, 1909 (final results) ("He resented familiarity on the part of his staff").

340 "There's so much ... a woman into it": Quoted in Talty, *Black Hand*, 24.

340 sixth-grade education ... Verdi: *NYT*, March 14, 1909, March 12, 1944; *WAPO*, June 28, 1914; Talty, *Black Hand*, xix, 5, 24.

340 "Send for the dago!": Talty, *Black Hand*, 26, 32.

340 "The gangsters who ... finished beating them": Petacco, *Joe Petrosino*, 31.

341 Carey held ... came in all shapes: Carey, xiii (ten thousand murder cases), 46–47, 122, 171, 211–12, 304–18.

341 held ... high regard: Carey, 115, 121.

341 disliked ... taken him ten years: *WAPO*, June 28, 1914; Talty, *Black Hand*, 14.

341 "in part ... probing mind": Humbert S. Nelli, *The Business of Crime: Italians and Syndicate Crime in the United States* (1976; repr., Chicago: University of Chicago Press, 1981), 95.

341 "Do you know ... some change": Petacco, *Joe Petrosino*, 32; Talty, *Black Hand*, 40–41.

342 Carey, arriving early ... spotted a sugar barrel: Carey, 113–14 (quotations); *World*, April 14, 1903 (night) (Petrosino translated); *NYT*, April 15, 16, 1903; *Sun*, April

15, 16 (description of café), 1903; *Tribune*, April 15, 16, 1903; Dash, *First Family*, 8–12. Some sources list the shipping lot number as G.233.

343 **Inzerillo was by turns . . . didn't recognize him**: Carey, 117; Dash, *First Family*, 19; *WAPO*, August 2, 1914 (photo of Petrosino diary); *NYT*, April 16, 1903; *Tribune*, April 16, 1903; *Sun*, April 16, 1903.

343 **US Secret Service . . . nabbed in Yonkers**: Flynn, *Barrel Mystery*, 18–20; Critchley, *Origin*, 39–42; Dash, *First Family*, 12–13; *Tribune*, April 16, 1903.

344 **Catania . . . bushes in Bay Ridge**: *NYT*, July 24, 25, 26, 27, 1902, April 16, 1903; *Tribune*, April 16, 1903; *World*, April 16, 1903 (night); Critchley, *Origin*, 42; Dash, *First Family*, 105–6.

344 **"as little compunction . . . killing a dog"**: *Sun*, April 16, 1903.

345 **Petrosino was convinced . . . same man**: *Tribune*, April 16, 1903; *Sun*, April 16, 1903; *World*, April 16, 1903 (night); *NYT*, April 16, 1903.

345 **Giuseppe Morello was a slight . . . "the Clutch Hand"**: Critchley, *Origin*, 36–38; Dash, *First Family*, "Rogues' Gallery" introduction (Giuseppe Morello), 4–5, 44–53; Joseph Bonanno, *A Man of Honor: The Autobiography of Joseph Bonanno*, with Sergio Lalli (New York: St. Martin's Paperbacks, 1983), 100 (nickname, physical description); 1910 US Census, South Bend, Fulton, Ga., Enum. Dist. 131 (Giuseppe Marello [Giuseppe Morello]); *WAPO*, June 7 (murders in Italy), July 12 (Petrosino diary notes of questioning of Morello), 1914; Flynn, *Barrel Mystery*, 244–59 (murders in Italy); Justin Cascio, "The Murder of Giovanni Vella," *Mafia Genealogy*, last modified February 8, 2016, https://mafiagenealogy.wordpress.com/2016/02/08/the-murder-of-giovanni-vella/.

345 **Stepson of Bernardo Terranova . . . the Sicilian for six years**: Critchley, *Origin*, 38–39, 51–52; Dash, *First Family*, 44–45, 54–65, 88–95; *Tribune*, June 12, 30, 1900 (Irish maid and arrests); *WAPO*, July 12, 1914 (Petrosino diary); Wallace, *Greater Gotham*, 592–93. The arrested woman may have been the Margaret Callahan listed in the 1905 New York State Census as living with her six children at 1935 Third Avenue in Manhattan, an address between 106th and 107th Streets in East Harlem.

346 **First Family . . . Genovese crime family**: Critchley, *Origin*, 36; Dash, *First Family*, 95–96, 294–95; Downey, *Gangster City*, 18; Ferrara, *Manhattan Mafia Guide*, 34–37 (Luciano), 60–66 (Genovese), 109–10 (Masseria), 117–21 (Morello), 201 (lineage); Mike Dickson, "Genovese Family: One of the 'Five Families,'" *American Mafia History: Chronicle of Events and Biographies Related to the American Mafia*, last modified August 31, 2015, https://americanmafiahistory.com/genovese-family/.

346 **"a continuous link . . . organized crime history"**: Critchley, *Origin*, 36.

346 **By 1902 . . . recommended by Corleone mafiosi**: Critchley, 38; *WAPO*, July 12, 1914 (Petrosino diary) (8 Prince Street); Dash, *First Family*, 96 (gang of thirty, related or recommended); *Sun*, April 16, 1903 (8 Prince); *NYT*, April 16, 1903 (thirty); Ferrara, *Manhattan Mafia Guide*, 119–20 (spaghetti saloon); Flynn, *Barrel Mystery*, 24–25 (8 Prince); Carey, 113, 117 (saloon-restaurant on Prince); *WAPO*, April 26, 1914 (restaurant description).

347 **Morello married . . . child's diaper**: Critchley, *Origin*, 52–53, 152; Dash, *First Family*, "Rogues' Gallery" introduction (Lina Morello), 101–3, 212–13; Flynn, *Barrel*

Mystery, 206 (letters in baby's diaper); *WAPO*, May 24, 1914 (in child's clothing), February 5, 1922 (same). The baby appears to have been one-year-old Carmela Morello. 1910 US Census, New York, N.Y., Ward 12, Dist. 345 (Carmela Morello).

347 **Ignazio Lupo . . . flashy presence:** US World War I Draft Registration Card for Ignazio Lupo, September 12, 1918 (Ancestry.com) (b. March 21, 1877); Jon Black, "Ignazio Lupo," *Gangrule: The History of the Mafia*, accessed December 29, 2020, https://www.gangrule.com/biographies/ignazio-lupo (8 and 9 Prince Street, Lupo police record); "Ignatius 'Lupo the Wolf' Lupo," Find a Grave, last modified November 20, 1999; Critchley, *Origin*, 42, 46–47, 52; Dash, *First Family*, 98–101; Flynn, *Barrel Mystery*, 28 (businessman, physical appearance); *NYT*, April 17, 1903 (9 Prince).

347 **By contrast, Morello . . . plain worker's garments:** Dash, *First Family*, 100; Flynn, *Barrel Mystery*, 28.

347 **"They say . . . if I could be one":** *WAPO*, July 12, 1914 (Petrosino diary).

347 **Lupo was a fugitive . . . last person seen with:** *NYT*, April 20, 1903; National Archives and Records Administration II, RG 87, Daily Reports of the US Secret Service Agents, 1875–1936, Publication no. T915A, reel 109, William Flynn, report (hereafter, Flynn Daily Reports) for April 19, 1903. Flynn typically completed his official report for a given day's activities on the following day and forwarded it to Thomas Wilkie, chief of the Secret Service in Washington, D.C. The citations to the Flynn reports in these notes correspond with the earlier of the two dates—in other words, the date for which the report was prepared, not the completion date.

348 **"only needed to touch you . . . poisoned":** *WAPO*, February 5, 1922.

348 **"they crossed themselves . . . priests for protection":** Carey, 111.

348 **series of grocery stores . . . target for blackmail:** Talty, *Black Hand*, 57; Dash, *First Family*, 98–100, 103–4; Flynn, *Barrel Mystery*, 27, 29; *WAPO*, May 3, July 12, 1914; Jon Black, "The Grocery Conspiracy," *Gangrule*, accessed December 29, 2020, https://www.gangrule.com/articles/the-grocery-conspiracy.

348 **barbershop and cobbler . . . laundered:** Flynn, *Barrel Mystery*, 27–29; Dash, *First Family*, 151–52; *WAPO*, April 26 (laundered money, $200,000), July 12, 1914 (Petrosino notes); Jon Black, "Giuseppe Morello," *Gangrule*, accessed December 29, 2020, https://www.gangrule.com/biographies/giuseppe-morello.

348 **He made it a habit . . . "do it for him":** *WAPO*, February 5, 1922.

348 **real estate company . . . Ignatz Florio Co-operative:** Dash, *First Family*, 152–54; Critchfield, *Origin*, 45–46; *WAPO*, July 12, 1914; Flynn, *Barrel Mystery*, 28–30, 183–84.

349 **Rather than print . . . inside olive oil cans:** *WAPO*, April 26, 1914 (notes imported); Flynn, *Barrel Mystery*, 18 (same); *NYT*, April 3, 1910 (olive oil cans); Carey, 119 (same).

349 **Stella Frauto . . . Vito Cascioferro:** Critchley, *Origin*, 39–41, 51 (Morello, Frauto, and Cascioferro), 68, 261n248 ("macaroni"); *Dickerman's United States Treasury Counterfeit Detector* 19, no. 6 (June 1902): 15 (Frauto and Cascioferro); *NYT*, November 28, 1902; Dash, *First Family*, 98, 144, 189; Thomas Hunt, *Wrongly Executed? The*

Long-Forgotten Context of Charles Sberna's 1939 Electrocution (Whiting, Vt.: Seven-Seven-Eight, 2016), 65–68; Jon Black, "Vito Cascioferro," *Gangrule,* accessed December 29, 2020, https://www.gangrule.com/biographies/vito-cascioferro; Flynn Daily Reports, reel 108, April 6 (Morello and Frauto gang), May 21 (Cascioferro arrested), 1902.

349 first two weeks . . . Cascioferro was often seen: Carey, 112; Dash, *First Family,* 15–16; Flynn Daily Reports, reel 109, April 6, 8, 9, 13, 1903 (Cascioferro with Morello).

CHAPTER 27: THE NEWCOMER

351 afternoon of April 13 . . . leaving the butcher shop: Flynn Daily Reports, reel 109, April 13 (talking earnestly), 14 (unusual activity), 1903; *Tribune,* April 16, 1903; *NYT,* April 16, 1903; *Sun,* April 16, 1903; *World,* April 16, 17, 1903 (night eds.); Flynn, *Barrel Mystery,* 9–10. Although the newspaper accounts are mostly consistent with one another, they vary from the Secret Service agents' daily reports. The discussion in text draws mainly from the latter.

In his 1919 book on the case, Flynn claimed to have personally participated in the surveillance on the night of the murder, which he placed erroneously on April 12. But neither the contemporary newspaper accounts nor his daily reports mentions his presence. See also *WAPO,* April 19, 1914, where Flynn makes the same claim.

352 Carey would write . . . went home: *Carey,* 112–17. Carey's version of events differs in significant detail from that of Flynn and the original newspaper accounts. According to Carey, the Newcomer answered to the description of a traveling agent for the Morello counterfeiting gang the Secret Service had been eager to locate. Although the newspapers quoted the Secret Service agents as insisting that they saw the Newcomer for the first time on April 13, Carey wrote that they'd seen him in the butcher shop the night before, talking to Lupo the Wolf and another gang member.

352 After a photograph . . . "Morello et al. last evening": *World,* April 14 (night) (photo of victim), 16 (morgue), 1903; Flynn Daily Reports, reel 109, April 14, 1903 (quotation); *NYT,* April 16, 1903 (morgue); *Tribune,* April 16, 1903 (same). See also Carey, 114–15; Flynn, *Barrel Mystery,* 9–10; Dash, *First Family,* 17–19. Flynn's claim that he recognized the man in the newspaper photo as the person he'd seen at the Stanton Street butcher shop (*WAPO,* April 19, 1914) is dubious, since he was not present for the surveillance.

352 Bertillon measurements . . . did not match: Flynn, *Barrel Mystery,* 8; *WAPO,* April 19, 1914.

352 thirteen of the gang's members . . . Tomasso "Thomas" Petto: *Sun,* April 16 ("murderous-looking"), 17, May 8 (Petto), 1903, October 24, 1905 (Petto); Dash, *First Family,* 4 (Petto), 23–29 (arrests); *World,* April 16 (initial arrests), 20 (thirteen total arrested), 25 (Petto), 1903 (night eds.); Flynn, *Barrel Mystery,* 10–11; *NYT,* April 16, 17, 1903; *Tribune,* April 16, 1903; Thomas Hunt, "Petto, Tomasso (1879–1905)," *The American Mafia: The History of Organized Crime in the United States,* last

modified 2018, http://mob-who.blogspot.com/2015/12/tomasso-petto-1879-1905.
html; Flynn Daily Reports, reel 109, April 20, 29, May 5, 6, 1903 (Petto/Perrino).

353 heavily armed . . . ill and bedridden: *Sun*, April 16, 1903. See also Flynn, *Barrel
Mystery*, 11–12; Flynn Daily Reports, reel 109, April 15, 16, 1903; *NYT*, April 16,
17, 1903; *Tribune*, April 16, 1903.

353 Inzerillo . . . bailed out by Big Tim: *Tribune*, April 16, 1903 (arrest); Flynn Daily
Reports, reel 109, April 26, 1903 (bailed out).

353 Cascioferro . . . returned to Sicily: Flynn Daily Reports, reel 109, April 16, 17, 18,
21, 23, 1903 (Cascioferro not found); Dash, *First Family*, 189 (escape to Sicily, Sicilian Mafia).

353 grudge against Joe Petrosino . . . in his wallet: Petacco, *Joe Petrosino*, 90.

353 Searches of . . . Carey visited: Flynn Daily Reports, reel 109, April 16, 17, 21, 23,
1903 (searches); *NYT*, April 16 (cigars), 17, 1903; *Sun*, April 16, 1903 ("M.U.R.L.");
Carey, 117 (scooped up sawdust).

354 jubilant . . . Flynn said he was certain: *Sun*, April 16, 1903 (New York police);
World, April 17, 1903 (night) (Flynn).

354 "the most desperate and bloodthirsty . . . East Side": *Tribune*, April 16, 1903.

354 "Poora feller . . . I no know him": Carey, 119–20. See also Flynn, *Barrel Mystery*, 12;
Sun, April 16, 23, 1903; *NYT*, April 23, May 8, 1903.

354 an anonymous letter . . . red ink: Flynn, *Barrel Mystery*, 13–14 (letter to Petrosino,
prison interview); Flynn Daily Reports, reel 109, April 20, 1903 (anonymous letter,
"can tell you all," red ink); *Sun*, April 21 ("That is my brother-in-law"), 23 (angry
letter), 1903; *World*, April 20, 21, 1903 (night eds.); *NYT*, April 21, 23 (letter from
Madonia, red ink), 1903; Dash, *First Family*, 25–28, 108. Some sources state that the
anonymous letter was addressed to McClusky, while Flynn writes that it was sent to
Petrosino. I have credited Flynn here based on his May 2, 1903, daily report, which
notes that Petrosino had just received another anonymous letter, "evidently from the
same person" who sent the earlier one naming Di Priemo.

355 Interviews by Petrosino . . . It was Madonia's wife: *World*, April 20, 21 (wife's fear,
sent telegram), 1903 (night eds.); *NYT*, April 21, 23, 1903; *Sun*, April 21, 23, 1903;
Carey, 115–16, 119 (Madonia letter); Dash, *First Family*, 107–8. According to Flynn,
the motive for the murder was revenge upon Di Priemo for squealing on the Morello
gang after he and other counterfeiters were arrested in Yonkers in January 1903.
Flynn, a relentless self-promoter, claims to have cleverly staged an interrogation of
Di Priemo to make it appear to the others that he confessed all he knew about the
gang. Because Di Priemo was in jail, the gang, "following the hereditary Sicilian
custom," proceeded to select his nearest male relative in America—Madonia—and
mark him for murder. Flynn, *Barrel Mystery*, 18–21. See also *WAPO*, April 26, 1914.
The theory finds little factual support, as the evidence suggests that Madonia was
killed because his own actions and demands antagonized Morello, not because he
was a substitute target.

355 "as sure as you live . . . batch we arrested": *World*, April 21, 1903 (night).

356 from the pocket of Petto . . . pawned on Tuesday: *World*, April 25, 26, 1903 (night eds.); *NYT*, April 26, 1903; *Tribune*, April 26, 1903; *Sun*, April 26, 1903 (gold watch); Carey, 118; see ibid., 46, 70, 83 (McCafferty). After Madonia's stepson identified the watch in New York, the Secret Service's Flynn claimed credit for having suggested the pawnshop visit the previous day. Flynn Daily Reports, reel 109, April 25, 1903.

357 Inspector McClusky . . . case solved: *Tribune*, April 26, 1903.

357 McCafferty . . . electric chair: *World*, April 25, 1903 (night).

357 As for Petto . . . John feared losing it: *Tribune*, April 26, May 9, 1903.

358 "obtained by the coroner . . . Mafia's vengeance": *NYT*, May 2, 1903.

358 coroner's jury found . . . accessories to the crime: *World*, May 8, 1903 (night); *Tribune*, May 9, 1903.

358 Petto was . . . indicted: *World*, June 25, 1903 (night).

358 Three key witnesses . . . suddenly clammed up: Carey, 120; *World*, May 1, 1903 (night); *NYT*, May 2, 8, 1903.

358 "There was a shuffling . . . fingers to his lips": Carey, 120.

358 One by one . . . Flynn blamed: Carey, 121; Flynn, *Barrel Mystery*, 14–16; *World*, January 29, 1904 (night) (Petto discharged); *Sun*, January 20, 1904 (coroner's physician).

359 "I was in hopes . . . keep them silent": *World*, January 29, 1904 (night).

359 Carey continued his work . . . heads of dead hogs: Carey, 126–29; *NYT*, December 14, 1952.

CHAPTER 28: THE BLACK HAND

360 "If you don't meet" . . . "Beware of Mano Nera": Nelli, *Business of Crime*, 75–76, quoting *Herald*, September 13, 1903.

361 Again Cappiello declined . . . "in constant expectation of death": Talty, *Black Hand*, 30–31 (quotation); Nelli, *Business of Crime*, 76. See also *NYT*, September 14, 27, 1903; *World*, September 18, 1903.

361 The method . . . considerable bank account: Nelli, *Business of Crime*, 76–77; Critchley, *Origin*, 22; Ferrara, *Manhattan Mafia Guide*, 18–19; *Tribune*, August 21, 1904 (illustrations); *World*, August 27, 1904 (night) ("Dear Madame"); *WAPO*, July 19, 1914.

362 perpetrators were usually wanted . . . compliant victims: *NYT*, January 6, 1908, March 3, 1907; *WAPO*, July 12, 1914; Nelli, *Business of Crime*, 79–80.

362 Explosive devices . . . dynamite sticks: *WAPO*, July 26, 1914.

362 The term "Black Hand" . . . championed the poor: Gaetano D'Amato, "The 'Black Hand' Myth," *North American Review* 187, no. 629 (April 1908): 544; Lindsay Denison, "The Black Hand," *Everybody's Magazine* 19, no. 3 (September 1908): 293; *NYT*, September 27, 1903; Nelli, *Business of Crime*, 71–72.

362 "a member of . . . Black Hand of Berlin": *NYT*, March 28, 1885.

362 "Scores of Italian murderers . . . running them down": *WAPO*, July 12, 1914.

363 first one in New York . . . attributed to the Black Hand: Nelli, *Business of Crime*, 75, 77; Talty, *Black Hand*, 31; Critchley, *Origin*, 22. The term "Black Hand" was applied to the Cappiello case in *Herald*, September 13, 1903; *World*, September 18, 1903 (night); and *NYT*, September 27, 1903.

363 Mafia "is not unknown . . . alternative is death": *World*, September 18, 1903 (night).

363 Barrel Murder case . . . crystallize New Yorkers' interest: Nelli, *Business of Crime*, 73.

363 became the preferred term . . . supplanting the word "Mafia": Nelli, 77.

363 Flynn . . . referred to the early New York Mafia: *WAPO*, April 19, May 10, 31, June 7, 14, 1914, February 5, 1922; Flynn, *Barrel Mystery*, 15; Critchley, *Origin*, 20–21, 29.

363 *The Black Hand* . . . "a Mafia melodrama": *Sun*, February 7, 9, 1904.

363 unlike the Mafia . . . modus operandi: Lardner and Reppetto, *NYPD*, 128; Reppetto, *American Mafia*, 37; Wallace, *Greater Gotham*, 589–92; Critchley, *Origin*, 21.

363 "There is no big central . . . 'Black Hand'": *NYT*, January 6, 1908. See also McAdoo, *Guarding a Great City*, 151; Denison, "The Black Hand," 291–301; "The Black Hand Scourge," *Cosmopolitan*, June 1909, 31–32.

363 Black Handers were small groups . . . They did not coordinate with: Critchley, *Origin*, 23, 26–30, 35; Nelli, *Business of Crime*, 77; *WAPO*, June 28, 1914.

363 Morello counterfeiting gang . . . Black Hand extortion methods: *Tribune*, May 27, 1906; Critchley, *Origin*, 30.

363 Lupo the Wolf . . . merchant failed to appear: Critchley, *Origin*, 31; Dash, *First Family*, 103–4; *Sun*, March 17, November 13, 18, 1909; *Tribune*, November 23, 1909 (released); *NYT*, March 8, 1906 (kidnapping); *World*, March 8, 1906 (night) (same). According to Dash, Morello was also likely involved in the kidnapping. *First Family*, 147.

364 Lupo claimed . . . cost of doing business: *Sun*, November 13, 1909 (Black Hand threats); Nelli, *Business of Crime*, 78–79 (same).

364 Petrosino was constantly urging . . . alarmist: *NYT*, October 15, 18, 1905, March 3, 1907; *WAPO*, July 19, August 9, 1914.

364 Ciro . . . murdered or disappeared: *World*, August 11, 1904 (evening). The newspaper transposed and misspelled his last name. See various contemporary references to Ciro Poggioreale at Ancestry.com.

364 panic . . . "epidemic of kidnapping and blackmail": *Tribune*, August 19, 1904 (quotation); Talty, *Black Hand*, 33.

364 Antonio Mannino . . . father had schooled him: *NYT*, August 11 ("Come along"), 12 ("I would rather"), 16, 18, 19, 20, 1904; *Sun*, August 12, 19, 1904; *Tribune*, August 18 ("Stop chasing"), 19 ("slowly cut"), 20 (father schooled), 1904; *World*, August 11, 1904 (evening) ($50,000); Talty, *Black Hand*, 33 (Petrosino discouraged father); Mele, *Italian Squad*, 16 (same).

366 connections to the Barrel Murder case . . . Vito Laduca: *NYT*, August 13, 14, 16, 17, 18, 1904; Critchley, *Origin*, 30–31; Dash, *First Family*, 97.

366 summer of 1904 . . . "Black Hand Fever": Mele, *Italian Squad*, 17.

366 Brooklyn candy store . . . suffocating: *Tribune*, August 21, 1904.

366 Bronx contractor's wife . . . liked the man: Talty, *Black Hand*, 36; *NYT*, November 24, 1904.

366 wives . . . to the countryside: *Tribune*, August 20, 1904.

366 One prominent banker . . . guarded by detectives: *Tribune*, August 21, 1904.

366 Joseph Graffi . . . stabbed to death: *NYT*, August 29, 1904.

366 Greenwich, Connecticut . . . pistols: *NYT*, August 31, 1904.

366 deputy sheriffs . . . carry firearms: *Tribune*, July 9, 1905.

366 Some patrolled . . . shotguns: Talty, *Black Hand*, xvi, 67–68; *Tribune*, July 9, 1905; *NYT*, October 15, 1905.

366 bodyguards . . . watchdogs: *NYT*, March 3, 1907.

367 thirteen-year-old . . . made up the story: *Tribune*, February 9, 1904.

367 "It has come to pass . . . and speedily": *Brooklyn Daily Eagle*, October 8, 1904. See also *NYT*, October 8, 1904.

367 Petrosino and others advocated . . . McAdoo turned down: Talty, *Black Hand*, 39–43; Whalen and Whalen, *First Fifty Years*, 41; Mele, *Italian Squad*, 17; *NYT*, September 14, 1904 ("moral movement"), September 22, 1905 ("If they would form"), January 6, 1908 ("The trouble is").

368 In September 1904 . . . the Italian Squad: *NYT*, September 14, 1904; *Sun*, September 14, 1904.

368 eight thousand NYPD officers . . . seventeen spoke Italian: *Tribune*, August 21, 1904.

368 incorruptible associates . . . Bonnoil . . . Cassidy: Petacco, *Joe Petrosino*, 59; Talty, *Black Hand*, 45–46; *Tribune*, February 16, 1896 (Bonnoil), October 28, 1905 (Bonnoil, Peter Dondero), January 15, 1906 (Bonnoil); *Sun*, July 14, 1903, August 12, October 15, 1904, September 29, 30, 1905, June 29, 1906 (all Bonnoil); *NYT*, July 20, 1895 (Bonnoil), December 20, 1906 (Dondero); New York, N.Y., Index to Birth Certificates, Morris [Maurice] Bonnoil, certif. no. 26176; 1910 US Census, New York, N.Y., Ward 12, Enum. Dist. 620 (Maurice Bonnoil). On Cassidy being Italian, see *Sun*, December 31, 1904. He was typically assigned to Italian sections. See, for example, ibid.; *Tribune*, November 27, December 13, 1902; *World*, October 14, 1902 (night). Other sources list different or additional original members of the Italian Squad. See Mele, *Italian Squad*, 38; *WAPO*, August 9, 1914.

368n Bat Masterson . . . better watch out: *Sun*, February 7, 1905.

368 a half million . . . ten thousand: *NYT*, March 3, 1907; Whalen and Whalen, *First Fifty Years*, 41.

368 "mysterious six" . . . Petrosino's own apartment: Talty, *Black Hand*, 46 (quotation); *WAPO*, August 9, 1914.

369 176 Waverly Place . . . found new quarters: *Sun*, October 4, 1905; *Tribune*, October 4, 1905. The raid probably took place around June, as O'Brien was transferred in June 1905. *NYT*, June 24, 1905. The sources are in conflict as to the office spaces used by the Italian Squad during this period. See *Sun*, October 4, 1905 (office in police headquarters); *NYT*, December 20, 1906 (room above a saloon on Centre Street); *WAPO*, August 9, 1914 (second-floor room on Lafayette Street).

369 Cerino Nizzari . . . "will look after him, all right": *Tribune*, September 11, 1905 (quotation); *NYT*, September 11, 1905. The newspapers misspelled the baker's name as Serrino Nizzarri.

369 Nizzari continued . . . years later: New York, N.Y., Extracted Death Index, Cerino Nizzari, March 3, 1915, certif. no. 6672; *Trow's for 1905–'06* (Cirillo [*sic*] Nizzari, macaroni, 98 Bayard Street); *R & L Polk & Co.'s Trow General Directory of New York City, 1917* (New York: Polk, 1917) (Nizzari widow, 98 Bayard Street).

369 February 1906 . . . slept upstairs: *Tribune*, February 15, 1906; *Sun*, February 15, 1906.

370 ingenious plan . . . Napoli's arrest: *Sun*, February 17, 1906.

370 his squad made hundreds: *NYT*, March 3, 1907. See also, for instance, *Tribune*, June 5, August 2, 1906, January 14, April 19, May 1, September 4, 1907, June 13, 1908; *Sun*, November 26, 1906.

370 size of his squad . . . Vachris: *Sun*, December 20, 1906; *WAPO*, August 9, 1914; Talty, *Black Hand*, 62, 96; Mele, *Italian Squad*, 41, 171–74.

370 "Gee. Dey've pinched . . . once a month!": *Tribune*, January 17, 1907.

371 "His exploits . . . everyone he passed": *NYT*, March 12, 1944.

371 Radin claimed . . . Enrico Caruso: *NYT*, March 12, 1944.

371 story has grown . . . cape and suit: See, for example, Talty, *Black Hand*, 98–99.

371 Caruso did, in fact, receive . . . Petrosino played no role: *NYT*, March 11, 1910; Sydney Reid, "The Death Sign," *Independent* 70, no. 3253 (April 6, 1911): 712. Petrosino was no longer alive at the time of the Caruso incident.

371 Black Hand cases . . . 33 Black Hand offenses: "Black Hand Scourge," 37–38; Nelli, *Business of Crime*, 85.

371 "When one remembers . . . edge of the city": "Black Hand Scourge," 38–39.

372 "a demoralizing disgrace . . . so indefinite an organization": Denison, "The Black Hand," 292, 300.

372 "at the same time denouncing . . . if it really existed": *Tribune*, February 7, 1908.

372 mass meeting . . . sue the city for damages: *Sun*, February 7, 1908.

372 "Are we not dagoes? . . . can blackmail us": *NYT*, June 28, 1908.

372 "raise hell": *NYT*, September 7, 1934 (Bingham obituary).

373 "Russian Hebrews" . . . "time of peace": Theodore A. Bingham, "Foreign Criminals in New York," *North American Review* 188, no. 634 (September 1908): 383–85.

373 he retracted . . . inaccurate statistics: *NYT*, September 17, 1908.

373 "The employment of Irish . . . capital of Italy": D'Amato, "'Black Hand' Myth," 546.

373 Bingham acknowledged . . . civil service exam: Bingham, "Foreign Criminals," 393.

373 "Petrosino has done good work . . . destroys their usefulness": *Tribune*, February 7, 1908.

373 The first thing . . . acquaint himself: Bingham, "Foreign Criminals," 394.

373 "Fresh *parsley* . . . beautiful *parsley*!": Talty, *Black Hand*, 11; Dash, *First Family*, 179, both citing Petacco, *Joe Petrosino*, 40; *NYT*, March 19, 1911 ("petrosello").

373 Mayor McClellan could . . . without being recognized: *Tribune*, July 15, 1908.

373 **Bingham proposed . . . secret police force:** *Tribune*, February 7, 1908; Bingham, "Foreign Criminals," 394; Talty, *Black Hand*, 166–69.

374 **But Big Tim Sullivan . . . refused to appropriate:** *NYT*, September 2, 1908; Talty, *Black Hand*, 167–71.

374 **"crooked politicians":** *NYT*, September 2, 1908.

374 **Bingham privately raised . . . headed by Petrosino:** *Tribune*, February 20, 1909; *NYT*, February 20, 1909; Talty, *Black Hand*, 171–72.

374 **The consensus . . . lax immigration laws:** "The Black Hand," editorial, *NYT*, April 5, 1908. See also "Italo-American," letter to the editor, *NYT*, June 2, 1908; "Black Hand Scourge," 41; D'Amato, "'Black Hand' Myth," 544, 546, 549; Arthur Woods, "The Problem of the Black Hand," *McClure's* 33, no. 1 (May 1909): 40–47.

374 **"The United States has become . . . and Calabria":** *NYT*, January 6, 1908.

374 **"I have already got . . . committed in Italy":** *NYT*, March 3, 1907.

374 **trip to Ellis Island:** *Tribune*, March 10, 1908.

374 **penal certificates . . . send someone directly:** *NYT*, March 16, 1909; Petacco, *Joe Petrosino*, 114–17; Dash, *First Family*, 181–82; Talty, *Black Hand*, 172.

375 **"lots of money . . . a 'monk' at that":** *Tribune*, February 20, 1909.

375 **Antonio Comito . . . Clutch Hand himself:** *WAPO*, May 10, 17, June 7, July 12, 1914; Dash, *First Family*, 154–75; *NYT*, March 17, 1909 (severe beating).

376 **"Tell me something" . . . "carogna":** *WAPO*, June 7, 1914. See also Downey, *Gangster City*, 29–30; Talty, *Black Hand*, 176–77, 229–30; Flynn, *Barrel Mystery*, 113n.

377 **February 9:** Talty, *Black Hand*, 174.

CHAPTER 29: ENDINGS

378 **mixed feelings . . . Jewish businessman:** Talty, *Black Hand*, 151–52, 165 (marriage, baby); Petacco, *Joe Petrosino*, 118–19 (poor mood); *World*, March 13, 1909 (final results) ("Some day").

378 **Traveling first-class . . . Hôtel de France:** *NYT*, March 14, 1909; Petacco, *Joe Petrosino*, 119–20, 126–35; Dash, *First Family*, 183–86; Thom L. Jones, "The Sun King of the Mafia," *Gangsters Inc.*, last modified November 10, 2010, http://gangstersinc.ning.com/profiles/blogs/the-sun-king-of-the-mafia.

379 **cover was blown already . . . disoriented there:** Nelli, *Business of Crime*, 97; Petacco, *Joe Petrosino*, 123–36; Talty, *Black Hand*, 182–90.

379 **The Italian authorities . . . unarmed:** Whalen and Whalen, *First Fifty Years*, 53 (500 lire); Talty, *Black Hand*, 191–93; Petacco, *Joe Petrosino*, 138–42 (quotation, 141); Dash, *First Family*, 186–88.

380 **in the habit . . . a colleague trail him:** *World*, March 13, 1909 (final results).

380 **March 12 . . . "dreaded criminal":** Petacco, *Joe Petrosino*, 145; Dash, *First Family*, 189.

380 **Around seven-thirty . . . "far from her daddy":** *World*, March 13, 1909 (final results); *NYT*, March 14, 15, 1909; *Sun*, March 14, 15, 1909; *Tribune*, March 14, 17 (gun in

hotel), 1909; Petacco, *Joe Petrosino*, 145–50 ("A kiss"); Talty, *Black Hand*, 106 (back to wall), 197–99.

382 **"Oh, my poor Joe!"** . . . *"il povero Petrosino!"*: *NYT*, March 14, 1909.

382 **American press . . . Bingham sought to downplay:** *NYT*, March 14, 15, 1909; *Tribune*, March 14, 15, 1909; *Sun*, March 14, 1909 (*La Tribuna*); Talty, *Black Hand*, 202–6 (reaction), 218–19, 225 (Bingham); Whalen and Whalen, *First Fifty Years*, 53 (Bingham); Petacco, *Joe Petrosino*, 180 (Bingham dismissal).

383 **funeral at old St. Patrick's . . . half-mast:** *NYT*, April 13, 1909; *Sun*, April 13, 1909; *Tribune*, April 13, 1909.

383 **"If Petrosino had died . . . manifested":** *NYT*, April 13, 1909.

383 **"Petrosino was a great . . . such a man as 'Joe' Petrosino":** *Tribune*, March 14, 1909.

383 **"most tragic . . . one of its bravest men":** Carey, 121.

383 **Big Tim Sullivan sponsored . . . $2,000 pension:** *WAPO*, June 28, 1914; Moses, *Unlikely Union*, 147.

383 **Petrosino's killers . . . Cascioferro for execution:** Talty, *Black Hand*, 219, 230, 243; Dash, *First Family*, 192–95; Petacco, *Joe Petrosino*, 165–84; Whalen and Whalen, *First Fifty Years*, 53; Downey, *Gangster City*, 31; Critchley, *Origin*, 66–69; *Tribune*, February 20, 1910.

384 **Comito recalled further . . . "it could never fail":** *WAPO*, June 7, 1914; Downey, *Gangster City*, 31. See also Jon Black, "Joe Petrosino Murder," *Gangrule*, accessed December 29, 2020, https://www.gangrule.com/events/petrosino-murder-1909.

384 **Carlo Costantino . . . Antonino Passananti:** *NYT*, April 7, 1909; Petacco, *Joe Petrosino*, 124–25, 152–53, 165–74; Jon Black, "Petrosino Murder" (and related entries for Costantino and Passananti); Dash, *First Family*, 189, 192–93; Critchley, *Origin*, 68–69; Jones, "Sun King"; *NYT*, December 31, 1911 ("whiskers").

384 **Cascioferro had an alibi . . . the gunman:** Petacco, *Joe Petrosino*, 170–71, 175–78, 187–95; Talty, *Black Hand*, 244; Critchley, *Origin*, 68; Nelli, *Business of Crime*, 97–98; Jones, "Sun King."

384 **Petrosino was the first . . . killed on foreign soil:** *NYT*, June 23, 2014.

384 **His positive legacy . . . "international crime and terrorism":** Anne T. Romano, *Italian Americans in Law Enforcement* (Bloomington, Ind.: Xlibris, 2010), 48–49 (quotation); Mele, *Italian Squad*, 72–73 (Bomb Squad); Talty, *Black Hand*, 153 (same).

385 **small triangular park . . . bronze relief portrait:** *NYT*, October 13, 2009; "Petrosino Square," New York City Department of Parks and Recreation online, accessed December 29, 2020, https://www.nycgovparks.org/parks/petrosino-square/history.

385 **police headquarters . . . rogues' gallery:** *NYT*, November 14, 1909; Frank Marshall White, "The Finest Police Headquarters in the World," *Harper's Weekly*, August 14, 1909, 27; Whalen and Whalen, *First Fifty Years*, 56.

386 **He took a job . . . Wall Street insurance company:** *Weekly Underwriter*, August 8, 1896, 70 (advertisement); *Baltimore Underwriter*, September 5, 1896, 118 (advertisement).

386 **private detective agency . . . "high-class service":** *Sun*, February 28, 1898 (quotation); *Trow's (formerly Wilson's) Business Directory of the Boroughs of Manhattan and the Bronx, City of New York* (New York: Trow, 1898), 350.

386 Manhattan real estate . . . potential candidate: *NYT,* May 8, 1910 (real estate, consulting); *World,* October 24, 1902 (night) (consulting); *Tribune,* January 29, 1900 (trotting), January 12, 1901 (potential candidate); *Sun,* January 15, April 17, 1900 (trotting); Inglis, "Celebrities at Home," 11–12 (investments, yachting).

386 "the incompetent head" . . . "police business": Inglis, "Celebrities at Home," 12.

387 New Jersey summer home . . . "precision, vigor, and balance": Inglis, 11–12.

387 stomach cancer . . . wife and five daughters: *NYT,* May 8, 1910; *Tribune,* May 8, 1910.

387 funeral . . . buried at Calvary Cemetery: *NYT,* May 11, 1910; *Tribune,* May 11, 1910.

387 "the greatest policeman . . . made the Detective Bureau famous": *NYT,* May 8, 1910 (quotations), October 14, 1933 (McLaughlin).

388 "last important figure" . . . "Supersede the Old": *NYT,* May 15, 1910.

388 Faurot's expert testimony . . . fingerprint evidence: Jeffery G. Barnes, "History," in *The Fingerprint Sourcebook,* ed. Alan McRoberts (Washington, D.C.: US Department of Justice), 1–17.

389 "The Work Inaugurated . . . Present System": *NYT,* May 15, 1910.

EPILOGUE

391 "Clubber" Williams . . . died in 1917: *NYT,* March 26, 1917.

391 Max Schmittberger . . . chief inspector: *NYT,* February 19, March 14, 1909, November 1, 1917.

391 returned to bribe taking . . . never proven: Dash, *Satan's Circus,* 107–11, 347; Murphy, *Scoundrels in Law,* 187, 302n122; Lardner and Reppetto, *NYPD,* 158; *NYT,* September 22, 25, December 15, 1906.

391 Big Bill Devery . . . June 1919: *NYT,* June 21, 1919.

391 Art Carey's being reassigned . . . December 13, 1952: Carey, 129–33; *NYT,* December 14, 1952; Lardner and Reppetto, *NYPD,* 222. For Woods, see Carey, 125–29, 141, 145–46; Reppetto, *American Police,* 158–63; Johnson, *Street Justice,* 107–13; *NYT,* May 13, 1942 (obituary). For the Rothstein case and Carey's involvement, see *NYT,* November 8, 16, 20, December 20, 22, 23, 1928; Lardner and Reppetto, *NYPD,* 222; Reppetto, *American Police,* 180–81; Whalen and Whalen, *First Fifty Years,* 143–48.

393 Thomas (the "Ox") Petto . . . knew too much: *Sun,* October 24, 1905; Carey, 121; *WAPO,* April 26, 1914; Dash, *First Family,* 122–23; Hunt, "Petto, Tomasso."

393 Morello and his partner Lupo . . . Calvary Cemetery: *NYT,* January 27, February 1, 2, 3, 20, 25, 1910; *Tribune,* February 20, 1910; *WAPO,* May 24, 31, June 7, 1914, February 5, 1922; Critchley, *Origin,* 47–50; 154–56, 180–81; Dash, *First Family,* "Rogues' Gallery" introduction, 208–27, 281–89, 304–11; Ferrara, *Manhattan Mafia Guide,* 37–39 (Terranova), 109–10, 193 (Masseria), 193–94 (Morello); Nelli, *Business of Crime,* 130–32, 197–98, 203; Reppetto, *American Mafia,* 77–78, 81; Jon Black, "The Morello and Lupo Trial," *Gangrule,* accessed December 29, 2020, https://www.gangrule.com/events/the-morello-lupo-trial-1910; Bonanno, *Man of Honor,* 98–107 (Morello).

394 Black Hand . . . factors: Talty, *Black Hand*, 221–22, 227–29, 231–43; Nelli, *Business of Crime*, 81–82, 98–100; Critchley, *Origin*, 29, 33–34; Frank Marshall White, "The Black Hand in Control in Italian New York," *Outlook*, August 16, 1913, 857–65; Frank Marshall White, "The Passing of the Black Hand," *Century*, January 1918, 331–37.

394 Paul Vaccarelli . . . labor-union leader: Ferrara, *Manhattan Mafia Guide*, 84–88; Hanson, *Heroic Gangster*, 127–28.

394 "dock strike conciliator . . . Big Tim Sullivan": *NYT*, April 5, 1936.

394 Monk Eastman . . . playing of taps: Hanson, *Heroic Gangster*, 137–38, 142–46, 204–5, 284–99; Arons, *Jews of Sing Sing*, 48–52; *Sun*, June 20, 1909; *NYT*, December 27, 31, 1920, January 2, 1921; *Brooklyn Daily Eagle*, December 27, 1920; *Herald*, December 27, 1920; *Tribune*, December 27, 1920, January 2, 1921.

395 "one of the toughest . . . violently": *Herald*, December 27, 1920.

395 Big Tim Sullivan . . . his confinement: *NYT*, September 14, 1913; Welch, *King of the Bowery*, 174–84.

395 Sullivan Act . . . others suspected: *NYT*, April 26, August 26, 1911; Welch, *King of the Bowery*, 144–46; Czitrom, "Underworlds and Underdogs," 556; Van Loan, "Disarming New York," 691–92.

396 sewing up their coat . . . carry their revolvers: Wallace, *Greater Gotham*, 601.

396 Jack Zelig . . . was scheduled to testify: Downey, *Gangster City*, 61–62; DeStefano, *Gangland New York*, 33–36; Keefe, *Starker*, 239–53.

396 Rosenthal was gunned down . . . Packard's running boards: The Becker-Rosenthal case has been the subject of numerous books and articles, among the more recent being Dash, *Satan's Circus*, and Keefe, *Starker*. See also Downey, *Gangster City*, 58–64; DeStefano, *Gangland New York*, 35–37; *NYT*, October 9, 1947 (obituary of Jacob "Baldy Jack" Rose, chief gambler witness against Becker).

SELECTED BIBLIOGRAPHY

BOOKS AND ARTICLES

Adams, Brewster. "The Street Gang as a Factor in Politics." *Outlook*, August 22, 1903.

Alexiou, Alice Sparberg. *Devil's Mile: The Rich, Gritty History of the Bowery*. New York: St. Martin's Press, 2018.

Ames, Daniel T. *Ames on Forgery: Its Detection and Illustration*. New York: Ames-Rollinson, 1900.

Anbinder, Tyler. *City of Dreams: The 400-Year Epic History of Immigrant New York*. Boston: Houghton Mifflin, 2016.

———. *Five Points: The Nineteenth-Century New York City Neighborhood That Invented Tap Dance, Stole Elections, and Became the World's Most Notorious Slum*. New York: Free Press, 2001.

Andrews, Avery D. "Theodore Roosevelt as Police Commissioner." *New-York Historical Society Quarterly* 42, no. 2 (April 1958): 117–41.

Arons, Ron. *The Jews of Sing Sing: Gotham Gangsters and Gonuvim*. Fort Lee, N.J.: Barricade Books, 2008.

Asbury, Herbert. *The Gangs of New York: An Informal History of the Underworld*. 1928. Reprint, New York: Vintage Books, 2008.

Axelrod, Alan. *The Gilded Age, 1876–1912: Overture to the American Century*. New York: Sterling, 2017.

Berman, Jay Stuart. *Police Administration and Progressive Reform: Theodore Roosevelt as Police Commissioner of New York*. Westport, Conn.: Greenwood Press, 1987.

———. "The Taming of the Tiger: The Lexow Committee Investigation of Tammany Hall and the Police Department of the City of New York." *Police Studies: The International Review of Police Development* 3, no. 4 (Winter 1981): 55–65.

Bingham, Theodore A. "Foreign Criminals in New York." *North American Review* 188, no. 634 (September 1908): 383–94.

Black, Jon. *Gangrule: The History of the Mafia*. Accessed December 29, 2020. https://www.gangrule.com/.

"The Black Hand Scourge." *Cosmopolitan*, June 1909, 31–41.

Blum, Deborah. *The Poisoner's Handbook: Murder and the Birth of Forensic Medicine in Jazz Age New York*. 2010. Reprint, New York: Penguin, 2011.

Bonanno, Joseph. *A Man of Honor: The Autobiography of Joseph Bonanno*. With Sergio Lalli. New York: St. Martin's Paperbacks, 1983.

Brands, H. W. *The Murder of Jim Fisk for the Love of Josie Mansfield*. New York: Anchor Books, 2011.

Burns, Ric, and James Sanders. *New York: An Illustrated History*. With Lisa Ades. New York: Knopf, 1999.

Burrows, Edwin G., and Mike Wallace. *Gotham: A History of New York City to 1898*. New York: Oxford University Press, 1999.

Byrnes, Thomas. "How to Protect a City from Crime." *North American Review* 159, no. 452 (July 1894): 100–107.

———. "The Menace of 'Coxeyism': Character and Methods of the Men." *North American Review* 158, no. 451 (June 1894): 696–701.

———. *Professional Criminals of America*. Revised ed. New York: G. W. Dillingham, 1895.

———. *Professional Criminals of America*. With introductions by Arthur M. Schlesinger Jr., and S. J. Perelman. 1886. Reprint, New York: Chelsea House, 1969.

Campbell, Helen. *Darkness and Daylight; or, Lights and Shadows of New York Life*. With additional material by Thomas W. Knox and Thomas Byrnes. 1892. Reprint, Hartford, Conn.: A. D. Worthington, 1897.

Carey, Arthur A. *Memoirs of a Murder Man*. In collaboration with Howard McLellan. Garden City, N.Y.: Doubleday, 1930.

Carr, Caleb. *The Alienist*. New York: Random House, 1994.

Collins, Holly. "A Study of Chateau Sur Mer, Part I: The Wetmore Family and Domestic Life at Chateau Sur Mer." Research report, Preservation Society of Newport County, June 14, 2000. https://www.newportmansions.org/documents/a_study_of _chateau_sur_mer_report_i_the_wetmore_family_and_their_domestics.pdf.

Collins, Paul. *The Murder of the Century: The Gilded Age Crime That Scandalized a City and Sparked the Tabloid Wars*. New York: Broadway Paperbacks, 2011.

Connable, Alfred, and Edward Silberfarb. *Tigers of Tammany: Nine Men Who Ran New York*. New York: Holt, Rinehart, 1967.

Costello, Augustine E. *Our Firemen: A History of the New York Fire Departments, Volunteer and Paid*. New York: Self-published, 1887.

———. *Our Police Protectors: History of the New York Police from the Earliest Period to the Present Time*. 2nd ed. [New York]: Self-published, 1885.

Crain, Esther. "The 'Bridge of Sighs' over a Downtown Prison." *Ephemeral New York*. (blog) January 4, 2012. https://ephemeralnewyork.wordpress.com/2012/01/04/the -bridge-of-sighs-over-a-downtown-prison.

———. *The Gilded Age in New York, 1870–1910*. New York: Black Dog & Leventhal, 2016.

Crapsey, Edward. *The Nether Side of New York; or, The Vice, Crime and Poverty of the Great Metropolis*. New York: Sheldon, 1872.

Critchley, David. *The Origin of Organized Crime in America: The New York City Mafia, 1891–1931*. New York: Routledge, 2009.

Cummings, Mary. *Saving Sin City: William Travers Jerome, Stanford White, and the Original Crime of the Century*. New York: Pegasus, 2018.

Czitrom, Daniel. *New York Exposed: The Gilded Age Police Scandal That Launched the Progressive Era*. New York: Oxford University Press, 2016.

———. "Underworlds and Underdogs: Big Tim Sullivan and Metropolitan Politics in New York, 1889–1913." *Journal of American History* 78, no. 2 (September 1991): 536–58.

D'Amato, Gaetano. "The 'Black Hand' Myth." *North American Review* 187, no. 629 (April 1908): 543–49.

Dash, Mike. *The First Family: Terror, Extortion, Revenge, Murder, and the Birth of the American Mafia*. New York: Random House, 2009.

———. *Satan's Circus: Murder, Vice, Police Corruption, and New York's Trial of the Century*. 2007. Reprint, New York: Three Rivers, 2008.

Denison, Lindsay. "The Black Hand." *Everybody's Magazine* 19, no. 3 (September 1908): 291–301.

DeStefano, Anthony M. *Gangland New York: The Places and Faces of Mob History*. Guilford, Conn.: Lyons Press, 2015.

DeVillo, Stephen Paul. *The Bowery: The Strange History of New York's Oldest Street*. New York: Skyhorse, 2017.

Donald, Aida D. *Lion in the White House: A Life of Theodore Roosevelt*. New York: Basic Books, 2007.

Downey, Patrick. *Gangster City: The History of the New York Underworld, 1900–1935*. Fort Lee, N.J.: Barricade Books, 2004.

Eldridge, Benjamin P., and William B. Watts. *Our Rival the Rascal: A Faithful Portrayal of the Conflict Between the Criminals of This Age and the Defenders of Society—the Police*. Boston: Pemberton, 1897.

English, T. J. *Paddy Whacked: The Untold Story of the Irish American Gangster*. 2005. Reprint, New York: HarperCollins, 2006.

Erroll, David, and John Erroll. *American Genius: Nineteenth-Century Bank Locks and Time Locks*. New York: Quantuck Lane Press, 2006.

Fales, William E., and George W. Curtis. "Chief Inspector Thomas Byrnes." *Harper's Weekly*, February 9, 1889.

Feather, Bill. "The Mustache Pete's [NYC]: Influential Italian Gangsters [pre Cosa Nostra]." *Mafia Membership Charts*. Last modified October 3, 2015. http://mafiamembershipcharts.blogspot.com/search?updated-max=2015-10-14T13:18:00-07:00&max-results=7.

Ferrara, Eric. *Manhattan Mafia Guide: Hits, Homes & Headquarters*. Charleston, S.C.: History Press, 2011.

Fisher, Jim. "Document Examination: The Molineux Case." *Jim Fisher—the Official Website*. Last modified January 7, 2008. http://jimfisher.edinboro.edu/forensics/mol1.html.

Flynn, William J. *The Barrel Mystery*. New York: James A. McCann, 1919.

Flynt, Josiah. *The World of Graft*. New York: McClure, Phillips, 1901.

Fosdick, Raymond B. "Passing of the Bertillon System of Identification." *Journal of the American Institute of Criminal Law and Criminology* 6, no. 3 (May 1915–March 1916): 363–69.

Freeland, David. *Automats, Taxi Dances, and Vaudeville: Excavating Manhattan's Lost Places of Leisure*. New York: NYU Press, 2009.

Fried, Albert. *The Rise and Fall of the Jewish Gangster in America*. 1980. Reprint, New York: Columbia University Press, 1993.

Gilfoyle, Timothy J. *City of Eros: New York City, Prostitution, and the Commercialization of Sex, 1790–1920*. 1992. Reprint, New York: W. W. Norton, 1994.

———. *A Pickpocket's Tale: The Underworld of Nineteenth-Century New York*. New York: W. W. Norton, 2007.

Goodheart, Adam. *1861: The Civil War Awakening*. New York: Knopf, 2011.

Goodwin, Doris Kearns. *The Bully Pulpit: Theodore Roosevelt, William Howard Taft, and the Golden Age of Journalism*. New York: Simon & Schuster, 2013.

Hall, Bruce Edward. *Tea That Burns: A Family Memoir of Chinatown*. New York: Free Press, 1998.

Hanson, Neil. *The Heroic Gangster: The Story of Monk Eastman, from the Streets of New York to the Battlefields of Europe and Back*. New York: Skyhorse, 2013.

Hapgood, Hutchins, ed. *The Autobiography of a Thief*. New York: Fox, Duffield, 1903.

Hartsfield, Larry K. *The American Response to Professional Crime, 1870–1917*. Westport, Conn.: Greenwood Press, 1985.

Hawthorne, Julian. *The Great Bank Robbery, from the Diary of Inspector Byrnes*. New York: Cassell, 1887.

———. *Section 558; or, The Fatal Letter*. New York: Cassell, 1888.

Headley, J. T. *The Great Riots of New York, 1712 to 1873*. New York: E. B. Treat, 1873.

Holub, Rona. "Fredericka Mandelbaum (1825–1894)." In *Immigrant Entrepreneurship: German-American Business Biographies, 1720 to the Present*. Edited by William J. Hausman. Vol. 2. German Historical Institute. Last modified October 15, 2013. http://www.immigrantentrepreneurship.org/entry.php?rec=160.

Howe, William, and Abraham Hummel. *Danger! A True History of a Great City's Wiles and Temptations*. Buffalo, N.Y.: Courier Company, 1886.

Hunt, Thomas. "Petto, Tomasso (1879–1905)." *The American Mafia: The History of Organized Crime in the United States*. Last modified 2018. http://mob-who.blogspot.com/2015/12/tomasso-petto-1879-1905.html.

———. *Wrongly Executed? The Long-Forgotten Context of Charles Sberna's 1939 Electrocution*. Whiting, Vt.: Seven-Seven-Eight, 2016.

Infamous New York: A Gangland Tour of New York City's Most Infamous Crime Scenes. Accessed March 18, 2020. https://infamousnewyork.com/.

Inglis, William. "Celebrities at Home: Thomas F. Byrnes, Former Chief of the New York Police." *Harper's Weekly*, November 14, 1908.

Inman, Keith, and Norah Rudin. *Principles and Practice of Criminalistics: The Profession of Forensic Science*. Boca Raton, Fla.: CRC Press, 2000.

Johnson, Marilynn S. *Street Justice: A History of Police Violence in New York* City. Boston: Beacon Press, 2003.

Jonakait, Randolph N. "*People v. Molineux* and Other Crime Evidence: One Hundred Years and Counting." *American Journal of Criminal Law* 30, no. 1 (Fall 2002): 1–43.

Jones, Thom L. "The Sun King of the Mafia." *Gangsters Inc.* Last modified November 10, 2010. http://gangstersinc.ning.com/profiles/blogs/the-sun-king-of-the-mafia.

Keefe, Rose. *The Starker: Big Jack Zelig, the Becker-Rosenthal Case, and the Advent of the Jewish Gangster.* Nashville: Cumberland House, 2008.

Kendrick, Bayard. "The Dolly Reynolds Case." In *New York Murders*, edited by Ted Collins, 85–108. New York: Duell, Sloan and Pearce, 1944.

Klaus, Samuel, ed. *The Molineux Case.* London: George Routledge, 1929.

Kuntz, Jerry. *Asbury's The Gangs of New York—Annotated: Re-Examinations of the Classic Sketch of Nineteenth-Century Underworld Life.* 2019–2020. https://gangsannotated.blog/page/1/.

———. *Professional Criminals of America—REVISED: Revised Biographies Based on NYPD Chief Thomas Byrnes' 1886 book, 'Professional Criminals of America.'"* (blog) 2018–2019. https://criminalsrevised.blog/.

Lamb, Bill. "Bill Devery." *Society for American Baseball Research online.* Accessed March 18, 2020. https://sabr.org/bioproj/person/500ba2d3#sdendnote6sym.

Lardner, James, and Thomas A. Reppetto. *NYPD: A City and Its Police.* New York: Henry Holt, 2000.

Lewis, Alfred Henry. *The Apaches of New York.* Chicago: M. A. Donohue, 1912.

———. "The Modern Robin Hood." *Cosmopolitan*, June 1905.

Locker, Maggie. "57 Great Jones Street." *Locker-Polding Index.* Last modified February 3, 2018. http://lockerpoldingindex.com/home/2018/2/3/57-great-jones-street.

Lyons, Sophie. *Why Crime Does Not Pay.* New York: J. S. Ogilvie, 1913.

Macintyre, Ben. *The Napoleon of Crime: The Life and Times of Adam Worth, Master Thief.* 1997. Reprint, New York: Broadway Paperbacks, 2011.

McAdoo, William. *Guarding a Great City.* New York: Harper & Brothers, 1906.

McCabe, James D., Jr. *Lights and Shadows of New York Life; or, The Sights and Sensations of the Great City.* Philadelphia: National Publishing, 1872.

McIllwain, Jeffrey Scott. *Organizing Crime in Chinatown: Race and Racketeering in New York City, 1890–1910.* Jefferson, N.C.: McFarland, 2004.

Mele, Andrew Paul. *The Italian Squad: How the NYPD Took Down the Black Hand Extortion Racket.* Jefferson, N.C.: McFarland, 2020.

Moore, Langdon W. *His Own Story of His Eventful Life.* Boston: Self-published, 1893.

Morris, Edmund. *The Rise of Theodore Roosevelt.* 1979. Reprint, New York: Random House, 2010.

Moses, Paul. *An Unlikely Union: The Love-Hate Story of New York's Irish and Italians.* New York: NYU Press, 2015.

Moss, Frank. *The American Metropolis: From Knickerbocker Days to the Present Time.* Vol. 3. New York: P. F. Collier, 1897.

Murphy, Cait. *Scoundrels in Law: The Trials of Howe & Hummel, Lawyers to the Gangsters, Cops, Starlets, and Rakes Who Made the Gilded Age*. New York: Smithsonian Books/HarperCollins, 2010.

Myers, Gustavus. *The History of Tammany Hall*. 2nd ed. New York: Boni and Liveright, 1917.

Nelli, Humbert S. *The Business of Crime: Italians and Syndicate Crime in the United States*. 1976. Reprint, Chicago: University of Chicago Press, 1981.

O'Connor, Richard. *Courtroom Warrior: The Combative Career of William Travers Jerome*. Boston: Little, Brown, 1963.

Oliver, Wesley MacNeil. "The Neglected History of Criminal Procedure, 1850–1940." *Rutgers Law Review* 62, no. 2 (2010): 447–525.

Parkhurst, Charles H. *Our Fight with Tammany*. New York: Charles Scribner's Sons, 1895.

Pejsa, Jane. *The Molineux Affair*. 1983. Reprint, New York: St. Martin's Press, 1987.

Petacco, Arrigo. *Joe Petrosino*. Translated by Charles Lam Markmann. 1972. Reprint, New York: Macmillan, 1974.

Pigott, Robert. *New York's Legal Landmarks: A Guide to Legal Edifices, Institutions, Lore, History and Curiosities on the City's Streets*. 2nd ed. New York: Attorney Street Editions, 2018.

Pinkerton, Allan. *The Bankers, Their Vaults, and the Burglars*. Chicago: Self-published, Fergus, 1873.

———. *Criminal Reminiscences and Detective Sketches*. New York: G. W. Dillingham, 1878.

———. *Professional Thieves and the Detective: Containing Numerous Detective Sketches Collected from Private Records*. New York: G. W. Carleton, 1883.

Pinkerton, William A. "Safe Burglary: Its Beginning and Progress." *National Police Journal* 6, no. 5 (August 1920): 10–11, 31, 33.

Reppetto, Thomas A. *American Mafia: A History of Its Rise to Power*. 2004. Reprint, Holt Paperbacks, 2005.

———. *American Police: The Blue Parade, 1845–1945*. 1978. Reprint, New York: Enigma, 2010.

Reynolds, Robert Grey, Jr. *Louis Pioggi: New York City Gang Leader*. Self-published, Smashwords, 2017.

Richardson, James F. *The New York Police: Colonial Times to 1901*. New York: Oxford University Press, 1970.

Riis, Jacob A. *How the Other Half Lives: Studies Among the Tenements of New York*. New York: Charles Scribner's Sons, 1890.

———. *The Making of an American*. New York: Macmillan, 1901.

———. *A Ten Years' War: An Account of the Battle with the Slum in New York*. Boston: Houghton Mifflin, 1900.

"Romances of the Day No. III: Organized Assassination." *Illustrated American* 4, no. 38 (November 8, 1890): 327–51.

Romano, Anne T. *Italian Americans in Law Enforcement*. Bloomington, Ind.: Xlibris, 2010.

Roosevelt, Theodore. *An Autobiography*. New York: Macmillan, 1913.

———. *The Letters of Theodore Roosevelt*. Edited by Elting E. Morison. Vol. 1, *The Years of Preparation, 1868–1898*. Cambridge, Mass.: Harvard University Press, 1951.

Salmon, Patricia M. *Staten Island Slayings: Murderers and Mysteries of the Forgotten Borough*. Charleston, S.C.: History Press, 2014.

Sante, Luc. *Low Life: Lures and Snares of Old New York*. New York: Farrar, Straus and Giroux, 1991.

Schechter, Harold. *The Devil's Gentleman: Privilege, Poison, and the Trial That Ushered in the Twentieth Century*. New York: Ballantine Books, 2007.

Schlesinger, Arthur M., Jr. "The Business of Crime." Introduction to Byrnes (1886), xiii–xxvi.

Schoenbein, Maximilian. *King of Burglars: The Heist Stories of Max Shinburn*. Edited with a foreword by Jerry Kuntz. Warwick, N.Y.: Wickham House, 2018.

Seligman, Scott D. *Tong Wars: The Untold Story of Vice, Money, and Murder in New York's Chinatown*. New York: Viking, 2016.

Shepp, James W., and Daniel B. Shepp. *Shepp's New York City Illustrated*. Chicago: Globe Bible, 1894.

Simmons, Oliver. "Passing of the Sullivan Dynasty." *Munsey's* 50, no. 3 (December 1913): 407–16.

Stead, W. T. *Satan's Invisible World Displayed; or, Despairing Democracy*. London: Mowbray House, 1898.

Steffens, Lincoln. *The Autobiography of Lincoln Steffens*. Vol. 1. New York: Harcourt Brace, 1931.

Swaine, Robert T. *The Cravath Firm and Its Predecessors, 1819–1947*. Vol. 1, *The Predecessor Firms, 1819–1906*. 1946. Reprint, Clark, N.J.: Lawbook Exchange, 2012.

Talty, Stephan. *The Black Hand: The Epic War Between a Brilliant Detective and the Deadliest Secret Society in American History*. 2017. Reprint, Boston: Mariner Books, 2018.

Train, Arthur. *Courts and Criminals*. New York: McKinlay, Stone & Mackenzie, 1912.

Turner, George Kibbe. "Tammany's Control of New York by Professional Criminals: A Study of a New Period of Decadence in the Popular Government of Great Cities." *McClure's* 33, no. 2 (June 1909): 117–34.

Underwood, Richard H. *Gaslight Lawyers: Criminal Trials and Exploits in Gilded Age New York*. Lexington, Ky.: Shadelandhouse Modern Press, 2017.

Vanderlin, Wolf. "The New York Affair, Part II." *Casebook: Jack the Ripper*. https://www.casebook.org/dissertations/rn-nya2.html. Reprinted from *Ripper Notes: The American Journal for Ripper Studies*, no. 17 (January 2004).

———. "The New York Affair, Part Three." *Ripper Notes: The American Journal for Ripper Studies*, no. 19 (July 2004): 8–57.

Van Every, Edward. *Sins of New York as "Exposed" by the Police Gazette*. New York: F. A. Stokes, 1930.

Van Loan, Charles E. "Disarming New York." *Munsey's* 46, no. 5 (February 1912): 687–92.

Wallace, Mike. *Greater Gotham: A History of New York City from 1898 to 1919*. New York: Oxford University Press, 2017.

Walling, George W. *Recollections of a New York Chief of Police*. New York: Caxton, 1887.

Welch, Richard F. *King of the Bowery: Big Tim Sullivan, Tammany Hall, and New York City from the Gilded Age to the Progressive Era*. 2008. Reprint, Albany: State University of New York Press, 2010.

Wellman, Francis L. *Luck and Opportunity: Recollections*. New York: Macmillan, 1938.

Werner, M. R. *It Happened in New York*. New York: Coward-McCann, 1957.

Whalen, Bernard J., Philip Messing, and Robert Mladinich. *Undisclosed Files of the Police: Cases from the Archives of the NYPD from 1831 to the Present*. New York: Black Dog & Leventhal, 2016.

Whalen, Bernard J., and Jon Whalen. *The NYPD's First Fifty Years: Politicians, Police Commissioners, and Patrolme*n. Lincoln, Neb.: Potomac Books, 2014.

Wheatley, Richard. "The New York Police Department." *Harper's New Monthly Magazine*, March 1887.

White, George M. (alias George Bliss). *From Boniface to Bank Burglar; or, The Price of Persecution*. Bellows Falls, Vt.: Self-published, Truax, 1905.

Willemse, Cornelius W. *A Cop Remembers*. New York: Dutton, 1933.

Woods, Arthur. "The Problem of the Black Hand." *McClure's* 33, no. 1 (May 1909): 40–47.

Young, Greg, and Tom Meyers. *The Bowery Boys: Adventures in Old New York—An Unconventional Exploration of Manhattan's Historic Neighborhoods, Secret Spots and Colorful Characters*. Berkeley, Calif.: Ulysses Press, 2016.

Zacks, Richard. *Island of Vice: Theodore Roosevelt's Quest to Clean Up Sin-Loving New York*. New York: Anchor Books, 2012.

GOVERNMENT REPORTS, TRANSCRIPTS, OFFICIAL RECORDS

Annual Report of the Adjutant-General of the State of New York for the Year 1862. Albany, N.Y.: C. Van Benthuysen, 1862.

Municipal Archives, New York City. D. A. Cases, Court of General Sessions, New York County, Grand Jury Indictments 1879–1893, Daniel Driscoll, 07/08/86, Murder, 1st Degree, Folder 2209, Box 225.

National Archives and Records Administration II, RG 87. Daily Reports of the US Secret Service Agents, 1875–1936, Publication no. T915A, reels 108, 109.

New York State Senate. *Report and Proceedings of the Senate Committee Appointed to Investigate the Police Department of the City of New York*. 5 vols. Albany, N.Y.: James B. Lyon, 1895.

People of the State of New York Against Daniel Driscoll, Case on Appeal. New York, 1886. Trial transcript, reprinted in https://books.google.com/books?id=opXbBzEKaHkC&printsec=frontcover#v=onepage&q&f=false.

People of the State of New York v. John Hope, Court of General Sessions, City and County of New York. Trial transcript. Reprinted in *Supreme Court, General Term, John Hope Against the People of the State of New York, Error Book*. New York, 1879. https://books.google.com/books?id=pXQkHnfhSiUC&pg=RA24-PP1#v=onepage&q=john%20hope&f=false.

People of the State of New York v. Samuel J. Kennedy, Trial #261, May 6, 1901, third trial transcript. John Jay College of Criminal Justice, Lloyd Sealy Library, Criminal Trial Transcripts of New York County Collection.

People of the State of New York v. William Delaney, Alias Monk Eastman, Court of General Sessions of the Peace in and for the County of New York. Trial transcript. 1904. http://www.crimeinnyc.org/sites/default/files/transcript-pdf-original/421.pdf.

People of the State of New York, Respondents, Against Roland B. Molineux, Appellant, Court of Appeals, State of New York, Case on Appeal. Vols. 2, 3, 4. New York: Martin B. Brown, 1901.

Report of the Police Department of the City of New York for the Year Ending December 31, 1895. New York: Martin B. Brown, 1897.

Report of the Police Department of the City of New York for the Year Ending December 31, 1896. New York: Martin B. Brown, 1897.

Report of the Police Department of the City of New York for the Year Ending December 31, 1898. New York: Martin B. Brown, 1899.

Report of the Police Department of the City of New York for the Year Ending December 31, 1904. New York: Martin B. Brown, 1906.

Roosevelt, Theodore. Papers. Library of Congress Manuscript Division.

Third Annual Report of the Bureau of Military Record of the State of New York. Albany, N.Y.: C. Wendell, 1866.

ILLUSTRATION CREDITS

All images are from public domain sources. Further credits are as follows:

Title page: Photograph of NYPD roll call, c. 1900. Getty Images.

Page

2 Arthur Carey, 1903. Library of Congress.

3 Illustration of Guldensuppe torso, from *New York Journal and Advertiser*, June 28, 1897.

7 Photograph of Thomas F. Byrnes, from Byrnes, *Professional Criminals of America* (1886).

14 Illustration of shooting of Jim Fisk, from *Frank Leslie's Illustrated Newspaper*, January 20, 1872.

17 Photograph of Tombs prison complex, 1896. Library of Congress.

27 Illustration of 1857 New York police riot, by Valerian Gribayedoff.

46 Rogues' gallery mug shots, from Byrnes, *Professional Criminals of America* (1886).

67 Illustration of Marm Mandelbaum, from Van Every, *Sins of New York* (1930).

71 Illustration of Mandelbaum's salon, from Walling, *Recollections* (1887).

93 Photograph of Byrnes watching mug shot session, 1880s. Jacob A. Riis/Museum of the City of New York.

96 Illustration of Byrnes's museum of crime, from Costello, *Our Police Protectors* (1885).

97 Photograph of Alexander "Clubber" Williams, c. 1885, by Benjamin J. Falk.

99 Photograph of Mike McGloin, c. 1882. Jacob A. Riis/Museum of the City of New York.

108 Photograph of Bandit's Roost, 1888, by Henry Granger Piffard and Richard Howe Lawrence for Jacob A. Riis/Museum of the City of New York.

116 Photograph of Danny Driscoll, 1880s. Jacob A. Riis/Museum of the City of New York.

121 Illustration of Olney, Mandelbaum, and Byrnes from cover of *Puck* magazine, August 12, 1884.

152 Photograph of Carrie Brown, c. 1890. NYC Municipal Archives.

ILLUSTRATION CREDITS

162 Photograph of Timothy Sullivan, with Larry Mulligan and Margaret Hickey, c. 1912. Library of Congress.

167 Photograph of Charles H. Parkhurst, c. 1896. Library of Congress.

173 Photograph of William Devery, c. 1905. Granger, NYC.

187 Photograph of George Appo, c. 1894. Courtesy of Timothy Gilfoyle.

206 Photograph of Max Schmittberger, c. 1910. Library of Congress.

222 Photograph of Theodore Roosevelt as police commissioner, c. 1895. Theodore Roosevelt Collection, Harvard College Library.

229 Photograph of Mulberry Street, NYC, 1900.

232 Cartoon of police and Roosevelt jack-o'-lantern. Theodore Roosevelt Center, Dickinson State University.

241 Photograph of NYPD bicycle squad, 1899. New York Public Library.

253 Cartoon of William Devery as police chief, from *Harper's Weekly*, September 6, 1902.

261 Illustration of Emeline "Dolly" Reynolds, from *New York Journal and Advertiser*, January 23, 1899.

262 Photograph of Samuel J. Kennedy, 1890s.

263 Photograph of Garfield National Bank check payable to Emeline Reynolds, 1898.

273 Photograph of Roland B. Molineux, early 1900s.

274 Photograph of package label sent to Harry Cornish, from *Ames on Forgery*, 1900.

295 Photograph of Edward "Monk" Eastman, c. 1903.

296 Photograph of Paul Kelly (Vaccarelli), c. 1903.

332 Photograph of Jack Zelig, c. 1912. Library of Congress.

336 Photograph of Joseph Petrosino, c. 1908. Granger, NYC.

344 Photograph of Giuseppe Morello, c. 1900. National Archives.

357 Photograph of Joseph Petrosino, Thomas Petto, and Arthur Carey, 1903. Library of Congress.

382 Photograph of funeral of Joseph Petrosino, 1909. Detroit Public Library.

INDEX

INDEX

Glennon, Edward, 180, 198, 250–51
Goatville precinct, 2–3, 143, 182, 256
Godfather, The (film), 383
Godfather Part II, The (film), 394
Goff, John W.
  and Battle of Rivington Street, 307
  and Becker-Rosenthal case, 396–97
  and Clubber Williams's testimony, 211–14
  and Eastman's assault trial, 321, 323–24
  and Kelly's conviction, 300–301
  and Lexow Committee hearings, 178–79,
    181, 183–84, 193–94, 196, 198–200,
    201–3, 205, 207, 209–10, 215–20
  and Molineux poisoning case, 283–84
  and Parkhurst's morality crusade, 176
Golden Rule Pleasure Club, 169
Goldman, Emma, 172–73
Goodie, Ed, 77, 78, 83–84
Goodwin, Isabella, 231
Gophers gang, 295
Gould, George, 216
Gould, Jay, 12, 15, 34, 102–3, 216, 224
Grady, John D. ("Traveling Mike"), 72–74,
  76–77, 80
Graffi, Joseph, 366
graffiti, 233
graft. *See* corruption and graft
Grand Central Hotel, 11, 13, *14*
Grand Hotel, 258, 260, 263–66,
  268, 340
Grant, Frederick, 221–22, 249
Grant, Hugh, 142, 199
Grant, Ulysses S., 12, 103
Great Diamond Robbery, The (melodrama), 126
Great Gatsby, The (Fitzgerald), 397
Great Poison Mystery, The (play), 290
Green, Patrick "Paddy," 117, 118, 317
Greene, Francis V., 312
green goods business, 184–85,
  186–93
Greenwall, John, 138
Greenwich, Charles, 330
Greenwich Village, 11, 204
growler gangs, 111
Guerin, Eddie, 85–86
Guldensuppe, William, 5–6, 7,
  256, 272
gun laws, 396

Hamilton, Schuyler, 128
handwriting analysis, 264, 267, 271–73, *274,*
  277–79, 281–82, 290–91
Hanier, Louis, 98–100, *99,* 110, 207, 357
Hanson, Neil, 303
Harper's Weekly, 34, 53, 89–90, 95, 149,
  253, 387
Harrington (murder victim), 327–28
Harriot, Lucy, 181–82
Hawthorne, Julian, 73, 146, 271
Haymarket, 142
Healy, John, 320
Hearst, William Randolph, 271
Heckman, Nicholas, 279–80
height requirements for police force,
  229–30, 229n
Hell's Kitchen, 5
Henderson, William, 17–18
Henry W. Jaehne Coterie, 127
Hermann, Matilda, 179, 180–81
Hewitt, Abram, 141
Hickey, Margaret, *162*
High Bridge Aqueduct, 1
Hill, Harry, 89
Hines, Josh, 145n
Hip Sings, 310
homelessness, 4, 243–44
Homicide Squad, 392
Hope, Harry, 84
Hope, Jimmy, *46*
  and Carey's background, 258
  and Grady's background, 73
  Leslie compared with, 56
  and Manhattan Savings robbery, 45–48, 58,
    63, 64, 77–79
  prison terms, 80–81
Hope, Johnny, 45–48, *46,* 77, 79–80, 130
horse racing, 262–63, 266
hotel thieves, 102
Howe, William, 69–70, 80, 85, 125, 147–48
Howe & Hummel law firm
  and Byrnes's public image, 147–49
  and Carlton, 138
  and decline of gangs, 144
  and dive crackdowns, 142
  and Driscoll's murder trial, 134–36
  and Hanier murder case, 100
  and Irving and Walsh killings, 85